Business Ethics

{ *Case Studies and Selected Readings* }

FOURTH 4 EDITION

Marianne M. Jennings

Professor of Legal and Ethical Studies in Business
Arizona State University
Member of the Arizona Bar

Australia · Canada · Mexico · Singapore · Spain · United Kingdom · United States

Business Ethics: Case Studies and Selected Readings, 4e
Marianne M. Jennings

Editor-in-Chief:
Jack W. Calhoun

Vice President, Team Director:
Michael P. Roche

Sr. Acquisitions Editor:
Rob Dewey

Developmental Editor:
Bob Sandman

Marketing Manager:
Steven Silverstein

Production Editor:
Starratt E. Alexander

Manufacturing Coordinator:
Rhonda Utley

Compositor & Production House:
Cover to Cover Publishing, Inc.

Printer:
Transcontinental Printing, Inc.
Louiseville, QC

Internal Designer:
Chris Miller

Cover Designer:
Chris Miller

Cover Illustrator:
Dave Cutler

Printed in Canada
1 2 3 4 5 04 03 02 01

For more information contact West Legal Studies in Business,
5191 Natorp Boulevard,
Mason, Ohio 45040.
Or you can visit our Internet site at: http://www.westbuslaw.com

Library of Congress Cataloging-in-Publication Data

Jennings, Marianne.
Business ethics : case studies and selected readings / Marianne M. Jennings.-- 4th ed.
p. cm.
Includes bibliographical references (p.) index.
ISBN 0-324-11080-4
1. Business ethics--United States--Case studies. I. Title.
HF5387.5.U6 J46 2002
174'.4--dc21
2002066835

Contents

UNIT 8

Business and Government 461

UNIT 9

Ethics and Nonprofits 483

Preface

"What is right is right even if no one is doing it. What is wrong is wrong even if everyone is doing it."

Source Unknown

"Goodness is the only investment that never fails."

Henry D. Thoreau

Walden; *Higher Laws*

"Three people can keep a secret if two are dead."

Hell's Angels

In 2000, KPMG, the international accounting firm, surveyed 3,075 working adults. Nearly half reported seeing unethical or illegal conduct of a serious nature at their jobs during the past year, and 76 percent said they had observed a "high level" of illegal or unethical conduct. The most common legal and ethical breaches reported by the survey respondents were deceptive sales practices, unsafe working conditions, and mishandling of confidential or proprietary information.[1] These are not small misdeeds. Nearly half of those employees surveyed also indicated that if members of the public were aware of these misdeeds, it would result in a loss of public trust.

Longitudinally, data on both attitudes about ethics and ethical breaches show that there is a steady increase in both ethical breaches as well as the tolerance for them occurring. In 1997, a Rutgers University survey revealed that 26 percent of undergraduate students engaged in plagiarism in writing papers for their courses. In May 2001,

[1] *KPMG, LLP,* 2000 Organizational Integrity Survey: A Summary, *published by the KPMG Integrity Management Services unit. For more information, go to http://www.us.kpmg.com or http://www.kpmgconsulting.com.*

that figure had increased to 54 percent, a doubling in four years.[2] Certainly the Internet has made the task of plagiarism easier, but the rate of increase in that form of dishonesty as well as others is indicative of a troubling trend.

The following events from the past few years offer some insight into the current issues in business ethics:

- The Securities and Exchange Commission (SEC) filed fraud charges against Sunbeam, its former CEO Albert J. Dunlap (often called "Chainsaw Al" for his career pattern of downsizing companies and making deep and swift cuts in the size of their work forces in order to quickly restore profitability), and its auditors for allegedly overstating earnings by, among other things, recording sales that did not really occur.[3] Mr. Dunlap has settled his case by agreeing to pay shareholders $15 million. Arthur Andersen settled with the shareholders for $110 million.[4]
- Jonathan G. Lebed began trading stock when he was 12 and through the Internet was able to pump and dump his way from an initial investment of $8,000 all the way to $800,000 until the SEC moved in and filed its first fraud charges against a minor, collecting almost $600,000 in gains and leaving his parents only with the funds to pay the income taxes on young Jonathan's 3-year run.[5]
- FINOVA, Inc., a financial corporation, and Enron, an energy trading firm, both consistently named one of the top ten companies to work for in the United States, had to issue corrected financial statements. The final fall-out from information about debts and write-downs not revealed to shareholders was that both companies now sit in Chapter 11 bankruptcy with their shares valued at under one dollar each, down from highs of $70–$80 per share. These are the largest and seventh largest bankruptcies in the history of the United States and their root causes for failure rest in ethical lapses.
- Both the stock exchanges and the SEC are exploring new codes of ethics for conflicts of interest among analysts and the companies they evaluate in light of the NASDAQ crash.
- General Motors lost a case on its Malibu car that exploded on impact and the jury awarded the family injured in the fiery crash over $4.9 billion (later reduced to $1.2 billion on appeal) because the evidence included internal memos with GM's knowledge of the defect in design centering around the gas tank and its placement that GM would not correct.[6]
- Nearly all dot-com firms are revamping, retooling, and recovering from an era in which financial statements have now been shown to be false, overstated, and creative in their approaches.[7]

Profits. High returns on investments. Earnings management. Product defects. Fraud. Each day brings news of another business with an ethical flaw. Businesses do exist to make a profit, but business ethics exists to set parameters for earning

[2] *The Rutgers study is conducted by Professor Donald McCabe on a regular basis. The survey had 4,500 student respondents. ESchool News Online, May 11, 2001, Edupage. See also http://www.rutgers.edu for more information on Professor McCabe and his work on academic integrity.*

[3] *Floyd Norris, "They Noticed the Fraud but Figured It Was Not Important,"* The New York Times, *May 18, 2001, p. C1.*

[4] *Michael Lewis, "Jonathan Lebed: Stock Manipulator, S.E.C. Nemesis—and 15,"* The New York Times, *February 25, 2001, at http://www.nytimes.com and also p. 24 of* The New York Times Sunday Magazine.

[5] *Kelly Greene, "Dunlap Agrees To Settle Suit Over Sunbeam,"* The Wall Street Journal, *January 15, 2002, p. A3.*

[6] *Milo Geyelin, "How an Internal Memo Written 26 Years Ago Is Costing GM Dearly,"* The Wall Street Journal, *September 29, 1999, pp. A1, A6.*

[7] *For example, Microstrategy's stock premiered in its IPO (initial primary offering) at $6 per share and climbed to $333 per share. When the SEC announced its investigation of the company for "accounting improprieties," the stock price fell 62 percent. Its share price was $3.59 in June 2000. Michael Schroeder, "SEC's Probe of Microstrategy Focuses on Auditor Independence Standards,"* The Wall Street Journal, *July 18, 2000, p. A3.*

that profit. This book of readings and cases explores those parameters and their importance.

In 1986, before Ivan Boesky was a household name and Michael Douglas was Gordon Gekko in *Wall Street*, I began teaching a business ethics course in the MBA program in the College of Business at Arizona State University. The course was an elective. I had trouble making the minimum enrollments. However, two things changed my enrollments and my fate. First, the American Association of Collegiate Schools of Business (AACSB) changed the curriculum for graduate and undergraduate business degree programs and required the coverage of ethics. The other event was actually a series of happenings. Indictments, convictions, and guilty pleas by major companies and their officers—from E.F. Hutton to Union Carbide to Beech-Nut to Exxon—brought national attention to the need to incorporate values in American businesses and business leaders.

Whether out of fear, curiosity, or the need for reaccreditation, business schools and students embraced the concept of studying business ethics. My course went from a little-known elective to the final required course in the MBA program. In the years since, the interest in business ethics has only increased. Today nearly 100 percent of the Fortune 500 companies have a code of ethics. Over half provide their employees with regular training in ethics.

Application of ethical principles in a business setting is a critical skill. Real-life examples are necessary. Over the past sixteen years, I have collected examples of ethical dilemmas, poor ethical choices, and wise ethical decisions from newspapers, business journals, and my experiences as a consultant and board member. Knowing that other instructors and students were in need of examples, I have turned my experiences into cases and coupled them with the most memorable readings in the field to provide a training and thought-provoking experience on business ethics.

The cases come not only from a quarter of a century of teaching and business experience, but also from my conviction that a strong sense of values is an essential management skill that can be taught. The cases apply theory to reality; hopefully, they will nurture or reinforce a needed sense of values in future business leaders.

The fourth edition continues the features students and instructors embraced in the first, second, and third editions, including both short and long cases, discussion questions, hypothetical situations, and up-to-the-moment current, ongoing, and real ethical dilemmas. Some of the longstanding favorites are back by popular demand—such as the Nestlé infant formula experience with its longstanding lessons in doing the right thing.

The fourth edition continues the classic readings in business ethics that provide insight into the importance of ethics in business and how to resolve ethical dilemmas. For this edition, the readings are integrated throughout the book to provide substantive thoughts on the particular areas covered in each section. The organizational structure and indexes, somewhat modified from the third edition, make material easy to locate. A case can be located using the table of contents, the topical index, or the product index, which lists both products and companies by name. An index for business disciplines groups the cases by accounting, management, and the other disciplines in colleges of business.

The instructor's manual is updated with more sample test objective- and essay-answer questions of varying lengths and structures. The questions have been coded for topic and even some for case-specific questions so that exams can be created by subject area. The transparency/ PowerPoint package, which includes illustrative charts to assist instructors in walking classes through the more complex cases, has been updated and expanded.

This book is not mine. It is the result of the efforts and sacrifices of many. I am grateful to the reviewers for their comments and insights. Their patience, expertise, and service are remarkable.

I am fortunate to have Bob Sandman as the editor for this edition. His calm and steady guidance make him an author's choice for editor-of-the-year. I am grateful to Rob Dewey for his continuing support of all my work. I continue to love editors. Where I see only deadlines, they see both the big picture of the book and its details: They have vision.

I am grateful to my parents for the values they inculcated in me. Their ethical perspective has been an inspiration, a comfort, and, in many cases, the final say in my decision-making processes. I am especially grateful to my father for his continual quest for examples of ethical and not-so-ethical behavior in action in the world of business. I am grateful for my family's understanding and support. I am most grateful for the reminder their very presence gives me of what is truly important.

Marianne M. Jennings
Professor of Legal and Ethical Studies in Business
College of Business
Arizona State University
Marianne.jennings@asu.edu

Introduction

"The reputation of a thousand years is determined by the conduct of one hour."

Japanese Proverb

"A quiet conscience makes one so serene."

Byron

"There is no pillow as soft as a clear conscience."

Kenneth Blanchard and Norman Vincent Peale
The Power of Ethical Management

"What once seemed black and white
Turns to so many shades of gray
We lose ourselves in work to do and bills to pay"

Bruce Springsteen, *Blood Brothers*[1]

Why Business Ethics?

A cover story in *Fortune* magazine, entitled "The Payoff from a Good Reputation" (*Fortune*, February 10, 1992), quotes a vice chairman of an advertising agency as saying, "The only sustainable competitive advantage any business has is its reputation." The same could be said about individual business persons. Reputation cannot be found in the annual 10K filing the Securities and Exchange Commission requires of a firm and won't be reflected in the net worth recorded on the firm's balance sheet. But its loss can be so devastating that if it were quantifiable, the failure of a firm to disclose that its ethical values were waning would constitute fraud under the federal securities laws. A business lacking an ethical commitment will, eventually, bring about its own demise.

A May 14, 2001, cover for *Fortune* magazine asks this question: "Can we ever trust again?" As we discover some of the creative accounting of the dot-com companies and the all-too-close relationships and conflicts among analysts, underwriters, and their clients, those who have invested are wondering how there could have been so many breaches of trust with so few people willing to express concerns. The burst of the dot-com bubble offers its share of ethical missteps that may have contributed to or exacerbated the scope of the economic downturn.

But the dot-coms with creative accounting and conflicts of interest are not unique. Examining the fates of companies such as Union Carbide, Beech-Nut, E.F. Hutton, Salomon Brothers, Johns-Manville, Exxon, Phar-Mor, Kidder Peabody, Bausch & Lomb, Sunbeam, FINOVA, Nike, Ford, Firestone, and others whose very public ethical mishaps resulted in tremendous losses supports the notion that a lack of commitment to ethical behavior is a lack of commitment to a firm's success.

Many people consider the term "business ethics" an oxymoron. Nonetheless, in keeping with the observations in *Fortune*, compelling reasons support choosing ethical behavior in a business setting. Courses in finance and accounting teach us that the primary purpose and obligation of a business is to earn a profit. The immediate pursuit of the bottom line occasionally can distort even the most conscientious perspective. The fear of losing business and consequently losing profits can lead individuals and companies to make decisions that, while not illegal, raise concerns about fairness, equity, justice, and honesty.

In their 1994 book *Built to Last*, James C. Collins and Jerry I. Porras noted that the common thread among companies with long-term growth and profits was a strong commitment to values. These successful companies had high standards for product quality, concern for employees and employee safety, and reputations for fairness and good service. In short, the ethical components of business were a common thread in their success.

A firm must pursue the positive figure for its bottom line with a long-term perspective in mind. Running a successful and ethical business is like running a marathon, not a sprint. Studies show that firms that perform better financially over time are those with a commitment to ethical behavior. A study by the Lincoln Center for Ethics and Professors Louis Grossman and Marianne Jennings at Arizona State University demonstrated that the fifteen U.S. corporations that have paid dividends for at least one hundred years without interruption also had a strong commitment to values. These companies knew what they had to do to be successful, but they also knew what they would *not* do to achieve that success.[2] What they would not do is compromise their values.

A 1997 study in the *Academy of Management Journal* concludes that firms involved in ethical difficulties (including criminal violations, regulatory citations, and product liability suits) experience earnings declines for at least five years following the public announcement of their problems.[3]

There is something to the correlation between business ethics and business success. While not every ethical person is guaranteed business success, every business that engages in unethical behavior is guaranteed a setback and the costs of trying to restore that invaluable reputation.

[2] *The results of this study will appear in the forthcoming book,* Building and Growing a Business: The Remarkable Stories of Fifteen Companies Each with 100 Years of Consistent Dividends, *Greenwood Press, 2002.*

[3] *Melissa S. Baucus and David A. Baucus, 40* Academy of Management Journal, *1997, p. 129.*

unit 1

Foundations of Business Ethics: Virtue, Values, and Business

1a

Defining Business Ethics

READING 1.1

What Is Business Ethics?

Society recognizes the value of ethics even as it realizes that companies and their employees may not perceive or properly resolve the ethical dilemmas that confront them. Many firms simply adopt a standard of complying with positive law, or any law enacted at any level of government that carries some sanction or punishment for noncompliance. While such compliance promotes many ethical values and moral principles, many actions that comply with positive law raise ethical issues. For example, several border guards formerly stationed at the East German border have been tried for manslaughter for killing East Germans as they attempted to escape into West Germany. In their defense, the former guards argued that they had been ordered to "shoot to kill." However, the judge, in sentencing the men, noted that not all activity that is legal is right. Still, the former guards had faced the dilemma of obeying orders under similar threats to their lives or following their moral standards with respect to the value of human life.

Recently, many Arizona businesses used a hastily passed state statute providing tax credit for vehicles with alternative fuel tanks. The statute and the tax credits were intended to create incentives for autos using non-polluting fuels, and the tax credits were so extensive that large and expensive sport utility vehicles (SUVs) could be purchased for the cost of a Geo. Further, dealers and others were just adding a 2-gallon propane tank to the vehicles, including Chevrolet Suburbans and Ford Expeditions, to meet the alternative fuel requirements. The statute produced a land office business for car dealers and businesses specializing in the installation of alternative fuel tanks. The results were that the environmental incentives of the statute were ignored and the total cost to the state for the tax credits was over $600 million before the program could be contained with meaningful requirements. No buyer or business did anything illegal, but the ethics of skirting the intent of law present a different question.

This Unit examines the role of basic virtues such as honesty, loyalty, and even compliance with the law. Conduct such as bribery, conflicts of interest, and puffing arise in various business settings. A good grasp of the issues in these basic virtues is critical for all business people. This section begins with a summary of the areas of ethical challenges that serves as the framework for the organization of the remainder of the book. Following is an excerpt from Marianne M. Jennings' book, *Business: Its Legal, Ethical and Global Environment, 6th Ed.* on the categories of ethical issues as well as a framework for resolving them. Albert Carr's piece, *Is Business Bluffing Ethical?* provides a different perspective on virtue ethics. Finally, Laura Nash provides a framework for integrating the decision-making process into a business organization. With these pieces you have differing perspectives on ethics as well as tools to apply in analyzing the cases in this Unit and those that follow.

READING 1.2

The Areas of Ethical Challenges[1]

The remaining pages of this book present more readings and cases that illustrate ethical dilemmas faced by businesses and business people. The cases require critical examination of one's moral standards and the impact poor ethical decisions can have on individuals and companies. The cases are divided into categories based on The Conference Board's groupings of ethical dilemmas in business. (The Conference Board is a private research and information group that focuses on corporate and business issues.) Each category represents a grouping of the types of ethical dilemmas that were ranked most important by CEOs in a 1991 survey conducted by the Ethics Resource Center. The topics in each category are listed here.

Individual Values and the Business Organization
- Employee Conflicts of Interest
- Inappropriate Gifts
- Security of Company Records
- Personal Honesty

Individual Rights and the Business Organization
- Corporate Due Process
- Employee Screening
- Employee Privacy
- Sexual Harassment
- Affirmative Action/Equal Employment Opportunity
- Employment at Will
- Whistle-Blowing
- Employee Rights
- Comparable Worth

Business Operations
- Financial and Cash Management Procedures
- Conflicts between the Corporation's Ethical Code and Accepted Business Practices in Foreign Countries
- Unauthorized Payments to Foreign Officials
- Workplace Safety
- Plant Closures and Downsizing

[1] *Used by permission of The Conference Board.*

Environmental Issues
Purchasing: Conflicts and Bribery
Business and Its Competition
Advertising Content
Appropriation of Others' Ideas
Product Pricing
Business and Its Product
Contract Relations
Product Safety
Product Quality
Customer Privacy
Business and Its Stakeholders
Shareholders' Interests
Executive Salaries
Corporate Contributions
Social Issues
Business and Government
Government Employees
Government Contracts
Government Responsibilities

READING 1.3

Recognizing Ethical Dilemmas: The Language[2]

Despite a strong value system, an individual facing the complexities of business needs help in recognizing ethical dilemmas. There are two ways an ethical dilemma can be spotted: by language and by category. This reading covers the language recognition technique and the following reading covers the categories.

The Language of Ethical Lapses

The first way to spot an ethical dilemma is by watching the language those involved use. There are key phrases of rationalization employed in ethical dilemmas.

"Everybody Else Does It"

Zoë Baird's nomination for attorney general in early 1993 met with opposition when an investigation revealed that Baird and her husband had employed illegal immigrants as a chauffeur and as a nanny for their child and had failed to pay the Social Security, Medicare, and unemployment taxes required of household employers. The response of many to the issue was that only 25 percent of all household employers paid such taxes; fully 75 percent or "everybody else" did not. Statistical support is not a valid basis for making ethical choices. The law had been violated. Everybody else was investing in those risky financial instruments, derivatives. The eventual and catastrophic losses from these instruments to Long-Term Capital, Procter & Gamble, Orange

[2] *From* Business: Its Legal, Ethical and Global Environment, *6th Ed., by Marianne M. Jennings, Chapter 2 , pp. 52–59.* *Copyright © 2003. Reprinted with permission of South-Western, a division of Thomson Learning.*

County, Barings Bank, Gibson Greetings, and Enron show how "everybody else" is often wrong. "Everybody else does it" is a rationalization for a poor ethical choice.

"If We Don't Do It, Someone Else Will"

The rationalization of competition is that since someone will do it and make money, it might as well be us. For Halloween 1994, there were O. J. Simpson masks and plastic knives and Nicole Brown Simpson masks and costumes complete with slashes and blood stains. When Nicole Simpson's family objected to this violation of the basic standard of decency, a costume-shop owner commented that if he didn't sell the items, someone down the street would. While nothing about the marketing of the costumes was illegal, the ethical issues that surround earning a profit from an event as heinous as the brutal murder of a young mother abound.

"That's the Way It Has Always Been Done"

Corporate or business history and business practices are not always sound. The fact that for years nothing has changed in a firm may indicate the need for change and an atmosphere that invites possible ethical violations. For example, until the Securities and Exchange Commission required corporate boards of directors compensation committees to make reports and to disclose the identities of their members, the sitting members of many of these committees had conflicts of interest. For example, a senior partner of a law firm who represented a given corporation often sat on that client's board and on its compensation committee. The result was that a lawyer whose firm was economically dependent on the corporation as a client was making salary determinations for the corporation's officers, who, of course, made the decisions about which law firm would represent their company. A conflict of interest existed, but everybody was doing it, and it was the way corporations had always been governed. Again, unquestioning adherence to a pattern of practice or behavior often indicates an underlying ethical dilemma.

"We'll Wait until the Lawyers Tell Us It's Wrong"

Lawyers are trained to provide only the parameters of the law. In many situations, they offer an opinion that is correct in that it does not violate the law. Whether the conduct they have passed judgment on as legal is ethical is a different question. Allowing law and lawyers to control a firm's destiny ignores the opportunity to make wise and ethical choices. For example, Orange County, California, filed for bankruptcy in 1994 because its investment strategy, involving heavy investments in financial derivative instruments, had failed, and it had lost sums so large that it was rendered insolvent. Were the derivative investments legal? Absolutely. Were the derivative investments reviewed by lawyers? Yes, for both buyers and sellers. Legality is often not a sufficient standard for ethical behavior. Following the positive law does not always guarantee that a firm will avoid legal difficulties. Analyzing issues of fairness, risk, and disclosure requires input beyond just a legal opinion.

"It Doesn't Really Hurt Anyone"

When we are the sole rubberneckers on the freeway, traffic remains unaffected. But if everyone rubbernecks, we have a traffic jam. All of us making poor ethical choices would cause significant harm. A man interviewed after he was arrested for defrauding insurance companies through staged auto accidents remarked, "It didn't really hurt anyone. Insurance companies can afford it." The second part of his statement is accurate. The insurance companies can afford it—but not without cost to someone else. Such fraud harms all of us because we must pay higher premiums to allow insurers to absorb the costs of investigating and paying for fraudulent claims.

"The System Is Unfair"

Often touted by students as a justification for cheating on exams, this rationalization eases our consciences by telling us we are cheating only to make up for deficiencies in the system. Yet just one person cheating can send ripples through an entire system. The credibility of grades and the institution come into question as students obtain grades through means beyond the system's standards. As we see events unfold in China, Italy, and Brazil, with government employees awarding contracts and rights to do business on the basis of payments rather than on the merits of a given company or its proposal, we understand how such bribery only results in greater unfairness within and greater costs to those countries. Many economists have noted that a country's businesses and economy will not progress without some fundamental assurance of trust.

"I Was Just Following Orders"

In many criminal trials and disputes over responsibility and liability, many managers will disclaim their responsibility by stating, "I was just following orders." There are times when individuals cannot follow the directions of supervisors, for they have been asked to do something illegal or immoral. Judges who preside over the criminal trials of war criminals often remind defendants that an order is not necessarily legal or moral. Values require us to question or depart from orders when others will be harmed or wronged.

READING 1.4

The Categories of Ethical Dilemmas[3]

The second method for spotting an ethical dilemma is to understand the categories of ethical dilemmas. The following twelve categories were developed and listed in *Exchange*, the magazine of the Brigham Young University School of Business:

Taking Things That Don't Belong to You

Everything from the unauthorized use of the Pitney Bowes postage meter at your office for mailing personal letters to exaggerations on travel expenses belongs in this category of ethical violations. Regardless of size, motivation, or the presence of any of the rationalizations discussed previously, the unauthorized use of someone else's property or taking property under false pretenses still means taking something that does not belong to you. A chief financial officer of a large electric utility reported that after taking a cab from LaGuardia International Airport to his midtown Manhattan hotel, he asked for a receipt. The cab driver handed him a full book of blank receipts and drove away. Apparently the problem of accurately reporting travel expenses involves more than just employees.

[3] *J. Own Cherrington and David J. Cherrington, "Ethics: A Major Business Problem,"* Exchange, *Fall 1989, p. 30.*

Saying Things You Know Are Not True

Often in their quest for promotion and advancement, fellow employees discredit their co-workers. Falsely assigning blame or inaccurately reporting conversations is lying. While "This is the way the game is played around here" is a common justification, saying things that are untrue is an ethical violation.

Giving or Allowing False Impressions

The salesman who permits a potential customer to believe that his cardboard boxes will hold the customer's tomatoes for long-distance shipping when he knows the boxes are not strong enough has given a false impression. A car dealer who fails to disclose that a car has been in an accident is misleading potential customers. A co-worker or supervisor who takes credit for another employee's idea has allowed a false impression.

Buying Influence or Engaging in Conflict of Interest

A company awards a construction contract to a firm owned by the father of the state attorney general while the state attorney general's office is investigating that company. A county administrator responsible for awarding the construction contract for a baseball stadium accepts from contractors interested in bidding on the project paid travel around the country to other stadiums that the contractors have built.

The wife of a state attorney general accepts trading advice from the corporate attorney for a highly regulated company and subsequently earns, in her first attempt at the market, over $100,000 in the commodities market in cattle futures.

These examples illustrate conflicts of interest. Those involved in situations such as these often protest, "But I would never allow that to influence me." The ethical violation is the conflict. Whether the conflict can or will influence those it touches is not the issue, for neither party can prove conclusively that a *quid pro quo* was not intended. The possibility exists, and it creates suspicion. Hence, conflicts of interest are to be avoided or, at a minimum, disclosed.

Hiding or Divulging Information

Taking your firm's product development or trade secrets to a new place of employment constitutes an ethical violation: divulging proprietary information. Failing to disclose the results of medical studies that indicate your firm's new drug has significant side effects is the ethical violation of hiding information that the product could be harmful to purchasers.

Taking Unfair Advantage

Many current consumer protection laws were passed because so many businesses took unfair advantage of those who were not educated or were unable to discern the nuances of complex contracts. Credit disclosure requirements, truth-in-lending provisions, and new regulations on auto leasing all resulted because businesses misled consumers who could not easily follow the jargon of long and complex agreements.

Committing Acts of Personal Decadence

While many argue about the ethical notion of an employee's right to privacy, it has become increasingly clear that personal conduct outside the job can influence performance and company reputation. Thus, a company driver must abstain from substance abuse because of safety issues. Even the traditional company Christmas party and picnic have come under scrutiny as the behavior of employees at, and following, these events has brought harm to others in the form of alcohol-related accidents.

Perpetrating Interpersonal Abuse

A manager sexually harasses an employee. Another manager is verbally abusive to an employee. Still another manager subjects employees to humiliating correction in the presence of customers. In some cases, laws protect employees. However, many situations are simply ethical violations that constitute interpersonal abuse.

Permitting Organizational Abuse

Many U.S. firms with operations overseas, such as Levi Strauss, The Gap, and Esprit, have faced issues of organizational abuse. The unfair treatment of workers in international operations appears in the form of child labor, demeaning wages, and too-long hours. While a business cannot change the culture of another country, it can perpetuate—or alleviate—abuse through its operations there.

Violating Rules

Many rules, particularly those in large organizations that tend toward bureaucracy from a need to maintain internal controls or follow lines of authority, seem burdensome to employees trying to serve customers and other employees. Stanford University experienced difficulties in this area of ethics as it used funds from federal grants for miscellaneous university purposes. Questions arose about the propriety of the expenditures, which quite possibly could have been approved through proper channels, but weren't. The rules for the administration of federal grant monies used for overhead were not followed. The result was not only an ethical violation but damage to Stanford's reputation and a new president for the university.

Condoning Unethical Actions

In this breach of ethics, the wrong results from the failure to report the wrong. What if you witnessed a fellow employee embezzling company funds by forging her signature on a check that was to be voided? Would you report that violation? A winking tolerance of others' unethical behavior is in itself unethical. Suppose that as a product designer you were aware of a fundamental flaw in your company's new product—a product predicted to catapult your firm to record earnings. Would you pursue the problem to the point of halting the distribution of the product? Would you disclose what you know to the public if you could not get your company to act?

Balancing Ethical Dilemmas

In these types of situations, there are no right or wrong answers; rather, there are dilemmas to be resolved. For example, Levi Strauss struggled with its decision about whether to do business in the People's Republic of China because of known human rights violations by the government there. Other companies debated doing business in South Africa when that country's government followed a policy of apartheid. In some respects, the presence of these companies would help by advancing human rights and, certainly, by improving the standard of living for at least some international operations workers. On the other hand, their ability to recruit businesses could help such governments sustain themselves by enabling them to point to economic successes despite human rights violations.

1b

Resolutions of Business Ethics Dilemma

The resolution of ethical dilemmas in business is often difficult, even in firms with a code of ethics and a culture committed to compliance with ethical models for decision making. Managers need guidelines for making ethical choices. Several prominent scholars in the field of business ethics have developed models for use in difficult situations. In this section you have the chance to read the views of two scholars in the field of business ethics whose perspectives offer different ends of the spectrum. Following their discussions are summaries of the views of others in business ethics for resolution of ethical dilemmas.

READING 1.5

Is Business Bluffing Ethical?[4]

In the following classic reading, Albert Carr compares business to poker and offers a justification for business bluffing. Mr. Carr provides a different perspective from the previous discussion with its various models and categories geared more toward absolutes.

Albert Z. Carr

A respected businessman with whom I discussed the theme of this article remarked with some heat, "You mean to say you're going to encourage men to bluff? Why, bluffing is nothing more than a form of lying! You're advising them to lie!"

I agreed that the basis of private morality is a respect for truth and that the closer a businessman comes to the truth, the more he deserves respect. At the same time, I suggested that most bluffing in business might be regarded simply as game strategy—much like bluffing in poker, which does not reflect on the morality of the bluffer.

I quoted Henry Taylor, the British statesman who pointed out that "falsehood ceases to be falsehood when it is understood on all sides that the truth is not expected

[4] *Reprinted by permission of* Harvard Business Review. *From "Is Business Bluffing Ethical?" by Albert Z. Carr, Vol. 46, January/February 1968. Copyright © 1968 by the Harvard Business School Publishing Corporation; all rights reserved.*

to be spoken"—an exact description of bluffing in poker, diplomacy, and business. I cited the analogy of the criminal court, where the criminal is not expected to tell the truth when he pleads "not guilty." Everyone from the judge down takes it for granted that the job of the defendant's attorney is to get his client off, not to reveal the truth; and this is considered ethical practice. I mentioned Representative Omar Burleson, the Democrat from Texas, who was quoted as saying, in regard to the ethics of Congress, "Ethics is a barrel of worms"[5]—a pungent summing up of the problem of deciding who is ethical in politics.

I reminded my friend that millions of businessmen feel constrained every day to say *yes* to their bosses when they secretly believe *no* and that this is generally accepted as permissible strategy when the alternative might be the loss of a job. The essential point, I said, is that the ethics of business are games ethics, different from the ethics of religion.

He remained unconvinced. Referring to the company of which he is president, he declared: "Maybe that's good enough for some businessmen, but I can tell you that we pride ourselves on our ethics. In thirty years not one customer has ever questioned my word or asked to check our figures. We're loyal to our customers and fair to our suppliers. I regard my handshake on a deal as a contract. I've never entered into price-fixing schemes with my competitors. I've never allowed my salesmen to spread injurious rumors about other companies. Our union contract is the best in our industry. And, if I do say so myself, our ethical standards are of the highest!"

He really was saying, without realizing it, that he was living up to the ethical standards of the business game—which are a far cry from those of private life. Like a gentlemanly poker player, he did not play in cahoots with others at the table, try to smear their reputations, or hold back chips he owed them.

But this same fine man, at that very time, was allowing one of his products to be advertised in a way that made it sound a great deal better than it actually was. Another item in his product line was notorious among dealers for its "built-in-obsolescence." He was holding back from the market a much-improved product because he did not want it to interfere with sales of the inferior item it would have replaced. He had joined with certain of his competitors in hiring a lobbyist to push a state legislature, by methods that he preferred not to know too much about, into amending a bill then being enacted.

In his view these things had nothing to do with ethics; they were merely normal business practice. He himself undoubtedly avoided outright falsehoods—never lied in so many words. But the entire organization that he ruled was deeply involved in numerous strategies of deception.

Pressure to Deceive

Most executives from time to time are almost compelled, in the interest of their companies or themselves, to practice some form of deception when negotiating with customers, dealers, labor unions, government officials or even other department[s] of their companies. By conscious misstatements, concealment of pertinent facts, or exaggeration—in short, by bluffing—they seek to persuade others to agree with them.

[5] The New York Times, *March 9, 1967.*

I think it is fair to say that if the individual executive refuses to bluff from time to time—if he feels obligated to tell the truth, the whole truth, and nothing but the truth—he is ignoring opportunities permitted under the rules and is at a heavy disadvantage in his business dealings.

But here and there a businessman is unable to reconcile himself to the bluff in which he plays a part. His conscience, perhaps spurred by religious idealism, troubles him. He feels guilty; he may develop an ulcer or a nervous tic. Before any executive can make profitable use of the strategy of the bluff, he needs to make sure that in bluffing he will not lose self-respect or become emotionally disturbed. If he is to reconcile personal integrity and high standards of honesty with the practical requirements of business, he must feel that his bluffs are ethically justified. The justification rests on the fact that business, as practiced by individuals as well as by corporations, has the impersonal character of a game—a game that demands both special strategy and an understanding of its special ethics.

The game is played at all levels of corporate life, from the highest to the lowest. At the very instant that a man decides to enter business, he may be forced into a game situation, as is shown by the recent experience of a Cornell honor graduate who applied for a job with a large company.

This applicant was given a psychological test which included the statement, "Of the following magazines, check any that you have read either regularly or from time to time, and double-check those which interest you most. *Reader's Digest, Time, Fortune, Saturday Evening Post, The New Republic, Life, Look, Ramparts, Newsweek, Business Week, U.S. News & World Report, The Nation, Playboy, Esquire, Harper's, Sports Illustrated.*"

His tastes in reading were broad, and at one time or another he had read almost all of these magazines. He was a subscriber to *The New Republic*, an enthusiast for *Ramparts*, and an avid student of the pictures in *Playboy*. He was not sure whether his interest in *Playboy* would be held against him, but he had a shrewd suspicion that if he confessed to an interest in *Ramparts* and *The New Republic*, he would be thought a liberal, a radical, or at least an intellectual, and his chances of getting the job, which he needed, would greatly diminish. He therefore checked five of the more conservative magazines. Apparently it was a sound decision, for he got the job.

He had made a game player's decision, consistent with business ethics.

A similar case is that of a magazine space salesman who, owing to a merger, suddenly found himself out of a job:

> This man was 58, and, in spite of a good record, his chance of getting a job elsewhere in a business where youth is favored in hiring practice was not good. He was a vigorous, healthy man, and only a considerable amount of gray in his hair suggested his age. Before beginning his job search he touched up his hair with a black dye to confine the gray to his temples. He knew that the truth about his age might well come out in time, but he calculated that he could deal with that situation when it arose. He and his wife decided that he could easily pass for 45, and he so stated his age on his résumé.

This was a lie, yet within the accepted rules of the business game, no moral culpability attaches to it.

The Poker Analogy

We can learn a good deal about the nature of business by comparing it with poker. While both have a large element of chance, in the long run the winner is the man who plays with steady skill. In both games ultimate victory requires intimate knowledge of the rules, insight into the psychology of the other players, a bold front, a considerable amount of self-discipline, and the ability to respond swiftly and effectively to opportunities provided by chance.

No one expects poker to be played on the ethical principles preached in churches. In poker it is right and proper to bluff a friend out of the rewards of being dealt a good hand. A player feels no more than a slight twinge of sympathy, if that, when—with nothing better than a single ace in his hand—he strips a heavy loser, who holds a pair, of the rest of his chips. It was up to the other fellow to protect himself. In the words of an excellent poker player, former President Harry Truman, "If you can't stand the heat, stay out of the kitchen." If one shows mercy to a loser in poker, it is a personal gesture, divorced from the rules of the game.

Poker has its special ethics, and here I am not referring to rules against cheating. The man who keeps an ace up his sleeve or who marks the cards is more than unethical; he is a crook, and can be punished as such—kicked out of the game or, in the Old West, shot.

In contrast to the cheat, the unethical poker player is one who, while abiding by the letter of the rules, finds ways to put the other players at an unfair disadvantage. Perhaps he unnerves them with loud talk. Or he tries to get them drunk. Or he plays in cahoots with someone else at the table. Ethical poker players frown on such tactics.

Poker's own brand of ethics is different from the ethical ideals of civilized human relationships. The game calls for distrust of the other fellow. It ignores the claim of friendship. Cunning deception and concealment of one's strength and intentions, not kindness and openheartedness, are vital in poker. No one thinks any the worse of poker on that account. And no one should think any the worse of the game of business because its standards of right and wrong differ from the prevailing traditions of morality in our society.

Discard the Golden Rule

This view of business is especially worrisome to people without much business experience. A minister of my acquaintance once protested that business cannot possibly function in our society unless it is based on the Judeo-Christian system of ethics. He told me:

> "I know some businessmen have supplied call girls to customers, but there are always a few rotten apples in every barrel. That doesn't mean the rest of the fruit isn't sound. Surely the vast majority of businessmen are ethical. I myself am acquainted with many who adhere to strict codes of ethics based fundamentally on religious teachings. They contribute to good causes. They participate in community activities. They cooperate with other companies to improve working conditions in their industries. Certainly they are not indifferent to ethics."

That most businessmen are not indifferent to ethics in their private lives, everyone will agree. My point is that in their office lives they cease to be private citizens; they become game players who must be guided by a somewhat different set of ethical standards.

The point was forcefully made to me by a Midwestern executive who has given a good deal of thought to the question:

> "So long as a businessman complies with the laws of the land and avoids telling malicious lies, he's ethical. If the law as written gives a man a wide-open chance to make a killing, he'd be a fool not to take advantage of it. If he doesn't, somebody else will. There's no obligation on him to stop and consider who is going to get hurt. If the law says he can do it, that's all the justification he needs. There's nothing unethical about that. It's just plain business sense."

This executive (call him Robbins) took the stand that even industrial espionage, which is frowned on by some businessmen, ought not to be considered unethical. He recalled a recent meeting of the National Industrial Conference Board where an authority on marketing made a speech in which he deplored the employment of spies by business organizations. More and more companies, he pointed out, find it cheaper to penetrate the secrets of competitors with concealed cameras and microphones or by bribing employees than to set up costly research and design departments of their own. A whole branch of the electronics industry has grown up with this trend, he continued, providing equipment to make industrial espionage easier.

Disturbing? The marketing expert found it so. But when it came to a remedy, he could only appeal to "respect for the golden rule." Robbins thought this a confession of defeat, believing that the golden rule, for all its value as an ideal for society, is simply not feasible as a guide for business. A good part of the time the businessman is trying to do unto others as he hopes others will *not* do unto him.[6] Robbins continued:

> "Espionage of one kind or another has become so common in business that it's like taking a drink during Prohibition—it's not considered sinful. And we don't even have Prohibition where espionage is concerned; the law is very tolerant in this area. There's no more shame for a business that uses a secret agent than there is for a nation. Bear in mind that there already is at least one large corporation—you can buy its stock over the counter—that makes millions by providing counterespionage service to industrial firms. Espionage in business is not an ethical problem; it's an established technique of business competition."

"We Don't Make the Laws."

Wherever we turn in business, we can perceive the sharp distinction between its ethical standards and those of the churches. Newspapers abound with sensational stories growing out of this distinction:

- We read one day that Senator Philip A. Hart of Michigan has attacked food processors for deceptive packaging of numerous products.[7]
- The next day there is a Congressional to-do over Ralph Nader's book, *Unsafe At Any Speed*, which demonstrates that automobile companies for years have neglected the safety of car-owning families.[8]
- Then another Senator, Lee Metcalf of Montana, and journalist Vic Reinemer show in their book, *Overcharge*, the methods by which utility companies elude regulating government bodies to extract unduly large payments from users of electricity.[9]

[6] *See Bruce D. Henderson, "Brinkmanship in Business,"* Harvard Business Review, *March–April 1967, p. 49.*

[7] The New York Times, *November 21, 1966.*

[8] *Grossman Publishers, Inc.: New York, 1965.*

[9] *David McKay Company, Inc.: New York, 1967.*

These are merely dramatic instances of a prevailing condition; there is hardly a major industry at which a similar attack could not be aimed. Critics of business regard such behavior as unethical, but the companies concerned know that they are merely playing the business game.

Among the most respected of our business institutions are the insurance companies. A group of insurance executives meeting recently in New England was startled when their guest speaker, social critic Daniel Patrick Moynihan, roundly berated them for "unethical" practices. They had been guilty, Moynihan alleged, of using outdated actuarial tables to obtain unfairly high premiums. They habitually delayed the hearings of lawsuits against them in order to tire out the plaintiffs and win cheap settlements. In their employment policies they used ingenious devices to discriminate against certain minority groups.[10]

It was difficult for the audience to deny the validity of these charges. But these men were business game players. Their reaction to Moynihan's attack was much the same as that of the automobile manufacturers to Nader, of the utilities to Senator Metcalf, and of the food processors to Senator Hart. If the laws governing their businesses change, or if public opinion becomes clamorous, they will make the necessary adjustments. But morally they have, in their view, done nothing wrong. As long as they comply with the letter of the law, they are within their rights to operate their businesses as they see fit.

The small business is in the same position as the great corporation in this respect. For example:

> In 1967 a key manufacturer was accused of providing master keys for automobiles to mail-order customers, although it was obvious that some of the purchasers might be automobile thieves. His defense was plain and straightforward. If there was nothing in the law to prevent him from selling his keys to anyone who ordered them, it was not up to him to inquire as to his customers' motives. Why was it any worse, he insisted, for him to sell car keys by mail, than for mail-order houses to sell guns that might be used for murder? Until the law was changed, the key manufacturer could regard himself as being just as ethical as any other businessman by the rules of the business game.[11]

Violations of the ethical ideals of society are common in business, but they are not necessarily violations of business principles. Each year the Federal Trade Commission orders hundreds of companies, many of them of the first magnitude, to "cease and desist" from practices which, judged by ordinary standards, are of questionable morality but which are stoutly defended by the companies concerned.

In one case, a firm manufacturing a well-known mouth-wash was accused of using a cheap form of alcohol possibly deleterious to health. The company's chief executive, after testifying in Washington, made this comment privately:

> "We broke no law. We're in a highly competitive industry. If we're going to stay in business, we have to look for profit wherever the law permits. We don't make the laws. We obey them. Then why do we have to put up with this 'holier than thou' talk about

[10] The New York Times, *January 17, 1967.*

[11] *Cited by Ralph Nader in "Business Crime,"* The New Republic, *July 1, 1967, p. 7.*

> ethics? It's sheer hypocrisy. We're not in business to promote ethics. Look at the cigarette companies, for God's sake! If the ethics aren't embodied in the laws by the men who made them, you can't expect businessmen to fill the lack. Why, a sudden submission to Christian ethics by businessmen would bring about the greatest economic upheaval in history!"

It may be noted that the government failed to prove its case against him.

Cast Illusions Aside

Talk about ethics by businessmen is often a thin decorative coating over the hard realities of the game:

> Once I listened to a speech by a young executive who pointed to a new industry code as proof that his company and its competitors were deeply aware of their responsibilities to society. It was a code of ethics, he said. The industry was going to police itself, to dissuade constituent companies from wrongdoing. His eyes shone with conviction and enthusiasm.
>
> The same day there was a meeting in a hotel room where the industry's top executives met with the "czar" who was to administer the new code, a man of high repute. No one who was present could doubt their common attitude. In their eyes the code was designed primarily to forestall a move by the federal government to impose stern restrictions on the industry. They felt that the code would hamper them a good deal less than new federal laws would. It was, in other words, conceived as a protection for the industry, not for the public.
>
> The young executive accepted the surface explanation of the code; these leaders, all experienced game players, did not deceive themselves for a moment about its purpose.

The illusion that business can afford to be guided by ethics as conceived in private life is often fostered by speeches and articles containing such phrases as, "It pays to be ethical," or, "Sound ethics is good business." Actually this is not an ethical position at all; it is a self-serving calculation in disguise. The speaker is really saying that in the long run a company can make more money if it does not antagonize competitors, suppliers, employees, and customers by squeezing them too hard. He is saying that oversharp policies reduce ultimate gains. That is true, but it has nothing to do with ethics. The underlying attitude is much like that in the familiar story of the shopkeeper who finds an extra twenty-dollar bill in the cash register, debates with himself the ethical problem—should he tell his partner?—and finally decides to share the money because the gesture will give him an edge over the s.o.b. the next time they quarrel.

I think it is fair to sum up the prevailing attitude of businessmen on ethics as follows:

> We live in what is probably the most competitive of the world's civilized societies. Our customs encourage a high degree of aggression in the individual's striving for success. Business is our main area of competition, and it has been ritualized into a game of strategy. The basic rules of the game have been set by the government, which attempts to detect and punish business frauds. But as long as a company does not transgress the rules of the game set by law, it has the legal right to shape its strategy without reference to anything but its profits. If it takes a long-term view of its profits, it will

preserve amicable relations, so far as possible, with those with whom it deals. A wise businessman will not seek advantage to the point where he generates dangerous hostility among employees, competitors, customers, government, or the public at large. But decisions in this area are, in the final test, decisions of strategy, not of ethics.

The Individual and the Game

An individual within a company often finds it difficult to adjust to the requirements of the business game. He tries to preserve his private ethical standards in situations that call for game strategy. When he is obliged to carry out company policies that challenge his conception of himself as an ethical man, he suffers.

It disturbs him when he is ordered, for instance, to deny a raise to a man who deserves it, to fire an employee of long standing, to prepare advertising that he believes to be misleading, to conceal facts that he feels customers are entitled to know, to cheapen the quality of materials used in the manufacture of an established product, to sell as new a product that he knows to be rebuilt, to exaggerate the curative powers of a medicinal preparation, or to coerce dealers.

There are some fortunate executives who, by the nature of their work and circumstances, never have to face problems of this kind. But in one form or another the ethical dilemma is felt sooner or later by most businessmen. Possibly the dilemma is most painful not when the company forces the action on the executive but when he originates it himself—that is, when he has taken or is contemplating a step which is in his own interest but which runs counter to his early moral conditioning. To illustrate:

- The manager of an export department, eager to show rising sales, is pressed by a big customer to provide invoices which, while containing no overt falsehood that would violate a U.S. law, are so worded that the customer may be able to evade certain taxes in his homeland.
- A company president finds that an aging executive, within a few years of retirement and his pension, is not as productive as formerly. Should he be kept on?
- The produce manager of a supermarket debates with himself whether to get rid of a lot of half-rotten tomatoes by including one, with its good side exposed, in every tomato six-pack.
- An accountant discovers that he has taken an improper deduction on his company's tax return and fears the consequences if he calls the matter to the president's attention, though he himself has done nothing illegal. Perhaps if he says nothing, no one will notice the error.
- A chief executive officer is asked by his directors to comment on a rumor that he owns stock in another company with which he has placed large orders. He could deny it, for the stock is in the name of his son-in-law and he has earlier formally instructed his son-in-law to sell the holding.

Temptations of this kind constantly arise in business. If an executive allows himself to be torn between a decision based on business considerations and one based on his private ethical code, he exposes himself to a grave psychological strain.

This is not to say that sound business strategy necessarily runs counter to ethical ideals. They may frequently coincide; and when they do, everyone is gratified. But the major tests of every move in business, as in all games of strategy, are legality and profit. A man who intends to be a winner in the business game must have a game player's attitude.

The business strategists's decisions must be as impersonal as those of a surgeon performing an operation—concentrating on objective and technique, and subordinating personal feelings. If the chief executive admits that his son-in-law owns the stock, it is because he stands to lose more if the fact comes out later than if he states it boldly and at once. If the supermarket manager orders the rotten tomatoes to be discarded, he does so to avoid an increase in consumer complaints and a loss of goodwill. The company president decides not to fire the elderly executive in the belief that the negative reaction of other employees would in the long run cost the company more than it would lose in keeping him and paying his pension.

All sensible businessmen prefer to be truthful, but they seldom feel inclined to tell the *whole* truth. In the business game truth-telling usually has to be kept within narrow limits if trouble is to be avoided. The point was neatly made a long time ago (in 1888) by one of John D. Rockefeller's associates, Paul Babcock, to Standard Oil Company executives who were about to testify before a government investigating committee: "Parry every question with answers which, while perfectly truthful, are evasive of *bottom* facts."[12] This was, is, and probably always will be regarded as wise and permissible business strategy.

For Office Use Only

An executive's family life can easily be dislocated if he fails to make a sharp distinction between the ethical systems of the home and the office—or if his wife does not grasp that distinction. Many a businessman who has remarked to his wife, "I had to let Jones go today" or "I had to admit to the boss that Jim has been goofing off lately," has been met with an indignant protest. "How could you do a thing like that? You know Jones is over 50 and will have a lot of trouble getting another job." Or, "You did that to Jim? With his wife ill and the all the worry she's been having with the kids?"

If the executive insists that he had no choice because the profits of the company and his own security were involved, he may see a certain cool and ominous reappraisal in his wife's eyes. Many wives are not prepared to accept the fact that business operates with a special code of ethics. An illuminating illustration of this comes from a Southern sales executive who related a conversation he had had with his wife at a time when a hotly contested political campaign was being waged in their state:

> "I made the mistake of telling her that I had had lunch with Colby, who gives me about half my business. Colby mentioned that his company had a stake in the election. Then he said, 'By the way, I'm treasurer of the citizens' committee for Lang. I'm collecting contributions. Can I count on you for a hundred dollars?'
>
> "Well, there I was. I was opposed to Lang, but I knew Colby. If he withdrew his business, I could be in a bad spot. So I just smiled and wrote out a check then and there. He thanked me, and we started to talk about his next order. Maybe he thought I shared his political views. If so, I wasn't going to lose any sleep over it.
>
> "I should have had sense enough not to tell Mary about it. She hit the ceiling. She said she was disappointed in me. She said I hadn't acted like a man, that I should have stood up to Colby.
>
> "I said, 'Look, it was an either-or situation. I had to do it or risk losing the business.'

[12] *Babock in a memorandum to Rockefeller (Rockefeller Archives).*

"She came back at me with, 'I don't believe it. You could have been honest with him. You could have said that you didn't feel you ought to contribute to a campaign for a man you weren't going to vote for. I'm sure he would have understood.'

"I said, 'Mary, you're a wonderful woman, but you're way off the track. Do you know what would have happened if I had said that? Colby would have smiled and said, "Oh, I didn't realize. Forget it." But in his eyes from that moment I would be an oddball, maybe a bit of a radical. He would have listened to me talk about his order and would have promised to give it consideration. After that I wouldn't hear from him for a week. Then I would telephone and learn from his secretary that he wasn't yet ready to place the order. And in about a month I would hear through the grapevine that he was giving his business to another company. A month after that I'd be out of a job.'

"She was silent for a while. Then she said, 'Tom, something is wrong with business when a man is forced to choose between his family's security and his moral obligation to himself. It's easy for me to say you should have stood up to him—but if you had, you might have felt you were betraying me and the kids. I'm sorry that you did it, Tom, but I can't blame you. Something is wrong with business!'"

This wife saw the problem in terms of moral obligation as conceived in private life; her husband saw it as a matter of game strategy. As a player in a weak position, he felt that he could not afford to indulge an ethical sentiment that might have cost him his seat at the table.

Playing to Win

Some men might challenge the Colbys of business—might accept serious setbacks to their business careers rather than risk a feeling of moral cowardice. They merit our respect—but as private individuals, not businessmen. When the skillful player of the business game is compelled to submit to unfair pressure, he does not castigate himself for moral weakness. Instead, he strives to put himself into a strong position where he can defend himself against such pressures in the future without loss.

If a man plans to take a seat in the business game, he owes it to himself to master the principles by which the game is played, including its special ethical outlook. He can then hardly fail to recognize that an occasional bluff may well be justified in terms of the game's ethics and warranted in terms of economic necessity. Once he clears his mind on this point, he is in a good position to match his strategy against that of the other players. He can then determine objectively whether a bluff in a given situation has a good chance of succeeding and can decide when and how to bluff, without a feeling of ethical transgression.

To be a winner, a man must play to win. This does not mean that he must be ruthless, cruel, harsh, or treacherous. On the contrary, the better his reputation for integrity, honesty, and decency, the better his chances of victory will be in the long run. But from time to time every businessman, like every poker player, is offered a choice between certain loss or bluffing within the legal rules of the game. If he is not resigned to losing, if he wants to rise in his company and industry, then in such a crisis he will bluff—and bluff hard.

Every now and then one meets a successful businessman who has conveniently forgotten the small or large deceptions that he practiced on his way to fortune. "God gave me my money," old John D. Rockefeller once piously told a Sunday school class. It would be a rare tycoon in our time who would risk the horse laugh with which such a remark would be greeted.

In the last third of the twentieth century even children are aware that if a man has become prosperous in business, he has sometimes departed from the strict truth in order to overcome obstacles or has practiced the more subtle deceptions of the half-truth or the misleading omission. Whatever the form of the bluff, it is an integral part of the game, and the executive who does not master its techniques is not likely to accumulate much money or power.

Discussion Questions

1. Do you agree or disagree with Carr's premise?
2. Does everyone operate at the same level of bluffing?
3. How is the phrase "sound ethics is good business" characterized?

READING 1.6

Ethics Without the Sermon[13]

Business ethicist and professor Laura Nash has developed a series of questions for resolving ethical dilemmas that are covered in the following article. Her insights are particularly helpful in those cases in which the conduct has already occurred and you will be providing some recommendations on how the business or individual could prevent these types of dilemmas from occurring again.

Laura L. Nash

As if via a network TV program on the telecommunications satellite, declarations such as these are being broadcast throughout the land:

> *Scene 1.* Annual meeting, Anyproducts Inc.; John Q. Moneypockets, chairman and CEO, speaking: "Our responsibility to the public has always come first at our company, and we continue to strive toward serving our public in the best way possible in the belief that good ethics is good business. . . . Despite our forecast of a continued recession in the industry through 1982, we are pleased to announce that 1981's earnings per share were up for the twenty-sixth year in a row."
>
> *Scene 2.* Corporate headquarters, Anyproducts Inc.; Linda Diesinker, group vice president, speaking: "Of course we're concerned about minority development and the plight of the inner cities. But the best place for our new plant would be Horsepasture, Minnesota. We need a lot of space for our operations and a skilled labor force, and the demographics and tax incentives in Horsepasture are perfect."

[13] *Reprinted by permission of* Harvard Business Review. *From "Ethics Without the Sermon," by Laura L. Nash, Vol. 59, November/December 1981. Copyright © 1981 by the Harvard Business School Publishing Corporation; all rights reserved.*

Scene 3. Interview with a financial writer; Rafe Shortstop, president, Anyproducts Inc., speaking: "We're very concerned about the state of American business and our ability to compete with foreign companies. . . . No, I don't think we have any real ethical problems. We don't bribe people or anything like that."

Scene 4. Jud McFisticuff, taxi driver, speaking: "Anyproducts? You've got to be kidding! I wouldn't buy their stuff for anything. The last thing of theirs I bought fell apart in six months. And did you see how they were dumping wastes in the Roxburg water system?"

Scene 5. Leslie Matriculant, MBA '82, speaking: "Join Anyproducts? I don't want to risk my reputation working for a company like that. They recently acquired a business that turned out to have ten class-action discrimination suits against it. And when Anyproducts tried to settle the whole thing out of court, the president had his picture in *Business Week* with the caption, 'His secretary still serves him coffee.'"

Whether you regard it as an unchecked epidemic or as the first blast of Gabriel's horn, the trend toward focusing on the social impact of the corporation is an inescapable reality that must be factored into today's managerial decision making. But for the executive who asks, "How do we as a corporation examine our ethical concerns?" the theoretical insights currently available may be more frustrating than helpful.

As the first scene in this article implies, many executives firmly believe that corporate operations and corporate values are dynamically intertwined. For the purposes of analysis, however, the executive needs to uncoil the business-ethics helix and examine both strands closely.

Unfortunately, the ethics strand has remained largely inaccessible, for business has not yet developed a workable process by which corporate values can be articulated. If ethics and business are part of the same double helix, perhaps we can develop a microscope capable of enlarging our perception of both aspects of business administration—what we do and who we are. . . .

What is needed is a process of ethical inquiry that is immediately comprehensible to a group of executives and not predisposed to the utopian, and sometimes anticapitalistic, bias marking much of the work in applied business philosophy today. So I suggest, as a preliminary solution, a set of twelve questions that draw on traditional philosophical frameworks but that avoid the level of abstraction normally associated with formal moral reasoning.

I offer the questions as a first step in a very new discipline. As such, they form a tentative model that will certainly undergo modifications after its parts are given some exercise.

To illustrate the application of the questions, I will draw especially on a program at Lex Service Group, Ltd., whose top management prepared a statement of financial objectives and moral values as a part of its strategic planning process.[14] Lex is a British company with operations in the United Kingdom and the United States. Its sales total

[14] *The process is modeled after ideas in Kenneth R. Andrew's book* The Concept of Corporate Strategy *(New York, McGraw-Hill Companies, Inc., 1980, revised edition) and in Richard F. Vancil's article "Strategy Formulation in Complex Organizations,"* Sloan Management Review, *Winter 1976, p. 4.*

about $1.2 billion. In 1978 its structure was partially decentralized, and in 1979 the chairman's policy group began a strategic planning process. The intent, according to its statement of values and objectives, was "to make explicit the sort of company Lex was, or wished to be."

Neither a paralegal code nor a generalized philosophy, the statement consisted of a series of general policies regarding financial strategy as well as such aspects of the company's character as customer service, employee-shareholder responsibility, and quality of management. Its content largely reflected the personal values of Lex's chairman and CEO, Trevor Chinn, whose private philanthropy is well known and whose concern for social welfare has long been echoed in the company's personnel policies.

In the past, pressure on senior managers for high profit performance had obscured some of these ideals in practice, and the statement of strategy was a way of radically realigning various competing moral claims with the financial objectives of the company. As one senior manager remarked to me, "The values seem obvious, and if we hadn't been so gross in the past we wouldn't have needed the statement." Despite a predictable variance among Lex's top executives as to the desirability of the values outlined in the statement, it was adopted with general agreement to comply and was scheduled for reassessment at a senior managers' meeting one year after implementation.

The Twelve Questions

1. Have you defined the problem accurately?

How one assembles the facts weights an issue before the moral examination ever begins, and a definition is rarely accurate if it articulates one's loyalties rather than the facts. The importance of factual neutrality is readily seen, for example, in assessing the moral implications of producing a chemical agent for use in warfare. Depending on one's loyalties, the decision to make the substance can be described as serving one's country, developing products, or killing babies. All of the above may be factual statements, but none is neutral or accurate if viewed in isolation.

Similarly, the recent controversy over marketing U.S.-made cigarettes in Third World countries rarely noted that the incidence of lung cancer in underdeveloped nations is quite low (from one-tenth to one-twentieth the rate for U.S. males) due primarily to the lower life expectancies and earlier predominance of other diseases in these nations. Such a fact does not decide the ethical complexities of this marketing problem, but it does add a crucial perspective in the assignment of moral priorities by defining precisely the injury that tobacco exports may cause. . . .

Extensive fact gathering may also help defuse the emotionalism of an issue. For instance, local statistics on lung cancer incidence reveal that the U.S. tobacco industry is not now "exporting death," as has been charged. Moreover, the substantial and immediate economic benefits attached to tobacco may be providing food and health care in these countries. Nevertheless, as life expectancy and the standards of living rise, a higher incidence of cigarette-related diseases appears likely to develop in these nations. Therefore, cultivation of the nicotine habit may be deemed detrimental to the long-term welfare of these nations.

According to one supposedly infallible truth of modernism, technology is so complex that its results will never be fully comprehensible or predictable. Part of the executive's frustration in responding to Question 1 is the real possibility that the "experts" will find no grounds for agreement about the facts.

As a first step, however, defining fully the factual implications of a decision determines to a large degree the quality of one's subsequent moral position. Pericles' definition of true courage rejected the Spartans' blind obedience in war in preference to the courage of the Athenian citizen who, he said, was able to make a decision to proceed in full knowledge of the probable danger. A truly moral decision is an informed decision. A decision that is based on blind or convenient ignorance is hardly defensible.

One simple test of the initial definition is the question:

2. How would you define the problem if you stood on the other side of the fence?

The contemplated construction of a plant for Division X is touted at the finance committee meeting as an absolute necessity for expansion at a cost saving of at least 25%. With plans drawn up for an energy-efficient building and an option already secured on a 99-year lease in a new industrial part in Chippewa County, the committee is likely to feel comfortable in approving the request for funds in a matter of minutes.

The facts of the matter are that the company will expand in an appropriate market, allocate its resources sensibly, create new jobs, increase Chippewa County's tax base, and most likely increase its returns to the shareholders. To the residents of Chippewa County, however, the plant may mean the destruction of a customary recreation spot, the onset of severe traffic jams, and the erection of an architectural eyesore. These are also facts of the situation, and certainly more immediate to the county than utilitarian justifications of profit performance and rights of ownership from an impersonal corporation whose headquarters are 1,000 miles from Chippewa County and whose executives have plenty of acreage for their own recreation.

The purpose of articulating the other side, whose needs are understandably less proximate than operational considerations, is to allow some mechanism whereby calculations of self-interest (or even of a project's ultimate general beneficence) can be interrupted by a compelling empathy for those who might suffer immediate injury or mere annoyance as a result of a corporation's decisions. Such empathy is a necessary prerequisite for shouldering voluntarily some responsibility for the social consequences of corporate operations, and it may be the only solution to today's overly litigious and anarchic world.

There is a power in self-examination: with an exploration of the likely consequences of a proposal, taken from the viewpoint of those who do not immediately benefit, comes a discomfort or an embarrassment that rises in proportion to the degree of the likely injury and its articulation. Like Socrates as gadfly, who stung his fellow citizens into a critical examination of their conduct when they became complacent, the discomfort of the alternative definition is meant to prompt a disinclination to choose the expedient over the most responsible course of action.

Abstract generalities about the benefits of the profit motive and the free market system are, for some, legitimate and ultimate justifications, but when unadorned with alternative viewpoints, such arguments also tend to promote the complacency, carelessness, and impersonality that have characterized some of the more injurious actions of corporations. The advocates of these arguments are like the reformers in Nathaniel Hawthorne's short story "Hall of Fantasy" who "had got possession of some crystal fragment of truth, the brightness of which so dazzled them that they could see nothing else in the whole universe."

In the example of Division X's new plant, it was a simple matter to define the alternate facts; the process rested largely on an assumption that certain values were commonly shared (no one likes a traffic jam, landscaping pleases more than an unadorned building, and so forth). But the alternative definition often underscores an inherent disparity in values or language. To some, the employment of illegal aliens is a criminal act (fact #1); to others, it is a solution to the 60% unemployment rate of a neighboring country (fact #2). One country's bribe is another country's redistribution of sales commissions.

When there are cultural or linguistic disparities, it is easy to get the facts wrong or to invoke a pluralistic tolerance as an excuse to act in one's own self-interest: "That's the way they do things over there. Who are we to question their beliefs?" This kind of reasoning can be both factually inaccurate (many generalizations about bribery rest on hearsay and do not represent the complexities of a culture) and philosophically inconsistent (there are plenty of beliefs, such as those of the environmentalist, which the same generalizers do not hesitate to question).

3. How did this situation occur in the first place?

Lex Motor Company, a subsidiary of Lex Service Group, Ltd., had been losing [market] share at a 20% rate in a declining market; and Depot B's performance was the worst of all. Two nearby Lex depots could easily absorb B's business, and closing it down seemed the only sound financial decision. Lex's chairman, Trevor Chinn, hesitated to approve the closure, however, on the grounds that putting 100 people out of work was not right when the corporation itself was not really jeopardized by B's existence. Moreover, seven department managers, who were all within five years of retirement and had 25 or more years of service at Lex, were scheduled to be made redundant.

The values statement provided no automatic solution, for it placed value on both employees' security and shareholders' interest. Should they close Depot B? At first Chinn thought not: Why should the little guys suffer disproportionately when the company was not performing well? Why not close a more recently acquired business where employee service was not so large a factor? Or why not wait out the short term and reduce head count through natural attrition?

As important as deciding the ethics of the situation was the inquiry into its history. Indeed, the history gave a clue to solving the dilemma: Lex's traditional emphasis on employee security *and* high financial performance had led to a precipitate series of acquisitions and subsequent divestitures when the company had failed to meet its overall objectives. After each rationalization, the people serving the longest had been retained and placed at Depot B, so that by 1980 the facility had more managers than it needed and a very high proportion of long-service employees.

So the very factors that had created the performance problems were making the closure decision difficult, and the very solution that Lex was inclined to favor again would exacerbate the situation further!

In deciding the ethics of a situation it is important to distinguish the symptoms from the disease. Great profit pressures with no sensitivity to the cycles in a particular industry, for example, may force division managers to be ruthless with employees, to short-weight customers, or even to fiddle with cash flow reports in order to meet headquarters' performance criteria.

Dealing with the immediate case of lying, quality discrepancy, or strained labor relations—when the problem is finally discovered—is only a temporary solution. A full examination of how the situation occurred and what the traditional solutions have been may reveal a more serious discrepancy of values and pressures, and this will illuminate the real significance and ethics of the problem. It will also reveal recurring patterns of events that in isolation appear trivial but that as a whole point up a serious situation.

Such a mechanism is particularly important because very few executives are outright scoundrels. Rather, violations of corporate and social values usually occur inadvertently because no one recognizes that a problem exists until it becomes a crisis. This tendency toward initial trivialization seems to be the biggest ethical problem in business today. Articulating answers to my first three questions is a way of reversing that process.

4. To whom and what do you give your loyalties as a person and as a member of the corporation?

Every executive faces conflicts of loyalty. The most familiar occasions pit private conscience and sense of duty against corporate policy, but equally frequent are the situations in which one's close colleagues demand participation (tacit or explicit) in an operation or a decision that runs counter to company policy. To whom or what is the greater loyalty—to one's corporation? superior? family? society? self? race? sex?

The good news about conflicts of loyalty is that their identification is a workable way of smoking out the ethics of a situation and of discovering the absolute values inherent in it. As one executive in a discussion of a Harvard case study put it, "My corporate brain says this action is O.K., but my noncorporate brain keeps flashing these warning lights."

The bad news about conflicts of loyalty is that there are few automatic answers to placing priorities on them. "To thine own self be true" is a murky quagmire when the self takes on a variety of roles, as it does so often in this complex modern world.

Supposedly, today's young managers are giving more weight to individual than to corporate identity, and some older executives see this tendency as being ultimately subversive. At the same time, most of them believe individual integrity is essential to a company's reputation.

The U.S. securities industry, for example, is one of the most rigorous industries in America in its requirements of honesty and disclosure. Yet in the end, all its systematic precautions prove inadequate unless the people involved also have a strong sense of integrity that puts loyalty to these principles above personal gain.

A system, however, must permit the time and foster the motivation to allow personal integrity to surface in a particular situation. An examination of loyalties is one way to bring this about. Such an examination may strengthen reputations but also may result in blowing the whistle (freedom of thought carries with it the risk of revolution). But a sorting out of loyalties can also bridge the gulf between policy and implementation or among various interest groups whose affiliations may mask a common devotion to an aspect of a problem—a devotion on which consensus can be built.

How does one probe into one's own loyalties and their implications? A useful method is simply to play various roles out loud, to call on one's loyalty to family and community (for example) by asking, "What will I say when my child asks me why I did that?" If the answer is "That's the way the world works," then your loyalties are clear and moral passivity inevitable. But if the question presents real problems, you have begun a demodulation of signals from your conscience that can only enhance corporate responsibility.

5. What is your intention in making this decision?

6. How does this intention compare with the likely results?

These two questions are asked together because their content often bears close resemblance and, by most calculations, both color the ethics of a situation.

Corporation Buglebloom decides to build a new plant in an underdeveloped minority-populated district where the city has been trying with little success to encourage industrial development. The media approve and Buglebloom adds another star to its good reputation. Is Buglebloom a civic leader and a supporter of minorities or a canny investor about to take advantage of the disadvantaged? The possibilities of Buglebloom's intentions are endless and probably unfathomable to the public; Buglebloom may be both canny investor and friend of minority groups.

I argue that despite their complexity and elusiveness, a company's intentions do matter. The "purity" of Buglebloom's motives (purely profit-seeking or purely altruistic) will have wide-reaching effects inside and outside the corporation—on attitudes toward minority employees in other parts of the company, on the wages paid at the new plant, and on the number of other investors in the same area—that will legitimize a certain ethos in the corporation and the community.

Sociologist Max Weber called this an "ethics of attitude" and contrasted it with an "ethics of absolute ends." An ethics of attitude sets a standard to ensure a certain action. A firm policy at headquarters of not cheating customers, for example, may also deter salespeople from succumbing to a tendency to lie by omission or purchasers from continuing to patronize a high-priced supplier when the costs are automatically passed on in the selling price.

What about the ethics of result? Two years later, Buglebloom wishes it had never begun Project Minority Plant. Every good intention has been lost in the realities of doing business in an unfamiliar area, and Buglebloom now has dirty hands: some of those payoffs were absolutely unavoidable if the plant was to open, operations have been plagued with vandalism—and language problems, and local resentment at the industrialization of the neighborhood has risen as charges of discrimination have surfaced. No one seems to be benefitting from the project.

The goodness of intent pales somewhat before results that perpetrate great injury or simply do little good. Common sense demands that the "responsible" corporation try to align the two more closely, to identify the probable consequences and also the limitations of knowledge that might lead to more harm than good. Two things to remember in comparing intention and results are that knowledge of the future is always inadequate and that overconfidence often precedes a disastrous mistake.

These two precepts, cribbed from ancient Greece, may help the corporation keep the disparities between intent and result a fearsome reality to consider continuously. The next two questions explore two ways of reducing the moral risks of being wrong.

7. Whom could your decision or action injure?

The question presses whether injury is intentional or not. Given the limits of knowledge about a new product or policy, who and how many will come into contact with it? Could its inadequate disposal affect an entire community? two employees? yourself? How might your product be used if it happened to be acquired by a terrorist radical group or a terrorist military police force? Has your distribution system or disposal plan ensured against such injury? Could it ever?

If not, there may be a compelling moral justification for stopping production. In an integrated society where business and government share certain values, possible injury is an even more important consideration than potential benefit. In policymaking, a much likelier ground for agreement than benefit is avoidance of injury through those "universal nos"—such as no mass death, no totalitarianism, no hunger or malnutrition, no harm to children.

To exclude *at the outset* any policy or decision that might have such results is to reshape the way modern business examines its own morality. So often business formulates questions of injury only after the fact in the form of liability suits.

8. Can you engage the affected parties in a discussion of the problem before you make your decision?

If the calculus of injury is one way of responding to limitations of knowledge about the probable results of a particular business decision, the participation of affected parties is one of the best ways of informing that consideration. Civil rights groups often complain that corporations fail to invite participation from local leaders during the planning stages of community development projects and charitable programs. The corporate foundation that builds a tennis complex for disadvantaged youth is throwing away precious resources if most children in the neighborhood suffer from chronic malnutrition.

In the Lex depot closure case I have mentioned, senior executives agonized over whether the employees would choose redundancy over job transfer and which course would ultimately be more beneficial to them. The managers, however, did not consult the employees. There were more than 200 projected job transfers to another town. But all the affected employees, held by local ties and uneasy about possibly lower housing subsidies, refused relocation offers. Had the employees been allowed to participate in the redundancy discussions, the company might have wasted less time on relocation plans or might have uncovered and resolved the fears about relocating.

The issue of participation affects everyone. (How many executives feel that someone else should decide what is in *their* best interest?) And yet it is a principle often forgotten because of the pressure of time or the inconvenience of calling people together and facing predictably hostile questions.

9. Are you confident that your position will be as valid over a long period of time as it seems now?

As anyone knows who has had to consider long-range plans and short-term budgets simultaneously, a difference in time frame can change the meaning of a problem as much as spring and autumn change the colors of a tree. The ethical coloring of a business decision is no exception to this generational aspect of decision making. Time alters circumstances, and few corporate value systems are immune to shifts in financial status, external political pressure, and personnel. (One survey now places the average U.S. CEO's tenure in office at five years.)

At Lex, for example, the humanitarianism of the statement of objectives and values depended on financial prosperity. The values did not fully anticipate the extent to which the U.K. economy would undergo a recession, and the resulting changes had to be examined, reconciled, and fought if the company's values were to have any meaning. At the Lex annual review, the managers asked themselves repeatedly whether hard times were the ultimate test of the statement or a clear indication that a corporation had to be able to "afford" ethical positions.

Ideally, a company's articulation of its values should anticipate changes of fortune. As the hearings for the passage of the Foreign Corrupt Practices Act of 1977 demonstrated, doing what you can get away with today may not be a secure moral standard, but short-term discomfort for long-term sainthood may require irrational courage or a rational reasoning system or, more likely, both. These twelve questions attempt to elicit a rational system. Courage, of course, depends on personal integrity.

Another aspect of the ethical time frame stretches beyond the boundaries of Question 9 but deserves special attention, and that is the timing of the ethical inquiry. When and where will it be made?

We do not normally invoke moral principles in our everyday conduct. Some time ago the participants in a national business ethics conference had worked late into the night preparing the final case for the meeting, and they were very anxious the next morning to get the class under way. Just before the session began, however, someone suggested that they all donate a dollar apiece as a gratuity for the dining hall help at the institute.

Then just as everyone automatically reached into his or her pocket, another person questioned the direction of the gift. Why tip the person behind the counter but not the cook in the kitchen? Should the money be given to each person in proportion to salary or divided equally among all? The participants laughed uneasily—or groaned—as they thought of the diversion of precious time from the case. A decision had to be made.

With the sure instincts of efficient managers, the group chose to forgo further discussion of distributive justice and, yes, appoint a committee. The committee doled out the money without further group consideration, and no formal feedback on the donation was asked for or given.

The questions offered here do not solve the problem of making time for the inquiry.

10. Could you disclose without qualm your decision or action to your boss, your CEO, the board of directors, your family, or society as a whole?

The old question, "Would you want your decision to appear on the front page of *The New York Times*?" still holds. A corporation may maintain that there's really no problem, but a survey of how many "trivial" actions it is reluctant to disclose might be interesting. Disclosure is a way of sounding those submarine depths of conscience and of searching out loyalties.

It is also a way of keeping a corporate character cohesive. The Lex Group, for example, was once faced with a very sticky problem concerning a small but profitable site with unpleasant (though in no way illegal) working conditions, where two men with 30 years' service worked. I wrote up the case for a Lex senior managers' meeting on the promise to disguise it heavily because the executive who supervised the plant was convinced that, if the chairman and the personnel director knew the plant's true location, they would close it down immediately.

At the meeting, however, as everyone became involved in the discussion and the chairman himself showed sensitivity to the dilemma, the executive disclosed the location and spoke of his own feelings about the situation. The level of mutual confidence was apparent to all, and by other reports it was the most open discussion the group had ever had.

The meeting also fostered understanding of the company's values and their implementation. When the discussion finally flagged, the chairman spoke up. Basing his views on a full knowledge of the group's understanding of the problem, he set the company's priorities. "Jobs over fancy conditions, health over jobs," Chinn said, "but we always *must disclose*." The group decided to keep the plant open, at least for the time being.

Disclosure does not, however, automatically bring universal sympathy. In the early 1970s, a large food store chain that repeatedly found itself embroiled in the United Farm Workers (UFW) disputes with the Teamsters over California grape and lettuce contracts took very seriously the moral implications of a decision whether to stop selling these products. The company endlessly researched the issues, talked to all sides, and made itself available to public representatives of various interest groups to explain its position and to hear out everyone else.

When the controversy started, the company decided to support the UFW boycott, but three years later top management reversed its position. Most of the people who wrote to the company or asked it to send representatives to their local UFW support meetings, however, continued to condemn the chain even after hearing its views, and the general public apparently never became aware of the company's side of the story.

11. What is the symbolic potential of your action if understood? if misunderstood?

Jones Inc., a diversified multinational corporation with assets of $5 billion, has a paper manufacturing operation that happens to be the only major industry in Stirville, and the factory has been polluting the river on which it is located. Local and national conservation groups have filed suit against Jones Inc. for past damages, and the company is defending itself. Meanwhile, the corporation has adopted plans for a new waste-efficient plant. The legal battle is extended and local resentment against Jones Inc. gets bitter.

As a settlement is being reached, Jones Inc. announces that, as a civic-minded gesture, it will make 400 acres of Stirville woodland it owns available to the residents for conservation and recreation purposes. Jones's intention is to offer a peace pipe to the people of Stirville, and the company sees the gift as a symbol of its own belief in conservation and a way of signaling that value to Stirville residents and national conservation groups. Should Jones Inc. give the land away? Is the symbolism significant?

If the symbolic value of the land is understood as Jones Inc. intends, the gift may patch up the company's relations with Stirville and stave off further disaffection with potential employees as the new plant is being built. It may also signal to employees throughout the corporation that Jones Inc. places a premium on conservation efforts and community relations.

If the symbolic value is misunderstood, however, or if completion of the plant is delayed and the old one has to be put back in use—or if another Jones operation is discovered to be polluting another community and becomes a target of the press—the gift could be interpreted as nothing more than a cheap effort to pay off the people of Stirville and hasten settlement of the lawsuit.

The Greek root of our word *symbol* means both signal and contract. A business decision—whether it is the use of an expense account or a corporate donation—has a symbolic value in signaling what is acceptable behavior within the corporate culture and in making a tacit contract with employees and the community about the rules of the game. How the symbol is actually perceived (or misperceived) is as important as how you intend it to be perceived.

12. Under what conditions would you allow exceptions to your stand?

If we accept the idea that every business decision has an important symbolic value and a contractual nature, then the need for consistency is obvious. At the same time, it is also important to ask under what conditions the rules of the game may be changed. What conflicting principles, circumstances, or time constraints would provide a morally acceptable basis for making an exception to one's non-normal institutional ethos? For instance, how does the cost of the strategy to develop managers from minority groups over the long term fit in with short-term hurdle rates? Also to be considered is what would mitigate a clear case of employee dishonesty.

Questions of consistency—if you would do X, would you also do Y?—are yet another way of eliciting the ethics of the company and of oneself, and can be a final test of the strength, idealism, or practicality of those values. A last example from the experience of Lex illustrates this point and gives temporary credence to the platitude that good ethics is good business. An article in the Sunday paper about a company that had run a series of racy ads, with pictures of half-dressed women and promises of free merchandise to promote the sale of a very mundane product, sparked an extended examination at Lex of its policies on corporate inducements.

One area of concern was holiday giving. What was the acceptable limit for a gift—a bottle of whiskey? a case? Did it matter only that the company did not *intend* the gift to be an inducement, or did the mere possibility of inducement taint the gift? Was the cut-off point absolute? The group could agree on no halfway point for allowing some gifts and not others, so a new value was added to the formal statement that prohibited the offering or receiving of inducements.

The next holiday season Chinn sent a letter to friends and colleagues who had received gifts of appreciation in the past. In it he explained that, as a result of Lex's concern with "the very complex area of business ethics," management had decided that the company would no longer send any gifts, nor would it be appropriate for its employees to receive any. Although the letter did not explain Lex's reasoning behind the decision, apparently there was a large untapped consensus about such gift giving: by return mail Chinn received at least twenty letters from directors, general managers, and chairmen of companies with which Lex had done business congratulating him for his decision, agreeing with the new policy, and thanking him for his holiday wishes. . . .

The situations for testing business morality remain complex. But by avoiding theoretical inquiry and limiting the expectations of corporate goodness to a few rules for social behavior that are based on common sense, we can develop an ethic that is appropriate to the language, ideology, and institutional dynamics of business decision making and consensus. This ethic can also offer managers a practical way of exploring those occasions when their corporate brains are getting warning flashes from their noncorporate brains.

Discussion Questions

1. What questions help resolve the issue of whether to accept gifts from suppliers at Christmas?
2. What is "ethics of attitude"? What is "ethics of absolute ends"?
3. Why are history and future important in the Laura Nash model?

READING 1.7

Other Models for Resolution of Business Ethics Dilemmas

There are others who have offered their insights on the resolution of ethical dilemmas. The following sections offer summaries of the thoughts and models of others in the field.

Blanchard and Peale

The late Dr. Norman Vincent Peale and management expert Kenneth Blanchard offer three questions that managers should ponder in resolving ethical dilemmas: Is it legal? Is it balanced? How does it make me feel?

If the answer to the first question, "Is it legal?" is no, a manager should not proceed any further. An examination of the Justice Department's antitrust case against some of the country's best and largest universities demonstrates that managers still fail to ask the basic ethical question of whether they are in compliance with the law. In that case, twenty-two large private northeastern universities had agreed to offer the same financial aid packages to students, so that students' decisions on which institution to attend were based on factors other than the level of financial aid. This loan package arrangement was nothing more than an agreement on price; antitrust laws prohibit such agreements.

Answering the second question, "Is it balanced?" requires a manager to step back and view a problem from other perspectives—those of other parties, owners, shareholders, or the community. For example, an M&M/Mars cacao buyer was able to secure a very low price on cacao for his company because of pending government takeovers and political disruption. M&M/Mars officers decided to pay more for the cacao than the negotiated figure. Their reason was that some day their company would not have the upper hand, and then they would want to be treated fairly when the price became the seller's choice.

Answering "How does it make me feel?" requires a manager to do a self-examination of the comfort level of a decision. Some decisions, though they may be legal and may appear balanced, can still make a manager uncomfortable. For example, many managers feel uncomfortable about the "management" of earnings when inventory and shipments are controlled to maximize bonuses or to produce a particularly good result for a quarter. Although they've done nothing illegal, managers who engage in such practices often suffer such physical effects as insomnia and appetite problems.

The Front-Page-of-the-Newspaper Test

One very simple ethical model requires only that a decision maker envision how a reporter would describe a decision on the front page of a local or national newspaper. For example, with regard to the NBC News report on the sidesaddle gas tanks in GM pickup trucks, the *USA Today* headline read: "GM Suit Attacks NBC Report: Says show faked fiery truck crash." Would NBC have made the same decisions about its staging of the truck crash if that headline had been foreseen?

When Salomon Brothers' illegal cornering of the U.S. government's bond market was revealed, the *Business Week* headline read: "How Bad Will It Get?"; nearly two years later, a follow-up story on Salomon's crisis strategy was headlined "The Bomb Shelter That Salomon Built." During the aftermath of the bond market scandal, the interim chairman of Salomon, Warren Buffet, told employees, "Contemplating any business act, an employee should ask himself whether he would be willing to see it immediately described by an informed and critical reporter on the front page of his local paper, there to be read by his spouse, children, and friends. At Salomon we simply want no part of any activities that pass legal tests but that we, as citizens, would find offensive."

Dow Corning might have made different decisions about disclosures on its silicone breast implants if it had envisioned such headlines as "Breast Implants: What Did the Industry Know, and When?" from *Business Week* shortly after a woman won a $4 million verdict for permanent injury resulting from her implants.

The Wall Street Journal Model

The Wall Street Journal model for resolution of ethical dilemmas consists of compliance, contribution, and consequences. Like the Blanchard-Peale model, any proposed conduct must first be in compliance with the law. The next step requires an evaluation of a decision's contributions to the shareholders, the employees, the community, and the customers. For example, furniture manufacturer Herman Miller decided both to invest in equipment that would exceed the requirements for compliance with the 1990 Clean Air Act and to refrain from using rain forest woods in producing its signature Eames chair. The decision was costly to the shareholders at first, but ultimately they, the community, and customers enjoyed the benefits.

Finally, managers are asked to envision the consequences of a decision, such as whether headlines that are unfavorable to the firm may result. The initial consequences for Miller's decisions were a reduction in profits because of the costs of the changes. However, the long-term consequences were the respect of environmental regulators, a responsive public committed to rain forest preservation, and Miller's recognition by *Business Week* as an outstanding firm for 1992.

Other Models

Of course, there are much simpler models for making ethical business decisions. One, the antithesis of the Carr model, stems from Immanuel Kant's categorical imperative, loosely similar to the Golden Rule of: "Do unto others as you would have them do unto you." Treating others or others' money as we would want to be treated is a powerful evaluation technique in ethical dilemmas. Another way of looking at issues is to apply your standards in all situations and think about whether you would be comfortable. In other words, if the world lived by your personal ethical standards, would you be comfortable or would you be nervous? Many of us are terribly shocked when someone dents our car in a parking lot and fails to leave a note, but would we leave a note when we are the ones who have done the damage?

1C

Applying the Foundations of Business Ethics

READING 1.8

Trying Out the Models and a Resolution Approach

While you now have a list of the categories of ethical breaches and many different models for resolution, you may still be wondering about the process for analyzing cases. What follows is a suggested approach for these cases so that you can provide an in-depth analysis from all perspectives.

Steps for Analyzing Ethical Dilemmas and Case Studies in Business

1. Make sure you have a grasp of all of the facts available.
2. List any information you would like to have but don't and what assumptions you would have to make, if any, in resolving the dilemma.
3. Take each person involved in the dilemma and list the concerns they face or might have. Be sure to consider the impact on those not specifically mentioned in the case. For example, product safety issues don't involve just engineers' careers and company profits; shareholders, customers, customers' families, and even communities supported by the business are affected by a business decision on what to do about a product and its safety issue.
4. Develop a list of resolutions for the problem. Apply the various models for reaching this resolution. You may also find that as you apply the various models to the dilemma you find additional insights for questions 1, 2, and 3. If the breach has already occurred, consider the possible remedies and develop systemic changes so that such breaches do not occur in the future.
5. Evaluate the resolutions for costs, legalities, and impact. Try to determine how each of the parties will react to and will be affected by each of the resolutions you have proposed.
6. Make a recommendation on the actions that should be taken.

In some of the cases you will be evaluating the ethics of conduct after the fact. In those situations, your recommendations and resolutions will center on reforms and perhaps recompense for the parties affected.

Each case in this book requires you to examine different perspectives and analyze the impact that the resolution of a dilemma has on the parties involved. Return to these models to question the propriety of the actions taken in each case. Examine the origins of the ethical dilemmas and explore possible solutions. As you work through the cases, you will find yourself developing a new awareness of values and their importance in making business decisions. Try your hand at a few before proceeding to the following sections. The two following, rather short, cases offer an opportunity for application of the materials from this section and give you the chance to hone your skills for ethical resolutions.

CASE 1.9

Barbara Walters and Her Andrew Lloyd Webber Conflict

Barbara Walters is a network correspondent for ABC News as well as a co-host of the ABC prime-time news show *20/20.* In December 1996, Ms. Walters interviewed British composer, Andrew Lloyd Webber, now Sir Andrew Lloyd Webber, and the interview aired the same month as a segment on *20/20.*

Two months after the interview aired, a report in the *New York Post* revealed that Ms. Walters had invested $100,000 in Webber's Broadway production of his musical, *Sunset Boulevard.* ABC News responded that had it known of the investment, it would have disclosed it before the interview aired. ABC does have a policy on conflicts that permits correspondents to cover "businesses in which they have a minority interest."

Webber's *Sunset* cost $10 million to produce and investors received back 85% of their initial investment. Ms. Walters' interest in *Sunset* was one percent.

Ms. Walters acknowledged a mistake, "In retrospect, I should have discussed it. I didn't even think about it."[15]

Discussion Questions

1. What interests are in conflict on the part of Ms. Walters?
2. When should she have disclosed her investment? When it was made, before she did the interview, or before the show aired?

[15] *Peter Johnson, "Walters Missed Her Cue to Disclose 'Sunset' Backing,"* USA Today, *February 20, 1997, 3D.*

3. In a recent *20/20* show, Ms. Walters, in announcing a segment on the *Jerry Springer* show said that her day-time program, *The View*, is seen opposite *Jerry Springer* and that she had no part in the idea for or production of the *20/20* segment. Why did Ms. Walters make this disclosure?

Some Help for You on the Barbara Walters Case

To help you in your analysis, consider the following list of the parties affected by this dilemma:

1. Ms. Walters—her credibility as a journalist is affected if there is an actual conflict or the appearance of a conflict.
2. ABC News and *20/20*—while the producers and others associated with the show and the news division may not have known of Ms. Walters' investment, they are affected by the post-show disclosure of it in terms of their credibility.
3. Viewers—even unintentional conflicts cause viewers to lose trust.
4. Mr. Webber, the new show, *Sunset Boulevard*, his investors—his credibility is affected by the undisclosed conflict and controversy.
5. Ticket holders for the new show—those who purchased tickets based on what they thought was news coverage may feel they were taken advantage of and future ticket holders may not be willing to purchase until they feel there is a more objective evaluation.

To assist you in your analysis, consider the following categories:

Conflict of interest—Ms. Walters has an economic interest in the show doing well and that interest was at odds with her journalistic role, which is one of objective reporting.

Giving or allowing false impression—Ms. Walters played the role of an objective journalist when she was really a journalist who had an investment in a critical project of the subject of her interview.

To assist you in your analysis, think about the following:

Because the conduct has already occurred, your role becomes one of recommendation. You need to provide a recommendation that affords protection to all the parties listed as affected by the conduct. For example, to protect the credibility of the news organization, there will need to be a policy on journalists' disclosures of conflicts of interest, including any investments they hold with the companies or projects of the subjects of their interviews. That policy may not only require disclosure but also withdrawal from certain stories if the conflict seems too difficult to overcome. There are two ways to fix a conflict of interest: don't do it or disclose it to those affected. Sometimes disclosure is insufficient and one party must not engage in the conduct. It seems as if Ms. Walters has begun adhering to such a policy as she made her disclosure on her other show and also declined to be part of the story.

Now, try your hand at this case, another one in which the conduct has already occurred and you will be making recommendations.

CASE 1.10

The Rigged Election

The Finance Club at Harvard University is a prestigious organization for Harvard MBA students. The student members have the opportunity to interact with public officials like Senator William Proxmire and business executives such as Bruce Wasserstein. The Finance Club also serves as a network for job hunting.

Each spring, the club holds elections for its officers, including two co-presidents. In the spring of 1992, after initial balloting, there was a tie between two teams of two co-presidents. Murry Gunty was one member of one of the teams and busily recruited students to vote in a run-off election. Two of the students he recruited voted under names of absentee members of the Finance Club. The new votes gave Mr. Gunty his victory. However, two of the votes were from students who were not members of the club, but used someone else's name to vote.[16]

After an anonymous tip, the elections were set aside and the runners-up installed as co-presidents. Mr. Gunty was required to write a paper on ethics.[17]

Discussion Questions

1. In the words of the school newspaper publisher, "Why would anyone do this? It's just a club."

2. Was anyone really hurt by the conduct?

3. Would you have reported the conduct anonymously or disclosed it publicly?

4. What are the long-term implications for Mr. Gunty?

In the following case, you are playing a different role in that you are analyzing from the perspective of offering a solution in a situation where the conduct has not already been undertaken (as in the first two cases).

CASE 1.11

The Loan Officer and the Debtors

Ben Garrison is a senior loan officer with First National Federal Bank, the second-largest financial institution in Wyoming. Ben, who has been with First National Federal for ten years, handles loan applications from all over the state.

[16] *Gilbert Fuchsberg, "Harvard Has Some Crimson Faces Over a Lesson in Practical Politics,"* The Wall Street Journal, *April 9, 1992, B1.*

[17] *"Harvard Student Rigging Election Must Write Paper,"* The Wall Street Journal, *April 24, 1992, A3.*

Following the savings and loan debacle of the late 1980s, First National Federal implemented many institutional changes. Some of the changes were operational; others involved the bank's lending policy. A change that Ben found frustrating was an increasing emphasis on ethics. Ben complained to one of his loan officers, "I don't get this ethics stuff. If it's legal, I'm ethical." One of the loan officers, Shelby Grant, a recent graduate of the University of Wyoming School of Business, replied, "Well, sometimes doing what's ethical helps you avoid legal problems." Ben replied, "Sometimes doing what's ethical just costs you more money!"

Later that morning, following their discussion, Ben appeared in Shelby's office with a loan application from Doug Whitton, a rancher in the northwestern part of the state. He told Shelby that they needed to take a trip to evaluate the proposed collateral for the loan. An on-site evaluation of collateral is a required procedure for loan processing at First National Federal. Ben added, "Whitton's paying our way up there for the evaluation." Shelby asked, "Shouldn't the bank pay our way, since we may not make the loan and we wouldn't want to be obligated to Whitton?" Ben responded, "Now why in the hell would I want to pay our way up there and increase my costs when he's offering to pay?" Shelby was uncertain about the propriety of the proposal.

Ben added that First National Federal's annual fundraiser picnic was coming up and that they were planning to have the usual prize drawing. "So," he told Shelby, "just get on the phone to all the customers whose loans you handle and see what prizes they're willing to donate for this year's drawings." Shelby asked, "Isn't it wrong for us to pressure our customers into donating prizes?" Ben replied angrily, "These prizes are not for us! The money is not for us! This is charity! What could be unethical about that?"

Shelby went home that evening to prepare for the trip to the ranch. She hadn't called any of her customers for donations, and she didn't want to go on the trip unless the bank paid. She was also $20,000 in debt from school, and it had taken her four months after graduation to find this job. "I guess this is just the way business is done," she concluded.

Discussion Questions

1. Is Shelby correct? Are both these issues "just the way business is done"?

2. Is the appearance of impropriety an important ethical constraint?

3. What problems arise in having the potential borrower pay for the collateral evaluation trip?

4. What problems arise in soliciting donations from loan customers?

5. How would it be different if a merchant offered to donate items without being asked?

6. If you were Shelby, would you pursue the donations issue or just follow the process the bank has always used?

unit 2

Foundations of Business Ethics: What Is the Role of Business in Society? Shareholders vs. Stakeholders

2a

The Role of Business in Society

The study of business ethics is not the study of what is legal but of the application of moral standards to business decisions. Moral standards are canons of personal behavior that are neither legislated nor changed by legislation. For example, regardless of legislative and regulatory requirements, we all are committed to safety and fairness for employees in the workplace. But what happens when several moral standards conflict? A company that manufactures athletic shoes finds cheap labor in developing nations. The company pays minimum wage for that country, but those wages wouldn't bring enough in one month to allow the workers to buy a pair of the company's shoes. Factory conditions meet that nation's standards but violate nearly all U.S. minimum standards. Without the cheap labor, the shoe manufacturer can't compete. Without the jobs, the nation can't develop, but children are working 50-hour weeks in these third world countries. Fair and just treatment in the workplace is an issue the company must face in making this foreign outsourcing of labor.

Employees hold moral standards of following instructions, doing an honest day's work for a day's pay, and being loyal to their employers. But what happens when their employers are producing products that, because of inadequate testing, will be harmful to users? To whom do employees turn if employers reject them and their concerns? Other moral standards—of not intentionally harming others and adequately testing products—will present those employees with a dilemma and force them to decide an appropriate course of action.

Businesses, consumers, and employees too often subscribe to the "what's good for GM is good for the country" theory of business ethics. Jeff Dachis, the founder and former CEO of Razorfish, once said when he was questioned about the lack of independence on his board, "My partner and I control 10 percent of the company. What's good for me is good for all shareholders. Management isn't screwing up. We've created enormous shareholder value."[1] He spoke when his stock was at $56 in June 1999. In May 2001, when he added three independent directors to his board and resigned as CEO, Razorfish stock was trading at $1.11 per share. No one at Razorfish did anything illegal, but it is the presence of perspective in a company through its board and also

[1] *Erick Schonfeld, "Doing Business the Dot-Com Way,"* Fortune, *March 20, 2000, p. 116.*

through the analytical framework of ethics that may save a company from its hubris. Businesses have now begun to realize that, contrary to Sir Alfred Coke's allegation that a corporation has no conscience, the corporation must develop a conscience. That conscience develops as firms and the individuals within them develop perspective on and guidelines for their respective conduct.

In defining business ethics, we are really defining the voluntary role of business: how does a business behave when the law does not dictate its conduct or the law permits conduct that might benefit shareholders but is harmful to others?

In the following readings, economist Milton Friedman, management expert Peter Drucker, and Professor Edward Freeman present different views on the role of ethics in business as well as the role of business in society. You can now add to your steps for resolving dilemmas the additional factor of your position and the position of the company and individuals involved in the role of business in society.

READING 2.1

The Social Responsibility of Business Is to Increase Its Profits[2]

Milton Friedman

When I hear businessmen speak eloquently about the "social responsibilities of business in a free-enterprise system," I am reminded of the wonderful line about the Frenchman who discovered at the age of 70 that he had been speaking prose all his life. The businessmen believe that they are defending free enterprise when they declaim that business is not concerned "merely" with profit but also with promoting desirable "social" ends; that business has a "social conscience" and takes seriously its responsibilities for providing employment, eliminating discrimination, avoiding pollution and whatever else may be the catchwords of the contemporary crop of reformers. In fact they are—or would be if they or anyone else took them seriously—preaching pure and unadulterated socialism. Businessmen who talk this way are unwitting puppets of the intellectual forces that have been undermining the basis of a free society these past decades.

The discussions of the "social responsibilities of business" are notable for their analytical looseness and lack of rigor. What does it mean to say that "business" has responsibilities? Only people can have responsibilities. A corporation is an artificial person and in this sense may have artificial responsibilities, but "business" as a whole cannot be said to have responsibilities, even in this vague sense. The first step toward clarity in examining the doctrine of the social responsibility of business is to ask precisely what it implies for whom.

Presumably, the individuals who are to be responsible are businessmen, which means individual proprietors or corporate executives. Most of the discussion of social

[2] *Source:* The New York Times Sunday Magazine, *September 13, 1970. Copyright © 1970 by The New York Times Company. Reprinted by permission.*

responsibility is directed at corporations, so in what follows I shall mostly neglect the individual proprietor and speak of corporate executives.

In a free-enterprise, private-property system, a corporate executive is an employee of the owners of the business. He has direct responsibility to his employers. That responsibility is to conduct the business in accordance with their desires, which generally will be to make as much money as possible while conforming to the basic rules of the society, both those embodied in law and those embodied in ethical custom. Of course, in some cases his employers may have a different objective. A group of persons might establish a corporation for an eleemosynary purpose—for example, a hospital or a school. The manager of such a corporation will not have money profit as his objective but the rendering of certain services.

In either case, the key point is that, in his capacity as a corporate executive, the manager is the agent of the individuals who own the corporation or establish the eleemosynary institution, and his primary responsibility is to them.

Needless to say, this does not mean that it is easy to judge how well he is performing his task. But at least the criterion of performance is straightforward, and the persons among whom a voluntary contractual arrangement exists are clearly defined.

Of course, the corporate executive is also a person in his own right. As a person, he may have many other responsibilities that he recognizes or assumes voluntarily—to his family, his conscience, his feelings of charity, his church, his clubs, his city, his country. He may feel impelled by these responsibilities to devote part of his income to causes he regards as worthy, to refuse to work for particular corporations, even to leave his job, for example, to join his country's armed forces. If we wish, we may refer to some of these responsibilities as "social responsibilities." But in these respects he is acting as a principal, not an agent; he is spending his own money or time or energy, not the money of his employers or the time or energy he had contracted to devote to their purposes. If these are "social responsibilities," they are the social responsibilities of individuals, not of business.

What does it mean to say that the corporate executive has a "social responsibility" in his capacity as businessman? If this statement is not pure rhetoric, it must mean that he is to act in some way that is not in the interest of his employers. For example, that he is to refrain from increasing the price of the product in order to contribute to the social objective of preventing inflation, even though a price increase would be in the best interests of the corporation. Or that he is to make expenditures on reducing pollution beyond the amount that is in the best interests of the corporation or that is required by law in order to contribute to the social objective of improving the environment. Or that, at the expense of corporate profits, he is to hire "hard-core" unemployed instead of better-qualified available workmen to contribute to the social objective of reducing poverty.

In each of these cases, the corporate executive would be spending someone else's money for a general social interest. Insofar as his actions in accord with his "social responsibility" reduce returns to stockholders, he is spending their money. Insofar as his actions raise the price to customers, he is spending the customers' money. Insofar as his actions lower the wages of some employees, he is spending their money.

The stockholders or the customers or the employees could separately spend their own money on the particular action if they wished to do so. The executive is exercising a distinct "social responsibility," rather than serving as an agent of the stockholders or the customers or the employees, only if he spends the money in a different way than they would have spent it.

But if he does this, he is in effect imposing taxes, on the one hand, and deciding how the tax proceeds shall be spent, on the other.

This process raises political questions on two levels: principle and consequences. On the level of political principle, the imposition of taxes and the expenditure of tax proceeds are governmental functions. We have established elaborate constitutional, parliamentary and judicial provisions to control these functions, to assure that taxes are imposed so far as possible in accordance with the preferences and desires of the public—after all, "taxation without representation" was one of the battle cries of the American Revolution. We have a system of checks and balances to separate the legislative function of imposing taxes and enacting expenditures from the executive function of collecting taxes and administering expenditure programs and from the judicial function of mediating disputes and interpreting the law.

Here the businessman—self-selected or appointed directly or indirectly by stockholders—is to be simultaneously legislator, executive and jurist. He is to decide whom to tax by how much and for what purpose, and he is to spend the proceeds—all this guided only by general exhortations from on high to restrain inflation, improve the environment, fight poverty and so on and on.

The whole justification for permitting the corporate executive to be selected by the stockholders is that the executive is an agent serving the interests of his principal. This justification disappears when the corporate executive imposes taxes and spends the proceeds for "social" purposes. He becomes in effect a public employee, a civil servant, even though he remains in name an employee of a private enterprise. On grounds of political principle, it is intolerable that such civil servants—insofar as their actions in the name of social responsibility are real and not just window-dressing—should be selected as they are now. If they are to be civil servants, then they must be selected through a political process. If they are to impose taxes and make expenditures to foster "social" objectives, then political machinery must be set up to guide the assessment of taxes and to determine through a political process the objectives to be served.

This is the basic reason why the doctrine of "social responsibility" involves the acceptance of the socialist view that political mechanisms, not market mechanisms, are the appropriate way to determine the allocation of scarce resources to alternative uses.

On the grounds of consequences, can the corporate executive in fact discharge his alleged "social responsibilities"? On the one hand, suppose he could get away with spending the stockholders' or customers' or employees' money. How is he to know how to spend it? He is told that he must contribute to fighting inflation. How is he to know what action of his will contribute to that end? He is presumably an expert in running his company—in producing a product or selling it or financing it. But nothing about his selection makes him an expert on inflation. Will his holding down the price of his product reduce inflationary pressure? Or, by leaving more spending power in the hands of his customers, simply divert it elsewhere? Or, by forcing him to produce less because of the lower price, will it simply contribute to shortages? Even if he could answer these questions, how much cost is he justified in imposing on his stockholders, customers and employees for this social purpose? What is his appropriate share and what is the appropriate share of others?

And, whether he wants to or not, can he get away with spending his stockholders', customers' or employees' money? Will not the stockholders fire him? (Either the present ones or those who take over when his actions in the name of social responsibility have reduced the corporation's profits and the price of its stock.) His customers and his employees can desert him for other producers and employers less scrupulous in exercising their social responsibilities.

This facet of "social responsibility" doctrine is brought into sharp relief when the doctrine is used to justify wage restraint by trade unions. The conflict of interest is naked and clear when union officials are asked to subordinate the interest of their members to some more general social purpose. If the union officials try to enforce wage restraint, the consequence is likely to be wildcat strikes, rank-and-file revolts and the emergence of strong competitors for their jobs. We thus have the ironic phenomenon that union leaders—at least in the U.S.—have objected to government interference with the market far more consistently and courageously than have business leaders.

The difficulty of exercising "social responsibility" illustrates, of course, the great virtue of private competitive enterprise—it forces people to be responsible for their own actions and makes it difficult for them to "exploit" other people for either selfish or unselfish purposes. They can do good—but only at their own expense.

Many a reader who has followed the argument this far may be tempted to remonstrate that it is well and good to speak of government's having the responsibility to impose taxes and determine expenditures for such "social" purposes as controlling pollution or training the hard-core unemployed, but that the problems are too urgent to wait on the slow course of political processes, that the exercise of social responsibility by businessmen is a quicker and surer way to solve pressing current problems.

Aside from the question of fact—I share Adam Smith's skepticism about the benefits that can be expected from "those who affected to trade for the public good"—this argument must be rejected on grounds of principle. What it amounts to is an assertion that those who favor the taxes and expenditures in question have failed to persuade a majority of their fellow citizens to be of like mind and that they are seeking to attain by undemocratic procedures what they cannot attain by democratic procedures. In a free society, it is hard for "good" people to do "good," but that is a small price to pay for making it hard for "evil" people to do "evil," especially since one man's good is another's evil.

I have, for simplicity, concentrated on the special case of the corporate executive, except only for the brief digression on trade unions. But precisely the same argument applies to the newer phenomenon of calling upon stockholders to require corporations to exercise social responsibility (the recent GM crusade, for example). In most of these cases, what is in effect involved in some stockholders trying to get other stockholders (or customers or employees) to contribute against their will to "social" causes favored by the activists. Insofar as they succeed, they are again imposing taxes and spending the proceeds.

The situation of the individual proprietor is somewhat different. If he acts to reduce the returns of his enterprise in order to exercise his "social responsibility," he is spending his own money, not someone else's. If he wishes to spend his money on such purposes, that is his right, and I cannot see that there is any objection to his doing so. In the process, he, too, may impose costs on employees and customers. However, because he is far less likely than a large corporation or union to have monopolistic power, any such side effects will tend to be minor.

Of course, in practice the doctrine of social responsibility is frequently a cloak for actions that are justified on other grounds rather than a reason for those actions.

To illustrate, it may well be in the long-run interest of a corporation that is a major employer in a small community to devote resources to providing amenities to that community or to improving its government. That may make it easier to attract desirable employees, it may reduce the wage bill or lessen losses from pilferage and sabotage or have other worthwhile effects. Or it may be that, given the laws about the deductibility of corporate charitable contributions, the stockholders can contribute more to charities they favor by having the corporation make the gift than by doing it themselves, since they can in that way contribute an amount that would otherwise have been paid as corporate taxes.

In each of these—and many similar—cases, there is a strong temptation to rationalize these actions as an exercise of "social responsibility." In the present climate of opinion, with its widespread aversion to "capitalism," "profits," the "soulless corporation" and so on, this is one way for a corporation to generate goodwill as a by-product of expenditures that are entirely justified in its own self-interest.

It would be inconsistent of me to call on corporate executives to refrain from this hypocritical window-dressing because it harms the foundations of a free society. That would be to call on them to exercise a "social responsibility"! If our institutions, and the attitudes of the public, make it in their self-interest to cloak their actions in this way, I cannot summon much indignation to denounce them. At the same time, I can express admiration for those individual proprietors or owners of closely held corporations or stockholders of more broadly held corporations who disdain such tactics as approaching fraud.

Whether blameworthy or not, the use of the cloak of social responsibility, and the nonsense spoken in its name by influential and prestigious businessmen, does clearly harm the foundations of a free society. I have been impressed time and again by the schizophrenic character of many businessmen. They are capable of being extremely far-sighted and clear-headed in matters that are internal to their businesses. They are incredibly short-sighted and muddle-headed in matters that are outside their businesses but affect the possible survival of business in general. This short-sightedness is strikingly exemplified in the calls from many businessmen for wage and price guidelines or controls or incomes policies. There is nothing that could do more in a brief period to destroy a market system and replace it by a centrally controlled system than effective governmental control of prices and wages.

The short-sightedness is also exemplified in speeches by businessmen on social responsibility. This may gain them kudos in the short run. But it helps to strengthen the already too prevalent view that the pursuit of profits is wicked and immoral and must be curbed and controlled by external forces. Once this view is adopted, the external forces that curb the market will not be the social consciences, however highly developed, of the pontificating executives; it will be the iron fist of government bureaucrats. Here, as with price and wage controls, businessmen seem to me to reveal a suicidal impulse.

The political principle that underlies the market mechanism is unanimity. In an ideal free market resting on private property, no individual can coerce any other, all cooperation is voluntary, all parties to such cooperation benefit or they need not participate. There are no "social" values, no "social" responsibilities in any sense other than the shared values and responsibilities of individuals. Society is a collection of individuals and of the various groups they voluntarily form.

The political principle that underlies the political mechanism is conformity. The individual must serve a more general social interest—whether that be determined by a church or a dictator or a majority. The individual may have a vote and a say in what is to be done, but if he is overruled, he must conform. It is appropriate for some to require others to contribute to a general social purpose whether they wish to or not.

Unfortunately, unanimity is not always feasible. There are some respects in which conformity appears unavoidable, so I do not see how one can avoid the use of the political mechanism altogether.

But the doctrine of "social responsibility" taken seriously would extend the scope of the political mechanism to every human activity. It does not differ in philosophy from the most explicitly collectivist doctrine. It differs only by professing to believe that collectivist ends can be attained without collectivist means. That is why, in my book *Capitalism and Freedom*, I have called it a "fundamentally subversive doctrine" in a free society, and have said that in such a society, "there is one and only one social responsibility of business—to use its resources and engage in activities designed to increase its profits so long as it stays within the rules of the game, which is to say, engages in open and free competition without deception or fraud."

Discussion Questions

1. How does Dr. Friedman characterize discussions on "social responsibilities of business"? Why?
2. What is the role of a corporate executive selected by stockholders?
3. What analogy does Dr. Friedman draw between trade union wages and corporations' decisions based on social responsibilities?
4. Would Dr. Friedman ever support voluntary actions on the part of a corporation (e.g., conduct not prohibited specifically or mandated by law)?

READING 2.2

The Ethics of Responsibility[3]

Peter Drucker

Countless sermons have been preached and printed on the ethics of business or the ethics of the businessman. Most have nothing to do with business and little to do with ethics.

One main topic is plain, everyday honesty. Businessmen, we are told solemnly, should not cheat, steal, lie, bribe, or take bribes. But nor should anyone else. Men and women do not acquire exemption from ordinary rules of personal behavior because of their work or job. Nor, however, do they cease to be human beings when appointed vice-president, city manager, or college dean. And there has always been a number of people who cheat, steal, lie, bribe, or take bribes. The problem is one of moral values and moral education, of the individual, of the family, of the school. But there neither is a separate ethics of business, nor is one needed.

All that is needed is to mete out stiff punishments to those—whether business executives or others—who yield to temptation. In England a magistrate still tends to hand down a harsher punishment in a drunken-driving case if the accused has gone to one of the well-known public schools or to Oxford or Cambridge. And the conviction still rates a headline in the evening paper: "Eton graduate convicted of drunken driving." No one expects an Eton education to produce temperance leaders. But it is still a badge of distinction, if not of privilege. And not to treat a wearer of such a badge more harshly than an ordinary workingman who has had one too many would offend the community's sense of justice. But no one considers this a problem of the "ethics of the Eton graduate."

The other common theme in the discussion of ethics in business has nothing to do with ethics.

Such things as the employment of call girls to entertain customers are not matters of ethics but matters of esthetics. "Do I want to see a pimp when I look at myself in the mirror while shaving?" is the real question.

It would indeed be nice to have fastidious leaders. Alas, fastidiousness has never been prevalent among leadership groups, whether kings and counts, priests or generals, or even "intellectuals" such as the painters and humanists of the Renaissance, or the "literati" of the Chinese tradition. All a fastidious man can do is withdraw personally from activities that violate his self-respect and his sense of taste.

Lately these old sermon topics have been joined, especially in the U.S., by a third one: managers, we are being told, have an "ethical responsibility" to take an active and constructive role in their community, to serve community causes, give of their time to community activities, and so on.

[3] *Submitted excerpt from* Management: Tasks, Responsibilities, Practices, *by Peter F. Drucker. Copyright © 1973, 1974 by Peter F. Drucker. Reprinted by permission of HarperCollins Publishers, Inc.*

There are many countries where such community activity does not fit the traditional mores; Japan and France would be examples. But where the community has a tradition of "voluntarism"—that is, especially in the U.S.—managers should indeed be encouraged to participate and to take responsible leadership in community affairs and community organizations. Such activities should, however, never be forced on them, nor should they be appraised, rewarded, or promoted according to their participation in voluntary activities. Ordering or pressuring managers into such work is abuse of organizational power and illegitimate.

An exception might be made for managers in businesses where the community activities are really part of their obligation to the business. . . .

But, while desirable, community participation of managers has nothing to do with ethics, and not much to do with responsibility. It is the contribution of an individual in his capacity as a neighbor and citizen. And it is something that lies outside his job and outside his managerial responsibility.

Leadership Groups but Not Leaders

A problem of ethics that is peculiar to the manager arises from the fact that the managers of institutions are *collectively* the leadership groups of the society of organizations. But *individually* a manager is just another fellow employee.

This is clearly recognized by the public. Even the most powerful head of the largest corporation is unknown to the public. Indeed most of the company's employees barely know his name and would not recognize his face. He may owe his position entirely to personal merit and proven performance. But he owes his authority and standing entirely to his institution. Everybody knows GE, the Telephone Company, Mitsubishi, Siemens, and Unilever. But who heads these great corporations—or for that matter, the University of California, the Ecole Polytechnique or Guy's Hospital in London—is of direct interest and concern primarily to the management group within these institutions.

It is therefore inappropriate to speak of managers as leaders. They are "members of the leadership group." The group, however, does occupy a position of visibility, of prominence, and of authority. It therefore has responsibility. . . .

But what are the responsibilities, what are the ethics of the individual manager, as a member of the leadership group?

Essentially being a member of a leadership group is what traditionally has been meant by the term "professional.". . . But as a member of a leadership group a manager stands under the demands of professional ethics—the demands of an ethic of responsibility.

Primum Non Nocere

The first responsibility of a professional was spelled out clearly, 2,500 years ago, in the Hippocratic oath of the Greek physician: *primum non nocere*—"Above all, not knowingly to do harm."

No professional, be he doctor, lawyer, or manager, can promise that he will indeed do good for his client. All he can do is try. But he can promise that he will not knowingly do harm. And the client, in turn, must be able to trust the professional not knowingly to do him harm. Otherwise he cannot trust him at all. The professional has to have autonomy. He cannot be controlled, supervised, or directed by the client. He has to be private in that his knowledge and his judgment have to be entrusted with the decision. But it is the foundation of his autonomy, and indeed its rationale, that he see himself as "affected with the public interest." A professional, in other words, is private in the sense that he is autonomous and not subject to political or ideological control. But he is public in the sense that the welfare of his client sets limits to his deeds and words. And *primum non nocere*, "not knowingly to do harm," is the basic rule of professional ethics, the basic rule of an ethics of public responsibility.

There are important areas where managers, and especially business managers, still do not realize that in order to be permitted to remain autonomous and private they have to impose on themselves the responsibility of the professional ethic. They still have to learn that it is their job to scrutinize their deeds, words, and behavior to make sure that they do not knowingly do harm.

The manager who fails to think through and work for the appropriate solution to an impact of his business because it makes him "unpopular in the club" knowingly does harm. He knowingly abets a cancerous growth. That this is stupid has been said. That this always in the end hurts the business or the industry more than a little temporary "unpleasantness" would have hurt has been said too. But it is also a gross violation of professional ethics.

But there are other areas as well. American managers, in particular, tend to violate the rule not knowingly to do harm with respect to:

- executive compensation;
- the use of benefit plans to impose "golden fetters" on people in the company's employ; and
- in their profit rhetoric.

Their actions and their words in these areas tend to cause social disruption. They tend to conceal healthy reality and to create disease, or at least social hypochondria. They tend to misdirect and to prevent understanding. And this is grievous social harm.

The Rhetoric of the Profit Motive

Managers, . . . through their rhetoric, make it impossible for the public to understand economic reality. This violates the requirement that managers, being leaders, not knowingly do harm. This is particularly true of the United States but also of Western Europe. For in the West, managers still talk constantly of the profit motive. And they still define the goal of their business as profit maximization. They do not stress the objective function of profit. They do not talk of risks—or very rarely. They do not stress the need for capital. They almost never even mention the cost of capital, let alone that a business has to produce enough profit to obtain the capital it needs at minimum cost.

common folk don't understand "profit" talk.

Managers constantly complain about the hostility to profit. They rarely realize that their own rhetoric is one of the main reasons for this hostility. For indeed in the terms management uses when it talks to the public, there is no possible justification for profit, no explanation for its existence, no function it performs. There is only the profit motive, that is, the desire of some anonymous capitalists—and why that desire should be indulged in by society any more than bigamy, for instance, is never explained. But profitability is a crucial *need* of economy and society.

Managerial practice in most large American companies is perfectly rational. It is the rhetoric which obscures, and thereby threatens to damage both business and society. To be sure, few American companies work out profitability as a *minimum* requirement. As a result, most probably underestimate the profitability the company truly requires (let alone the inflationary erosion of capital). But they, consciously or not, base their profit planning on the twin objectives of ensuring access to capital needed and minimizing the cost of capital. In the American context, if only because of the structure of the U.S. capital market, a high "price/earnings ratio" is indeed a key to the minimization of the cost of capital; and "optimization of profits" is therefore a perfectly rational strategy which tends to lower, in the long run, the actual cost of capital.

But this makes it even less justifiable to keep on using the rhetoric of the profit motive. It serves no purpose except to confuse and to embitter.

These examples of areas in which managers do not hold themselves to the rule "not knowingly to do harm" are primarily American examples. They apply to some extent to Western Europe. But they hardly apply to Japan. The principle, however, applies in all countries, and in the developing countries as much as in developed ones. These cases are taken from business management. The principle, however, applies to managers of all institutions in the society of organizations.

In any pluralist society responsibility for the public good has been the central problem and issue. The pluralist society or organizations will be no exception. Its leaders represent "special interests," that is, institutions designed to fulfill a specific and partial need of society. Indeed the leaders of this pluralist society of organizations are the servants of such institutions. At the same time, they are the major leadership group such a society knows or is likely to produce. They have to serve both their own institution and the common good. If the society is to function, let alone if it is to remain a free society, the men we call managers will remain "private" in their institutions. No matter who owns them and how, they will maintain autonomy. But they will also have to be "public" in their ethics.

In this tension between the private functioning of the manager, the necessary autonomy of his institution and its accountability to its own mission and purpose, and the public character of the manager, lies the specific ethical problem of the society of organizations. *Primum non nocere* may seem tame compared to the rousing calls for "statesmanship" that abound in today's manifestos on social responsibility. But, as the physicians found out long ago, it is not an easy rule to live up to. Its very modesty and self-constraint make it the right rule for the ethics manager's need, the ethics of responsibility.

Discussion Questions

1. How does Professor Drucker see the relationship between business and personal ethics?
2. What problems do leadership groups create for ethics in business?
3. In what three areas does Professor Drucker see managers violating the principle of *primum non nocere*?

4. What is the rhetoric of the profit motive?
5. Does Professor Drucker believe ethical standards vary from country to country?

READING 2.3

Principles of Social Responsibility in Business

This reading is a summary of several of the more widely adopted voluntary codes of social responsibility that businesses have adopted as their posture on the issue of social responsibility. To assist companies in positioning their role in society, some organizations have developed standards and statements of principles. The purpose of these standards is to provide businesses with resolutions in advance of dilemmas. Those companies that adopt these types of lists of standards have already resolved certain ethical dilemmas in advance. These standards are also a means for looking at ethical dilemmas presented in this book. You can use these standards as a means of developing resolutions.

Referred to as SA 8000, the Council on Economic Priorities (CEP) models its standards after ISO (International Standards Organization) 9000 and ISO 14000—the two standards for quality control and environmental management systems.

SA 8000 is also an employment-focused stakeholder standard providing guidelines in the following areas: child labor, forced labor, health and safety, freedom of association, discrimination, disciplinary practices, working hours, compensation, and management.

The CEP does offer SA 8000 certification following a company audit for compliance. The SA 8000 guidelines are available at http://www.cepaa.org.

The Caux Round Table Principles of Business provide a broad look at stakeholder accountability, going beyond labor requirements. The general stakeholder definition in the Principles covers customers, employees, and shareholders and also lists the following as business responsibilities: accountability beyond shareholders; innovation, justice, and respect for the world community; business beyond the letter of the law; respect for rules; support for multilateral trade; respect for the environment; and avoidance of illicit operations. The principles found at http://www.cauxroundtable.org then establish stakeholder principles such as treating customers with dignity, providing customers with high-quality goods, treating customers fairly, improving living conditions for workers, ensuring health and safety of workers while at work, communicating honestly and openly with employees, not discriminating, assisting in training for employees, exercising fair pricing policies, avoiding unnecessary litigation, bringing suppliers into their processes, paying suppliers on time, conserving the environment, opening markets, promoting competition, and respecting intellectual property. The guidelines do include providing a return to shareholders.

The Interfaith Center's guidelines for business focus on 16 areas: ecosystems; national communities; local communities; indigenous communities; the employed; women in the workforce; minority groups; persons with disabilities; child labor; forced labor; suppliers; financial integrity; ethical integrity; shareholders; joint ventures and partnerships; and customers and consumers. Each area then has guidelines. The Interfaith Center also publishes an annual report on shareholder proxy proposals (which tend to focus on these 16 areas) and their fate at annual meetings. The Interfaith Principles also incorporate by reference other shareholder standards such as CERES principles, available through Interfaith Center on Corporate Responsibility, 475 Riverside Drive, Room 550, NY, NY 10015, (212) 870-2295.

The Society for International Business Ethics (IBE) focuses on 13 areas: political activities; health and safety; gifts; conflicts of interest; insider dealing; equal opportunity and discrimination; alcohol and drug abuse; sexual harassment; disclosure of company information; financial transactions; fair competition; environment; and software copying.

The IBE code is available at http://www.ibe.org.uk.

The Clarkson Principles of Stakeholder Management evolved from the intersection of these codes and can be found at http://www.rotman.utoronto.ca/ccbe/. The seven Clarkson Principles are as follows:[4]

Principle 1 Managers should **acknowledge** and actively **monitor** the concerns of all legitimate stakeholders, and should take their interests appropriately into account in decision making and operations.

Principle 2 Managers should **listen** to and openly **communicate** with stakeholders about their respective concerns and contributions, and about the risks that they assume because of their involvement with the corporation.

Principle 3 Managers should **adopt** processes and modes of behavior that are sensitive to the concerns and capabilities of each stakeholder constituency.

Principle 4 Managers should **recognize the interdependence** of efforts and rewards among stakeholders, and should attempt to achieve a fair distribution of the benefits and burdens of corporate activity among them, taking into account their respective risks and vulnerabilities.

Principle 5 Managers should **work cooperatively** with other entities, both public and private, to ensure that risks and harms arising from corporate activities are minimized and, where they cannot be avoided, appropriately compensated.

Principle 6 Managers should **avoid altogether** activities that might jeopardize inalienable human rights (e.g., the right to life) or give rise to risks which, if clearly understood, would be patently unacceptable to relevant stakeholders.

Principle 7 Managers should **acknowledge the potential conflicts** between (a) their own role as corporate stakeholders, and (b) their legal and moral responsibilities for the interests of stakeholders, and should address such conflicts through open communication, appropriate reporting and incentive systems and, where necessary, third-party review.

[4] *Clarkson Centre for Business Ethics. 1999.* Principles of Stakeholder Management. *Toronto: CCBE. (p. 4).*

Schools of Thought on Social Responsibility[5]

The following excerpt deals with the various schools of thought on social responsibility. These postures can be found across industries and can be used as a framework for analysis of dilemmas.

Ethical Postures, Social Responsibility, and Business Practice

The ethical perspective of a business often sets the tone for its operations and employees' choices. Historically, the philosophical debate over the role of business in society has evolved into four schools of thought on ethical behavior based on the responses to two questions: (1) Whose interest should a corporation serve? and (2) To whom should a corporation be responsive in order to best serve that interest? There are only two answers to these questions—"shareholders only" and "the larger society"—and the combination of those answers defines the school of thought.

Inherence

According to the **inherence** school of thought, managers answer only to shareholders and act only with shareholders' interests in mind. This type of manager would not become involved in any political or social issues unless it was in the shareholders' best interests to do so, and provided the involvement did not backfire and cost the firm sales. Milton Friedman's philosophy, as previously expressed, is an example of inherence. To illustrate how a business following the inherence school of thought would behave, consider the issue of a proposed increase in residential property taxes for school-funding purposes. A business that subscribes to the inherence school would support a school-tax increase only if the educational issue affected the company's performance and only if such a position did not offend those who opposed the tax increase.

Enlightened Self-Interest

According to this school of thought, the manager is responsible to the shareholders but serves them best by being responsive to the larger society. **Enlightened self-interest** is based on the view that, in the long run, business value is enhanced if business is responsive to the needs of society. In this school, managers are free to speak out on societal issues without the constraint of offending someone, as in inherence. Businesses would anticipate social changes and needs and be early advocates for change. For example, many corporations today have instituted job sharing, child-care facilities, and sick-child care in response to the changing structure of the American family and workforce. This responsiveness to the needs of the larger society should also be beneficial to shareholders, because it enables the business to retain a quality workforce.

The Invisible Hand

The **invisible hand** school of thought is the opposite of enlightened self-interest. According to this philosophy, business ought to serve the larger society and it does

[5] *From* Business: Its Legal, Ethical and Global Environment*, 6th Ed., by Marianne M. Jennings, pp. 46–47. Copyright © 2003. Reprinted with permission of South-Western, a division of Thomson Learning.*

this best when it serves the shareholders only. Such businesses allow government to set the standards and boundaries for appropriate behavior and simply adhere to these governmental constraints as a way of maximizing benefits to their shareholders. They become involved in issues of social responsibility or in political issues only when society lacks sufficient information on an issue to make a decision. Even then, their involvement is limited to presenting data and does not extend to advocating a particular viewpoint or position. This school of thought holds that it is best for society to guide itself and that businesses work best when they serve shareholders within those constraints.

Social Responsibility

In the **social responsibility** school of thought, the role of business is to serve the larger society, and that is best accomplished by being responsive to the larger society. This view is simply a reflection of the idea that businesses profit by being responsive to society and its needs. A business following this school of thought would advocate full disclosure of product information to consumers in its advertising and would encourage political activism on the part of its managers and employees on all issues, not just those that affect the corporation. These businesses believe that their sense of social responsibility contributes to their long-term success.

2b

Stakeholder vs. Shareholder Accountability

Should corporations serve larger society or do they serve large society best when they are accountable to their shareholders? Or are corporations best accountable to their shareholders when they are accountable to larger society? There is a longstanding and continuing debate on the accountability of businesses. The readings in this section provide background for you as you consider the responsibility of businesses to their various constituencies.

One of the difficulties with the theory that managers should be accountable to others beyond their shareholders is answering these questions: To which group am I accountable? How do they make their wishes known? What happens if the groups have conflicting interests?

There is a significant debate among academics and businesspeople as to who stakeholders are and what role they should play in working with business managers. In the following readings, you gain insight into the scope of the stakeholder concept as well as a view of the various organizations that have tried to provide concrete principles of stakeholder theory.

READING 2.5

Stakeholder Theory and the Coase Theorem[6]

Marianne M. Jennings and Stephen K. Happel

This reading is included to help you with not only resolving the issue of business accountability, but also to offer you some perspective in terms of listing those who are affected by a particular ethical dilemma. Understanding the notion of who constitutes

[6] *Marianne M. Jennings and Stephen K. Happel, "The Avoidable Unhappiness in CSR: An Examination of Stakeholder Accountability, Property Rights and Application of the Coase Theorem to Corporate Governance," unpublished manuscript.*

a stakeholder can help not only in listing the stakeholders in a dilemma but in understanding their perspectives and concerns.

The following are definitions of "stakeholder" that have appeared in the literature:

"groups or individuals who affect or are affected by organizational performance," R. Edward Freeman, *Strategic Management: A Stakeholder Approach*, iv (1984); "those groups without whose support the organization would cease to exist with the original list including shareowners, employees, customers, suppliers, lenders and society," Stanford Research Institute Internal memo as cited in R. Edward Freeman and David L. Reed, *Stockholders and Stakeholders: A New Perspective on Corporate Governance*, 25 CAL. MGMT. REV. 88, 89 (1983); "any identifiable group or individual who can affect the achievement of an organization's objectives or who is affected by the achievement of an organization's objectives," "public interest groups, protest groups, government agencies, trade association, competitors, unions"; "employees, customer segments, shareowners"; Freeman and Reed, at 91; "any identifiable group or individual on which the organization is dependent for its continued survival," (Defined to include "employees, customer segments certain suppliers, key government agencies, shareowners, certain financial institutions as well as others"), Freeman and Reed, at 91.

One scholar has written:

"The precise origins of stakeholder theory are impossible to determine," Frederick Sturdivant, *Executives and Activists: A Test of Stakeholder Management*, 22 CAL. MGMT. REV. 53 (1979).

But there are still those who attempt a definition:

"While as we shall see later, 'responsibilities' and 'objectives' are not synonymous, they have been made one in a 'stakeholder theory' of objectives. This theory maintains that the objectives of the firm should be derived by balancing the conflicting claims of various 'stakeholders' in the firm: managers, workers, stockholders, suppliers, vendors," Igor Ansoff, *Corporate Strategy*, 33 (1965); "an individual or group that asserts to have one or more stakes in a business," Archie B. Carroll, *Business and Society: Ethics and Stakeholder Management*, 60 (2d ed., 1993); "any individual or group who feel that they have a stake in the consequences of management's decisions and who have the power to influence current or future decisions," Frederick D. Sturdivant and Heidi Vernon-Wortzel, *Business and Society: A Managerial Approach*, 64 (4th ed., 1990); "an individual, a coalition of people, or an organization whose support is essential or whose opposition must be negated if major strategic change is to be successfully implemented," Ian C. Macmillan and Patricia E. Jones, *Strategy Formulation: Power and Politics*, 60 (2d ed., 1986); "persons that have, or claim, ownership, rights, or interests in a corporation and its activities, past, present, or future," M.E. Clarkson and M. Deck, *The Stakeholder Theory of the Corporation*, Proceedings of a Workshop on the Stakeholder Theory of the Firm and the Management of Ethics in the Workplace, U. Toronto, May 9, 1993, 20–21; "stakeholders are persons or groups with legitimate interests in procedural and/or substantive aspects of corporate activity," Thomas Donaldson and Lee E. Preston, at the same Toronto Conference. Paper #37.

Discussion Questions

1. The city of Phoenix, because of its rapid growth, has reached a point where its airport is not large enough to accommodate all incoming and outgoing air traffic. Managers for the city indicate the airport needs two new runways as well as additional flight paths over the city in order to meet the growing demands of commercial airlines for use of Phoenix as an international hub. List all who will be affected and/or benefit from the expansion of the airport.
2. Suppose that there are objections to the airport expansion. List categories of those you believe might object. Are they stakeholders of commercial airlines? Should they have a say in whether the airlines expand service to Phoenix? Should they have a say in whether the airlines pay for the expansion of the Phoenix airport?

READING 2.6

Appeasing Stakeholders with Public Relations[7]

This reading provides a different perspective on the stakeholder vs. shareholder debate. The author questions its wisdom and precision.

Robert Halfon

The problem in today's era of corporate pseudo-ethics is that the pendulum has shifted too far. From genuine philanthropy, . . . 'corporate responsibility' has mutated into a dangerous form of political correctness. The enlightened, entrepreneurial philanthropy of old has, through activist agitation, become the burden of today's so-called 'corporate responsibility.' At least four distinct trends are in evidence here: the rise of single issue activist groups; the targeting of companies with dealings in specific countries or specific industries; a rise in public sympathy for such actions; and a seal of approval guaranteed by many Western governments today.

Corporations have an obligation to anticipate and deal with these threats. This can be done in a number of ways. First, every important commercial activity should be rigorously assessed for its political risk. This means the risks or threats a business may face (from pressure groups, governments, *et al.*) in undertaking a particular activity. Business needs to inform itself at the highest level of the political environment in which it operates. As one commentator on these matters argues without hesitation:

> The lessons that need to be understood are simple. It does not matter where you are, or how big you are, if you are not prepared, pressure groups have the ability to make your company a member of the endangered species. You cannot respond effectively in six minutes to a campaign that has probably taken six months to organize. . . . Our first option is to ignore the increasing threat of pressure groups and lose everything. Our

[7] *Robert Halfon,* Corporate Irresponsibility: Is Business Appeasing Anti-business Activists? *Great Britain: The Social Affairs Unit, 1998, p. 7.*

second option is to fight back, challenge and probably win. We have the opportunity to deliver results by promoting morality; challenging credibility; setting policy and practices; offering solutions and advice.[8]

Once the political risks are evaluated, then two actions are required: first, for businesses to mount an efficient public relations campaign, arguing the case for corporate capitalism and stressing how their activities are benefiting the national—or global—economy in which they operate. All businesses, forewarned, should be proactive, not reactive. They must be prepared to fight fire with fire and, if necessary, should be prepared to take their case all the way to the courts. Secondly, companies across the spectrum must band together and act in unison to limit the unaccountable, undemocratic and often extra-legal activities of the activist groups they are up against.

Discussion Questions

1. What does Halfon see as the proper tools for handling stakeholder objections?
2. Can you describe a situation in which his tool may not be effective? What are the costs to the company if his tools fail to halt the opposition of stakeholders to a proposed corporate action?

[8] *Tony Meehan, "The Art of Media Manipulation,"* The Herald, *May 10, 1997.*

2C

Applying Social Responsibility and Stakeholder Theory

The following cases illustrate dilemmas in which there are many stakeholders with conflicting interests and provide you with an opportunity to apply the model for analysis provided in Unit 1 along with the various approaches to stakeholder theory described in the readings.

CASE 2.7

SUVs, the Environment, Safety, and Stakeholders

The SUV Market

In 1990, the SUV/light truck market consisted of approximately 4,000,000 units sold out of 14,000,000 of total vehicle sales in the United States. By 1999, the percentage of the total market had increased and total sales were higher. SUVs/light truck sales were 8,200,000 of 16,400,000 units sold.[9] 47.6 percent of Ford Motor Company's sales are of SUVs, primarily its Ford Explorer and larger Expedition, but also of its even larger Excursion. These vehicles took the place of the truck-like Bronco and smaller Bronco II.

The largest players in the SUV market (with the number of units sold in 2000) are as follows:[10]

Ford Expedition	203,412
Jeep Grand Cherokee	181,908
Dodge Durango	139,811
Ford Explorer	93,710
Chevrolet Suburban	48,982
Chevrolet Tahoe	47,103

[9] *Jerry Flint, "GM Discovers Sport Utilities,"* Forbes, *August 7, 2000, p. 68 (citing Wards' AutoInfo Bank data).*

[10] *Micheline Maynard, "Plush Sport Utility Sales Soar,"* USA Today, *December 9, 1998, p. 3B; "The History of Small Cars in America,"* USA Today, *July 2, 1999, p. 3B.*

In 1997, most auto manufacturers entered the luxury SUV market. These SUVs, with prices around $50,000, featured in-vehicle televisions and VCRs, leather interiors, and all the amenities of luxury cars. The new market entrants are listed below:

GM	Cadillac Escalade
	GMC Yukon Denali
	271 Tahoe
	Lincoln Navigator
Mercedes	M Class SUV
BMW	BMW X5
Lexus	RX300
Toyota	Landcruiser

The U.S. segment of the luxury SUV market is 80.5 percent.[11]

In 2000, SUV purchases constituted one of every five auto sales in the United States and are the highest margin products in all the automakers' lineups.[12] Profits per SUV average $10,000 per unit. Profits on the Ford Excursion are $18,000 per unit. Twenty percent of all of Ford's vehicle sales are of SUVs and comprise the majority of Ford's profits.[13]

Market data on SUV buyers indicate that the primary reason for their purchase of an SUV is safety (44 percent) followed by need (due to family size—33 percent) followed by a desire to go off-roading (10 percent) and finally by "wanted to be with the latest trend" (10 percent).[14]

By the summer of 2001, there were some indications of a slow-down in the SUV market. Many attributed the decrease in sales to the price of gasoline and its escalation. However, vehicles that are crossover SUVs, part-auto and part-truck, appeared to be enjoying an increase in sales by mid-2001.[15]

The SUV has proven to be a lightening rod in public discussion in the areas of environmentalism and safety.[16] There has been intense media coverage of SUVs and a resulting emotionalism on all sides about the ethics of owning, driving, and manufacturing SUVs. These issues and attitudes are explored in the following sections.

The SUV and the Environment

Among industrialized nations, the United States emits the greatest amount of carbon dioxide, the greenhouse gas (GHG) most often mentioned in connection with the phenomenon known as global warming. As of 1998, one-third of the United States GHGs come from motor vehicles. That figure was one-fourth in 1992 when the

[11] *Micheline Maynard, "Plush Sport Utility Sales Soar,"* USA Today, *December 9, 1998, p. 3B.*

[12] Id.

[13] *Robert H. Frank, "Feeling Crash-Resistant in an S.U.V.,"* The New York Times, *May 16, 2000, p. A31; "The Unsung Comeback of the Large Car,"* The New York Times, *October 3, 1999, p. MB1, 8.*

[14] *Jeffrey Ball and Sholnn Freeman, "SUV Love Going Strong,"* The Tribune, *August 27, 2000, pp. B1, B2; Jeffrey Ball and Sholnn Freeman, "Driving Sports Utility Sales,"* USA Today, *November 18, 1998, p. 1B.*

[15] *Joseph B. White, Stephen Power, and Milo Geyelin, "America's Love Affair with Sport's Utilities Is Now Cooling Off,"* The Wall Street Journal, *May 30, 2001, pp. A1, A8.*

[16] *Ellen Goodman, "SUV Backlash Promises to Be Big, Dirty,"* Arizona Republic, *May 11, 1999, p. B7.*

Framework Convention on Climate Change was agreed upon at the Earth Summit in Rio de Janeiro in 1992.[17]

Between 1992 and 1997, the nations in attendance at the Rio summit engaged in negotiations over both voluntary and binding emissions standards. Those negotiations could be charitably described as contentious. At the Kyoto meeting in 1997 and the Buenos Aires meeting in 1998, the U.S. delegation argued for developing nations to make commitments for reduction in their GHG emissions. The position of the developing nations is that GHGs have resulted from the expansion and industries of countries such as the United States and that the United States and other industrial countries should bear the greatest burden when it comes to reduction of GHGs.

Since the 1992 Earth Summit, CO_2 emissions from motor vehicles have outpaced all other U.S. sources. The largest growth in auto sales has been in sport utility vehicles (SUVs) and light trucks. Both of these vehicles are covered under more lenient government fuel efficiency standards. Trucks, busses, and vehicles in excess of 8,000 pounds are not subject to federal fuel efficiency standards at all. Sample weights of SUVs follow:[18]

Toyota LandCruiser	5,115 pounds
GM Tahoe	4,828 pounds
Lincoln Navigator	5,390 pounds
GM Suburban	4,914 pounds
Toyota 4-Runner	3,885 pounds

A Lincoln Towne Car, a four-door luxury sedan, weighs 4,156 pounds.

In 1997, *The New York Times* ran a report that concluded that because of a loophole, these vehicles, including SUVs, had emissions 20 to 100 percent higher than cars.[19] The article noted that if Americans had continued buying just cars instead of light trucks and SUVs, then CO_2 emissions would have been "down by 9.3%."

Later in 1997, California air quality officials revealed a proposal to require trucks, minivans, and most SUVs to meet the same emissions standards as passenger cars by the year 2004. That proposal is now law.

Following the Kyoto treaty of December 12, 1997, in which the United States agreed (subject to ratification by the Senate) to reduce its emissions to its 1990 levels by the year 2012, Ford and Chrysler announced on January 5, 1998, that they would cut the emissions of their SUVs and minivans. At a cost of $100 per vehicle or $100 million per year, Ford announced that its Windstar vans would immediately meet the same emissions standards as its passenger vehicles. *The New York Times* reported on the Ford decision as follows:

> . . . Jacques Nasser [Ford's president of worldwide automotive operations] made clear in an interview that Ford wanted to maintain the acceptability of sports utility

[17] *Donald O. Mayer, "Greenhouse Gas Emissions and the Social Responsibility of Automakers,"* Business and Society Review, *Vol. 105, Number 3, pp. 347–360.*

[18] *Toyota, GM, Ford, Lincoln Web sites.*

[19] *Keith Bradsher, "Light Trucks Increase Profits but Foul Air More than Cars," The New York Times, November 30, 1997, p. A1.*

> vehicles as alternatives to cars, while gaining an advantage over rival automakers in catering to environmentally aware families. 'Anybody who has concerns about the environment can set them aside,' Nasser said adding that Ford was also influenced by recent articles in *The New York Times* on the environmental problems of light trucks.[20]

USA Today ran a series of articles during 1999 on the following topics: the disadvantages of driving a small car in an SUV-dominated market and road; the high center of gravity in small SUVs and the danger of rollovers; and the car makers' detours around CAFÉ rules. CAFÉ (Corporate Average Fuel Economy) rules are the mileage standards the federal government requires each automaker to attain when the fuel economies of all the vehicles they sell in a model year are averaged together. The standard for cars is 27.5 miles per gallon in combined city and highway driving and the standard for trucks and SUVs is 20.7 miles per gallon. The fine for failing to meet CAFÉ is $5.50 for each 0.1 miles per gallon short of the CAFÉ standard. If an automaker sells 1 million cars that average 27 miles per gallon instead of 27.5 miles per gallon, then the fine is $27.5 million.

Foreign automakers generally ignore the CAFÉ standards and simply pay the fines as they say "as a cost of doing business." U.S. automakers are in compliance because criminal sanctions include prison time for officers and managers. *USA Today* concluded, however, that U.S. automaker compliance was meaningless because the automakers are permitted to carry credits forward when they exceed CAFÉ and juggling model years, by mid-year introduction of vehicles, can result in exclusion of large chunks of sales of larger vehicles that would decrease the miles per gallon.

Following the series in *The New York Times* and *USA Today*, Ford announced that it would escalate its emissions standards for its trucks and SUVs. Jacques Nasser announced on May 17, 1999, that Ford's trucks, including its Explorer and Expedition, would meet EPA (Environmental Protection Agency) emissions standards for 2004 by the year 2000. Nasser said he wants customers to have the choice of a full range of Ford products and not have to choose "between the one that is environmentally friendly and the one that isn't."[21]

In early 2000, Ford released its social responsibility report, called "Corporate Citizenship Report," and its chairman announced it to the shareholders at Ford's annual meeting in May 2000. William Clay Ford, Jr. read the Sierra Club's description of the Ford Excursion at the meeting as, "a gas-guzzling rolling monument to environmental destruction." Mr. Ford promised that his company would do better. Sales of the Excursion in 1999 were 15,838 units, in excess of the 15,000 produced. There was a waiting list for buyers.

The following day, *The Detroit Free Press* carried the story of the Ford announcement with the following headline in its business section, "Ford admits its trucks hurt the earth." The Associated Press headline was, "Ford admits dilemma: SUVs vs. environment." Environmental groups said that they would use the report for lobbying in Washington for more stringent regulations. Debbie Zemke, director of Ford's corpo-

[20] *Fara Warner, "Ford's SUVs in 2000 to Meet 2004 Standards,"* The Wall Street Journal, *May 18, 1999, p. B22.*

[21] Id.

rate governance, said Ford still stood by its decision to be forthright, "We just said: 'For heaven's sake, everybody else is talking about it, so why shouldn't we?'"[22]

While environmental groups praised the admission, others questioned the wisdom of such a step. A member of the Michigan congressional delegation said, "It does make it more difficult for us to propose reasonable standards. The company is trying to find itself right now, and we're not sure where it is."[23]

GM and DaimlerChrysler announced that while they would not be accelerating their emissions reductions programs, they were working on alternative fuel vehicles. "We have different objectives on how we get to lower emissions," was the DaimlerChrysler response. GM noted, "It is taking its own path to lower vehicle emissions in the U.S. and around the world."

Since 1996, the automakers have funded ($1.6 billion to date) the Partnership for a New Generation of Vehicles (PNGV). The goal is to develop an 80 miles per gallon family car. There have been alliances with fuel cell technology firms as part of the project, but there are not results as yet and there is no pledge that anything developed there will be brought to the market.

By 2001, the industry average of miles per gallon for sport utility vehicles was at 21.2 miles per gallon, which exceeds the mandatory federal standard of 20.7. Automakers point to the achievement as an indication of their good faith. Environmentalists point to the achievement as an indication that Congress needs to raise the miles per gallon standard.[24] However, by the end of 2001, executives of all of the Big Three auto manufacturers were expressing doubts about Ford's ability to meet its pledge of improving fuel economy from 20 miles per gallon to 25 miles per gallon by 2005. Dieter Zetsche, CEO of the Chrysler Group, said, "Taking 25 percent out in five years is very ambitious."[25]

A recent poll reveals that 66 percent of U.S. citizens believe global warming is a reality, and 72 percent support an agreement among nations to cut CO_2 emissions. Other studies show that drivers may love their SUVs, but also feel some guilt. Some have quoted the 1960's activist Eldridge Cleaver and concluded that they "are not part of the solution, but part of the problem."[26]

Near the end of 2000, several environmental groups began a project of tagging SUVs. The bumper stickers are placed, stealth fashion on parked SUVs, and they read, "I'm changing the environment. Ask me how!" Those participating indicated the bumper stickers are a form of public shame designed to modify behaviors. The bumper sticker includes the name of a Web site, http://www.changingtheclimate.com, which provides instructions for the removal of the bumper sticker.[27]

[22] *Keith Bradsher, "Ford's Admission Perplexes the Neighbors in Henry's Hometown,"* The New York Times, *April 13, 2000, pp. B1, B4.*

[23] Id.

[24] *James R. Healey, "Fuel Efficiency Fires Renewed Public Debate,"* USA Today, *July 27, 2001, pp. 1B, 2B.*

[25] *Danny Hakim, "Fuel Targets for Sports Utilities Pose Difficulties for Automakers,"* The New York Times, *November 23, 2001, pp. C1, C5.*

[26] *Matthew L. Wald, "Even S.U.V. Drivers Can Find Ways to Hug a Tree,"* The New York Times, *January 30, 2000, p. BU12.*

[27] *Karen Gaudette, "'Mad Taggers' Take Aim at SUVs,"* The Tribune, *December 26, 2000, p. A10.*

SUV owners have formed their own group for advocacy. The Sport Utility Vehicle Owners Association of America, Inc. was started in 2000 and is self-described as an advocacy group for life, liberty, and the right to drive a large vehicle. The association charges $50 for membership and has not been given any funding by automakers. A spokesman for DaimlerChrysler said, "To some extent, he's (William D. Brouse, the president) got more credibility if he's not supported by the auto industry."[28] The association has taken the approach of educating policy makers and the public on the virtues of SUVs, including safety and their ability to carry significant numbers of passengers at one time.

The SUV and Safety

At the same time that the Kyoto coverage and SUV emissions issues arose, questions about SUV safety erupted. Data from the U.S. Department of Transportation showed that the death rate for accidents involving smaller cars is 3 per 10,000 registered vehicles. The death rate for SUVs is 1.3 per 10,000 registered vehicles.[29] A study of fatalities revealed that over half of the deaths of small car drivers and occupants resulted from collisions with other cars, not SUVs. SUV collisions with smaller vehicles that resulted in deaths of the occupants of smaller cars constituted 7 percent of the total vehicle fatalities.[30] The conclusion of the study by the Insurance Institute for Highway Safety was that small cars do not provide sufficient protection for their occupants. The data also show that large SUVs are three times as likely as large cars or minivans to kill occupants of the other vehicle in a crash.[31]

A 2001 study by the Insurance Institute for Highway Safety concluded that it was the height of the SUV that was a critical factor in the amount of damage and types of injuries in other cars struck by SUVs. This study was particularly critical of the Mercedes M-Class SUV, a product of DaimlerChrysler, which was, oddly, promoted as the first SUV to minimize damage to other vehicles in the event of a collision. Also, by lowering the vehicles the Institute found that the SUVs caused greater damage, but the damage to persons in other vehicles was to the legs and lower parts of the body. Injuries to the torso and head are more dangerous. The Institute report stressed the need for lower vehicles.[32]

Further data focused on the rollover risk of SUVs. A series in *The New York Times* on rollover risk concluded:

> The number of people in all types of vehicles dying in crashes has remained relatively steady over the last decade, as has the number dying in crashes involving rollovers. But the number of people in sports utility vehicles dying in crashes has grown almost as fast as the number of SUVs on the road, and most of the deaths have been in rollovers.[33]

[28] *Keith Bradsher, "In Proud Defense of the S.U.V.,"* The New York Times, *March 25, 2001, p. BU2.*

[29] *Gary Stoller, "SUVs' Roll Risk Called Greatest,"* USA Today, *July 17, 2000, p. 1A.*

[30] *Jayne O'Donnell, "Smaller Cars; Trucks Aren't Biggest Worry,"* USA Today, *February 10, 1998, p. 1B.*

[31] *Laurie McGinley, "Gas Savings vs. Safety Stirs Debate,"* The Wall Street Journal, *September 6, 1990, pp. B1, B8.*

[32] *Keith Bradsher, "Study Says Height Makes S.U.V.'s Dangerous in Collisions,"* The New York Times, *May 16, 2001, p. C4.*

[33] *Keith Bradsher, "Congress Appears Ready to Tackle Vehicle Rollover Problem,"* The New York Times, *September 21, 2000, pp. C1, C12.*

Total deaths of SUV drivers per million registered vehicles in 1998 were 550 for all SUVs, 641 for small vehicles, 472 for trucks, and 348 for cars. Also, in 62 percent of the fatal accidents involving SUVs, a rollover was involved.[34]

As a result of the various reports, the National Highway Traffic Safety Administration proposed requiring rollover-warning labels in all SUVs. Phil Haseltine, the president of the American Coalition for Highway Safety, a group funded by the auto industry, responded to the NHTSA proposal, "The vast majority of rollover fatalities results from high-risk behavior, not vehicle design. Colorful warning stickers aren't going to make a difference."[35] The 1998 statistics show that 62 percent of all deaths in SUVs were the result of rollovers. That rate is three times the rollover death rate for cars. Deaths in 1998 from SUV rollovers were 1,705. The warning stickers were eventually required to be placed in vehicles and included the following:

> WARNING: Higher Rollover Risk
> Avoid Abrupt Maneuvers and Excessive Speed
> See Owner's Manual for Further Information[36]

However, a study from Rutgers University indicates that since SUVs have been on the road, single-driver fatalities have decreased by 7.5 percent.[37] Overall, since the upward swing in the sale of SUVs, there has been a 50 percent decline in traffic fatalities per vehicle.[38] The authors of the study do note other factors such as increased penalties for driving under the influence, seat belt laws, and air bags. However, even after controlling for these factors statistically, the professors believe that SUV ownership carries substantial safety benefits for both drivers and passengers. The authors refer to their results as a "net savings in lives," with this conclusion, "The increased safety to occupants of light trucks outweighs potential increases in fatalities to occupants of other vehicles."[39]

Later in 1998, *The New York Times* ran a series on the danger of the headlights of SUVs. The series concluded:

> As sport-utility vehicles get higher, their headlights have reached the level of the side mirrors of the cars, producing a blinding glare when cars are in front of them.[40]

The head of the society for automotive engineers said of the glare problem, "My feeling is that it's debilitating; it wears you down." Robert C. Lange, vehicle safety director for GM responded, "I suspect there are very few if any collision events associated with glare."[41] Sonja L. Bultnyck, a spokeswoman for Chrysler, said that the problem is that drivers do not keep sufficient space between their vehicles when they are driving and that the headlight problem is not one of vehicle design but inconsiderate drivers.

[34] *Gregory L. White, "Auto Makers Rush to Improve Safety of SUVs,"* The Wall Street Journal, *May 16, 2000, pp. B1, B4.*

[35] *Anna Wilde Mathews, "Industry Finds Devil in the Details of Plan for Bolder SUV Labels,"* The Wall Street Journal, *February 24, 1999, pp. A1, A8.*

[36] *Jayne O'Donnell, "Rollover Rules Expected for SUVs,"* USA Today, *May 7, 1999, p. 1A.*

[37] *Jayne O'Donnell, "Feds Plan New Warning on Sports Utilities,"* USA Today, *February 17, 1999, p. 1B.*

[38] *Brock Yates, "SUVs Mean Safer Roads,"* The Wall Street Journal, *April 5, 2001, p. A22.*

[39] Id.

[40] *Keith Bradsher, "Larger Vehicles Are Hampering Visibility,"* The New York Times, *November 22, 1998, p. Y17.*

[41] Id.

In 1996, an auto industry task force, comprised of engineers from all the auto manufacturers, had issued a report recommending that the headlights on trucks and SUVs should be lower. Their report recommended that the maximum allowable height be reduced from 54 inches to either 36 or 40 inches. Twenty years ago the headlight height on a Jeep Wagoneer was 33 inches. Today's GM Suburban's headlights are at 39 inches.

The headlight battle took a new turn in 2001 as drivers complained about the brightness and color of headlights, and an ongoing investigation into the safety issues focuses on all headlights and not just those of SUVs.[42]

In September 2000, Congress held hearings on rollover deaths. The hearings released information indicating that of 35,806 deaths that occurred in vehicles in 1999, rollovers were a factor in 10,657. Ninety-two percent of all rollovers occurred because the vehicle was "tripped," which means that it happened because the vehicle struck another car, a curb, a guard rail, or other large object that caused it to teeter onto one side. Legislation with bipartisan support would require all vehicles to carry a rollover rating given by the National Academy of Sciences following their studies of the vehicles and attributed risk factors for rollover.[43] The insurance and auto industry support the proposed rating system. Consumers Union, publisher of *Consumer Reports*, opposes the rating system on the grounds that standards for the rating are too lax.

At least one class action suit is pending on SUV rollovers (*Connick v. Suzuki Motor Co.*, 675 N.E.2d 584 (Ill. 1997)). An appeals court has ruled that there was a sufficient basis for pursuing the plaintiffs' theory that there was a failure to warn about the rollover risk. Trial in the case is now pending. Other cases are pending and an increase in the number of suits is likely.[44]

In March 2000, all the automakers announced that they would redesign their SUVs by placing steel rails two inches lower inside their underbodies to reduce the risk of their overriding cars' bumpers and doorsills in collisions.[45] The change in design came from complaints of small car drivers who pointed to the data on SUVs actually driving over cars following collisions.

Despite the intense media coverage of the safety and environmental issues, sales of SUVs indicate a strong love affair between these vehicles and the American public. Auto industry analyst Maryann Keller notes that consumers' car purchases "are dictated by their desires for performance, comfort, and safety, not by an ecological standard." A Detroit consultant notes that the SUV has enjoyed a particular connection with customers, "The SUV is such a close connector with their values. They're not going to give it up easily." A GM spokeswoman noted, "We're hell-bent on continuing momentum in SUVs and trucks."[46]

[42] *James R. Healey, "Bright Lights, Big Controversy,"* USA Today, *June 7, 2001, pp. 1B, 2B.*

[43] *James R. Healey, "Deaths by the Gallon,"* USA Today, *July 2, 1999, pp. 1B, 2B.*

[44] *Gary Stoller, "Popularity of SUVs Likely to Mean More Lawsuits,"* USA Today, *July 17, 2000, p. 3B.*

[45] *Keith Bradsher, "Automakers Modifying S.U.V.'s to Reduce Risk to Other Drivers,"* The New York Times, *March 21, 2000, pp. A1, C4.*

[46] *Brock Yates, "Pecksniffs Can't Stop the SUV,"* The Wall Street Journal, *May 17, 2000, p. A26.*

Running parallel to these safety issues has been the Ford Explorer/Firestone Tire controversy (see Case 5.31). Both companies were defendants in class action lawsuits brought against them for those injured or killed in rollover accidents involving Ford Explorers equipped with certain brands of Firestone tires. The cause of the accidents and ultimate accountability remains questionable, but the accidents have been lumped together by the public with the general SUV safety concerns.[47]

While the Ford Explorer/Firestone Tire issue has had a dramatic impact on the sales of the Ford Explorer, there has not been any impact on other SUV sales. Ford released data showing that the death rate for its Explorer is lower than the death rates for smaller SUVs of other manufacturers. However, Ford continues to feel the sting from the questions about SUVs, and its CEO, Jacques Nasser, resigned in October 2001 following questions by the Ford board about his management style and approach to issues and employees.

Discussion Questions

1. List all of the stakeholders in the SUV controversy and explain their desires and interests in whether auto manufacturers continue to produce SUVs.
2. What do you think is driving the demands for the SUV?
3. How do you resolve conflicts among the various stakeholder groups in the SUV controversy?
4. Assume the role of a senior manager at one of the major U.S. automakers. What steps would you take to resolve the controversy?

CASE 2.8

Ice-T, The Body Count Album, and Shareholder Uprisings

Ice-T (Tracy Morrow), a black rap artist signed under the Time Warner label, released an album called *Body Count* in 1992 that contained a controversial song, "Cop Killer." The lyrics included: "I've got my twelve-gauge sawed-off . . . I'm 'bout to dust some cops off . . . die, pig, die."

The song set off a storm of protest from law enforcement groups. At the annual meeting of Time Warner at the Beverly Wilshire Hotel, 1,100 shareholders, as well as police representatives and their spokesman, Charlton Heston, denounced Time Warner executives in a five-hour session on the album and its content. Heston noted that the compact disc had been shipped to radio stations in small replicas of body bags.

[47] *Milo Geyelin and Timothy Aeppel, "For Firestone, Tire Trial Is Mixed Victory,"* The Wall Street Journal, *August 28, 2001, pp. A3, A4.*

One police officer said the company had "lost its moral compass, or never had it." Others said that Time Warner seemed to cultivate these types of artists. One shareholder claimed that Time Warner was always "pushing the envelope" with its artists, such as Madonna with her *Sex* book, and its products, such as the film *The Last Temptation of Christ*, which drew large protests from religious groups. Another shareholder pointed out that Gerald Levin, Time Warner president, promised a stuttering-awareness group that the cartoon character Porky Pig would be changed after they made far fewer vocal protests.

Levin responded that the album would not be pulled. He defended it as "depicting the despair and anger that hang in the air of every American inner city, not advocating attacks on police." Levin announced Time Warner would sponsor a TV forum for artists, law enforcement officials, and others to discuss such topics as racism and free speech. At the meeting, Levin also announced a four-for-one stock split and a 12 percent increase in Time Warner's dividend.

The protests continued after the meeting. Philadelphia's municipal pension fund decided to sell $1.6 million in Time Warner holdings to protest the Ice-T song. Said Louis J. Campione, a police officer and member of the city's Board of Pensions and Retirement, "It's fine that somebody would express their opinions, but we don't have to support it."

Several CEOs responded to Levin's and Time Warner's support of the song.[48] Roger Salquist, CEO of Calgene, Inc., noted:

> I'm outraged. I think the concept of free speech has been perverted. It's anti-American, it's antihumanity, and there is no excuse for it.
>
> I hope it kills them. It's certainly not something I tolerate, and I find their behavior offensive as a corporation.
>
> If you can increase sales with controversy without harming people, that's one thing. [But Time Warner's decision to support Ice-T] is outside the bounds of what I consider acceptable behavior and decency in this country.

David Geffen, chairman of Geffen Records, who refused to release Geto Boys records because of lyrics, said:

> The question is not about business, it is about responsibility. Should someone make money by advocating the murder of policemen? To say that this whole issue is not about profit is silly. It certainly is not about artistic freedom.
>
> If the album were about language, sex or drugs, there are people on both sides of these issues. But when it comes down to murder, I don't think there is any part of society that approves of it. . . . I wish [Time Warner] would show some sensitivity by donating the profits to a fund for wounded policemen.

Jerry Greenfield, co-founder of Ben & Jerry's Homemade, Inc., responded that "songs like 'Cop Killer' aren't constructive, but we as a society need to look at what

[48] *Wall Street Journal. Eastern Edition (Staff Produced Copy Only) by Wall Street Journal News Round Up. Copyright 1992 by Dow Jones & Co. Inc. Reproduced with permission of Dow Jones & Co. Inc. in the format textbook via Copyright Clearance Center.*

we've created. I don't condone cop killing. [But] to reach a more just and equitable society everyone's voice must be heard."

Neal Fox, CEO of A. Sulka & Company (an apparel retailer owned by Luxco Investments), said:

> As a businessperson, my inclination is to say that Time Warner management has to be consistent. Once you've decided to get behind this product and support it, you can't express feelings of censorship. They didn't have recourse.
>
> Also, they are defending flag and country for the industry. If they bend to pressures regarding the material, it opens a Pandora's box for all creative work being done in the entertainment industry.
>
> On a personal basis, I abhor the concept, but on a corporate basis, I understand their reasoning.

John W. Hatsopoulos, executive vice president of Thermo Electron Corporation, had this to say:

> I think the fact that a major U.S. corporation would almost encourage kids to attack the police force is horrible. Time Warner is a huge corporation. That they would encourage something like this for a few bucks. . . . You know about yelling fire in a crowded theater.
>
> I was so upset I was looking at [Thermo Electron's] pension plan to see if we owned any Time Warner stock [in order to sell it]. But we don't own any.

Bud Konheim, CEO of Nicole Miller, Ltd., weighed in with:

> I don't think that people in the media can say that advertising influences consumers to buy cars or shirts, and then argue that violence on television or in music has no impact. The idea of media is to influence people's minds, and if you are inciting people to riot, it's very dangerous.
>
> It's also disappointing that they chose to defend themselves. It was a knee-jerk reaction instead of seizing the role to assert moral leadership. They had a great opportunity. Unfortunately, I don't think they will pay for this decision because there is already so much dust in people's eyes.

George Sanborn, CEO of Sanborn, Inc., said: "Would you release the album if it said, 'Kill a Jew or bash a fag'? I think we all know what the answer would be. They're doing it to make money."

Mark Nathanson, CEO of Falcon Cable Systems Company, responded: "If you aren't happy with the product, you don't have to buy it. I might not like what [someone like Ice-T] has to say, but I would vigorously defend his right to express his viewpoint."

Stoney M. Stubbs, Jr., chairman of Frozen Food Express Industries, Inc., commented: "The more attention these types of things get, the better the products sell. I don't particularly approve of the way they play on people's emotions, but from a business standpoint [Time Warner is] probably going to make some money off it. They're protecting the people that make them the money . . . the artists."[49]

[49] The Wall Street Journal, *"Time Warner's Ice-T Defense Is Assailed," July 23, 1992, pp. B1, B8.*

Despite the flap over the album, sales were less than spectacular. It reached number 32 on the Billboard Top 200 album chart and sold 300,000 copies.[50]

Levin had defended Time Warner's position:

> Time Warner is determined to be a global force for encouraging the confrontation of ideas. We know that profits are the source of our strength and independence, of our ability to produce and distribute the work of our artists and writers, but we won't retreat in the face of threats of boycotts or political grandstanding. In the short run, cutting and running would be the surest and safest way to put this controversy behind us and get on with our business. But in the long run, it would be a destructive precedent. It would be a signal to all the artists and journalists inside and outside Time Warner that if they wish to be heard, then they must tailor their minds and souls to fit the reigning orthodoxies.
>
> In the weeks and months ahead, Time Warner intends to use the debate engendered by the uproar over this one song to create a forum in which we can bring together the different sides in this controversy. We will invest in fostering the open discussion of the violent tensions that Ice-T's music has exposed.
>
> We're under no illusions. We know all the wounds can't be healed by such a process or all the bitterness—on both sides—talked out of existence. But we believe that the future of our country—indeed, of our world—is contained in the commitment to truth and free expression, in the refusal to run away.[51]

By August 1992, protests against the song had grown and sales suffered. Ice-T made the decision himself to withdraw "Cop Killer" from the *Body Count* album. Time Warner asked music stores to exchange the *Body Count* CDs for ones without "Cop Killer." Some store owners refused, saying there were much worse records. Former Geto Boys member, Willie D., said Ice-T's free speech rights were violated. "We're living in a communist country and everyone's afraid to say it," he said.

Following the flap over the song, the Time Warner board met to establish general company policies to bar distribution of music deemed inappropriate. By February 1993, Time Warner and Ice-T agreed that Ice-T would leave the Time Warner label because of "creative differences." The split came after Time Warner executives objected to Ice-T's proposed cover for his new album, which showed black men attacking whites.

By May 1993, Time Warner's board was steering the company into more family-oriented entertainment. It began its transition with the 1993 release of such movies as *Dennis the Menace*, *Free Willy*, and *The Secret Garden*.

In June 1995, presidential candidate, Senator Robert Dole, pointed to Time Warner's rap albums and movies as societal problems. Public outcry against Time Warner resulted.

In June 1995, C. DeLores Tucker, 67, and head of the National Political Congress of Black Women handed Chairman of Time Warner Michael J. Fuchs the following lyrics from a Time Warner label recording:

[50] *Mark Landler, "Time Warner Seeks a Delicate Balance in Rap Music Furor,"* The New York Times, *June 5, 1995, p. 1B.*

[51] *Wall Street Journal. Eastern Edition (Staff Produced Copy Only) by Holman W. Jenkins, Jr. Copyright 1996 by Dow Jones & Co. Inc. Reproduced with permission of Dow Jones & Co. Inc. in the format textbook via Copyright Clearance Center.*

Her body's beautiful,
so I'm thinkin' rape.
Grabbed the bitch by her mouth,
slam her down on the couch.
She begged in a low voice:
"Please don't kill me."
I slit her throat
and watch her shake like on TV.

—Geto Boys, *Mind of a Lunatic*

and asked Mr. Fuchs the following, "Read this out loud. I'll give you $100 to read it." Mr. Fuchs declined.

Mrs. Tucker was joined by William Bennett, a GOP activist and former Education Secretary. Mrs. Tucker believes Time Warner is "pimping pornography to children for the almighty dollar. Corporations need to understand: What does it profit a corporation to gain the world but lose its soul? That's the real bottom line."

In June 1995, following Mrs. Tucker's national campaign, Time Warner fired Doug Morris, the chairman of domestic music operations. By July, Morris and Time Warner were in litigation. Morris had been a defender of gangsta rap music and had acquired the Interscope label that produced albums for Tupac Shakur and Snoop Doggy Dogg. Mr. Fuchs said the termination had nothing to do with the rap controversy.

Rap accounts for less than 10 percent of total sales in the record industry. Total sales are about $12 billion with rock music bringing in $4 billion of the sales. Some retail chains, including Wal-Mart, refuse to carry the gangsta rap albums and some radio stations refuse to play the songs. The songs cited included the following:

"I'd rather use my gun 'cause I get the money quicker . . . got them in the frame—Bang! Bang! . . . blowing [expletive] to the moon."

—Tupac Shakur, "Strugglin"

These lyrics contain slang expressions for using an AK-47 machine gun to murder a police officer:

"It's 1-8-7 on a [expletive] cop . . . so what the [expletive] does a nigger like you gotta say? Got to take trip to the MIA and serve your ass with a [expletive] AK.

—Snoop Doggy Dogg, "Tha' Shiznit"

Discussion Questions

1. Was Ice-T's song an exercise of free speech or sensationalism for profit?
2. Would you have taken Levin's position?
3. Is Time Warner morally responsible for its artists?
4. Does screening lyrics set a dangerous precedent?
5. Would shareholder objections influence your response to such a controversy?

6. What was Time Warner's purpose in firing Morris? By November 1995, Time Warner's Levin fired Michael Fuchs. What message is there for executives in controversial products?

Guns 'n Social Responsibility

The issues of the manufacture and sale of guns continues to be an issue of social responsibility. While the issues surrounding guns are complex and are progressing through both legislatures and courts, all of the issues can be grouped into two broad categories: the issues affecting retail sales and issues affecting production and distribution.

Retail Issues, Guns, and Social Responsibility

(1) Criminal Activity Using Purchased Guns

At the retail level, there is significant activity and liability for the sale of weapons that are then used in the commission of crimes.

During the early 1990s, there was a substantial increase in the number of such cases and resulting litigation. For example, in October 1993, a court ordered Kmart Corporation to pay $12.5 million to Deborah Kitchen, who was left a quadriplegic after her boyfriend, Thomas Knapp, shot her point-blank in the neck with a rifle he purchased at Kmart. The trial records show he was so drunk at the time of purchase that he could not legibly complete the federal firearms forms, so a clerk did it for him. The family of a couple slain by their schizophrenic son with a .38 caliber handgun he had purchased at Wal-Mart sued Wal-Mart in December 1993.[52]

By the end of 1993, both Wal-Mart and Kmart announced they would no longer sell any handguns at their retail stores. Firearm sales for the two discounters totaled $158 million. A Wal-Mart spokesman said, "A majority of our customers tell us they would prefer not to shop in a retail store that sells handguns."[53]

Both retailers were the last to stop selling guns. Montgomery Ward and Sears, Roebuck and Co. stopped in 1981; Ward's felt the sales were too problematic, and Sears cited burdensome paperwork.

(2) The Toy Gun Controversy

The retail issues were not limited, however, to actual weapons. There were a number of incidents involving toy guns within the same time frame. In September 1994, a thirteen-year-old boy was fatally shot by a police officer in the stairwell of a New York City housing project because he was carrying a toy gun the officer assumed to be real. A similar incident occurred when another officer shot and wounded a 16-year-old youth who was also carrying a toy gun.

52 *Robert Davis, "Gun Sales All 'Supply and Demand,'"* USA Today, *April 19, 1994, p. 1B.*

53 *Andrea Gerlin, "Wal-Mart Stops Handgun Sales Inside Its Stores,"* The Wall Street Journal, *December 23, 1993, pp. B1, B8.*

By October 1994, both Kay-Bee Toy Stores, now K•B Toys, and Toys 'R' Us announced that they would no longer carry realistic-looking military- or police-style weapons. They would sell only brightly colored, oversized toy guns or those with logos or decals that clearly distinguish them from real weapons.

Said Ann Iverson, president and CEO of K•B, which has a chain of 1,100 stores nationwide, "This step is just a part of K•B's strategy to re-evaluate our merchandise mix and address what families need today in terms of fun, safe, and developmentally sound toys."[54] Toy guns represent 2 percent of K•B's inventory.

CEO Michael Goldstein of Toys 'R' Us has led an industry initiative to eliminate the realistic-looking guns. He said, "The issue is the potential harm that these products pose to children and others. We believe that by taking this step we can help raise awareness and encourage manufacturers and other retailers to join us in this effort."[55]

A Toys 'R' Us shopper commented, "If it saves a couple kids' lives, I think it's a good thing. Actually, it's a courageous move. They're going to lose business."[56]

The sales policies adopted by the stores and companies in the wake of these incidents have changed, and the year 2001 saw a reemergence of litigation related to how retailers conduct their sales of guns and their responsibility when the purchaser is not checked adequately.

Kmart returned to selling guns in its stores and in the fall of 2001 lost a lawsuit brought against it by the parents of a teen for wrongful death. The jury awarded $1.5 million in damages and another $1.5 million in punitive damages in the wrongful death suit.

Ryan Eslinger, who was 19 at the time, bought a shotgun at a Kmart in Kimball Junction, Utah. Eslinger had been declared mentally incompetent by a court, but when he filled out the questionnaire for the Bureau of Alcohol, Tobacco and Firearms (ATF) that is required prior to gun purchases, he offered a "no" answer to the form's question on mental illness.

The Kmart clerk accepted Eslinger's passport as identification because Eslinger did not have a driver's license. However, the passport did not have Eslinger's current address.

Eslinger returned the next day to the Kmart with the gun, which had been completely disassembled. He asked for assistance in putting the gun back together. At that point Kmart's store security pulled the ATF application that Eslinger had completed. When he saw that the application noted that there was no proof of current address, the security guard called Kmart's legal department, but no one returned the call. The security guard refused to give the gun back to Eslinger, but he was overruled by the store manager.

The gun was reassembled and Eslinger took the gun home and shot and killed himself.

[54] *Joseph Pereira and Barbara Carton, "Toys 'R' Us to Banish Some 'Realistic' Toy Guns,"* The Wall Street Journal, *October 14, 1994, pp. B1, B9.*

[55] Id.

[56] Id.

The lawyer for Eslinger argued that Kmart had not adequately trained its personnel on the sale of guns. Kmart's video for training on gun sales indicates that the most important sale is the "one you don't make."[57] At the time Eslinger purchased the gun there was testimony that indicated he was drooling and that he had self-inflicted injuries. Kmart argued that he looked clean cut.

(3) Retail Regulatory Circumvention

As the litigation battles over purchased guns continued, more regulations were being passed, particularly at the federal level, that limited the types of guns that could be manufactured and sold in the United States. Congress placed controls on assault weapons with a resulting impact on retail gun stores that sold the weapons as part of their core business.

Sylvia Daniel of Ducktown, Tennessee, is known as "Machine Gun Mama" and the "First Lady of Firearms." She still sells machine guns outlawed under President Ronald Reagan in 1986 because they were made before the ban went into effect. In 1985, she sold them for $185; now, she sells them for $3,000. She and her husband specialize in selling weapons by finding loopholes in gun control laws. Wayne Daniel said, "If there is a dollar to be made, make it. It may be immoral but not illegal. The bottom line is money. This is a legal business."[58]

The Daniels sell their semiautomatic M-11/9 pistol nationwide. An agent of the Bureau of Alcohol, Tobacco and Firearms noted that this weapon is good for only two things: the firing range and killing. Sylvia Daniel agreed, but added, "It's not the gun, it's the people. We sell to federally licensed dealers. They sell it to you. Did you take it home and put it under your bed and your son got it and killed with it? Is that my fault? I know kids are killed every day. But the problem is not the gun. . . . It's not about gun control. It's about crime control."[59]

The Daniels also sell a "Mac-in-a-sack" for $160, which consists of fifty-two parts for the M-11/9. Excluded are the barrel and frame where the serial number would be, so buyers can make guns with no serial number. The Daniels also sell a briefcase that holds a Mac and has a switch to fire the pistol. The ATF labels the briefcase, one of the Daniels' best-sellers, an assassination device.

Manufacture and Distribution, Guns and Social Responsibility

There are also several issues in the manufacture and distribution of weapons. These extend beyond the retail level and the issue of selling guns to whether companies should manufacture guns and whether their distribution systems and types of guns exacerbate social problems.

(1) Cheap Handguns

One of the principal targets of anti-gun activists has been the so-called "Saturday Night Special," a gun that costs about $13 to make and then retails for between $59

[57] *Margaret Cronin Fisk, "Kmart to pay $3 million for selling gun to suicidal teen,"* National Law Journal, *October 1, 2001, p. B1.*

[58] *Robert Davis, "Gun Sales All 'Supply and Demand,'"* USA Today, *April 19, 1994, p. 2A.*

[59] Id.

and $70. The gun has a long history that traces back to the Jennings family of California, a family that focused on the successful sales of handguns.

Three gun manufacturers in California evolved from the Jennings family. George Jennings founded Raven Arms, Inc., in 1970 and made the Raven .25. George's son, Bruce Jennings, left Raven in 1978 to form Jennings Firearms, Inc., which manufactures another Saturday Night Special, the Jennings .22, which costs $13 to make and retails for $75 to $89.

George's son-in-law, Jim Davis, left Raven in 1982 to start Davis Industries, Inc., which makes a third Saturday Night Special, the Davis .38; this gun costs $15 to make and retails for $95 to $100.

Based on Bureau of Alcohol, Tobacco and Firearms data on handguns sold after 1986, the leading handguns used in crimes are the Davis, the Raven, and the Jennings.

Many criminologists, prosecutors, and gun-sale reform advocates maintain that the availability of cheap weapons escalates crime and killing. Josh Sugarmann of the Violence Policy Center, which studies violence prevention, said of the Saturday Night Specials: "We have a fire burning, and these companies are throwing gasoline on it. These people know what the inner-city gun buyer wants."[60]

Dave Brazeau, the general manager of Raven Arms, responded, "If it wasn't a gun, it would just be something else—a rock, a bow and arrow, or a baseball bat."[61]

Only a few states ban the cheap handguns. Maryland, for example, has banned the Jennings .22 and the Raven .25 as "unreliable as to safety." South Carolina and Illinois have banned the three California companies' brands because the zinc-alloy frames melt at less than 800 degrees.[62]

Smith & Wesson holds the top slot in gun sales, but the three Jennings-related companies together account for 22 percent of all handguns sold and 27 percent of all handguns used in crimes across the country.[63]

The Saturday Night Specials are often sold in bulk in states where gun laws are lax and then smuggled to urban areas for sale. An illegal gun dealer in Harlem commented, "Here, where I live, every young kid has a .22 or a .25. It's like their first Pampers."[64]

Congress passed the Brady Bill in 1993, which mandates a five-day waiting period for handgun purchases. Other proposals on gun bans have passed and some remain on the table to ban the sale of Saturday Night Specials altogether.

A number of states also proposed regulations of Saturday Night Specials. Some note that firecrackers are regulated but firearms are not.

[60] *Alix M. Freedman, "A Single Family Makes Many of Cheap Pistols That Saturate Cities,"* The Wall Street Journal, *February 28, 1992, p. A1.*

[61] Id.

[62] Id.

[63] Id.

[64] Id.

(2) Generic Liability and Distribution

With legislation carrying political and emotional battles, many gun control advocates have used litigation as a means of controlling the number of guns available. Imposing liability is seen as a means for curbing both production as well as the number of gun manufacturers.

For example, the Department of Housing and Urban Development (HUD) long rumbled about the possibility of suing gun manufacturers in order to hold them liable for security costs at federally funded public housing complexes where shootings are common. HUD's reasoning would begin a series of cases by cities that focused not on a defect in the gun's design, but in their distribution to those who are likely to abuse them in such a way as to cause harm to others.[65]

Cities around the country adopted the HUD theory as well as one from the tobacco litigation. The cities brought suit against the gun manufacturers to seek reimbursement for the costs they incur in treating gun shot victims as well as the costs of investigation and other related expenses that come from the use of guns in the commission of crime. The suits, while filed around the country, have not done well in the courts. The city of Cincinnati had its suit against several gun manufacturers dismissed.[66] The court warned of a slippery slope, "Were we to decide otherwise, we would open a Pandora's box. For example, the city could sue the manufacturers of matches for arson, or automobile manufacturers for traffic accidents, or breweries for drunken driving."[67]

The Smith & Wesson Deal and Social Responsibility

In the meantime, Smith & Wesson, a gun manufacturer, concerned about proposed Massachusetts regulation and the pending litigation, was struggling as to how to handle all the potential liability. Additionally, its parent company, Tomkins, P.L.C., a British firm, was trying to sell the 157-year-old Massachusetts company and was not having much luck given the status of the pending litigation.

Tomkins had purchased Smith & Wesson in 1987 for $112.5 million. As a manufacturer of plumbing supplies and lawn mowers, it was unprepared for the litigation and very public controversy surrounding gun manufacturers in the United States. Further, the British attitude toward handguns (they are outlawed in Britain) created considerable controversy for Tomkins at home as it began experiencing protests and boycotts over its ownership.

To find a way out of the situation, Smith & Wesson decided to break rank with its fellow gun manufacturers and it reached a settlement with the federal government that included substantial restrictions on the production and distribution of handguns. On March 17, 2000, Smith & Wesson signed an agreement with the federal government that provided for the following:

In the 21-page settlement, Smith & Wesson agreed to change the way its guns are designed, marketed, and distributed. Under the key provisions of the pact, the company will:

65 *Paul M. Barrett, "HUD May Join Assault on Gun Makers,"* The Wall Street Journal, *July 28, 1999, p. A3.*

66 City of Cincinnati v. Beretta U.S.A. Corp., *2000 Ohio App. Lexis 3601 at * 1 (Aug. 11, 2000).*

67 Id.

- equip all handguns with external safety locks within 60 days;
- equip all pistols with internal locking devices within two years;
- devote 2 percent of its gross revenues to the development of "smart," personalized guns that can only be fired by an authorized user;
- design firearms so that they cannot be readily operated by a child under age six;
- include chamber-load indicators on all pistols within one year; and
- stop producing firearms that accept large-capacity ammunition magazines.

The company has also agreed to add a hidden serial number on every gun to make it easier for law enforcement authorities to trace guns used by criminals.

Sales and Distribution

Within six months, Smith & Wesson must include in the packaging of each firearm sold a warning on risks of guns in the home and information about proper home storage. In addition, the gun maker agreed not to sell firearms that are resistant to fingerprints or that can be readily converted to illegal fully automatic weapons.

All authorized dealers and distributors of Smith & Wesson's products will be required to abide by a "code of conduct" to eliminate the sale of firearms to criminals, unauthorized juveniles, or "straw purchasers." Specifically, dealers and distributors must agree that they will:

- deny guns to purchasers unless they have completed a background check, even if the check takes longer than the current legal standard of three business days;
- make no sales to anyone who has not passed a certified firearms safety course or exam;
- require purchasers of multiple handguns to take only one gun on the day of sale and the rest two weeks later; and
- implement a security plan to prevent gun thefts.

Under the code of conduct, dealers must also agree not to allow children under 18 access, without an adult, to gun shops or sections of stores where guns are sold.[68]

In exchange, the federal government would see that all gun litigation was dismissed. There were approximately 30 such suits pending around the country.

The reaction to the settlement was mixed. While the British hailed the decision as brilliant and many business ethicists heralded it as a socially responsible decision, Charlton Heston, president of the National Rifle Association (NRA), said, "Smith & Wesson is a good company and a fine old American name, but they're owned by the Brits. I don't really relish the idea of the Brits telling us how to deal with one part of our Bill of Rights."[69]

There was significant customer backlash, and the CEO of Tomkins, Ed Shultz, received used tea bags in his mail from U.S. customers to remind him of the Boston Tea Party.[70] There was a boycott of Smith & Wesson guns by both customers and retailers, with many retailers refusing to carry Smith & Wesson guns in their inventory.

68 *Gary Fields, "For Smith & Wesson, Blanks Instead of a Magic Bullet,"* The Wall Street Journal, *August 24, 2000, p. A24; Paul M. Barrett, Joe Mathews, and Vanessa O'Connell, "Arms Deal,"* The Wall Street Journal, *March 21, 2000, p. A1.*

69 *Christine W. Westphal and Susan M. Wheeler, "When Ethical Decisions Alienate Stakeholders: Smith & Wesson as a Case Study," Paper presented at the Academy of Legal Studies, August 8, 2001, Albuquerque, New Mexico, citing,* The Guardian *(London), August 5, 2000, Guardian City pages, p. 24.*

70 Id.

The result was that Smith & Wesson was forced to close plants in Maine and Massachusetts, and, by September of 2000, it was forced to lay off a substantial number of workers.

In May 2001, Tomkins sold Smith & Wesson for $15 million to an Arizona gun lock company, Saf-T-Hammer Lock Corporation of Scottsdale. As part of the sale, Saf-T-Lock got $97 million in assets, including a 660,000-square-foot plant in Springfield, Massachusetts; a production facility in Houlton, Maine; Smith & Wesson patents; trademarks; intellectual property; distribution rights; inventory; equipment; and machine drawings.

The Bush Administration announced in August 2001 that it was not bound by the Smith & Wesson agreement and considered the agreement to be only a "Memorandum of Agreement," but not a binding and final contract. However, by the time the announcement was made, Smith & Wesson's sales had fallen off by one-third and it had a loss year-to-date of $57 million.[71]

The Constitutional Issues

While the gun safety, liability, and regulation issues continue, the major opposition comes from those who are concerned about the Second Amendment to the U.S. Constitution and the right to keep and bear arms. Groups such as the National Rifle Association (NRA) and Gun Owners of America, Inc. (GOA) have engaged in extensive lobbying and worked with gun manufacturers to help them in the ongoing litigation. "To bring the right to bear firearms under consumer safety is just one more element in a scheme to destroy private ownership of firearms," was a comment by Dennis Fusaro of GOA, and he added, "Putting all these bells and whistles on firearms is . . . the first step."[72]

Those against the litigation and regulation present emotionally charged arguments to counter the safety issues and discussions about children's safety that are part of the regulation advocates' presentations.

The constitutional issue centers around the interpretation of the Second Amendment and whether it means that there is a right to have a militia or whether it is an individual right of each citizen to own firearms and the extent of that right as well as how much can be regulated without infringing on constitutional rights.

The nature of the constitutional argument is summarized in the following excerpt from a law review piece written by Professor Sanford Levinson for the *Yale Law Journal* entitled, "The Embarrassing Second Amendment."[73] The piece is a commentary on the unwillingness of scholars to debate the issue of the right to keep and bear arms as well as a discussion about the history of the amendment and its framers' intentions (footnotes omitted).

> A standard move of those legal analysts who wish to limit the Second Amendment's force is to focus on its "preamble" as setting out a restrictive purpose. Recall Laurence

[71] *Tish Durkin, "Good Deeds Can Misfire: Consider a Gunmaker's Tumble,"* National Law Journal, *April 28, 2001, p. 1207.*

[72] Id.

[73] *Reprinted by permission of The Yale Law Journal Company and William S. Hein Company from* The Yale Law Journal, *Vol. 99, pp. 637–659.*

Tribe's assertion that that purpose was to allow the states to keep their militias and to protect them against the possibility that the new national government will use its power to establish a powerful standing army and eliminate the state militias. This purposive reading quickly disposes of any notion that there is an "individual" right to keep and bear arms. The right, if such it be, is only a state's right. The consequence of this reading is obvious: the national government has the power to regulate—to the point of prohibition—private ownership of guns, since that has, by stipulation, nothing to do with preserving state militias. This is, indeed, the position of the ACLU, which reads the Amendment as protecting only the right of "maintaining an effective state militia. . . . [T]he individual's right to bear arms applies only to the preservation or efficiency of a well-regulated [state] militia. Except for lawful police and military purposes, the possession of weapons by individuals is not constitutionally protected."

This is not a wholly implausible reading, but one might ask why the Framers did not simply say something like "Congress shall have no power to prohibit state-organized and directed militias." Perhaps they in fact meant to do something else. Moreover, we might ask if ordinary readers of late 18th Century legal prose would have interpreted it as meaning something else. The text at best provides only a starting point for a conversation. In this specific instance, it does not come close to resolving the questions posed by federal regulation of arms. Even if we accept the preamble as significant, we must still try to figure out what might be suggested by guaranteeing to "the people the right to keep and bear arms;" moreover, as we shall see presently, even the preamble presents unexpected difficulties in interpretation.

One might argue (and some have) that the substantive right is one pertaining to a collective body—"the people"—rather than to individuals. Professor Cress, for example, argues that state constitutions regularly used the words "man" or "person" in regard to "individual rights such as freedom of conscience," whereas the use in those constitutions of the term "the people" in regard to a right to bear arms is intended to refer to the "sovereign citizenry" collectively organized. Such an argument founders, however, upon examination of the text of the federal Bill of Rights itself and the usage there of the term "the people" in the First, Fourth, Ninth, and Tenth Amendments.

Consider that the Fourth Amendment protects "[t]he right of the people to be secure in their persons," or that the First Amendment refers to the "right of the people peaceably to assemble, and to petition the Government for a redress of grievances." It is difficult to know how one might plausibly read the Fourth Amendment as other than a protection of individual rights, and it would approach the frivolous to read the assembly and petition clause as referring only to the right of state legislatures to meet and pass a remonstrance directed to Congress or the President against some governmental act. The Tenth Amendment is trickier, though it does explicitly differentiate between "states" and "the people" in terms of retained rights. Concededly, it would be possible to read the Tenth Amendment as suggesting only an ultimate right of revolution by the collective people should the "states" stray too far from their designated role of protecting the rights of the people. This reading follows directly from the social contract theory of the state. (But, of course, many of these rights are held by individuals.)

Although the record is suitably complicated, it seems tendentious to reject out of hand the argument that one purpose of the Amendment was to recognize an individual's right to engage in armed self-defense against criminal conduct. Historian Robert

E. Shalhope supports this view, arguing in his article "The Ideological Origins of the Second Amendment" that the Amendment guarantees individuals the right "to possess arms for their own personal defense". It would be especially unsurprising if this were the case, given the fact that the development of a professional police force (even within large American cities) was still at least a half century away at the end of the colonial period. I shall return later in this essay to this individualist notion of the Amendment, particularly in regard to the argument that "changing circumstances," including the development of a professional police force, have deprived it of any continuing plausibility. But I want now to explore a second possible purpose of the Amendment, which as a sometime political theorist I find considerably more interesting.

Assume, as Professor Cress has argued, that the Second Amendment refers to a communitarian, rather than an individual, right. We are still left the task of defining the relationship between the community and the state apparatus. It is this fascinating problem to which I now turn.

Consider once more the preamble and its reference to the importance of a well-regulated militia. Is the meaning of the term obvious? Perhaps we should make some effort to find out what the term "militia" meant to 18th century readers and writers, rather than assume that it refers only to Dan Quayle's Indiana National Guard and the like. By no means am I arguing that the discovery of that meaning is dispositive as to the general meaning of the Constitution for us today. But it seems foolhardy to be entirely uninterested in the historical philology behind the Second Amendment.

I, for one, have been persuaded that the term "militia" did not have the limited reference that Professor Cress and many modern legal analysts assign to it. There is strong evidence that "militia" refers to all of the people, or at least all of those treated as full citizens of the community. Consider, for example, the question asked by George Mason, one of the Virginians who refused to sign the Constitution because of its lack of a Bill of Rights: "Who are the Militia? They consist now of the whole people." Similarly, the Federal Farmer, one of the most important Anti-Federalist opponents of the Constitution, referred to a "militia, when properly formed, as in fact the people themselves." We have, of course, moved now from text to history. And this history is most interesting, especially when we look at the development of notions of popular sovereignty.

It has become almost a cliche of contemporary American historiography to link the development of American political thought, including its constitutional aspects, to republican thought in England, the "country" critique of the powerful "court" centered in London.

One of this school's important writers, of course, was James Harrington, who not only was influential at the time but also has recently been given a certain pride of place by one of the most prominent of contemporary "neo-republicans," Professor Frank Michelman. One historian describes Harrington as having made "the most significant contribution to English libertarian attitudes toward arms, the individual, and society." He was a central figure in the development of the ideas of popular sovereignty and republicanism. For Harrington, preservation of republican liberty requires independence, which rests primarily on possession of adequate property to make men free from coercion by employers or landlords. But widespread ownership of land is not sufficient. These independent yeoman should also bear arms. As Professor Morgan puts it, "[T]hese independent yeomen, armed and embodied in a militia, are also a popular government's best protection against its enemies, whether they be aggressive foreign monarchs or scheming demagogues within the nation itself."

A central fear of Harrington and of all future republicans was a standing army, composed of professional soldiers. Harrington and his fellow republicans viewed a standing army as a threat to freedom, to be avoided at almost all costs. Thus, says Morgan, "A militia is the only safe form of military power that a popular government can employ; and because it is composed of the armed yeomanry, it will prevail over the mercenary professionals who man the armies of neighboring monarchs."

Scholars of the First Amendment have made us aware of the importance of John Trenchard and Thomas Gordon, whose Cato's Letters were central to the formation of the American notion of freedom of the press. That notion includes what Vincent Blasi would come to call the "checking value" of a free press, which stands as a sturdy exposer of governmental misdeeds. Consider the possibility, though, that the ultimate "checking value" in a republican polity is the ability of an armed populace, resumptively motivated by a shared commitment to the common good, to resist governmental tyranny. Indeed, one of Cato's Letters refers to "the Exercise of despotick Power as the unrelenting War of an armed Tyrant upon his unarmed Subjects. . . ."

Cress persuasively shows that no one defended universal possession of arms. New Hampshire had no objection to disarming those who "are or have been in actual rebellion," just as Samuel Adams stressed that only "peaceable citizens" should be protected in their right of "keeping their own arms." All these points can be conceded, however, without conceding as well that Congress—or, for that matter, that States—had the power to disarm these "peaceable citizens." Surely one of the foundations of American political thought of the period was the well-justified concern about political corruption and consequent governmental tyranny. Even the Federalists, fending off their opponents who accused them of foisting an oppressive new scheme upon the American people, were careful to acknowledge the risks of tyranny. James Madison, for example, speaks in Federalist Number Forty-Six of "the advantage of being armed, which the Americans possess over the people of almost every other nation." The advantage in question was not merely the defense of American borders; a standing army might well accomplish that. Rather, an armed public was advantageous in protecting political liberty. It is therefore no surprise that the Federal Farmer, the nom de plume of an anti-federalist critic of the new Constitution and its absence of a Bill of Rights, could write that "to preserve liberty, it is essential that the whole body of the people always possess arms, and be taught alike, especially when young, how to use them. . . ." On this matter, at least, there was no cleavage between the pro-ratification Madison and his opponent.

In his influential Commentaries on the Constitution, Joseph Story, certainly no friend of Anti-Federalism, emphasized the "importance" of the Second Amendment. He went on to describe the militia as "the natural defence of a free country" not only "against sudden foreign invasions" and "domestic insurrections," with which one might well expect a Federalist to be concerned, but also against "domestic usurpations of power by rulers." "The right of the citizens to keep and bear arms has justly been considered," Story wrote, "as the palladium of the liberties of a republic; since it offers a strong moral check against the usurpation and arbitrary power of rulers; and will generally, even if these are successful in the first instance, enable the people to resist and triumph over them."

We also see this blending of individualist and collective accounts of the right to bear arms in remarks by Judge Thomas Cooley, one of the most influential 19th century constitutional commentators. Noting that the state might call into its official militia only "a small number" of the eligible citizenry, Cooley wrote that "if the right [to keep and bear arms] were limited to those enrolled, the purpose of this guaranty might be defeated altogether by the action or neglect to act of the government it was meant to hold in check." Finally, it is worth noting the remarks of Theodore Schroeder, one of the most important developers of the theory of freedom of speech early in this century. "[T]he obvious import of the constitutional guarantee to carry arms," he argues, "is to promote a state of preparedness for self-defense even against the invasions of government, because only governments have ever disarmed any considerable class of people as a means toward their enslavement."

Discussion Questions

1. Would any employees or owners of the Jennings-related companies be morally responsible for crimes committed with the weapons they make?
2. Would a gun dealer be morally or legally responsible for a crime committed by someone to whom he or she sold a gun?
3. The Jennings-related companies have found a very successful market niche in selling guns at affordable prices. Is it ethical to capitalize on this market factor?
4. If the price of the weapon were increased, would the gun makers' moral responsibility be reduced?
5. If you owned a sporting goods or gun store, would you carry Saturday Night Specials?
6. Describe the Daniels' ethical standards.
7. Are the Daniels persuasive in disclaiming responsibility for what guns do?
8. Aren't the Daniels just fulfilling a market need?
9. Could you work for the Daniels?
10. Are the Kmart and Wal-Mart decisions on gun sales rooted in ethics or potential liability?
11. Do retailers have a potential liability in selling toy guns?
12. Did the ban on realistic toy weapons earn publicity for the toy store chains? Do you believe that was partially their motivation? Consider the following comment by a spokeswoman for Target, which has never carried the realistic-looking guns: "The only guns we have are neon plastic toy guns. We cater to the family, and we don't really consider realistic toy guns to be a family toy."
13. If you were a toy retailer, would you carry realistic-looking toy guns?
14. If you were a retailer, would you sell guns? If no retailers sell guns, have consumers lost a fundamental constitutional right?

15. Consider the following analysis by Professors Christine Westphal and Susan Wheeler about the Smith & Wesson experience and then evaluate the stakeholder vs. shareholder debate in that scenario:

> A number of editorial writers have characterized Smith & Wesson's agreement with the government as an ethical decision that was not necessarily good business, and certainly there is some justification for that position. The agreement might also be seen as a conflict among stakeholders where Smith & Wesson betrayed its customers in order to satisfy the demands of its financiers and community.[74]

Did Smith & Wesson betray its employees too? Did Smith & Wesson violate trust for selfish ends, as the National Shooting Sports Foundation said?

CASE 2.10

Shock Jock: Howard Stern

"Shock Jock" Howard Stern's radio talk show, which originates at Infinity Broadcasting Corporation's flagship New York station, is number one in its time slot in New York, Philadelphia, Los Angeles, Boston, and several other cities. A total of 20 million listeners tune in each week. Stern is known for his banter that borders on, and occasionally is, indecent.[75] His on-the-air routines involve such subjects as "Butt Bongo" and "Lesbian Dial-a-Date." Infinity has been fined $1.67 million by the Federal Communications Commission (FCC) for Stern's material that allegedly violated federal on-the-air decency standards.[76] Since the fines have not deterred the violations, one commissioner has cited ongoing complaints as the basis for conducting an FCC hearing into whether Infinity's licenses for its eleven stations should be revoked.

Stern's book, *Private Parts*, published by Simon & Schuster in October 1993, had such chapter titles as "Yes, I am Fartman"; Stern appears semi-clothed on the cover. Twelve days after its release, the book was in its seventh printing, having sold more than 1 million copies.

Stern has enjoyed continued success with his 1997 critically acclaimed movie, *Private Parts*, and a 1998 CBS television contract.[77]

Discussion Questions

1. Does Infinity have an obligation to monitor and control Stern?

2. Does Simon & Schuster have an obligation to establish editorial standards?

[74] *Christine W. Westphal and Susan M. Wheeler, "When Ethical Decisions Alienate Stakeholders: Smith & Wesson as a Case Study," Paper presented at the Academy of Legal Studies, August 8, 2001, Albuquerque, New Mexico, citing,* The Guardian *(London), August 5, 2000, Guardian City pages, p. 24.*

[75] *Kurt Anderson, "Big Mouths,"* Time, *November 1, 1993, pp. 60–66.*

[76] *"FCC Gets Complaints on 'Shock Jock,'"* Mesa Tribune, *March 19, 1994, p. A3.*

[77] *Julie Tilsner, "From Radio Rage, Raging Best-Sellers,"* Business Week, *November 1, 1993, p. 42.*

3. Do you think shareholders of Infinity or Simon & Schuster would be concerned about standards of decency, given Stern's success?

4. Would you publish Stern's book? Would you hire him as a radio talent?

CASE 2.11

Dayton-Hudson and Its Contributions to Planned Parenthood

Dayton-Hudson Corporation is a multistate department store chain. In 1990, its charitable foundation gave $18,000 to Planned Parenthood and other contributions to Children's Home Society, the Association for the Advancement of Young Women, and the Young Women's Christian Association. It had contributed to Planned Parenthood for twenty-two years.

Anti-abortion groups have vocally criticized corporate foundations that support Planned Parenthood and have persuaded JCPenney Company and American Telephone and Telegraph to stop their contributions to the organization. After Pioneer Hi-Bred International's foundation gave $25,000 to Planned Parenthood of Greater Iowa for rural clinics that did not perform abortions, Midwest farmers began circulating a flyer headlined, "Is Pioneer Hi-Bred Pro-Abortion?" CEO Thomas Urban canceled the donation, saying, "We were blackmailed, but you can't put the core business at risk."[78] When anti-abortion groups raised their objections with the Dayton-Hudson foundation, the foundation's board decided to halt its contributions to Planned Parenthood.

Pro-choice supporters responded strongly by boycotting Dayton-Hudson stores, writing letters to newspaper editors and closing charge accounts. Pickets appeared outside Dayton-Hudson stores, and picketers cut up their charge cards for media cameras.

A trustee for the New York City Employees Retirement System, which owned 438,290 Dayton shares, commented: "By antagonizing consumers, they've threatened the value of our investment."[79]

Dayton-Hudson decided to resume its funding of Planned Parenthood, even though anti-abortion groups announced plans to boycott the company's stores.[80]

Discussion Questions

1. Is there any way for a corporation to meet all demands in formulating policies on philanthropic giving?

[78] *Richard Gibson, "Boycott Drive Against Pioneer Hi-Bred Shows Perils of Corporate Philanthropy,"* The Wall Street Journal, *June 10, 1992, p. B1.*

[79] *Kevin Kelly, "Dayton-Hudson Finds There's No Graceful Way to Flip-Flop,"* Business Week, *September 24, 1990, p. 50.*

[80] *Fern Portnoy, "Corporate Giving Creates Tough Decisions, Fragile Balances,"* Denver Business Journal, *November 15, 1991, p. 15.*

2. Should contributions be considered simply an extension of marketing and made accordingly?
3. Should contributions be consistent with the firm's culture and values?
4. Is giving in to objections to certain donations by special-interest groups ethical?

CASE 2.12

Bayer, Anthrax, Cipro, Patents, and Half-Price

Following the deadly September 11, 2001, attacks on the World Trade Center, the United States experienced the first cases of anthrax it had seen since 1978. The anthrax spores were found in letters sent to the American Media, Inc. building in Florida (publishing home of the *National Enquirer* and the *Globe*); the offices of Tom Brokaw of NBC News and Dan Rather of CBS News; and the offices of Senators Tom Daschle, Patrick Leahy, and Edward Kennedy in the United States Senate. There were a series of deaths, cutaneous infections, and hundreds of employees at these organizations who tested positive for exposure to the anthrax spores. In addition, there were at least two anthrax deaths for which the source of the anthrax was not readily located.

As a result of these exposures, from letters that were mailed on September 18, 2001, the most effective antibiotic for treating anthrax, ciprofloxacin, was in high demand. Bayer AG, a German company, owns the patent for this antibiotic, which it calls Cipro. The patent expires in December 2003.

However, executives at headquarters for the company remained silent for weeks about the company's ability to manufacture sufficient amounts of the patented antibiotic. Executives indicated that the company was concerned that if it appeared in the media it would give the appearance of taking advantage of the dire circumstances.

Bayer's history made it wary of any involvement in international battles. Bayer AG had to pay reparations following World War II and its patent for its world-famous aspirin, Bayer, was stripped from it and awarded to a U.S. company. It was not until 2000 that Bayer was once again permitted to use its name. The company's low profile during the fall 2001 anthrax scares was deliberate and explained by executives as a desire to avoid appearing "exploitive of the problem" of the infections and illnesses.[81]

Frustrated with the lack of communication from Bayer, Canada suspended Bayer's patent in Canada and ordered other drug manufacturers to begin production of their pending generic formulas for Cipro. The Canadian national health service purchased one million of the Cipro-generic from another manufacturer.[82] Other drug companies do have their own formulas developed and ready to go, but could not produce these generics so long as Bayer AG held its patent protection. One company, Apotex,

[81] *Edmund L. Andrews, "Drug Makers Seem Uncertain in Response to Cipro Frenzy,"* The New York Times, *October 20, 2001, pp. A1, B8.*

[82] *Amy Harmon and Robert Pear, "Canada Overrides Patent for Cipro to Treat Anthrax,"* The New York Times, *October 19, 2001, pp. A1, B7.*

indicated its production method would not infringe on Bayer's patent, but Bayer threatened litigation and indicated it would deliver all the Cipro needed and/or ordered by both the United States and Canadian governments. Health officials were skeptical and one stated, "There's no way you can tell me getting it from six companies is going to be slower than getting it from one company."[83]

There has been antitrust and patent litigation surrounding Cipro. In 1997 Bayer entered into a settlement with Barr Laboratories, Inc. in which Bayer agreed to pay Barr and another generic manufacturer of ciprofloxacin $24.55 million each to not produce the drug.[84] Barr agreed to drop its challenge to Bayer's patent to Cipro in exchange for the payment. Now there are antitrust suits against Barr, Bayer, and another drug company for this agreement, which the suits contend served to eliminate competition for the sale and production of ciprofloxacin.[85]

The production levels needed in order to supply Cipro for the anthrax cases as well as for those who had been exposed to the sources (about 20,000 Americans) required a significant ramp-up.[86] Bayer AG's United States unit went into 24-hour shifts following the anthrax breakouts.[87] Mr. Brokaw held up a bottle of Cipro on his program, "NBC Nightly News," and calmed a jittery public by saying, "In Cipro we trust." Workers at one of Bayer's U.S. plants cheered with the coverage.[88]

On October 23, 2001, the following content appeared in a full-page ad in *The New York Times*:

> A Message From Bayer Corporation to the American People
>
> **Our Commitment to You**
>
> In response to the attacks on America and as part of the fight against bioterrorism, the people of Bayer are substantially increasing production of Cipro (ciprofloxacin).
>
> Our commitment to the American public is clear: We will meet this threat head on. Bayer is now working 24 hours a day, seven days a week to assure that Americans are equipped to fight this threat.
>
> In the last few weeks, we have shipped tens of millions of Cipro tablets, have tripled production and have committed to shipping 200 million tablets over the next three months.
>
> We will continue to work with the nation's healthcare professionals to ensure appropriate use of our antibiotics. We stand ready to support the United States government in providing Cipro to meet emergency needs.

[83] Id.

[84] *Margaret Cronin Fisk, "Cipro maker fighting trust suits,"* National Law Journal, *October 29, 2001, p. A11.*

[85] In re Ciprofloxacin Hydrochloride Antitrust Litigation *(No. MDL 001383 (E.D.N.Y.)).*

[86] *Melody Petersen and Robert Pear, "Anthrax Fears Send Demand for a Drug Far beyond Output,"* The New York Times, *October 16, 2001, pp. A1, B7.*

[87] *Keith Bradsher, "Bayer Insists Cipro Supply Is Sufficient; Fights Generic,"* The New York Times, *October 21, 2001, p. B7.*

[88] *Vanessa Fuhrmans and Ron Winslow, "Its Image Under Fire, Bayer AG Scrambles To Meet Cipro Demand,"* The Wall Street Journal, *October 22, 2001, pp. A1, A8.*

As a world leader in health care, we take seriously our responsibility to help protect and improve your welfare. We will face this latest challenge together . . . and we will succeed.

You have our commitment.

Bayer

For more information, go to www.CiproUSA.com[89]

The U.S. Congress was considering suspension of the Cipro patent in the U.S. in order to ramp-up production even more.[90] The legislation would permit federal judges to suspend patents on the basis of public health issues. Secretary of Health and Human Services, Tommy Thompson, also issued a public threat of suspending Bayer AG's patent in order to meet the increasing demands.[91]

In response to some panic in the United States, pharmacies in Mexico, permitted to sell Cipro without a doctor's prescription, as required in the United States, were ordering large amounts of Cipro, increasing their prices and doing a great deal of profitable business from U.S. orders. For example, the Zipp Pharmacy, located in Ciudad Juarez, a border town, said its orders for Cipro increased 15 times what they were before the anthrax infections. A nurse buying doses of Cipro for her entire family said, "What if there are mad runs on it? It's nice to have it around just in case."[92]

The Internet business for Cipro via online prescription services was booming.[93] MedicalWeb.com is a company that was found at the root of most Web sites providing Cipro information, which included the following:

2-buy-cipro.com
Cipro-for-anthrax.com
Cipro-antibiotics-anthrax-vaccines.com
1-cipro-4-anthrax.com
Cipropharmacy.com
Ciprostockpile.com
Gas-masks-israeli-gasmasks.com
Cipro-for-less.com

A subsidiary of MedicalWeb.com is MedicalGroup.com, a service that connects patients with doctors who will write prescriptions for them. MedicalGroup.com has 35 physicians with whom it works who write prescriptions for patients after interacting with the patients online. The prescription is then filled by 1stOnline-Pharmacy.com, another subsidiary of MedicalWeb.com.

The company's business jumped from filling 6 to 10 Cipro orders per day to over 100 per day. The increase in activity and national attention brought regulatory

[89] The New York Times, *October 23, 2001, p. B12.*

[90] *Holman W. Jenkins, Jr., "Of Germs and Geopolitics,"* The Wall Street Journal, *October 24, 2001, p. A23.*

[91] *Julie Appleby, "HHS chief wants Cipro price cut,"* USA Today, *October 24, 2001, p. 3B.*

[92] *Greg Winter, "Si We Have Cipro; the Panicky and Profiteers Head to Mexico,"* The New York Times, *October 20, 2001, pp. B1, B8.*

[93] *"The Cipro Circus,"* The Wall Street Journal, *October 25, 2001, p. A20.*

attention to MedicalWeb, a company based in North Carolina. The company had already rankled professional organizations, and the newfound earnings only exacerbated the tense relationships. CEO Tania Malik of MedicalWeb.com said, "It's almost, 'Be Careful what you wish for.' We did want people to know about Virtual-Medical-Group, but my fear is people see the press and think we're arrogant."[94]

The U.S. Government began a program for purchasing Cipro from Bayer and negotiated a price of $1.00 per tablet, a discount from the usual $1.83 per tablet. The first 100 million tablets would cost only 95 cents each.[95] The government negotiated the price by using its bargaining position of suspending the patent, as the Canadian government had done. The price Bayer charges wholesalers is $5.00 per pill.[96]

Bayer refused to grant interviews on the discount program but its CEO for American operations, Helge H. Wehmeier, said, "I was smiling going in because how often in your life do you and your company have an opportunity to make a difference."[97] Bayer would also not respond to a question on whether it was making a profit. But drug industry analysts indicated the price was perhaps enough to cover costs but little more.

Three other drug manufacturers offered their drugs for free if the federal government would approve them for the treatment of anthrax. In addition, all of the drug manufacturers formed a task force so that they could work jointly with the federal government to provide vaccines and treatments needed because of the threats of bioterrorism.[98] There is precedent for such cooperation. During World War II the pharmaceutical companies worked together to develop both penicillin as well as drugs for the treatment of malaria that affected troops in the Pacific as well as in Africa.[99]

Physicians at the Center for Disease Control (CDC) were concerned about the Mexico purchases and use of the drug without physician prescription. They note the following problems: (1) some people are allergic to Cipro and can become quite ill with just one dose; (2) Cipro has side effects for almost everyone including nausea, vomiting, and loss of appetite; (3) Cipro does have an effect on the brain including possible seizures and hallucinations or simply mood changes and insomnia; and (4) Cipro damages cartilage in the joints, especially when taken by children, and is given to children only when there is the absolute need (i.e., there is an infection ongoing). The CDC has advised use of Cipro only upon determination of exposure or infection from anthrax.

Bayer continued to struggle with its position, promises, and public perception as the anthrax infections increased. Bayer's corporate policy is as follows:

[94] *Julia Angwin, "Demand for Cipro Brings Sales—and Scrutiny—to Online Supplier,"* The Wall Street Journal, *October 22, 2001, pp. B1, B6.*

[95] *Keith Bradsher and Edmund L. Andrews, "U.S. Says Bayer Will Cut Costs of Its Anthrax Drug,"* The New York Times, *October 24, 2001, p. B7.*

[96] *Gina Kolata, "Cipro Isn't the Only Drug That Can Be Prescribed,"* The New York Times, *October 17, 2001, p. B7.*

[97] *Keith Bradsher, "Bayer Halves Price for Cipro, But Rivals Offer Drugs Free,"* The New York Times, *October 26, 2001, pp. A1, B8.*

[98] *Andrew Pollack, "Drug Makers Wrestle With World's New Rules,"* The New York Times, *October 21, 2001, Section 3-1, 3-10 (Money and Business).*

[99] *Chris Adams, "Drug Firms Fought Efforts for Global Pact on Bioterrorism,"* The Wall Street Journal, *October 25, 2001, p. A22.*

We offer our customers a wide variety of products and services in areas ranging from health care and agriculture to plastics and specialty chemicals. Bayer is research-based and is aiming for technological leadership in its core activities.

Our goals are to steadily increase corporate value and generate a high value added for the benefit of our stockholders, our employees and the community in every country in which we operate. We believe that our technical and commercial expertise involves responsibility to work for the common good and contribute to sustainable development.

Bayer: Success through Expertise with Responsibility.

Last updated: August 2, 2001

For more information on anthrax, Cipro, and the ethical issues, visit the following Web sites:

http://www.bayer.com
http://www.cdc.gov
http://www.cptech.org

The last Web site is one for Ralph Nader's Consumer Project on Technology and provides information on the patents and sale of Cipro.

Discussion Questions

1. What decisions do you think Bayer should make in this situation?

2. Should Bayer suspend its patent voluntarily? Professor John W. Dienhart, a business ethics professor at Seattle University, stated that Bayer should be a "good corporate citizen." He added, "This is not breaking a patent but adjusting a patent to meet a particular need." And "We're dealing with life and death itself, not Post-it Notes."[100]

   Professor Gerald C. Meyers, formerly the chairman of American Motors, encouraged Bayer to license Cipro, "They can't do anything other than license. They'll take such a hit if they refuse."[101] Professor Thomas Donaldson of the Wharton School of the University of Pennsylvania adds that companies must see the "psychology as well as the objective facts." Professor John R. Boatright of Loyola University of Chicago suggested that if Bayer can make enough Cipro, there is no ethical issue related to the patent or licensing and that sufficient production is the key question.[102]

3. Should Bayer suspend profits on the sale? Professor Donaldson said, "Extraordinary events sometimes call for extraordinary corporate compassion. The company cannot just look at profits but must look at the face of the victims."[103]

[100] *Andrew Pollack, "Drug Makers Wrestle With World's New Rules,"* The New York Times, *October 21, 2001, Section 3-1, 3-10 (Money and Business).*

[101] Id.

[102] Id.

[103] Id.

4. What recommendations should Bayer make on taking Cipro? Should it back up the warning from the CDC?

5. What do you think of the ethics and social responsibility of the Mexican pharmacies and online pharmacies profiting from selling Cipro? Are they different from Bayer or do the same ethical issues apply?

CASE 2.13

The Chicago Inner-City School Experiment

A group of Chicago businesses pooled funds to create a privately owned and operated elementary school in a Chicago inner-city neighborhood because of their concerns about the quality of education. Observing that American businesses spend $4 to $5 billion annually in training just to bring their workers to very basic skill levels, these businesses determined that they would help improve public education. They incorporated business notions on pay and accountability in the most challenging environment—an inner-city school.[104]

The school is free for neighborhood children ages two to twelve. At the school, students get breakfast, lunch, and snacks, as well as after-school care.

Teachers in the school are paid 10 percent more than their public school counterparts. The school is run like a private corporation, and the administrators and teachers understand that a lack of improvement in the students can result in termination of employment.

If it achieves its goals, this project could be a model for other schools. The founders of this Chicago experiment believe the future success of their businesses lies in the skills of their employees.[105]

Discussion Questions

1. Would Milton Friedman support the school founders' endeavor as a proper use of shareholder funds?

2. A shareholder of one of the businesses has protested: "Why are my funds being used for an inner-city school? We have taxes for that. I invested in a distribution firm, not an education firm. Your job is to earn my dividend, not spend it on things you think are important."

   If you were the director of shareholder relations for the firm, how would you respond to the shareholder?

[104] *Alex Kotlowitz, "A Businessman Turns His Skills to Aiding Inner-City Schools,"* The Wall Street Journal, *February 25, 1992, pp. A1, A8.*

[105] *"Why Business Should Invest in Literacy,"* Business Week, *July 20, 1992, p. 102.*

unit 3

Individual Values and the Business Organization

The conscience that is dark
with shame for his own deeds or for another's,
may well, indeed, feel harshness in your words;

Nevertheless, do not resort to lies,
let what you write reveal all you have seen,
and let those men who itch scratch where it hurts.

Though when your words are taken in at first
they may taste bitter, but once well-digested
they will become a vital nutrient.

Dante, *Paradisio* XVII.124–132

unit 3

At times, an individual who has become part of a larger organization feels that his or her personal values are in conflict with those of the organization. The types of ethical dilemmas that arise between an individual and his or her company include conflicts of interests and issues of honesty, fairness, and loyalty. One who negotiates contracts for an organization may find that contract bidders are willing to offer personally beneficial incidental benefits that would tend to cloud his or her judgment with respect to which vendor is best for the company. Elsewhere, an employee may find information indicating that the company is not addressing the correctable dangers of one of its products. The individual must confront such issues, pitting concerns about continuing employment and livelihood against moral standards and safety concerns.

These concerns represent the most common and difficult dilemmas businesspeople face. Studying them, reviewing alternatives, and carefully establishing values will prepare you for the dilemmas that we all must ultimately confront. This section begins with a famous *Harvard Business Review* piece by former investment banker Bowen "Buzz" McCoy. In the reading he examines his own values, the values of business, and his role in a business organization in light of a personal experience.

3a

Personal Values in Business Decisions

READING 3.1

The Parable of the Sadhu[1]

Bowen H. McCoy

[In 1982], as the first participant in the new six-month sabbatical program that Morgan Stanley has adopted, I enjoyed a rare opportunity to collect my thoughts as well as do some traveling. I spent the first three months in Nepal, walking 600 miles through 200 villages in the Himalayas and climbing some 120,000 vertical feet. On the trip my sole Western companion was an anthropologist who shed light on the cultural patterns of the villages we passed through.

During the Nepal hike, something occurred that has had a powerful impact on my thinking about corporate ethics. Although some might argue that the experience has no relevance to business, it was a situation in which a basic ethical dilemma suddenly intruded into the lives of a group of individuals. How the group responded I think holds a lesson for all organizations no matter how defined.

The Sadhu

The Nepal experience was more rugged and adventure-some than I had anticipated. Most commercial treks last two or three weeks and cover a quarter of the distance we traveled.

My friend Stephen, the anthropologist, and I were halfway through the 60-day Himalayan part of the trip when we reached the high point, an 18,000-foot pass over a crest that we'd have to traverse to reach the village of Muklinath, an ancient holy place for pilgrims.

[1] *Reprinted by permission of* Harvard Business Review. *From "The Parable of the Sadhu" by Bowen H. McCoy, September/October 1983. Copyright © 1983 by the Harvard Business School Publishing Corporation; all rights reserved.*

Six years earlier I had suffered pulmonary edema, an acute form of altitude sickness, at 16,500 feet in the vicinity of Everest base camp, so we were understandably concerned about what would happen at 18,000 feet. Moreover, the Himalayas were having their wettest spring in 20 years; hip-deep powder and ice had already driven us off one ridge. If we failed to cross the pass, I feared that the last half of our "once in a lifetime" trip would be ruined.

The night before we would try the pass, we camped at a hut at 14,500 feet. In the photos taken at that camp, my face appears wan. The last village we'd passed through was a sturdy two-day walk below us, and I was tired.

During the late afternoon, four backpackers from New Zealand joined us, and we spent most of the night awake, anticipating the climb. Below we could see the fires of two other parties, which turned out to be two Swiss couples and a Japanese hiking club.

To get over the steep part of the climb before the sun melted the steps cut in the ice, we departed at 3:30 a.m. The New Zealanders left first, followed by Stephen and myself, our porters and Sherpas, and then the Swiss. The Japanese lingered in their camp. The sky was clear, and we were confident that no spring storm would erupt that day to close the pass.

At 15,500 feet, it looked to me as if Stephen were shuffling and staggering a bit, which are symptoms of altitude sickness. (The initial stage of altitude sickness brings a headache and nausea. As the condition worsens, a climber may encounter difficult breathing, disorientation, aphasia, and paralysis.) I felt strong, my adrenaline was flowing, but I was very concerned about my ultimate ability to get across. A couple of our porters were also suffering from the height, and Pasang, our Sherpa sirdar (leader), was worried.

Just after daybreak, while we rested at 15,500 feet, one of the New Zealanders, who had gone ahead, came staggering down toward us with a body slung across his shoulders. He dumped the almost naked, barefoot body of an Indian holy man—a sadhu—at my feet. He had found the pilgrim lying on the ice, shivering and suffering from hypothermia. I cradled the sadhu's head and laid him out on the rocks. The New Zealander was angry. He wanted to get across the pass before the bright sun melted the snow. He said, "Look, I've done what I can. You have porters and Sherpa guides. You care for him. We're going on!" He turned and went back up the mountain to join his friends.

I took a carotid pulse and found that the sadhu was still alive. We figured he had probably visited the holy shrines at Muklinath and was on his way home. It was fruitless to question why he had chosen this desperately high route instead of the safe, heavily traveled caravan route through the kali Gandaki gorge. Or why he was almost naked and with no shoes, or how long he had been lying in the pass. The answers weren't going to solve our problem.

Stephen and the four Swiss began stripping off outer clothing and opening their packs. The sadhu was soon clothed from head to foot. He was not able to walk, but he was very much alive. I looked down the mountain and spotted below the Japanese climbers marching up with a horse.

Without a great deal of thought, I told Stephen and Pasang that I was concerned about withstanding the heights to come and wanted to get over the pass. I took off after several of our porters who had gone ahead.

On the steep part of the ascent where, if the ice steps had given way, I would have slid down about 3,000 feet, I felt vertigo. I stopped for a breather, allowing the Swiss to catch up with me. I inquired about the sadhu and Stephen. They said that the sadhu was fine and that Stephen was just behind. I set off again for the summit.

Stephen arrived at the summit an hour after I did. Still exhilarated by victory, I ran down the snow slope to congratulate him. He was suffering from altitude sickness, walking fifteen steps, then stopping, walking fifteen steps, then stopping, walking fifteen steps, then stopping. When I reached them, Stephen glared at me and said: "How do you feel about contributing to the death of a fellow man?"

I did not fully comprehend what he meant.

"Is the sadhu dead?" I inquired.

"No," replied Stephen, "but he surely will be!"

After I had gone, and the Swiss had departed not long after, Stephen had remained with the sadhu. When the Japanese had arrived, Stephen had asked to use their horse to transport the sadhu down to the hut. They had refused. He had then asked Pasang to have a group of our porters carry the sadhu. Pasang had resisted the idea, saying that the porters would have to exert all their energy to get themselves over the pass. He had thought they could not carry a man down 1,000 feet to the hut, reclimb the slope, and get across safely before the snow melted. Pasang had pressed Stephen not to delay any longer.

The Sherpas had carried the sadhu down to a rock in the sun at about 15,000 feet and had pointed out the hut another 500 feet below. The Japanese had given him food and drink. When they had last seen him he was listlessly throwing rocks at the Japanese party's dog, which had frightened him.

We do not know if the sadhu lived or died.

For many of the following days and evenings Stephen and I discussed and debated our behavior toward the sadhu. Stephen is a committed Quaker with deep moral vision. He said, "I feel that what happened with the sadhu is a good example of the breakdown between the individual ethic and the corporate ethic. No one person was willing to assume ultimate responsibility for the sadhu. Each was willing to do his bit just so long as it was not too inconvenient. When it got to be a bother, everyone just passed the buck to someone else and took off. Jesus was relevant to a more individualist stage of society, and how do we interpret his teaching today in a world filled with large, impersonal organizations and groups?"

I defended the larger group, saying, "Look, we all cared. We all stopped and gave aid and comfort. Everyone did his bit. The New Zealander carried him down below the snow line. I took his pulse and suggested we treat him for hypothermia. You and the Swiss gave him clothing and got him warmed up. The Japanese gave him food and water. The Sherpas carried him down to the sun and pointed out the easy trail toward the hut. He was well enough to throw rocks at a dog. What more could we do?"

"You have just described the typical affluent Westerner's response to a problem. Throwing money—in this case food and sweaters—at it, but not solving the fundamentals!" Stephen retorted.

"What would satisfy you?" I said. "Here we are, a group of New Zealanders, Swiss, Americans, and Japanese who have never met before and who are at the apex of one of the most powerful experiences of our lives. Some years the pass is so bad no one gets over it. What right does an almost naked pilgrim who chooses the wrong trail have to disrupt our lives? Even the Sherpas had no interest in risking the trip to help him beyond a certain point."

Stephen calmly rebutted, "I wonder what the Sherpas would have done if the sadhu had been a well-dressed Nepali, or what the Japanese would have done if the sadhu had been a well-dressed Asian, or what you would have done, Buzz, if the sadhu had been a well-dressed Western woman?"

"Where, in your opinion," I asked instead, "is the limit of our responsibility in a situation like this? We had our own well-being to worry about. Our Sherpa guides were unwilling to jeopardize us or the porters for the sadhu. No one else on the mountain was willing to commit himself beyond certain self-imposed limits."

Stephen said, "As individual Christians or people with a Western ethical tradition, we can fulfill our obligations in such a situation only if (1) the sadhu dies in our care, (2) the sadhu demonstrates to us that he could undertake the two-day walk down to the village, or (3) we carry the sadhu for two days down to the village and convince someone there to care of him."

"Leaving the sadhu in the sun with food and clothing, while he demonstrated hand-eye coordination by throwing a rock at a dog, comes close to fulfilling items one and two," I answered. "And it wouldn't have made sense to take him to the village where the people appeared to be far less caring than the Sherpas, so the third condition is impractical. Are you really saying that, no matter what the implications, we should, at the drop of a hat, have changed our entire plan?"

The Individual vs. the Group Ethic

Despite my arguments, I felt and continue to feel guilt about the sadhu. I had literally walked through a classic moral dilemma without fully thinking through the consequences. My excuses for my actions include a high adrenaline flow, a superordinate goal, and a once-in-a-lifetime opportunity—factors in the usual corporate situation, especially when one is under stress.

Real moral dilemmas are ambiguous, and many of us hike right through them, unaware that they exist. When, usually after the fact, someone makes an issue of them, we tend to resent his or her bringing it up. Often, when the full import of what we have done (or not done) falls on us, we dig into a defensive position from which it is very difficult to emerge. In rare circumstances we may contemplate what we have done from inside a prison.

Had we mountaineers been free of physical and mental stress caused by the effort and the high altitude, we might have treated the sadhu differently. Yet isn't stress the real test of personal and corporate values? The instant decisions executives make under pressure reveal the most about personal and corporate character.

Among the many questions that occur to me when pondering my experience are: What are the practical limits of moral imagination and vision? Is there a collective or institutional ethic beyond the ethics of the individual? At what level of effort or commitment can one discharge one's ethical responsibilities?

Not every ethical dilemma has a right solution. Reasonable people often disagree; otherwise there would be no dilemma. In a business context, however, it is essential that managers agree on a process for dealing with dilemmas.

The sadhu experience offers an interesting parallel to business situations. An immediate response was mandatory. Failure to act was a decision in itself. Up on the mountain we could not resign and submit our résumé to a headhunter. In contrast to philosophy, business involves action and implementation—getting things done. Managers must come up with answers to problems based on what they see and what they allow to influence their decision-making processes. On the mountain, none of us but Stephen realized the true dimensions of the situation we were facing.

One of our problems was that as a group we had no process for developing a consensus. We had no sense of purpose or plan. The difficulties of dealing with the sadhu were so complex that no one person could handle it. Because it did not have a set of preconditions that could guide its action to an acceptable resolution, the group reacted instinctively as individuals. The cross-cultural nature of the group added a further layer of complexity. We had no leader with whom we could all identify and in whose purpose we believed. Only Stephen was willing to take charge, but he could not gain adequate support to care for the sadhu.

Some organizations do have a value system that transcends the personal values of the managers. Such values, which go beyond profitability, are usually revealed when the organization is under stress. People throughout the organization generally accept its values, which, because they are not presented as a rigid list of commandments, may be somewhat ambiguous. The stories people tell, rather than printed materials, transmit these conceptions of what is proper behavior.

For twenty years I have been exposed at senior levels to a variety of corporations and organizations. It is amazing how quickly an outsider can sense the tone and style of an organization and the degree of tolerated openness and freedom to challenge management.

Organizations that do not have a heritage of mutually accepted, shared values tend to become unhinged during stress, with each individual bailing out for himself. In the great takeover battles we have witnessed during past years, companies that had strong cultures drew the wagons around them and fought it out, while other companies saw executives, supported by their golden parachutes, bail out of the struggles.

Because corporations and their members are interdependent, for the corporation to be strong the members need to share a preconceived notion of what is correct behavior, a "business ethic," and think of it as a positive force, not a constraint.

As an investment banker I am continually warned by well-meaning lawyers, clients, and associates to be wary of conflicts of interest. Yet if I were to run away from every difficult situation, I wouldn't be an effective investment banker. I have to feel my way through conflicts. An effective manager can't run from risk either; he or she has to confront and deal with risk. To feel "safe" in doing this, managers need the guidelines of an agreed-on process and set of values within the organization.

After my three months in Nepal, I spent three months as an executive-in-residence at both Stanford Business School and the Center for Ethics and Social Policy at the Graduate Theological Union at Berkeley. These six months away from my job gave me time to assimilate twenty years of business experience. My thoughts turned often to the meaning of the leadership role in any large organization. Students at the seminary thought of themselves as antibusiness. But when I questioned them they agreed that they distrusted all large organizations, including the church. They perceived all large organizations as impersonal and opposed to individual values and needs. Yet we all know of organizations where people's values and beliefs are respected and their expressions encouraged. What makes the difference? Can we identify the difference and, as a result, manage more effectively?

The word "ethics" turns off many and confuses more. Yet the notions of shared values and an agreed-on process for dealing with adversity and change—what many people mean when they talk about corporate culture—seem to be at the heart of the ethical issue. People who are in touch with their own core beliefs and the beliefs of others and are sustained by them can be more comfortable living on the cutting edge. At times, taking a tough line or a decisive stand in a muddle of ambiguity is the only ethical thing to do. If a manager is indecisive and spends time trying to figure out the "good" thing to do, the enterprise may be lost.

Business ethics, then, has to do with the authenticity and integrity of the enterprise. To be ethical is to follow the business as well as the cultural goals of the corporation, its owners, its employees, and its customers. Those who cannot serve the corporate vision are not authentic business people and, therefore, are not ethical in the business sense.

At this stage of my own business experience I have a strong interest in organizational behavior. Sociologists are keenly studying what they call corporate stories, legends, and heroes as a way organizations have of transmitting the value system. Corporations such as Arco have even hired consultants to perform an audit of their corporate culture. In a company, the leader is the person who understands, interprets, and manages the corporate value system. Effective managers are then action-oriented people who resolve conflict, are tolerant of ambiguity, stress, and change, and have a strong sense of purpose for themselves and their organizations.

If all this is true, I wonder about the role of the professional manager who moves from company to company. How can he or she quickly absorb the values and culture of different organizations? Or is there, indeed, an art of management that is totally transportable? Assuming such fungible managers do exist, is it proper for them to manipulate the values of others?

What would have happened had Stephen and I carried the sadhu for two days back to the village and become involved with the villagers in his care? In four trips to Nepal my most interesting experiences occurred in 1975 when I lived in a Sherpa home in the Khumbu for five days recovering from altitude sickness. The high point of Stephen's trip was an invitation to participate in a family funeral ceremony in Manang. Neither experience had to do with climbing the high passes of the Himalayas. Why were we so reluctant to try the lower path, the ambiguous trail? Perhaps because we did not have a leader who could reveal the greater purpose of the trip to us.

Why didn't Stephen with his moral vision opt to take the sadhu under his personal care? The answer is because, in part, Stephen was hard-stressed physically himself, and because, in part, without some support system that involved our involuntary and episodic community on the mountain, it was beyond his individual capacity to do so.

I see the current interest in corporate culture and corporate value systems as a positive response to Stephen's pessimism about the decline of the role of the individual in large organizations. Individuals who operate from a thoughtful set of personal values provide the foundation of a corporate culture. A corporate tradition that encourages freedom of inquiry, supports personal values, and reinforces a focused sense of direction can fulfill the need for individuality along with the prosperity and success of the group. Without such corporate support, the individual is lost.

That is the lesson of the sadhu. In a complex corporate situation, the individual requires or deserves the support of the group. If people cannot find such support from their organization, they don't know how to act. If such support is forthcoming, a person has a stake in the success of the group, and can add much to the process of establishing and maintaining a corporate culture. It is management's challenge to be sensitive to individual needs, to shape them, and to direct and focus them for the benefit of the group as a whole.

For each of us the sadhu lives. Should we stop what we are doing and comfort him; or should we keep trudging up toward the high pass? Should I pause to help the derelict I pass on the street each night as I walk by the Yale Club en route to Grand Central Station? Am I his brother? What is the nature of our responsibility if we consider ourselves to be ethical persons? Perhaps it is to change the values of the group so that it can, with all its resources, take the other road.

Discussion Questions

Consider the closing questions Mr. McCoy poses. How do they apply to you personally and to businesses?

READING 3.2

The Moving Line

George Lefcoe

George Lefcoe, former commissioner of the Los Angeles County Regional Planning Commission on his retirement and the seduction of public office:

I really missed the cards from engineers I never met, the wine and cheese from development companies I never heard of, and the honeybaked ham from, of all places,

Forest Lawn Cemetery, even though the company was never an applicant before the commission when I was there.

My first Christmas as a commissioner—when I received the ham—I tried to return it, though for the record, I did not since no one at Forest Lawn seemed authorized to accept the ham, apparently not even for burial. My guess is that no one of the many public servants who received the ham had ever tried to return it.

When I received another ham the next Christmas, I gave it to a worthy charity. The next year, some worthy friends were having a party so I gave it to them. The next year I had a party and we enjoyed the ham.

In the fifth year, about the tenth of December, I began wondering, where is my ham?[2]

[2] The Wall Street Journal, *"Notable, Quotable," December 18, 1998, p. A14.*

3b

Personal Honesty

Is your résumé accurate, or does it cross the line of demarcation in exaggeration? How far would you go to win a prestigious office in a college club? Is it acceptable to "puff" when you are a reference? Personal standards of behavior often come into play as we confront dilemmas of qualifications and landing that important job or title.

CASE 3.3

Puffing in the Résumé

The résumé is a door opener for a job seeker. What's on them can get you in the door or cause the door to be slammed in your face. With that type of pressure, it is not surprising to learn that one 1997 study by a group of executive search firms showed that 25 percent of all résumés contain misstatements. A 1988 Equifax study (Equifax is a credit-reporting agency often used by employers for background checks) also found the following:

Eleven percent of all applicants lied about their reasons for leaving a previous job;
Four percent fudged job titles on their resumes;
Three percent listed fake employers;
Three percent fabricated jobs; and
Three percent pretended to have a college degree.[3]

Ed Andler, an expert in credential verification, says that one-third of all résumés contain some level of "creative writing." Mr. Andler notes that assembly-line workers don't mention misdemeanor convictions and middle-managers embellish their educational background. One reference-checking firm looked into the background of a security guard applicant and found he was wanted for manslaughter in another state.

Vericon Resources, Inc., a background check firm, has found that 2 percent of the applicants they investigate are hiding a criminal past. Vericon also notes, however, that potential employers can easily discover whether job candidates are lying about previous employment by requesting W-2s from previous employers.

In one résumé "puffing" case, according to Michael Oliver, a former executive recruiter who is presently director of staffing for Dial Corporation, a strong candidate

[3] *Dan Barry, "Cheating Hearts and Lying Resumes,"* The New York Times, *December 14, 1997, pp. WK1, WK4.*

for a senior marketing management position said he had an MBA from Harvard and four years' experience at a previous company, where he had been a vice president of marketing. Actually, Harvard had never heard of him, he had worked for the firm for only two years, and he had been a senior product manager, not a vice president.

In a wrongful firing case brought against Honeywell by a former employee, a federal court permitted Honeywell to use the defense that the employee had lied on her résumé (over eight years before the litigation) by stating that she had a college degree when she had taken only six courses (two as audits) and that she had managed property during a time when she owned no property and was unemployed. Her discharge had nothing to do with the puffing on her résumé, but the court ruled that "an employer may defend a wrongful discharge claim on the basis of facts unknown at the time of discharge." A subsequent court decision has held that a previously unknown fact is not a defense to discrimination, but it can always be used as grounds for termination.[4]

In 1997, Dianna Green, a senior vice president at Duquesne Light, left her position at that utility. The memo from the CEO described her departure as one that would allow Ms. Green to pursue "other career interests she has had for many years." While the memo expressed sadness at her departure, Ms. Green had been fired for lying on her résumé by stating that she had a master's degree in business administration when, in fact, she had no master's degree.[5]

Ms. Green had worked her way up through the company and had been responsible for handling the human resources issues in Duquesne's nine years of downsizing. At the time of her termination, she was a director at Pennsylvania's largest bank and known widely for her community service.

On the day following her termination, Ms. Green was found dead of a self-inflicted gunshot wound.[6]

Discussion Questions

1. Would it be wrong to engage in résumé puffing and then disclose the actual facts in an interview?
2. Suppose that you had earned but, due to a hold on your academic record because of unpaid debts, had never been formally awarded a college degree. Would you state on your résumé that you had a college degree?
3. Suppose that, in an otherwise good career track, you were laid off because of an economic downturn and remained unemployed for thirteen months. Would you attempt to conceal the thirteen-month lapse in your résumé?

[4] Id.

[5] *The information was revealed after Ms. Green was deposed in a suit by a former subordinate for termination. Because Ms. Green hesitated in giving a year for her degree, the plaintiff's lawyer checked and found no degree and notified Duquesne officials. Duquesne officials then negotiated a severance package.*

[6] *It should be noted that Ms. Green was suffering from diabetes to such an extent that she could no longer see well enough to drive. Also, during the year before her termination, her mother had died of a stroke and her youngest brother also had died. Carol Hymowitz and Raju Narisetti, "A Promising Career Comes to a Tragic End, And a City Asks Why,"* The Wall Street Journal, *May 9, 1997, pp. A1, A8.*

4. Won't complete candor prevent you from ever getting a job?
5. Is puffing a short-term solution in a tight job market?
6. Was the tragedy of Ms. Green avoidable? Was Duquesne Light justified in terminating her?
7. What dangers arise if applicants are not honest?

CASE 3.4
Radar Detectors and the Law

Just recently the state of Connecticut legalized the use of radar detectors, reversing a previous statute that permitted state police to fine motorists for using the devices.[7] Representative Alex Knopp, one of the legislators who objected to the legalization of the devices, stated, "The bottom line is that speeding kills and that radar detectors will cause more speeding in the state of Connecticut." In 1993, Congress passed a law banning the use of radar detectors by tractor-trailer drivers. Senator Frank R. Lautenberg of New Jersey stated, "It's unacceptable to have devices designed to thwart the law. I want to get rid of these things."[8]

Discussion Questions

1. Are radar detectors a means of breaking the law and avoiding getting caught?
2. Is it morally wrong to speed?
3. Is it morally wrong to use a radar detector?
4. Is it possible that speeding laws constitute positive law but do not reflect any ethical or moral standard?
5. New technology has allowed the development of photo radar along with license plate shields so that the automatic cameras cannot photograph the offending driver's license plate. Do these license plate covers facilitate breaking the law?

CASE 3.5
The Ethics of Looking Busy

"Some bosses just like you to be there, whether you need to be there or not. So I've come up with ways to look like a workaholic," Jane Nugent said. "I can be off shopping or on a two-hour lunch, and everyone back at the office thinks I'm still there," she noted, smiling. Jane then listed her strategies:

[7] *Kirk Johnson, "Connecticut Lawmakers Legalize Radar Detectors,"* The New York Times, *June 23 1992, p. A6.*

[8] *"U.S. Acts to Ban Radar Detectors in Big Trucks,"* The New York Times, *November 12, 1993, pp. A1, A16.*

- Before leaving, place a fresh, steaming cup of coffee on your desk; people will assume you'll be right back;
- Always leave the lights on and the computer running;[9]
- Hang around at the office until the last supervisor leaves—then go;
- Arrive early and let them see you, your car, and your office up and running, and then leave for the morning;
- Go in on Saturday and stay for a few hours—you don't need to work, just make sure someone sees you;
- If you leave early, call back in and ask someone to look something up in your office—they'll assume you're at an out-of-office meeting;
- If you must make personal calls, always have a pad in front of you, write on it frequently and speak firmly (the rest of the office will think you're negotiating); and
- Leave personal belongings (coat, jacket) in your office to give the impression that you're returning.[10]

Discussion Questions

1. Evaluate Jane's strategies from an ethical perspective.
2. Should Jane consider flexible hours?
3. Does Jane have enough to keep her busy at her job? Is it dishonest for her to continue her facade?
4. How should Jane's secretary respond to being asked to go in and jump around in Jane's office so that Jane can be gone?
5. Are Jane's actions just a response to management's basis of evaluation that time spent in the office equals performance?

CASE 3.6

The Employment Application Lie That Haunts the Applicant

Susan Weissman was hired by Crawford and worked for the company for approximately 18 months. Weissman had several ongoing disputes with her supervisor including one between Weissman, her supervisor, and the Department of Labor over the number of breaks she was entitled to take. Weissman wanted lunch, restroom, drink, and rest breaks with the rest breaks not involving any of the other activities. With the break issue yet to be resolved, Weissman requested a personal leave day. Weissman's supervisor denied her request because Weissman had failed to follow Crawford's policy of asking for personal leave days at least two weeks in advance.

[9] *Note: Some offices have motion-detector energy savers. When activity in the office ceases, the lights go off. Therefore, Jane notes, instruct your secretary to go into your office periodically and jump around while you're gone.*

[10] *Sue Shellenbarger, "How to Look Like a Workaholic While Still Having a Life,"* The Wall Street Journal, *December 28, 1994, p. B1.*

Weissman did not show up for work on the day she had requested and she was terminated for insubordination. Weissman then filed suit against Crawford for breach of contract, promissory estoppel, outrageous conduct, and wrongful discharge. During the course of discovery in the case, Crawford discovered that Weissman had omitted one place of employment from her application for employment at Crawford. Weissman had failed to list a former employer who had also terminated her and against whom she had filed suit. Weissman had signed the application to Crawford below the following declaration:

> The information I am presenting in this application is true and correct to the best of my knowledge, and I understand that any falsification or misrepresentation herein could result in my discharge and in the event I am hired by Crawford & Company.[11]

Discussion Questions

1. Should Weissman be terminated?
2. Was her warning adequate?
3. Was her conduct ethical?

CASE 3.7

Travel Expenses: A Chance for Extra Income

The New York Times Magazine profiled the problems with employees' submissions for travel and entertainment expenses reimbursement. American Express reported that employees spend $156 billion annually on travel and entertainment related to business. Internal auditors at companies listed types of expenses for which employees have sought reimbursement: hairdresser, traffic tickets, and kennel fees.

While the IRS raised the amount allowable for undocumented expenses to $75, most companies keep their limit for employees at $25. One company auditor commented that all taxi cab rides now cost $24.97 and if the company went with the IRS limit, the cab fares would climb to $74.65.

Some of the horror stories submitted by auditors on travel and entertainment expenses submitted by employees:

> One employee submitted a bill for $12 for a tin of cookies. When questioned, he could not explain how it had been used but asked for reimbursement anyway because all he would have to do is "make up" a couple of taxi rides to get it back anyway;
>
> $225 for three hockey tickets, except that the names on the tickets were the employee's family members;

[11] Crawford Rehabilitation Services, Inc. v. Weissman, *1997 Wl 304917 (Colo. 1997).*

$625 for wallpapering. The employee had included it with her other travel expenses and even had the wallpaper receipt written in a different language in order to throw off any questions; and

$275 sports jacket submitted as a restaurant bill. The travel office called the number listed on the receipt and asked if food was sold there. The response was, "No, we're a men's clothing store."[12]

Discussion Questions

1. The auditors noted that employees who are confronted often respond with similar justifications:

   "The company owes it to me."
   "It doesn't really hurt anyone."
   "Everybody does this."

   Are these justifications or rationalizations?

2. Why do employees risk questionable expenses?
3. Who is harmed by dishonest expense submissions?

CASE 3.8

Do Cheaters Prosper?

In a new book entitled *Cheaters Always Prosper: 50 Ways to Beat the System Without Being Caught*,[13] James Brazil (a pen name), a college student from the University of California at Santa Barbara, has provided 50 ways to obtain a "free lunch." One suggestion is to place shards of glass in your dessert at a fancy restaurant and then "raise hell." The manager or owner will then come running with certificates for free meals and probably waive your bill.

Another suggestion is, rather than spend $400 on new tires for your car, rent a car for a day for $35 and switch the rental car tires with your tires. So long as your car tires are not bald, the rental car company employees will not notice, and you will have your new tires for a mere $35.

Discussion Questions

1. Are these suggestions ethical?
2. Was publishing the book with the suggestions ethical?
3. Do any of these suggestions cost anyone any money?

[12] *Paul Burnham Finney, "Hey, It's on the Company!"* The New York Times Magazine, *March 8, 1998, pp. 99–100.*
[13] *Citadel Press, October 1996.*

3C

Trust and Employment

Information is a powerful business tool and often a competitor's edge. Inside information released too early to the press can harm both a company and its personnel. Employees must recognize the value and ownership of company information.

CASE 3.9

General Motors, Volkswagen, and the Traveling Executive

Jose Ignacio Lopez de Arriortua was a vice president with General Motors Corporation's GM Espana, Opel, and GM Europe AG Division (GM). Shortly after his promotion to vice president in February 1993, Mr. Lopez resigned from GM and took a position as part of the management board of Volkswagen AG, a German corporation (VW) on March 16, 1993.[14]

Joining Mr. Lopez at VW by March 22, 1993, were GM's executive director of purchasing for GM Espana, Jorge Alvarez, a platform manager for the S-Car, O-car and Opel, Rosario Piazza, a sourcing specialist for Opel, Hugo Van der Auwera, executive director of worldwide purchasing for GM Continential (based out of Belgium), Francisco Garcia-Sanz, executive director of worldwide purchasing for GM's electrical commodity group, Andries Versteeg, manager-European liaison for advance purchasing and global sourcing, and William Admiraal, an employee of GM who is also married to Lopez's daughter, Irene.

GM filed suit under the Lanham Act (protection against the taking of trade secrets) and alleged that Mr. Lopez, from as early as August 1992 until his departure in March 1993, secretly communicated with VW representatives about a job and promised to bring along with him to his new job at VW business plans and trade secrets.[15] Specifically, the suit alleges that Mr. Lopez was to bring along confidential documents, transparencies, and computer diskettes that contained the following information:[16]

[14] *William M. Carley, "Secret Suit: What Did He Know?"* The Wall Street Journal, *January 19, 1988, pp. B1, B8.*

[15] General Motors Corporation v. Ignacio Lopez de Arriortua, *948 F.Supp. 656 (E.D. Mich. 1996).*

[16] *"Judge Sets Michigan Venue for GM Suit Against VW,"* The Wall Street Journal, *October 18, 1996, p. B5.*

- Listings of GM and Opel components by worldwide supplier, price, terms, conditions, and delivery schedules
- A copy of GM's Product Purchasing System (PPS)
- A copy of GM Europe's European Purchasing Optimization System (EPOS)
- Plans for "Plant X," the factory of the future
- Future auto plans to the year 2003
- Future strategies for purchasing[17]

GM alleged that Lopez and those GM employees who went with him to Volkswagen took over 20 cartons of stolen documents, entered the data on computers over a month-long period at VW, and had the documents transferred to a third party for shredding in order to destroy the evidence of the documents being taken from GM. An audit by KPMG Peat Marwick, commissioned by GM, concluded that the documents had been taken.[18] Following an initial denial in which VW's CEO, Ferdinand Piech, referred to the GM charges as "mudslinging," VW admitted in August 1993 that the former GM employees had indeed taken the documents but that they were destroyed shortly after they began their work at VW and that VW never had access to the information. In a statement admitting the document theft, VW said that GM employees "destroyed documents which could possibly be attributed to GM and could contain critical information, in order to remove any danger of distribution at Volkswagen."[19] The release also added that its own internal investigation found nothing "which could warrant the accusation of industrial espionage." The statement also added that the "young men didn't act correctly toward their former employer."[20]

In June 1993, German officials discovered four boxes of trade secret documents in the home of one of the associates of Lopez, as well as others in Lopez's home.[21] Those boxes were seized and German authorities ultimately indicted Mr. Lopez and three others who transferred to VW. German authorities continued with their prosecution despite VW's press release because the destruction did not mean the information was not ultimately used and the company had not used a third party to conduct the internal investigation.

These circumstances ultimately resulted in 11 different legal proceedings, including the German charges and the suit by GM for violations of the Lanham Act as well as RICO violations. Mr. Lopez was indicted on six counts of wire fraud and interstate transportation of stolen property in May 2000. The indictment alleges that in the four months preceding his departure from GM, Mr. Lopez and his assistants made an extraordinary number of requests for confidential documents.

Mr. Lopez was indicted, not under the Economic Espionage Act (EEA) because that act was passed largely because of the Lopez/VW scenario and was enacted after the fact. *Ex post facto* laws cannot be applied to conduct occurring before the passage, but

[17] *John Templeman and Peggy Salz-Trautman, "VW Figures Its Best Defense May Be a Good Offense,"* Business Week, *August 19, 1993, p. 29.*

[18] *Ferdinand Protzman, "VW Sets a Board Meeting on G.M. Dispute,"* The New York Times, *October 5, 1993, p. C4.*

[19] *"VW, GM 'Spy' Feud,"* Arizona Republic, *July 30, 1993, p. B1.*

[20] *Audrey Choi, "VW Discloses GM Documents Were Destroyed,"* The Wall Street Journal, *August 9, 1993, p. A3.*

[21] *Ferdinand Protzman, "German Prosecutors Link Lopez to Secret GM Papers,"* The New York Times, *July 23, 1993, pp. C1, C2.*

under computer fraud statutes.[22] The EEA makes it a crime for employees to download, copy, e-mail, transfer, or in any way provide information about their current companies to their new companies.

VW settled the suit by GM in 1997 by agreeing to pay $100 million. VW did not, however, admit any wrongdoing as part of that settlement. Mr. Lopez settled his criminal charges by the German government by agreeing to pay $224,000 to charity. Mr. Lopez left VW in 1996, largely because the company did not fulfill what he said was its promise to him to allow him to build a "dream factory." Mr. Lopez works as an auto consultant while living in the Basque region of Spain. In 1998 he was in an auto accident and suffered brain damage which has resulted in memory lapses. Of the whole GM/VW scenario, Mr. Lopez was disappointed that VW did not build his dream factory, "If I had known that, I wouldn't have changed jobs. It was my error."[23]

Discussion Questions

1. Do you think what the GM employees did was wrong?
2. Wouldn't Mr. Lopez have most of the keys to the supply chain management system of GM in his head anyway?
3. Don't competitors hire employees from their competitors with the hope of bringing in experience? Is there a line between sharing experience and sharing systems?
4. Would you have taken the documents?
5. Does it make a difference that the documents are related to the supply chain and not new products or ideas?

CASE 3.10

The Sale of Sand to the Saudis

Joe Raymond's position as sales manager for Granite Rock and Sand was in jeopardy. His unit had been low performer in terms of sales for the last seven quarters. Joe's supervisor, vice president Tom Haws, told Joe that he had through the next quarter to pull his unit out of last place. Haws also told Joe that Joe would have to be replaced if the improvement did not occur.

Joe and his wife had just purchased their first home. With their mortgage payments totaling $1,100 per month, the loss of Joe's salary would mean the loss of their home.

Following Tom's warning, Joe began interviewing candidates for a vacant sales position in his unit. Joe had conducted three interviews when the final candidate, Jessica Morris, arrived. During the interview with Morris, Joe learned that she was the victim

[22] *Keith Bradsher, "Former G.M. Executive Indicted on Charges of Taking Trade Secrets,"* The New York Times, *May 23, 2000, pp. C1, C2.*

[23] Id.

of a layoff by a competitor, Silt, Sand, and Such. Joe was not terribly impressed with Morris, but just before she left, she opened her briefcase and offered Joe a sheet of paper bearing the name of an official in the Saudi Arabian government. Morris explained:

> When I was with Silt, Sand, and Such, we started a program for finding innovative markets for our products. You know, we wanted to tap markets no one had ever thought of. After a lot of research, we discovered that Saudi desalinization plants need a particular type of sand they don't have over there, but we have here. We're the only firm that knows about this. If you hire me, I can see the sale through for Granite.

Morris added:

> Look, I need this job. You need your sales up. Think about it and call me.

After Morris left, Joe sat in his office and felt his problems were solved. Or were they?

Discussion Questions

1. If you were Joe, would you hire Morris?
2. Would anyone be harmed if you hired Morris?
3. What long-term problems could you foresee if Morris were hired?
4. Would using the information from Morris be illegal? Would Morris be committing a crime?
5. Would you be able to trust Morris if you hired her?

CASE 3.11

The Compliance Officer Who Strayed

Marisa Baridis, 29, was the legal compliance officer at Morgan Stanley, Dean Witter, Discover and Company. Ms. Baridis was in charge of what is commonly referred to as the "Chinese wall" in brokerage houses. Her job was to be certain that sensitive information did not cross from the side of the house putting together deals to the side of the house that buys stock. Her responsibilities included making certain that confidential information about Morgan Stanley clients did not leak to the brokerage side of the business so that Morgan Stanley brokers would not use inside information for trading.

Ms. Baridis met Jeffrey Streich, 31, in the summer of 1997. Mr. Streich was a broker who specialized in speculative stocks. Over a six-month period, Ms. Baridis allegedly provided Mr. Streich with information in exchange for $2,500 for each tip. However, late in October 1997, Mr. Streich and Ms. Baridis would have their last meeting when Mr. Streich went to their meeting wearing a hidden recorder, and there was a camera across the street that videotaped them both sitting in the window of a restaurant. The tape shows Mr. Streich handing Ms. Baridis $2,500 in one-hundred-dollar bills.

Ms. Baridis, who was indicted on charges of trading on inside information to make a profit, was fired from her $70,000-a-year job. Her father posted her $250,000 bail. Her indictment included statements by her obtained on a surveillance tape. When asked if she understood the implications of the tips and their scheme to profit she said, "It's the most illegalest thing you can do."[24] Ms. Baridis received kickbacks totaling $40,000. In another segment of the tape she is asked if she understands what would happen if they were caught, "We'd be interviewed in every magazine. We'd be in like . . . we'd be, who were the people of the '80s? Boesky? Michael Milken. We'd be bigger than that."[25] She added, "It's fun. If you don't get greedy."[26]

Prior to her indictment, Ms. Baridis had an upscale Manhattan apartment with rent of $2,400 per month. The extra money from the sale of information had afforded her a comfortable New York lifestyle. Her assets were frozen and prosecutors obtained $100,000 in a seizure of those assets. Overall, the insider tips involved thirteen companies and netted those involved in the trading over $1,000,000.[27]

Ms. Baridis entered a guilty plea in exchange for a lighter sentence contingent upon her cooperation. A college friend of Ms. Baridis also entered a guilty plea in federal court to charges of insider trading. Mr. Mitchell Sher, 32, admitted that he made cash payments to Ms. Baridis in exchange for her furnishing confidential information about pending events such as mergers for Morgan Stanley clients.[28]

Mr. Sher admitted that he used information provided to him by Ms. Baridis to trade in shares of Georgia-Pacific Corp., Burlington Resources, and two other companies. Unlike the ten other individuals charged in the case, Mr. Sher was not a broker but rather a vice president for a book distributor. He also admitted in his plea that Ms. Baridis had fed him confidential information in exchange for cash when she worked for Smith Barney earlier in her career.

When asked to comment on the Baridis case, an executive with Smith Barney said, "We had trusted the individual with great responsibility and that trust was misplaced."[29]

Discussion Questions

1. What is troublesome about insiders using information in advance of public disclosure to make money?

[24] *Dean Starkman, "Three Indicted for Insider Trading Tied to Ex-Morgan Stanley Aide,"* The Wall Street Journal, *November 26, 1997, p. B2.*

[25] *Elise Ackerman, "Remember Boesky? Many Gen Xers Don't,"* U.S. News & World Report, *November 22, 1999, p. 52.*

[26] *Peter Truell, "Lessons of Boesky and Milken Go Unheeded in Fraud Case,"* The New York Times, *November 26, 1997, pp. C1, C10.*

[27] *Peter Truell, "Sparring for Pieces of the Wall Street Action,"* The New York Times, *December 26, 1997, pp. C1, C2.*

[28] *Dean Starkman, "Five Brokers Indicted for Insider Trades Linked to Ex-Morgan Stanley Officer,"* The Wall Street Journal, *December 23, 1997, p. B9.*

[29] *Peter Truell, "An Employee on Wall Street Is Arrested,"* The New York Times, *November 7, 1997, p. C8.*

2. Why do regulators police such exchanges of information?
3. What does this case say about compliance programs and officers?

CASE 3.12

Espionage and Job-Hopping

Employees throughout a company have access to proprietary information, including customer lists, management techniques, and future plans.

What happens when those employees want to leave their current employer and go to work for a competitor? Or what happens when employees use or sell proprietary information?

Steven L. Davis, a lead process control engineer with Wright Industries, Inc., was part of a team working on the development and fabrication of equipment for Gillette Co.'s secret new shaving system. The new Gillette shaving system, predicted to be revolutionary, had been kept a very closely held secret. Wright Industries had been hired by Gillette. Mr. Davis was indicted by a federal grand jury on ten counts of wire fraud and theft of trade secrets. The indictment alleged Mr. Davis sent five faxes and electronic mail messages to Gillette's competitors with language intended to solicit interest in the purchase of Gillette's new technology. The messages included Mr. Davis's complaint that he had been passed over for a promotion.[30]

One of the competitors that received the fax alerted Gillette. Gillette contacted federal authorities and after an undercover investigation, Mr. Davis was charged. Mr. Davis then sent follow-up messages to the companies he had originally contacted complaining that someone "had betrayed him."

Discussion Questions

1. Is Mr. Davis's situation different because he did not work directly for Gillette?
2. If you had been one of the competitors Mr. Davis allegedly contacted, would you have notified Gillette?
3. Is there any irony in Mr. Davis's comment about betrayal?
4. What are the pros and cons of covenants in employee contracts that prohibit them (for a period of time) from working for a competitor? Some examples of recently enforced covenants:
   - Daniel O'Neill, the former head of Campbell Soup Co.'s soup division, could go to work for H.J. Heinz Co., but not in its soup division until August 1998 (a one-year ban).
   - Kevin R. Donohue, a former executive vice president with Kodak, was prohibited from working for a competitor (Fuji had hired him and Kodak sued for breach of contact) for one year.

[30] *Mark Maremont and Joseph Pereira, "Engineer Indicted on Charges He Stole Trade Secrets on Gillette Shaving System,"* The Wall Street Journal, *September 26, 1997, p. B2.*

- William Redmond, a soft-drink marketing executive with PepsiCo, was prohibited from going to work for the beverage division of Quaker Oats for six months.[31]

5. Are employees such as the executives in Question 4 capable of working for a competitor without divulging information? Consider the perspective of one executive, "It's difficult to have a competitive advantage over other companies unless there's something that you can call sacred to your company."[32]

CASE 3.13

The Glowing Recommendation[33]

Randi W. is a 13-year-old minor who attended the Livingston Middle School where Robert Gadams served as vice principal. On February 1, 1992, while Randi was in Gadams's office, Gadams sexually molested Randi.

Gadams's had previously been employed at the Mendota Unified School District (from 1985 to 1988). During his time of employment there, Gadams had been investigated and reprimanded for improper conduct with female junior high students, including giving them back massages, making sexual remarks to them, and being involved in "sexual situations" with them.

Gilbert Rossette, an official with Mendota, provided a letter of recommendation for Gadams in May 1990. The letter was part of Gadams's placement file at Fresno Pacific College, where he had received his teaching credentials. The recommendation was extensive and referred to Gadams's "genuine concern" for students, his "outstanding rapport" with everyone, and concluded, "I wouldn't hesitate to recommend Mr. Gadams for any position."

Gadams had also previously been employed at the Tranquility High School District and Golden Plains Unified District (1987–1990). Richard Cole, an administrator at Golden Plains, also provided a letter of recommendation for the Fresno placement file that listed Gadams's "favorable" qualities and concluded that he "would recommend him for almost any administrative position he wishes to pursue." Cole knew, at the time he provided the recommendation, that Gadams had been the subject of various parents' complaints, including that he "led a panty raid, made sexual overtures to students, sexual remarks to students." Cole also knew that Gadams had resigned under pressure because of these sexual misconduct charges.

Gadams's last place of employment (1990–1991) before Livingston was Muroc Unified School District, where disciplinary actions were taken against him for sexual harassment. When allegations of "sexual touching" of female students were made, Gadams was forced to resign from Muroc. Nonetheless, Gary Rice and David Malcolm, officials at Muroc, provided a letter of recommendation for Gadams that described him as "an upbeat, enthusiastic administrator who relates well to the students," and who was responsible "in large part," for making Boron Junior High School

[31] *"Non Compete Clauses are Serious,"* The Wall Street Journal, *December 10, 1996, p. A1.*

[32] Id.

[33] *Adapted from* Randi W. v. Muroc Joint Unified School District, *929 P.2d 582 (Cal. 1997).*

(located in Muroc) "a safe, orderly and clean environment for students and staff." The letter concluded that they recommended Gadams "for an assistant principalship or equivalent position without reservation."

All of the letters provided by previous administrators of Gadams were sent in on forms that included a disclosure that the information provided "will be sent to prospective employers."

Through her guardian, Randi W. filed suit against the districts, alleging that her injuries from Gadams's sexual touching were proximately caused by their failure to provide full and accurate information about Gadams to the placement service.

Discussion Questions

1. If you were a former administrator to whom Gadams reported, what kind of recommendation would you give?
2. Should the previous administrators have done something about Gadams prior to being placed in this dilemma?
3. Do administrators owe their loyalty to employees ? to students? to the school district? to the parents?
4. Is this type of recommendation commonly given to get rid of employees?
5. Should friendship have a higher value than honesty?
6. Why do you think the administrators said nothing?

READING 3.14

The Ethics of Confrontation[34]

Marianne M. Jennings

I. Introduction

Studying a recent California court decision brought to mind the issue of the ethics of confrontation and the underlying question of why there is such hesitancy to confront truth at appropriate times and take the actions necessary to remedy its consequences. The California case, *Randi W. v. Muroc Unified School District*,[35] involves Robert Gadams, an educational administrator for the junior high/middle school years, who had been accused of improper touching or sexual conduct with students at four schools where he had served as an administrator.

[34] *"The Ethics of Confrontation: The Virtues and Vice in Remaining Silent,"* Corporate Finance Review *6(4): 42–46 (2002). Reprinted from Corporate Finance Review by RIA, 395 Hudson Street, New York, NY 10014.*

[35] *929 P.2d 582 (Cal. 1997).*

Apparently the principals of the first three schools, the district administrators and school boards wanted no more than to be rid of him and the confrontation that would be necessary to revoke his certification. Each passed him along to other schools, with glowing letters of recommendation. One former principal wrote that Gadams made his junior high a "safe, orderly and clean environment for students and staff." Another wrote that he would recommend Gadams "for an assistant principalship or equivalent position without reservation."

It was at the fourth school where this problematic administrator perpetrated real harm against a young girl that his history emerged, but only because of litigation filed by her parents.

The case raises the question that is a universal one in business: why is there such a hesitancy to bring to a head evolving problems? Why is there such a fear of confrontation? The reasons are many, as noted in the following sections, but the justifications are few and the benefits virtually nonexistent.

II. Examples in Business of Confrontation Avoidance

While the case that has piqued this discussion is one from the field of education, business with all its respect for the bottom line and performance results, certainly has no dearth of examples of avoiding confrontation until the result is the same messy litigation evident in the *Muroc* case.

One could begin with performance evaluations. Businesses have finally migrated to rankings and grades as a means of evaluating employees and sorting the wheat from the chaff because the nature of evaluation content was grounded in confrontation avoidance. Annual evaluations of marginal employees were often difficult to distinguish from those of stellar performers because managers avoided the confrontation of candid performance reviews with employees, fearing the reaction and possible process of appeals involving everything from company reviews to allegations of discrimination.

However, rather than confront the often messy issues in disparate performance, candid feedback and justified termination or reprimand, employers have resorted to rankings as a means of annual performance evaluations. For example, Ford Motor Company has 18,000 managers who are grouped into sets of 30-50. Of each group, 10% must be assigned an "A" grade, 80% must be assigned a "B" grade and 10% must be given a "C" grade. Those with the bottom grades are then eased out of the company. Those with a "C' grade cannot be given a pay raise and those with a "C" grade for two years in a row are demoted or terminated. There are no exceptions made for any of the groups, but Ford did cut back on the "C" requirement to 5% for 2001.

The companies hide the issues within a number system. At Sun Microsystems, employees given a "C" there are given 90 days to improve. If they do not improve, they are given a chance to resign and take a severance package or risk termination. Cisco Systems has established a goal of getting rid of 1 of every 20 employees with the focus being on employees given substandard performance evaluations. GE has a 20-70-10 plan for ranking employees. GE follows a carrot approach in that it rewards the top 20% so well that few ever leave the company. GE uses the 10% group to terminate employees and it terminates about 8,000 management and professional employees each year. Jack Welch has noted that those in the 10% would end up leaving the company anyway because they are unhappy in not performing and GE just makes the inevitable decision for them early.[36] While the system may ease the employee hassles, it never really confronts the issues the employees and their supervisors should be grappling with as part of the evaluation. The numbers are a substitute for analysis and feedback, the most painful aspects of performance evaluation.

In financial performance, employees, managers and auditors have all been engaged in a well-choreographed ritual of confrontation avoidance. FINOVA, the Phoenix-based company that was once a darling of Wall Street for its double-digit growth and named consistently one of the top ten companies in America to work for, had at least one year of confrontation avoidance over its accounting practices. During that time employees expressed reservations, concern and even outrage over the company's failure to write down a $70 million loan to a California computer firm (among other issues) and both the concerns and some employees were dismissed. Their managers understood their concerns and many agreed, but they were unwilling to confront senior management over the issues. The auditors were unwilling to do the same until after the company's initial 1999 annual report had gone to press. The result was a public confrontation, a dismissal of the auditors, new auditors and the eventual disclosure of all that the employees and managers had avoided confronting senior managers about.

There are other examples of this financial avoidance that have appeared in these discussions over the past five years: the slippery slope of earnings management; Al Dunlap and the booking of a sale of parts that they are charged with knowing would be reversed once the quarterly earnings goals were met, Joseph Jett, Nick Leeson and other rogue traders who were not confronted by their managers despite their unrealistic returns to the firms until outsiders demanded such, and the list goes on with every business sharing the common thread of avoiding or postponing confrontation.

III. Why We Avoid Confrontation

The "don't rock the boat" attitude is frequently seen as the virtuous road. Confrontation is messy—there are often hurt feelings. There are embarrassing revelations. There are destroyed careers. There are costs. Whether confrontation involves sexual misconduct by an assistant school principal or cooking the books by a manager or bond trader, the impact is the same.

Human nature flees from such situations. Further, there is within human nature that rationalization that avoiding confrontation is being "nice," and nice is associated with ethics.

There are also the harsh realities of confrontation. To confront the assistant school principal with allegations and carry through with a disciplinary process for the loss of a license to teach is time consuming and reflects on the school and administrators who hired him in the first place. There is exposure to liability.

The same is true with the business scenarios presented. A good employee evaluation means that the employee is happy, there are no reviews, no messy discussions and no allegations of discrimination. Not confronting a rogue trader means enjoying the ride of their performance and earnings and worrying about consequences at another

[36] *Del Jones, "More Firms Cut Workers Ranked at the Bottom to Make Way for Talent,"* USA Today, *May 30, 2001, pp. 1B, 2B.*

time when perhaps something else will come along to counterbalance any of their harmful activities. Not insisting that a loan be written down carries with it the comfort of steady growth and earnings and a hope that future financial performance can make up for the loss when it eventually must be disclosed.

There is a great deal of rationalization that goes into the avoidance of confrontation. There is a comfort in maintaining status quo. There is at least a postponement of legal issues and liabilities. Often, avoiding confrontation is a painless road that carries with it the hope that whatever lies beneath does not break through and reveal its ugliness. Often confrontation carries with it the hope that a problem will solve itself or become a moot issue.

IV. The Harms of Avoiding Confrontation

Postponing confrontation does not produce a better result when the issue at the heart of the needed confrontation inevitably emerges. Those harms include liability, individual harms, reputational damage and the loss of income as the issue chugs along without resolution.

A. Physical Harm

In the *Muroc* case, all of the districts were liable for their failure to take action and then issuing glowing letters of recommendation. Had the issue of sexual misconduct and the assistant principal been confronted the first time there was misconduct, there would not have been the remaining 3 schools and victims.

B. Loss of Reputation and Income

In FINOVA's case, a $3 billion company can survive the write-down of a $70 million loan. It cannot, as FINOVA's bankruptcy has shown, survive that write-down when the investment community loses trust as the disclosure of the bad loan and its write-down are withheld until there is a confrontation that must necessarily be public because the change in auditors.

In Joseph Jett's case, there were a number of employees who questioned the earnings Jett was posting in managing the government bonds section of Kidder Peabody. They raised the impossibility of Jett's earnings curve in the bond market. Instead of confronting Jett, the managers continued to enjoy the ride. The longer the ride, the greater the fall-out and Kidder Peabody was destroyed as a result of the eventual confrontation with Jett's fabricated sales and revenues.[37]

C. Liability Increased

Another example is the eventual confrontation between Ford and Firestone over who and what was responsible for the Ford Explorer debacle and the accidents and deaths. The two companies' longstanding business relationship and an unwillingness to deal with data and questions accomplished little. With more information percolating on a regular basis, both companies acknowledged, even as they battled with each other in a media confrontation, that neither has emerged with its reputation intact in the public eye. Civil litigation and an investigation by the federal government as well as depositions of top executives in the companies were trickled out to the public. Those

[37] *Sylvia Nasar, "Kidder Scandal Tied to Failure of Supervisors,"* The New York Times, *July 26, 1994, pp. C1, C14.*

depositions have had some inconsistencies with the some of the public statements by Bridgestone/Firestone.

For example, Bridgestone/Firestone has issued public statements that it was not aware of peeling issues with its tires used on the Ford Explorer. However, a deposition of Firestone's chief of quality reveals that he believes he discussed the issue of the tires with the company's CEO in 1999, a full year before the issue became public with the resulting recall. David Laubie, who retired from the company in May 2000, said that he handled consumer claims and quality control issues for the company and had received complaints which he passed along to the CEO in memo form as well as in their regular meetings.

In testimony before Congress in September, 2000, Firestone's executive vice president, Gary Crigger, testified that the company only became aware of the problem in July or August of 2000.

Another issue in the case has been Firestone's allegation that Ford did not put the proper tire pressure instructions with the Ford Explorer. Firestone said that Ford's recommendation of an unusually low tire pressure, 26 pounds per square inch, caused the sidewalls to flex and get hot which then weakened the tires. However, both the depositions of Mr. Laubie and the current quality control chief of Firestone indicate that no one from Firestone ever discussed the low tire pressure issue with anyone at Ford.[38] The lack of confrontation before, during and after the public revelations about some issue, whatever that may prove to be, surrounding the Ford Explorer and its tires, cost both companies in terms of reputation and perhaps liability.

V. The Deceptive Lull of "Being Nice"

One of the faulty assumptions in avoiding confrontation is that the "niceness" benefits the individuals affected. A good performance evaluation is beneficial to the employee. Not taking disciplinary action permits a teacher or administrator to continue his career and earn a living. Not raising a financial reporting issue means that shareholders can continue to enjoy returns and market value. Not questioning an employee's unusual success means that the earnings figures stand unscathed. Many are protected when confrontation is avoided.

The difficulty with the protection argument is that it presumes that the truth will not emerge. When it does, the preservation of a career in light of information introduces greater liability. Termination of an employee for cause may carry with it the difficulties of challenge and even litigation. Not terminating an employee for cause who goes on later to do more harm exposes the company to liability. The difficulty with not disclosing matters that affect earnings is that when those matters do emerge, there is not just the resulting restatement of earnings but the accompanying lack of investor trust and resulting reduction in market value. The greatest harm in avoiding confrontation is that what the confrontation could have minimized is exacerbated by the postponement.

VI. The Ethics of Confrontation

While not widely accepted as a principle of virtue, there is an ethical duty of confrontation. Edmund Burke was a proponent of such a duty with his admonition of two

[38] *James R. Healey and Sara Nathan, "Depositions in Tire Lawsuits Don't Match Company's Lines,"* USA Today, *December 11, 2000, p. 3B.*

centuries ago, "All that is necessary for evil to triumph is for good men to do nothing." There is the more modern phraseology that holds that if there is a legal or ethical problem in a company and an employee or manager or executive says nothing, they become part of the problem.

However, one of the reasons for the hesitancy in confrontation not discussed earlier is a certain degree of ineptness on the part of those who must do the confronting. If confrontation is indeed a virtue, are there guides for its exercise? The following offers a model for confrontation.

A. Determine the facts.

An underlying disdain for confrontation arises because too often those who do the confronting are wrong. Prior to confrontation, prepare as if you were working on a budget, a product launch or a financing. Know what is happening or what has happened and obtain as much background information as possible. Preparation also serves as protection for any fears of liability from taking action. Employers need to understand that well-documented personnel actions are not a basis for discrimination suits. And termination of employees who are harming others is not actionable if the harm is established.

B. If you don't know the facts, or can't know the facts, present the issue to those involved and affected.

Ford and Firestone will perhaps not know the issues of liability and accountability for years to come with regard to the Explorer and the tires. However, their lack of information should not have prevented them from confronting each other or confronting the customers and public with the information they did have.

In the case of allegations or when an employee has raised a question about how a particular matter is being carried on the books, you may only be presented with one side. That lack of information need not preclude you from raising the question. In the case of the school administrator, the students made an allegation against the assistant principal. The principal has no way of knowing whether the allegation is true or false, but he can go to the assistant principal and raise the issue and then can proceed with the types of hearings or inquiries that can provide the information or at least constitute the confrontation.

A financial officer can hear from employees a number of views on carrying certain items on the books. The very definition of materiality opens the door to that type of disagreement. But a good financial officer knows that an open discussion of the issue, and confrontation of the issue with those who tout various views, is the solution that serves the company best in the long run. Without such confrontation, the failure to listen to an employee's view exacerbates the eventual fall-out from a bad decision. The public confrontation of the issue is, in and of itself, insurance against the fall-out should that decision prove to be wrong.

C. Always give the opportunity for self-remedy.

One of the reasons confrontation enjoys such universal disdain is that very often the confrontation is done circuitously. If your attorney has done something questionable, confront him or her first and then report them to the state bar for discipline. If an employee has engaged in misconduct, tell them and don't let him or her hear it from someone else. If earnings are overstated, employees should work within the company for self-remedy before heading to the SEC.

One of the virtue constraints in the ethics of confrontation is having the courage to discuss the issues and concerns with those who are involved in creating them. An end run is not a confrontation. It is an act of cowardice that can result in the liability discussed earlier.

D. Don't fear the fall-out and hassle.

The reasons for the lack of confrontation discussed earlier included the realistic observation that many avoid confrontation because it is too much trouble. However, as also noted earlier, if there is a problem that remains unconfronted, it does not improve with age. Indeed, the failure to make a timely confrontation often proves to result in more costs in the long run. Hassles don't dissipate as confrontation is postponed or avoided.

VII. Conclusion

The ethics of confrontation are quite simply that confrontation is a necessary part of managing an honest business. Confrontation openly airs disagreement. Confrontation prevents the damage that comes from concealed truth. Confrontation preserves reputations when it produces the self-remedies that are nearly always cheaper than those imposed from the lack of confrontation. Niceness is rarely the ethical route when issues and facts need to be aired. Confrontation, while not always pleasant, is often the only resolution of a problem.

Discussion Questions

1. What are the consequences of the failure to raise an issue, whether legal or ethical, when it first arises?
2. What factors contribute to the failure to confront an issue?
3. What steps could a business take to encourage confrontation?

3d

Taking Advantage

What happens when you have the upper hand when it comes to knowledge and information? Do you have an obligation to share with the other side in your negotiations that they are making incorrect assumptions? Do you let them know that there are downsides to your product? Do you use technology to circumvent privacy and property rights issues? The ethical category of taking unfair advantage is one in which one party has a superior bargaining, knowledge, information or power position and uses it to cause the other side to lose something in the process. Sometimes parties take advantage of others just by their philanthropic position. Their goodness in cause is used to justify unfairness in treatment.

CASE 3.15

Napster: The Ethics of "Peer-to-Peer File Sharing"

Napster, Inc., a company founded by Shawn Fanning and Sean Parker, operates an online service for "peer-to-peer file sharing" (http://www.napster.com) so that users can, free of charge, download recordings via the Internet through a process known as "ripping," which is the downloading of digital MP3 files. MP3 is the abbreviated term for audio recordings in a digital format known as MPEG-3. This compressed format allows for rapid transmission of digital audio files from one computer to another.[39]

Napster's online service provides a search vehicle for files stored on others' computers and permits the downloading of the recordings from the hard drives of other Napster users. Napster provides technical support as well as a chat room for users to exchange information. The result is that users, who register and have a password through Napster, can download single songs and complete CDs or albums, via the peer-to-peer file sharing.

A & M Records and others, including Geffen Records, Sony Music, MCA Records, Atlantic Recording, Motown Records, and Capital Records, are in the business of the

[39] A & M Records, Inc. v. Napster, Inc., *239 F.3d 1004 (9th Cir. 2001).*

commercial recording, distribution, and sale of copyrighted musical compositions and sound recordings. They filed suit against Napster, Inc. (Napster) as a contributory and vicarious copyright infringer. Related copyright suits were filed by Metallica and Andre Young (Dr. Dre). Metallica demanded that Napster deregister its music from its file-sharing service. Dr. Dre indicated, "I don't like people stealing my music," when he was asked about his litigation.[40] Mike Stoller, a songwriter since age 17 whose portfolio includes "Hound Dog," "Jailhouse Rock," and "Love Potion No. 9," also filed suit against Napster and wrote the following in an opinion piece for *The New York Times*:

> I fear for the 17-year-old songwriter looking forward to a career in the music business today. Napster and companies like it are not only threatening my retirement, but the future of music itself. In fact, by taking the incentive out of songwriting, Napster may be pushing itself closer to a time when there won't be any songs for its users to swap.[41]

Professor Paul Kedrosky of the University of British Columbia wrote the following in his call for an injunction shutting down Napster:

> Let's be blunt: Napster-style file sharing is theft. But for some reason commentators don't see it that way. Instead we hear all sorts of tripe about waves of change, the inevitability of the Internet, and so on.
>
> Why do so-called opinion leaders so smirkingly dismiss theft? In a nutshell, it's because aging would-be hipsters are trying to demonstrate their technology bona fides to amoral technologists.
>
> Opioneers aside, the rest of us should know better. So why don't we treat online music theft the same way we treat offline theft? In part, because it doesn't feel like theft. After all, you're just sitting at home downloading files. It's not as if you slipped a CD from Sam Goody into your coat pocket, then scrambled out the door.
>
> Napster has done little to dissuade people from thinking otherwise. After standing blithely by while millions of dollars in pirated music flowed over its servers. Napster is now insisting that it has a role to play. It has, it insists, market presence and could be a new means of distribution for music. In other words, it is saying, "Just pay us!" Sound familiar? It should. It's a classic shakedown right out of Mafia 101.[42]

The controversy over Napster created fierce media and Congressional battles among and between artists, fans, and music companies. Recording artists and record companies called "peer-to-peer file sharing" nothing more than copyright infringement. "It's a technology no one anticipated and the law doesn't apply," was the observation of one legal expert. Don Henley, formerly of The Eagles, and Alanis Morissette both testified before Congress that Napster deprived them of their royalty income and their rights in their intellectual property. Members of the rock group Metallica complained that fans who downloaded music via Napster exhibited a lack of morals.

Other artists were busily establishing Internet strategies. Lance Bass, of the teen band 'N Sync, developed strategies for digital music. By participating in teen chat

[40] *Holman W. Jenkins, Jr., "Let's Give It Up for Metallica,"* The Wall Street Journal, *May 10, 2000, p. A27.*

[41] *Mike Stoller, "Songs That Won't Be Written,"* The New York Times, *October 7, 2000, p. A29.*

[42] *Paul Kedrosky, "Napster Should Be Playing Jailhouse Rock,"* The Wall Street Journal, *July 31, 2000, p. A32.*

rooms, Bass learns which songs his fans take a liking to and has been selling his songs over the Internet. He makes about $1 per CD sold because the record companies have monopolies on distribution and spend large amounts on marketing. One of the executives for TransContinental Records, the company that has 'N Sync under contract, notes, "An awful lot of established bands out there are looking at their digital strategy and looking at record companies and saying, 'Why do I need you?'"[43]

Others noted that if Napster were liable under the law for the downloading so also were the phone companies and cable companies that furnish the lines that permit Internet access and the resulting downloading of the music. And the Napster users' arguments could be summed up as one *Time* magazine reader wrote, "Using Napster is like inviting 100,000 friends over for *Monday Night Football*—not what the network intended, but not illegal." In an interview with *The New York Times Magazine*, Mr. Fanning said, "Thirty-seven million users can't all be criminals."[44]

The Recording Industry Association of America (RIAA) began tracing the origins of file-sharing sites and tipped off law enforcement authorities. A number of 18- and 19-year-old freshmen around the country were arrested in their dorm rooms as they facilitated music downloading.[45]

As the controversy over the file-sharing/infringement issues continued, Napster began to experience some issues with its logo. File sharers were downloading and copying the Napster logo and it was even showing up on t-shirts. Napster filed suit against those using the trademark without authorization for infringement, seeking an injunction as well as damages.

When the suit was filed by the record companies, the district court granted a preliminary injunction to the plaintiffs enjoining Napster from "engaging in, or facilitating others in copying, downloading, uploading, transmitting, or distributing plaintiffs' copyrighted musical compositions and sound recordings, protected by either federal or state law, without express permission of the rights owner."[46]

The federal court of appeals for the ninth circuit entered a temporary stay of the injunction to review the case. Both the trial court and the appellate court struggled with the issues of what Napster was and what it actually allowed computer users to do and whether it was a violation of the law or simply a question of ethics.

The evidence at the trial showed that a majority of Napster users use the service to download and upload copyrighted music. Napster users also upload file names to the search index so that others can make copies of the same music once they have gone to the trouble of downloading the various songs.

Napster owner Shawn Fanning, who was 18 at the time he created the Napster technology, and his lawyer, David Boies (who represented the Justice Department in its litigation against Microsoft, and former vice president Albert Gore, Jr. in his litigation over the Florida recounts) argue that Napster users do not directly infringe plaintiffs' copyrights because the users are engaged in fair use of the material. They

[43] *Amy Kover, "Digital Artists Want Control,"* Fortune, *June 26, 2000, p. 134.*

[44] *David D. Kirkpatrick, "Napster,"* The New York Times Magazine, *June 10, 2001, p. 73.*

[45] *Jenny Eliscu, "Freshman Busted for MP3 Piracy,"* Rolling Stone, *November 9, 2000, p. 33.*

[46] *114 F. Supp.2d 896 (N.D. Cal. 2000).*

identified three specific alleged fair uses: sampling, where users make temporary copies of a work before purchasing (using the service to listen to a song before purchasing the CD); space-shifting, where users access a sound recording through the Napster system that they already own in audio CD format (they own the Beatles' White Album in record, tape, or CD form and want it in MP3 technology; and permissive distribution of recordings by both new and established artists (artists permit the downloading of their songs and performances).

However, the evidence at the trial showed that permissive uses were the exception and not the rule and that there were repeated and exploitative unauthorized copies of copyrighted works made, for the most part, to save the expense of purchasing authorized copies.

The federal copyright laws do permit "fair use" of copyrighted materials. Fair use, when properly applied, is limited to copying by others that does not materially impair the marketability of the work which is copied. The evidence at the district court level showed that Napster harms the market in "at least" two ways: it reduces audio CD sales among college students and it "raises barriers to plaintiffs' entry into the market for the digital downloading of music."[47]

However, Napster did present evidence from its own expert, Dr. Peter S. Fader, who concluded in his report that Napster is beneficial to the music industry because MP3 music file-sharing stimulates more audio CD sales than it displaces. However, the trial court judge dismissed most of Dr. Fader's report because Dr. Fader played a minimal role in overseeing the administration of the survey and that there was a general lack of objective data in his report.

The district court also found that both the market for audio CDs and the market for online distribution are adversely affected by Napster's service. Once a user lists a copy of music he already owns on the Napster system in order to access the music from another location, the song becomes "available to millions of other individuals," not just the original CD owner.

Napster argued that it could not be held liable for copyright infringement because it was not participating in the downloading and could not supervise the use of its system. However, the court ruled that Napster knew how its system was being used even if it was not aware of each specific instance. In fact, Napster's founders were aware of their vulnerability. During the proceedings in district court, the music companies proffered a document authored by Napster co-founder Sean Parker that mentioned "the need to remain ignorant of users' real names and IP addresses 'since they are exchanging pirated music'"; and (2) The RIAA informed Napster of more than 12,000 infringing files, some of which are still available.

Napster was eventually shut down by the federal court. Several interim steps were taken as the companies tried to get their songs de-registered. Any slight difference in title spelling or phrasing meant users could circumvent the blocks. However, the German record company, BMG, purchased Napster and has begun doing marketing surveys of former Napster users to determine how much they would be willing to pay for subscription services to copyrighted music.

[47] *114 F. Supp.2d 896, 911.*

Discussion Questions

1. Do you think that downloading the music was legal? Do you think it was ethical?
2. Why do some use the term *peer-to-peer file sharing* while others refer to the downloading as theft?
3. Congress passed the Digital Millennium Copyright Act of 1998, an act that prohibited the circumvention of encryption devices on copyrighted materials in order to make copies. The DMCA also held those who provided the means, such as software programs, for circumvention of encryption devices liable for copyright infringement. Further, those who provide server access, such as colleges and universities, are required to do periodic checks to verify that their systems are not being used for such circumvention. What are these complex laws attempting to do?
4. What is the difference between downloading and theft?
5. Must morals and ethics change because technology has made things so different?
6. What happens if there are no protections for intellectual property?
7. Hilary Rosen, the CEO of RIAA, said the following in an interview with *USA Today*, "The Napster battle was classic. People took their free music really seriously. It was amazing how strongly people felt about their principled right to someone else's property."[48] What does her statement reflect in terms of her ethical values? About those of the downloaders?

CASE 3.16

The Dot-Coms and Finance

The new economy was often touted as one that offered a different way of doing business, complete with new values. The following piece takes a look at how some of the new values backfired on the businesses that used them.[49]

I. Introduction

This was a ride, this journey with the dot-coms and their IPOs. As we watch former millionaires look for work, their fortunes vanished as quickly as they were lavished, we are left with the post-mortem analysis. What went wrong and how did it go so wrong so quickly? While the dot-coms gave us new technology, new ways of doing business, new decision-making processes and even new dress codes, they exit reminding us of some very old lessons about business. Post-mortem is never easy for the defeated champions, but the analysis is important for next year's team. As we clean up the burst bubble, we find the lessons of the new economy were ages old. And the bottom line in

[48] *"Rosen Weighs in on Napster, Lyrics—and Her CDs,"* USA Today, *May 2, 2001, p. 3D.*

[49] *Marianne M. Jennings, "A Post Mortem on the Dot-Com Economy: Basic Values Forgotten,"* Corporate Finance Review *6(2): 42–48 (2001). Reprinted from Corporate Finance Review by RIA, 395 Hudson Street, New York, NY 10014.*

all of the analyses is that there are certain irrevocably decreed values in business that cannot be ignored, no matter what the product or how bullish the market.

II. The Fall-Out From the Dot-Coms

The following factors are descriptive of the financial cycle we just completed:

- High price earnings multipliers
- Economic disturbances abroad
- High levels of optimism
- Insiders selling their shares
- Insider trading
- Options abound
- Speculation
- A false security in a feeling of invincibility

This descriptive list was actually taken from readings on the Holland Tulip market of the 1600's, the 1929 stock market and the California Gold Rush.[50]

There was a false sense of invincibility that fueled the players in the new economy because they lacked historical perspective. Many had never witnessed the down side of an economic cycle in their young lives. The nature of their new businesses contributed to the hubris. They perceived themselves to be somehow above the basic rules of business and economics. Whether you discussed little issues such as sales and earnings or big issues such as insider trading and earnings management turned into cooking books, many of the new economy companies and their officers felt they were above the fray. Their perception was that they need not bother with the worldly issues of accounting improprieties. There is certainly sufficient blame to go around in the post-mortem analyses. There were investors who should have known better who were dropping everything they owned into IPOs without having seen a financial statement let alone a dime in earnings.

The end results are evidenced by a look at three companies that have experienced some of the worst falls. Their attitudes, experience and consequences are generally applicable and universally instructive.

III. Razorfish: A Little Adult Supervision and If It Sounds Too Good to be True . . .

Jeff Dachis, the former CEO of Razorfish, saw his company's stock premier at $56 per share in 1999. Razorfish reached its earnings peak in 1999 when it had net income of $14,000,000. In 2000, the company posted a $148,000,000 revenue loss and by May 2001, the shares were trading at $1.11. Mr. Dachis, you may recall, was quoted in this column as saying that he did not see the need for outside directors on his board for, "Management isn't screwing up. What's good for me is good for all shareholders." No matter how good a digital technology company is, it still needs business expertise to run smoothly. Mr. Dachis and his board not only lacked that experience, they did not acknowledge it as important until it was too late. Brilliant with the Web and still in their 30's, the executive team failed to understand that expertise in product is not the same as expertise in finance or management. They were not familiar with one of the key

[50] *Mike Dash,* Tulipomania: The Story of the World's Most Coveted Flower & the Extraordinary Passions It Aroused, *Three Rivers Press: New York, 1999; Harold Bierman, Jr.,* The Causes of the 1929 Stock Market Crash, *Greenwood Press: Westport, CT, London, 1999; and "California Gold Rush,"* Encyclopedia Britannica, *1998.*

tenets of business ethics which is that good business decisions, operations and financials come from companies with disagreement through a diverse management team. Singular in age and background, the company lacked the depth for disagreement.

No more evident is the lack of disagreement than in the company's overly optimistic press releases and earnings statements and projections. A company at ethical risk is one that not only boasts of it double-digit earnings growth but also promises more or at least a continuation. The pressure on employees is acute and the result is that many will cut corners, whether it is in the treatment of customers as a cost reduction measure or in the reporting of income under creative interpretation of FASB rules. Below are excerpts from the earnings release statements that Razorfish made over the course of the new economy. The releases appear with their respective dates.

> New York, New York, May 17, 1999—Razorfish, Inc. (NASDAQ: RAZF), a cutting-edge global digital communications solutions provider, today reported financial results for the quarter ended March 31, 1999.
>
> Revenues rose to $12.4 million, a 483% increase over the first quarter of 1998 and a 161% increase over the fourth quarter of 1998. At the same time, gross margin improved to 47.5% from 33.6% in the first quarter of 1998 and 43.3% in the fourth quarter of 1998. Razorfish believes that gross margin improved because utilization of billable employees increased to 65%, compared with 51% in the first quarter of 1998, and 54% in the fourth quarter of 1998.
>
> Earnings Before Interest, Taxes, Depreciation, and Amortization (EBITDA) on a percentage basis were 18.0%, compared with 7.7% in the first quarter of 1998 and 21.9% in the fourth quarter of 1998. Basic earnings per share increased to $0.03 from $0.00 in the first quarter of 1998, and $0.01 in the fourth quarter of 1998.
>
> On a pro forma basis, revenues totaled $6.9 million for the first quarter of 1998 and $9.2 million for the fourth quarter of 1998. Revenue in the first quarter of 1999 increased by 78.7% compared with pro forma revenue for the first quarter of 1998 and increased by 34.8% compared with pro forma revenue for the fourth quarter of 1998. Gross margin increased to 47.5% for the first quarter of 1999 compared with pro forma gross margin of 30.5% for the first quarter of 1998 and pro forma gross margin of 30.7% for the fourth quarter of 1998.
>
> EBITDA increased to 18.0% for the first quarter of 1999 compared with pro forma EBITDA of 9.8% for the first quarter of 1998 and pro forma EBITDA of 8.1% for the fourth quarter of 1998. Basic earnings per share increased to $0.03 for the first quarter of 1999 compared with a pro forma basic earnings per share loss of $0.01 for the first quarter of 1998.
>
> In April 1999, Razorfish completed an Initial Public Offering of 3.45 million shares at $16 per share. Net proceeds to Razorfish from the offering totaled approximately $48 million, which will be used for general corporate purposes, including expanding its human resources department and hiring additional personnel, developing a formal sales and marketing department, and strategic acquisitions or investments.[51]

[51] *Press release on http://www.razorfish.com (last visited November 17, 2001).*

Note the following critical elements:

(1) The focus on the percentage increase in earnings growth
(2) The promise of more or equal earnings growth
(3) The focus on EBITDA (not bad in and of itself) ignores some of the market realities and hits to earnings that the company might face

Despite a market that had already begun changing, Razorfish released the following in April 2000:

> New York, April 25, 2000—Razorfish, Inc. (NASDAQ: RAZF), the global digital solutions provider, today reported record financial results for the quarter ended March 31, 2000. The company also announced the appointment of John Roberts as its new chief financial officer (See related announcement of April 25, 2000).
>
> Razorfish 2000 first quarter revenues rose to $64,116,000, a 97% increase over the revenue for the same period a year ago of $32,612,000, and an increase of 22% over the revenue for the previous quarter of $52,705,000.
>
> 2000 first quarter net income (before amortization of intangibles, and non-cash compensation expense) was $6,479,000 or cash EPS of $0.07, compared to $3,739,000 or cash EPS of $0.04 in the first quarter of 1999. Net income for the quarter (including the above costs) totaled $4,493,000 or $0.05 per share, compared to net income of $3,100,000 or $0.04 per share for the first quarter of 1999.
>
> "Our strong sequential, quarter-over-quarter growth of 22% has Razorfish hitting on all cylinders now that we have successfully integrated our acquisitions and built global, scaleable capabilities that will harness the wireless and broadband explosion and keep Razorfish at the forefront of the digital revolution," said Jeff Dachis, chief executive officer and president of Razorfish. "Razorfish is winning because we continue to invent new businesses and reinvent Fortune 1000 businesses with cutting-edge solutions executed through the passion and talent of over 1,600 of the industry's brightest leaders. Through the deep technology capabilities, creative skills and business strategy of our employees, we are able to transform businesses that are committed to winning through a focus on user design."[52]

Note the following:

(1) Percentages are down, but still the focus on the phenomenal growth remains
(2) Dachis is still in charge and convinced that talent alone will see them through

How things change in just one year, as the following press release shows:

> New York, May 3, 2001—Razorfish, Inc. (NASDAQ: RAZF), a global digital solutions provider, today reported its results for the quarter ended March 31, 2001 and announced that Jean-Philippe Maheu, former Chief Operating Officer has been promoted to the role of Chief Executive Officer.
>
> For the first quarter 2001, revenues were $42.7 million, which compares to $50.1 million in the fourth quarter 2000. Pro forma net loss (before amortization of intangibles and non-recurring expenses) for the first quarter 2001 was ($6.6 million) or

[52] Id.

($0.07) per share, which compares to pro forma net loss of ($19.8 million) or ($.20) per share in the fourth quarter 2000 and pro forma net income of $6.5 million or $0.07 per share for the first quarter 2000.

"Our primary goal is to manage our return to profitable operations and positive cash flow while successfully serving the expectations of our clients, shareholders and employees," said Mr. Maheu, Chief Executive Officer of Razorfish. "These financial results reflect this direction and we continue to gain traction with new and current clients, including Cisco, Ford, and Natwest and we are beginning to see the benefits of our cost reduction efforts."[53]

Notice the following:

(1) They are now minimizing losses
(2) They are now cutting costs
(3) They have now replaced Mr. Dachis
(4) They now have 3 outsiders on their board

In short, Razorfish returned to the basic principles of business: watch your costs, make and market a good product and get input from those outside your business to help you see the issues. From an ethics perspective, we could add one more: be honest and accurate in your financial statements and predictions about future earnings. It is simply not possible to sustain growth in the 400% range and nothing acknowledged that reality until the market did it for Razorfish, something now reflected in its $1.11 share price, quite a dive from a $56 premier in 1999.

IV. MicroStrategy: Creative Accounting

MicroStrategy 's share price at the time of its IPO was $6 and it climbed to $333 per share by March 2000 largely due to profits posted for 1999. By December 2000, the SEC announced that it was investigating MicroStrategy for "accounting improprieties." The share price dropped 62% in one day following Dachis's sale of a large amount of MicroStrategy stock. In late 1999, PricewaterhouseCoopers demanded that MicroStrategy restate its earnings for 1999. Those earnings were restated with a resulting loss as the earnings noted for earlier years were reversed. MicroStrategy agreed to change its accounting practices to spread revenues for software sales and services over the lives of the contracts rather than in lump sums as it had been booking them. Its explanation follows:

The Company has concluded that certain of its software sales that include service relationships will be accounted for using contract accounting, which spreads the recognition of revenues over the entire contract period as opposed to separating it between the software and services components. The effect of these revisions is to defer the time when revenue is recognized for large, complex contracts that combine both products and services.

The Company, with the concurrence of PricewaterhouseCoopers LLP, its auditors, will reduce its 1999 reported revenue from $205.3 million to between approximately $150.0 million and $155.0 million, and its results of operations from diluted net income per share of $0.15 to a diluted loss per share of between approximately $(0.43)

[53] Id.

and $(0.51). Correspondingly, deferred revenue at December 31, 1999 will increase from $16.8 million to between approximately $66.5 million and $76.5 million. The Company will also reduce its reported revenues for 1998 from $106.4 million to between approximately $95.9 million and $100.9 million.[54]

In May 2001, PricewaterhouseCoopers settled a lawsuit against it by MicroStrategy shareholders for $51 millions. The shareholders had filed suit against PricewaterhouseCoopers for its original certification of those 1999 financials. MicroStrategy's share price hovered at $3.59 as of June 2001.

MicroStrategy's mistakes, in addition to the mistakes of Razorfish on earnings expectations and business inexperience, included the problem with creative accounting. The result of any borderline accounting decision on reporting revenues (and it is arguable that this decision on booking revenues was not even borderline) is a betrayal of trust and the impact in the market is devastating. When in doubt, disclosure is the best long-term policy, but that sense of invincibility and a conscious choice to ignore conventional wisdom because of a new economy that seemed to have no limits resulted in the release of income statements that were deceptive. In addition to the general economic recovery, MicroStrategy faces the uphill battle of restoring its credibility in its financial reports and disclosures.

V. Three Companies, Five Lessons, Old Values

The lessons from a quick glance at three companies that rode the wave of the new economy was old and simple:

1. The basics of business, from cost management to true earnings, will always apply no matter how novel the product;
2. If it sounds too good to be true, it is too good to be true. Companies simply cannot sustain double and triple digits growth over sustained periods of times and often succumb to pressures in financial reporting and income sources in order to achieve those growth rates;
3. Compliance with the rules remains important for long-term market trust. Creative use of accounting rules may provide a temporary reprieve on meeting unrealistic growth goals, but when the eventual disclosure comes, the loss of trust and resulting impact on shareholder value are devastating;
4. The perspective of outsiders, via board participation and audits, remains important in business as a means of checks and balances as well as a reality check for those who believe that talent is mightier than a knowledge of business and experience in it; and
5. History repeats itself.

What happened with these companies and many others is no different from the fall-out of the 1929 market or the deflation of Holland's tulip bonanza and California's gold rush. Exuberance drives an economy of new ideas. Wise choices, measured progress and honesty in potential and performance sustain it. As we live through the adjustment from overly exuberant to honest and rational business, we would be wise to remember that there is nothing new in business operations, reporting and values. While the products may change and the enthusiasm wane, the firms with sustained

[54] *http://www.microstrategy.com*

growth are those that take the routes of sound business practice and historical wisdom and perspective.

CASE 3.17

Nestlé Infant Formula

While the merits and problems of breast-feeding versus using infant formula are debated in the United States and other developed countries, the issue is not so balanced in third world nations. Studies have demonstrated the difficulties and risks of bottle-feeding babies in such places.

First, refrigeration is not generally available, so the formula, once it is mixed or opened (in the case of premixed types), cannot be stored properly. Second, the lack of purified water for mixing with the formula powder results in diarrhea or other diseases in formula-fed infants. Third, inadequate education and income, along with cultural differences, often lead to the dilution of formula and thus greatly reduced nutrition.

Medical studies also suggest that regardless of the mother's nourishment, sanitation, and income level, an infant can be adequately nourished through breast-feeding.

In spite of medical concerns about using their products in these countries, some infant formula manufacturers heavily promoted bottle-feeding.

These promotions, which went largely unchecked through 1970, included billboards, radio jingles, and posters of healthy, happy infants, as well as baby books and formula samples distributed through the health care systems of various countries.

Also, some firms used "milk nurses" as part of their promotions. Dressed in nurse uniforms, "milk nurses" were assigned to maternity wards by their companies and paid commissions to get new mothers to feed their babies formula. Mothers who did so soon discovered that lactation could not be achieved and the commitment to bottle-feeding was irreversible.

In the early 1970s, physicians working in nations where milk nurses were used began vocalizing their concerns. For example, Dr. Derrick Jelliffe, the then-director of the Caribbean Food and Nutrition Institute, had the Protein-Calorie Advisory Group of the United Nations place infant formula promotion methods on its agenda for several of its meetings.

Journalist Mike Muller first brought the issue to public awareness with a series of articles in the *New Internationalist* in the 1970s. He also wrote a pamphlet on the promotion of infant formulas called "The Baby Killer," which was published by a British charity, War on Want. The same pamphlet was published in Switzerland, the headquarters of Nestlé, a major formula maker, under the title "Nestlé Kills Babies." Nestlé sued in 1975, which resulted in extensive media coverage.

In response to the bad publicity, manufacturers of infant formula representing about 75 percent of the market formed the International Council of Infant Food Industries to establish standards for infant formula marketing. The new code banned the milk nurse commissions and required the milk nurses to have identification that would eliminate confusion about their "nurse" status.

The code failed to curb advertising of formulas. In fact, distribution of samples increased. By 1977, groups in the United States began a boycott against formula makers over what Jelliffe called "comerciogenic malnutrition."

One U.S. group, Infant Formula Action Coalition (INFACT), worked with the staff of Senator Edward Kennedy of Massachusetts to have hearings on the issue by the Senate Subcommittee on Health and Human Resources, which Kennedy chaired. The hearings produced evidence that 40 percent of the worldwide market for infant formula, which totaled $1.5 billion at the time, was in third world countries. No regulations resulted, but Congress did tie certain forms of foreign aid to the development by recipient countries of programs to encourage breast-feeding.

Boycotts against Nestlé products began in Switzerland in 1975 and in the United States in 1977. The boycotts and Senator Kennedy's involvement heightened media interest in the issue and led to the World Health Organization (WHO) debating the issue of infant formula marketing in 1979 and agreeing to draft a code to govern it.

After four drafts and two presidential administrations (Carter and Reagan), the 118 member nations of WHO finally voted on a code for infant formula marketing. The United States was the only nation to vote against it; the Reagan administration opposed the code being mandatory. In the end, WHO made the code a recommendation only, but the United States still refused to support it.

The publicity on the vote fueled the boycott of Nestlé, which continued until the formula maker announced it would meet the WHO standards for infant formula marketing. Nestlé created the Nestlé Infant Formula Audit Commission (NIFAC) to demonstrate its commitment to and ensure its implementation of the WHO code.

In 1988, Nestlé introduced a new infant formula, Good Start, through its subsidiary, Carnation. The industry leader, Abbott Laboratories, which held 54 percent of the market with its Similac brand, revealed Carnation's affiliation: "They are Nestlé," said Robert A. Schoellhorn, Abbott's chairman and CEO.[55] Schoellhorn also disclosed that Nestlé was the owner of Beech-Nut Nutrition Corporation, officers of which had been indicted and convicted (later reversed) for selling adulterated apple juice for babies.[56]

Carnation advertised Good Start in magazines and on television. The American Academy of Pediatrics (AAP) objected to this direct advertising, and grocers feared boycotts.

The letters "H.A." came after the name"Good Start," indicating the formula was hypoallergenic. Touted as a medical breakthrough by Carnation, the formula was made from whey and advertised as ideal for babies who were colicky or could not tolerate milk-based formulas.

Within four months of Good Start's introduction in November 1988, the FDA was investigating the formula because of six reported cases of vomiting due to the formula.

[55] *Rick Reiff, "Baby Bottle Battle,"* Forbes, *November 28, 1988, pp. 222–224.*

[56] *For details of the apple juice case, see Case 4.16.*

Carnation then agreed not to label the formula hypoallergenic and to include a warning that milk-allergic babies should be given Good Start only with a doctor's approval and supervision.

In 1990, with its infant formula market share at 2.8 percent, Carnation's president, Timm F. Crull, called on the AAP to "examine all marketing practices that might hinder breast-feeding."[57] Crull specifically cited manufacturers' practices of giving hospitals education and research grants, as well as free bottles, in exchange for having exclusive rights to supply the hospital with formula and to give free samples to mothers. He also called for scrutiny of the practice of paying pediatricians' expenses to attend conferences on infant formulas.

The AAP looked into prohibiting direct marketing of formula to mothers and physicians' accepting cash awards for research from formula manufacturers.

The distribution of samples in third world countries continued during this time. Studies by the United Nations Children's Fund found that a million infants were dying every year because they were not breast-fed adequately. In many cases, the infant starved because the mother used free formula samples and could not buy more, while her own milk dried up. In 1991, the International Association of Infant Food Manufacturers agreed to stop distributing infant formula samples by the end of 1992.

In the United States in 1980, the surgeon general established a goal that the nation's breast-feeding rate be 75 percent by 1990. The rate remains below 60 percent, however, despite overwhelming evidence that breast milk reduces susceptibility to illness, especially ear infections and gastrointestinal illnesses. The AAP took a strong position that infant formula makers should not advertise to the public but, as a result, new entrants into the market (such as Nestlé with its Carnation Good Start) were disadvantaged because long-time formula makers Abbott and Mead Johnson were well-established through physicians. In 1993, Nestlé filed an antitrust suit alleging a conspiracy among AAP, Abbott, and Mead Johnson.

Some 200 U.S. hospitals have voluntarily stopped distributing discharge packs from formula makers to their maternity patients because they felt it "important not to appear to be endorsing any products or acting as commercial agents."[60] A study at Boston City Hospital showed that mothers who receive discharge packs are less likely to continue nursing, if they nurse at all. UNICEF and WHO offer "Baby Friendly" certification to maternity wards that take steps to eliminate discharge packs and formula samples.

Discussion Questions

1. If you had been an executive with Nestlé, would you have changed your marketing approach after the boycotts began?

2. Did Nestlé suffer long-term damage because of its third world marketing techniques?

[57] *Julia F. Siler and D. Woodruff, "The Furor over Formula Is Coming to a Boil,"* Business Week, *April 9, 1990, pp. 52–53.*

3. How could a marketing plan address the concerns of the AAP and WHO?
4. Is anyone in the infant formula companies morally responsible for the deaths of infants described in the United Nations study?
5. Is the moratorium on distributing free formula samples voluntary? Would your company comply?
6. If you were a hospital administrator, what policy would you adopt on discharge packs?
7. Should formula makers advertise directly to the public? What if their ads read, "Remember, breast is best"?

Sources

"Breast Milk for the World's Babies," *The New York Times*, March 12, 1992, p. A18.

Burton, Thomas B., "Methods of Marketing Infant Formula Land Abbott in Hot Water," *The Wall Street Journal*, May 25, 1993, pp. A1, A6.

Freedman, Alix M., "Nestlé's Bid to Crash Baby-Formula Market in the U.S. Stirs a Row," *The Wall Street Journal*, February 6, 1989, pp. A1, A10.

Garland, Susan B., "Are Formula Makers Putting the Squeeze on the States?" *Business Week*, June 18, 1990, p. 31.

Meier, Barry, "Battle over the Market for Baby Formula," *The New York Times*, June 15, 1993, pp. C1, C15.

"Nestlé Unit Sues Baby Formula Firms, Alleging Conspiracy with Pediatricians," *The Wall Street Journal*, June 1, 1993, p. B4.

Post, James E., "Assessing the Nestlé Boycott: Corporate Accountability and Human Rights," *California Management Review* 27, 1985, pp. 113–31.

Star, Marlene G., "Breast Is Best," *Vegetarian Times*, June 1991, pp. 25–26.

"What's in a Name?" *Time*, March 29, 1989, p. 58.

unit 4

Individual Rights and the Business Organization

"Good intentions are not a substitute for good actions."

Marianne Jennings

In this section, the focus moves from how the individual treats the organization to how the organization treats the individual. How much privacy should employees have? What pre-employment tests and screening are appropriate? What obligations does an employer have with respect to the workplace atmosphere? Should employees have job security? The conflicts between employers and their employees' rights take many forms.

4a

Corporate Due Process

Should fairness be a criterion in employer decisions? Must employers provide a forum for employee grievances?

CASE 4.1

Ann Hopkins, Price Waterhouse, and the Partnership

Ann Hopkins was a senior manager in the Price Waterhouse Office of Government Services in Washington, D.C. She started working there in 1977 and by 1982 had been proposed as a candidate for partnership along with eighty-eight other Price Waterhouse employees.

At that time, Price Waterhouse was a nationwide professional accounting partnership. A senior manager became a candidate for partnership when the partners in her office submitted her name for partnership status.

In 1982, Price Waterhouse had 662 partners, 7 of whom were women. Hopkins was responsible for bringing to Price Waterhouse a two-year, $25 million contract with the Department of State.

All of the firm's partners were invited to submit written comments regarding each candidate on either "long" or "short" evaluation forms. Partners chose a form according to their exposure to the candidate. All partners were invited to submit comments, but not every partner did so. Of the thirty-two partners who submitted comments on Hopkins, one stated that "none of the other partnership candidates at Price Waterhouse that year [has] a comparable record in terms of successfully procuring major contracts for the partnership."[1]

After reviewing the comments, the firm's Admissions Committee made recommendations about the partnership candidates to the Price Waterhouse Policy Board. The recommendations consisted of accepting the candidate, denying the promotion,

[1] Price Waterhouse v. Hopkins, *490 U.S. 228 (1989).*

or putting the application on hold. The Policy Board then decided whether to submit the candidate to a vote, reject the candidate, or hold the candidacy.

There were no limits on the number of persons to whom partnership could be awarded and no guidelines for evaluating positive and negative comments about candidates.

Of the eighty-eight candidates for partnership in 1982, Hopkins was the only woman. Thirteen of the thirty-two partners who submitted comments on Hopkins supported her; three recommended putting her "on hold"; eight said they did not have enough information; and eight recommended denial.

The partners in Hopkins' office praised her character as well as her accomplishments, describing her in their joint statement as "an outstanding professional" who had a "deft touch," a "strong character, independence and integrity." Clients appear to have agreed with these assessments. One official from the State Department described her as "extremely competent, intelligent," "strong and forthright, very productive, energetic and creative." Another high-ranking official praised Hopkins' decisiveness, broadmindedness, and "intellectual clarity"; she was, in his words, "a stimulating conversationalist."[2] Hopkins "had no difficulty dealing with clients and her clients appear to have been very pleased with her work."[3] She "was generally viewed as a highly competent project leader who worked long hours, pushed vigorously to meet deadlines and demanded much from the multidisciplinary staffs with which she worked."[4]

On too many occasions, however, Hopkins' aggressiveness apparently spilled over into abrasiveness. Staff members seem to have borne the brunt of Hopkins' brusqueness. Long before her bid for partnership, partners evaluating her work had counseled her to improve her relations with staff members. Although later evaluations indicate an improvement, Hopkins' perceived shortcomings in this important area eventually doomed her bid for partnership. Virtually all of the partners' negative remarks about Hopkins—even those of partners who supported her—concerned her "interpersonal skills." Both "[s]upporters and opponents of her candidacy indicated that she was sometimes overly aggressive, unduly harsh, difficult to work with and impatient with staff."[5]

Clear signs indicated, though, that some of the partners reacted negatively to Hopkins' personality because she was a woman. One partner described her as "macho," while another suggested that she "overcompensated for being a woman"; a third advised her to take "a course at charm school."[6] Several partners criticized her use of profanity. In response, one partner suggested that those partners objected to her swearing only "because it[']s a lady using foul language."[7] Another supporter explained that Hopkins "ha[d] matured from a tough-talking somewhat masculine hardnosed manager to an authoritative, formidable, but much more appealing lady partner candidate."[8] In order for Hopkins to improve her chances for partnership,

[2] Price Waterhouse v. Hopkins, *490 U.S. 228 (1989), at 234.*

[3] Id.

[4] Id.

[5] Price Waterhouse v. Hopkins, *490 U.S. 228 (1989), at 235.*

[6] Id.

[7] Id.

[8] Id.

Thomas Beyer, a partner, suggested that she "walk more femininely, talk more femininely, dress more femininely, wear make-up, have her hair styled, and wear jewelry."[9]

Dr. Susan Fiske, a social psychologist and associate professor of psychology at Carnegie-Mellon University, reviewed the Price Waterhouse selection process and concluded that it was likely influenced by sex stereotyping. Dr. Fiske indicated that some of the partners' comments were gender-biased, while others that were gender-neutral were intensely critical and made by partners who barely knew Hopkins. Dr. Fiske concluded that the subjectivity of the evaluations and their sharply critical nature were probably the result of sex-stereotyping.[10]

Of the eighty-eight candidates, forty-seven were admitted to partnership, twenty-one were rejected, and Hopkins and nineteen others were put on hold for the following year. Later, two partners withdrew their support for Hopkins, and she was informed that she would not be reconsidered the following year. Hopkins then resigned.[11]

Ms. Hopkins, who litigated the Price Waterhouse denial of her partnership as a violation of Title VII of the Civil Rights Act of 1964 (which prohibits discrimination in employment practices), has stated she filed the suit to find out why Price Waterhouse made "such a bad business decision."[12] She did not learn of the partners' comments until discovery during the case. The Supreme Court found for Ms. Hopkins. In 1990, on remand, Ms. Hopkins was awarded her partnership[13] and $350,000 in damages.

Today at Price Waterhouse offices in Washington, D.C., 44 percent of the professional staff are women and 22 percent are minorities.[14] In accounting firms generally, the number of female principals has grown from 1 percent in 1983 to 18 percent today. Ms. Hopkins became a partner at Price Waterhouse following her U.S. Supreme Court victory.

Discussion Questions

1. What ethical problems do you see with the Price Waterhouse partnership evaluation system?
2. Suppose that you were a partner and a member of either the Admissions Committee or the Policy Board. What objections, if any, would you have made to any of the comments by the partners? What would have made it difficult for you to object? How might your being a female partner in that position have made objection more difficult?

[9] Id.

[10] *Cynthia Cohen, "Perils of Partnership Reviews: Lessons from Price Waterhouse v. Hopkins,"* Labor Law Journal, *October 1991, pp. 677–682.*

[11] Price Waterhouse v. Hopkins, *490 U.S. 228, at 233.*

[12] *Interview with Ann Hopkins, June 18, 1993.*

[13] *Technically, Ms. Hopkins was made a principal, a title reserved for those reaching partner status who do not hold CPA licenses. Ms. Hopkins has a master's degree in mathematics.*

[14] *"More Women Become Partners in Accounting,"* The Wall Street Journal, *August 10, 1993, p. B1.*

3. In what ways, if any, do you find the subjectivity of the evaluation troublesome? What aspects of the evaluation would you change?

4. To what extent did the partners' comments reflect mixed motives (i.e., to what extent did their points express legal factors while others expressed illegal ones)?

5. Ms. Hopkins listed three factors to help companies avoid what happened to her: (a) clear direction from the top of the enterprise, (b) diversity in management, and (c) specificity in evaluation criteria. Give examples of how a company could implement these factors.

4b

Employee Screening

What can an employer do to check an employee's background, personality, and potential? How do we know such tests are accurate? Could they destroy opportunities?

CASE 4.2

Handwriting Analysis and Employment

Thomas Interior Systems, Inc., employs analysts to examine candidates' handwriting. President Thomas Klobucher says, "At first I thought [handwriting analysis] was hocus-pocus. But I've learned to depend on it."[15] "It has been said handwriting is civilization's casual encephalogram."[16] Following the surfacing of anthrax-laced letters at government and media offices in late 2001, the FBI released its profile of the person who addressed the envelope. One portion of the analysis indicated that the person who addressed the envelopes with the anthrax was not a native English speaker. The conclusion was drawn from the carefully executed, crude printing with block-style letters.

Though much more prevalent in Europe and Israel, graphology is used in two to three thousand U.S. organizations. Companies that have used graphology in personnel selection include Ford, General Electric, Mutual of Omaha, H&R Block, Firestone, USX Corp., and Northwest Mutual Life Insurance Company. In 1980, the Library of Congress changed the classification of graphology from "occult" to "psychology" under the Dewey Decimal System.[17]

Views on the accuracy of handwriting analysis vary. Psychologist John Jones says, "No body of research shows that handwriting consistently predicts job behavior."[18] James Crumbaugh, a retired clinical psychologist, notes that although traditional personality tests, such as the inkblot test, are hard to validate, their use continues.

[15] *Michael J. McCarthy, "Handwriting Analysis as Personnel Tool,"* The Wall Street Journal, *August 25, 1988, p. 19.*

[16] *David L. Kurtz, et al., "CEOs: A Handwriting Analysis,"* Business Horizons, *January/February 1989, pp. 41–43.*

[17] *William Kennen, Jr., "Handwriting Analysis—What Can It Tell You?"* Sales and Marketing Management, *April 1990, pp. 44–47.*

[18] *Kurtz, "CEOs: A Handwriting Analysis," pp. 41–43.*

Handwriting analysis is growing in popularity as a means of screening potential employees. A Honeywell manager explains, "I'm looking for any means that I think is credible to avoid a hiring mistake."[19]

The same manager adds, "I don't know if [prospective employees are] mass murderers or not; I simply learn if they'll operate well as sales representatives."[20]

Among other handwriting factors, a graphologist will analyze

> [t]he height of the signature. Those people with signatures above 1/4" in height, particularly when placed on the far right, are enterprising and motivated by prestige. They are good salespeople. Those with small signatures (less than 1/8" in height) are objective, cool, good listeners and negotiators. Those with medium signatures are team players. The dots on "i's", the bars on "t's", loops and hooks are all linked by graphologists to various personality traits. The absence of "i" dots, for example, can be indications of wandering attention and disregard for detail. Variances in pen pressure can demonstrate those same personality traits. A light pen pressure means the person is not aggressive. Rounded letters and variations in letter forms suggest listener more than persuader. Inconsistent legibility is linked with a lack of patience.[21]

Graphologists charge between $150 and $500 for an analysis. Traditional areas of examination, apart from handwriting size, include slant, regularity, margins, pressure, lines, connection between letters, and word and line spacing.[22]

Problems have accompanied the use of handwriting samples. One applicant for a truck driving position had his wife write his sample. Some applicants change their handwriting when providing a sample for analysis, and experts have raised the issue of discrimination in the use of graphology. A test by *The Wall Street Journal* in which the same writing sample was submitted to three graphology firms yielded often conflicting results among the firms. Richard Klimoski, professor of psychology at Ohio State University, says, "The better the studies [of handwriting analysis] have been, the less support they offer to proponents. My reading of the evidence is that there is nothing there that's worth your time and money."[23]

Discussion Questions

1. What concerns would you have about the relevancy of handwriting analysis?

2. Would you impose handwriting analysis as a requirement for employment?

3. Are you comfortable with the accuracy of handwriting analysis?

4. One employer states that graphology has revealed so much to him that he feels as if such analysis constitutes an invasion of privacy. How might this employer

[19] *Kurtz, "CEOs: A Handwriting Analysis," pp. 41–43.*

[20] *McCarthy, "Handwriting Analysis as Personnel Tool," p. 19.*

[21] *Guy Webster, "Job Applicants' Fate Written in the Script,"* Arizona Republic, *September 1, 1991, p. F2.*

[22] *Kathryn K. Sackheim,* Handwriting Analysis and the Employee Selection Process, *Westport, CT: Quorum Books, 1990.*

[23] *Webster, "Job Applicants' Fate Written in the Script," p. F2.*

balance his concerns regarding this "invasion" with his concerns regarding the accuracy of graphology?

5. If handwriting analysis produced disparate statistics in terms of male/female hires, would you still continue to use it?

6. An employer that had conducted a national search for a key executive had Phoenix graphologist Mark Hopper perform handwriting analysis on the top candidate. Mr. Hopper's analysis confirmed what the company's top officers believed about the candidate based on their interviews: bright, talented, and motivated. However, Hopper also cautioned that there was a high risk of substance abuse in the candidate. The company raised the issue with the candidate and he confessed to being a recovering alcoholic. He was hired but the bar in the executive suite was removed. What issues do you see in this use of handwriting analysis?[24]

CASE 4.3

Health and Genetic Screening

During the past decade, biologists have made significant strides in the field of genetics. Media attention has focused on gene splicing, the creation of new forms of life, and the increase in the quality, size, and disease resistance of agricultural products.

However, this new technology is also enabling biologists to delve into complex genetic information. DNA tests provide full physical and mental profiles of human beings. Apart from the issues that such testing will present for parents-to-be, complexities could develop in the workplace as well.

The Office of Technology Assessment of the House Committee on Science and Technology surveyed the five hundred largest U.S. industrial companies, fifty private utilities, and eleven unions and found that seventeen had used genetic testing to screen employees for the sickle-cell trait or enzyme deficiencies.

Genetic screening also could reveal an individual's tolerance for or susceptibility to chemicals used in the workplace. With health insurance costs increasing exponentially, employers are trying to improve employee health with routine medical screening, the creation of smoke-free environments, and drug testing. Genetic profile tests could be used to hire only those individuals who meet certain minimum health requirements and are thus likely to keep health insurance costs down.

Insurers have used AIDS screening as a prerequisite for medical insurance coverage; similarly, genetic tests could predict susceptibility to heart disease and cancer. Genetic tests allow insurers to screen applicants and either deny coverage or create higher-risk pools for those in high risk groups.

Scientist Robert Weinberg has stated:

> A belief that each of us is ultimately responsible for our own behavior has woven our social fabric. Yet in the coming years, we will hear more and more from those who

[24] *Ken Western, "Firms Turning to Graphology in Screening,"* Arizona Republic, *December 8, 1996, pp. D1, D4.*

write off bad behavior to the inexorable forces of biology and who embrace a new astrology in which alleles rather than stars determine individuals' lives. It is hard to imagine how far this growing abdication of responsibility will carry us.

> As a biologist, I find this prospect a bitter pill. The biological revolution of the past decades has proven extraordinarily exciting and endlessly fascinating, and it will, without doubt, spawn enormous benefit. But as with most new technologies, we will pay a price unless we anticipate the human genome project's dark side. We need to craft an ethic that cherishes our human ability to transcend biology, that enshrines our spontaneity, unpredictability, and individual uniqueness. At the moment, I find myself and those around me ill equipped to respond to the challenge.[25]

Starting in 1972, DuPont screened its black employees for sickle-cell anemia, which affects one in every four hundred to six hundred black Americans. Requested by the Black DuPont Employees Association to perform the genetic screening, DuPont administered the voluntary test not to deny jobs, but to offer employees relocation to chemical-free areas where the disease would not be triggered.

Critics of DuPont said the testing allowed the company to transfer workers rather than clean up its work environment. DuPont's medical director responded,

> This is a very naive view. No one can operate at zero emissions, exposures—zero anything. There has to be an agreed-upon practical, safe limit. But there are some employees who are more susceptible to certain diseases than others. It's only common sense to offer them the opportunity to relocate.[26]

In the 1960s, certain workers at an Israeli dynamite factory became ill with acute hemolytic anemia, which causes the walls of the red blood cells to dissolve, thus decreasing the cells' ability to circulate oxygen throughout the body. The workers were transferred to other parts of the plant, but genetic screening revealed that all of them had a G-6-PD deficiency, which causes hemolytic anemia upon exposure to chemicals. The information allowed the factory to place workers properly and led it to reduce chemical levels in the plant.[27]

Discussion Questions

1. What impact does genetic screening have on an employee's privacy?
2. In what ways should employers regard genetic screening as necessary?
3. Is DuPont's sickle-cell anemia screening program justifiable? Explain.
4. Discuss how genetic screening might lead to discrimination.
5. Will genetic screening help employers increase safety in the workplace?
6. What impact might the Americans with Disabilities Act have on genetic screening?

[25] *Robert Weinberg, "Genetic Screening,"* Technology Review, *April 1991, p. 51.*

[26] *William P. Patterson, "Genetic Screening,"* Industry Week, *June 1, 1987, p. 48.*

[27] *Thomas H. Murray, "Genetic Testing at Work: How Should It Be Used?"* Personnel Administrator, *September 1985, pp. 90–92.*

4C

Employee Privacy

Does a line separate my private life from my employment? How much can I be watched at work? Are mandatory drug tests a violation of my privacy or necessary for safety in my field?

CASE 4.4

Employee and Technology Privacy: Is the Boss Spying?

Technology has permitted employees to work more quickly, efficiently, and even from home as telecommuting has become an option for many companies and their employees. The interesting dichotomy is that while technology makes employees' work much easier, it also provides tracking for employers of virtually everything employees do while at work. One company posted this motto, "In God we trust. All others we monitor." Following are the various forms of technology and their use in the workplace. In each of these forms of technology there are issues of employees' privacy and rights as well as employers' rights with regard to business property and employees' use of time.

Surveillance by Employers

Internal theft, liability for harm to customers, the need to ensure good driving records, and customer service are a few of the reasons businesses give for keeping a secret eye on employees.[28] From the well-known secret shoppers of the retail industry to phone company monitoring of operator performance, employers gather data on employee performance and wrongdoing.

Safeway Stores, Inc., a large multistore grocery chain, has dashboard computers in its 782 delivery trucks. The computers monitor speed, oil pressure, engine RPMs and idling, and the length of stops. Safeway touts the program for its efficacy with regard to driver safety and truck maintenance.

[28] *Christina E. Garza, "The Touchy Ethics of Corporate Anthropology,"* Business Week, *September 30, 1991, p. 78.*

In other businesses, high-tech developments enable employers to eavesdrop on employees' telephone and office conversations, while small cameras monitor employee work habits and behavior through pinholes in office walls.[29]

The electronic surveillance of phone conversations has increased as employers seek to monitor productivity, accuracy, and courtesy. Such monitoring is permissible if the monitored party (the employee) consents. Legislation proposed at the state level would require employers to sound a beeping tone when monitoring begins to alert the employee under observation. But an AT&T official notes that employers need the ability to monitor without notice: "Factory supervisors don't blow whistles to warn assembly-line workers they're coming."[30]

In contrast, Barbara Otto, the director of *9 to 5*, a national association of working women, maintains that monitoring affects personal calls: "Employers start catching non-work-related information. They discover that employees are spending weekends with a person of the same sex or talking about forming a union."[31]

The American Civil Liberties Union objects to monitoring because of the current lack of required notice and also because employees lack access to the information employers gather about them via electronic means.

The Internet at Work and Employee Privacy

How employees use their computers and online access at work is a subject of much study as well as surveillance by employers. Vault.com conducted a survey of workers and asked how they use the Internet at work for nonwork-related activity and found the following:[32]

News reading	72%
Travel arrangements	45%
Shopping	40%
Job searching	37%
Special interests (hobbies)	37%
Stock-checking	34%
Planning social events	28%
Instant messaging	26%
Music downloads	13%
Games	11%
Chatting	9%
Pornography	4%

Employers have software that enables them to see which Web sites employees have visited, when they visited, and how long they stayed there. Many employers have been issuing reports that indicate which employees are spending large amounts of time "surfing the net." One employer warned an employee about too much online shopping during working hours and then blocked the sites so that the employee could not access them.

[29] *Jeffrey Rothfeder, et al., "Is Your Boss Spying on You?"* Business Week, *January 15, 1990, pp. 74–75.*

[30] *Richard Lacayo, "Nowhere to Hide,"* Time, *November 11, 1991, p. 34.*

[31] Id., *p. 39.*

[32] *Alan Cohen, "Worker Watchers,"* Fortune, *Summer 2001 (special issue* Fortune/CNET Technology Review*), p. 70.*

While employees are concerned about privacy, employers are concerned about productivity and the fact that downloading music, for example, can result in the employer's network jamming. Also, employers are concerned that the types of sites being visited, such as pornographic sites, may result in liability for the employer for an atmosphere of harassment.[33]

The same Vault.com survey found that 90 percent of all employees surf the net during work hours for things unrelated to their jobs and 37 percent have used their computers at work to access the Internet to look for another job. About 13 percent say that they spend two or more hours per working day surfing the net for things unrelated to their jobs. Ten percent say that they receive 21 or more e-mails that are personal per day at work. However, 53 percent say that they limit their nonwork Internet access to 30 minutes per working day.[34]

There are also companies that will police employee use for employers. Websense, Inc. serves this function for 12,000 companies, including 239 of the Fortune 500. The cost is approximately $15 per employee per year.

E-Mail and Employee Privacy

Other issues of employee privacy center around electronic mail systems. Electronic mail (e-mail) systems enable employees to communicate and interact by typing messages on their personal computers. E-mail is often described as a cross between a telephone conversation and a memo. The result is a means of communication, more casual than a memo, that allows users to relax and say more. On the other hand, unlike a telephone conversation, e-mail produces a written record of often casual conversations.

Employers have access to employee files and e-mail messages; moreover, employers can retain backup files of such messages even when users have deleted them. Courts have ruled that e-mail messages belong not to the employee but to the employer and are discoverable in litigation, whereupon they must be turned over to the opposing party. In one case an e-mail message from a corporate president to an employee's manager, deleted from the president's and manager's files but saved on the company's hard drive, read, "I don't care what it takes. Fire the _____ bitch." After the message was produced during discovery in the employee's suit, the result was an immediate $250,000 settlement.[35]

In addition to the litigation issues of e-mail, there are the employee usage issues. Employees often use company e-mail systems for sending along jokes, lists, and even electronic forms of chain letters and messages. Not only are these e-mails discoverable, employers can be held liable for their content in terms of defamation and sexual harassment if the messages serve to create an atmosphere of harassment for employees. For example, Michelle Murphy, a former customer-service representative at The Principal Financial Group, was fired after she used company e-mail to send jokes such as "A Few Good Reasons Cookie Dough is Better Than Men" and "Top 10 Reasons Why Trick-or-Treating Is Better Than Sex." Principal Financial's employee handbook included the following:

[33] *Ann Carrns, "Those Bawdy E-Mails Were Good for a Laugh—Until the Axe Fell,"* The Wall Street Journal, *February 4, 2000, pp. A1, A8.*

[34] *Cohen, "Worker Watchers," p. 70.*

[35] *Richard Behar, "Who's Reading Your E-Mail?"* Fortune, *February 3, 1997, pp. 57–70.*

> The corporation's electronic mail system is business property and is to be used for business purposes. The corporation reserves the right to monitor all electronic messages.[36]

Murphy has appealed her termination, but the court again made it clear that the e-mail system belongs to the employer and can be used as the employer directs and employees can be subject to disciplinary action for violation of the employer's policies on e-mail usage. Employers are also liable for content in e-mails that amounts to sexual harassment.[37]

Michael Smyth, a manager for Pillsbury in Pennsylvania, sent an e-mail to his supervisor complaining about company executives and threatening to "kill the back-stabbing bastards."[38] Shortly after, he was fired. He sued for wrongful discharge. Again, however, the employer would have the right to terminate for the use of foul language in the e-mail along with the management issues created by such conduct and words.

E-Mail, Privacy, Technology, and Purging

Employers and employees are now keenly aware that the "Delete" button on an e-mail system does not delete messages completely.[39] The messages could be backed up in the employer's system and there is the possibility of key-stroking technology that can be used to reconstruct messages that employees drafted but never sent.

In response to employees' concerns about their e-mail being monitored as well as concerns of businesses regarding espionage via e-mail and the types of uses of e-mails by employees, several companies have been working to develop technology that can eliminate e-mail messages. SafeMessage has unveiled a new software product that can make e-mail messages self-destruct in as little as ten seconds. Once e-mail is sent, the sender, using the SafeMessage program, can set a time frame after the message is opened for it to self-destruct, thereby removing it from the hard drive forever. It has been referred to as a shredder for computers.[40]

There is a troublesome aspect to this technology for law enforcement because messages could be sent without a trace. Also, law enforcement officials rely on e-mail to reconstruct crimes. These types of programs eliminate the back-up as well as any copies of the messages that might be floating about because e-mail messages are forwarded so easily.

In addition to the "shredding technique," the market for privacy programs for e-mail messages has grown substantially, thanks in large part to the e-mail messages of Bill Gates and other Microsoft officers used extensively in the government's antitrust case against Microsoft.[41]

Observing that an e-mail message "is about as secure as a postcard," many companies have developed software to help companies with the lack of privacy. E-mail messages generally make about twelve stops as they journey from the sender to the

[36] *Mark P. Couch, "E-Mail Can Return to Haunt Employers, Workers,"* Mesa Tribune, *February 2, 1997, pp. E1, E5; David C. Jacobson, et al., "Peril of the E-Mail Trail,"* National Law Journal, *January 16, 1995, pp. C1, C22.*

[37] *Lisa Guernsey, "You've Got Inappropriate Mail,"* The New York Times, *April 5, 2000, pp. C1, C10.*

[38] *Brenda Sandburg, "Web Postings Not Libel,"* National Law Journal, *March 12, 2001, pp. B1, B4.*

[39] *Michael J. McCarthy, "You Assumed 'Erase' Wiped Out that Rant Against the Boss? Nope,"* The Wall Street Journal, *March 7, 2000, pp. A1, A16.*

[40] *Jeffrey Beard, "E-Mail that Evaporates,"* National Law Journal, *July 17, 2000, p. B11.*

[41] *Steve Lohr, "Antitrust Case Is Highlighting Role of E-Mail,"* The New York Times, *November 2, 1998, pp. C1, C4.*

recipient. One of those stops is the company server, which makes a back-up copy of the message that remains on the server for anywhere from one to three years at most companies. The data from servers has been subject to discovery by the courts when e-mail messages could prove relevant in a court case.[42]

Tumbleweed Communications, Inc. offers software that handles privacy with encryption devices. Recipients are notified that there is a message for them on the company server, which they can only obtain with access codes. The encrypted document can also be placed on a Web site to which only the recipient has access.

Hush Mail is another company with a program that is so secure that even Hush employees cannot read e-mail when it is protected by the HushMail program.

These companies had a boost in business when there was a 2000 scandal regarding the ability of the White House to archive messages. The White House revealed that it failed to turn over e-mails requested as part of the investigation into fund-raising during the 1996 election because of "a software glitch." The glitch was revealed when a contractor for Northrup Grumman who was working at the White House revealed in a civil suit that she had been threatened if she revealed the e-mails or the problem with the server. The glitch resulted in 100,000 e-mails generated by 500 computer users never being turned over to the special counsel pursuant to a federal grand jury subpoena. The employee and others from Northrup claimed that they were threatened with "jail" if they spoke about the problem to their employer or spouses.

The problem was referred to as Project X and all the e-mails not turned over were labeled as "Classified." Sheryl Hall, chief of White House Computer Operations has said that at least 4,000 of the e-mails were related to Monica Lewinsky, the White House intern who became the center of a presidential scandal.[43]

Based on past White House experience, President George W. Bush sent an e-mail to 42 of his friends on January 17, 2001, just three days before his inauguration with the following:

> My lawyers tell me that all correspondence by e-mail is subject to open record requests. Since I do not want my private conversations looked at by those out to embarrass, the only course of action is not to correspond in cyberspace. This saddens me. I have enjoyed conversing with each of you.[44]

In response to the Microsoft case and White House e-mail issues, a company called Disappearing, Inc. is working to develop an encryption system that would enable senders to control whether their e-mail can be forwarded and another encryption system that would enable senders to set a date when their mail would not longer be readable.[45]

More e-mail control is also now available on the new Microsoft software. There is the now-available recall feature, available on Microsoft's Outlook 2002. Access code re-

[42] *Bob Tedeschi, "E-Commerce Report: Wary of Hackers and the Courts, E-Mail Users are Turning to Services that Keep Their Messages Secure,"* The New York Times, *January 31, 2000, p. C11.*

[43] *Joe Matthews, "Burton Seeks Special Counsel in E-Mail Probe,"* The Wall Street Journal, *March 28, 2000, p. A6.*

[44] *Richard L. Berke, "The Last (E-Mail) Goodbye, From 'gwb' to His 42 Buddies,"* The New York Times, *March 17, 2001, pp. A1, A8.*

[45] *Amy Harmon, "E-Mail is Treacherous. So Why Do We Keep Trusting It?"* The New York Times, *March 26, 2000, p. WK3; see also Jerry Seper, "Northrop Officials: White House Hid Subpoenaed E-Mail,"* Washington Times, *March 13–19, 2000 (weekly edition), p. 22.*

quirements are also taking hold. With this type of e-mail system, the sender can encode e-mails and anyone who wants to read the message must have a password. There are also systems that delete e-mail messages after 24 hours.[46]

Visit the following Web sites for companies offering this technology:

http://www.authentica.com
http://www.disappearinginc.com

For more information on e-mail security, visit

http://anon.efga.org/Remailers

For information on an e-mail encryption software, visit

http://www.Ziplip.com

E-Mail and Theft

Yet another problem with e-mail comes from unauthorized access by hackers. Employees should exercise caution about the type of information sent via e-mail because hackers use information for corporate espionage, insider trading, and even just mischief. For a 1997 article in *Fortune*, and with the company's permission, hackers hired by the magazine were able to access the company's system within a 16-hour period. With access, the hackers obtained a $5,000 bonus authorization from the CEO for an employee. Their access allowed them to read, modify, and destroy files or plant a destructive virus.[47]

Voice Mail and Privacy

Voice mail or telephone messaging is a technological convenience used by nearly 100 percent of all companies with five or more employees. In many situations, such companies do business and enter into contracts using only voice mail. However, voice mail carries with it the same privacy issues as e-mail. Employers can review the voice mail of employees and the messages and their content is discoverable in litigation.

Fax

Faxed documents reduce mailing costs and facilitate rapid negotiations and deal refinements. However, fax technology can also facilitate dishonesty. It would be difficult, for example, to determine the lack of authenticity of a signature transferred from another document to a fax. Facsimile machine technology has not evolved to the point where we can tell whether a fax has been sent, received, or sent or received in its entirety. Finally, centrally located fax machines present privacy problems as faxed materials are pulled off the machines by others and then delivered to the intended recipient.

Discussion Questions

1. Do you think employees should be able to use the Internet for personal items while they are at work?

[46] *Jon Swartz, "Software Can Make E-Mail Disappear Without a Trace,"* USA Today, *September 20, 2000, p. 1B.*

[47] *Behar, "Who's Reading Your E-Mail?" pp. 57–70.*

2. Does it perhaps save time and money to allow employees to do errands via the Internet instead of taking longer lunches and breaks?
3. Is it a breach of privacy for employers to monitor employee use?
4. Is corporate spying necessary?
5. How does secret or electronic monitoring differ from a manager's decision to, without notice, walk around an office to observe behavior and work?
6. Does privacy protection apply in the case of law enforcement? What about warrants for e-mails?
7. To what extent does an employee have a right to privacy in the workplace?
8. How would disclosure of monitoring activities lessen their invasion of employee privacy?
9. How does electronic surveillance differ from going through an employee's desk?
10. How would the nature of a given business affect your decision regarding surveillance?
11. What ethical standards should businesses adopt with respect to e-mail, voice mail, and fax technology?
12. What procedures might eliminate some of the ethical dilemmas noted here?
13. Should employers disclose to potential and current employees their ability to access e-mail and voice mail?
14. Is it fair that all e-mails and voice mail generated in the workplace belong to the employer? Why or why not?
15. What policies would you adopt with regard to subject matter in your employees' voice and e-mail?
16. How do voice mail and e-mail provide opportunities for dishonesty in contracts? How might companies guarantee the authenticity of messages that utilize these devices?

CASE 4.5

The Athlete Role Model

On August 20, 1996, the North Texas Toyota Dealers Association filed suit against Michael Irvin, the Dallas Cowboys player who entered a no contest plea to charges of cocaine possession earlier in the month. The Toyota dealers' suit alleges Mr. Irvin represented himself as a moral person when he signed an endorsement contract with the Association and that, with the drug plea, he can no longer be used as a spokesperson. The suit also asks for the return of the Toyota Land Cruiser (valued at $50,000) that Mr. Irvin was given as part of the endorsement contract.[48]

[48] *Randall Lane, "Nice Guys Finish First,"* Forbes, *December 16, 1996, pp. 236–242.*

Mr. Irvin returned the car voluntarily and has received a sentence of four years, deferred adjudication, a fine of $10,000, and 800 hours of community service. He was also suspended by the NFL for the first five games of the 1996–1997 season for his involvement with drugs.[49]

The lawsuit also asks for the costs of the aborted campaign and $1.2 million in lost sales. The total damages requested are $1.4 million.[50]

Discussion Question

1. Do you think Mr. Irvin breached his endorsement contract?
2. Is morality a condition for being a spokesperson?
3. Is it implied in the contract?
4. Is illegal conduct a grounds for termination of an endorsement contract?

CASE 4.6
Drug Testing of Employees

John Lawn, the former director of the Drug Enforcement Administration (DEA), supported mandatory drug testing, calling it "critical [i]n those occupations where either the public trust or public safety is involved."[51] He listed doctors, lawyers, airline pilots, truck drivers, and teachers as examples and urged the professions to develop their own rules and regulations for drug testing.

The percentage of employers who test employees for drugs increased from 22 percent in 1987 to 67 percent in 2001. However, some employees have questioned the accuracy of the tests and have filed suit challenging the tests and their resulting termination. And some employers note that employees can tamper with the test results.

Because of the accusations and confusion, the Department of Health and Human Services is expected to issue its employee drug-testing guidelines by the end of the year. The guidelines will dictate certain types of jobs for which employees must always be tested (pilots, conductors) and also provide procedures for conducting the tests that will then become prima facie evidence of accuracy of the test results.[52]

The federal government has Supreme Court approval for 113 drug testing programs, but state law regulates private employers in the administration of their tests. Some states limit testing to safety-sensitive jobs; other states require probable cause as a prerequisite for testing employees. Courts continue to address issues of employer need and employee privacy, along with questions involving drug test reliability.

[49] *Christine Biederman, "Irvin Given Probation in Plea Deal,"* The New York Times, *July 18, 1996, p. B7.*

[50] *"Irvin Sued by Car Dealers He Endorsed,"* The New York Times, *August 21, 1996, p. B12.*

[51] *David Hess, "Drug Tests Urged in Jobs Dealing with Public Trust,"* Arizona Republic, *August 19, 1986, p. A1.*

[52] *Stephanie Armour, "Accused Workers Challenge Drug-Test Results in Court,"* USA Today, *July 16, 2001, p. 1B.*

A Seattle equipment company worker complains: "I am so tired of hearing that I have a right to privacy. What about our right to safety?"[53]

J. F. Spencer, a production manager for Pennwalt Pharmaceutical of Rochester, New York, expresses his feelings as follows:

> People at work who are illegally using drugs are infringing on the rights of law-abiding individuals. It is an invasion of privacy, but until someone comes up with a better way to keep people on drugs out of high-risk jobs, I will put up with it.[54]

But a Boston executive maintains, "Individual rights are too precious to be compromised by this route. Other ways must be found to combat drug problems in the workplace."[55] New Jersey Superior Court Judge Donald A. Smith, Jr., wrote in a decision striking down the discharge of an employee who tested positive for marijuana and Valium, "Whether it be a private or public employer, a free-for-all approach to drug testing cannot be tolerated."[56]

Kim Haggart, a quality-assurance manager at Dragon Valves, Inc., adopts the following position: "If the job is high-risk or safety-sensitive, testing should be required because impairment can affect the health and safety of others."[57]

Discussion Questions

1. What steps do you think an employer should take to ensure the validity of the drug tests?
2. Is there a difference between drug tests for new employees and using company-wide ongoing drug testing?
3. Is ongoing drug testing necessary?
4. You are the manager of a pizzeria that operates solely as a pizza delivery business. As you contemplate drug testing for your drivers, consider the following questions.
    a. What safety issues are involved with your drivers?
    b. Will your testing be random or scheduled? Explain your choice.
    c. Will you test all employees or just your drivers? Explain.
    d. Will you test employees who are in an accident? Why? Why not?
    e. Why do you think you should—or should not—test your employees?
    f. Will you test only suspicious drivers?
    g. What penalties will you impose on employees who test positive?
    h. What opportunities for rehabilitation will you offer for employees who test positive?
    i. How will you ensure the accuracy of the tests?
    j. Will you inform drivers of your testing policy before hiring them? Why? Why not?

53 *"Test Workers for Drugs?"* Industry Week, *December 14, 1987, p. 17.*

54 Id.

55 Id.

56 *Wayne A. Green, "Drug Testing Becomes Corporate Mine Field,"* The Wall Street Journal, *November 21, 1989, p. B1.*

57 *"Test Workers for Drugs?" p. 18.*

4d

Sexual Harassment

Sexual harassment became the topic of the 1990s when the 1991 Senate confirmation hearings of Supreme Court Justice Clarence Thomas captured the nation's attention. While the Anita Hill accusations against Justice Thomas brought the issue to the forefront, the 1998 allegations by Paula Jones and Kathleen Willey against President Clinton caused a re-examination of what constitutes sexual harassment. Employers are responsible for eliminating not just the *quid pro quo* forms of sexual harassment but also controlling the atmosphere of their places of employment. Jokes, pictures, comments, and attitudes are all issues of sexual harassment in the workplace.

CASE 4.7

Seinfeld in the Workplace

Jerold J. Mackenzie was hired by Miller Brewing Company in 1974 as an area manager of Miller distributors with a salary grade level of 7. In 1982 he had progressed to grade level 14, and he attained the position of Sales Services and Development Manager reporting to Robert L. Smith in 1987. In late 1987 Miller undertook a corporate reorganization, which led to a transfer of many of Mackenzie's responsibilities.[58]

Concerned, Mackenzie asked Smith whether the reorganization affected his grade level. Smith responded that it did not. In 1989 Miller reevaluated the grade levels of 716 positions, including Mackenzie's. As a result, Mackenzie's position was downgraded to grade level 13. The reevaluation, however, was prospective and applied to the position, not the employee. Therefore, Mackenzie was grandfathered as a grade level 14, even though his position was a grade level 13. That same year, Mackenzie's secretary, Linda Braun, made a sexual harassment complaint against him. She made another sexual harassment complaint against him in 1990.

In August of 1992 Miller sent a memo to employees whose positions had been downgraded but who had been grandfathered to their current grade level informing them that they would be downgraded to their position grade level. Therefore, as of January 1, 1993, Mackenzie would be at grade level 13. He would receive the same

[58] *James L. Graff and Andrea Sachs, "It Was a Joke!"* Time, *July 28, 1997, p. 62.*

salary and benefits of a grade level 14, but he would not be entitled to any future grants of stock options.

On March 23, 1993, Patricia Best, a Miller distributor services manager who had previously reported to Mackenzie, told her supervisor, Dave Goulet, that Mackenzie had told her about a sexually suggestive episode of the "Seinfeld" television show, which made her uncomfortable. The *Seinfeld* episode is one in which Jerry forgets the first name of a woman he is dating but does recall that her name rhymes with a part of the female anatomy (Dolores was the woman's name). Ms. Best said she didn't "get it," and Mackenzie made a photocopy of the word clitoris from the dictionary. Best reported the incident to her supervisor. Miller immediately investigated the matter, and Mackenzie denied sexually harassing Ms. Best. After concluding its investigation, Miller fired Mackenzie for "unacceptable managerial performance" and "exercising poor judgment."

Mackenzie filed suit against Miller on September 29, 1994. He alleged four causes of action in tort against Miller, Smith, and Best: (1) intentional misrepresentation against Smith and Miller, (2) tortious interference with prospective contract against Smith, (3) tortious interference with contract against Best, and (4) wrongful termination against Miller. His theory supporting the intentional misrepresentation torts against Smith and Miller was that Miller had a duty to disclose after the 1987 reorganization that his position had been grandfathered and that Smith misrepresented to Mackenzie that he would not be affected by the reorganization. In support of the tortious interference claim against Best, he contended that she improperly induced Miller to terminate Mackenzie by fraudulently misrepresenting to Miller that she felt harassed by his discussion of the *Seinfeld* program. The circuit court denied the defendants' motion to dismiss.

On June 23, 1997, a jury trial began and resulted in a verdict three weeks later. The jury awarded $6,501,500 in compensatory damages and $18,000,000 in punitive damages against Miller on the intentional misrepresentation claim. The jury also awarded $1,500 in compensatory damages and $500,000 in punitive damages against Smith on the same tort. The jury found Smith liable for tortious interference with Mackenzie's promotion and awarded him compensatory damages of $100,000. Finally, the jury failed to award Mackenzie any compensatory damages for tortious interference with contract against Best, but did award him $1,500,000 in punitive damages. The jurors in the case (10 women and 2 men) said the *Seinfeld* story did not offend them and they wanted to send a message with the size of the award that "sexual harassment has to be more important" than a story from a TV show.

The circuit court reduced the punitive damages against Smith to $100,000—giving Mackenzie the option to take the reduction or risk a new trial on the issue of damages—and dismissed Mackenzie's claim against Best because the jury failed to award compensatory damages. Miller and Smith appealed.

In an exhaustive opinion, the court of appeals reversed the judgment of the circuit court.[59] Mackenzie appealed and the Wisconsin Supreme Court affirmed the appellate court's decision.[60]

[59] Mackenzie v. Miller Brewing Co., *2000 Wis. App 48, 234 Wis.2d 1, 608 N.W.2d 331 (2000).*

[60] Mackenzie v. Miller Brewing Co., *241 Wis.2d 700, 623 N.W.2d 739 (Wis. 2001).*

Discussion Questions

1. Do you think Mackenzie's conduct was sexual harassment?
2. Do you think Mackenzie's conduct was professional?
3. Was the award excessive? Was the court of appeals correct in reversing the decision?
4. Do you think Mackenzie was wrongfully terminated? Was he already having difficulty at work? What about the previous allegations of harassment? Should Miller have taken action then to prevent the so-called "*Seinfeld* episode"?

CASE 4.8

Hooters: More Than a Waitress?

Hooters is a successful chain of restaurants and bars that features waitresses in tight shirts and very short shorts. Hooters also markets T-shirts that bear its name as well as its slogan, "More Than a Mouthful."

Former Hooters waitresses have filed a class action lawsuit, alleging that the atmosphere Hooters created in its restaurants allowed them to be sexually harassed. One waitress noted on a talk show: "We thought it was a family restaurant. [The uniforms] made us look stupid."[61] The former waitresses have noted that Hooters hired no male wait staff, and that all of the waitresses at its restaurants are very young and mostly blonde. Customers, cooks, and managers, according to the women, made lewd comments and, on occasion, touched them. The women contend that Hooters' atmosphere, their mandatory uniforms, and all-male management caused them to be sexually harassed. The EEOC and Hooters settled the litigation. Hooters' dress policy and its slogans and practices remain the same.[62]

Discussion Questions

1. Should the women have known of the problems when they agreed to work at Hooters? What bearing should such knowledge have on their right to allege harassment?
2. What ethical obligations does an employer such as Hooters owe its employees in the creation of its atmosphere?
3. What role should managers play in minimizing customer harassment?
4. Would you work for and/or patronize Hooters?
5. Every Wednesday, the Chicago-area Hooters restaurants donate half of what they earn selling spicy chicken wings to the Holy Family Lutheran church. Between

[61] *Andrew Blum, "Hooter Suit Lawyer Faces Ethics Complaint,"* National Law Journal, *November 15, 1993, p. 13.*

[62] Id.

1993 and 1995, the Hooters restaurant gave $15,000 to the church. On one Wednesday, Hooters brought in calendar girls and a Playboy Playmate for autographs in order to increase business. When asked about the combination of Hooters and religion, Pastor Charles Infelt responded, "We're not asking people to go there. I live in a larger Lutheran world. We try not to get into that side of life. We just accept their money. We don't evaluate. Our role is to be gracious and thankful. I don't want to get into negative thoughts." Evaluate this relationship.[63]

CASE 4.9

Navy Top Guns and Sexual Harassment

In September 1991, the Tailhook Association, a private group of retired and active-duty naval aviators, held its 35th annual convention at the Las Vegas Hilton in Las Vegas, Nevada. Over 1,500 current and former aviators attended the three-day meeting. Navy funds in excess of $190,000 were used to fly the officers on military aircraft to the Las Vegas gathering.

The Tailhook convention is known for its rowdiness. During the evenings, the officers occupied twenty hospitality suites on the third floor of the Hilton. Strippers and scantily clad bartenders worked the suites, and the alcohol bill for three days was estimated at $7,000 per suite. Pornographic films were shown in the suites, and the aviators traveled from suite to suite down a 140-foot hallway. One officer, describing the scene as a "hot, drunken, messy mass of humanity,"[64] later noted that the hallway became so crowded that going from one end to the other took twenty minutes.

It was in the hallway that a pattern of sexual harassment developed over the three days. Groups of officers in civilian clothes shoved both female officers and civilians down "the gauntlet," while grabbing at their breasts and buttocks and stripping off their clothes. Many of the women were ambushed at the elevator and shoved down the long hallway of arms. Two of the women, who were civilians, filed complaints with the Las Vegas police, but the complaints were dropped for a lack of evidence.

One of the women who was forced down the gauntlet was an aide to Admiral John W. Snyder. When she complained of the treatment to Snyder, he replied, "That's what you get for going to a hotel party with a bunch of drunk aviators."[65] However, the Admiral did report the complaint, which eventually reached then-Secretary of the Navy H. Lawrence Garrett, who launched (so to speak) an investigation.

The investigators encountered difficulties because of the officers' refusals to talk about the three-day gauntlet or identify those involved. Garrett then ordered the scope of the investigation broadened to include senior officers who did not participate in the gauntlet but who were in the nearby suites and did nothing to prevent the harassment of women. The investigation targeted seventy officers and identified harassment inci-

[63] *Richard Gibson, "Hooters Tries to Do Good Works By Selling Lots of Chicken Wings,"* The Wall Street Journal, *February 8, 1995, p. B1.*

[64] *"Top Guns Dogfight with Sex Scandal,"* Arizona Republic, *June 14, 1992, p. A17.*

[65] Id.

dents involving 26 women. A videotape of the gauntlet discovered during the investigation shows a seventeen-year-old girl being fondled and undressed.

In June 1992, the Navy added sexual harassment training to its "Top Gun" training program and started an awareness campaign for the prevention of sexual harassment. A poster on sexual harassment titled "Not in Our Navy" is required to be placed on all Navy base bulletin boards.

At the end of June 1992, Navy Secretary H. Lawrence Garrett resigned abruptly. In his resignation letter to President George Bush, Garrett wrote that he accepted "full responsibility" for his "leadership failure" with respect to the incidents at the Tailhook convention.[66] Admiral Frank B. Kelso 2d, Chief of Naval Operations, resigned as well, two months prior to his scheduled retirement.

The Tailhook convention for 1992 was canceled. Acting Navy Secretary Daniel Howard, vowing to purge the Navy of its "hard-drinking, skirt-chasing, anything-goes philosophy"[67] evidenced by Tailhook, imposed a requirement of one day of sexual harassment training for all naval officers and enlisted persons. Howard blamed Tailhook on a "decaying culture" and the "tolerance of Stone Age attitudes about warriors returning from the sea."[68]

Following Garrett's resignation, a party at the Miramar Naval Air Station Officers' Club in California included an annual revue known as the "Tomcat Follies." In the flyers for the revue were pictures of scantily clad women holding a poster that made reference to Colorado Representative Patricia Schroeder and oral sex. Schroeder was, at that time, a member of the House Armed Services Committee who criticized the Navy for Tailhook and demanded an investigation. Two officers involved in the Follies at Miramar were relieved of their command. Congressional hearings on the sexual harassment of women in the armed services began, and Sean O'Keefe, the Pentagon comptroller, was appointed Secretary of the Navy.

Shortly after Sean O'Keefe's appointment, Lieutenant Paula Coughlin, one of the twenty-six women sexually molested at the Tailhook Las Vegas convention, said that an agent of the Naval Investigative Service assigned to her case invited her to dinner and a drive in the country in November 1991. The agent, Laney Spigener, also called Coughlin "Sweetcakes" and pawed her as she sorted through photographs in an attempt to identify officers who took part in the Tailhook gauntlet. Spigener was removed from the case and suspended for three days.

In September 1992, four women sued both the Navy and Hilton Hotels for more than $2.5 million for their sexual assault in the hotel corridor gauntlet at the Las Vegas Hilton during the Tailhook convention. Coughlin was awarded $1.7 million by a federal jury in her suit against Hilton for the Las Vegas Hilton's failure to provide adequate security at the 1991 convention. Coughlin settled her claim against the Tailhook organization. A later hearing on punitive damages resulted in an additional $5 million award from the Las Vegas Hilton to Coughlin, who has since resigned from the Navy.

[66] *Andy Pasztor, "Garrett's Leaving Isn't Seen Protecting Administration from Scandal Fallout,"* The Wall Street Journal, *June 29, 1992, p. A14.*

[67] *"Navy Orders Training on Sex Harassment,"* Arizona Republic, *July 3, 1992, p. A8.*

[68] Id.

After the Navy investigation, 140 Navy and Marine Corps pilots were implicated in the assaults of 83 women at the Tailhook convention. There were no court-martials, but 60 officers were fined or disciplined. The charges against the remaining officers were dropped for lack of evidence.

Discussion Questions

1. Was the gauntlet sexual harassment or just "party fun"? How might the officers who participated in the gauntlet justify their conduct? What conditions of employment or environment might seem to justify such behavior?
2. Would you say that such treatment at a party in which drinking has been going on for three days is deserved, if not to be expected?
3. What action, if any, should the senior officers have taken to stop the gauntlet?
4. What action should hotel management have taken?
5. Would you be reluctant to identify your fellow officers if you had been involved in or had witnessed the Tailhook incidents? Why or why not?
6. Evaluate the conduct of Naval Investigator Laney Spigener.
7. In what ways was the "tone at the top" partially responsible for Tailhook?
8. Prior to Kelso's resignation, a military judge ruled that Admiral Kelso was present at Tailhook and did nothing to stop the conduct in the gauntlet. Further, the judge stated that Kelso's control of the investigation deflected inquiry into his presence and behavior. Why might it be said that a cover-up often is worse than the conduct it's covering?

Sources

Castaneda, Carol J., and Andrea Stone, "Girl's Ordeal Reignites Scandal," *USA Today*, July 30, 1992, p. 4A.

"Choppy Waters," *Time*, July 6, 1992, p. 17.

"Citing Scandal, Navy Chief Says He'll Quit Early," *The New York Times*, February 16, 1994, p. A16.

"Grounded," *Time*, June 29, 1992, p. 31.

Jolidon, Laurence, "Harassment Is on the Front Burner," *USA Today*, July 8, 1992, pp. 1A, 2A.

"Hotel to Pay $1.7 Million in Tailhook," *Mesa Tribune*, October 29, 1994, pp. A1, A12.

"Punitive Award in Tailhook Case—$5 M," *USA Today*, November 1, 1994, p. 3A.

Rohter, Larry, "The Navy Alters Its Training to Curb Sexual Harassment," *The New York Times*, June 22, 1992, p. A11.

Schmitt, Eric, "Officials Say Navy Balked at Report," *The New York Times*, July 8, 1992, pp. A1, A10.

Smolowe, Jill, "An Officer, Not a Gentleman," *Time*, July 13, 1992, p. 36.

Stone, Andrea, "Military Sex Harassment Charged," *USA Today*, September 11, 1992, p. 3A.

Stone, Andrea, "Scandal Could be Agent of Change," *USA Today*, July 30, 1992, p. 4A.

Stone, Andrea, and Carol J. Castaneda, "Military Brass on Hill Today," *USA Today*, July 30, 1992, p. 1A.

"Swabbing the Deck," *Time*, July 20, 1992, p. 15.

"Tailhook Victim Quitting Navy," *USA Today*, February 11, 1994, p. 2A.

"Whistleblower on Tailhook to Quit Navy," *Mesa Tribune*, February 11, 1994, p. A6.

4e

Diversity, Equal Employment, and Affirmative Action

Diversity in the workplace continues to be a stated goal, yet we still face difficult dilemmas, such as fetal endangerment when a prospective mother takes a higher-paying but higher-risk job. When has an employer done enough in terms of employee diversity and safety? Are current goals sufficient?

READING 4.10

The Benefits of Diversity—Doug Daft, CEO of Coca-Cola, Inc.

Remarks of CEO Douglas Daft on the Importance of Diversity at Coca-Cola

Coca-Cola, Inc. entered into a settlement with the EEOC in order to dismiss complaints of 2,000 employees for racial discrimination. The total settlement amount is $191.5 million (plus costs), the largest settlement ever in a discrimination case, topping the Texaco settlement (see Case 4.13) in 1996 of $176 million.[69]

The payments will be made to current and former African-American employees of Coke and as follows:

- $92.4 million in compensatory damages to employees
- $20.6 million in attorneys' fee
- $43.5 million to promote pay equity within the company
- $35 million invested in diversity reform programs[70]

[69] *Theresa Howard, "Coke Settles Bias Lawsuit for $192.5 Million,"* USA Today, *November 17, 2000, p. 1B.*

[70] *Betsy McKay, "Coke Settles Bias Suit for $192.5 Million,"* The Wall Street Journal, *November 17, 2000, p. A3.*

Coke also agreed to link management pay to diversity efforts by managers and form a seven-member independent panel to oversee diversity efforts at Coke and measure progress.

The settlement with the EEOC does not dispose of individual employee claims in a $1.5 billion racial bias class action suit still pending, which employees who benefit from this settlement may still join.

The following speech by the CEO indicates a new commitment to diversity by Coca-Cola.[71]

Good evening everyone and welcome.

Thank you, Ralph, for your kind words and thanks to everyone here at King and Spalding for inviting me to speak tonight. The link between The Coca-Cola Company and King & Spalding certainly predates my thirty-year career with Coca-Cola. A number of our Directors and General Counsels have hailed from King & Spalding, including Sam Nunn, Joe Gladden, Jimmy Sibley and his father John Sibley . . . just to name a few. I am honored to be here.

Tonight, I have been asked to share a few thoughts with you about diversity . . . diversity is a simple word, but a complex subject. Complex, in part, because it is rooted in deeply personal and emotional attitudes connected to race and gender. Complex, too, because there are so many things that come together to make every individual unique, and at the same time a part of an interdependent community.

What sort of characteristics am I talking about? Ones that go well beyond race and gender . . . characteristics like professional experiences, educational backgrounds, working styles and career aspirations. Also family values, our childhood communities and the books we have read and the people we have met.

There is a near endless list of factors that help shape our perspectives. And each individual's perspective—like every individual—is indeed unique.

But that's both the beauty and the power of diversity . . . Bringing those unique perspectives together to solve a problem or capture an opportunity is what managing diversity is all about.

And as we look at the changed world after the tragedies of September 11, we can only be reminded that diversity of different peoples, with different experiences and opinions not only made this country great, but also made it a prime target of the terrorists who seek to destroy our way of life.

These terrible events remind us of the importance of understanding and embracing diversity in our country, our communities and our companies.

The reality is that managing diversity . . . simply understanding diversity . . . requires an investment on our part. An investment of time . . . an investment of focus . . . and more than anything, an investment in people. If you take anything away from my remarks this evening, I hope it will be that such investment is well worth making.

[71] *http://www.cocacola.com*

Diversity is a subject I am continually learning more about. I have spent much of my working career in places and situations where I was one of the persons who brought diversity to the team . . . including my current role as an Australian CEO of a worldwide corporation, headquartered here in Atlanta.

During my years with Coca-Cola, I have lived and worked in communities throughout Asia, Europe and the United States. Most of the time, I was a minority learning to operate with respect and consideration in a societal culture very different from my own.

These experiences have helped me to appreciate the complexity of diversity and have given me an opportunity to experience its enormous power.

My commitment to diversity is rooted in seeing how a rich mosaic of perspectives builds a brand that transcends demographics . . . A brand that makes more than a billion people feel just a little bit better, a little more refreshed, and a little more connected to one another every day . . . A brand that is as at home in Brussels, as it is in Buckhead.

I am fortunate to work for The Coca-Cola Company . . . because we have a brand that lives and breathes the paradox of diversity. It is the same simple formula all over the world. And yet each individual . . . each community . . . each culture, experiences this wonderful beverage in a unique way.

I hope the beliefs I share tonight will be useful to you in your own organizations.

For us, at Coca-Cola we have a company built on relationships.

We created the world's leading brand by establishing a deep and lasting bond with our consumers. From there, we built a global marketing and distribution system second to none. We wove a global web of interconnected relationships. But all those relationships are local.

And diversity is at the core of those relationships. When we connect with consumers locally, our brands—particularly Coca-Cola—have become significantly stronger and more relevant . . . and our business has flourished.

People like to talk about Coca-Cola as a global brand . . . But the reality is that no one drinks a Coke globally . . . Local people in every market get thirsty, go to their local retailer, and buy locally-produced Cokes.

So our communication to consumers . . . their interaction with the brand . . . has to address their local needs and wants. Only if we understand them can we address them. And that understanding comes from devoting ourselves to recognizing, respecting, and celebrating the diversity of those local needs and wants.

At one point, we struggled with our advertising in China. We just could not seem to get traction. Well, when we talked to the Chinese about our advertising, we learned that we were not connecting with them culturally. Needless to say, we changed our processes, and now we have successful advertising in China. Here's another example . . . In Japan, we have a ready-to-drink coffee brand called Georgia. I am proud to say that it is the number one coffee brand in Japan. When we talked to Japanese consumers about growing the brand, we learned that they wanted variety.

So, we responded to their needs and wants by introducing multiple flavors of Georgia Coffee. We now have Georgia original, Espresso, Cappuccino and Café au-lait . . . and we now have dramatic growth of the brand.

We would not be able to grow our business the way we have around the world if we didn't open ourselves up to the perspectives of others. Genuinely expressed interest in another's point of view in a way to build bridges and mutual respect . . . it is about the power of relationships.

One more example illustrates how one product can be viewed differently by different people in different parts of the world.

Here in the U.S., you may have noticed the relaunch of POWERade, which is producing truly spectacular results . . . our overall volume for POWERade is up 17% this year! In our home country, the brand is aimed at athletes—from the professional to the weekend warrior. We tap into the desire for a beverage that replenishes you while you are working out.

However, in Japan, sports drinks are viewed very differently. They are a component of relaxation. Japanese consumers might enjoy a sports beverage, not during their workout, but after it, while they bathe. Understanding that difference has helped us make our Aquarius brand the biggest selling sports drink in Japan.

Understanding diversity has led to innovation for our carbonated brands too. For example, I hope that all of you will try our newest brand extension, diet Coke with Lemon.

Sometime ago, some of our people came up with an idea . . . In the U.S., they said, "People sit at cafes and restaurants and enjoy diet Coke with a lemon in their drink." They asked, "Why don't we put that flavor into the beverage itself, so that consumers can enjoy the same taste while they are on the go?"

As a result, diet Coke with Lemon is currently being introduced in the Midwest to rave reviews and will be rolled out nationwide later this month.

These are all a result of listening to new and different perspectives—from inside and outside our Company—and incorporating them into our decision-making to grow our business. In short . . . diversity marketing.

Why do we talk about diversity this way? Why don't we discuss, first and foremost, zero-tolerance policies against discrimination, or how to help sensitize our workforces to respect others of different racial or ethnic backgrounds?

At Coca-Cola, we certainly do all these things. We believe that diversity is not merely about compliance . . . it is about values; it is about relationships. Taking advantage of diversity is a critical key to who we are and to our business success.

And even if you don't operate in two hundred countries around the world, any organization will be more successful if it can access a broader array of perspectives and then channel them towards the organization's mission. Those perspectives can be driven not only by race or gender, but also by functional background or professional expertise.

Put simply . . . you are not taking advantage of your diversity if, in developing a new strategy, you gather a group of people with the same perspective or business expertise, say a group of marketers, or a group of accountants, or even lawyers . . . sorry . . . You'll get limited, narrow points of view.

We all must, recognize, respect, value and celebrate the uniqueness of all members of our organizations as we embrace diversity as one of our fundamental values.

At Coca-Cola, we value a workforce that mirrors the consumers we serve, and we continue to build towards that objective. And let's be clear about what that means. Yes, it is including African-Americans, Latinos, and Asian-Americans. And it is also bringing together young people with those closer to my age . . . It's single parents . . . It's liberals and conservatives. It is working diligently to maintain a workforce that possesses the experiences, backgrounds and influences that can enrich our lives and enhance our business.

How does that get translated into the workplace? Well, it means that we encourage innovative thinking, by everyone at every level, and taking calculated risks to develop our business to meet changing consumer tastes. Again, it's a role that must be embraced by senior management.

It starts with education. All of us, from myself on, have participated in strategic diversity management sessions—to educate ourselves, to understand how we can best leverage our diversity to support our business, and to apply what we learn to our operations.

But it also involves ensuring that the lessons we learn in these sessions are reinforced in the everyday life of our corporation . . . and that, of course, is the objective.

This commitment to bring diversity to the way we do business extends beyond the Company and into society at large, through the communities of which we are a part. Through our local people and those of our bottling partners, we are part of the community connecting with local residents through local marketing and local civic programs. We create opportunities for our consumers to[o.] For example, our Urban Economic Partnership in Harlem developed with our largest U.S. bottler, Coca-Cola Enterprises, has expanded to several other communities in the Northeast. Many of the people hired in those new jobs have been promoted from account managers to district managers and sales managers.

As we continue our long history of being part of the communities we serve, we are continually seeking opportunities to partner with our neighbors and use innovative diversity initiatives to help other organizations develop their own benefit from diversity.

Last fall we donated $1.5 million to the American Institute of Managing Diversity for the establishment of the Diversity Leadership Academy, right here in Atlanta.

The Diversity Leadership Academy is designed to build diversity management skills and capabilities in leaders from various sectors within the community—including government, non-profits, education and business—so they all can benefit from better diversity management.

Our grant will enable 300–400 leaders to participate in this innovative program. The first classes began on October 4.

In addition, last week, I announced that our vice president of Diversity Strategies, Juan Johnson, has become the president of the Diversity Leadership Academy. While remaining a vice president of our company, Juan will lead the Atlanta Academy to serve as a model for other communities across the nation and the world. Charlene Crusoe-Ingram will succeed him as vice president for Diversity Strategy and Culture, reporting directly to [. . .] Realizing the full potential of diversity is essential to our business . . . from the communities we serve, to the decisions we make every day about our operations. Diversity has a direct impact on The Coca-Cola Company:

- It improves our understanding of local markets;
- It makes us a better employer and business partner;
- It helps us compete more effectively;
- It makes us better neighbors in our communities; and ultimately,
- It builds value for our shareowners.

Respecting and benefiting from diversity in our businesses and in our communities is not only a guiding principle but also a core value of The Coca-Cola Company.

That's why our success demands that we continue to develop a worldwide team rich in its diversity of thinking, perspectives, backgrounds and culture.

Only when we do that can we keep developing a unique intellectual and physical system throughout the world, a system with the people and assets to refresh consumers in local communities in over 200 countries.

Enjoy tonight's dinner, and I know that the diverse perspectives that each of you will bring to your conversations will be fascinating.

Thank you.

Discussion Questions

1. Why does Mr. Daft believe diversity is important?
2. What personal experiences does he have with the issue of diversity?
3. What are the five components of Coke's diversity program?
4. Do you think the program was put into place because of the EEOC issues? Do you think the program will prevent future EEOC issues?

CASE 4.11

On-the-Job Fetal Injuries

Johnson Controls, Inc., is a battery manufacturer. In the battery manufacturing process, the primary ingredient is lead. Exposure to lead endangers health and can harm a fetus carried by a female who is exposed to lead.

Before Congress passed the Civil Rights Act of 1964, Johnson Controls did not employ any women in the battery manufacturing process. In June 1977, Johnson

Controls announced its first official policy with regard to women who desired to work in battery manufacturing, which would expose them to lead:

> Protection of the health of the unborn child is the immediate and direct responsibility of the prospective parents. While the medical professional and the company can support them in the exercise of this responsibility, it cannot assume it for them without simultaneously infringing their rights as persons.
>
> Since not all women who can become mothers wish to become mothers (or will become mothers), it would appear to be illegal discrimination to treat all who are capable of pregnancy as though they will become pregnant.[72]

The policy stopped short of excluding women capable of bearing children from jobs involving lead exposure but emphasized that a woman who expected to have a child should not choose a job that involved such exposure.

Johnson Controls required women who wished to be considered for employment in the lead exposure jobs to sign statements indicating that they had been told of the risks lead exposure posed to an unborn child: ". . . that women exposed to lead have a higher rate of abortion . . . not as clear as the relationship between cigarette smoking and cancer . . . but medically speaking, just good sense not to run that risk if you want children and do not want to expose the unborn child to risk, however small."

By 1982, however, the policy of warning had been changed to a policy of exclusion. Johnson Controls was responding to the fact that between 1979 and 1982, eight employees became pregnant while maintaining blood lead levels in excess of thirty micrograms per deciliter, an exposure level that OSHA categorizes as critical. The company's new policy was as follows:

> It is Johnson Controls' policy that women who are pregnant or who are capable of bearing children will not be placed into jobs involving lead exposure or which would expose them to lead through the exercise of job bidding, bumping, transfer or promotion rights.[73]

The policy defined women capable of bearing children as "all women except those whose inability to bear children is medically documented."[74] The policy defined unacceptable lead exposure as the OSHA standard of thirty micrograms per deciliter in the blood or thirty micrograms per cubic centimeter in the air.

In 1984, three Johnson Controls employees filed suit against the company on the grounds that the fetal-protection policy was a form of sex discrimination that violated Title VII of the Civil Rights Act. The three employees included Mary Craig, who had chosen to be sterilized to avoid losing a job that involved lead exposure; Elsie Nason, a fifty-year-old divorcee who experienced a wage decrease when she transferred out of a job in which she was exposed to lead; and Donald Penney, a man who was denied a leave of absence so that he could lower his lead level because he intended to become a father. The trial court certified a class action that included all past, present, and future Johnson Controls' employees who had been or would continue to be affected by the fetal-protection policy Johnson Controls implemented in 1982.

[72] International Union v. Johnson Controls, Inc., *499 U.S. 187, 191 (1991).*

[73] Id., *at 191.*

[74] Id., *at 192.*

At the trial, uncontroverted evidence showed that lead exposure affects the reproductive abilities of men and women and that the effects of exposure on adults are as great as those on a fetus, although the fetus appears to be more vulnerable to exposure. Johnson Controls maintained that its policy was a product of business necessity.

The employees argued in turn that the company allowed fertile men, but not fertile women, to choose whether they wished to risk their reproductive health for a particular job. Johnson Controls responded that it had based its policy not on any intent to discriminate, but rather on its concern for the health of unborn children. Johnson Controls also pointed out that inasmuch as more than forty states recognize a parent's right to recover for a prenatal injury based on negligence or wrongful death, its policy was designed to prevent its liability for such fetal injury or death. The company maintained that simple compliance with Title VII would not shelter it from state tort liability for injury to a parent or child.

Johnson Controls also maintained that its policy represented a bona fide occupational qualification and that it was requiring medical certification of non-childbearing status to avoid substantial liability for injuries.

Discussion Questions

1. As the director of human resources for Johnson Controls, would you support or change the policy on women performing lead-exposure tasks? Why?

2. Why should women be given—or not given—the choice to accept the risk of exposure?

3. To what extent should a woman have the right to make decisions that will affect not only her health but the health of her unborn child? To what extent should a woman's consent to or acknowledgment of danger mitigate an employer's liability? What if a child born with lead-induced birth defects sues? Should the mother's consent apply as a defense?

4. The U.S. Supreme Court eventually decided Johnson Controls' policy was discriminatory and a violation of Title VII (*International Union v. Johnson Controls, Inc.*, 499 U.S. 187 (1991)). What steps would you take as director of human resources to create a "policy-free" work setting?

5. At what times, if any, should discrimination issues be subordinate to other issues, such as the risk of danger to unborn children?

CASE 4.12

Denny's: Discriminatory Service with a Smile

On March 24, 1993, a group of minority customers filed a lawsuit in San Jose, California, against the Denny's restaurant chain. Denny's was requiring its minority customers to pay cover charges and to prepay for meals. In April, Denny's settled the charges with the Justice Department.[75]

On May 24, 1993, six African-American secret service agents filed suit against Denny's, claiming the wait staff at the Annapolis, Maryland, Denny's had been deliberately slow in serving them (the agents had waited 55 minutes), thereby effectively denying them service. Their white colleagues had been served in a timely fashion.[76]

Other Denny's customers who are black complained that they were told they would have to pay first if they wanted to eat at Denny's.

In July 1993, Denny's signed a $1 billion pact to settle the secret service case and all other claims. In the pact, Denny's agreed to:[77]

- Buy nearly $700 million in food, paper, and supplies from black-owned businesses.
- Launch a training and recruitment program to increase black representation in Flagstar's[78] management ranks from 4.4 percent to 12 percent.
- Add 53 black-run franchises. Denny's had 1,485 restaurants, only one of which was operated by a black franchisee.
- Funnel Flagstar business to black accountants, lawyers, ad agencies, and banks.[79]

Denny's also agreed to pay $46 million to black patrons and $8.7 million for legal fees. An additional $28 million was paid to California customers to settle civil rights cases there. The six agents in the Annapolis restaurant will split $17.7 million. The customers in the class action suit each received about $180 each as their part of the settlement.[80]

Denny's now buys $50 million in supplies from minority contractors and one in four of its store managers is black.[81] At the time of the settlement, Denny's had only two minority contractors. In 1997, Denny's began a $5 million ad campaign that features black families entering Denny's restaurants.[82] Denny's CEO now tells employees, "I will fire you if you discriminate."[83]

Discussion Questions

1. In what ways could you say that Denny's is an example of a firm failing to monitor its practices?
2. How costly was Denny's discrimination?

[75] *Chuck Hawkins, "Denny's: The Stain That Isn't Coming Out,"* Business Week, *June 28, 1993, pp. 98–99.*

[76] *Anne Faircloth, "Denny's Changes Its Spots,"* Fortune, *May 13, 1996, pp. 133–142*

[77] *Blair S. Walker, "Denny's, NAACP Sign $1 Billion Pact,"* USA Today, *July 2, 1993, pp. 1B, 2B.*

[78] *Flagstar is the parent company for Denny's.*

[79] Id.

[80] *Del Jones, "Denny's Checks Smaller than Plaintiffs Expected,"* USA Today, *December 12, 1995, p. 1B.*

[81] *Eleena de Lisser and Benjamin A. Holden, "Denny's Begins Repairing Its Image—and Its Attitude,"* The Wall Street Journal, *March 1, 1994, pp. B1, B3.*

[82] *Laura Bird, "Denny's TV Ad Seeks to Mend Bias Image,"* The Wall Street Journal, *June 21, 1993, p. B6; see also Melanie Wells, "Denny's Serves Up $5M Ad Campaign to Fix Racist Image,"* USA Today, *May 23, 1997, p. 1B.*

[83] *Emory Thomas, Jr., "Denny's Shines Its Bad Image with New Deal,"* The Wall Street Journal, *November 9, 1994, pp. B1, B7.*

3. How effective would encouraging employees to report discrimination be as a step in changing the corporate culture at Denny's and other service organizations?
4. Denny's includes the following information on its Web site about diversity:[84]

- Forty-eight percent of Advantica's more than 46,221 company employees are minorities; 11 percent are African-Americans and 31 percent are Hispanic-American. Thirty-two percent of Advantica's restaurant and multi-restaurant supervisory positions are held by minorities.
- Minority employees represent 32 percent of Denny's parent company Advantica's management; African-Americans, Hispanic-Americans, and Asian-Pacific Americans account for 12 percent, 14 percent and 6 percent, respectively, of Advantica's management.
- *Working Woman* magazine ranked Advantica, Denny's parent company, 12th in its 2001 survey of the "Top 25 Companies for Women Executives."
- *Fortune* magazine ranked Advantica, Denny's parent company, number 1 in its list of "America's 50 Best Companies for Minorities" for two consecutive years—2000 and 2001.
- Advantica, Denny's parent company, received the 1997 Fair Share Corporate Award for Minority Business Development from the National Association for the Advancement of Colored People (NAACP) in June 1997.
- Jim Adamson, former chairman and CEO of Advantica, Denny's parent company, received the "CEO of the Year" Award from Kweisi Mfume, President and CEO of the National Association for the Advancement of Colored People (NAACP) in June of 1996. He also received the national "Humanitarian of the Year" Award from the prestigious American Jewish Committee in February 1997 for his work in the diversity arena.

Since October 1994, Denny's has been Save the Children's largest corporate sponsor. Through the enthusiastic support of its employees, franchisees and customers, Denny's has contributed over $2,500,000 and has positively impacted the lives of more than 75,000 disadvantaged children in over 100 U.S. communities. Denny's goal continues to be to raise $1,000,000 annually for Save the Children. Donations to Save the Children are primarily the result of in-store coin canister donations, a 10-cent donation from each All-American Slam and kids' menu Smiley-Face Hotcakes plate sold, as well as raffles, car washes, etc.

The partnership has been a win-win for both parties. As Denny's national charity, Save the Children receives annual contributions from the nation's largest family restaurant chain for its domestic Web of Support programs. Web of Support programs are committed to increasing quality, out-of-school time for children at-risk to the influence of drugs, teenage pregnancy, and dropping out of high school. In return, this initiative provides an opportunity for local restaurant employees, franchisees, and customers to get more involved with the programs in their individual communities.

Denny's commitment to Save the Children is more than just a financial relationship. In the first half of 1998, Denny's donated more than 2,700 Harlem Globetrotter basketball game tickets to Save the Children, enabling disadvantaged

[84] *Used with permission of DFO, Inc.*

children nationwide to attend these entertaining events and pre-game basketball demonstrations. Additionally, more than 100 Save the Children youth received complimentary admission to a five-day Harlem Globetrotters summer basketball camp held in markets across the country.

Do you think the progress was the result of the discrimination cases? Do you think Denny's will experience discrimination cases in the future? Why or why not? Are there similarities between Denny's programs and philosophies and Coca-Cola's (see Reading 4.10)?

5. Denny's has security cameras in every restaurant. Those cameras, while intended to help deter and solve crimes, also videotape employees' interactions with customers. The cameras have proven to be a help in suits that claim discrimination. For example, in 2000, two African-American males filed suit against Denny's (Advantica Restaurant Group, Inc. is Denny's owner) for alleged discrimination in one restaurant's failure to seat them. The lawyer for Advantica asked to see the videotape from the restaurant. The two plaintiffs were only in the Denny's waiting area for 10 minutes before leaving. And during the time they were waiting, the host had seated Hispanics, African-Americans and others, in the order in which they entered the restaurant. The plaintiffs withdrew their suit.[85]

   Is the use of these tapes and cameras ethical? Is their use for non-security reasons ethical?

CASE 4.13

Texaco: The Jelly Bean Diversity Fiasco

In November 1996, Texaco, Inc. was rocked by the disclosure of tape-recorded conversations among three executives about a racial discrimination suit pending against the company. The suit, seeking $71 million, had been brought by 6 employees, on behalf of 1,500 other employees, who alleged the following forms of discrimination:

- I have had KKK printed on my car. I have had my tires slashed and racial slurs written about me on bathroom walls. One co-worker blatantly called me a racial epithet to my face.
- Throughout my employment, three supervisors in my department openly discussed their view that African-Americans are ignorant and incompetent, and, specifically, that Thurgood Marshall was the most incompetent person they had ever seen.
- Sheryl Joseph, formerly a Texaco secretary in Harvey, Louisiana, was given a cake for her birthday which occurred shortly after she announced that she was pregnant. The cake depicted a black pregnant woman and read, "Happy Birthday, Sheryl. It must have been those watermelon seeds."[86]

The suit also included data on Texaco's workforce:

1989	Minorities as a percentage of Texaco's workforce	15.2%
1994	Minorities as a percentage of Texaco's workforce	19.4%

85 *David E. Rovella, "Denny's Serves Up a Winning Video,"* National Law Journal, *August 28, 2000, p. A17.*

86 *Kurt Eichenwald, "Behind the Two Faces of Texaco,"* The New York Times, *November 10, 1996, pp. 3-1, 3-10.*

# of Years to Promotion by Job Classification

Minority Employees	*Job*	*Other Employees*
6.1	Accountant	4.6
6.4	Senior Accountant	5.4
12.5	Analyst	6.3
14.2	Financial Analyst	13.9
15.0	Assistant Accounting Supervisor	9.8

Senior Managers[87]

	White	*Black*
1991	1,887	19
1992	2,001	21
1993	2,000	23
1994	2,029	23

Racial Composition (% of Blacks) by Pay Range[88]

Salary	*Texaco*	*Other Oil Companies*
$51,100	5.9%	7.2%
$56,900	4.7%	6.5%
$63,000	4.1%	4.7%
$69,900	2.3%	5.1%
$77,600	1.8%	3.2%
$88,100	1.9%	2.3%
$95,600	1.4%	2.6%
$106,100	1.2%	2.3%
$117,600	0.8%	2.3%
$128,800	0.4%	1.8%

(African-Americans make up 12% of the U.S. population)

The acting head of the EEOC wrote in 1995, "Deficiencies in the affirmative-action programs suggest that Texaco is not committed to insuring comprehensive, facility by facility, compliance with the company's affirmative-action responsibilities."[89]

Faced with the lawsuit, Texaco's former treasurer, Robert Ulrich, senior assistant treasurer, J. David Keough, and senior coordinator for personnel services, Richard A. Lundwall, met and discussed the suit. A tape transcript follows:[90]

They look through evidence, deciding what to turn over to the plaintiffs.

Lundwall Here, look at this chart. You know, I'm not really quite sure what it means. This chart is not mentioned in the agency, so it's not important that we even have it in there. . . . They would never know it was here.

87 *Adam Bryant, "How Much Has Texaco Changed?"* The New York Times, *November 2, 1997, pp. 3-1, 3-16.*

88 *Eichenwald, "Behind the Two Faces of Texaco," p. 3-10.*

89 *Richard W. Stevenson, "Texaco Is Said to Set Payment Over Sex Bias,"* The New York Times, *January 6, 1999, pp. C1, C4.*

90 *Kurt Eichenwald, "Texaco Executives, On Tape, Discussed Impeding a Bias Suit,"* The New York Times, *November 4, 1996, pp. A1, C4.*

Keough They'll find it when they look through it.

Lundwall Not if I take it out they won't.

The executives decide to leave out certain pages of a document; they worry that another version will turn up.

Ulrich We're gonna purge the [expletive deleted] out of these books, though. We're not going to have any damn thing that we don't need to be in them—

Lundwall As a matter of fact, I just want to be reminded of what we discussed. You take your data and . . .

Keough You look and make sure it's consistent to what we've given them already for minutes. Two versions with the restricted and that's marked clearly on top—

Ulrich But I don't want to be caught up in a cover-up. I don't want to be my own Watergate.

Lundwall We've been doing pretty much two versions, too. This one here, this is strictly my book, your book . . .

Ulrich Boy, I'll tell you, that one, you would put that and you would have the only copy. Nobody else ought to have copies of that.

Lundwall O.K.?

Ulrich You have that someplace and it doesn't exist.

Lundwall Yeah, O.K.

Ulrich I just don't want anybody to have a copy of that.

Lundwall Good. No problem.

Ulrich You know, there is no point in even keeping the restricted version anymore. All it could do is get us in trouble. That's the way I feel. I would not keep anything.

Lundwall Let me shred this thing and any other restricted version like it.

Ulrich Why do we have to keep the minutes of the meeting anymore?

Lundwall You don't, you don't.

Ulrich We don't?

Lundwall Because we don't, no, we don't because it comes back to haunt us like right now—

Ulrich I mean, the pendulum is swinging the other way, guys.

The executives discuss the minority employees who brought the suit.

Lundwall They are perpetuating an us/them atmosphere. Last week or last Friday I told . . .

Ulrich [Inaudible.]

Lundwall Yeah, that's what I said to you, you want to frag grenade? You know, duck, I'm going to throw one. Well, that's what I was alluding to. But the point is not, that's

not bad in itself but it does perpetuate us/them. And if you're trying to get away and get to the we . . . you can't do that kind of stuff.

Ulrich [Inaudible.] I agree. This diversity thing. You know how black jelly beans agree . . .

Lundwall That's funny. All the black jelly beans seem to be glued to the bottom of the bag.

Ulrich You can't have just we and them. You can't just have black jelly beans and other jelly beans. It doesn't work.

Lundwall Yeah. But they're perpetuating the black jelly beans.

Ulrich I'm still having trouble with Hanukkah. Now, we have Kwanza (laughter).[91]

The release of the tape prompted the Reverend Jesse Jackson to call for a nationwide boycott of Texaco.[92] Sales fell 8 percent, Texaco's stock fell 2 percent, and several institutional investors were preparing to sell their stock.[93]

Texaco did have a minority recruiting effort in place and the "jelly bean" remark was tied to a diversity trainer the company had hired.[94] The following are excerpts from Texaco's statement of vision and values:

Respect for the Individual

Our employees are our most important resource. Each person deserves to be treated with respect and dignity in appropriate work environments, without regard to race, religion, sex, age, national origin, disability or position in the company. Each employee has the responsibility to demonstrate respect for others.

The company believes that a work environment that reflects a diverse workforce, values diversity, and is free of all forms of discrimination, intimidation, and harassment is essential for a productive and efficient workforce. Accordingly, conduct directed toward any employee that is unwelcome, hostile, offensive, degrading, or abusive is unacceptable and will not be tolerated.[95]

A federal grand jury began an investigation at Texaco to determine whether there had been obstruction of justice in the withholding of documents.[96]

Within days of the release of the tape, Texaco settled its bias suit for $176.1 million, the largest sum, at that time, ever allowed in a discrimination case. The money allowed a 11 percent pay raise for blacks and other minorities who joined in the lawsuit.[97]

[91] *Del Jones, "Oil Giant Argues Tapes Didn't Contain Racial Slur," November 12, 1996, p. 1B; see also Kurt Eichenwald, "Blowing the Whistle, and Now Facing the Music,"* The New York Times, *March 16, 1997, pp. 3-1, 3-12, 3-13.*

[92] *Kurt Eichenwald, "Rights Groups Urge Boycott of Texaco,"* The New York Times, *November 13, 1996, pp. C1, C6.*

[93] *Allanna Sullivan and Peter Fritsch, "Texaco's Bijur Says Company Is Trying to Settle Bias Suit,"* The Wall Street Journal, *November 13, 1996, p. A12; see also Del Jones, "Jackson Calls for Boycott of Texaco,"* USA Today, *November 13, 1996, p. 1A.*

[94] *Kurt Eichenwald, "U.S. Inquiring Into Texaco's Actions in Suit,"* The New York Times, *November 5, 1996, pp. C1, C2.*

[95] *Eichenwald, "Behind the Two Faces of Texaco," pp. 3-1, 3-10.*

[96] *Ellen Neubourne, "Texaco Race-Bias Tapes: Were Erasures Intended?"* USA Today, *July 11, 1997, p. 1B.*

[97] *"Texaco to Pay $176 Million to End Bias Suit,"* Arizona Republic, *November 16, 1996, pp. A1, A15.*

Texaco's chairman and CEO at that time, Peter I. Bijur, issued the following statement after agreeing to a settlement:

> Texaco is facing a difficult but vital challenge. It's broader than any specific words and larger than any lawsuit. It is one we must and are attacking head-on.
>
> We are a company of 27,000 people worldwide. In any organization of that size, unfortunately, there are bound to be people with unacceptable, biased attitudes toward race, gender and religion.
>
> Our goal, and our responsibility, is to eradicate this kind of thinking wherever and however it is found in our company. And our challenge is to make Texaco a company of limitless opportunity for all men and women.
>
> We are committed to begin meeting this challenge immediately through programs with concrete goals and measurable timetables.
>
> I've already announced certain specific steps, including a redoubling of efforts within Texaco to focus on the paramount value of respect for the individual and a comprehensive review of our diversity programs at every level of our company.
>
> We also want to broaden economic access to Texaco for minority firms and increase the positive impact our investments can have in the minority community. This includes areas such as hiring and promotion; professional services such as advertising, banking, investment management and legal services; and wholesale and retail station ownership.
>
> To assist us, we are reaching out to leaders of minority and religious organizations and others for ideas and perspectives that will help Texaco succeed in our mission of becoming a model of diversity and workplace equality.
>
> It is essential to this urgent mission that Texaco and African-Americans and other minority community leaders work together to help solve the programs we face as a company—which, after all, echo the problems faced in society as a whole.
>
> Discrimination will be extinguished only if we tackle it together, only if we join in a unified, common effort.
>
> Working together, I believe we can take Texaco into the 21st century as a model of diversity. We can make Texaco a company of limitless opportunity. We can make Texaco a leader in according respect to every man and woman.[98]

Even after the announcement, Texaco stock was down $3 per share, a loss of $800 million total, and the boycott was continued. Texaco's proposed merger with Shell Oil began to unravel as Shell's CEO expressed concern about Texaco's integrity. However, after the settlement, additional information about the case began to emerge.[99]

Holman W. Jenkins, Jr. wrote the following piece for *The Wall Street Journal*:

> Quietly, corporate America is debating whether Texaco's Peter Bijur did the right thing.

[98] *Peter I. Bijur, "Texaco Will Wipe Out Bias,"* USA Today, *November 14, 1996, p. 14A.*

[99] *Bari-Ellen Roberts and Jack E. White, "Portrait of a Company Behaving Badly,"* Time, *March 16, 1998, pp. 46–51.*

Mr. Bijur gets paid to make the hard calls, and with the airwaves aflame over "nigger" and "black jelly beans," Texaco took a battering in the stock and political markets. He had every reason for wanting to put a stop-loss on the media frenzy. "Once the taped conversations were revealed," he says, settling was "reasonable and honorable." So now Texaco is betting $176 million that paying off minority employees and their lawyers is the quickest way out of the news.

But as the company's own investigation showed, the truly inflammatory comments reported in the media never took place. They were purely a fabrication by opposing lawyers, and trumpeted by a credulous New York Times. And some digging would have shown this problem cropping up before in the career of Mike Hausfeld, lead attorney for the plaintiffs.

In an antitrust case years ago, he presented a secret recording that he claimed showed oil executives conspiring to threaten gasoline dealers. But a check by the same expert who handled the Nixon Watergate tapes showed no such thing. Says Larry Sharp, the Washington antitrust lawyer who opposed Mr. Hausfeld: "To put it generously, he gave himself the benefit of the doubt in making the transcript."

But this time the lie has been rewarded, and the broader public, unschooled in legal cynicism, heads home believing Texaco an admitted racist.

The catechism of corporate crisis management says you can't fight the media. Mr. Bijur had to consider that Jesse Jackson was threatening a boycott if Texaco failed to "regret, repent and seek renewal." Mr. Jackson pointedly added that "any attempt to shift to denial would add insult to injury"—a warning against trying to spread some egg to the faces of those who were fooled by the fake transcript.

There may have been wisdom, if not valor, in Mr. Bijur's decision to run up the white flag. But he also evinced symptoms of Stockholm Syndrome, telling CNN that Texaco was just the "tip of the iceberg" of corporate racism. Ducking this fight so ignominiously may yet prove a penny-wise, pound-foolish strategy. The City of Philadelphia has decided to dump its Texaco holdings anyway, partly out of fear of more litigation.

What else could Texaco have done? It could have apologized for any offense, but stuck up for its former treasurer Bob Ulrich, who was wronged by the phony transcript and stripped of his medical benefits by Texaco. And the company could have vowed to fight the lawsuit like the dickens, arguing that Texaco is not the cause of society's racial troubles but has tried to be part of the solution.

Start with the tapes: A fair listening does not necessarily reveal a "racist" conversation by executives at Texaco, but certainly a candid conversation about the problems of race at Texaco. They spoke of "jelly beans" dividing into camps of "us" and "them," an honest representation of life at many companies, not just in the oil patch.

Mr. Bijur could have made this point, starting with the New York Times, which has been embroiled in its own discrimination lawsuit with Angela Dodson, once its top-ranking black female. In a complaint filed with New York City's Human Rights Commission, she claims the paper was "engaged in gender-based harassment and disability-based discrimination . . . because The Times no longer wanted me, as a black person, to occupy a position as Senior editor."

Her deepest ire is reserved for Times veteran Carolyn Lee, who is white and more accustomed to being lauded as a champion of women and minorities. Ms. Dodson told the Village Voice: "It got to the point that whenever I was in her presence or earshot she made remarks [about other black people] that could only be taken as negative."

This sounds remarkably like the anecdotes filed in the Texaco complaint. All an outsider can safely conclude is that race makes everything more complicated, as sensitivity begets sensitivity. Mr. Bijur would have done more for racial understanding had he used his platform to open up this subject.

Yes, the cartoonist racists are out there, he might have said, but the Times coverage of Texaco only found cartoonist racists. The paper could have looked to its own experience for another story—a story about how garden-variety interpersonal conflict can land even decent people in the snares of racial mistrust.

This is what affirmative action, by throwing people together, was supposed to get us past. And it may be no accident that our most quota-ridden newspaper, USA Today, jumped off the bandwagon on the Texaco tapes, noting the ambiguity of whether the "jelly bean" remarks were meant to be hostile or friendly to blacks.

And McPaper kept on asking intelligent questions, like whether the New York Times had been "used by plaintiffs in the case to promote a faulty but more inflammatory transcript?" ("Not unless the court was used," answered Times Business Editor John Geddes, sounding like a lawyer himself.)

So Mr. Bijur was not facing a uniformly hopeless media torrent. The truth, even a complicated truth, catches up with the headlines eventually.

In time, he might have found surprising allies drifting to his side. The New Republic and the New Yorker have run thoughtful articles arguing that businesses should be allowed to use quotas but shouldn't be subject to harassment litigation if they don't. Right now, we do the opposite: Forbid companies to promote by quota, then sue them under federal "adverse impact" rules when they don't.

In effect, liberal voices are arguing that business could do more for minorities with less conflict if freedom of contract were restored. The world is changing, and companies have their own reasons nowadays for wanting minorities around. They need input from different kinds of people on how to deal with different kinds of people. No doubt this is why McPaper feels free to thumb its nose at the conformity crowd on stories like Texaco and church-burnings. (See September's Harvard Business Review for what business is thinking about diversity now.)

If companies were set free to assemble the work forces most useful to them, they could sweep away a heap of excuses for recrimination. Whites couldn't feel cheated out of jobs. Blacks wouldn't end up at companies that want them only for window-dressing. And the world could go back to feeling OK about being an interesting place. We might even allow that cultural patterns other than racism may explain why so many rednecks, and so few blacks, become petroleum engineers.

Mr. Bijur may have made the best of a bad deal for his shareholders. Whether it was best for America is a different judgment.[100]

[100] *Wall Street Journal. Eastern Edition (Staff Produced Copy Only) by Gerald M. Levin. Copyright 1992 by Dow Jones & Co. Inc. Reproduced with permission of Dow Jones & Co. Inc. in the format textbook via Copyright Clearance Center.*

Richard Lundwall, the executive who taped the sessions with the other executives, was charged with one count of obstruction of justice. Lundwall had turned over the tapes of the conversations to lawyers for the plaintiffs in the discrimination suit on October 25, 1996. Lundwall had been terminated.

Texaco hired attorney Michael Armstrong to investigate the underlying allegations. Mr. Armstrong found the tapes had not been transcribed correctly.

As part of its settlement, Texaco agreed to, at a cost of $55 million, assign a task force to police hiring and promotion as well as requiring mentors for black employees and sensitivity training for white employees.[101]

The following interview with CEO Bijur appeared in *Business Week*:

Q: *How did your legal strategy change once the news of the tapes was printed?*

A: When I saw [the story], I knew that this lawsuit was pending and moving forward. I made the judgment that we needed to accelerate the settlement process. And those discussions on settlement commenced almost immediately.

Q: *It has been reported that you didn't get the board of directors involved with the settlement talks and other issues. Why not?*

A: You're drawing conclusions that are erroneous. The board was fully involved throughout the entire process. I talked to numerous directors personally. We had several board and executive committee meetings. The board was fully supportive of our actions.

Q: *Have you met with shareholders?*

A: Yes, of course. I went down to [New York] and met with the Interfaith Center on Corporate Responsibility, which is a group of religious shareholders. I expressed our position on this and listened carefully to their position and got some good counsel and guidance. But I wanted to provide our side of the issue as well. I have met with [New York State Comptroller] Carl McCall and [New York City Comptroller] Alan Hevesi about concerns that they had, and I will continue to meet with other shareholders as I normally do.

Q: *Why do you think the oil industry has such a poor reputation on issues of racial diversity and gender equality? How does Texaco stack up against the others?*

A: The percentage of minorities within Texaco is just about average for the petroleum industry. We have made really significant progress in the last several years in improving the percentage. But there are some very interesting points that need to be examined to place in context what may be going on in this industry. I just read a study that showed that in 1995, there were only nine petroleum engineering minority graduates that came out of all engineering schools in the United States—only nine. That's not an excuse. But it is indicative of why it is difficult for this industry to have a lot of people in the pipeline. Now, of course, that does not apply to accountants, finance people, and anybody else. But we are a very technically oriented industry.

[101] *"Texaco: Lessons from a Crisis in Progress,"* Business Week, *December 2, 1996, p. 44.*

Q: *Have you personally witnessed discrimination at Texaco?*

A: In the nearly 31 years I have been with Texaco, I have never witnessed an incident of racial bias or prejudice. And had I seen it, I would have taken disciplinary action. I've never seen it.

Q: *Is there a widespread culture of insensitivity at Texaco?*

A: I do not think there is a culture of institutional bias within Texaco. I think we've got a great many very good and decent human beings, but that unfortunately we mirror society. There is bigotry in society. There is prejudice and injustice in society. I am sorry to say that, and I am sorry to say that probably does exist within Texaco. I can't do much about society, but I certainly can do something about Texaco.

Q: *What are your views on affirmative action?*

A: Texaco's views on affirmative action have not changed a bit. We have supported affirmative action, and we will continue to support affirmative action.

Q: *This is your first big trial since taking over. What have you learned?*

A: I've learned that as good as our programs are in the company—and they really are quite good, even in this area—there's always more we can do. We've got to really drill down into the programs. We've got to make certain that they're meeting the objectives and goals we've set for them.

Q: *Are there other lessons in terms of your style of management?*

A: I don't think I would do anything different the next time than what I did this time.

Q: *How will you make sure the spirit as well as the letter of the policy is followed at Texaco?*

A: We're going to put more and more and more emphasis on it until we get it through everybody's head: Bigotry is not going to be tolerated here.[102]

Robert W. Ulrich was indicted in 1997.[103] Mr. Lundwall entered a "not guilty" plea on July 8, 1997, and J. David Keough has sued Texaco for libel. Texaco named Mary Bush, a financial consultant, as its first black female board member.[104]

As Lundwall's prosecution has proceeded, new discoveries have been made. For example, "purposeful erasures" have been found on the tapes.[105]

In an interim report on its progress toward the settlement goals, Texaco revealed the following:

Polishing the Star

As part of its settlement of a discrimination lawsuit brought by black employees, Texaco has moved on a half-dozen fronts to alter its business practices.

[102] *Tim Smart, "Texaco: Lessons from a Crisis-in-Progress." Reprinted from December 2, 1996, issue of* Business Week *by special permission, © 1997 by McGraw Hill, Inc.*

[103] *Terzan Ewing, "Ex-Texaco Official Is Indicted in Case Tied to Bias Suit,"* The Wall Street Journal, *June 30, 1997, p. A9.*

[104] *"Texaco Board Names First Black Woman,"* USA Today, *July 8, 1997, p. 2B.*

[105] *Mike France and Tim Smart, "The Ugly Talk on the Texaco Tape,"* Business Week, *November 18, 1996, p. 58.*

Hiring Asked search firms to identify wider arrays of candidates. Expanded recruiting at historically minority colleges. Gave 50 scholarships and paid internships to minority students seeking engineering or technical degrees.

Career Advancement Wrote objective standards for promotions. Developing training program for new managers. Developing a mentoring program.

Diversity Initiatives Conducted two-day diversity training for more than 8,000 of 20,000 U.S. employees. Tied management bonuses to diversity goals. Developing alternative dispute resolution and ombudsman programs.

Purchasing Nearly doubled purchases from minority- or women-owned businesses. Asking suppliers to report their purchases from such companies.

Financial Services Substantially increased banking, investment management and insurance business with minority- and women-owned firms. A group of such firms underwrote a $150 million public financing.

Retailing Added three black independent retailers, 18 black managers of company-owned service stations, 12 minority or female wholesalers, 13 minority- or women-owned Xpress Lube outlets and 6 minority- or women-owned lubricant distributors.[106]

In May 1998, the Texaco executives were acquitted of all criminal charges.[107] Lawyers argued successfully that the tapes were interrupted over 500 times and were "utterly untrustworthy"[108] and that the executives had not been adequately instructed by their lawyers on document production.

Mr. Bijur's conduct in the "Jelly Bean Fiasco" was heralded by managers and academics worldwide. He was in demand at virtually all large conferences as a guest speaker. However, Texaco did not perform as well as other oil companies during his tenure. For example, Texaco and Chevron each had revenues of $50 million in 2000, but Texaco's profits were $2.5 billion, as compared to Chevron's $5.2 billion. Near the end of 2000, the Texaco board agreed to merge the company with Chevron.

Before that merger occurred, Mr. Bijur resigned abruptly from Texaco after being summoned by the Texaco board to a meeting at which the board announced that it had lost confidence in him. There had been a series of issues such as the $2 million remodeling of the corporate suite at New York City's Carlyle Hotel, the use of the company jet, and his romance with a subordinate whom he eventually married in the summer of 2000. Texaco and Mr. Bijur have declined to discuss the issues, but an audit concludes that while there may have been bad judgment in Mr. Bijur's behavior and decisions, there was nothing illegal or even "serious."[109]

Discussion Questions

1. Provide a summary of the players and their concerns.

[106] *Bryant, "How Much Has Texaco Changed?" pp. BU1, BU16.*

[107] *David E. Rovella, "Texaco Execs' Verdicts Roil Prosecution,"* National Law Journal, *May 25, 1998, pp. B1, B2.*

[108] *Steve Liesman, "Texaco Bias Case Leads to Acquittals,"* The Wall Street Journal, *May 13, 1998, p. A3.*

[109] *Thaddeus Herrick and Nikhil Deogun, "Insiders Assert Behavior an Issue with Texaco CEO,"* The Wall Street Journal, *March 16, 2001, pp. B1, B4.*

2. Discuss the ethics of the recording.
3. Why do you think the executives discussed document destruction?
4. What ethical issues surround diversity training and affirmative action?
5. Evaluate Texaco's performance and Mr. Bijur's behavior since the time of the settlement of this case. Consider that Texaco's spending with minority firms was at $528 million, just 2 years into its 5-year-$1 billion promise.[110]
6. Read the following and discuss whether Mr. Bijur acted in the shareholders' interests.

A Texaco Chairman Who Believed the N.Y. Times[111]

Paul Craig Roberts

Texaco and its shareholders are the first victims of the 1991 Civil Rights act. This legislation permits plaintiffs in job-discrimination cases to be awarded compensatory and punitive damages in addition to back pay.

Before the 1991 act, class-action suits threatened companies that lacked race and gender proportion in their work force with having to fork over years of back pay to preferred minorities who had not been hired. Since there was seldom any evidence that the companies had actually discriminated against any of the individuals, the companies would sometimes fight these suits rather than settle them.

This rankled the sharp lawyers who make tens of millions of dollars off such lawsuits and civil rights groups that need voluntary settlements of discrimination suits as proof of institutionalized racism. They wanted a bigger club over the companies to force faster and easier settlements, and the Bush administration gave it to them by adding compensatory and punitive damages.

This tripled the cost to a company of losing a discrimination suit in court, thereby making settlement instead of trial a near certainty. Since the accused company just wants to settle, the accuser does not need evidence that would have to stand up in court.

The Texaco case illustrates this perfectly. Michael Hausfeld, the lawyer for the black employees, claimed to have an audio tape of Texaco executives using racial slurs while conspiring to hide evidence of Texaco's discrimination. He gave what he said was a transcript of the incriminating tape to Kurt Eichenwald of the New York Times. Mr. Eichenwald was not sufficiently professional to recognize Mr. Hausfeld's vested interest ($38.3 million is his and co-counsel Dan Berger's share of the settlement), and he did not ask to listen to the tape and to check the transcript against it. He quoted on trust from the inflammatory transcript that was handed to him.

[110] *"Texaco's Spending with Minority Firms Ahead of Five-Year Plan,"* The Wall Street Journal, *March 17, 1999, p. B6.*

[111] *Paul Craig Roberts, "A Texaco Chairman Who Believed The N.Y. Times,"* The Washington Times, *December 15, 1996, p. 32. Reprinted by permission of Paul Craig Roberts and Creators Syndicate, Inc.*

The next mistake in the farce was made by Texaco Chairman Peter I. Bijur. He believed the New York Times still had reportorial integrity and was horrified by what he read about his executives. He quickly announced a generous settlement and placed financial sanctions on the presumed guilty executives. All of this happened before anyone listened to the tapes. When the tapes were finally transcribed by disinterested professionals, it turned out that Mr. Eichenwald's report, the catalyst for the record settlement, was inaccurate. No one had used a racial epithet, and the reference to black employees as jelly beans was an innocent multicultural metaphor that diversity trainers had taught the company to use. All Texaco employees are jelly beans, and the different colors are supposed to be appropriately mixed in the jar. What the company executives are actually protesting in the taped conversation is the "us-them" attitude of black employees: "You can't have just we and them. You can't just have black jelly beans and other jelly beans. It doesn't work," said Texaco treasurer Robert Ulrich.

The outcome is that the New York Times reporter's predisposition to believe in a racist corporate America made it easy for a sharp lawyer to use him to win a big case and establish a precedent: Companies that established quotas for hiring now will have to establish them for promotions. If they do not, every one of the preferred minorities on their payrolls can use the club of compensatory and punitive damages to extort large settlements.

But this is the least of it. Texaco's abject surrender to a lie has cemented into the belief system the image of racist America that civil rights plaintiffs have labored to establish. Corporate America is in a dither. Quotas are not more important to success than marketing, finance, or manufacturing. There is talk of providing boards of directors with full-time staffs to implement and monitor "diversity goals."

The ultimate casualty may be California's Civil Rights Initiative (already, a federal judge temporarily has blocked its implementation). The initiative, which passed comfortably in the November elections, seeks to reestablish equality before the law in California state and local government employment and university admissions. But it will prove difficult to admit students and to hire and promote government employees by individual merit alone when group rights are the rule in corporate America.

CASE 4.14

Hunter Tylo: Pregnancy Is Not a BFOQ

Hunter Tylo was hired by Spelling Entertainment Group to play a character who would "strut in a bikini to steal actress Heather Locklear's husband" on the television show *Melrose Place.* Ms. Tylo never began work on the contract because she was fired after she disclosed to the show's executives that she was pregnant.[112]

Mr. Spelling, the owner of the Spelling Entertainment Group, explained that Ms. Tylo was fired because he did not think it was fair to have scripts rewritten around a character and actress who had not yet appeared on the show. Mr. Spelling noted that

[112] *Maureen Dowd, "Civil Rights Siren,"* The New York Times, *December 24, 1997, p. A13.*

he had worked with Ms. Locklear during her pregnancy, using various camera angles to avoid revealing Ms. Locklear's pregnancy.

In a letter to Mr. Spelling from actress Gabrielle Carteris, who plays a character on Mr. Spelling's other show, *Beverly Hills 90210*, Ms. Carteris expressed support for Mr. Spelling, "I just had to let you know how sorry I am with regards to the trial. It was particularly upsetting, when for me you were so very supportive of my getting pregnant."[113]

Mr. Spelling also said that following Ms. Tylo's termination, he offered her a contract for the following season that would have paid more than her fee of $13,500 per episode that was provided on the terminated contract and that the new contract would have run for more episodes. Ms. Tylo refused the offer and filed suit. She was awarded $4 million by a jury for emotional distress and $894,601 for economic loss.[114]

Discussion Questions

1. Is there a distinction between Ms. Tylo's circumstances and Ms. Locklear's?
2. Is not being pregnant a BFOQ (bona fide occupational qualification) for playing a "vixen" on a television series?
3. Did Mr. Spelling give sufficient justification for Ms. Tylo's termination?

[113] *Ann Oldenburg, "'Hurt' Spelling Says Tylo's Pregnancy Wasn't Issue,"* USA Today, *December 26, 1997, p. 1D.*

[114] *Ann Oldenburg, "Actress Fired for Being Pregnant Wins Lawsuit,"* USA Today, *December 23, 1997, p. 1D.*

4f

Whistle-Blowing

In a true confrontation between personal values and company policy, employees are often faced with the knowledge that their employer is acting unethically in a way that does or could hurt someone else. How should they react? What should they do? Why do employers often ignore employees' concerns?

READING 4.15

The Options for Whistle-Blowers

Employees who are faced with a situation at work in which their values are at odds with the actions of their employers are grappling with their sense of loyalty to the company and their co-workers as well as their own value system. For example, an employee who knows that her company's product is defective is torn between her concern for customers who buy the product and her loyalty to the company and her fellow workers, who may also be her friends. She is concerned about her livelihood, her co-workers' livelihood, and the safety of others. Table 1 on the following page illustrates the options available to those who find their values at odds with the company's conduct.

Discussion Questions

1. What choices do whistle-blowers have?

2. As you read the following cases, decide which type of whistle-blower was involved.

CASE 4.16

Beech-Nut and the No-Apple-Juice Apple Juice

Jerome J. LiCari was the director of research and development for Beech-Nut Nutrition Corporation. Beech-Nut, at the time of LiCari's employment (in the late 1970s and early 1980s), was the second-largest baby food manufacturer in the United

unit 4
section f

Table 1
Employee Concerns and Employee Dissent

	nature of the perceived activity triggering the concern			
	illegal, immoral, or illegitimate		*not illegal, immoral, or illegitimate*	
Expression of the concern (voice)	*Exit dimension*			
	Stay	*Go*	*Stay*	*Go*
External dissent to someone who can take action	External whistle-blowing	Exit with public protest	Secret sharing	Exit with secret sharing
Internal dissent to someone who can take action	Internal whistle-blowing	Protest during exit interview	Employee participation, grievance	Explain reason for resignation in exit
Dissent in some other form	Discussion, confrontation with wrongdoer	Exit with notice to wrongdoer	Sabotage, strikes	Sabotage, strikes with exit
No expressed dissent	Inactive observation	Inactive departure	Silent disgruntlement	Silent departure

From: Peter B. Jubb, "Whistleblowing: A Restrictive Definition and Interpretation," 21 Journal of Business Ethics *77, 80 (1999). Reprinted with kind permission of Kluwer Academic Publishers.*

States. Beech-Nut is a subsidiary of Nestlé, the international food producer based in Switzerland.

In 1977, Beech-Nut entered into an agreement with Interjuice Trading Corporation (the Universal Juice Corporation) for apple juice concentrate. The deal was a lifesaver for Beech-Nut because Interjuice's prices were 20 percent below market and Beech-Nut was heavily in debt, had only 15 percent of the baby food market, and was operating out of a badly maintained eighty-year-old plant in Canajoharie, New York.

Beech-Nut had once had a profitable product line with its chewing gum, but its parent, Squibb Corp., sold the chewing gum segment and the Beech-Nut name in 1973. The baby food division had never been a profitable part of Squibb's business and, by 1978, creditors and debts were mounting.

With apple concentrate in 30 percent of Beech-Nut's baby food products, the 1977 Interjuice contract marked the company's turnaround point. Nestlé was attracted and bought Beech-Nut in 1979. However, because of its substantially increased marketing costs, Beech-Nut's money pressures remained.

Rumors of adulteration (or the addition or substituted use of inferior substances in a product) were flying in the apple juice industry at the time of the Beech-Nut/Interjuice contract. Chemists in LiCari's department were suspicious. At that time, accurate tests for adulteration did not exist, but LiCari and his chemists devised tests that revealed added ingredients, such as corn sugar, in the concentrate.

In October 1978, Dr. LiCari received additional information suggesting that that concentrate might be adulterated, that is, might be made of syrups and edible substances other than, and cheaper than, apples. LiCari reported this information to John Lavery. As vice president for operations, Lavery was responsible for the purchasing and processing of apple juice concentrates used in Beech-Nut's apple juice and in its "mixed juice" products. When Neils Hoyvald became Beech-Nut's president and chief executive officer in April 1981, Lavery reported directly to him.

In response, Lavery sent two employees to inspect Universal's blending operation. What the employees found, however, was only a warehouse without any blending facility. Lavery did not attempt to determine the location of the blending operation and pursue an inspection. Instead, he required Universal to give the company a "hold harmless" agreement which was intended to protect Beech-Nut from legal claims related to the juice.

Thereafter, as a result of tests, LiCari continued to express to Lavery his concerns about the quality of the concentrate supplied by Universal; he argued that a supplier willing to adulterate the concentrate in the first place would likely have little compunction about continuing to supply adulterated product after signing a hold-harmless document. Lavery's response was that the agreement would adequately protect the company even if the juice was adulterated.

Lavery told LiCari that Universal's price to Beech-Nut for the concentrate was 50 cents to a dollar per gallon below the price charged by the company's previous supplier. He stated that, because of the tremendous economic pressure under which the company was operating, he would not change suppliers unless LiCari's tests were sufficient to prove in a court of law that the concentrate was adulterated. He directed LiCari to give the testing low priority.

In 1979, LiCari had the concentrate analyzed by an outside laboratory. The test results showed that the concentrate consisted primarily of sugar syrup. Lavery was informed of these results but took no action. In July 1979, Lavery received a memorandum from the company's plant manager in San Jose, California, advising him that approximately 95,000 pounds of concentrate inventory was "funny" and "adulterated," in that it was "almost pure corn syrup." The plant manager suggested that Beech-Nut demand its money back from the supplier. Instead, Lavery, who did not dispute the accuracy of these reports, instructed the manager to use the tainted concentrate in the company's mixed juices. These, too, were labeled 100 percent pure juice. The company continued to purchase its apple juice concentrate from Universal.

On numerous occasions thereafter, Beech-Nut's scientists advised Lavery of their concerns that the apple juice concentrate was adulterated. In August 1981, LiCari sent a memorandum to Charles Jones, the company's purchasing manager, with a copy to Lavery, stating that although the scientists had not proven that the concentrate was adulterated there was "a tremendous amount of circumstantial evidence" to that effect, "paint[ing] a grave case against the current supplier." LiCari's memorandum concluded that "[i]t is imperative that Beech-Nut establish the authenticity of the Apple Juice Concentrate used to formulate our products. If the authenticity cannot be established, I feel that we have sufficient reason to look for a new supplier."[115]

Lavery took no action to change suppliers. Rather, he instructed Jones to ignore LiCari's memorandum, criticized LiCari for not being a "team player," and called his scientists "Chicken Little." He threatened to fire LiCari.[116]

[115] *Chris Welles, "What Led Beech-Nut Down the Road to Disgrace,"* Business Week, *February 22, 1988, pp. 124–128.*

[116] U.S. v. Beech-Nut, Inc., *871 F.2d 1181 (2nd Cir. 1989), at 1185; 925 F.2d 604 (2nd Cir. 1991);* cert. denied, *493 U.S. 933 (1989).*

In late 1981, the company received, unsolicited, a report from a Swiss laboratory concluding that Beech-Nut's apple juice product was adulterated, stating, "[t]he apple juice is false, can not see any apple."[117] Lavery reviewed this report, and one of his aides sent it to Universal. Universal made no response, and Beech-Nut took no action.

Both before and after becoming president of Beech-Nut in April 1981, Hoyvald received information from several sources about the adulteration problem. In November, purchasing manager Jones raised the problem. Hoyvald took no action in response to any of these communications. Rather, he told Lavery that, for budgetary reasons, he would not approve a change in concentrate suppliers until 1983.[118]

In the spring of 1982, Paul Hillabush, the company's director of quality assurance, advised Hoyvald not to be surprised by adverse publicity concerning Beech-Nut's purchases of apple juice concentrate. This information was passed along because on June 25, 1982, a detective hired by the Processed Apple Institute had visited Lavery at the Beech-Nut manufacturing facility in Canajoharie, New York, and advised him that Beech-Nut was about to be involved in a lawsuit as a result of its use of adulterated juice.

LiCari continued to take his evidence to Hoyvald. Hoyvald told LiCari he would take up the issue. Several months later, after no action had been taken, LiCari resigned. In his evaluation of LiCari's performance for 1981, John Lavery had written that LiCari had great technical ability but that his judgment was "colored by naivete and impractical ideals."[119]

After leaving Beech-Nut, LiCari wrote an anonymous letter to the Food and Drug Administration (FDA) disclosing the juice adulteration at Beech-Nut. He signed the letter, "Johnny Appleseed."

After LiCari left, the pressure at Beech-Nut to continue using the adulterated apple juice increased because of operating losses. In 1982, a private investigator for the Processed Apples Institute, Inc., showed Canajoharie plant operators documents from the Interjuice dumpster and new tests indicating that the juice was adulterated. The institute invited Beech-Nut to join its lawsuit against Interjuice.

Beech-Nut did not join the suit (which eventually closed Interjuice) but did cancel its contracts. However, Beech-Nut continued to sell the juice and juice products it had on hand until 1983 when the FDA ordered it to issue a juice recall. Beech-Nut had $3.5 million in apple-juice-product inventory.

An FDA investigator observed:

> They played a cat-and-mouse game with us. When FDA would identify a specific apple juice lot as tainted, Beech-Nut would quickly destroy it before the FDA could seize it, an act that would have created negative publicity.[120]

When New York state government tests first revealed that a batch contained little or no apple juice, Beech-Nut had the juice moved during the night using nine tanker

[117] Id.

[118] Id.

[119] *Welles, "What Led Beech-Nut Down the Road to Disgrace," p. 128.*

[120] Id.

trucks. Hoyvald realized that an inability to sell this inventory would be financially crippling to the company, and so he began delaying tactics designed to give the company time to sell it.

To avoid seizure of the inventory in New York by state officials in August 1982, Hoyvald had this juice moved out of state during the night. It was transported from the New York plant to a warehouse in Secaucus, New Jersey, and the records of this shipment and others were withheld from FDA investigators until the investigators independently located the carrier Beech-Nut had used. While the FDA was searching for the adulterated products but before it had discovered the Secaucus warehouse, Hoyvald ordered virtually the entire stock in that warehouse shipped to Beech-Nut's distributor in Puerto Rico; the Puerto Rico distributor had not placed an order for the product and had twice refused to buy the product even at great discounts offered personally by Hoyvald.

Similarly, in September 1982, Hoyvald ordered a rush shipment of the inventory of apple juice products held at Beech-Nut's San Jose plant, and took a number of unusual steps to get rid of the entire stock. He authorized price discounts of 50 percent; the largest discount ever offered theretofore had been 10 percent. Hoyvald insisted that the product be shipped "fast, fast, fast," and gave a distributor in the Dominican Republic only two days, instead of the usual thirty, to consider and respond to this product promotion. Further, in order to get the juice out of the warehouse and out of the country as quickly as possible, the company shipped it to the Dominican Republic on the first possible sailing date, which was from an unusually distant port, thereby raising the freight cost to a level nearly equal to the value of the goods themselves. Finally, this stock was shipped before Beech-Nut had received the necessary financial documentation from the distributor, which, as one Beech-Nut employee testified, was "tantamount to giving the stuff away."[121]

Hoyvald also used Beech-Nut's lawyers to help delay the government investigation, thereby giving the company more time to sell its inventory of adulterated juice before the product could be seized or a recall could be ordered. For example, in September 1982, the FDA informed Beech-Nut that it intended to seize all of Beech-Nut's apple juice products made from Universal concentrate; in October, New York State authorities advised the company that they planned to initiate a local recall of these products. Beech-Nut's lawyers, at Hoyvald's direction, successfully negotiated with the authorities for a limited recall, excluding products held by retailers and stocks of mixed juice products. Beech-Nut thus eventually agreed to conduct a nationwide recall only of apple juice, and by the time of the recall Hoyvald knew that more than 97 percent of the earlier stocks of apple juice had been sold. In December 1982, in response to Hoyvald's request, Thomas Ward, a member of a law firm retained by Beech-Nut, sent Hoyvald a letter that summarized the events surrounding the apple juice concentrate problem as follows:

> From the start, we had two main objectives:
>
> 1) to minimize Beech-Nut's potential economic loss, which we understand has been conservatively estimated at $3.5 million, and
>
> 2) to minimize any damage to the company's reputation.

[121] U.S. v. Beech-Nut, Inc., *871 F.2d, at 1186. This segment of the case was adapted from the judicial opinion.*

> We determined that this could be done by delaying, for as long as possible, any market withdrawal of products produced from the Universal Juice concentrate. . . .
>
> . . . In spite of the recognition that FDA might wish to have Beech-Nut recall some of its products, management decided to continue sales of all such products for the time being. . . . The decision to continue sales and some production of the products was based upon the recognition of the significant potential financial loss and loss of goodwill, and the fact that apple juice is a critical lead-in item for Beech-Nut.
>
> Since the mixed fruit juices and other products constituted the bulk of the products produced with Universal concentrate, one of our main goals became to prevent the FDA and state authorities from focusing on these products, and we were in fact successful in limiting the controversy strictly to apple juice.[122]

In November 1986, Beech-Nut, Hoyvald, and Lavery, along with Universal's proprietor Zeev Kaplansky and four others ("suppliers"), were indicted on charges relating to the company's sale of adulterated and misbranded apple juice products. Hoyvald and Lavery were charged with (1) one count of conspiring with the suppliers to violate the FDCA, 21 U.S.C. §§ 331(a), (k), and 333(b) (1982 & Supp. IV 1986), in violation of 18 U.S.C. § 371; (2) 20 counts of mail fraud, in violation of 18 U.S.C. §§ 1341 and 2; and (3) 429 counts of introducing adulterated and misbranded apple juice into interstate commerce, in violation of 21 U.S.C. §§ 331(a) and 333(b) and 18 U.S.C. § 2. The suppliers were also charged with introducing adulterated concentrate into interstate commerce; Hoyvald and Lavery were not charged with any substantive offense regarding the concentrate itself, either directly or as aiders and abettors.

Hoyvald and Lavery pleaded not guilty to the charges against them. Eventually, Beech-Nut pleaded guilty to 215 felony violations of §§ 331(a) and 333(b); it received a $2,000,000 fine and was ordered to pay $140,000 to the FDA for the expenses of its investigation. Kaplansky and the other four supplier-defendants also eventually pleaded guilty to some or all of the charges against them. Hoyvald and Lavery thus went to trial alone. LiCari testified at the trials, "I thought apple juice should be made from apples."[123]

Prior to trial, Hoyvald and Lavery made various motions, including (1) a motion to dismiss the substantive FDCA counts against them on the ground that none of the acts on which those counts were based occurred in the Eastern District of New York, and hence venue was improper; and (2) a motion to dismiss the conspiracy count on the ground that it pleaded two conspiracies rather than a single conspiracy. In an opinion reported at 659 F.Supp. 1487 (1987), the district court denied both motions. It denied the venue motion on the ground that, since transportation is necessary for the "introduction" of goods into commerce, the FDCA offenses were continuing crimes under 18 U.S.C. § 3237(a) (1982 & Supp. IV 1986) and venue was thus proper in any district in which the offenses were begun, continued, or completed. It denied the motion to dismiss the conspiracy count, finding that the indictment adequately alleged a single conspiracy albeit with multiple objectives.

The trial began in November 1987 and continued for three months. The government's evidence included that previously discussed. Hoyvald's principal defense was

[122] Id. *at 1186–1187.*

[123] *Welles, "What Led Beech-Nut Down the Road to Disgrace," p. 128.*

that all of his acts relating to the problem of adulterated concentrate had been performed on the advice of counsel. For example, there was evidence that the Beech-Nut shipment of adulterated juices from its San Jose plant to the Dominican Republic followed the receipt by Hoyvald of a telex sent by Sheldon Klein, an associate of the law firm representing Beech-Nut, which summarized a telephone conference between Beech-Nut officials and its attorneys as follows:

> We understand that approximately 25,000 cases of apple juice manufactured from concentrate purchased from Universal Juice is [sic] currently in San Jose. It is strongly recommended that such product and all other Universal products in Beech-Nut's possession anywhere in the US be destroyed before a meeting with [the FDA] takes place.[124]

Hoyvald and Klein testified that they had a follow-up conversation in which Klein told Hoyvald that, as an alternative, it would be lawful to export the adulterated apple juice products.

The jury returned a verdict of guilty on all of the counts against Lavery. It returned a verdict of guilty against Hoyvald on 359 counts of adulterating and misbranding apple juice, all of which related to shipments after June 25, 1982. It was unable to reach a verdict on the remaining counts against Hoyvald, which related to events prior to that date.

The federal district court sentenced Hoyvald to a term of imprisonment of a year and a day, fined him $100,000, imposed a $9,000 special assessment, and ordered him to pay the costs of prosecution. In March 1989, the federal court of appeals for the second circuit reversed the conviction on the ground that venue was improperly laid in the Eastern District instead of the Northern District of New York. The case was remanded to the district court for a new trial.[125] In August 1989 Hoyvald was retried before Chief Judge Platt on 19 of the counts on which a mistrial had been declared during his first trial. After four weeks of trial, the jury was unable to agree on a verdict and a mistrial was declared.

Rather than face a third trial Hoyvald entered into a plea agreement with the government on November 7, 1989. It was agreed that the government would recommend that the court impose a suspended sentence; five years probation, including 1,000 hours of community service; and a $100,000 fine. On November 13, 1989, the district court accepted the plea and imposed sentence. At that plea proceeding Judge Platt agreed, at Hoyvald's request, to defer the beginning of his community service to give him three weeks time to travel to Denmark to visit his 84-year-old mother.

Six months later, in May 1990, Hoyvald again requested permission from his probation officer to return to Denmark to visit his mother, and then to be permitted to visit "East and West Germany, Switzerland, Hungary, Czechoslovakia, and Greece" on business, a journey that would take slightly more than three weeks. The Probation Department expressed no opposition to the trip so long as he "supplies an appropriate itinerary and documentation as to the business portions of his trip." The United States Attorney did not oppose the request. On May 22, 1990, Hoyvald requested

[124] U.S. v. Beech-Nut, Inc., *871 F.2d 1181, at 1194. Again, this material is adapted from the case.*

[125] United States v. Beech-Nut Nutrition Corp., *871 F.2d 1181 (2nd Cir.)*, cert. denied, *493 U.S. 933, 110 S.Ct. 324, 107 L.Ed.2d 314 (1989).*

permission to travel to the other European countries to "look for a job and to investigate business opportunities" in those countries. The district court ruled that Hoyvald could visit his mother in Denmark but denied the request to travel to other countries.

Discussion Questions

1. No one was ever made ill or harmed by the "fake" apple juice. Was LiCari justified in his concern?
2. Did LiCari follow the lines of authority in his efforts? Is this important for a "whistle-blower"? Why?
3. LiCari had only circumstantial evidence at one point. Is this type of evidence sufficient?
4. What pressures contributed to Beech-Nut's unwillingness to switch suppliers?
5. When no change was made in the supply contract, could LiCari have stayed with Beech-Nut?
6. Why did LiCari write anonymously to the FDA?
7. Is it troublesome that Hoyvald and Lavery escaped sentences on a technicality? Is the sentence too light?
8. Is the judge being unreasonable in denying Mr. Hoyvald's travel requests?

CASE 4.17

NASA and the Space Shuttle Booster Rockets

Morton Thiokol, Inc., an aerospace company, manufactures the solid propellent rocket motors for the Peacekeeper missile and the missiles on Trident nuclear submarines. Thiokol also worked closely with the National Aeronautics and Space Administration (NASA) in developing the *Challenger*, one of NASA's reusable space shuttles.

Morton Thiokol served as the manufacturer for the booster rockets used to launch the *Challenger*. NASA had scheduled a special launch of the *Challenger* for January 1986. The launch was highly publicized because NASA had conducted a nationwide search for a teacher to send on the flight. For NASA's twenty-fifth shuttle mission, teacher Christa McAuliffe would be on board.

On the scheduled launch day, January 28, 1986, the weather was cloudy and cold at the John F. Kennedy Space Center in Cape Canaveral, Florida. The launch had already been delayed several times, but NASA officials still contacted Thiokol engineers in Utah to discuss whether the shuttle should be launched in such cold weather. The temperature range for the boosters, as specified in Thiokol's contract with NASA, was between 40° F and 90° F.

The temperature at Cape Canaveral that January morning was below 30° F. The launch of the *Challenger* proceeded nevertheless. A presidential commission later concluded, "Thiokol management reversed its position and recommended the launch of [the *Challenger*] at the urging of [NASA] and contrary to the views of its engineers in order to accommodate a major customer."[126]

Two of the Thiokol engineers involved in the launch, Allan McDonald and Roger Boisjoly, later testified that they had opposed the launch. Boisjoly had done work on the shuttle's booster rockets at the Marshall Space Flight Center in Utah in February 1985, at which time he noted that at low temperatures, an O-ring assembly in the rockets eroded and, consequently, failed to seal properly. Though Boisjoly gave a presentation on the issue, little action was taken over the course of the year. Boisjoly conveyed his frustration in his activity reports. Finally, in July 1985, Boisjoly wrote a confidential memo to R. K. (Bob) Lund, Thiokol's vice president for engineering. An excerpt follows:

> This letter is written to insure that management is fully aware of the seriousness of the current O-ring erosion problem. . . . The mistakenly accepted position on the joint problem was to fly without fear of failure. . . . [This position] is now drastically changed as a result of the SRM [shuttle recovery mission] 16A nozzle joint erosion which eroded a secondary O-ring with the primary O-ring never sealing. If the same scenario should occur in a field joint (and it could), then it is a jump ball as to the success or failure of the joint. . . . The result would be a catastrophe of the highest order—loss of human life. . . .
>
> It is my honest and real fear that if we do not take immediate action to dedicate a team to solve the problem, with the field joint having the number one priority, then we stand in jeopardy of losing a flight along with all the launch pad facilities.[127]

In October 1985, Boisjoly presented the O-ring issue at a conference of the Society of Automotive Engineers and requested suggestions for resolution.[128]

On January 27, 1986, the day before the launch, Boisjoly attempted to halt the launch. Mr. McDonald also offered his insights to a group of NASA and Thiokol engineers, However, four Thiokol managers, including Lund, voted unanimously to recommend the launch. One manager had urged Lund to "take off his engineering hat and put on his management hat."[129] The managers then developed the following revised recommendations. Engineers were excluded from the final decision and the development of these findings.[130]

- Calculations show that SRM-25 [the designation for the *Challenger's* January 28 flight] O-rings will be 20° colder than SRM-15 O-rings
- Temperature data not conclusive on predicting primary O-ring blow-by
- Engineering assessment is that:
  - Colder O-rings will have increased effective durometer [that is, they will be harder]

[126] *Judith Dobrzynski, "Morton Thiokol: Reflections on the Shuttle Disaster,"* Business Week, *March 14, 1988, p. 82.*

[127] *Russell Boisjoly, et al., "Roger Boisjoly and the* Challenger *Disaster: The Ethical Dimensions,"* Journal of Business Ethics *8, 1989, pp. 217–230.*

[128] *"No. 2 Official Is Appointed at Thiokol,"* The New York Times, *June 12, 1992, p. C3; "Whistle-blowing: Not Always a Losing Game,"* EE Spectrum, *December 1990, pp. 49–52.*

[129] *Boisjoly, "Roger Boisjoly and the* Challenger *Disaster," pp. 217–230.*

[130] *Paul Hoversten, "Engineers Waver, then Decide to Launch,"* USA Today, *January 22, 1996, p. 2A.*

- "Harder" O-rings will take longer to seat
- More gas may pass primary [SRM-25] O-ring before the primary seal seats (relative to SRM-15)
- Demonstrated sealing threshold [on SRM-25 O-ring] is 3 times greater than 0.038" erosion experienced on SRM-15
- If the primary seal does not seat, the secondary seal will seat
- Pressure will get to secondary seal before the metal parts rotate
- O-ring pressure leak check places secondary seal in outboard position which minimizes sealing time
- MTI recommends STS-51L launch proceed on 28 January 1986
- SRM-25 will not be significantly different from SRM-15[131]

After the decision was made, Boisjoly returned to his office and wrote in his journal:

> I sincerely hope this launch does not result in a catastrophe. I personally do not agree with some of the statements made in Joe Kilminster's [Kilminster was one of the four Thiokol managers who voted to recommend the launch] written summary stating that SRM-25 is okay to fly.[132]

Seventy-four seconds into the *Challenger* launch, the low temperature caused the seals at the booster rocket joints to fail. The *Challenger* exploded, killing Christa McAuliffe and the six astronauts on board.[133]

The subsequent investigation by the presidential commission placed the blame for the faulty O-rings squarely with Thiokol. Charles S. Locke, Thiokol's CEO, maintained, "I take the position that we never agreed to the launch at the temperature at the time of the launch. The *Challenger* incident resulted more from human error than mechanical error. The decision to launch should have been referred to headquarters. If we'd been consulted here, we'd never have given clearance, because the temperature was not within the contracted specs."[134]

Both Boisjoly and McDonald testified before the presidential panel regarding their opposition to the launch and the decision of their managers (who were also engineers) to override their recommendation. Both Boisjoly and McDonald also testified that following their expressed opposition to the launch and their willingness to come forward, they had been isolated from NASA and subsequently demoted. Since testifying, McDonald has been assigned to "special projects." Boisjoly, who took medical leave for post-traumatic stress disorder, has left Thiokol, but receives disability pay from the company. Currently, Mr. Boisjoly operates a consulting firm in Mesa, Arizona. He speaks frequently on business ethics to professional organizations and companies.[135]

In May 1986, then-CEO Locke stated, in an interview with *The Wall Street Journal*, "This shuttle thing will cost us this year 10¢ a share."[136] Locke later protested that his statement had been taken out of context.[137]

[131] *Boisjoly, "Roger Boisjoly and the* Challenger *Disaster," pp. 217–230.*

[132] *Interview with Roger Boisjoly, June 28, 1993.*

[133] *Paul Hoversten, Patricia Edmonds, and Haya El Nasser, "Debate Raged Night Before Doomed Launch,"* USA Today, *January 22, 1996, pp. A1, A2.*

[134] *Dobrzynski, "Morton Thiokol," p. 82.*

[135] *Interview with Roger Boisjoly.*

[136] *Dobrzynski, "Morton Thiokol," p. 82.*

[137] *"No. 2 Official Is Appointed at Thiokol," p. C3; "Whistle-blowing," pp. 49–52.*

In 1989, Morton Norwich separated from Thiokol Chemical Corporation. The two companies had previously merged to become Morton Thiokol. Following the separation, Thiokol Chemical became Thiokol Corporation. Morton returned to the salt business, and Thiokol, remained under contract with NASA through 1999, redesigned its space shuttle rocket motor to correct the deficiencies. No one at Thiokol was fired following the *Challenger* accident. Because of this incident and defense contractor indictments, the Government Accountability Project was established in Washington, D.C. The office provides a staff, legal assistance, and pamphlets to help whistle-blowers working on government projects.

Discussion Questions

1. Who is morally responsible for the deaths that resulted from the *Challenger* explosion?

2. If you had been in Allan McDonald's or Roger Boisjoly's position on January 28, 1986, what would you have done?

3. Evaluate Locke's comment on the loss of ten cents per share.

4. Should the possibility that the booster rockets might not perform below 30° F have been a factor in the decision to allow the launch to proceed?

5. Roger Boisjoly offers the following advice on whistle-blowing:

   a. You owe your organization an opportunity to respond. Speak to them first verbally. Memos are not appropriate for the first step.
   b. Gather collegial support for your position. If you cannot get the support then make sure you are correct.
   c. Spell out the problem in a letter.

   Mr. Boisjoly acknowledges he did not gather collegial support. How can such support be obtained? Where would you start? What would you use to persuade others?

6. Scientist William Lourance has written, ". . . a thing is safe if its attendant risks are judged to be acceptable."[138] Had everyone, including the astronauts, accepted the risks attendant to the *Challenger's* launch?

7. Groupthink is defined as

   > . . . a mode of thinking that people engage in when they are deeply involved in a cohesive in-group, when the members' strivings for unanimity override their motivation to realistically appraise alternative courses of action. . . . Groupthink refers to the deterioration of mental efficiency, reality testing, and moral judgment that results from in-group pressures.[139]

   Is this what happened when Thiokol's management group took off its "engineering hats"?

[138] *Joseph R. Herkert, "Management's Hat Trick: Misuse of 'Engineering Judgment' in the* Challenger *Incident,"* Journal of Business Ethics *10, 1991, p. 617.*

[139] *Irving L. Janis,* Victims of Groupthink, *Houghton, Mifflin, Boston, MA: 1972.*

CASE 4.18

Dow Corning and the Silicone Implants: Questions of Safety and Disclosure

The Development of the Silicone-Filled Breast Implant

In the early 1960s, Dow Corning and other manufacturers began marketing silicone-filled implants for use in breast enlargement procedures. The silicone implants are breast-shaped bags filled with silicone gel. The bag itself is made of another form of silicone that is like a heavy plastic; this latter material is the same substance used in sealant and the children's toy, Silly Putty.

The other companies that manufactured the implants included Heyer-Schulte Corporation, to which several Dow Corning scientists and salesmen had migrated along with their silicone gel implant knowledge, and McGhan Medical Corporation, an offspring corporation resulting from the subsequent departure of the Dow migrants from Heyer-Schulte. Much of the attention regarding the implants has focused on Dow Corning because the Heyer-Schulte and McGhan implants simply duplicated the Dow Corning product, and these other manufacturers relied upon Dow's implant tests.

Transfers of the ownership of implant firms have exacerbated the complexity of implant liability. That complexity is somewhat simplified in Figure 1.

In the mid-1970s, Dow Corning conducted animal studies regarding problems with leakage from the implants. Though Dow furnished the studies to the FDA, it did so under a confidentiality procedure that prevented their disclosure under the Freedom of Information Act.

In the course of conducting its research, Dow Corning found that laboratory animals exposed to silicone gels developed tumors. A panel of research experts examined the Dow Corning studies and concluded that 80 percent of the exposed animals had developed tumors. The figure was so high that the panel deemed the research suspect and labeled the study "inconclusive." A 1975 study eventually discovered during litigation in 1994 explained that silicone implants harmed the immune systems of mice. A lawyer representing women in a class action suit against Dow found the study among Dow documents.

Internal Studies and Safety Questions

Thomas D. Talcott, a Dow materials engineer, disputed the panel's conclusions and resigned from the firm in 1976 after a dispute with his supervisors over the safety of the implants. Internal documents from Dow Corning, revealed later in ongoing litigation, indicate that Mr. Talcott was not a lone dissenter on the safety issue. Also in 1976, the chairman of the Dow Corning task force working on the new implants wrote, "We are engulfed in unqualified speculation. Nothing to date is truly quantitative. Is there something that migrates out or off the mammary prosthesis? Yes or no? Does it continue for the life of the implant or is it limited or controlled for a period of time? What is it?"[140] According to a Dow Corning salesperson's 1980 characterization, "[the Dow

[140] *"Records Show Firm Delayed Breast Implant Safety Study,"* Mesa Tribune, *January 13, 1992, p. A1.*

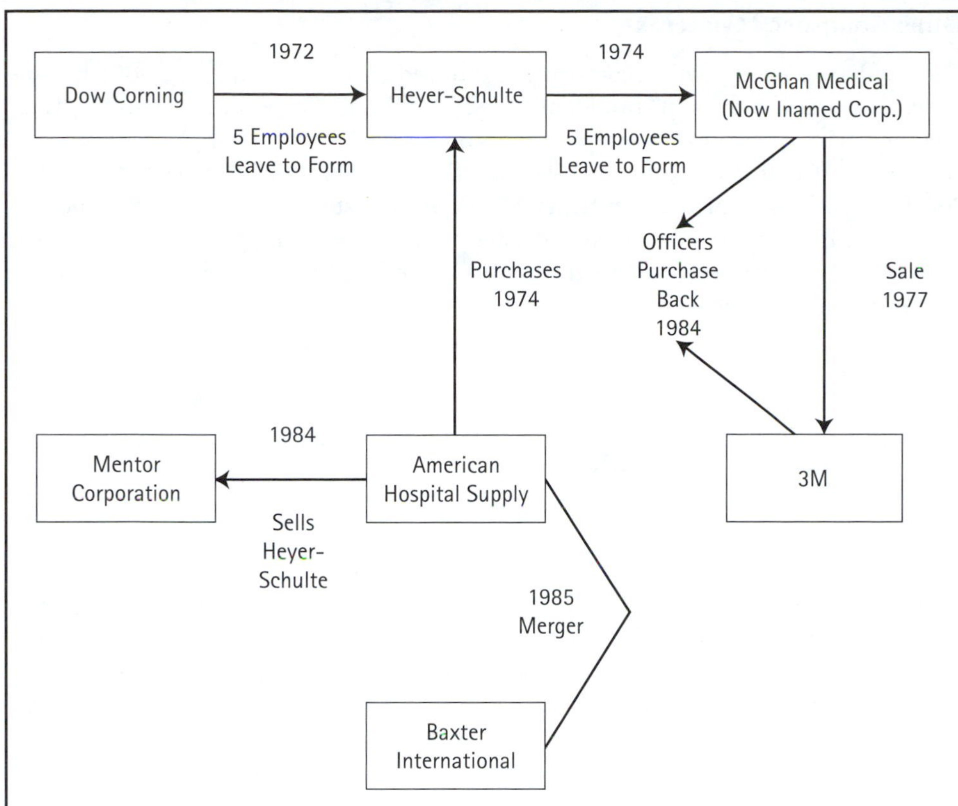

Figure 1
History and Ownership of Silicone Implant Manufacturers

Corning decision to sell a] questionable lot of mammaries on the market has to rank right up there with the Pinto gas tank."[141] Other internal documents revealed in litigation verified that early on, the company had known that the silicone gel could "bleed" and "migrate" into women's bodies.

In a deposition in an implant case against 3M, a Heyer-Schulte chemist disclosed that "[t]his phenomenon [gel bleeding] started to become of interest in the mid '70s."[142] He indicated that a breast implant placed on a blotter would leave a mark, especially if you applied pressure to the implant and allowed time to pass.

In 1983, a Dow Corning scientist, Bill Boley, wrote in an internal memo, "I want to emphasize that, to my knowledge, we have no valid long-term implant data to substantiate the safety of gel for long-term implant use."[143] There was, at that time, strong demand in the medical community for the silicone implant because of its great potential for reconstructive purposes.

Mr. Jan Varner, a former Dow Corning employee who currently is president of McGhan Medical (Inamed), maintains that very few implants leaked and any leakage was "very, very small."[144]

[141] *"Silicone Blues,"* Time, *February 24, 1992, p. 65.*

[142] *Thomas Burton, "Several Firms Face Breast-Implant Woes,"* The Wall Street Journal, *January 23, 1992, p. B1.*

[143] *Judy Foreman, "Choice on Breast Implants Divide Women,"* Arizona Republic, *January 21, 1992, p. C1.*

[144] *Burton, "Several Firms Face Breast-Implant Woes," p. B1.*

Other Companies' Concerns

Outside Dow Corning, other companies expressed their own concerns about silicone implants. James Rudy, then-president of Heyer-Schulte Corporation, wrote a "Dear Doctor" letter in 1976 to inform physicians about the risk of the implants rupturing. Between 1976 and 1978, Congress gave the FDA its first authority to regulate medical "devices" such as implants. Nevertheless, despite the studies and warnings, the implants continued to be sold to approximately 150,000 women per year. It was also at this time that a two-year Dow Corning study found malignant tumors in 80 percent of the laboratory animals exposed to silicone gels.

The study concluded:

> As you will see, the conclusion of this report is that silicone can cause cancers in rats; there is no direct proof that silicone causes cancer in humans; however, there is considerable reason to suspect that silicone can do so.[145]

In response, the FDA noted:

> The sponsor [of the study], Dow Corning, does not dispute the results of the current bioaesay, i.e., Dow Corning agrees that silicone gel is sarcomagenic. However, this sponsor contends that induction of sarcoma in rats is due to solid-state carcinogenesis (Oppenheimer effect). This is uniquely a rodent phenomenon. Therefore, that it is of no human health consequence as a solid-state cancer in man has not been documented. In support of these contentions, an epidemiological study by Delpco, et. al. [sic], has been cited and shows no increased incidence of cancer in breast implant recipients.[146]

FDA staff members added the following comment in their report on the studies:

> Solid-state tumor has been reported in rats, mice, chickens, rabbits and dogs. It is biologically unconvincing that man is a uniquely resistant species.[147]

At the time of the report, the FDA proposed reclassification of the gel implants as medical devices required to be proven safe before they could be sold. The agency imposed the stricter classification over the objections of both surgeons and sellers of the implants. Data regarding the safety of the implants was not required, however, until April 1991.

Problems with the Implants Begin

As the regulatory arena for the implants changed, product liability suits by women experiencing implant-related side effects began. Their problems included rupturing of the silicone sacs, which then spilled the silicone gel into their bodies, causing painful inflammations as their bodies' autoimmune systems tried to combat the invading foreign substance. Other autoimmune disorders appeared in women who experienced leakage or ruptures:

- scleroderma: a disorder which thickens and stiffens the skin and results in the build-up of fibrous tissue in the body's organs;

[145] Id.

[146] *Tim Smart, "Breast Implants: What Did the Industry Know, and When?"* Business Week, *June 10, 1991, p. 94; Tim Smart, "This Man Sounded the Silicone Alarm in 1976,"* Business Week, *January 27, 1992, p. 34.*

[147] Id.

- lupus erythematosus: a disease characterized by chronic joint pain and rashes; and
- rheumatoid arthritis: a disease of stiffening of the joints.[148]

In a 1984 landmark case, a federal district court, in awarding Maria Stern of Nevada $1.5 million in punitive damages, held that Dow Corning had committed fraud in marketing the implants as safe. In ruling on a post-trial motion, U.S. District Judge Marilyn Hall Palel wrote that although Dow Corning's own studies "cast considerable doubt on the safety of the product, the company had not disclosed those studies to patients, including Stern, an act that she labeled "highly reprehensible."[149]

Following the Stern case, in 1985 Dow began to place in its implant packages inserts that mentioned the possibility of "immune system sensitivity and possible silicone migration following rupture."[150]

In a 1987 position statement, Dow Corning did not dispute the possibility of implant leakage but did discount the linkage between those leaks and immune-system problems. A 1982 medical study that the company cited in the statement supported Dow Corning's assertion that there was no connection between implants and breast cancer. Also, the statement indicated that any leaked silicone would be picked up by the lymph system and excreted or stored. The position statement discounted the immune-system problems, maintaining that only silicone of lesser purity would cause such problems.

Following Dow Corning's position statement, litigation activity increased as the FDA received 2,500 reports of illnesses or injuries associated with the implants.[151] By the end of 1991, nearly 1,000 implant lawsuits were pending against manufacturers.[152]

Early in the year, a New York jury awarded $4.5 million, nearly three times the Stern award, to a woman who alleged that her 1983 silicone implant with a polyurethane-foam covering had caused her breast cancer.

Regulatory Action

While Dow Corning appealed the New York case, Bristol-Myers withdrew its implant following the FDA's confirmation of a study that linked the foam used to coat the implant with a cancer-causing agent known as 2-toluene diamine (TDA). In the 1970s, the FDA banned the foam, used primarily in air and auto filters, from use in hair dyes because of the risk of birth defects. The FDA's order requiring manufacturers to prove the safety of their implant products or withdraw them from the market became effective in May 1991 and mandated that the proof from the manufacturers be forthcoming within a decade.

At the same time, Ralph Nader's group, the Public Citizen Health Research Group, met in Washington, D.C., with trial lawyers, women who had had the implants, and others. The group called for the full release of all implant-related safety data to date.

[148] *Andrew Purvis, "A Strike Against Silicone,"* Time, *January 20, 1992, pp. 40–41.*

[149] *Smart, "Breast Implants," p. 98.*

[150] Id.

[151] *Hal Mattern, "New Concerns About Breast Implants,"* Arizona Republic, *January 7, 1992, pp. C1, C4.*

[152] *Michele Galen, John Byrne, Tim Smart, and David Woodruff, "Debacle at Dow Corning: How Bad Will It Get?"* Business Week, *March 2, 1992, p. 36.*

Sybil Goldrich, one of the women leading the movement against implants, had received implants in 1983, following her bilateral mastectomy for breast cancer. Nearly a decade of medical problems, including the removal of her ovaries and uterus, resulted; her doctors attributed those problems to the implants. Ms. Goldrich has commented, "There is no way to detoxify from this chemical." Her suit was dismissed in 1994 because the statute of limitations on product liability and negligence had run. She was unable to establish fraud.[153]

In September 1991, the FDA required implant manufacturers to provide risk information to women considering implant surgery. The agency, which specified the information required to be disclosed, issued the rule as an interim measure while it reviewed data on implant safety. These were the risks required to be disclosed:

- hardening of tissue around the implant,
- interference with mammography and tumor detection, and
- the possibility of leakage, autoimmune diseases, and cancer.

The FDA began its hearings on the silicone implants in October 1991. Speakers on both sides of the issue offered impassioned testimony. Manufacturers had boxes of data to support their claims that their products were harmless. Nearly four hundred women from thirty-seven states traveled to Washington to testify in favor of the implants. Recruited by plastic surgeons, the women testified about the importance of the implants to their physical and mental well-being and their freedom of choice. The women spoke of how the implants had helped them to recapture their self-esteem and gain psychological boosts in their battles with breast cancer.[154]

Physicians and professors of pharmacology and toxicology offered testimony to the contrary. Sybil Goldrich, by now the founder of Command Trust Network, a group advocating further study, asked of the women who testified:

> Do they know that silicone is bleeding into their bodies steadily? Do they know that implants are only good for a limited time and they will have to have surgery again and again?[155]

Speaking from a different perspective, Sharon Green, the executive director of the Y-ME National Organization for Breast Cancer Information, supported implant sales:

> Who are these women and why have so many of them rebuilt their bodies? As can be expected, many of our callers are breast cancer survivors. They have faced breast loss, a year or two of chemotherapy, and some have had their chests radiated. They face each day hoping that they have overcome cancer. Many no longer want to be reminded every morning and night of the cancer that played havoc with their bodies.
>
> It is estimated that one-third of current breast cancer patients are having reconstruction, most often with silicone implants. Saline implants can be an alternative, but they are not as aesthetically pleasing. An estimated 20% of implants are performed to reconstruct the breast; the rest, for augmentation. Y-ME's most recent survey (October 1991) of its own Hotline counselors—all breast cancer survivors—showed that among

[153] Goldrich v. Dow Corning, *31 Cal.Rptr.2d 162 (1994).*

[154] *"Women State Case for Breast Implants,"* Mesa Tribune, *October 21, 1991, p. A3.*

[155] Id.

the respondents who had implants, the overwhelming majority were satisfied with their implants and 87% believed the devices helped their emotional recovery.

Y-ME's position is clear and simple. If silicone breast implants can be scientifically proved dangerous, then this information should be made available to women. If the data are inconclusive, we demand full disclosure of all information so women can make decisions based on fact and not on unscientific claims and anecdotes. We also understand that no medical device can be guaranteed 100% safe and that some people are willing to take greater risks to improve the quality of their lives. However, it should be a personal choice based on all the medically verified evidence as it is known today.

To ban or severely limit silicone breast implants based on inconclusive data would be one more insult to women by taking away their right to make informed decisions regarding their own bodies. For others to deny the right of a woman to implants because they fundamentally believe implants are unnecessary is arrogance in its ugliest form.[156]

After the hearings, the panel recommended unanimously that implants stay on the market but also called for continuing safety tests, concluding that the tests conducted by the four largest manufacturers had been inadequate. The panel cited the following hazards, offered during the hearings, for specific testing:

Scarring and hardening of breast tissue,
Implant leakage,
Reduced effectiveness of mammograms,
Autoimmune reactions,
Infections, and
Cancer.

Impact on Corning

In December 1991, another plaintiff, Mariann Hopkins, was awarded $7.3 million by a San Francisco jury that found Dow Corning had knowingly sold her a defective implant. The court of appeals for the ninth circuit affirmed the decision in 1994.

On December 30, 1991, the FDA sent Dow Corning a warning letter regarding the information Dow Corning was providing via a toll-free telephone number carried in ads about the safety of the implants. The FDA stated in the letter that the hotline information was used in a "confusing or misleading context."

On January 6, 1992, the FDA asked the medical device industry to halt the sale of silicone-gel implants until the agency could review new safety studies. FDA commissioner David Kessler asked all plastic surgeons to discontinue their use of the implants until the FDA could review information from Dow Corning that came to light in two product liability suits against a Dow Corning subsidiary. There was, however, no substitute in terms of natural look and texture for the silicone implants, and demand remained strong.

Following the disclosure of the information in the product liability suits, by mid-January 1992, Corning's stock had dropped $10 to $68.375 per share, while Dow Chemical's stock had fallen 87.5 cents per share. The two companies are joint venturers

[156] *Testimony of Sharon Green, Food and Drug Administration hearings on Silicone Breast Implants, Fall 1991.*

in manufacture and sale of breast implants. Within days of the stock price slip, investors had filed suits against the company. Ten suits were pending by March.

In February 1992, the General and Plastic Surgery Devices Panel of the FDA recommended that the use of implants for cosmetic enlargement be restricted but that implants be made available to women with breast cancer and "anatomical defects."[157]

By March, Dow Corning had announced its intent to withdraw from the implant market. Class action suits by women with immune-system disorders were pending around the country, and Ira Reiner, the Los Angeles County district attorney, began a criminal probe into whether Dow Corning concealed health risks associated with the implants. Reiner proceeded under California's new so-called "be-a-manager-go-to-jail" law, which holds executives criminally liable for product defects that cause harm to either a company's employees or its customers. Reiner has observed, "There's no deterrent like a clank of a jail cell closing behind you."[158] Mr. Reiner left office before the criminal cases were completed.

In early 1992, two women were hospitalized after using razors to remove their implants because they could not afford surgery for removal. Both were suffering from autoimmune diseases. Both had complications from the attempted self-removals and had to undergo surgery to complete the implant removals.[159] By the summer of 1992, Dow Corning reported that its second-quarter earnings had dropped 84.4 percent because of a $45 million pretax charge for eliminating its silicone gel breast-implant business. Even without the one-time charge, Dow Corning's earnings were down 19 percent.[160]

Ongoing Warnings

In mid-1992, the Department of Health and Human Services established a Breast Implant Information Service that offered information and study enrollment for women with implants. The following is an excerpt:

UPDATE ON SILICONE GEL-FILLED BREAST IMPLANTS[161]

> On April 16, 1992, FDA announced that, in keeping with the recommendations of its outside advisory panel, it would allow silicone gel-filled breast implants to be available, but only under special conditions.
>
> Since FDA continues to be concerned about the safety of these devices, all patients to receive breast implants must be enrolled in clinical studies. FDA recognizes that there is a public health need for the implants among patients who have lost a breast because of cancer or trauma, or who have a serious malformation of the breast requiring reconstruction. Thus any woman who needs the implant to reconstruct the breast will be permitted access to such studies. Implants for the purpose of augmentation (breast enlargement) will be available only to a very limited number of women

[157] *Jeff Nesmith, "Scientific Panel Suggests Breast Implant Restrictions,"* Mesa Tribune, *February 21, 1992, pp. A1, A12.*

[158] *Ronald Grover, "The L.A. Lawman Gunning for Dow Corning,"* Business Week, *March 2, 1992, p. 38.*

[159] *"Woman Cuts Breast to Get Implant Aid,"* Mesa Tribune, *May 15, 1992, p. A1; "Woman Claims She Removed Her Own Implants,"* Phoenix Gazette, *April 17, 1992, p. A2.*

[160] *"Dow Corning's Profits Down 84.4% in Quarter,"* The New York Times, *July 28, 1992, p. C2.*

[161] *FDA's Breast Implant Information Service, issued May 25, 1992.*

who are enrolled in controlled clinical studies approved by FDA and designed to study specific safety questions relevant to the device.

The following should help to answer questions about how FDA's decision will affect women, and what they should know about the implants.

Under what circumstances will the implants be available?

Silicone gel-filled implants will be available for clinical studies in three stages.

Stage 1:

Since FDA's April 16 decision, women with an urgent need for reconstruction with the implants have been allowed access to them. This category includes:

- women with temporary tissue expanders in place for breast reconstruction following mastectomy, who need to complete their reconstruction with gel-filled implants;
- women with silicone gel-filled implants who need replacement for medical reasons, such as rupture, gel leakage or severe contracture; and
- women having mastectomies before the studies are in place and for whom immediate reconstruction at the time of mastectomy is medically and surgically more appropriate than implantation at a later time. For women in this category, physicians must document that saline-filled implants are not a satisfactory alternative.

In order for a woman to get the implants in Stage 1, her doctor must first certify that she falls into one of the above three categories. She will have to sign a special form certifying that she has been told about the risks of the implants, and agree to enroll in a registry so that she can be notified in the future, if necessary, about new information on the implants.

Stage 2:

In this stage, breast implant manufacturers will set up studies which will enroll any woman who needs the gel-filled implants for breast reconstruction. FDA must approve these studies before they can begin.

Eligible women will include those who have had breast cancer surgery, severe injury to the breast, or a medical condition causing a severe breast abnormality. Women who must have an existing implant replaced for medical reasons will also be eligible.

As in Stage 1, all women will have to be told about the risks, provide informed consent, and be enrolled in a registry. It will probably take until mid-summer until plans are in place for these studies.

Stage 3:

In addition to the Stage 2 studies, FDA will require carefully controlled research studies for each model of silicone implant that manufacturers wish to continue marketing. These Stage 3 studies will include both reconstruction and augmentation patients and will be focused on specific safety questions about the implants, such as how often rupture and hardening of the scar tissue around the implants occur. They will also evaluate the psychological benefits of the implants. The studies will be limited to the number of patients required to answer the safety questions.

As in Stages 1 and 2, women will have to be told about the risks, provide informed consent, and be enrolled in a registry. In addition, women in the Stage 3 studies will be followed more extensively to check for problems related to the implants.

Designing these Stage 3 studies will take time, and so they cannot begin as quickly as the Stage 2 studies.

How can a woman get enrolled in these studies?

She should contact the doctor who would be performing the implant surgery. The doctor can then contact the manufacturer of the implants to find out which hospitals or doctors' offices are taking part in the studies in that particular area.

The Settlement

In April 1994, Dow (along with Bristol-Myers Squibb and Baxter Healthcare Corp.) reached a $4.2 billion[162] settlement with women who claimed to have health problems resulting from the implants. 3M, Union Carbide, Inamed, Wilshire Foam, and Applied Silicone, all suppliers of silicone to implant manufacturers, settled with the women for approximately $500 million.

In February 1995, a jury in a case in Houston, Texas, held Dow Chemical Company liable in a breast implant litigation case. Dow Chemical has appealed the case which awarded $5.2 million to two female plaintiffs.

By October 1995, the global $4.2 billion settlement had fallen apart and Bristol-Myers Squibb, Baxter, and 3M joined together to make their own settlement proposal. Since then, Bristol, Baxter, and 3M have settled with two-thirds of the women who have brought claims, paying between $10,000 and $250,000 each. Bristol also won two jury verdicts in August 1997.

In 1997, a Mayo Clinic study found that 25 percent of women with implants required reoperations to fix problems such as abnormal tissue growth or chronic pain. The rate for reoperation was higher (34 percent) among post-cancer patients with implants. The early science, upon which the class action suits relied, has been labeled "junk science." Most studies conclude that the reactions to implants will occur in about 5 percent of women, about the percentage of the population that will have some reaction to prescription drugs once they are on the market.

In February 1996, a Harvard medical school study of 10,830 women with silicone implants concluded that there was a "small but statistically significant increased risk" of contracting immune-system illnesses once a woman has the implants.

Dow faced 19,000 product liability lawsuits and proposed a reorganization plan for emerging from Chapter 11 bankruptcy. Under the plan $600 million would be set aside for women to settle their lawsuits and another $1.4 billion would go to women with implants if a jury trial found causation between the presence of the implants and immune-system illnesses. About 1,000,000 women have implants. Creditors, under the proposal, would receive $1 billion.

[162] *Thomas M. Burton, "Frequency of Reoperations for Woman with Breast Implants Put at Nearly 25%,"* The Wall Street Journal, *March 6, 1997, p. B6.*

Also during this time, it was revealed that John E. Swanson, an executive at Dow Corning for 27 years who had helped shape its ethics program, concluded that his wife Colleen's devastating illnesses were caused by her Dow Corning implants. Colleen Swanson had sued Dow Corning in 1992.

Colleen settled her suit in 1993, and three months later Swanson left Dow Corning. Swanson then cooperated with senior writer for *Business Week*, John A. Byrne, for Byrne's book, *Informed Consent: A Story of Personal Tragedy and Corporate Betrayal . . . Inside the Silicone Breast Implant Crisis.*

In August 1997, Dow Chemical lost its first class action suit, involving 1,800 women in federal district court in New Orleans. The case held the parent responsible. Two other verdicts were rendered previously against Dow Chemical, but they were not class action suits. The verdicts were overturned by the trial judge and the appellate court.[163]

Also in 1997, a federal district judge appointed a panel of scientists to review articles and studies to assist him with evidentiary rulings. The issue the parties disputed at length was whether the cases could be consolidated for trial. The federal court of appeals consolidated 10,000 cases into one trial in federal district court in Detroit. Baxter, Bristol-Myers Squibb, and 3M were unsuccessful in getting their cases consolidated with Dow Corning's in Detroit.[164] Eventually, nearly 200,000 women filed claims. In 1999, Dow Corning received approval for the $4.5 billion settlement with what was, by then, 300,000 women. After attorneys' fees, the amount available for the women was $3.2 billion.[165] The plan provided for settlements of $10,000 to $250,000, depending upon the severity of the illnesses. However, anyone could accept a $2,000 "no-questions asked" payment.[166] Presently, the FDA is grappling with the safety of saline implants.[167]

Discussion Questions

1. Who is morally responsible for the harms alleged from the implants? Should the information from the 1975 study have been disclosed?
2. Did Thomas Talcott act ethically in resigning in 1976?
3. If you had been Talcott, what would you have done?
4. Is the freedom of choice issue a moral standard?
5. Did members of the FDA staff have moral responsibilities with respect to the women with implants?

[163] Spitzfaden v. Dow Corning, *708 So.2d 777 (La. App. 1998).*

[164] Hall v. Baxter, *947 F. Supp. 1387 (D. Or. 1996).*

[165] *Thomas Burton, "Dow Corning Bankruptcy Plan Approved,"* The Wall Street Journal, *December 1, 1999, pp. A3, A16.*

[166] Id.

[167] *Rita Ruben, "Saline Implants Studied for Safety,"* USA Today, *March 1, 2000, pp. 1D, 2D.*

6. Did James Rudy relieve himself of any responsibility through his "Dear Doctor" letter?
7. What would you have done if you were Swanson?

Sources

Blakeslee, Sandra, "Lawyers Say Dow Study Saw Implant Danger," *The New York Times*, April 7, 1994, pp. A1, A9.

Burton, Thomas M., "3M, Four Others Join Implant Settlement," *The Wall Street Journal*, April 12, 1994, p. B8.

Burton, Thomas M., "Dow Chemical, for First Time, Is Found Liable in a Trial Over Breast Implant," *The Wall Street Journal*, February 16, 1995, p. B8.

"Dow Corning Prevails in Breast Implant Suit," *National Law Journal*, September 26, 1994, p. B2.

Hopkins v. Dow Corning Corp., 1994 WL 460 325 (9th Cir. 1994).

Taylor, Gary, "Implant Plaintiffs Reach Into a Deep Pocket," *National Law Journal*, January 23, 1995, p. A8.

Taylor, Gary, "Jurors Fault Dow Units on Implants," *National Law Journal*, February 27, 1995, p. A1.

CASE 4.19

The Changing Time Cards

John Michael Gravitt was hired in 1980 at the General Electric jet engine plant as a machinist for $9.69 per hour. A Vietnam veteran, Gravitt was pleased to be among the 18,000 people working at GE's mile-long plant in Cincinnati, Ohio. The plant, which produced engines for both military and commercial aircraft, manufactured the engine for the U.S. military's B-1 bomber.

Gravitt had an excellent performance record. After eleven weeks as a machinist, he was promoted to the supervisory position of foreman. As a foreman, he was in a position to see workers' time cards. Gravitt discovered that workers' training and idle time were being charged to defense jobs. He also noticed that time cards were being altered so that work on projects that had overrun their budgets was being charged to other projects. To facilitate making the changes, the foremen received, in their mailboxes, "hot sheets" listing the projects that were in cost overruns.

Gravitt himself was encouraged to alter his workers' time cards, and during his first year as foreman, he did as he was told, charging his machinists' time to specified contracts. (For example, he was told to charge the workers' nonproductive time to expensive contracts.)[168] After the first year, however, he began to question the prac-

[168] *Personal interview with John M. Gravitt, June 24, 1993.*

tice. Sometimes overruns were charged to projects that weren't even in the plant yet. Gravitt first complained to his unit manager, who sent him to a plant supervisor, who gave Gravitt a "this-happens-everywhere-in-the-real-world" speech. Concerned because GE was dealing with the federal government, Gravitt went to a private attorney. The attorney also gave him the "real world" speech. Gravitt went on with his work but ignored the "hot sheets" and refused to alter time cards. His supervisor did it for him.

John F. Tepe Jr., a foreman who worked with Gravitt, followed orders and altered 50 to 60 percent of his workers' daily time cards. When Gravitt confronted Tepe and told him he could go to jail for altering the cards, Tepe replied that he was "just carrying out orders and there wasn't any chance of getting caught."[169]

By early 1983, Gravitt had decided to gather proof of the time card alterations. For two months, on weekend shifts, he went into the office of his supervisor's secretary, Karen Kerr, who had prepared the "hot sheets," and photocopied both "hot sheets" and time cards. Gravitt also wrote an eight-page letter, which he delivered, along with his documentation, to Brian H. Rowe, a senior vice president at the Cincinnati plant, on June 29, 1983. Gravitt was fired that day.

An internal audit by GE showed that 80 percent of Gravitt's allegations were true and 20 percent could not be disproved.

Gravitt testified before the Senate Subcommittee on Administrative Practice and Procedure and filed suit against GE under the 1863 False Claims Act, which allows private citizens to bring suit against profiteers and recover part of the bounty collected. Fines under the False Claims Act are $5,000 to $10,000 per violation, with 30 percent going to those who successfully bring the case. Gravitt felt that the fines would have an impact on future conduct at GE and at other businesses: "It's the only way people will know they can do something to correct what isn't right."[170] Others argued that the False Claims Act encourages employees not to talk first with employers about problems they spot.[171] Mr. Gravitt settled his suit with GE in 1989 for an undisclosed amount.

Discussion Questions

1. Did altering the cards harm anyone?
2. Did Mr. Gravitt make an ethical choice in reporting the time card alterations?
3. Did Mr. Gravitt have to violate Ms. Kerr's privacy to collect documentation?
4. Was Mr. Tepe correct in saying that he was not responsible because he was just following orders?

[169] *Gregory Stricharchuk, "Ex-Foreman May Win Millions for His Tale About Cheating at GE,"* The Wall Street Journal, *June 23, 1988, p. 16.*

[170] Id.

[171] *Amal Kumar Naj, "GE's Drive to Purge Fraud Is Hampered by Workers' Mistrust,"* The Wall Street Journal, *July 22, 1992, p. A1.*

5. Mr. Gravitt commented that a GE executive who spoke at his foreman's training session explained "how to succeed at GE." The executive's advice was that if a superior asks what 2 + 2 is, your answer should be "whatever you want it to be." What effect would such a philosophy have on a firm's ethical climate?

6. Mr. Gravitt noted that foremen's bonuses at GE were tied to time cards and vouchers. Does such an incentive send the wrong signal to employees?

7. Mr. Gravitt has been unable to find work with any GE contractor in Cincinnati, but he remains proud of his actions, his suit, and the money the federal government recovered. His advice for companies: "Listen to the honest people. Protect them. Transfer them or promote them and clean up the problem."[172] What would GE need to change to implement Mr. Gravitt's ideas?

[172] *Since the time of Mr. Gravitt's testimony GE has implemented a program* The Wall Street Journal *describes as a "remarkable effort" to encourage employees to act ethically and report any wrongdoing. For example, managers can spring pop quizzes on employees by asking questions such as "What are the three ways to report wrongdoing?" Employees who respond correctly get a gift such as a coffee mug.*

4g

Employee Rights

Compliance with labor laws. International operations and plants. These issues affect employees' attitudes at work and the reputation of a business.

CASE 4.20

Cheap Labor: Children, Sweatshops, Human Rights, and the Fifty-Hour Work Week

With the passage of GATT and NAFTA, a world-wide market has been emerging. In addition to the international market for goods, there is also an international market for labor. Many U.S. firms have subcontracted the production of their products to factories in China, Southeast Asia, and Central and South America.

The National Labor Committee (NLC), an activist group, periodically releases information on conditions in foreign factories and the companies utilizing those factories. In 1998, the NLC issued a report that Liz Claiborne, Wal-Mart, Ann Taylor, Esprit, Ralph Lauren, JCPenney, and Kmart were using subcontractors in China that use Chinese women (between the ages of 17 and 25) to work 60–90 hours per week for as little as 13–23 cents per hour. The Chinese subcontractors do not pay overtime, house the workers in crowded dormitories, feed them a poor diet, and operate unsafe factories.[173]

Levi Strauss pulled its manufacturing and sales operations out of China in 1993 because of human rights violations, but announced in 1998 that it would expand its manufacturing there and begin selling clothing there. Peter Jacobi, the president of Levi Strauss, indicated that it had the assurance of local contractors that they would adhere to Levi's guides on labor conditions. Jacobi stated, "Levi Strauss is not in the human rights business. But to the degree that human rights affect our business, we care about it."[174, 175]

[173] *Jon Frandsen, "Chinese Labor Practices Assailed,"* Mesa Tribune, *March 19, 1998, p. B2.*

[174] *Mark Landler, "Reversing Course, Levi Strauss Will Expand Its Output in China,"* The New York Times, *April 9, 1998, p. C1.*

[175] *G. Pascal Zachary, "Levi Tries to Make Sure Contract Plants in Asia Treat Workers Well,"* The Wall Street Journal, *July 28, 1994, pp. A1, A5.*

The Mariana Islands is currently a site of investigation by the Department of Interior for alleged indentured servitude of children as young as 14 in factories there.[176] Wendy Doromal, a human rights activist, issued a report that workers there have tuberculosis and oozing sores. Approximately $820 million worth of clothing items are manufactured each year on the islands, which are a U.S. territory. Labels manufactured there include The Gap, Liz Claiborne, Banana Republic, JCPenney, Ralph Lauren, and Brooks Brothers.[177]

U.S. companies' investments in foreign manufacturing in major developing nations like China, Indonesia, and Mexico have tripled in 15 years to $56 billion, a figure that does not include the subcontracting work. In Hong Kong, Singapore, South Korea, and Taiwan, where plants make apparel, toys, shoes, and wigs, national incomes have risen from 10 percent to 40 percent of American incomes over the past 10 years. In Indonesia, since the introduction of U.S. plants and subcontractors, the portion of malnourished children in the country has gone from one-half to one-third.[178]

In a practice that is widely accepted in other countries, children, ages 10 to 14, labor in factories for 50 or more hours per week. Their wages enable their families to survive. School is a luxury, and a child attends only until he or she is able to work in a factory. The Gap, Levi Strauss, Esprit, and Leslie Fay have all been listed in social responsibility literature as exploiting their workers.[179] In 1994, the following appeared in a quarter-page ad in *The New York Times*:

The Price of Corporate Greed at Leslie Fay

> Marie Whitt is fighting to keep the job she has held for 17 years at a Leslie Fay plant in Wilkes-Barre. Marie earns $7.80 an hour—hardly a fortune. On June 1st, she and 1,800 co-workers were forced to strike because Leslie Fay plans to dump them. Ninety percent are women whose average age is 50. They have given their whole working lives to the company and losing their jobs would be a disaster. Marie knows she will never find a comparable job in today's economy. Without her union benefits, she and her husband won't be able to pay for his anti-cancer medication. "What Leslie Fay wants to do is so rotten," she says. "You've got to draw the line somewhere and fight."
>
> Dorka Diaz worked for Leslie Fay in Honduras, alongside 12- and 13-year-old girls locked inside a factory where the temperature often hits 100° and where there is no clean drinking water. For a 54-hour week, including forced overtime, Dorka was paid a little over $20. With food prices high—a quart of milk costs 44 cents—Dorka and her three-year-old son live at the edge of starvation. In April, Dorka was fired for trying to organize a union. "We need jobs desperate," she says, "but not under such terrible conditions."[180]
>
> Leslie Fay executives claim they can only "compete" by producing in factories like Dorka's. But identical skirts—one made by Dorka, the other by Marie—were recently

[176] *Zachary, "Levi Tries to Make Sure Contract Plants in Asia Treat Workers Well," pp. A1, A5.*

[177] *John McCormick and Marc Levinson, "The Supply Police,"* Newsweek, *February 15, 1993, pp. 48–49.*

[178] *Allen R. Myerson, "In Principle, a Case for More 'Sweatshops,'"* The New York Times, *June 22, 1997, p. E5.*

[179] *Dana Canedy, "Peering Into the Shadows of Corporate Dealings,"* The New York Times, *March 25, 1997, pp. C1, C6.*

[180] *From Ms. Diaz's testimony before a hearing of the Subcommittee on Labor-Management Relations, Committee on Education and Labor, U.S. House of Representatives, Wilkes-Barre, Pennsylvania, June 7, 1994.*

purchased at a big retail chain here. Both cost $40. Searching the world for ever-cheaper sources of labor is not the kind of competition America needs. Leslie Fay already does 75% of its production overseas. If it really wants to compete successfully in the global economy, it would modernize its facilities here in the U.S. as many of its competitors have done. But Leslie Fay wants to make a fast buck by squeezing every last drop of sweat and blood out of its workers. Marie Whitt and Dorka Diaz don't think that's right. And they know it's a formula for disaster—for all of us.

You can help by not buying Leslie Fay products—until Leslie Fay lives up to its corporate responsibilities at home and overseas.

Don't buy Leslie Fay! Boycott all clothing made by Leslie Fay and sold under these labels: Leslie Fay, Joan Leslie, Albert Nipon, Theo Miles, Kasper, Le Suit, Nolan Miller, Castleberry, Castlebrook.[181]

In the United States, the issue of sweatshops came to the public's attention when it was revealed that talk-show host Kathie Lee Gifford's line of clothing at Wal-Mart had been manufactured in sweatshops in Guatemala, and CBS ran a report on conditions in Nike subcontractor factories in Vietnam and Indonesia.[182] The reports on Nike's factories issued by Vietnam Labor Watch included the following: women required to run laps around the factory for wearing non-regulation shoes to work; payment of subminimum wages; physical beatings, including with shoes, by factory supervisors; and most employees are women between the ages of 15 and 28. Philip Knight, CEO of Nike, included the following in a letter to shareholders:

Q: Why on earth did NIKE pick such a terrible place as Indonesia to have shoes made?

A: Effectively the US State Department asked us to. In 1976, when zero percent of Nike's production was in Taiwan and Korea, Secretary of State Cyrus Vance asked Charles Robinson . . . to start the US-ASEAN Business Council to fill the vacuum left by the withdrawal of the American military from that part of the world . . . Chuck Robinson accepted the challenge, put together the council and served as Chairman of the US side for three years. Mr. Robinson was a Nike Board member at that time as he is today . . . "Nike's presence in that part of the world," according to a senior state department official at that time, "is American foreign policy in action."[183]

Nike sent former U.N. Ambassador Andrew Young to its overseas factories in order to issue a report to Knight, the board, and the shareholders.[184] Young did tour factories but only with Nike staff and only for a few hours. Young issued the following findings:

- Factories that produce Nike goods are "clean, organized, adequately ventilated, and well-lit"
- No evidence of a "pattern of widespread or systematic abuse or mistreatment of workers"
- Workers don't know enough about their rights or about Nike's own code of conduct

[181] *From a statement published by the International Ladies Garment Workers Union in* The New York Times, *June 9, 1994, p. A16.*

[182] *Jeff Ballinger and Claes Olsson,* Beyond the Swoosh: The Struggle of Indonesians Making Nike Shoes, *ICDA/Global Publications Foundations, Uppsala Sweden 1997.*

[183] *Sharon R. King, "Flying the Swoosh and Stripes,"* The New York Times, *March 19, 1998, pp. C1, C6.*

[184] *Ellen Neuborne, "Nike to Take a Hit in Labor Report,"* USA Today, *March 27, 1997, p. 1A.*

- Few factory managers speak the local language, which inhibits workers from lodging complaints or grievances
- Independent monitoring is needed because factories are controlled by absentee owners and Nike has too few supervisors on site[185]

On October 18, 1997, there were international protests against Nike in 13 countries and 70 cities. On October 13, 1997, 6,000 Nike workers went on strike in Indonesia followed by a strike of 1,300 in Vietnam.[186]

On November 8, 1997, an Ernst & Young audit about unsafe conditions in a Nike factory in Vietnam was leaked to *The New York Times* and made front-page news.[187]

Michael Jordan, NBA and Nike's superstar endorser, agreed to tour Nike's factories in July 1998, stating, "the best thing I can do is go to Asia and see for myself. The last thing I want to do is pursue a business with a negative over my head that I don't have an understanding of. If there are issues . . . if it's an issue of slavery or sweatshops, [Nike executives] have to revise the situation."[188]

From June 1997 to January 1998, Nike distributed 100,000 plastic "code of conduct" cards to plant workers. The cards list workers' rights. Nike's performance has dropped. It's stock price has dropped from a 1996 high of $75.75 per share to a March 1998 low of $43 per share.[189] (Its share price rebounded to $62 by March 2002.)

Retailers have been canceling orders so that sales decreased 3 percent in 1997. Nike planned to reduce its labor force by 10 to 15 percent, or 2,100 to 3,100 positions.[190,191]

Press for Change and Global Exchange, an activist group, made the following demands of Nike in 1998:

1. **Accept independent monitoring by local human rights groups to ensure that Nike's Code of Conduct is respected by its subcontractors.** The GAP has already accepted independent monitoring for its factories in El Salvador, setting an important precedent in the garment industry. If Nike were to accept such monitoring in Indonesia, it would set a similar positive precedent in the shoe industry, making Nike a true leader in its field.
2. **Settle disputes with workers who have been unfairly dismissed for seeking decent wages and work conditions.** There are dozens of Indonesian workers who have been fired for their organizing efforts, and thousands who have been cheated out of legally-promised wages. Nike must take responsibility for the practices of its subcontractors, and should offer to reinstate fired workers and repay unpaid wages.
3. **Improve the wages paid to Indonesian workers.** The minimum wages in Indonesia is $2.26 a day. Subsistence needs are estimated to cost at least $4 a day.

[185] *"Nike Tries to Quell Exploitation Charges,"* The Wall Street Journal, *June 25, 1997, p. A16.*

[186] *Patricia Seller, "Four Reasons Nike's Not Cool,"* Fortune, *March 30, 1998, pp. 26–28.*

[187] *Bob Herbert, "Brutality in Vietnam,"* The New York Times, *March 28, 1997, p. A19.*

[188] *Bill Richards, "Tripped Up By Too Many Shoes, Nike Regroups,"* The Wall Street Journal, *March 3, 1998, pp. B1, B15.*

[189] *Tom Lowry and Bill Beyers, "Earnings Woes Trip Nike; Layoffs Loom,"* USA Today, *February 25, 1998, p. 1B.*

[190] Id.

[191] *"Nike Refuses to 'Just Do It,'"* Business Ethics, *January/February 1998, p. 8.*

> While Nike claims to pay double the minimum wage, this claim includes endless hours of overtime. We call on Nike to pay a minimum of $4 a day for an eight-hour day, and to end all forced overtime.[192, 193]

The American Apparel Manufacturers Association (AAMA), which counts 70 percent of all U.S. garment makers in its membership, has a database for its members to check labor compliance by contractors.[194] The National Retail Federation has established the following statement of Principles on Supplier Legal Compliance (now signed by 250 retailers):

1. We are committed to legal compliance and ethical business practices in all of our operations.
2. We choose suppliers that we believe share that commitment.
3. In our purchase contracts, we require our suppliers to comply with all applicable laws and regulations.
4. If it is found that a factory used by a supplier for the production of our merchandise has committed legal violations, we will take appropriate action, which may include canceling the affected purchase contracts, terminating our relationship with the supplier, commencing legal actions against the supplier, or other actions as warranted.
5. We support law enforcement and cooperate with law enforcement authorities in the proper execution of their responsibilities.
6. We support educational efforts designed to enhance legal compliance on the part of the U.S. apparel manufacturing industry.[195]

The U.S. Department of Labor has recommended the following to improve the current situation:

1. All sectors of the apparel industry, including manufacturers, retailers, buying agents and merchandisers, should consider the adoption of a code of conduct.
2. All parties should consider whether there would be any additional benefits to adopting more standardized codes of conduct [to eliminate confusion resulting from a proliferation of different codes with varying definitions of child labor].
3. U.S. apparel importers should do more to monitor subcontractors and homeworkers [the areas where child labor violations occur].
4. U.S. garment importers—particularly retailers—should consider taking a more active and direct role in the monitoring and implementation of their codes of conduct.
5. All parties, particularly workers, should be adequately informed about codes of conduct so that the codes can fully serve their purpose.[196]

By 2000, Nike, still experiencing campus protests for its overseas plant conditions, began to experience economic impact as the students protested their colleges and universities signing licensing agreements with Nike. For example, Nike ended negotiations

[192] *Lowry and Beyers, "Earnings Woes Trip Nike," p. 1B.*

[193] *"Nike Refuses to 'Just Do It,'" p. 8.*

[194] *"Slave Labor,"* Fortune, *December 9, 1996, p. 12.*

[195] *Martha Nichols, "Third-World Families at Work: Child Labor or Child Care?"* Harvard Business Review, *January–February 1993, pp. 12–23.*

[196] *Daniela Deane, "Senators to Hear of Slave Labor on U.S. Soil,"* USA Today, *March 31, 1998, p. 9A.*

with the University of Michigan for a six-year multi-million dollar licensing agreement because Michigan joined the consortium. And Phil Knight withdrew a pledge to make a $30 million donation to the University of Oregon because the university joined the consortium.

Nike continues to support the Fair Labor Association, an organization backed by the White House with about 135 colleges and universities as members, but its membership there has not halted the consortium's activities.[197]

Discussion Questions

1. One executive noted, "We're damned if we do because we exploit. We're damned if we don't because these foreign economies don't develop. Who's to know what's right?"

Levi Strauss & Company, discovering that youngsters under the age of 14 were routinely employed in its Bangladesh factories, could either fire 40 underage youngsters and impoverish their families or allow them to continue working. Levi compromised and provided the children both access to education and full adult wages.

Nike has shoe factories in Indonesia, and the women who work in those factories net $37.46 per month. However, as Nike points out, their wages far exceed that of other factory workers. Nike's Dusty Kidd notes, "Americans focus on wages paid, not what standard of living those wages relate to."

Economist Jeffrey D. Sachs of Harvard has served as a consultant to developing nations such as Bolivia, Russia, Poland, and Malawi. He observes that the conditions in sweatshops are horrible, but they are an essential first step toward modern prosperity. "My concern is not that there are too many sweatshops, but that there are too few. These are precisely the jobs that were the stepping stone for Singapore and Hong Kong, and those are the jobs that have to come to Africa to get them out of their backbreaking rural poverty."[198]

Business executives respond as follows:

"If someone is willing to work for 31 cents an hour, so be it—that's capitalism. But throw in long hours, abusive working conditions, poor safety conditions, and no benefits, and that's slavery. It was exactly those same conditions that spawned the union movement here in the U.S." John Waldron

"If the wages of 31 cents per hour were actually fair wages, adults would gladly do the work instead of children." Wesley M. John

"Just when you think the vile remnants of those who would build empires on the blood and bones of those less fortunate than ourselves have slithered off into the history books, you come across this kind of tripe. For shame for rationalizing throwing

[197] *Steven Greenhouse, "Anti-Sweatshop Group Invites Input by Apparel Makers,"* The New York Times, *April 29, 2000, p. A9.*

[198] *"Slave Labor," p. 12.*

crumbs to your fellow human beings so that you and your ilk can benefit at their expense." Jose Guardiola

Discuss the economic, social and ethical issues of plants and wages in developing countries. Consider the following excerpt from *The Economist*:

If a Chinese manufacturing worker can be hired for only 25 cents an hour, compared with $17 in America or $32 in Germany, surely it makes sense for western firms to shift all their production to China? International comparisons of labour costs often provoke such a question. They also provoke protests by trade unions and others in the rich world, who fear that unless governments do something, workers there will either see their wages driven down to third-world levels too, or face a jobless future. That "something" could mean blocking cheap imports or subsidizing exports.

Some jobs are inevitably being sucked out of the rich world and into the poorer one as western firms seek to cut their costs. Yet the threat that low-wage countries pose to employment in the rich countries is greatly exaggerated. After all, if cheap labour guaranteed economic success, nations such as Bangladesh or Mozambique would dominate global output.

So why don't they? One reason is that wages largely reflect international differences in productivity: cheap labour in emerging economies goes hand in hand with lower productivity. Cassandras draw little comfort from this. As poor countries get hold of the latest production techniques, they argue, richer ones will lose their traditional advantage. Third-world producers will be able to combine low wages with first-world technology—and hence productivity levels—making themselves super-competitive. This is nonsense. In the long run, increases in productivity will be offset by higher wages or a stronger exchange rate. Witness the experience of South Korea, where wages have risen from less than one-tenth to more than two-fifths of American levels over the past ten years.[199]

2. Would you employ a twelve-year-old in one of your factories if it were legal to do so?
3. Would you limit hours and require a minimum wage even if it were not legally mandated?
4. Would you work to provide educational opportunities for these child laborers?
5. Why do you think the public seized on the Kathie Lee Gifford and Nike issues?

Sources

Gibbs, Nancy, "Suffer the Little Children," *Time*, March 26, 1990, p. 18.

Mitchell, Russell, and Michael O'Neal, "Managing by Values," *Business Week*, August 1, 1994, pp. 40–52.

[199] *From "Invasion of the Job Snatchers,"* The Economist, *November 2, 1996, p. 18. © 1996 The Economist Newspaper Group Inc. Reprinted with permission. Further reproduction prohibited. www.economist.com*

"Nike's Workers in Third World Abused, Report Says," *Arizona Republic*, March 28, 1997, p. A10.

"Susie Tompkins," *Business Ethics*, January/February 1995, pp. 21–23.

READING 4.21

Human Rights Declarations and Company Policies

The issue of international labor has become a focus for nongovernmental entities as well as companies with international operations. In this reading you will review the corporate human rights and labor policies of ChevronTexaco, Levi Strauss & Co., and Unocal. You will also review the Sullivan Principles and the United Nations position on human rights.

ChevronTexaco Statement on Human Rights and Labor[200]

The ChevronTexaco Way explicitly states the company's "support for universal human rights." We are proud to have been among the early endorsers of The Global Sullivan Principles, a code of corporate conduct formulated by Rev. Leon H. Sullivan in 1999. These principles set high standards that are well aligned with the values shared by all ChevronTexaco employees.

We will be transparent in our implementation of these principles and provide information which demonstrates publicly our commitment to them.

Partnerships between ChevronTexaco and the local communities in which it operates are based on more than philanthropy. Only where both the business and the community make progress through mutual understanding and respect can either side hope to succeed.

We've learned to listen to the needs of the local community first and then engage in mutually beneficial partnerships where together we can become a greater force for positive community change. This includes employment and training opportunities as well as the improvement of local facilities and care for the environment.

Our community involvement, always geared to local needs, has taken many different forms. For example:

- In Venezuela, we built 10 schools where 4,500 students are now receiving a higher quality education.
- In Angola, where many children have been displaced and orphaned by civil war, we support a center for the homeless that educates and trains young women for entry into the work force.
- In Kazakhstan, we've provided mobile health clinics in remote areas where local populations previously had little or no health care.
- In the United States, we've contributed to music programs that help youngsters perform better in math and the sciences.

[200] *http://www.chevrontexaco.com*

- In Singapore, we help promising local university students through relevant work experience and assignments.

Resource: The Global Sullivan Principles[201]

Preamble

The objectives of the Global Sullivan Principles are to support economic, social and political justice by companies where they do business; to support human rights and to encourage equal opportunity at all levels of employment, including racial and gender diversity on decision making committees and boards; to train and advance disadvantaged workers for technical, supervisory and management opportunities; and to assist with greater tolerance and understanding among peoples; thereby, helping to improve the quality of life for communities, workers and children with dignity and equality. I urge companies large and small in every part of the world to support and follow the Global Sullivan Principles of corporate social responsibility wherever they have operations.

1 Feb 1999 *The Rev. Leon H. Sullivan*

Principles

As a company, which endorses the Global Sullivan Principles we will respect the law, and as a responsible member of society we will apply these Principles with integrity consistent with the legitimate role of business. We will develop and implement company policies, procedures, training and internal reporting structures to ensure commitment to these principles throughout our organization. We believe the application of these Principles will achieve greater tolerance and better understanding among peoples, and advance the culture of peace.

Accordingly, we will:

- Express our support for universal human rights and, particularly, those of our employees, the communities within which we operate, and parties with whom we do business.
- Promote equal opportunity for our employees at all levels of the company with respect to issues such as color, race, gender, age, ethnicity or religious beliefs, and operate without unacceptable worker treatment such as the exploitation of children, physical punishment, female abuse, involuntary servitude, or other forms of abuse.
- Respect our employees' voluntary freedom of association.
- Compensate our employees to enable them to meet at least their basic needs and provide the opportunity to improve their skill and capability in order to raise their social and economic opportunities.
- Provide a safe and healthy workplace; protect human health and the environment; and promote sustainable development.
- Promote fair competition including respect for intellectual and other property rights, and not offer, pay or accept bribes.
- Work with governments and communities in which we do business to improve the quality of life in those communities—their educational, cultural, economic and social well-being—and seek to provide training and opportunities for workers from disadvantaged backgrounds.

Promote the application of these principles by those with whom we do business.

[201] *Global Sullivan Principles, Rev. Leon H. Sullivan. http://www.globalsullivanprinciples.org*

Levi Strauss & Co. Global Sourcing and Operating Guidelines[202]

Success Stories

Inspiring Change

During a follow-up visit to a contractor in central Mexico, a Levi Strauss & Co. assessor determined that the increased size of the workforce and the changes in physical layout of the factory required additional emergency exits. The contractor, hesitant at first, made the necessary changes and conducted evacuation drills to prepare workers for various emergencies. Four months later, the area in which the factory was located suffered a massive earthquake. Because of the new exits and the emergency drills, the facility's 800 employees were able to evacuate quickly and safely.

Motivating Improvement

A supplier in India who failed Levi Strauss & Co.'s initial assessment due to wage violations and health and safety conditions that did not meet our guidelines requested a reassessment four months later. The assessor was pleased to see a dramatic improvement at the facility. Not only had the supplier corrected the violations, but there was a noticeable improvement in employee morale. The supplier noted that the changes he made in order to meet Levi Strauss & Co. guidelines contributed significantly to lower turnover, improved product quality and higher efficiency at his facility.

Protecting the Environment

Levi Strauss & Co. suppliers around the world have made efforts to improve and protect the environment in line with our Terms of Engagement and in locally appropriate ways. Contractors in Israel, Croatia and Turkey have installed innovative technologies that not only clean their wastewater, but also use less energy and reduce the amount of treatment chemicals required. Suppliers in Greece and Tunisia have received local and national prizes for their environmental improvement efforts.

A Leader in Socially Responsible Worldwide Sourcing

Levi Strauss & Co. is recognized as a leader in corporate citizenship, including ethical practices in sourcing production around the world.

In 1991, we became the first multinational company to establish a comprehensive ethical code of conduct for manufacturing and finishing contractors working with the company. This code, known as the *Global Sourcing and Operating Guidelines*, directs business practices, such as fair employment, worker health and safety, and environmental standards, among others. Our groundbreaking code earned the company the America's Corporate Conscience Award for International Commitment from the Council on Economic Priorities.

Evaluation & Compliance

Levi Strauss & Co. is committed to ensuring compliance with our code of conduct at all facilities that manufacture or finish our products around the world. Our goal is to achieve positive results and effect change by working with our business partners to find long-term solutions that will benefit the individuals who make our products and

[202] *http://www.levi.com*

will improve the quality of life in local communities. We work on-site with our contractors to develop strong alliances dedicated to responsible business practices and continuous improvement.

If Levi Strauss & Co. determines that a business partner is not complying with our Terms of Engagement, we require that the partner implement a corrective action plan within a specified time period. If a contractor fails to meet the corrective action plan commitment, Levi Strauss & Co. will terminate the business relationship.

We also work with non-governmental organizations (NGOs) for input and recommendations to improve our worldwide internal monitoring process. Levi Strauss & Co. actively participates in the *Fair Labor Association (FLA)*, a collaborative effort between the business, NGO and university communities aimed at protecting workers' rights and improving independent monitoring systems. In addition, we also participate in the *Ethical Trading Initiative (ETI)*.

Our Global Sourcing and Operating Guidelines help us to select business partners who follow workplace standards and business practices that are consistent with our company's values. These requirements are applied to every contractor who manufactures or finishes products for Levi Strauss & Co. Trained inspectors closely audit and monitor compliance among approximately 600 cutting, sewing, and finishing contractors in more than 60 countries.

The Levi Strauss & Co. Global Sourcing and Operating Guidelines include two parts:

I. **The Country Assessment Guidelines**, which address large, external issues beyond the control of Levi Strauss & Co.'s individual business partners. These help us assess the opportunities and risks of doing business in a particular country.

II. **The Business Partner Terms of Engagement**, which deal with issues that are substantially controllable by individual business partners. These Terms of Engagement are an integral part of our business relationships. Our employees and our business partners understand that complying with our Terms of Engagement is no less important than meeting our quality standards or delivery times.

Country Assessment Guidelines

The numerous countries where Levi Strauss & Co. has existing or future business interests present a variety of cultural, political, social and economic circumstances.

The Country Assessment Guidelines help us assess any issue that might present concern in light of the ethical principles we have set for ourselves. The Guidelines assist us in making practical and principled business decisions as we balance the potential risks and opportunities associated with conducting business in specific countries. Specifically, we assess whether the:

- **Health and Safety Conditions** would meet the expectations we have for employees and their families or our company representatives;
- **Human Rights Environment** would allow us to conduct business activities in a manner that is consistent with our Global Sourcing and Operating Guidelines and other company policies;
- **Legal System** would provide the necessary support to adequately protect our trademarks, investments or other commercial interests, or to implement the Global Sourcing and Operating Guidelines and other company policies; and

- **Political, Economic and Social Environment** would protect the company's commercial interests and brand/corporate image. We will not conduct business in countries prohibited by U.S. laws.

Terms of Engagement

- **Ethical Standards**
  We will seek to identify and utilize business partners who aspire as individuals and in the conduct of all their businesses to a set of ethical standards not incompatible with our own.
- **Legal Requirements**
  We expect our business partners to be law abiding as individuals and to comply with legal requirements relevant to the conduct of all their businesses.
- **Environmental Requirements**
  We will only do business with partners who share our commitment to the environment and who conduct their business in a way that is consistent with Levi Strauss & Co.'s Environmental Philosophy and Guiding Principles.
- **Community Involvement**
  We will favor business partners who share our commitment to improving community conditions.
- **Employment Standards**
  We will only do business with partners who adhere to the following guidelines:

  Child Labor: Use of child labor is not permissible. Workers can be no less than 15 years of age and not younger than the compulsory age to be in school. We will not utilize partners who use child labor in any of their facilities. We support the development of legitimate workplace apprenticeship programs for the educational benefit of younger people.

  Prison Labor/Forced Labor: We will not utilize prison or forced labor in contracting relationships in the manufacture and finishing of our products. We will not utilize or purchase materials from a business partner utilizing prison or forced labor.

  Disciplinary Practices: We will not utilize business partners who use corporal punishment or other forms of mental or physical coercion.

  Working Hours: While permitting flexibility in scheduling, we will identify local legal limits on work hours and seek business partners who do not exceed them except for appropriately compensated overtime. While we favor partners who utilize less than sixty-hour workweeks, we will not use contractors who, on a regular basis, require in excess of a sixty-hour week. Employees should be allowed at least one day off in seven.

  Wages and Benefits: We will only do business with partners who provide wages and benefits that comply with any applicable law and match the prevailing local manufacturing or finishing industry practices.

  Freedom of Association: We respect workers' rights to form and join organizations of their choice and to bargain collectively. We expect our suppliers to respect the right to free association and the right to organize and bargain collectively without unlawful interference. Business partners should ensure that workers who make such decisions or participate in such organizations are not the object of discrimination or punitive disciplinary actions and that the representatives of such organizations have access to their members under conditions established either by local laws or mutual agreement between the employer and the worker organizations.

  Discrimination: While we recognize and respect cultural differences, we believe that workers should be employed on the basis of their ability to do the job, rather than on the basis of personal characteristics or beliefs. We will favor business partners who share this value.

  Health & Safety: We will only utilize business partners who provide workers with a safe and healthy work environment. Business partners who provide residential facilities for their workers must provide safe and healthy facilities.

Unocal's Policies on Human Rights[203]

Note: Unocal has had perhaps the greatest public relations challenges of the three companies because of its presence in Myanmar (Burma), its planned presence in Afghanistan, and the related human rights issues.

At Unocal, we recognize our responsibility to support fundamental human rights and to advance the development of civil society.

Human rights are not just a matter for governments. They have become business issues, in part, because advocacy groups and the media have highlighted abuses in countries where multinational corporations are operating. Today, every multinational corporation is challenged to promote human rights, including freedom from discrimination, the right to life and security, freedom of expression and religion, freedom from slavery, and the right to fair working conditions.

Basic human values and high standards of ethical conduct have always been a central part of Unocal's approach to business and critical to our company's success. An American company that is more than a century old, Unocal is proud of its global reputation. We deeply believe in our core values: *honesty, integrity, excellence and trust.* And we take to heart our commitment "to improve the lives of people wherever we work."

Unocal's Code of Ethics and Compliance Guidelines states: "*We are committed to meeting the highest ethical standards in all our operations, whether at home or abroad. This includes treating everyone fairly and with respect, maintaining a safe and healthful workplace, and improving the quality of life wherever we do business. It also means conducting our business in a way that engenders pride in our employees and respect from the world community.*"

As a global corporation, we have a responsibility to promote and protect human rights in all of our activities. But what precisely does this responsibility entail? Should the company be expected to use its influence to address human rights issues in local communities and host countries at large? And if so—how?

What, if anything, is the role of the multinational corporation in supporting human rights?

Unocal, as a U.S. company operating in many different foreign countries, has a legal and ethical obligation to remain politically neutral. Our economic impact, however, is far from neutral. We have seen time and again how our presence has improved the quality of life for people—regardless of politics. And history suggests that economic progress typically promotes increasing respect for human rights.

Our energy development operations have clear human rights implications. We generate economic growth that gives political confidence and influence to a rising middle class. We hire, train and provide advancement opportunities for the citizens of our host countries. We introduce modern values and concepts, such as equal employment opportunity regardless of sex, race, ethnic background or religious preference. We provide a supportive working environment in which all employees may freely contribute. We introduce safety training and environmental programs into the workplace, and offer health care and educational opportunities that further empower communi-

[203] *Reprinted by permission of Unocal. http://www.unocal.com*

ties. And, in keeping with our commitment to improve people's lives wherever we work, we support a wide variety of humanitarian and philanthropic initiatives.

These are not simply by-products of our commercial activities. Rather, they constitute what we see as our **responsibility** and **commitment** to the people and the countries where we work.

Moreover, the nature of our business also creates long-term relationships with host country leaders and other key decision makers. Often, in the context of discussing our energy development activities with government officials, Unocal is able to raise concerns about human rights issues and privately present our views.

We know that it is not enough to set high standards of business conduct, we must also live by them. This is especially true of our investments in developing countries. Our experiences in Southeast Asia during the past 30 years demonstrate the value of economic engagement and the important benefits to communities that come from our health care, education, sanitation and other local initiatives.

A more recent case in point is our involvement in the Yadana natural gas development project offshore Myanmar (Burma), where we have taken a leadership role in ensuring that no human rights abuses have occurred in the project's activities. The main difference between our activities in other countries decades ago and in Myanmar now, is that Myanmar has become highly politicized, even though our approach has remained the same.

Unocal has been the subject of considerable attack over alleged human rights violations in conjunction with the Yadana project. Our critics have accused us of using forced labor in building the pipeline across Myanmar to the Thai border. These accusations are absolutely false. From the onset of the project, Unocal has carefully monitored the labor practices followed by the project operator, Total, a French energy company. We have sent our own fact-finding teams to the pipeline area.

Two internationally known human rights experts visited the project and the nearby villages in January 1998. Their report stated that *"not only are [the project operators] paying fair wages, well above the market price, but they are keeping their employees happy and the inhabitants of the 13 villages near the pipeline have experienced great improvement in their lives."*

Several U.S. Embassy officials also visited the pipeline region and reported similar findings. No credible source has ever called our attention to evidence that any forced labor was used on the project.

In 1996, the U.S. State Department issued a report on human rights in Burma. The report noted that "during 1996 there were repeated allegations that forced labor was used on a project to build a pipeline across the Tenasserim Region. The preponderance of evidence indicated that the pipeline project has paid its workers at least a market wage."

In September 1998, the U.S. Department of Labor issued its "Report on Labor Practices in Burma." Although Labor Department officials did not visit Burma to prepare this report, the document discusses issues related to Unocal's investment in the Yadana Project and attempts to tie alleged labor abuses in other parts of Burma to the Yadana Project. Unocal sent a letter to the Secretary of Labor questioning the authorship and research methods of this report and requested a formal investigation into the bias reflected in the report's sections on the Yadana project.

A recently released State Department cable reported that "If charges are made that the pipeline was built with forced labor, we would find such charges very difficult to believe." The same cable further states that "It appears that the pipeline project operators have made a concerted effort to improve the living conditions of residents in the vicinity of the pipeline, and that at least for the short term, the pipeline has raised the socio-economic level in the area."

Unocal would not tolerate the use of forced labor or other human rights abuses on any of our projects. We are proud of our record of improving the lives of people wherever we work. We are equally proud of the benefits provided to the people of Myanmar through our investment in the Yadana project. The project has created high-paying jobs for thousands of workers. It has supported a wide variety of educational, medical and economic programs for nearly 35,000 villagers living near the pipeline route. The Yadana project has built roads, schools, health centers and sanitation systems, and introduced a number of successful economic development initiatives for local farmers. These include poultry, pig and cattle farming, as well as other agricultural and small enterprise activities that have made the region a thriving, inter-related area.

The impact of the various socio-economic programs on local citizens is significant and lasting. Already, babies are being born healthier, with far better life expectancy, as a direct result of the doctors, clinics and health care programs that have been introduced into a region where previously there were none. Infant mortality rate in the villages in the pipeline vicinity has dropped by more than half the national average—to 46 deaths per 1,000 live births, compared with 95 deaths per 1,000 live births for the country overall.

Another important measure of achievement is education. In the pipeline area, thanks to new (or refurbished) schools and supplies, 77 percent of children now attend and complete school. Elsewhere in Myanmar, the U.S. State Department has reported that although education is compulsory, almost 40 percent of children never enroll in school, and only 25 to 35 percent complete primary school.

For all these reasons, the Yadana energy development project is helping to promote peace and prosperity through the Myanmar-Thailand region. We offer this project as a model of corporate responsibility in a developing country.

The United Nations' Universal Declaration of Human Rights[204]

UN DECLARATION

Universal Declaration of Human Rights

Adopted and proclaimed by the United Nations General Assembly resolution 217 A (III) of 10 December 1948.

Preamble

Whereas recognition of the inherent dignity and of the equal and inalienable rights of all members of the human family is the foundation of freedom, justice and peace in the world,

[204] *http://www.un.org*

Whereas disregard and contempt for human rights have resulted in barbarous acts which have outraged the conscience of mankind, and the advent of a world in which human beings shall enjoy freedom of speech and belief and freedom from fear and want has been proclaimed as the highest aspiration of the common people,

Whereas it is essential, if man is not to be compelled to have recourse, as a last resort, to rebellion against tyranny and oppression, that human rights should be protected by the rule of law,

Whereas it is essential to promote the development of friendly relations between nations,

Whereas the peoples of the United Nations have in the Charter reaffirmed their faith in fundamental human rights, in the dignity and worth of the human person and in the equal rights of men and women and have determined to promote social progress and better standards of life in larger freedom,

Whereas Member States have pledged themselves to achieve, in cooperation with the United Nations, the promotion of universal respect for and observance of human rights and fundamental freedoms,

Whereas a common understanding of these rights and freedoms is of the greatest importance for the full realization of this pledge,

Now, therefore,

The General Assembly,

Proclaims this Universal Declaration of Human Rights as a common standard of achievement for all peoples and all nations, to the end that every individual and every organ of society, keeping this Declaration constantly in mind, shall strive by teaching and education to promote respect for these rights and freedoms and by progressive measures, national and international, to secure their universal and effective recognition and observance, both among the peoples of Member States themselves and among the peoples of territories under their jurisdiction.

Article 1

All human beings are born free and equal in dignity and rights. They are endowed with reason and conscience and should act towards one another in a spirit of brotherhood.

Article 2

Everyone is entitled to all the rights and freedoms set forth in this Declaration, without distinction of any kind, such as race, color, sex, language, religion, political or other opinion, national or social origin, property, birth or other status.

Furthermore, no distinction shall be made on the basis of the political, jurisdictional or international status of the country or territory to which a person belongs, whether it be independent, trust, non-self-governing or under any other limitation of sovereignty.

Article 3

Everyone has the right to life, liberty and security of person.

Article 4

No one shall be held in slavery or servitude; slavery and the slave trade shall be prohibited in all their forms.

Article 5

No one shall be subjected to torture or to cruel, inhuman or degrading treatment or punishment.

Article 6

Everyone has the right to recognition everywhere as a person before the law.

Article 7

All are equal before the law and are entitled without any discrimination to equal protection of the law. All are entitled to equal protection against any discrimination in violation of this Declaration and against any incitement to such discrimination.

Article 8

Everyone has the right to an effective remedy by the competent national tribunals for acts violating the fundamental rights granted him by the constitution or by law.

Article 9

No one shall be subjected to arbitrary arrest, detention or exile.

Article 10

Everyone is entitled in full equality to a fair and public hearing by an independent and impartial tribunal, in the determination of his rights and obligations and of any criminal charge against him.

Article 11

Everyone charged with a penal offence has the right to be presumed innocent until proved guilty according to law in a public trial at which he has had all the guarantees necessary for his defence.

No one shall be held guilty of any penal offence on account of any act or omission which did not constitute a penal offence, under national or international law, at the time when it was committed. Nor shall a heavier penalty be imposed than the one that was applicable at the time the penal offence was committed.

Article 12

No one shall be subjected to arbitrary interference with his privacy, family, home or correspondence, nor to attacks upon his honor and reputation. Everyone has the right to the protection of the law against such interference or attacks.

Article 13

Everyone has the right to freedom of movement and residence within the borders of each State.

Everyone has the right to leave any country, including his own, and to return to his country.

Article 14

Everyone has the right to seek and to enjoy in other countries asylum from persecution.

This right may not be invoked in the case of prosecutions genuinely arising from non-political crimes or from acts contrary to the purposes and principles of the United Nations.

Article 15

Everyone has the right to a nationality.

No one shall be arbitrarily deprived of his nationality nor denied the right to change his nationality.

Article 16

Men and women of full age, without any limitation due to race, nationality or religion, have the right to marry and to found a family. They are entitled to equal rights as to marriage, during marriage and at its dissolution.

Marriage shall be entered into only with the free and full consent of the intending spouses.

The family is the natural and fundamental group unit of society and is entitled to protection by society and the State.

Article 17

Everyone has the right to own property alone as well as in association with others.

No one shall be arbitrarily deprived of his property.

Article 18

Everyone has the right to freedom of thought, conscience and religion; this right includes freedom to change his religion or belief, and freedom, either alone or in community with others and in public or private, to manifest his religion or belief in teaching, practice, worship and observance.

Article 19

Everyone has the right to freedom of opinion and expression; this right includes freedom to hold opinions without interference and to seek, receive and impart information and ideas through any media and regardless of frontiers.

Article 20

Everyone has the right to freedom of peaceful assembly and association.

No one may be compelled to belong to an association.

Article 21

Everyone has the right to take part in the government of his country, directly or through freely chosen representatives.

Everyone has the right to equal access to public service in his country.

The will of the people shall be the basis of the authority of government; this will shall be expressed in periodic and genuine elections which shall be by universal and equal suffrage and shall be held by secret vote or by equivalent free voting procedures.

Article 22

Everyone, as a member of society, has the right to social security and is entitled to realization, through national effort and international co-operation and in accordance with the organization and resources of each State, of the economic, social and cultural rights indispensable for his dignity and the free development of his personality.

Article 23

Everyone has the right to work, to free choice of employment, to just and favorable conditions of work and to protection against unemployment.

Everyone, without any discrimination, has the right to equal pay for equal work.

Everyone who works has the right to just and favorable remuneration ensuring for himself and his family an existence worthy of human dignity, and supplemented, if necessary, by other means of social protection.

Everyone has the right to form and to join trade unions for the protection of his interests.

Article 24

Everyone has the right to rest and leisure, including reasonable limitation of working hours and periodic holidays with pay.

Article 25

Everyone has the right to a standard of living adequate for the health and well-being of himself and of his family, including food, clothing, housing and medical care and necessary social services, and the right to security in the event of unemployment, sickness, disability, widowhood, old age or other lack of livelihood in circumstances beyond his control.

Motherhood and childhood are entitled to special care and assistance. All children, whether born in or out of wedlock, shall enjoy the same social protection.

Article 26

Everyone has the right to education. Education shall be free, at least in the elementary and fundamental stages. Elementary education shall be compulsory. Technical and professional education shall be made generally available and higher education shall be equally accessible to all on the basis of merit.

Education shall be directed to the full development of the human personality and to the strengthening of respect for human rights and fundamental freedoms. It shall promote understanding, tolerance and friendship among all nations, racial or religious groups, and shall further the activities of the United Nations for the maintenance of peace.

Parents have a prior right to choose the kind of education that shall be given to their children.

Article 27

Everyone has the right freely to participate in the cultural life of the community, to enjoy the arts and to share in scientific advancement and its benefits.

Everyone has the right to the protection of the moral and material interests resulting from any scientific, literary or artistic production of which he is the author.

Article 28

Everyone is entitled to a social and international order in which the rights and freedoms set forth in this Declaration can be fully realized.

Article 29

Everyone has duties to the community in which alone the free and full development of his personality is possible.

In the exercise of his rights and freedoms, everyone shall be subject only to such limitations as are determined by law solely for the purpose of securing due recognition and respect for the rights and freedoms of others and of meeting the just requirements of morality, public order and the general welfare in a democratic society.

These rights and freedoms may in no case be exercised contrary to the purposes and principles of the United Nations.

Article 30

Nothing in this Declaration may be interpreted as implying for any State, group or person any right to engage in any activity or to perform any act aimed at the destruction of any of the rights and freedoms set forth herein.

Discussion Questions

1. Make a list of all of the factors the statements of principles and company policies have in common.
2. What omissions are there in the company policies when compared with the principle statements?
3. If you were developing a policy for your company on human rights and international labor operations, how would you go about doing so?
4. What is the position in each of the statements on child labor?

unit 5

Business Operations

"If we were making that decision now in light of the press scrutiny we have been receiving, we probably would not have taken that risk."

Robert C. Winters
Former Chairman, Prudential Insurance

"Cookies." "Cookies with raisins."

The code words at Phar-Mor for a second set of books and false entries, respectively.

From cash and internal controls to "grease" payments in foreign operations, businesses face continuing dilemmas about the propriety of the use and flow of funds.

From production to shutdown, everything a business does affects its workers, their well being, the environment, and the community. Decisions in these areas require a careful balancing of many interests.

5a

Earnings, Transparency, and Management

Control of funds offers opportunities for misuse of funds. A lack of careful supervision can present tempting opportunities for personal and business gain that later could serve to destroy the firm. Who's in charge? How much information do they have? Can misuse be controlled? As you review these cases, think of how better management and ethical codes could have helped these firms.

READING 5.1

Earnings Management: The Ethical Issues Remain[1]

Marianne M. Jennings

Arthur Levitt recently made his position on earnings management clear at an address at New York University. "Too many corporate managers, auditors, and analysts are participants in the game of nods and winks. In the zeal to satisfy consensus earnings estimates and project a smooth earnings path, wishful thinking may be winning the day over faithful representation . . . Managing may be giving way to manipulation; integrity may be losing out to illusion."[2]

In addition to making his feelings clear, Mr. Levitt has created a blue ribbon panel to make recommendations on strengthening audit committees in their role as overseers of financial reporting.[3] One member of the panel noted that the U.S. capital markets are the most successful in the world because of integrity in capital formation. Issues on financial reporting and earnings management are at the heart of that

[1] Corporate Finance Review *3(5): 39–41 (March/April 1999). Reprinted from Corporate Finance Review by RIA, 395 Hudson Street, New York, NY 10014.*

[2] *"The Numbers Game," speech of Arthur Levitt, Chairman, Securities and Exchange Commission, NYU Center for Law and Business, September 28, 1998.*

[3] *The panel consists of representatives from the NYSE, NASD, and the legal community and is cochaired by John C. Whitehead, retired senior partner of Goldman, Sachs and Ira Millstein, senior partner, Weil Gotshal & Manges.*

integrity-based system. As the panel begins its work, it is important to understand the issue of earnings management: What is it? How is it done? How effective is it? How do accountants and managers perceive it from an ethical perspective?

What is Earnings Management?

Earnings management consists of actions by managers used to increase or decrease current reported earnings without a resulting increase or decrease in long-term economic profitability. No one in accounting literature points to a standard definition for earnings management but it consists of activities by managers to meet or exceed earnings projections in order to increase capitalization through increased stock value.

Anecdotally, companies make clear in their annual reports that increases in earnings are important. Tenneco's 1994 annual report provides this explanation in the management discussion section, "All of our strategic actions are guided by and measured against this goal of delivering consistently high increases in earnings over the long term." Eli Lilly noted it had 33 years of earnings without a break. Bank of America's annual report notes, "Increasing earnings per share was our most important objective for the year."

How Do Firms Manage Earnings?

The methods for managing earnings are varied and limited only by manager creativity within the fluid accounting rules. The common techniques are:

- Write down inventory
- Write up inventory product development for profit target
- Record supplies or next year's expenses ahead of schedule
- Delay invoices
- Sell excess assets
- Defer expenditures

Chairman Levitt noted 5 popular methods for earnings management.

(1) Large-charge restructuring which helps clean up the balance sheet (often referred to as the "big bath")
(2) Creative acquisition accounting—acquisition price is designated as "in-process" research and can then be written off in a "one-time" charge to avoid future earnings drag
(3) Cookie jar reserves—the use of unrealistic assumptions to estimate sales returns, loan losses or warranty costs. Accruals are stashed in good times and used when needed in bad times
(4) Materiality—recordings in error are not a problem so long as they are immaterial
(5) Revenue recognition–recognizing sales before delivery or final acceptance

Some of the literature breaks earnings management into categories. Operations earnings management would involve delaying or accelerating R&D, maintenance or sales. Finance earnings management is the early retirement of debt. Investment earnings management consists of sales of securities or fixed assets. Accountings earnings management could include the selection of accounting methods (straight-line vs. accelerated depreciation), LIFO and the use of reserving income etc. noted above as one of Levitt's five types of earnings management.

How Effective Is Earnings Management?

Earnings management is effective in increasing shareholder value. A consistent pattern of earnings increases results in higher price-to-earnings ratios. That ratio is larger the longer the series of consistent earnings. Firms that break patterns of consistent earnings experience an average 14% decline in stock returns for the year in which the earnings pattern is broken. However, the discovery of earnings manipulation at a company results in a stock price drop of 9%.

How Do Accountants and Managers Perceive Earnings Management?

There are certain incentives for managers to engage in earnings management. For example, compensation contracts may provide dramatic incentives for managing earnings. Bausch & Lomb, Sears and Cendant are all examples of companies whose managers operationally and financially manipulated earnings to the detriment of these companies. Incentives for earnings management can also come from sources other than compensation incentives for executives. Covenants in debt contracts, pending proxy contests, pending union negotiations, pending external financing proposals and pending matters in the political/regulatory processes can all be motivational factors for earnings management. Many managers perceive earnings management as a strategic tool to be used to impact pending matters.

Research indicates that the more seasoned auditors and managers are more likely to accept earnings management as appropriate in a wide variety of circumstances and methods. Indeed, there is an overriding rationalization that such management is necessary to increase the value of the stock of the company. Earnings management is perceived as a tool for influencing investors' perceptions about the company's value.

The Ethics of Earnings Management

The question that fails to arise in the context of management decisions on managing earnings is whether the financial statements of the company emerge with a sleight-of-hand. In a system dependent upon reliable and transparent financial information, the practice of earnings management conceals relevant information about financial performance. Indeed, research shows that firms that engage in earnings management are more likely to have boards with no independence and eventually higher costs of capital. So obvious are the ethical issues and the betrayal of full and fair disclosure standards that the SEC, in addition to creation of the blue ribbon panel, is proposing a plan to force confrontation of the ethical issues in earnings management.

The plan includes a new "before and after" representation; that is, the financials will reflect the impact of changes in accounting assumptions. New SEC guidelines will require the consideration of qualitative factors in making the decisions on materiality for purposes of disclosure. In other words, the size of the adjustment will no longer be the sole determinant for disclosure. Accounting rules on restructuring and revenue recognition will be reviewed by FASB, AICPA and SEC.

In short, the SEC's new attention to earnings management focuses on the ethical notion of balance: if you were the investor instead of the manager, what information about earnings management would you want disclosed? If you were on the outside looking in, how would you feel about the decision to book extra expenses this year in order to even out earnings in a year not so stellar? The problem with discussing the ethics of earnings management is that it has been done so long, so often and by so many that it is no longer perceived to be an ethical issue. Over the past year, *Fortune* magazine has even offered a feature piece on the "how to's" and the importance of doing it. It remains an unassailable proposition, based on the financial research, that a firm's stock price attains a quality of stability through earnings management. However, the financial issues in the decision to manage earnings are but one block in the decision tree. In focusing on that one block, firms are losing sight of the impact such activities have on employees, conduct and eventually on the company and its shareholders.

Discussion Questions

1. Is there a gradual increase in the level of earnings management?
2. What are the motivations for moving expenses and revenues around in quarters and years?
3. Don't shareholders benefit by earnings management? Who is really harmed by earnings management?

READING 5.2

That "M" Word: To Disclose or Not to Disclose—Materiality and Ethics in Financial Reporting[4]

Marianne M. Jennings

I. Introduction

The "if it's not 5% or more, we don't disclose" standard for materiality has long been the unwritten code in financial reporting.[5] Research dating back to 1984 indicates that the prevailing attitude among auditors was that the quantitative measure for financial reporting was controlling for disclosure standards, not qualitative factors.[6] That same research reveals that many auditors and managers subscribed to the notion that even

[4] Corporate Finance Review *4(5): 43–46 (2000). Reprinted from Corporate Finance Review by RIA, 395 Hudson Street, New York, NY 10014.*

[5] *FASB has required that an earnings per share dilution of 3% or more be disclosed (Accounting Principles Board No. 15 (APB15) (1969)) and whether 10% or more of consolidated revenue is from a separate subsidiary (Statement of Financial Accounting Standard No. 14 (SFAS 14) (1976)). The Canada Institute of Certified Accountants (CICA) does use a sliding scale for materiality disclosures based on gross profit. Australia uses 10% of the base (income, assets, profit) as material; less than 5% as immaterial. In the United Kingdom, an earnings dilution of 5% or more is material. Donald A. Leslie,* Materiality: The Concept and Its Application to Auditing, *Canadian Institute of Chartered Accountants, 1985, pp. 7–8.*

[6] *Marianne M. Jennings, Philip M. Reckers, and Daniel C. Kneer, "A Source of Insecurity: A Discussion and an Empirical Examination of Standards of Disclosure and Levels of Materiality in Financial Statements,"* 10 J. Corp. Law *639 (1985) and Jennings, Reckers, and Kneer, "The Adequacy of Auditor Disclosures in Financial Statements: Does More Disclosure Mean Less Liability? Does Acknowledgment of Non-Disclosure Alleviate Liability?"* 8 J. Law & Com. *283 (1988).*

items such as bribes need not be disclosed, despite their obvious revelations about the nature of company operations and management, so long as the amount of the bribes was below the quantitative materiality threshold. For some time such attitudes and disclosure standards have been troublesome to users, regulators, and certainly business ethicists. Recent SEC actions demonstrate that both the ethics and law relating to materiality in financial statements are changing.

II. The History of Materiality in Auditing

Auditors have traditionally been held liable only for material misstatements or omissions in the financial statements they audit. Users of audited financial statements who relied on the auditor's judgment in making investment and credit decisions have been permitted to recover for material omissions. The materiality standard for liability has been one adopted and used by the profession to prevent user misconceptions that the auditor's role is one of full disclosure or that of warrantor.[7]

The concept of materiality is similar to the concept of negligence, requiring case by case examination, with courts offering different definitions of the concept and reaching different results.[8] The result has often been a 20/20 hindsight review by users (and courts) of auditors' disclosure decisions made in the preparation of financial reports.[9] Despite the uncertainties, the use of audited financial statements in statutorily mandated reports is extensive, and when there are material inaccuracies in these types of reports, auditors have faced statutorily imposed liability.[10]

The adherence to generally accepted auditing standards has been no guarantee of liability protection for the auditor.[11] Indeed, in some cases, the adherence to such

[7] *AICPA, through the auditing standards board, has recommended the use of the following language to clarify the auditor's role: "In our opinion, the financial statements referred to above are, in all material respects, fairly presented in conformity with generally accepted accounting principles." Codification of Accounting Standards and Procedures, Statement in Auditing Standards No. 58 (Am. Inst. Of Certified Pub. Accountants 1988).*

[8] *A number of definitions have been offered in the course of the definitional struggle over materiality.* See TSC Indus., Inc. v. Northway, Inc., *426 U.S. 438, 449 (1976) (any fact affecting the investor's decision to buy, sell, or retain securities);* Mills v. Electric Auto-Lite Co., *396 U.S. 375, 384 (1970) any fact influencing the reasonable and prudent man in an investment decision);* Chelsea Assoc. v. Rapanos, *527 F.2d 1266 (6th Cir. 1975) (any omission of facts which has a substantial likelihood of affecting the average prudent investor's decision);* Cooke v. Teleprompter Corp., *334 F.Supp. 467 (S.D.N.Y. 1971) (materiality standards vary according to situations, contexts and companies);* Kardon v. National Gypsum Co., *73 F.Supp. 798, 800 (E.D. Pa. 1947) (any fact materially affecting the judgment of the other party to the transaction).* See also *§256(6)(1) (1978) of the Federal Securities Code. The Federal Securities Code was drafted and revised by Professor Louis Loss and several consultants and advisers through the American Law Institute. A draft was proposed each year from 1972 through 1978;* see also *W. Painter,* The Federal Securities Code and Corporate Disclosure *(1979). For background on the Code, see* Loss, The American Law Institute's Federal Securities Code Project, *25 Bus. Law. 27 (1969) and 1 Fed. Sec. Code 13 (Supp. II 1981). For a judicial reference* see Affiliated Ute Citizens v. United States, *406 U.S. 128, 193 (1972).*

[9] See *Schoenbaum,* The Relationship Between Corporate Disclosure and Corporate Responsibility, *40 Fordham L. Rev. 565 (1972).*

[10] *The statutory filings in which auditors participate include SEC registration statements for securities offerings, proxy solicitation materials, quarterly and informational reports such as the 10-K, 8-K, and 10-Q, and annual reports filed with the SEC. For reports, the liability of the auditor is the same as that of the primary parties involved in the issuance in the event there are misstatements or omissions in the financial materials.*

[11] Rhode Island Hosp. Trust Nat'l Bank v. Swartz, Bresenoff, Yavner & Jacobs, *455 F.2d 847, 852 (4th Cir. 1972) (Accounting standards are the minimum test of liability, not the maximum test.).* See SEC v. Arthur Young & Co., *590 F.2d 785, 788-89 (9th Cir. 1979) (Accountant not protected by Generally Accepted Accounting Principles (GAAP) if "he fails to reveal material facts which he knows or which, but for a deliberate refusal to become informed, he should have known.");* United States v. Simon, *425 F.2d 796, 805-06 (2d Cir. 1969),* cert. denied, *397 U.S. 1006 (1970) ("Proof*

principles does not provide the users with an accurate picture of the firm's financial status and, in such cases, auditors have been held liable for the failure to present an accurate picture in spite of such adherence.[12]

The SEC has, over the years, developed a list of specific types of disclosures an auditor is expected to make regardless of their size or impact on earnings because the SEC has taken the position that, certain items, if revealed, demonstrate problems with management integrity. For example, while the Foreign Corrupt Practices Act[13] made bribes abroad illegal, there remain certain types of sensitive payments still permissible. The disclosure of these payments is critical, not because of their amount, but because of their relevance to the operation of the corporation and the conduct of corporate management.[14] Similarly, the disclosure of material items in an inconspicuous place also seems to offer a clear-cut area of auditor liability because the disclosure in something-less-than-a-forthright manner gives the appearance of some intent to disguise a relevant and/or material item.[15]

III. The SEC Steps in More Definitively on Materiality

With sufficient evolving concerns about these pure quantitative standards for materiality, and the challenges of case-by-case determinations, the SEC began a process of redefining materiality for financial reporting because it appeared that qualitative issues were not going to emerge voluntarily as part of the standards for disclosure. In August, 1999, the SEC issued its Staff Accounting Bulletin (SAB) on the concept of materiality in the preparation of financial statements. While the SAB offers no bright line standards on disclosure, it does offer some new insights on the types of circumstances in which the qualitative measure for materiality is met even when the traditional quantitative 5% standard is not involved.

The following sections cover the fundamentals of the SEC's new position on materiality and provide some ethical insights into materiality and the ease with which those standards can be applied to escape the over analytical approach of the SAB and as well as the purely quantitative traditional notions of materiality.

A. The Basics of New SEC Materiality

The SAB makes clear that the SEC standard for materiality is not quantitative. Threshold standards are irrelevant, for example, when there has been an intentional

of compliance with generally accepted standards was evidence which may be very persuasive but not necessarily conclusive that he acted in good faith").

[12] *For example in* Gerstle v. Gamble-Skogmo, Inc., *298 F.Supp. 66 (E.D.N.Y. 1969), the auditors prepared financial statements for proxy materials with assets carried at book value (per GAAP) but did not disclose pending sales of the assets at far greater prices (a relevant factor to shareholders who would be voting on a merger).*

[13] *15 U.S.C. §§ 78dd-1, 78dd-2 (1999).*

[14] See Bryan v. Aston, *No. C75-0350 L (W.D. Ky. Aug. 13, 1976) (Westlaw, 1976 WL 828) (political contribution);* SEC V. United Brands Co., *Cir. No. 75-0509 (D.D.C. Jan. 27, 1976) (Westlaw, 1976 WL 756 (D.D.C)) (political contribution);* Meer v. United Brands Co., *No. 75 Cir. 1788 (S.D.N.Y. July 6, 1976) (Westlaw, 1976 WL 802 (D.C.N.Y.)) (bribe to foreign official).*

[15] See SEC v. Braniff Airways, Inc., *Litigation Release No. 7327, 9 S.E.C. Docket 292 (D.D.C. March 24, 1976) ($900,000 in a secret fund);* SEC v. Phillips Petroleum Co., *Litigation Release No. 6711, 6 S.E.C. Docket 419 (D. Minn. Jan. 31, 1975) ($634,000 in a secret fund);* SEC v. Gulf Oil Corp., *Litigation Release No. 6780, 6 S.E.C. Docket 464 (D.D.C. March 11, 1975) ($10 million passed through a subsidiary and then used for political contributions); and* SEC v. Ashland Oil, Inc., *Litigation Release No. 6890, 7 S.E.C. Docket 49 (D.D.C. May 19, 1975) ($700,000 in a secret fund).*

For a more complete historical discussion of standards for auditor liability see note 6 supra.

misstatement of sales or expenses. Following the research-based notion that such intentional acts are reflective of the character of management and the company as well as predictors of success, the SEC takes a near-absolute approach on intentional conduct and its disclosure. The SAB also takes great effort to remind auditors and officers of their reporting and disclosure obligations in the event the company issuing the financials is engaged in activity in violation of 10b.

Under the SAB, the fact that a market will react to information is a means of measuring materiality, regardless of amount. For example, with the issuance of the recent Microsoft decision, even at just the findings-of-fact stage in which Judge Jackson outlined monopolistic practices, the market reacted immediately, not even waiting for the conclusions of law or sanctions portions of the decision, which would be unveiled subsequently in parts. There is no way to know the actual impact of the findings of fact on Microsoft nor could we know which way the reaction would take the market. Initially, there was a drop in Microsoft's share price, which had rebounded by the following Monday. The impact of a judicial or regulatory finding on competitive markets and structure could be favorable as with the announcement of the Lucent technologies spin-off from AT&T. The impact could also be negative, as with several of the recent regulatory rulings on competitive market structures in the electric utility industry. However, the uncertainty centers around direction of market movement and degree, not whether the market is affected by the information. The information on monopolistic practices and market structure is material information that should be disclosed as part of the data for evaluating price.

The SAB also clarifies the cumulative effect issue in materiality. One misstatement in financial reports might be immaterial, in the sense of being below the threshold of 5%, but if such misstatements are part of a series over several quarters or years, financial reports should include the qualitative disclosure of ongoing issues regardless of their individual quantitative materiality.

B. Applying The New SEC Test to Situations

The SAB makes it pointedly clear that the 5% "bright line test" is but a starting point for the analysis on disclosure with financial reports requiring much deeper examination prior to make the "to disclose, or not to disclose" decision. The SAB provides a list of factors for that examination:

1. Whether the misstatement was the result of a natural lack of precision in measurement or the result of other factors;
2. Whether the misstatement affects earnings, trends, returns;
3. Whether the misstatement serves to conceal from analysts and investors the failure of the company to meet financial expectations and goals;
4. Whether the misstatement turns what was income into a loss;
5. Whether the misstatement centers around a portion of the company's business that is particularly critical for earnings and success;
6. Whether the misstatement means that the company was not in compliance with regulatory requirements;
7. Whether the misstatement means that the company's ratios, for example, were not met for purposes of loan covenants or any other contractual obligations tied to financial performance ratios;

8. Whether the misstatement had the effect of awarding or increasing bonuses to management and other employees as part of the company's incentive system; and
9. Whether the misstatement involved a violation of law, concealment or any other regulatory issues.

The SAB makes it clear that the list is not exhaustive and that there is no quick method for determining whether information is or is not material. The nine detailed and complex factors establish that there is a high level of expectation among SEC regulators for a very deliberative process in the determination of materiality. Any decision by management and auditors or either alone will require a new threshold to be met: that of careful consideration of all factors surrounding the decision which includes everything from these factors to market reaction.

Further, the SEC will take an aggregate approach. One factor may justifiably be found to be immaterial, but grouped with other factors creates an atmosphere or integrity problem. Paul Gerlach, an SEC associate director of enforcement noted in the *Wall Street Journal*, "There is effectively no safe harbor; a simple numerical test is not sufficient."[16] Chairman Arthur Levitt has noted that managers and auditors clearly understand the notions of materiality, "In markets where missing an earnings projection by a penny can result in a loss of millions of dollars in market capitalization, I have a hard time accepting that some of these so-called nonevents simply don't matter."[17]

IV. The Accounting Profession's Work to Date

Since March 1998, the Big Six (now Big Five) accounting firms have been working in the form of a task force to address the issue of materiality. The task force examined those companies' financial restatements that were initiated by the SEC in order to determine whether the SEC standards were different from those of the profession. The group compared financial restatements undertaken voluntarily by companies as well and concluded that there were no differences in the materiality standards being applied by the profession and those being followed by the SEC staff. However, the task force developed the following recommendations with respect to the materiality issue:

1. Auditors should adopt audit requirements aimed at encouraging audit clients to record adjustments to eliminate misstatements regardless of their quantitative materiality.
2. Auditors should develop guidance for the auditor's qualitative considerations for the audit process. A possible list was also developed as part of the report.
3. Auditors should be certain there are adequate consultation processes in place for the discussion of materiality issues among audit staff as well as management and board audit committees.
4. The firms agreed to sponsor audit research to better understand the issue of materiality and the role of the auditor in disclosure.

In short, the auditing profession was more general in its recommendations and has established a plan for implementation of the SEC standards, but offered little guidance

[16] *Elizabeth MacDonald, "Accounting Gets Two-Sided Overhaul,"* The Wall Street Journal, *September 8, 1999, p. A2.*

[17] Id.

for the profession. The SEC has removed the assurance, comfort, safe harbor and ease of the 5% threshold. Auditors and financial executives are left with the implementation task.

V. The Ethics of Materiality in Financial Disclosure

A. Confronting Disclosure

One of the typical issues in all ethical dilemmas is disclosure. Disclosure can resolve conflicts and prevent misrepresentation. It would help auditors, managers and users if a set of standards could be employed. Disclosure of the company's standards of disclosure might also help financial reporting.

Standards development on disclosure however, has not been successful, as illustrated by the Big 5 task force. Although many arguments can be marshaled for and against fully disclosed quantifiable and qualitative materiality standards, two arguments against them tend to prevail: Infeasibility and too much legal risk. Fears that significant new legal risks would be created by adoption of explicit materiality standards are real. Nonetheless, there have been proposals in the academic literature to opt for a voluntary disclosure of materiality standards. Informing the user of the auditor's materiality standard via explicit definition of materiality within the context of the financial report has been proposed since the 1980s. Given the SEC's strong position, the feasibility problem has been solved and the legal risk now lies in nondisclosure.

B. Confronting the Standard

Assuming that the materiality standard would be offered generically to users of the financial statement, the question still remains: What should that standard be?

There is the usual concern of many managers and auditors about their inability to predict how markets will react and their lack of experience in judging what an investor deems material. These managers and auditors have labored far too long in the comfort of the law without giving serious consideration to the adequacy of their disclosures. There are some misstatements that affect an investor's decision to buy, sell or hold. Follow a simple ethical standard such as, If it were your stock, would you want to know? The implementation of the new qualitative aspects of materiality should be quite simple under this type of review. The notion of materiality is facile when ethical standards are applied; it becomes complex only when the law is used as a shelter for nondisclosure.

Following this simple standard for disclosure, there are clearly issues that should be disclosed, even when the impact is positive. In the SEC's ongoing goal of preserving the transparency of U.S. financial statements, the element of integrity is being brought to the forefront with regulatory oversight. Below is a list of the types of information that should be disclosed ethically regardless of the amount because the information serves to provide a window into the soul of a company and that information has an impact on investors' decision-making process. The following list is a form of a qualitative safe harbor in the sense that if auditors find these factors present in a company, there must be disclosure, even if the amount is well below the traditional quantitative 5%.

1. Regulatory sanctions and actions against the company or individuals within the company. A charge of fraud that amounts to less than 5% of income is still a charge of fraud. For some time, environmental issues have been at the forefront of man-

agement discussion and disclosure even though the quantitative amounts could be material or zero. It is the unknown that mandates disclosure, coupled with the impact of negative information about company actions. Very few companies acknowledge, for example, the simple significance of consumer complaints filed with the Consumer Product Safety Commission. Yet those complaints, obtained by class action lawyers through Freedom of Information Act requests, form the basis of class action product liability suits. There is no quantitative figure associated with the complaint itself, but it is the beginning of class action liability.

2. Sales, inventory and other misstatements that served to place employees, at any level, in a position of earning bonuses, incentives, options, etc. It has long been established that earnings reversals are not the result of one-time poor choices on the part of management. Rather, there is an evolving pattern that begins with small issues and escalates. Because there are issues of character intertwined with amounts, regardless of materiality levels, the disclosure is necessary for investor evaluation. Manipulation of earnings is always material. Irregularities to "meet the numbers" even if immaterial should be disclosed.
3. Litigation that involves whistle-blowers. It is rare that these cases reach levels of materiality and those that do generally follow large-scale government sanctions as in the case of Columbia Health Care. However, a company with ongoing whistle-blower litigation once again carries some baggage with respect to the issues of its ethical culture and perhaps its character.
4. Whether the irregularity was related to loan covenant ratios and meeting such ratios.
5. Whether the irregularities were related to foreign operations where such irregularities could conceal everything from money laundering to violations of FCPA.

The SEC policy statement is not difficult to understand nor implement. The SEC policy is along the lines of the Supreme Court's position on pornography: You know it when you see it. There are certain types of activities within a company so revealing in their nature about the financial health and state of compliance and integrity of the company that disclosure is warranted, whether the amount is $1.00 or $6,000,000. And the ethical test which would satisfy the new legal standard is quite simple: if you as an investor would want this information, then it is material.

The impacts of ongoing and readily accepted earnings management are the introduction of unilateral, as opposed to universal reporting standards, the entrance into the gray area of manipulation and resulting questions about where the line of prohibition actually rests, and a refocus of management efforts on managing earnings as opposed to managing to earn. This last impact produces an atmosphere in which management's strategic plan is simply meeting goals, at whatever cost. Long-term planning, customer relations, and attention to strategy suffer. Such a short-term focus breeds an atmosphere in which ethical melt down becomes more likely than not. In every case of earnings reversal by a publicly-traded firm, there is one common factor: the managers were managing earnings and got creative. Their creativity crossed them over into the field of fiction.

In effect, the SEC's recent steps mean that, once again, laws and regulations are being used as a substitute for what should be an ethical issue. Laws will now impose ethics upon earnings management. The result will be protests, cries of woe, and complaints, but there will also be the disclosure and less sleight-of-hand.

Bibliography

Burgstanler, David and Ilia Dichev, "Earnings Management to Avoid Earnings Decreases and Losses," *Journal of Accounting and Economics* 24: 1997, p. 99.

Dechow, Patricia M., Richard G. Sloan, and Amy P. Sweeney, "Causes and Consequences of Earnings Manipulation: An Analysis of Firms Subject to Enforcement Actions by the SEC," *Contemporary Accounting Research* 13(1), 1996, p. 1.

Jiabalbo, James, "Discussion of 'Causes and Consequences,'" *Contemporary Accounting Research* 13(1), 1996, p. 37.

Merchant, Kenneth A. and Joanne Rockness, "The Ethics of Managing Earnings: An Empirical Investigation," *Journal of Accounting and Public Policy* 13, 1994, pp. 79–94.

Remarks by Arthur Levitt, "The Numbers Game," September 28, 1998, New York University. http://www.sec.gov/news/speeches/spch220.txt

Zweig, Kenneth Rosen and Marilyn Fischer, "Is Managing Earnings Ethically Acceptable?" *Management Accounting*, March 1994, p. 31.

Discussion Questions

1. What is the difference between quantitative materiality and qualitative materiality?
2. Are there some items that are always material and must be disclosed? Can you give examples?
3. Who makes the decisions on whether an item is material?

READING 5.3

Chainsaw Al and the Ethics of Materiality in Financial Reporting[18]

Marianne M. Jennings

I. Introduction

Al Dunlap was once Mr. Fix-it. He turned Scott Paper around and then moved on to Sunbeam. He used the same approach there that he had in the past, that approach that won him the moniker, "Chainsaw Al." He slashed employees, reduced costs and sent the stock price soaring. He was a Wall Street darling as he slashed employee payrolls while touting the need for efficiency. His 1996 book, *Mean Business: How I Save Bad*

[18] Corporate Finance Review *(forthcoming, 2001). Reprinted from Corporate Finance Review by RIA, 395 Hudson Street, New York, NY 10014.*

Companies and Make Good Companies Great (with Bob Andelman) was a business favorite.[19] When business managers uttered "Chainsaw Al," they did so with a knowing smile. So renown was his reputation that just the announcement in 1996 that he was Sunbeam's new CEO caused a 50 percent jump of the company's stock price in just one day. Sunbeam was at $12.50 per share on the day before the announcement of Mr. Dunlap's hiring and closed at over $18 by the end of day of the announcement.

Mr. Dunlap had a history of achievement; he had gone into Scott Paper and slashed its work force and size and then sold it to Kimberly-Clark for a substantial gain for the shareholders. That same strategy was planned for Sunbeam.

But Sunbeam was not as amenable to the Scott slash-and-sell format of recovery. In fact, Mr. Dunlap was dismissed as CEO of Sunbeam by 1998. The underlying reasons for that dismissal were issues related to the earnings stated for Sunbeam's 1997 financials. But it would be years before anyone understood how bad those misstatements were. In February 2001, Sunbeam filed for bankruptcy. In May 2001, the SEC announced fraud charges against Mr. Dunlap and 4 other former Sunbeam executives. The charges stem from accounting issues; the SEC takes issue with the booking of certain items and the auditors claim immateriality as a defense. At the heart of the Sunbeam accounting dispute with the SEC is a key question on financial reporting: if materiality is the standard for disclosure, when are items material? And at the heart of the issue of materiality is not the law, but ethics and the ethics of financial reporting.

II. The Sunbeam Books

Understanding what happened with Sunbeam is the first step to addressing what is not a new issue in accounting and auditing, that of materiality, but which is sure to receive continuing attention and direction because of this high-profile case.

In 1996, when Mr. Dunlap first came on board, Sunbeam took huge write-offs from the plant closings and layoffs that Mr. Dunlap ordered. However, for 1997, Sunbeam showed a profit, and Mr. Dunlap told analysts via conference call that Sunbeam had "an amazing year" and "We are winning in every aspect of our business." The Board gave Mr. Dunlap a $2 million raise in his base salary as well as stock options for his quick turnaround of their ailing company.

The result of the financial reports and Mr. Dunlap's optimistic statements was that Sunbeam's stock rose to its peak of $52 in the first quarter of 1998. With its credit riding high, Sunbeam undertook, under Mr. Dunlap's direction, the acquisition of Coleman, Inc., First Alert, Inc. and Mr. Coffee. The fits were logical because Coleman sold camping equipment, including lanterns; First Alert sold home smoke alarms, and Mr. Coffee was a premier home coffee machine producer.

However, it soon became obvious that Sunbeam did not have the funds for the acquisitions. In fact, within the first quarter of 1998, revelations about the 1997 financials began to emerge. A summary of the accounting and audit issues, which resulted in what the SEC has said was $62 million in mythical income of the $189 million reported, appears below.

[19] *There is another book that is non-autobiographical: John Byrne,* Chainsaw: The Notorious Career of Al Dunlap in the Era of Profit-at-Any-Price, *1999.*

- Sunbeam, Inc., a maker of home appliances such as electric blankets, the Oster line of blenders, mixers, can openers and electric skillets, has a rather large inventory of parts it needs for the repair of these appliances when they come back while under warranty. Sunbeam used a warehouse owned by EPI Printers to store the parts, which were then shipped out as needed. Sunbeam proposed selling the parts to EPI for $11,000,000 and then booking an $8,000,000 profit. However, EPI was not game for the transaction because its appraisal of the parts came in at only $2,000,000. To overcome the EPI objection, Sunbeam let EPI enter into an agreement to agree at the end of 1997. The "agreement to agree" would have EPI buy the parts for $11,000,000, which Sunbeam would then book as a sale with the resulting profit. However, the agreement to agree allowed EPI to back out of the deal in January 1998. The deal was booked, the revenue recognized, Mr. Dunlap viewed as a recovery artist, the share price went up and all was well. And all without EPI ever spending a dime.
- The value of Sunbeam's inventory was substantially reduced in 1996 so that when sales of it were recorded in 1997, the profits were unusually high.
- Sunbeam took additional write-downs in 1996 that the SEC alleges became a "cookie jar" of reserves that then would permit the appearance of higher profits in 1997.
- Sunbeam engaged in what is known as "channel stuffing" which is when inventory is shipped out before delivery is required or, in some cases, even requested, so that it can be reflected as sales for that quarter. For example, Sunbeam shipped electric blankets to a distributor and asked it to hold the blankets until the retailer was ready for shipment and promised the distributor a portion of the profits as a reward for taking the shipment so that Sunbeam could book a sale.
- Sunbeam also shipped orders to retailers that had not actually been placed with the idea of "cleaning up" in the next quarter or year once the company was past its recovery mode.

The SEC complaint accused Sunbeam and five of its executives, including its CFO and Mr. Dunlap, of "orchestrating a fraudulent scheme to create the illusion of a successful restructuring of Sunbeam and facilitate the sale of the company at an inflated price." The SEC director of enforcement called the fraud accusations part of the SEC's ongoing efforts to prevent "fraudulent earnings-management practices."[20]

III. The Auditor's Role

With such obvious issues of accounting improprieties, where were the auditors? Arthur Anderson served as the outside auditor for Sunbeam during this time, and its managing partner, Phillip E. Harlow, did see the questions and didn't particularly care for the Sunbeam executives' responses. Mr. Harlow asked the executives to restate earnings reflecting changes he deemed necessary. Management refused and the financials were certified anyway.

Further, Mr. Harlow did not see some of the issues and changes as "material" and required no action on the part of Sunbeam executives in terms of restating earning prior to his certification. For example, the "agreement to agree" with EPI while nothing more than a sham transaction was not "material" with regard to Sunbeam's level of income. Mr. Harlow defined materiality only in the sense of percentage of income and did not see such a disclosure as a reflection of management integrity. The total amount of the items Mr. Harlow permitted that the SEC now challenges amounted to 16 percent of Sunbeam's profits for 1997.

[20] *Jonathan Weil, "Five Sunbeam Ex-Executives Sued by SEC,"* The Wall Street Journal, *May 16, 2001, pp. A3, A4.*

Mr. Harlow hired PricewaterhouseCoopers to go over Sunbeam's books and his judgment calls and those auditors agree that Mr. Harlow certified "materially accurate financial statements."[21]

IV. The Role of Materiality

Mr. Harlow and PricewaterhouseCoopers are correct in their interpretation of the FASB and AICPA rules. The amounts involved in many of the noted improprieties were not "material" in a percentage-of-income sense. The problem is that an individual auditor's definition of materiality is the cornerstone of a certified audit. All an auditor does is certify that the financial statements "present fairly, in all material respects, the financial position of ________________, in conformity with generally accepted accounting principles."

There is no definition of materiality for the accounting profession. My research shows that most auditors use a rule of thumb of 5 to 10 percent as a threshold level of disclosure, such as 5 percent of net income or 10 percent of assets or vice versa.[22] They may also use a fixed dollar amount or an index of time and trouble in relation to the amount in question.[23]

However, it is clear just from the amount of regulatory action, shareholder litigation and judicial definitions, that the standard for materiality employed by auditors is not the same as the standard other groups would use in deciding which information should be disclosed. Table 1 on the following page, adapted from research previously published, shows this expectations gap.

V. The Role of Ethics in Materiality

The data and litigation demonstrate that there is something about the expectations of investors and those who ultimately determine liability for non-disclosure that differ from the standards employed by corporations and the auditing profession in making decisions on whether items must be disclosed and when they should be disclosed. Also, given that there are no definitive rules on what is and is not material and the pressures that audit firms feel, as in the Sunbeam case, to sign off on financials, the leadership role on materiality belongs to the financial executives of a company. Those who present the figures for audit and eventually disclosure should establish clear standards for what will be disclosed and when it will be disclosed.

A. Who sets the rules for materiality and disclosure and why?

The CEO and CFO, along with the support of the board, and particularly the audit committee, should establish clear rules for disclosure that reflect the values of the company. Such a collection of rules, grounded in values, is a means of not only preventing the types of poor judgment calls in the Sunbeam case, but a means of ensuring that disappointed shareholders do not take advantage of the expectation gap on

[21] *Anderson has settled the suit brought against it by shareholders for $110 million. Floyd Norris, "S.E.C. Accuses Former Sunbeam Official of Fraud,"* The New York Times, *May 16, 2001, pp. A1, C2.*

[22] *Marianne M. Jennings, Philip M. Reckers, and Daniel C. Kneer, "A Source of Insecurity: A Discussion and an Empirical Examination of Standards of Disclosure and Levels of Materiality in Financial Statements," 10* J. Corp. L. *639 (1985).*

[23] *Jeffries, "Materiality as Defined by the Courts," 51* CPA J. *13 (1981).*

Table 1
Reflections on the Expectations Gap

type of event	*% of judicial who would not disclose*	*% of CPAs who would not disclose*
Inventory reduction (5%)	54.7%	80.5%
Inventory reduction (10%)	47%	63%
Lawsuit (5% of net income and 75% probability of success)	24%	63%
Lawsuit (5% of net income and 50% probability of success)	36%	77%
Lawsuit (10% of net income and 75% probability of success)	16%	25%
Lawsuit (10% of net income and 50% probability of success)	25%	54%
Bribe (5% net income)	15%	10%
Bribe (10% net income)	-0-	4%

disclosure and place the company and its auditors in the unforgiving and costly arena of litigation.

B. What types of materiality standards should be adopted?

The table gives a fairly clear starting point for adopting standards and rules for materiality in a company's financial reports. In the table, there is little disagreement about the need to disclose a bribe, regardless of the amount. This meeting of legal (and hence SEC) minds and accounting minds illustrates the common grounds on materiality. First, the standard is not necessarily always monetary. There are issues, such as a company engaging in bribery, that reflect the nature of management and its operations. This type of information affects the investment decision for it is a fairly accurate predictor of how a company will perform if management integrity, or in this case compliance with the law, is missing.

With that beginning, that management integrity seems universally important; we can proceed with a checklist for disclosure. There are some items that must always be disclosed: bribe, criminal conduct on the part of the company or officers, regulatory sanctions, and any other types of matters, regardless of amount, that reflect on the quality of management, although not in an income-material fashion.[24]

With that outside parameter, managers should move to the more difficult questions that surround conduct such as that in the Sunbeam case: issues of earnings management, perhaps pushed to the extreme there. The human imagination knows no limits in the methods that have and will be developed for booking or not booking items in a creative fashion. It would be impossible to develop a chart that provided a "yes, disclose" or "no, no need to disclose" on every possible nuance of earnings man-

[24] *In fact, the SEC issued a Staff Accounting Bulletin (SAB) in August 1999 that clearly establishes some "musts" for materiality. One of those is whether there is an issue of the violation of the law, any concealment or the nondisclosure of regulatory action. And the SEC has noted, "There is effectively no safe harbor; a simple numerical test [for materiality] is not sufficient." Elizabeth MacDonald, "Accounting Gets Two-Sided Overhaul,"* The Wall Street Journal, *September 8, 1999, p. A2.*

agement. But, there can be a definitive model for getting to the heart of an accounting issue in which there is a question about its disclosure, non-disclosure or the timing of either. As a company establishes its ethical standards for materiality and disclosure, it should adopt the following questions as a framework for resolution:

- What historically has happened in cases in which these types of items are not disclosed? In our company? In other companies?
- What are the financial implications if this item is not disclosed now?
- What are our motivations for not disclosing this item?[25]
- What are our motivations for booking this item in this way?
- What are our motivations for not booking this item?
- How do we expect this issue to be resolved?
- Are our expectations consistent with the actions we are taking vis-à-vis disclosure?
- If I were a shareholder on the outside would this be the kind of information I would want to know?

For each of these questions, there is an illustration that can help everyone involved understand the significance of the inquiry and the decision.

1. What has happened historically?

The failure to disclose information, the overbooking of losses, and other forms of earnings management have not served any companies well. Sunbeam, Cendant, FINOVA, ConAgra, and W.R. Grace are all examples of companies that thought they could manage earnings and hang on until the next quarter brought better news. In the cases of FINOVA (a failure to write down a $70 million loan that had gone bad and challenging the auditors on its disclosure) and Sunbeam, the result was bankruptcy. Cendant, ConAgra and W.R. Grace continue to pay the price in terms of squandered trust.

As this question is contemplated it is perhaps best to assume that the laws of probability don't apply. These matters have a way of percolating to the surface and the longer the truth percolates, it not only doesn't get any better, its fallout becomes more significant for the company.

2. What are the financial implications if this item is not disclosed?

If non-disclosure translates into meeting market expectations, then there is an issue of pressure. For Sunbeam, the nondisclosure of creative booking of sales meant that its stock price soared and that it was in a position to begin an acquisition program that would see its fate become that of Scott Paper with all the returns that brought to its shareholders.

It is within this question that managers and auditors feel the greatest pressure. In the case of Sunbeam, it is not difficult to imagine that those who saw the issues of nondisclosure and their relevance were thinking, "But this is Al Dunlap running the show!" There was no reason to doubt his judgment call on these accounting matters because of his track record. However, precisely because of a stellar track record, officers are subject to the temptation of excessive management of earnings.

[25] *In thinking about this question, the words of outgoing SEC chairman Arthur Levitt are instructive, "In markets where missing an earnings projection by a penny can result in a loss of millions of dollars in market capitalization, I have a hard time accepting that some of these so-called nonevents simply don't matter."* Id.

Under this question are the close calls of accounting. For example, America Online (AOL) capitalized its advertising expenses in 1996 under an accounting rule that permitted such if the company could show, by some formula, that such an investment was necessary and would yield results. AOL had developed a formula for the customer and revenue results from advertising dollars and had capitalized its advertising costs, rather than expensed them. The SEC disputed the judgment call and AOL paid a fine. However, hindsight shows that AOL was correct in its formula and in sinking funds into advertising dollars because its heavy advertising netted it its customer base that thrives today.[26] While AOL proved to be right in hindsight on the efficacy of advertising dollars, it did release income statements that were over-inflated because they did not indicate the dollars of income being expended for advertising purposes. While AOL settled the charges with the SEC, it admitted no wrongdoing.

For those handling such close call issues, perhaps there is a non-either/or answer to the question. For example, AOL could capitalize the ad dollars but include an explanation of that approach in the financials so that investors understand the true financial picture of the company.

3. and 4. What are our motivations for booking or not booking this item?

As a means of checks and balances for the temptation of the moment and the process of group think in the management decision-making process, this question forces those involved to understand their motivation because that motivation may provide insight into whether the booking or non-booking of the item is ethically correct. Motivations that cloud judgment include bonuses tied to earnings goals, option rights, pending retirements and other types of personal rewards that tempt the soul and strain the values. Look also to pride in achievement. Mr. Dunlap certainly had monetary motivation, but with his book and reputation, there was a certain pride in achievement that he was loathe to lose.

5. How do we expect this issue to be resolved?

If your resolution is to "make it up next quarter," or "hang on until _______," then there is a problem. Timing is everything and, using the lack of presence of the laws of probability, don't count on timing to be impeccable. There are plenty of good intentions in all reporting decisions. This question asks you to focus on resolution if you decide to disclose or not disclose a particular issue or item. For example, California Micro Devices, Inc. inflated its sales and earnings figures by booking bogus sales to fake companies. Not a bad source of revenue, if you can fake it. Fully one-third of its 1994 revenue was bogus and by 2000, even the auditors were being investigated for fraud because everyone had the good intentions of keeping the company afloat and the employees working.[27]

6. Is the resolution you anticipate consistent with the actions you are taking?

In the case of FINOVA, the company had no resolution for the write-down of $70 million. The decision was just to postpone it hoping that other areas of the company could make up for the loss over time. If the non-disclosure has to be resolved by some-

[26] *Floyd Norris, "AOL Pays a Fine to Settle a Charge That It Inflated Profits,"* The New York Times, *May 16, 2000, p. C1.*

[27] *Elizabeth MacDonald, "Auditors Miss a Fraud and SEC Tries to Put Them Out of Business,"* The Wall Street Journal, *January 6, 2000, pp. A1, A8.*

thing unrelated to the issue, you perhaps have a fairly good indication that you are pushing the envelope on materiality.

7. If you were a shareholder on the outside, would you want to know what is being withheld from you?

This question is perhaps the most telling and the one that will give employees a clear indication of management expectations on materiality. This question asks that you put yourself in the position of someone who has invested or is about to invest in the company. Is this the type of information that investor would deem important and relevant in making that investment decision to buy, sell or hold your stock? Campbell's Soup faced 5 class action lawsuits by shareholders for its alleged inflation of the value of its stock by reporting inflated product sales to distributors when, in reality, no product had ever been shipped to them, let alone sold.[28] In short, how would you want to be treated as a shareholder with regard to this information? Once you know the answer to that question, the issue of materiality is not as difficult as CPAs or judges make it. In fact, it is this shareholder perspective that prevents the eventual shareholder suits that follow the failure to take into account this view.

Truth doesn't get better with time. If the company has sales, performance and write-down issues, withholding that information with the hope that things will get better seems to be the beginning of the decline. Truth withheld means reputational capital squandered when the truth is eventually revealed, as it always is under the non-probability laws of financial reporting. To avoid the fate of Sunbeam and its executives, begin with the 7-point analysis of financial reporting. The seven factors leave little doubt as to the definition of this confusing concept of materiality.

Discussion Questions

1. Were the shareholders of Sunbeam ultimately served in the best way by the decision to enter into the sham contract?
2. Why does "making it up in the next quarter" not work?
3. Do you think there are other ways for a company to survive beyond earnings management? If you were a manager and you were not going to meet quarterly goals, what would you do and say?

CASE 5.4

Creative Medical Billing

Billie Jean Young is the administrator for Los Lomas, a private hospital located in Palm Springs, California. Los Lomas serves patients who carry insurance in 95 percent of the procedures the hospital performs. Los Lomas' noninsurance procedures tend to be plastic surgery; all plastic surgery patients pay in advance. The nature of the medical business at Los Lomas is largely the result of the hospital's location in an upper-middle class retirement/resort area.

28 *"Campbell's in the Soup?"* National Law Journal, *February 7, 2000, p. B3.*

Young has just read a recent study that shows that 98 percent of all hospital bills contain errors. Internal data for Los Lomas shows that the hospital receives complaints of errors on approximately 20 percent of the bills it issues.

The study indicates that doctors are "fudging" on insurance claims. All the players in the health care system follow a billing system based on 500 groups of 3,500 medical procedures and 12,574 diagnostic codes. How an illness is coded can make a substantial difference in the amount of reimbursement the medical provider receives for the care of the patient. For example, coding the removal of a mole as a larger procedure (known as "upcoding") will bring additional funds from an insurer. Breaking down surgeries (or "unbundling" them) into segments such as exploration, removal, and repair of scar tissue will substantially increase claims. Itemizing each test in a battery of tests ("exploding" the battery) can triple the cost of a single blood sample. Doctors accomplish all these billing strategies by savvy use of the coding process.

Insurers do have computer programs to check for "code creeps" (increased billing by coding), but often reject such claims in a report to the patient that explains how the charges exceed "usual and customary limits." The patient must then pay personally the amounts considered excessive.[29]

In many cases, miscoding is done to help provide patients with insurance coverage when coverage might not otherwise be available. For example, a patient's insurance might not cover routine tests as part of a physical but would cover those same tests if they were coded "to rule out cancer." Infertility procedures would not be covered, but diagnostic surgery to determine the presence of endometriosis would.

Most medical care providers hire consultants to help them with "upcoding." One consultant noted, "Every hospital does it or they die." Still another consultant noted, "Why shouldn't they go for the higher one?" But another consultant noted, "Oh, I grant you, there are shades of gray, but when hospitals cross the line, they know it." He also labeled the art of upcoding a "pathetic commentary on our times. These guys should be figuring out how to better treat patients in their hospitals."[30]

Many of these practices result from the inability to collect bills from uninsured patients who are simply unable to pay. Hospitals often use billings for insured patients to cover the costs they must absorb in providing care for uninsured patients. For example, one Florida hospital charged an insured patient $15 for one ounce of petroleum jelly. However, the five-digit CPT coding system is complex, confusing, and fraught with ambiguities. Some errors are the result of these factors.

Medicare recently announced a "bundling" payment policy for heart surgeries, under which it will pay a package price for coronary bypass procedures. The price will include all charges for both hospitals and doctors. Medicare officials maintain that "unbundled" bills encourage doctors to perform more procedures. Doctors maintain that the policy will sacrifice quality of care and their autonomy in making treatment decisions.[31]

[29] *Steve Marshall, "Overcharges Force New Rx in Fla. Hospitals,"* USA Today, *July 6, 1992, p. 1A.*

[30] *Rhonda Rundle, "How Doctors Boost Bills by Misrepresenting the Work They Do,"* The Wall Street Journal, *December 6, 1989, p. A1.*

[31] *Ron Winslow, "Medicare Tries to Save With One-Fee Billing for Some Operations,"* The Wall Street Journal, *June 10, 1992, pp. A1, A5.*

As these issues were unfolding, Ms. Young noted the evolving story of Columbia Health Care. Columbia/HCA Healthcare Corporation, Inc., the nation's largest hospital chain (342 hospitals), was investigated by the FBI for upcoding. The investigation began with an early-morning FBI raid on Columbia offices.[32] A Columbia newsletter once noted that the difference between coding a hip vs. a femur procedure is $4,493.[33]

Columbia began its own internal probe as the FBI investigated. Three executives were indicted in July 1997 on charges of defrauding the government by overbilling. In September 1997 Columbia warned its profits would decline with earnings per share dropping from 46 cents per share to 20 or 25 cents per share. Columbia fired its top executives and began a process of downsizing that included the reduction of the number of its hospitals from 345 to 220.

By October 1997, the FBI filed an affidavit in its investigation describing the fraud at Columbia/HCA as "systemic." The FBI unearthed a system in which expenses were overstated in order to take advantage of the fact that government oversight was lax because of low staffing and sheer complexity of the accounting and billing systems. Intent was alleged because Columbia waited two to three years before counting profits from these additional expenses to be certain that there were no audits or federal disputes with the expenses booked. The usual practice if a government agent found overstated expenses was to simply repay the amount. Generally there were no fines or interest. The FBI alleged that Columbia established its bookkeeping and accounting procedures in order to maximize its benefits from such a system.

The three executives that had been fired, plus one additional executive who was indicted later, Jay Jarrell, Robert Whiteside, Michael Neeb, and Carl Lynn Dick, went to trial in Florida in July 1999. Both Mr. Jarrell and Mr. Whiteside were convicted of defrauding the federal government. Mr. Neeb was acquitted. The jury was unable to reach a verdict in Mr. Dick's case, and his trial ended with a hung jury. Mr. Jarrell was sentenced in December 1999 to 33 months in prison and a $10,000 fine and was ordered to pay $1.7 million in restitution to the federal government.

Shareholder lawsuits began against Columbia all around the country. Between March 1997 and August 1997, the value of Columbia's stock dropped by one-third. Columbia's auditor, KPMG Peat Marwick, was also named as a defendant in the suits.[34] By 2000, Columbia had spent over $200 million in attorneys' fees and internal investigation costs.[35]

Several whistle-blowers initially filed suit against Columbia and then were joined by the Justice Department. They had been assisting the FBI. U.S. Attorney James Sheehan said that the whistle-blowers were invaluable to the investigation, "The whistle-blowers get you inside, share the company's intent and knowledge and provide

[32] *Julie Appleby, "Columbia Agrees to $745M Penalty,"* USA Today, *May 19, 2000, p. 1B; Kurt Eichenwald, "Hospital Company Agrees to Pay $745 Million in U.S. Fraud Case,"* The New York Times, *May 19, 2000, p. B1.*

[33] *In May 2000, Columbia changed its name to HCA—the Healthcare Co., as part of its effort to remove any taint from its image that resulted from the investigation, criminal charges, settlement, and criminal trials of its former executives. "Columbia/HCA Changes Name,"* The New York Times, *May 26, 2000.* New York Times Archives.

[34] *Kurt Eichenwald, "Accounting Firm Is Named In Medicare Fraud Lawsuit,"* The New York Times, *May 29, 1999, p. B5.*

[35] *Holman W. Jenkins, Jr., "A Hospital Chain's Lemonade Man,"* The Wall Street Journal, *May 24, 2000, p. A27.*

a road map for routines and systems."[36] Under federal whistle-blower protection statutes, those who report violations of federal laws by their companies are entitled to a percentage of the fine if the company settles or is found guilty of the violation and is required to pay a fine as part of either disposition. For example, for his role in reporting the billing issues at Olsten Home Health Care Service, Inc., Donald McLendon was given 24 percent of the $41 million penalty Olsten agreed to pay in order to settle the case. Olsten was once a business partner of Columbia.

One of the whistle-blowers at Columbia was James Alderson, a hospital accountant, who had been with Columbia for a number of years and at one hospital was asked to create two sets of books. At all the locations where he worked, he suspected that his employer was inflating expenses in its submissions to Medicare.[37]

By 2000, Columbia agreed to a settlement of $745 million on Medicare fraud charges, the largest settlement in the history of Medicare. The settlement covered only the criminal charges and three of the five sets of civil charges. By March of 2001, the Justice Department had filed a new set of charges against Columbia.[38] The new charges allege more inflation of Medicare cost reports as well as the payment of kickbacks to physicians. The Justice Department is asking for $400 million more in false claims reimbursements with these charges.[39]

At the same time the additional charges were filed, Michael Chertoff, the lead outside defense lawyer for Columbia HCA in these health care charges, was nominated by President George W. Bush and confirmed by the Senate to head the criminal division of the Justice Department. Some analysts reacted positively to his appointment because of their belief that it was a signal that the Bush administration would not be pursuing health care providers as vigorously as the Clinton Justice Department had.[40]

Ms. Young thought of what happened to Columbia and its executives and the charges that were still pending and wondered how she could develop a policy for her hospital. She also knew that she had the same types of systemic and structural issues as Columbia. For example, her hospital had physicians working there who had an ownership interest in the hospital. She wondered if she would be able to suggest policies given their ownership and authority.

Discussion Questions

1. If everyone was doing their billing in the same fashion, why is there a concern about ethics or possible illegality?

[36] *Kurt Eichenwald, "He Blew the Whistle and Health Giants Quaked,"* The New York Times, *October 18, 1998, pp. MB1, 13 (Section 3).*

[37] Id.

[38] *Lucette Lagnado, "HCA Faces New U.S. Filing on Medicare,"* The Wall Street Journal, *March 19, 2001, p. B13.*

[39] *"U.S. to Seek $400 Million More at HCA,"* The New York Times, *March 16, 2001, p. C5.*

[40] *Mr. Chertoff was the chief counsel for the Senate Whitewater Investigation during the Clinton years and has been the chief architect of the country's antiterrorism program, including expanding changes in the authority of federal agents for wiretaps and investigations.*

2. If there are shades of gray in diagnosing, is there any problem with always taking the higher code?
3. Do hospitals exist to make money or treat the ill?
4. How did shades of gray turn into allegations of systemic fraud and criminal indictments?
5. Why are there whistle-blowers in this case?
6. Should Ms. Young commission a study of the billing practices at Los Lomas and implement any changes that would correct the overbilling described?
7. Will Ms. Young be able to affect physicians' conduct in coding?
8. Do fudging, upcoding, exploding, and unbundling really harm anyone? Aren't many patients helped by these practices?
9. If patients are not complaining, is it a wise use of resources to audit bills?
10. In many cases, hospitals and physicians maintain these billing practices in order to shift costs. That is, they receive payment from insured patients to make up for the lack of payment from the uninsured who are unable to pay. Is this fair? Is it honest? Should it be disclosed?

CASE 5.5

MiniScribe and the Auditors

MiniScribe, founded in 1980 and based in Longmont, Colorado, was a disk drive manufacturer. When MiniScribe hit a slump in the mid-1980s because it had lost its largest customer, IBM, the board of directors brought in Q. T. Wiles. Called the "Mr. Fix-It" of high technology industries, Wiles had turned around Adobe Systems, Granger Associates, and Silicon General, Inc.[41]

When Wiles took over at MiniScribe, he engaged the venture-capital and investment banking firm of Hambrecht & Quist to raise the capital needed for the firm's turnaround. Hambrecht & Quist raised $20 million in 1987 through the sale of debentures. Wiles was, at that time, the chairman of Hambrecht & Quist. Hambrecht & Quist purchased $7.5 million of the debentures and also purchased a 17 percent interest in MiniScribe.

With new capital and simultaneous cost cuts, MiniScribe's sales went from $113.9 million in 1985 to a projected $603 million in 1988. In 1987, MiniScribe's board asked Wiles to stay on for another three years. That year, MiniScribe's stock climbed to $14 per share.

During 1988, the computer industry underwent another slump, and by May, Wiles and other officers were selling stock. Wiles sold 150,000 shares for between $11 and $12 per share, and seven other officers sold 200,000 shares.

[41] *"ITT Qume Chief Named President at MiniScribe,"* Electronic News, *November 5, 1984, pp. 20–21.*

By the time the shares were sold, MiniScribe held the unenviable position of having high inventory and high receivables. Industry sales were down, and MiniScribe customers were not paying their bills. In early 1989, MiniScribe announced a $14.6 million loss for the final quarter of 1988. MiniScribe's ratio of inventory to sales was 33 percent (the industry average was 24 percent), and its receivables were ninety-four days behind (the industry average was seventy days). The amount of receivables went from $109 million to $173 million in the last quarter of 1988.[42]

MiniScribe's release of the new financial information resulted in an in-house audit, shareholder lawsuits, and an investigation of stock trading by the Securities and Exchange Commission (SEC).[43] Scrutiny by regulators, outside directors, and the SEC revealed that Wiles, through his unrealistic sales goals, had created a high-pressure environment for managers.[44] In interviews, managers described "dash meetings" in which Wiles spouted his management philosophies. In one such meeting, Wiles had two controllers stand as he fired them, saying, "That's just to show everyone I'm in control of the company."[45] Wiles' attorney described him as "fairly autocratic and very demanding of the people who work for him."[46]

The in-house audit uncovered that, by late 1986, financial results had become the sole criterion for performance evaluations and bonuses at MiniScribe.[47] To be sure that they hit their quotas, MiniScribe sales personnel had used creative accounting maneuvers.[48] For example, in one case a customer was shipped twice as many disk drives as had been ordered—at a value of $9 million. Although the extra drives were returned, the sale for all the drives had already been booked.[49]

The investigation also revealed that, in some orders, sales were booked at the time of shipment even though title would not pass to the customer until completion of shipment. An examination of MiniScribe's financial records showed that the company had manipulated its reserves to offset its losses.[50] MiniScribe posted only 1 percent as reserves, whereas the industry range was 4 to 10 percent. In some of the transactions the audit uncovered, shipments sent to MiniScribe warehouses were booked as sales when, in fact, customers were not even invoiced until the drives were shipped from the warehouse.[51]

Through these creative manipulations and others, MiniScribe officers kept up a rosy fiscal appearance for the firm's auditors, Coopers & Lybrand. For example, for the 1987 audited financials, company officials packaged and shipped construction bricks (pretend inventory valued at $3.66 million) so that these products would count as re-

[42] *Michelle Schneider, "Firm's Execs 'Perpetrated Mass Fraud,' Report Finds,"* Rocky Mountain News, *December 12, 1989, pp. 1-B, 2-B.*

[43] *"Internal Probe Underway by Directors at MiniScribe,"* Electronic News, *May 29, 1989, p. 19.*

[44] *Peter Sleeth, "Audit to Compound MiniScribe's Troubles,"* The Denver Post, *August 6, 1989, pp. 1H–7H.*

[45] *Andy Zipser, "Recipe for Sales Led to Cooked Books,"* The Denver Post, *August 14, 1989, pp. 2B–3B.*

[46] Id.

[47] *Stuart Zipper, "Filings Reveal MiniScribe Struggle,"* Electronic News, *January 15, 1990, pp. 38, 40.*

[48] *Peter Sleeth, "MiniScribe Details 'Massive Fraud,'"* The Denver Post, *September 12, 1989, pp. 1C, 4C.*

[49] *Michelle Schneider, "MiniScribe Execs Rigged Huge Fraud, Audit Says,"* Rocky Mountain News, *September 12, 1989, pp. 1B–2B.*

[50] Id.

[51] Id.

tail sales. When bricks were returned, the sales were reversed but inventory increased. Obsolete parts and scraps were rewrapped as products and shipped to warehouses to be counted in inventory.

It was discovered during the 1986 audit by Coopers & Lybrand that company officials broke into trunks containing the auditors' work papers and increased year-end inventory figures.[52]

With the disclosure of the internal audit and the discovery of these creative accounting practices and inventory deceptions, MiniScribe's stock continued to drop, selling for $1.31 per share by September 1989. By 1990, MiniScribe had filed for bankruptcy and was purchased by Maxtor Corporation.[53]

Lawsuits against Hambrecht & Quist, Wiles, and Coopers & Lybrand were brought by Kempner Capital Management, the U.S. National Bank of Galveston, and eleven other investors in the debentures sold by Hambrecht & Quist. In February 1992, a jury awarded the investors $28.7 million in compensatory damages and $530 million in punitive damages.[54] Coopers & Lybrand was held responsible for $200 million, Wiles for $250 million, Hambrecht & Quist for $45 million, and Mr. Hambrecht for $35 million.[55]

Discussion Questions

1. What types of pressures led managers to "cook the books" at MiniScribe?
2. Were the auditors, Coopers & Lybrand, morally responsible for the investors' losses?
3. Suppose you were a manager who was asked to wrap construction bricks in disk drive packaging. Would you ask, "Why?" Would you be able to continue your employment? Would you be morally responsible for investors' losses by wrapping the bricks?
4. Were the internal control people (internal auditors) at MiniScribe morally responsible for the investors' losses?
5. Were the auditors just duped? Should deceived auditors be held responsible for investors' losses?

CASE 5.6

FINOVA and the Loan Write-Off

The FINOVA Group, Inc. was formed as a commercial finance firm in 1992. It was created as a spin-off from the Greyhound Financial Corporation (GFC). GFC

52 Peter Sleeth, *"MiniScribe Stock Plunges 36%,"* The Denver Post, *September 13, 1989, p. 1D.*

53 Stuart Zipper, *"MiniScribe Seeks Chapter 11 Sale of Firm for $160M,"* Electronic News, *January 8, 1990, pp. 1, 54.*

54 Andrew Pollack, *"Large Award in MiniScribe Fraud Suit,"* The New York Times, *February 5, 1992, p. C1.*

55 Andrew Pollack, *"The $550 Million Verdict,"* The New York Times, *February 9, 1992, p. C2.*

underwent a complete restructuring at that time and other spin-offs included the Dial Corporation.

FINOVA, headquartered in Phoenix, Arizona, quickly became a Wall Street darling. Its growth was ferocious. By 1993, its loan portfolio was over $1 billion both through its own loans as well as the acquisition of U.S. Bancorp Financial, Ambassador Factors, and TriCon Capital. In 1994, FINOVA had a successful $226 million stock offering. By 1995, its loan portfolio was $4.3 billion. Standard & Poors rated the company's senior debt as "A" and Duff & Phelps upgraded its rating to "A" in 1995 when FINOVA issued $115 million in convertible preferred shares and its portfolio reached $6 billion. FINOVA's income went from $30.3 million in 1991 to $117 million by 1996 to $13.12 billion in 1999. *Forbes* named FINOVA to its Platinum 400 list of the fastest-growing and most profitable companies in January 2000.

FINOVA was consistently named as one of the top companies to work for in the United States (it debuted as #12 on the list published by *Fortune* magazine in 1998 and subsequent years). Its benefits included an on-site gym for employee workouts and tuition for the children of FINOVA employees (up to $3,000 per child) who attended any one of the three Arizona state universities under what FINOVA called the "Future Leaders Grant Program."[56] FINOVA also had generous bonus and incentive plans tied to the stock price of the company. *Fortune* magazine described the 500 stock options each employee is given when hired, the free-on-site massages every Friday, concierge services, and unlimited time off with pay for volunteer work as a "breathtaking array of benefits."[57]

The name FINOVA was chosen as a combination of "financial" and "innovators." However, some with language training pointed out that FINOVA is a Celtic term that means "pig with lipstick." FINOVA took pride in its strategic distinction from other finance companies. It was able to borrow cheaply and then make loans to businesses at a premium. Its borrowers were those who were too small, too new, or too much in debt to qualify at banks.[58] Its 1997 annual report included the following language from FINOVA's CEO and chairman of the board, Sam Eichenfeld:

> FINOVA is, today, one of America's largest independent commercial finance companies. We concentrate on serving midsize business—companies with annual sales of $10 million to $300 million—with arguably the industry's broadest array of financing products and services. The goals we set forth in our first Annual Report were to:
>
> - grow our income by no less than 10% per year;
> - provide our shareholders with an overall return greater than that of the S & P 500;
> - preserve and enhance the quality of our loan portfolios;
> - continue enjoying improved credit ratings
>
> We have met those goals and, because they remain equally valid today, we intend to continue meeting or surpassing them in the future. Many observers comment on FINOVA's thoughtfulness and discipline and, indeed, FINOVA prides itself on its focus.

[56] *Dawn Gilbertson, "Finova's Perks Winning Notice,"* Arizona Republic, *December 22, 1998, pp. E1, E9.*

[57] *"The 100 Best Companies to Work For,"* Fortune, *January 11, 1999, p. 122.*

[58] *Riva D. Atlas, "Caught in a Credit Squeeze,"* The New York Times, *November 2, 2000, pp. C1, C21.*

FINOVA also had a reputation for its generous giving in the community. Again, from its 1997 annual report:

> FINOVA believes that it has a responsibility to support the communities in which its people live and work. Only by doing so can we help guarantee the future health and vitality of our clients and prospects, and only by doing so can we assure ourselves of our continuing ability to attract the best people.
>
> Over the years, not only have FINOVA and its people contributed monetarily to a broad range of charitable, educational and cultural causes, but FINOVA people have contributed their time and energy to a variety of volunteer efforts.
>
> In 1996, FINOVA contributed more than $1.5 million and thousands of volunteer hours to educate and develop youth, house the homeless, feed the hungry, elevate the arts, and support many other deserving causes around the country.

FINOVA's ascent continued in the years following the 1997 report. Its stock price climbed above $50 per share and management continued to emphasize reaching the income goals and the goals for portfolio growth. Throughout the company many spoke of the unwritten goal of reaching a stock price of $60 per share. That climb in stock price was rewarded. The stock traded in the $50 range for most of 1998 and 1999, reaching a high of $54.50 in July of 1999.

At the end of 1998, FINOVA reported that Mr. Eichenfeld's compensation for the year was $6.5 million, the highest for any CEO of firms headquartered in Phoenix. More than half of the compensation consisted of bonuses. Mr. Eichenfeld and his wife purchased a $3 million home in Paradise Valley shortly following the year-end announcement in 1998 of his compensation.[59] Mr. Eichenfeld was named the 1999 Fabulous Phoenician by *Phoenix Magazine* which included the following description:

> A true mensch in every sense of the word, Sam casually says, "I do what I can," referring to the community for which he has done so much. While he maintains a modest air on the outside, Sam admits, "I take a lot of pride in having created a lot of opportunity for a lot of people." As long as Sam is head of FINOVA and lives in this community, we're sure there will be many more people who will benefit from his kindness and his generosity.[60]

It was sometime during the period from 1996 through 1998 that issues regarding financial reporting arose within the company. FINOVA had a decentralized management structure that created autonomous units. There were at least sixteen different finance divisions such as Commercial Equipment Finance, Commercial Real Estate Finance, Corporate Finance, Factoring Services, Franchise Finance, Government Finance, Healthcare Finance, Inventory Finance, Transportation Finance, and Rediscount Finance. Each of these units had its own manager, credit manager, and financial manager. In many cases, the failure of one unit to meet prescribed goals resulted in another unit making up for that shortcoming through some changes in that unit's numbers that they would report for the consolidated financial statements of FINOVA.

[59] *"Finova Chief Splurges on $3 Million Mansion,"* Arizona Republic, *January 23, 1998, pp. E1, E7.*

[60] Phoenix Magazine, *1999.*

The Resort Finance division was a particularly high-risk segment of the company. Resort Finance was the term used to describe what were time-share interests that FINOVA was financing.[61] Time-share financing is a particularly risky form of financing because lenders are loaning money to borrowers who live in France for property located in the Bahamas that has been built by a company from the Netherlands and is managed by a firm with its headquarters in Britain. The confluence of laws, jurisdiction, and rights makes it nearly impossible to collect should the borrowers default. And the default rate is high because time-sharing interests are a luxury item that are the first payments to be dropped when households experience a drop in income because of illness or the loss of a job.

Resort Finance would prove to be a particularly weak spot in the company and an area in which questions about FINOVA's financial reporting would arise. For example, FINOVA had a time-share property loan for an RV park in Arkansas that had a golf course and restaurant. The idea, when first acted on in 1992, was that folks could pay for a place to park their RV in beautiful Arkansas for a week or two in a time-share RV resort. When the loan was made in 1992, the property had a book value of $800,000. At the time of the default in 1995, the property was worth $500,000. FINOVA took back the property but did not write down the loan. It did, however, continue to report the loan as an earning asset even as it capitalized the expenses it incurred to maintain the golf course and restaurant. By 1997, FINOVA was carrying the Arkansas time-share resort on its books as a $5.5 million earning asset. One manager remarked, "You couldn't sell all of Arkansas and get $5.5 million and we were carrying a bad loan at that amount."[62]

Because of its lending strategies, FINOVA had higher risk in virtually all of its lending divisions. For example, it was highly invested in high-tech companies because they fit the category of too new and too risky for banks.

However, FINOVA edged into the *Fortune* 1000 and built new company headquarters in Scottsdale, Arizona, as part of a revitalization project there. Its headquarters housed 380 employees, cost $50 million to construct, and was located just north of the tony Scottsdale Fashion Square shopping mall. FINOVA had about 1,000 other employees at offices around the world.

In the first quarter of 1999, FINOVA again caught national attention for the cover of its annual report that would soon be released. The cover featured a robot, but the head of the robot had an underlying wheel that readers could rotate. There were six heads to the robot, all photos of FINOVA employees. The torso of the robot was a safe and the arms and legs were made of symbols of the various industries in which FINOVA had lending interests. "When you have innovators in your name, you can't do a generic annual report," was the description from a FINOVA PR spokesman.[63]

However, the buzz over the annual report cover was small compared to what happened when the cover, printed ten weeks in advance of the content, was to be coupled with the numbers inside the report. FINOVA announced that its annual report would

[61] *Interviews with Jeff Dangemond, former finance/portfolio manager, FINOVA, 1996–2000.*

[62] Id.

[63] *"Cover of Finova's '98 Report Turns Heads,"* Arizona Republic, *April 9, 1999, p. E1.*

be delayed. It was unclear what was happening until its longstanding auditors, Deloitte and Touche, were fired. Mr. Eichenfeld explained that FINOVA fired its auditors because they had waited so long to discuss their concerns and issues with management. He indicated that he felt they should have raised the issues much earlier than on the eve of the release of the numbers.[64]

FINOVA then hired Ernst & Young, but when the annual report was finally released the company also announced that it would be restating earnings for the year. The price of the company's stock began to decline. FINOVA worked diligently to restore credibility, with its officers noting that the auditors' disagreements with management's numbers were often because the company was too conservative in its accounting and that there were counterbalances for decisions on aggressive vs. conservative accounting practices.[65] However, with a shift in economic conditions and the end of the high-tech market run, the asset quality of FINOVA's portfolio was deteriorating. FINOVA's acquisition of the Fremont Financial Group of California for $765 million only increased investors' concerns about the direction of the company and the quality of its management. By the end of 1999, its stock price had dipped to $34 per share.

In early 2000, when it was again time for the release of the annual report, there was to be another announcement about FINOVA's financial position. FINOVA announced that it was writing down a $70 million loan to a California computer manufacturer. Ernst & Young refused to certify the financial statements until the write-off was taken and the resulting shake-up followed.[66] At the same time as the announcement of the write-off, the FINOVA board announced Sam Eichenfeld's retirement with a compensation package of $10 million.[67]

FINOVA had to take an $80 million hit, or $0.74 per share, in one day to cover the loan write-off of $70 million plus the compensation package. FINOVA's stock, which had dipped to $32 per share when the 1998 issues on the annual report delay first surfaced, dropped to $19.88 in one day of heavy trading. The 38 percent dip in stock value was the largest for any stock that day on the New York Stock Exchange, March 27, 2000.[68] As analysts noted, there was a downward spiral because the trust had been breached in 1998; confidence was not regained and this latest write-off and its delay served to shake investor confidence. Two rating agencies immediately lowered FINOVA's credit ratings and the costs of its funds jumped dramatically.[69]

Shareholder lawsuits began in May 2000 with several alleging that the $70 million loan had been in default eight months earlier but that, because of bonus and compensation packages tied to the share price, the officers and managers opted not to write the loan off in order to maximize their compensation packages, which were computed at the end of December before the write-off was taken.

[64] *Dawn Gilbertson, "Finova Record Smudged,"* Arizona Republic, *April 18, 1999, pp. D1, D2.*

[65] *Max Jarman, "Finova Group's Stock Sinks,"* Arizona Republic, *December 10, 1999, pp. E1, E2.*

[66] *Anne Brady, "Shareholders Sue Finova Executives,"* The Tribune, *May 20, 2000, p. B1.*

[67] *Dawn Gilbertson, "Surprises at Finova,"* Arizona Republic, *March 28, 2000, pp. B1, B9.*

[68] Id.

[69] *Rhonda L. Rundle, "Finova Retains Credit Suisse Unit to Assess Operations,"* The Wall Street Journal, *May 10, 2000, p. A12.*

Also during May 2000, Credit Suisse First Boston, hired to aid the company strategically, announced that FINOVA had lost a $500 million line of credit from banks. Such a loss was seen as mandating the sale of the company because commercial loan companies must have $1 in a credit line as back-up for every $1 in commercial paper. FINOVA's stock fell to $12.62 on May 9, 2000.[70] Analysts noted that FINOVA's aggressive growth strategy placed it in a particularly vulnerable situation because, as credit lines dried up, it had more exposure on its large loan portfolios. Further, the nature of those portfolios was such that its default rate was higher than other commercial lenders. Analysts valued its loan portfolio at $0.58 on the dollar.[71]

By early 2001, FINOVA was reporting that it had lost $1 billion for the year.[72] It declared Chapter 11 bankruptcy on March 7, 2001. Its default on its bond debt was the largest since the Great Depression. Its bankruptcy is the eighth largest in history, with Enron now ranking number one (see Case 5.9). Its stock price fell to $1.64 per share on April 2, 2001. The stock would fall to $0.88 per share until Warren Buffett's Berkshire Hathaway Company and Leucadia National Corporation made a buy-out proposal for FINOVA, which caused the stock to jump to $2.13 in March 2001.[73] Berkshire Hathway owns $1.4 billion of FINOVA's debt including $300 million in bank debt and $1.1 billion in public bonds.

GE Capital and Goldman Sachs then countered the Buffett offer, but the bankruptcy court approved the Buffett offer.[74] However, pursuant to its rights under the agreement, the Buffett team backed out of the purchase and FINOVA remains in bankruptcy.

Discussion Questions

1. Why do you think the officers and managers waited until the auditors required it to write off the $70 million loan?
2. Do you think the incentive plans had any effect on the reported earnings? Why or why not?
3. Was FINOVA too generous with a resulting loyalty that was blinding? What impact would the types of perks FINOVA offered have on you as an employee?
4. Was FINOVA forthcoming about the level of risk in its business?
5. Most of the FINOVA employees are gone or have been laid off. What impression do you think their time at FINOVA makes as prospective employers read their résumés?

[70] *Donna Hogan, "Finova Finances May Force Sale,"* The Tribune, *May 9, 2000, pp. B1, B2.*

[71] *Atlas, "Caught in a Credit Squeeze," pp. C1, C21.*

[72] *Max Jarman, "Finova Posts $1 Billion Loss,"* Arizona Republic, *April 3, 2001, p. D1.*

[73] *Paul M. Sherer and Devon Spurgeon, "Finova Agrees to a Bailout by Berkshire and Leucadia,"* The Wall Street Journal, *February 28, 2001, pp. C1, C18.*

[74] *Edward Gately, "Bankruptcy Court OKs Finova Plan,"* The Tribune, *August 11, 2001, p. B1.*

CASE 5.7

Phar-Mor Earnings

Founded in 1982, Phar-Mor, the discount drug store chain, enjoyed a decade of phenomenal financial success. From 1982 to 1992, its sales grew to $3 billion. In that same period, Phar-Mor expanded from a single store to 305 stores in 33 states. It employed 23,000 workers in 1992. Phar-Mor's concept was to use warehouse-size-and-style stores that offered prescription drugs as well as items ranging from spaghetti sauce to videotapes.[75]

Founders Michael I. Monus and David S. Shapira utilized the concept of low margins to infiltrate even those markets where discount pharmacies were already operating. Opening nearly sixty stores each year, Phar-Mor was ranked as the forty-ninth largest privately held company in the United States in 1991.

Monus, a sports fan, started the World Basketball League (WBL) for short players (those six feet, seven inches or less in height) and also was a part owner and promoter of the Colorado Rockies. The WBL had only ten teams in midsize towns like Erie, Pennsylvania, but Mr. Monus spared no expense in running the league. League officials enjoyed limousine service, and the perks for the WBL commissioner included a Cadillac.[76]

On July 20, 1992, Phar-Mor officers were told (anonymously) of a transfer of Phar-Mor funds to the WBL in the amount of $100,000. An internal audit examination didn't find the $100,000 but did uncover several questionable transactions.[77]

By July 28, 1992, Mr. Monus, who was Phar-Mor's president, had been demoted to vice chairman. On July 31, 1992, Mr. Monus was fired, and the remaining Phar-Mor officers alerted federal authorities.[78] Additionally, Phar-Mor's chief financial officer, Patrick Finn, and its outside auditor, Coopers & Lybrand, were dismissed.[79]

David S. Shapira was appointed as Phar-Mor's chief executive officer.[80] In a statement, Mr. Shapira said that about $10 million in Phar-Mor funds had been funneled to the WBL. Mr. Shapira also stated that Mr. Finn and Mr. Monus had engaged in a "fraudulent scheme to cover up failures in the company and operating losses." As a result, Phar-Mor had had, in reality, no profits for the last three years: The company had overstated its profits by $350 million. Mr. Shapira referred to the work of Mr. Monus

[75] *Gabriella Stern, "Chicanery at Phar-Mor Ran Deep, Close Look at Discounter Shows,"* The Wall Street Journal, *January 20, 1994, pp. A1, A4.*

[76] *George Anders, "Phar-Mor Scandal Clouds Corporate Partners,"* The Wall Street Journal, *August 6, 1992, pp. C1, C19.*

[77] *Gabriella Stern and Clare Ansberry, "A Founder Embezzles Millions for Basketball, Phar-Mor Chain Says,"* The Wall Street Journal, *August 5, 1992, pp. A1, A8.*

[78] *Calmetta Y. Coleman, "Phar-Mor's Haft Agrees to Quit His Position,"* The Wall Street Journal, *August 25, 1997, p. B7.*

[79] *Gabriella Stern, "Phar-Mor Hires President, Shuffles Its Top Executives,"* The Wall Street Journal, *February 5, 1993, p. B2.*

[80] *Gabriella Stern, "Phar-Mor Fiasco Puts Shapira in Hot Seat,"* The Wall Street Journal, *August 7, 1992, p. B1.*

and Mr. Finn as "intricate criminal activity to defraud the company and its investors." Phar-Mor took a one-time reduction in earnings of $350 million in fiscal year 1993.

Mr. Monus was tried for fraud and embezzlement. In an earlier trial, there was a hung jury and investigations for jury tampering. Mr. Monus was convicted of 109 felony counts of fraud and embezzlement in 1995 and was sentenced to 235 months in prison. Mr. Monus said at his sentencing,

> In the 10 years I was at Phar-Mor, Phar-Mor grew to 300 stores in some 35 states and 20,000 employees. The important thing is not the numbers to me . . ., but the employees—all those dedicated, loyal and highly motivated people.
>
> I want them to know the sorrow and regret that I have. The sorrow and regret will live with me for the rest of my life.[81]

In response to the news of the company's problems and earnings reductions, many suppliers stopped shipping goods to Phar-Mor, except on a C.O.D. basis. Banks began filing liens on Phar-Mor properties, and the company contemplated a proposal to close 100 stores. By August 17, 1992, Phar-Mor had filed for Chapter 11 bankruptcy. The general counsel for Coopers & Lybrand issued a statement saying that Phar-Mor had showed "no remorse for the hiring, retaining and promoting of this senior management the board now claims are 'crooks.' Responsible boards have oversight of their management and knowledge of their company's operations. Phar-Mor is a closely held non-public company in which the owners, managers and the board are closely allied. Collusion and fraud at the senior management level did not occur in a vacuum."[82]

A lawyer of the American Institute of Certified Public Accountants (AICPA) stated that "if the fraud involves collusion among a number of people, the ordinary auditing procedures wouldn't necessarily uncover it."[83]

The final independent examiner's report on the Phar-Mor losses, completed in January 1994, revealed that those involved had kept two sets of books: the official books, which contained false entries, and a second set of records (called "cookies"), where the false entries (called "raisins") were monitored. The final loss figure due to insider fraud was $1 billion: Phar-Mor had had no earnings during the five-year period preceding the 1992 Chapter 11 filing.[84]

The court-appointed auditor discovered the following:

- a memo from general counsel warning Mr. Shapira of a lack of financial controls and conflicts of interest involving top executives;
- the back-dating of promissory notes by officers to exercise expired stock options;
- executives hiring (with company funds) cheerleaders in hot pants to escort them around Las Vegas;
- an internal memo questioning the expenditure of $30,000 for Nicole Miller neckties;
- the purchase by Phar-Mor of costume jewelry for sale in its stores from a firm in which Monus's brother was a part owner; Phar-Mor would have saved $2.1 million by purchasing the jewelry from another vendor; and

[81] *"Monus, Co-Founder of Phar-Mor, Gets a 20-Year Sentence,"* The Wall Street Journal, *December 4, 1995, p. B8.*

[82] *Milt Freudenheim, "Phar-Mor and Its Ex-Auditor Clash on Fraud Case,"* The New York Times, *August 6, 1992, p. C3.*

[83] *Milt Freudenheim, "Phar-Mor Says Profit Was Faked,"* The New York Times, *August 5, 1992, pp. C1, C4.*

[84] *Stephen D. Williger, "Phar-Mor—A Lesson in Fraud,"* The Wall Street Journal, *March 28, 1994, p. A14.*

- the fact that in 1989, Phar-Mor had adopted an essentially invisible code of ethics: officers questioned by the examiner were unaware of its existence.

Phar-Mor emerged from Chapter 11 bankruptcy in 1995 with a new CEO, David Schwartz, and board.[85] Its annual revenues were at that time $1.1 billion, down from its 1992 high of $3.1 billion. The number of employees was reduced by two-thirds and the company was closely held with Robert Haft holding a 31 percent share. Phar-Mor was to have merged with Shopko Stores in 1996, but it was acquired by Avatex in 1997.[86]

Discussion Questions

1. List the ethical violations by the various parties at Phar-Mor.
2. What elements in the company allowed such a large fraud to occur?
3. Was the company treated as a personal asset of the officers? What problems resulted from this attitude?
4. Suppose you had drafted the internal memo that expressed concerns about internal controls and conflicts of interest. What would you have done if the company took no action in response? What would you do next?
5. If you, as a Phar-Mor employee, had discovered the two sets of books, whom would you tell?
6. List those who have been harmed by the collusion at Phar-Mor.

Sources

Ansberry, Clare, "Phar-Mor's Problems May Give Boost to Rest of Drug Discount Industry," *The Wall Street Journal*, August 6, 1992, p. A4.

"Hard Pills to Swallow," *Time*, August 17, 1992, p. 16.

Murray, Matt, "Wounded Phar-Mor Found a Healer in Antonio Alvarez," *The Wall Street Journal*, May 26, 1995, p. B1.

"Phar-Mor Dismisses 2 More," *The New York Times*, August 7, 1992, p. C4.

Schiller, Zachary, "Wait a Minute—Phar-Mor Is Still Kicking," *Business Week*, March 8, 1993, pp. 60, 61.

Stern, Gabriella, "Phar-Mor, Embattled Chain, Is Trying to Stem Panic Among Vendors, Lenders," *The Wall Street Journal*, August 12, 1992, p. A3.

[85] *"Phar-Mor, Inc. Plan for Reorganization Is Cleared by Judge,"* The Wall Street Journal, *August 30, 1995, p. A8; see also "2 New Plans for Phar-Mor in Revamping,"* The New York Times, *April 25, 1995, p. C2.*

[86] *Matt Murray, "Phar-Mor to Merge with Shopko Stores,"* The Wall Street Journal, *September 10, 1996, p. A3.*

CASE 5.8

Overstated Earnings: Bausch & Lomb

The Hong Kong division of Bausch & Lomb enjoyed double-digit growth during the 1980s and 1990s. In some years earnings increased 25 percent; by 1993, the Hong Kong operation had total revenues of $100 million.

Earnings on contact lenses sales seemed to be absolutely unbeatable with sales increasing at double-digit pace.

It was in 1994 that Bausch & Lomb's twelve continuous years of double-digit growth in both sales and earnings (excluding one-time events) came to a halt with a company announcement that excessive distributor inventories would result in a significant reduction in 1994 earnings. The final result was a decline of 54 percent in earnings to $88.5 million. Sales were down only slightly to $1.9 billion. The following table reflects the shortfalls:[87]

		millions of dollars	
division	*1993*	*planned 1994*	*actual 1994*
TOTAL BAUSCH & LOMB			
Sales	1872.2	2051.9	1850.6
Operating Earnings	300.9	344.7	168.8
US EYEWEAR			
Sales	190.1	200.0	153.5
Operating Earnings	42.3	48.6	19.7
US CONTACT LENS			
Sales	151.0	176.0	85.8
Operating Earnings	16.8	20.5	-61.7
ASIA-PACIFIC			
Sales	148.9	169.7	107.8
Operating Earnings	34.6	46.8	4.0
ORAL CARE			
Sales	68.8	73.0	50.8
Operating Earnings	2.6	4.2	-10.3
MIRACLE EAR*			
Sales	–	57.9	37.3
Operating Earnings	–	2.3	-12.9
CANADA AND LATIN AMERICA			
Sales	126.1	154.0	113.4
Operating Earnings	17.8	27.3	6.4
EUROPE, MIDDLE EAST, AFRICA			
Sales	246.5	249.0	240.6
Operating Earnings	60.7	60.3	53.0

**Acquired during 1993.*

[87] *Mark Maremont, "Blind Ambition,"* Business Week, *October 23, 1995, pp. 78–92.*

An SEC investigation, as well as one by *Business Week*, revealed some underlying problems in operations of Ray-Ban Sunglasses. For example, the Hong Kong unit was faking sales to real customers but then dumping the glasses at discount prices to gray markets. The contact lens division shipped products that were never ordered to doctors in order to boost sales. Some distributors had up to two years of unordered inventories. The U.S., Latin, and Asian contact lens divisions also dumped lenses on the gray market, forcing Bausch & Lomb to compete with itself.

The SEC charged Bausch & Lomb with violation of federal securities law for overstatement of earnings. Bausch & Lomb settled the charges with the SEC in 1997. Without admitting or denying the allegations, Bausch & Lomb agreed to a cease and desist order and John Logan, a regional sales director for the contact lens division, agreed to pay a $10,000 fine. The cease and desist order also named the former president of Bausch & Lomb's contact lens division, the former controller, the vice president of finance, and the former director of distributor sales.[88, 89]

Bausch & Lomb emphasized that the SEC found no evidence that top management knew of the overstatement of profits at the time it was made. However, the SEC's associate director of enforcement said, "That's precisely the point. Here is a company where there was tremendous pressure down the line to make the numbers. The commission's view is that senior management has to be especially vigilant where the pressure to make the numbers creates the risk of improper revenue recognition."[90]

Former employees testified they were given a target number each year by operating unit and no excuses were accepted. One division manager, expecting a shortfall, said he was told to make the numbers but "don't do anything stupid." The manager said, "I'd walk away saying, 'I'd be stupid not to make the numbers.'" Another manager said that in order to meet targets they did 70% of their shipments in the last three days of the month.[91]

Bausch & Lomb also settled a shareholder lawsuit over the overstatement of earnings for $42 million.[92] Following this settlement and with the SEC charges behind it, Bausch & Lomb began its climb back from its tarnished image. It has, as the analysts prone to make puns have noted, lost its focus and has had trouble seeing the vision of the future clearly and sharpening its image. Its overseas operations have been a drain because those sales account for $1.8 billion in sales, but the devaluation of other currencies has been costly.[93] It tried to enter the two-week contact lens market but found that Johnson & Johnson had beat it there and had it fairly cornered.[94]

88 *Mark Maremont, "Judgment Day at Bausch & Lomb,"* Business Week, *December 25, 1995, p. 39.*

89 *Floyd Norris, "Bausch & Lomb and SEC Settle Dispute on '93 Profits,"* The New York Times, *November 18, 1997, p. C2.*

90 Id.

91 *Maremont, "Blind Ambition," pp. 78–92.*

92 *Mark Maremont, "Bausch & Lomb's Board Puts on Its Glasses,"* Business Week, *November 6, 1995, p. 41.*

93 *"Bausch & Lomb to Introduce New Contacts,"* The Wall Street Journal, *March 18, 1999, pp. B1, B9.*

94 *Claudia H. Deutsch, "New Chief Inherits a Bausch & Lomb That Is Listing Badly,"* The New York Times, *November 17, 2001, pp. C1, C2.*

The 148-year-old company that was once synonymous with eye care and quality has had a rugged climb back up and it has not yet reached its former levels of success in sales, revenues, or earnings.[95]

Discussion Questions

1. What went wrong with the Bausch & Lomb culture?
2. How was the company affected? Financially? Competitively?
3. Why are all those named in the consent decree "former" employees?
4. What changes would you make to prevent these types of issues?
5. Why do you think Bausch & Lomb has struggled for so many years to make a recovery that seems to elude it?

CASE 5.9

Enron—The CFO, Conflicts, and Cooking the Books with Natural Gas and Electricity

I. Introduction

Enron Corp. is an energy company, which was incorporated in Oregon in 1985 with its principal executive offices located in Houston, Texas. By the end of 2001, Enron Corp. was the world's largest energy company, holding 25 percent of all of the world's energy trading contracts.[96] Enron's own public relations materials describe it as "one of the world's leading electricity, natural gas and communications companies" that "markets electricity and natural gas, delivers physical commodities and financial and risk management services to companies around the world, and has developed an intelligent network platform to facilitate online business."[97] Enron was also one of the world's most admired corporations, holding a consistent place in *Fortune* magazine's 100 best companies to work for. The sign in the lobby of Enron's headquarters reads, WORLD'S LEADING COMPANY.[98] Employees at Enron's headquarters had access to an on-site health club, subsidized Starbucks coffee, concierge service that included massages, and car washes, all for free.[99] Those employees with Enron Broadband received free Palm Pilots, free cell phones, and free wireless laptops.[100]

[95] *Zina Moukheiber, "Eye Strain,"* Forbes, *October 4, 1999, pp. 58–60;* see also *Erile Norton, "CEO Gill to Retire From Bausch & Lomb; Carpenter Is Seen As Possible Successor,"* The Wall Street Journal, *December 14, 1995, p. B3.*

[96] *Noelle Knox, "Enron to Fire 4,000 from Headquarters,"* USA Today, *December 4, 2001, p. 1B.*

[97] *From the class action complaint filed in the Southern District of Texas,* Kaufman v. Enron.

[98] *Bethany McClean, "Why Enron Went Bust,"* Fortune, *December 24, 2001, pp. 59–72.*

[99] *Alexei Barrionuevo, "Jobless in a Flash, Enron's Ex-employees Are Stunned, Bitter, Ashamed,"* The Wall Street Journal, *December 11, 2001, pp. B1, B12.*

[100] Id.

In November 2001, a week following credit agencies' downgrading of its debt to "junk" grade, Enron filed for bankruptcy, the largest bankruptcy ($62 billion) in the history of the United States.[101] There are a significant number of stories between Enron's role as a darling of Wall Street to a national debacle that has resulted in Congressional hearings, accounting reform, class action securities litigation, and criminal investigations.

II. Background on Enron

Enron began as the merger of two gas pipelines, Houston Natural Gas and Internorth, orchestrated by Kenneth Lay, and emerged as an energy trading company. Poised to ride the wave of deregulation of electricity, Enron would be a power supplier to utilities. It would trade in energy and offer electricity for sale around the country by locking in supply contracts at fixed prices and then hedging on those contracts in other markets. There are few who dispute that its strategic plan at the beginning showed great foresight and that its timing for market entry was impeccable. It was the first mover in this market and it enjoyed phenomenal growth. It became the largest energy trader in the world, with $40 billion in revenue in 1998, $60 billion in 1999, and $101 billion in 2000. Its internal strategy was to grow revenue by 15 percent per year.[102]

When Enron rolled out its online trading of energy as a commodity, it was as if there had been a Wall Street created for energy contracts. Enron itself had 1,800 contracts in that online market. It had really created a market for weather futures so that utilities could be insulated by swings in the weather and the resulting impact on the prices of power. It virtually controlled the energy market in the United States. By December 2000 Enron's shares were selling for $85 each. Its employees had their 401(k)s heavily invested in Enron stock, and the company had a matching program in which it contributed additional shares of stock to savings and retirement plans when employees chose to fund them with Enron stock.

When competition began to heat up in energy trading, Enron began some diversification activities that proved to be disasters in terms of producing earnings. It acquired a water business that collapsed nearly instantaneously. It also had some international investments, particularly power plants in Brazil and India that had gone south. Its $1 billion investment in a 2,184-megawatt power plant in India was an ongoing dispute as its political and regulatory relations in that country had deteriorated and the state utility stopped paying its bills for the power.[103]

In 1999, it announced its foray into fiber optics and the broadband market. Enron overanticipated the market in this area and experienced substantial losses related to the expansion of its broadband market. Like Corning and other companies that overbuilt, Enron began bleeding quickly from losses related to this diversification.[104]

[101] *Richard A. Oppel, Jr. and Riva D. Atlas, "Hobbled Enron Tries to Stay On Its Feet,"* The New York Times, *December 4, 2001, pp. C1, C8.*

[102] *"Why John Olson Wasn't Bullish on Enron," from http://knowledge.Wharton.upenn.edu/013002_ss3.*

[103] *Saritha Rai, "New Doubts on Enron's India Investment,"* The New York Times, *November 21, 2001, p. W1.*

[104] *Proposed complaint, class action litigation, November 2001, http://www.kaplanfox.com.*

III. The Financial Reporting Issues

Enron followed the Financial Accounting Standards Board's (FASB's) rules for energy traders, which permit such companies to include in current earnings those profits they expect to earn on energy contracts and related derivative estimates.[105] The result is that many energy companies have been posting earnings, quite substantial, for non-cash gains that they expect to realize some time in the future.

However, the problem with such 'mark-to-market' accounting is that the numbers that the energy companies carry for earnings on these future contracts are subjective. The numbers they carry depend upon assumptions about market factors. Those assumptions used in computing future earnings booked in the present are not revealed in the financial reports and investors have no way of knowing the validity of those assumptions or even whether they are conservative or aggressive assumptions about energy market expectations. It becomes difficult for investors to cross-compare financial statements of energy companies because they are unable to compare what are apples and oranges in terms of earnings because of the futuristic nature of the income and the possibility that those figures may never come to fruition. One analyst also noted the pressure that comes with wide reporting discretion:

> Whenever there's a considerable amount of discretion that companies have in reporting their earnings, one gets concerned that some companies may overstate those earnings in certain situations where they feel pressure to make earnings goals.[106]

For example, the unrealized gains portion of Enron's pretax profit for 2000 was about 50 percent of the total $1.41 billion profit originally reported. That amount was one-third in 1999. Dynegy, another Houston energy company that was poised to buy Enron until it realized the extent of the financial issues, also had about one-half of its $762 million in pretax profits in unrealized gain. The two companies' litigation following Dynegy's withdrawal of its offer to purchase was settled in January 2002.

Most energy companies do not even disclose what percentage of their earnings comes from mark-to-market accounting. Pinnacle West Capital Corporation, the parent for Arizona Public Service and its energy-trading arm, does disclose that 27 percent of its earnings are from mark-to-market bookings. The contracts on which those earnings are booked range in length from two to seven years.[107] Duke Energy does not disclose its percentage of mark-to-market earnings but will do so in the future because of investor demands.

A number of Wall Street analysts complained throughout the period from 1995 through 2001 that Enron's financial statements were difficult to read and that its disclosures on officer relationships were not clear. Another has said that Enron managed to operate as a "giant hedge fund" without disclosing that risk in its SEC documents.[108] Jeffrey Skilling, in an interview in December 2001 said, "We're all trying to

[105] *Jonathan Weil, "After Enron, 'Mark to Market' Accounting Gets Scrutiny,"* The Wall Street Journal, *December 4, 2001, pp. C1, C2.*

[106] Id.

[107] *Matt Krantz, "Accounting Rule Eyed,"* USA Today, *December 3, 2001, p. 4B.*

[108] *Jonathan Weil, "What Enron's Financial Reports Did—and Didn't—Reveal,"* The Wall Street Journal, *November 5, 2001, pp. C1, C2.*

figure out what happened. This was a tragedy. I had no idea the company was in anything but excellent shape."[109]

Under "mark-to-market" accounting, under Financial Accounting Standards Board (FASB) rules, companies can include in present earnings portions of the profits they expect to realize for energy contracts that may not bring in those actual earnings for some time. This rule of "mark-to-market" applies to energy contracts and other forms of derivative investments.[110] Those within the company set the "fair value" of the contracts. For example, Enron may have had an energy contract that would run for five years and required delivery of power to a California utility. The California utility might not draw on the power, in which case it would still pay under what was usually a "take-or-pay" provision in the contract, or it might need all of the power and pay a premium. All of these events would occur sometime in the future and it was impossible to know how much the sale of power under the contract to the California utility would bring. Enron and other energy companies are permitted to place, internally, a value on the contract and book that amount as present earnings.[111]

This practice of "mark-to-market" accounting proved to be particularly hazardous for Enron management because their bonuses and performance ratings were tied to meeting earnings goals. The result was that their judgment on the fair value of these energy contracts, some as long as 20 years into the future, was greatly biased in favor of present recognition of substantial value.[112] The value of these contracts is dependent upon assumptions and variables, which are not discussed in the financial statements, not readily available to investors and shareholders, and include wild cards such as the weather, the price of natural gas, and market conditions in general. One analyst has noted, "Whenever there's a considerable amount of discretion that companies have in reporting their earnings, one gets concerned that some companies may overstate those earnings in certain situations where they feel pressure to make earnings goals."[113] A FASB study showed that when a hypothetical example on energy contracts was given at a conference, the valuations by managers for the contracts ranged from $40 million to $153 million.[114]

Some analysts were concerned about this method of accounting because these are noncash earnings. Some noted that Enron's noncash earnings were over 50 percent of its revenues. Others discovered the same issues when they noted that Enron's margins and cash flow did not match up with its phenomenal earnings records.[115] For example, Jim Chanos, of Kynikos Associates, noted that no one was really sure how Enron

[109] *Richard A. Oppel, Jr., "Former Head of Enron Denies Wrongdoing,"* The New York Times, *December 22, 2001, p. C1.*

[110] *Weil, "After Enron, 'Mark to Market' Accounting Gets Scrutiny," pp. C1, C2.*

[111] *American Electric Power, Duke Energy, El Paso, and Entergy are other companies with unrealized gains reported in their earnings, with some now willing to disclose that percentage and others not inclined to do so.* Id.

[112] *Susan Lee, "Enron's Success Story,"* The Wall Street Journal, *December 26, 2001, p. A11.*

[113] Id.

[114] *Weil, "After Enron, 'Mark to Market' Accounting Gets Scrutiny," p. C2.*

[115] *McClean, "Why Enron Went Bust," pp. 62–63. Ms. McLean had written a story in the summer of 2001 entitled, "Is Enron Overpriced?" for* Fortune. *The lead line to the story was, "How exactly does Enron make its money?" The story was buried. It enjoyed little coverage or attention until November 2001. Ms. McClean is now an analyst on the Enron case for NBC and has been featured on numerous news shows. Felicity Barringer, "10 Months Ago, Questions on Enron Came and Went With Little Notice,"* The New York Times, *January 28, 2002, p. A11. Ms. McClean has signed a multimillion dollar book contract.*

made money and that its operating margins were very low for the reported revenue. Mr. Chanos concluded that Enron was a "giant hedge fund sitting on top of a pipeline."[116] Mr. Chanos notes that Wall Street loved Enron because it consistently met targets, but he was skeptical because of off-the-balance sheet transactions.[117] Mr. Chanos and others who brought questions to Enron were readily dismissed. For example, *Fortune* reporter Bethany McClean experienced pressure in 2000 when she began asking questions about the revenues and margins and Mr. Lay called her editor to request that she be removed from the story. The Enron CEO at the time, Jeffrey Skilling, refused to answer her questions and labeled her line of inquiry as "unethical."[118] During an analysts' telephonic conference with Mr. Skilling in which Mr. Chanos asked why Enron had not provided a balance sheet, Mr. Skilling called Mr. Chanos, an "a___h____."[119] Mr. Chanos opted for selling Enron shares short and declined to disclose the amount of money he has made as a result of his position.

John Olson, an analyst with a Houston company, reflected that most analysts were unwilling to ask questions. When Mr. Olson asked Mr. Skilling questions about how Enron was making money, Mr. Skilling responded that Enron was part of the new economy and that Olson, "didn't get it."[120] Mr. Olson advised his company's clients not to invest in Enron because, as he explained to them, "Never invest in something you can't understand."[121]

When *U.S. News & World Report* published Mr. Olson's analysis and advice, Kenneth Lay sent Mr. Olson's boss a handwritten note with the following:

> John Olson has been wrong about Enron for over 10 years and is still wrong. But he is consistant (sic).

Upon reading the note sent to his boss, Mr. Olson responded, "You know that I'm old and I'm worthless, but at least I can spell consistent."[122]

IV. Enron's Related Party Transactions

Enron's books not only suffered from the problem of "mark-to-market" accounting, it has become clear that the company had made minimal disclosures about its related party transactions as well as the resulting off-the-balance sheet liabilities that it was carrying.[123] These problems, coupled with the FASB-sanctioned fair value of the energy contracts, permitted Enron's financial statements to paint a picture that did not adequately reflect the risk investors had.

Enron's "related party transactions" were substantial, but Enron's financial statements did not disclose those transactions and its resulting exposure because Enron had structured its ownership interests in these "off-the-books" transactions so that its

[116] Id.

[117] *Cassell Bryan-Low and Suzanne McGee, "Enron Short Seller Detected Red Flags in Regulatory Filings,"* The Wall Street Journal, *November 5, 2001, pp. C1, C2.*

[118] Id., *p. 60.*

[119] Id., *p. C2.*

[120] *"Why John Olson Wasn't Bullish on Enron," http://www.knowledge.wharton.upenn.edu/013002_ss3.*

[121] Id.

[122] Id.

[123] *Richard A. Oppel, Jr. and Andrew Ross Sorkin, "Enron Corp. Files Largest U.S. Claim For Bankruptcy,"* The New York Times, *December 3, 2001, pp. A1, A16.*

interests never exceeded 49 percent. Disclosure requirements under GAAP and FASB kick in at 50 percent ownership. When a company owns 50 percent or more of a company, it must disclose transactions with that company in the financials as "related party transactions."

Enron was forced, following its accounting reversals in October 2001, to reveal certain "off-the-balance sheet" transactions and companies that caused certain information about the activities of Enron's officers came to light. The focus shifted from "mark-to-market" accounting to Enron's "related party transactions" and whether its disclosures under accounting rules regarding the company's transactions with organizations in which it has an interest were adequate.

Enron created a complex network of subsidiaries and self-dealing that began at the end of 1999 when Enron announced that it had transferred by private agreement 1,999,999 shares from its affiliate, Sundance Assets, to another affiliate, SE Thunderbird.

Enron did not, however, disclose that Sundance Assets was partially owned and controlled by Enron's unconsolidated subsidiary, New Power. Enron owned 45 percent of New Power, and New Power was created to sell electricity and natural gas to residential and small load customers throughout deregulated markets in the United States. None of these ownership interests or Enron's contracts with these companies was disclosed in Enron's financial statements.[124]

Enron also did a substantial amount of business with LJM Cayman, L.P. (LJM), a private investment company that specializes in energy futures contracts. Enron's Chief Financial Officer (CFO), Andrew Fastow, who held an MBA from Northwestern's Kellogg School of Business, managed LJM. The disclosure in Enron's 1999 10K on this relationship was as follows:

> In June 1999, Enron entered into a series of transactions involving a third party and LJM Cayman, L.P. (LJM). LJM is a private investment company, which engages in acquiring or investing in primarily energy-related investments. A senior officer of Enron is the managing member of LJM's general partner.[125]

Mr. Fastow was also a principal in New Power. These complex interrelationships and the lack of a required disclosure enabled Enron to transfer assets into LJM, thereby increasing Enron's equity position and its market worth. For example, in June 2000, Enron transferred, through Mr. Fastow, sufficient shares to LJM to permit Enron to report an increase in its equity of $171 million while also reporting the assets that LJM transferred in exchange for the shares represented $500 million in proceeds.

During 2000, Fastow facilitated the sale of Enron's "dark fiber cable" to LJM for $30 million in cash and a $70 million note, a gross margin of $53 million reported as earnings for the quarter. These earnings were subsequently reduced in October 2001.

In March 2001, a senior officer who reported to Mr. Fastow, Michael Kopper, facilitated a $35 million deal between Enron and Chewco Investments, LP. Chewco had

[124] *John R. Emshwiller and Rebecca Smith, "Murky Waters: A Primer on Enron Partnerships,"* The Wall Street Journal, *January 21, 2002, pp. C1, C14.*

[125] *Enron Corp. 10K, Filed December 31, 1999, at 16.*

been formed by Enron executives and was run by Enron officers, primarily Mr. Kopper. Mr. Kopper was also listed as a principal in LJM and described as "manages the general partner of Chewco, an investment fund with approximately $400 million in capital commitments that was established in 1997 to purchase from Enron an interest in a defined pool of Enron assets."[126] No one is able to say how Enron paid the $35 million to Chewco and whether Chewco or Mr. Kopper benefited from the transaction. However, the LJM partnership reported that the company earned $7 million in management fees and $3 million in investment income in 2000.

Chewco was a partnership formed to buy the California Public Employees' Retirement System's (Calpers) interest in a joint venture it had with Enron called Joint Energy Development Investments, LP (JEDI). Calpers and Enron formed the joint venture for purposes of making energy-related investments. Both the partners are believed to have put in $250 million each into JEDI. This affiliation permitted Enron to undertake large amounts of debt without reflecting it on its own books (the consolidation issue again). Both Mr. Kopper and Mr. Fastow worked extensively in JEDI.

In 1997 when Calpers wanted out of JEDI, Enron could not simply buy back Calpers' share because it would have meant reflecting a debt load of $1.6 billion on its balance sheets because it would have meant 100 percent ownership of JEDI. Kopper and Fastow formed Chewco (believed to be named after Chewbacca of "Star Wars" fame) to purchase Calpers' share. Chewco borrowed money to purchase Calpers' share, which it sold to Chewco for $375 million.[127]

The effect of all of these partnerships was to allow Enron to transfer an asset from its books, along with the accompanying debt, to the partnership. An outside investor would fund as little as 3 percent of the partnership, with Enron occasionally providing even the front money for the investor. Enron would then guarantee the bank loan to the partnership for the purchase of the asset. Enron would pledge shares as collateral for these loans it guaranteed in cases where the bank felt the asset transferred to the partnership was insufficient collateral for the loan amount.[128] Enron had approximately 3,500 subsidiaries and affiliates that were limited partnerships or limited liability companies.

To add to the complexity of these off-the-books loans and the transfer of Enron debt, many of the entities formed to take the asset and debt were corporations in the Cayman Islands. Enron had 881 such corporations, with 700 formed in the Cayman Islands and, in addition to transferring the debt off its balance sheet, it enjoyed a substantial number of tax benefits because corporations operate tax-free there. The result is that Enron paid little or no federal income taxes between 1997 and 2000.[129]

In addition to these limited liability company and limited partnership asset transfers, there were apparently a series of transactions authorized by Mr. Lay in which Enron did business with companies owned by Mr. Lay's son, Mark, and his sister,

[126] *John R. Emshwiller and Rebecca Smith, "Behind Enron's Fall, A Culture of Operating Outside Public View,"* The Wall Street Journal, *December 5, 2001, pp. A1, A10.*

[127] *John R. Emshwiller, "Enron Transaction Comes Under Scrutiny,"* The Wall Street Journal, *November 5, 2001, pp. A3, A6.*

[128] *Emshwiller and Smith, "Murky Waters," p. C1.*

[129] *David Gonzalez, "Enron Footprints Revive Old Image of Caymans,"* The New York Times, *January 28, 2002, p. A10.*

Sharon Lay. Jeffrey Skilling had hired Mark Lay in 1989 when Mr. Lay graduated with a degree in economics from UCLA. However, Mr. Lay left Enron feeling that he needed to "stand on his own and work outside of Enron."[130] Enron eventually ended up acquiring Mr. Lay's son's company and hired him as an Enron executive with a guaranteed pay package of $1,000,000 over three years as well as 20,000 stock options for Enron shares.[131] There was a criminal investigation into the activities of one of the companies founded by Mark Lay, but he was not charged with wrongdoing. He did pay over $100,000 to settle a civil complaint in the matter, but admitted no wrongdoing. Mark Lay has entered a Baptist seminary in Houston and plans to become a minister.[132]

Sharon Lay owns a Houston travel agency and has received over $10 million in revenue from Enron during the past 3 years, one-half of her company's revenue during that period.[133] Both Ms. and Mr. Lay say that they made all the necessary disclosures to the board and regulators about their business with Enron.

V. Enron's Demise

Enron's slow and steady decline began in the November/December 2000 time frame when its share price was at $85 per share. By the time Jeffrey Skilling announced his departure as CEO on August 14, 2001, with no explanation, the share price was at about $43. Mr. Skilling says that he left the company simply to spend more time with his family, but his departure raised questions among analysts even as Kenneth Lay returned as CEO.[134] *The Wall Street Journal* raised questions about Enron's disclosures on August 28, 2001, even as Enron was beginning an aggressive movement for selling off assets.[135] By October, Enron disclosed that it was reporting a third quarter loss and it took a $1.2 billion reduction in shareholder equity. Within days of those announcements, CFO Andrew Fastow was terminated and in less than 2 weeks, Enron restated its earnings dating back to 1997, a $586 million, or 20 percent reduction.

Following these disclosures and the announcement of Enron's liability on a previously undisclosed $690 million loan, CEO Kenneth Lay left the company as CEO, but remained as chairman of the board.[136] Mr. Lay waived any rights to his parachute, reportedly worth $60 million and also agreed to repay a $2 million loan from the company.[137] Mr. Lay's wife, Linda, appeared on NBC with correspondent Lisa Meyer on January 28, 2002, and indicated that she and Mr. Lay were "fighting for liquidity."[138] She indicated that all their property was for sale, but a follow-up check by Ms. Meyer

[130] *David Barboza and Kurt Eichenwald, "Son and Sister Of Enron Chief Secured Deals,"* The New York Times, *February 2, 2002, pp. A1, B5.*

[131] Id.

[132] Id.

[133] Id.

[134] *Emshwiller and Smith, "Behind Enron's Fall," pp. A1, A10.*

[135] *John E. Emshwiller, Rebecca Smith, Robin Sidel, and Jonathan Weil, "Enron Cuts Profit Data of 4 Years by 20%,"* The Wall Street Journal, *November 9, 2001, p. A3.*

[136] Id.

[137] *Richard A. Oppel, Jr. and Floyd Norris, "Enron Chief Will Give Up Severance,"* The New York Times, *November 14, 2001, pp. C1, C10.*

[138] *Alessandra Stanley and Jim Yardley, "Lay's Family Is Financially Ruined, His Wife Says,"* The New York Times, *January 29, 2002, pp. C1, C6.*

found only one of a dozen homes owned by the Lays were for sale. Mr. Lay consulted privately with the Rev. Jesse Jackson for spiritual advice, according to Mrs. Lay.[139]

Litigation is pending on all of these issues, and the SEC is investigating a number of the financial disclosure issues. Enron's stock price dropped dramatically following these discoveries and disclosures.

VI. The Enron Culture

Enron was a company with a swagger. It had an aggressive culture in which a rating system required that 20 percent of all employees be rated at below performance and encouraged to leave the company. As a result of this policy, no employee wanted to be the bearer of bad news.

Margaret Ceconi, an employee with Enron Energy Services, wrote a five-page memo to Kenneth Lay on August 28, 2001 stating that losses from Enron Energy Services were being moved to another sector in Enron in order to make the Energy Service arm look profitable. One line from her memo read, "Some would say the house of cards are falling."[140] Mr. Lay did not meet with Ms. Ceconi, but she was contacted by Enron Human Resources and counseled on employee morale. When she raised the accounting issues in her meeting with HR managers, she was told they would be investigated and taken very seriously, but she was never contacted by anyone about her memo. Her memo remained dormant until January 2002 when she sent it to the U.S. House of Representatives' Energy and Commerce Committee, the body conducting a series of hearings on the Enron collapse.

Ms. Ceconi's memo followed two weeks after Sherron Watkins, a former executive, wrote of her concerns about "accounting scandals" at Enron. Ms. Watkins was a former Andersen employee who had been hired into the executive ranks by Enron. Ms. Watkins wrote a letter to Kenneth Lay on August 15, 2001, that included the following, "I am incredibly nervous that we will implode in a wave of accounting scandals. I have heard from one manager-level employee from the principal investments group say, 'I know it would be devastating to all of us, but I wish we would get caught. We're such a crooked company.'"[141] She also warned that Mr. Skilling's swift departure would raise questions about accounting improprieties and that "It sure looks to the layman on the street that we are hiding losses in a related company."[142] In her memo she listed J. Clifford Baxter as someone Mr. Lay could talk to in order to verify her facts and that her concerns about the company were legitimate. Ms. Watkins wrote the memo anonymously on August 15, 2001, but by August 22, and after discussing the memo with former colleagues at Andersen, she told her bosses that she was the one who had written the memo.

In the months prior to Enron's collapse, employees became suspicious about what was called "aggressive accounting" in online chat rooms.[143] Clayton Verdon was fired

[139] Id.

[140] *Julie Mason, "Concerned Ex-worker Was Sent to Human Resources,"* Houston Chronicle, *January 30, 2002, http://www.chron.com.*

[141] *Michael Duffy, "What Did They Know and When Did They Know It?"* Time, *January 28, 2002, pp. 16–27.*

[142] Id.

[143] *Alex Berenson, "Enron Fired Workers For Complaining Online,"* The New York Times, *January 21, 2002, pp. C1, C8.*

in November 2001 for his comments about "overstating profits," made in an employee chat room. A second employee was fired when he revealed in the chat room that the company had paid $55 million in bonuses to executives on the eve of its bankruptcy.[144] Enron indicated that the terminations were necessary because the employees had breached company security.

VII. The Enron Board

Some institutional investors have raised questions about conflicts and the lack of independence in Enron's board.[145] Members of Enron's board were well compensated with a total of $380,619 paid to each director in cash and stock for 2001. One member of the board was Dr. Wendy L. Gramm, the former chairwoman of the Commodity Futures Trading Commission and wife of Senator Phil Gramm, the senior U.S. senator from Texas, who received campaign donations from Enron employees and its PAC. Dr. Gramm opted to own no Enron stock and accepted payment for her board service only in a deferred compensation account.

Dr. John Mendelsohn, the president of the University of Texas M.D. Anderson Cancer Center in Houston, also served on the Enron board, including its audit committee. Dr. Mendelsohn's center received $92,508 from Enron and $240,250 from Linda and Ken Lay since Dr. Mendelsohn joined the Enron board in 1999. [146]

VIII. After the Fall

Litigation is pending on all of these issues and the SEC is investigating a number of the financial disclosure issues, an investigation begun on October 31, 2001. Enron fired 5,100 of its 7,500 employees by December 3, 2001. Each employee will receive a $4,500 severance package, if the bankruptcy court approves it. However, the employees are more concerned about their financial futures. Many held Enron stock and were compensated with Enron stock options. The stock was trading at $0.40 per share on December 3, 2001. Enron employees' 401(k) plans, funded with Enron stock, lost $1.2 billion in 2001. "Almost everyone is gone. Upper management is not talking. No managing directors are around, and police are on every floor. It's so unreal," said one departing employee.[147] One employee, George Kemper, a maintenance foreman, who is part of a suit filed against Enron related to the employees' 401(k) plans, whose plan was once worth $225,000 and is now worth less than $10,000, said, "How am I going to retire now? Everything I've worked for the past 25 years has been wiped out."[148]

Just prior to declaring bankruptcy, Enron paid $55 million in bonuses to executives described as "retention executives," or those the company needs to stay on board in order to continue operations.[149]

[144] Id.

[145] *Reed Abelson, "Enron Board Comes Under a Storm of Criticism,"* The New York Times, *December 16, 2001, p. BU4.*

[146] *Jo Thomas and Reed Abelson, "How a Top Medical Researcher Became Entangled With Enron,"* The New York Times, *January 28, 2002, pp. C1, C2.*

[147] *Oppel, Jr. and Atlas, "Hobbled Enron Tries to Stay On Its Feet," pp. C1, C8.*

[148] *Christine Dugas, "Enron Workers Sue Over Retirement Plan,"* USA Today, *November 27, 2001, p. 5B.*

[149] *Richard A. Oppel, Jr. and Kurt Eichenwald, "Enron Paid $55 Million for Bonuses,"* The New York Times, *December 4, 2001, pp. C1, C4.*

Tragically, J. Clifford Baxter, a former Enron vice chairman, and one Ms. Watkins suggested Mr. Lay talk with, took his own life in his 2002 Mercedes Benz about a mile from his $700,000 home in Sugar Land, Texas, a suburb 25 miles from Houston. Mr. Baxter, who earned his MBA at Columbia, had left Enron in May 2001, following what some employees say was his voicing of concerns over the accounting practices of Enron and its disclosures.[150] SEC records disclose that Mr. Baxter sold 577,000 shares of Enron stock for $35.2 million between October 1998 and early 2001.[151] He had been asked to appear before Congress to testify, was a defendant in all the pending litigation, and was last seen in public at his yacht club where he took his yacht out for a sail. Those who saw him indicated that his hair had become substantially grayer since October when the public disclosures about Enron's condition began. Mr. Baxter was depicted as a philanthropist in the Houston area, having raised money for charities such as Junior Achievement and other organizations to benefit children. He had created the Baxter Foundation with $200,000 from Enron and $20,000 of his own money to assist charities such as Junior Achievement, American Cancer Society, and the American Diabetes Association.[152]

As noted, Enron had a matching plan for its employees on the 401(k). However, 60 percent of their plan was invested in Enron stock. Between October 17 and November 19, 2001, when the issues surrounding Enron's accounting practices and related transactions began to surface, the company put a lock down on the plan so that employees could not sell their shares.[153] Prior to the lockdown, most of the executives had sold off large blocks of Enron stock. For example, Jeffrey Skilling, who left the company in August 2001, sold off 500,000 shares on September 17, 2001.[154] He had sold 240,000 shares in early 2001 and at the time of Enron's bankruptcy owned 600,000 shares and an undisclosed number of options.[155] Mr. Lay also sold a substantial amount of stock in August 2001, but his lawyer had indicated the sale of the stock was necessary in order to repay loans.[156]

In addition to the impact on Enron, its employees, and Houston, there is a worldwide ripple effect. Enron has large stakes in natural gas pipelines in the United States and around the world as well as interests in power plants everywhere from Latin America to Venezuela. It is also a partial owner of utilities, including telecommunications networks. Congressional hearings will begin as the House Energy and Commerce Committee investigates the company's collapse. Representative Billy Tauzin of Louisiana is scheduling the investigation and has noted, "How a company can sink so far, so fast, is very troubling. We need to find out if the company's accounting practices masked severe underlying financial problems."[157] Senator Jeff Bingham, chairman of

[150] *Elissa Gootman, "Hometown Remembers Man Who Wore Success Quietly,"* The New York Times, *January 30, 2002, p. C7.*

[151] *Mark Babineck, "Deceased Enron Executive Earned Respect in the Ranks,"* Houston Chronicle, *http://www.houstonchronicle.com, January 26, 2002.*

[152] Id.

[153] Id.

[154] *Oppel, Jr., "Former Head of Enron Denies Wrongdoing," pp. C1, C2.*

[155] Id.

[156] *Richard A. Oppel, Jr., "Enron Chief Says His Sale of Stock Was To Pay Loans,"* The New York Times, *January 21, 2002, pp. A1, A13.*

[157] *Richard A. Oppel, Jr. and Andrew Ross Sorkin, "Ripples Spreading From Enron's Expected Bankruptcy,"* The New York Times, *November 30, 2001, pp. C1, C6, C7.*

the Senate Energy Committee, has said, "I believe that our committee is keenly aware of the need for enhanced oversight and market monitoring."[158]

Enron's bankruptcy filing included a list of creditors 54 pages long. While the bankruptcy filing showed $24.76 billion in assets and $13.15 billion in debt, these figures do not include those off-the-balance sheet obligations, estimated to be about $27 billion.[159] Among the creditors exposed in the Enron bankruptcy, because of derivative transactions on energy contracts, are JPMorganChase and Chubb.

The effect also extends to Enron's energy customers, which include Pepsico, the California state university system, JCPenney, Owens-Illinois, and Starwood Hotels & Resorts. Enron had contracts with 28,500 customers. These customers are now revisiting their contracts for loopholes on both sides and ensuring that they have contingency plans in place. California's state universities were in negotiations for renewal of their 1998 contract with Enron, but those talks are now in a stalemate.[160]

Trammell Crow has halted the groundbreaking ceremony for its planned construction of new Enron headquarters; a building that would have been 50 stories high and included offices, apartments, and stores.[161]

The ripple effect even stretches into unrelated investments. Five major Japanese money market funds with heavy Enron investments fell below their face value by December 3, 2001.[162] These losses will have an impact primarily on retirees because the five funds were seen as "safe haven" funds for investors.

As the bankruptcy proceeds, the Enron board has hired Stephen F. Cooper as CEO, to replace Mr. Lay. Mr. Cooper is a specialist in leading companies through bankruptcy, including TWA and Federated Department Stores.[163]

Enron's collapse also appears to be raising concerns among state regulators about the entire deregulation issue in the utility industry. Several members of Congress have noted that lawmakers and regulators cannot leave energy products in the regulatory shadows if the companies involved in the industry are harming both consumers and investors.[164]

Other political ramifications included desperate calls from Mr. Lay to officials in the Bush administration asking for help as the company neared collapse.[165] The various media have covered all of Enron's substantial political donations to President

[158] *"Financial Threat from Enron Failure Continues to Widen,"* Financial Times, *December 1, 2001, p. 1.*

[159] *Rebecca Smith and Mitchell Pacelle, "Enron Files for Chapter 11 Bankruptcy, Sues Dynegy,"* The Wall Street Journal, *December 3, 2001, p. A2.*

[160] *Rhonda L. Rundle, "Enron Customers Seek Backup Suppliers,"* The Wall Street Journal, *December 3, 2001, p. A10.*

[161] *Allen R. Myerson, "With Enron's Fall, Many Dominoes Tremble,"* The New York Times, *December 2, 2001, pp. 3-1, MB1.*

[162] *Ken Belson, "Enron Causes 5 Major Japanese Money Market Funds to Plunge,"* The New York Times, *December 4, 2001, p. C9.*

[163] *Shaila K. Dewan and Jennifer 8. Lee, "Enron Names an Interim Chief to Oversee Its Bankruptcy,"* The New York Times, *January 30, 2002, p. C7.*

[164] *Joseph Kahn and Jeff Gerth, "Collapse May Reshape the Battlefield of Deregulation,"* The New York Times, *December 4, 2001, pp. C1, C8.*

[165] *Elisabeth Bumiller, "Enron Contacted 2 Cabinet Officers Before Collapsing,"* The New York Times, *January 11, 2002, pp. A1, C4.*

George W. Bush ($650,000 from Enron officials and its PAC over the course of his political career), as well as governors and members of Congress, noting that Republican officials received more donations than Democrats.[166]

An ongoing question is the role Enron played in Vice President Dick Cheney's energy policy committee. Aides to Mr. Cheney indicate that they met with Enron officials six times during their policy development and meetings with energy companies and officials throughout the country.[167]

The SEC has opened an investigation and a national team of lawyers is handling the Justice Department investigation.[168]

A shareholder class action lawsuit filed in November 2001 includes the following descriptions of Enron's practices:

> One of Andrew Fastow's "innovative" accounting techniques was to create entities (trusts) to which Enron would issue millions of dollars in mandatory convertible debentures or depreciated assets. The trust would then use the assets as collateral to receive billions of dollars in financing for Enron projects, including Broadband. Although Enron, Corp. officially owned less than fifty percent of these entities, Enron controlled them. Defendants, improperly, did not consolidate these entities into Enron's disclosed financials; rather, Defendants hid the true nature of all of these transactions from the public. This meant Enron was engaged in business deals, risky hedging, self-dealing transactions that were never disclosed to the SEC.[169]

Many have noted that "evidence of fraud may well be elusive" as the SEC and prosecutors investigate.[170] Professor Douglas Carmichael, a professor of accounting at Baruch College, is one who agrees, "It's conceivable that they complied with the rules. Absent a smoking-gun e-mail or something similar, it is an issue of trying to attack the reasonableness of their assumptions."[171] Some in the accounting profession continue to support the decision to allow "mark-to-market" valuation despite the fact that the rule allows for the creative gamemanship of Enron. One auditor said that it never occurred to him that anyone would "use models to try and forecast energy prices for 10 years, and then use those models to report profits, but that the rule had not placed a limit on such trades."[172] When asked about the accounting practices of Enron, Mr. Skilling said, "We are on the side of angels."[173]

When Dynegy backed out of its deal to acquire Enron, employees who had been laid off from Enron celebrated the news in a Houston bar, "At least we're going to be part of the biggest bankruptcy ever."[174]

[166] *Jeanne Cummins and Mike Schroeder, "Enron's Lay Lobbied White House for Aid,"* The Wall Street Journal, *January 11, 2002, p. A3.*

[167] *Pete Yost, "Cheney, Aides met with Enron Officials 6 Times,"* The Tribune, *January 9, 2002, p. A16.*

[168] *Jo Thomas, "A Specialist in Tough Cases Steps Into the Legal Tangle,"* The New York Times, *January 21, 2002, p. C8.*

[169] *Complaint, shareholder class action, November 5, 2001, N.D. California.*

[170] *Floyd Norris and Kurt Eichenwald, "Fuzzy Rules Of Accounting and Enron,"* The New York Times, *January 30, 2002, pp. C1, C6.*

[171] Id.

[172] Id.

[173] *Neil Weinberg and Daniel Fisher, "Power Player,"* Forbes, *December 24, 2001, pp. 53–58.*

[174] *Barrionuevo, "Jobless in a Flash, Enron's Ex-Employees Are Stunned, Bitter, Ashamed," pp. B1, B12.*

IX. Enron and the Auditor: Arthur Andersen

One focus in the many hearings and investigations is the role of Arthur Andersen as the outside auditor for Enron. Andersen certified Enron's financial statements during the time frames in question. The questions center on the accounting rules discussed earlier. But the questions also focus on the auditor's independence. Andersen employees who were working as auditors had permanent office space at Enron headquarters.[175] Andersen employees participated with Enron employees in birthday parties, office trips, and charity events. "People just thought they were Enron employees."[176] So many Andersen employees were making the transition to being hired as Enron employees that the Andersen Houston office asked Enron to put a cap on the number of solicitations and hires it would take from the Andersen employees assigned to Enron headquarters for the audit function.

Following the fall of Enron, there was a change of focus to Andersen and its role. Congress zeroed in on David Duncan, the partner in the Houston office of Andersen, who handled the Enron account. Mr. Duncan took the Fifth Amendment when he was subpoenaed to testify before Congress.

Early in 2002, employees revealed that Andersen had been shredding documents. In testimony before the House Committee on Energy and Commerce, Andersen's lawyer, Nancy Temple, discussed an October 12, 2001 e-mail that she received from Duncan regarding the company policy on destruction of documents. Ms. Temple laid out the company policy and then asked that her name be removed from the e-mail so that the chances of her being called as a witness would not be so great—"I prefer to avoid. . . ."[177]

Mr. Duncan began an "accelerated" document destruction program on October 23, 2001. When the document shredding became public, Mr. Duncan was fired shortly thereafter by Andersen on January 15, 2002, after it investigated internally and admitted on January 10, 2002, that, in fact, there had been accelerated shredding of documents. Shortly thereafter, Enron fired Andersen as its auditor.

Andersen has been reeling since the Enron problems emerged. It has hired public relations officials to operate from its headquarters in Chicago and a conference call in October reveals that its knowledge about Enron's shaky finances was clear enough that they contemplated dropping Enron as a client.[178] Andersen's fees from Enron were $50 million per year. It is named as a defendant in a number of lawsuits and has disclosed that it is losing clients.

In a full page ad placed in *The Wall Street Journal* on January 29, 2002, Joe Berardino, the managing partner and CEO of Andersen wrote:

> The past couple of months have been challenging times for Andersen. As we continue to work diligently to understand what happened in the Enron case and why, we are

[175] *Thaddeus Herrick and Alexei Barrionuevo, "Were Enron, Andersen Too Tightly Knit?"* The Wall Street Journal, *January 21, 2002, pp. C1, C14.*

[176] Id.

[177] *Michael Duffy and John F. Dickerson, "Enron Spoils the Party,"* Time, *February 4, 2002, pp. 19–26.*

[178] Id.

> also working just as hard with our clients, employees, public officials and the public to maintain the trust that you have put in Andersen for 88 years.
>
> As you may know, Andersen has discovered two issues related to Enron. In December we voluntarily appeared before a Congressional committee and acknowledged that an error in judgment had been made with respect to the accounting on one of Enron's partnerships.
>
> As our own internal investigation into the matter proceeded, we learned that our lead partner on our Enron account directed the destruction of a large number of documents. These activities were of such a nature and on such a scale as to remove any doubt that a gross error in judgment was made.
>
> These matters are the subject of much speculation. We are conducting a full scale internal investigation. Let one thing be clear—we will not tolerate unethical behavior or willful violation of our policies.
>
> We are well aware that the salience and significance of these Enron-related problems, which Andersen has voluntarily reported to the American public, our clients, government officials and the media, have the potential to erode confidence in our company across-the-board. That is why we want you to know the full story, not just about Enron, but about Andersen, our people, our work and our values.
>
> . . .
>
> "Think straight and talk straight" was Arthur Andersen's motto when he founded our firm 88 years ago. And because that is exactly how we intend to continue meeting the challenges we face today, it will be our pledge for another 88 years and beyond.[179]

On March 15, 2002, the Justice Department indicted Andersen on one felony count of obstruction of justice.[180] As a result, Andersen continued to experience a loss of clients and by April 2002, had lost nearly 100 clients, including the federal government, Sara Lee Corp., Northeast Utilities, Brunswick Corporation, and Abbott Laboratories.[181]

There was a significant impact on the stock market as the details in the Enron matter emerged. Investors began looking more skeptically at company financial statements, particularly those with Enron accounting issues and even those in which Andersen has served as the auditor.[182] There was a 247-point drop in the Dow Industrial on January 30, 2002, as more companies came forward with questions about their financial statements and their confidence in their auditors.[183] One analyst said, "Institutions are dumping stock because they don't want to be caught with an unexploded bomb like Enron."[184]

[179] The Wall Street Journal, *January 29, 2002, p. B5.*

[180] *Kurt Eichenwald, "Andersen Charged,"* The New York Times, *March 16, 2002, pp. A1, C1.*

[181] *Jonathan D. Glater, "Longtime Clients Abandon Auditor,"* The New York Times, *March 16, 2002, p. B1.*

[182] *Daniel Kadlec, "Under the Microscope,"* Time, *February 4, 2002, pp. 29–34.*

[183] *Gregory Zuckerman, "Stocks Tumble Amid Accounting Fears,"* The Wall Street Journal, *January 30, 2002, pp. C1, C18.*

[184] Id.

Discussion Questions

1. Can you see that Enron broke any laws?
2. Do you think that Enron's financial reports gave a false impression?
3. Does it matter that most investors in Enron were relatively sophisticated financial institutions? What about the employees' ownership of stock and their 401(k) plans?
4. What do you think will happen in a regulatory sense following Enron's bankruptcy?
5. Do you think Enron was fair in its financial reporting and with its employees?
6. Do you think Enron did anything unethical?
7. Did Mr. Fastow and Mr. Kopper have conflicts?
8. How should their relationships with Enron's partially owned subsidiaries been handled in terms of disclosure?
9. Was the means of operation in compliance with accounting principles?
10. Was it ethical to not consolidate the financial statements?
11. Evaluate Enron's culture.
12. Was Ms. Watkins a whistleblower?
13. Discuss the systemic effects of Enron.

5b

Personal Ambition and Hubris

CASE 5.10

Jonathan Lebed: The Middle School Tycoon

Jonathan Lebed, a 15-year-old New Jersey middle-school student, shocked the investment world when the Securities and Exchange Commission (SEC) came knocking at his parents' door with a charge of securities fraud. It seems that Jonathan had turned his $8,000 in savings and gifts from family members into nearly $900,000 in gains on stocks traded using a pump-and-dump strategy. Jonathan did so without ever missing a day of school.

Master Jonathan, using over 20 screen names on a computer his parents had given him as a gift, would buy shares of stock and then post positive information about the stock around the Internet in various chat rooms. When the price of his chosen stock would rise, he would then sell it and move on to another stock. He did the bulk of his "pump and dump" trading between September 1999 and February 2000. During that time he traded, on average, 60,000 shares per day; his smallest gain in a day was $12,000 and his largest was $74,000.

Mrs. Lebed said that Jonathan had always been fascinated with the market and would often sit by the TV and watch the stock prices go across the screen on MSNBC and CNN. His mother also indicated he was not a bad stock picker, having given some of her friends and family members some good investment advice on stock.

When the SEC stepped in to halt his trading and take his computer, Jonathan became the first minor ever prosecuted by the SEC for securities fraud. His father noted that his son did nothing more than what others in the market do and yet the SEC chose to come after "a kid." Mr. Lebed stated during a *60 Minutes* interview, "I'm proud of my son. It's not like he was out stealing the hubcaps off cars or peddling drugs to the neighbors."[185] Mr. Lebed also noted that analysts behaved in the same fashion and that his son had been singled out for prosecution.

[185] *Michael Lewis, "Jonathan Lebed: Stock Manipulator, S.E.C. Nemesis—and 15,"* The New York Times, *February 25, 2001, pp. 1–18.*

Michael Lewis, who conducted an investigation into the case, interviewed Richard Walker, the head of enforcement for the SEC, and asked what was different about Master Lebed's conduct from that of analysts. The following is their exchange:

> "Jonathan Lebed was seeking to manipulate the market,"said Walker.
>
> But that only begs the question. If Wall Street analysts and fund managers and corporate CEOs who appear on CNBC and CNNfn to plug stocks are not guilty of seeking to manipulate the market, what on earth does it mean to manipulate the market?
>
> "It's when you promote a stock for the purpose of artificially raising its price."
>
> But when a Wall Street analyst can send the price of a stock of a company that is losing billions of dollars up 50 points in a day, what does it mean to "artificially raise" the price of a stock? The law sounded perfectly circular.[186]

The Lebeds entered into a consent decree.[187] They repaid all of the money Jonathan had made except for $273,000, a sum equal to about what is no doubt owed by his parents as taxes on the gains Jonathan made in his trading activity.[188]

Discussion Questions

1. Do you think Master Lebed violated the law? Why or why not?
2. Can you distinguish his conduct from a CEO or analyst plugging a particular stock?
3. Did Master Lebed take unfair advantage or should investors be more wary of information they get over the Internet?
4. Do you think Master Lebed's conduct was ethical? Why or why not? Was it honest? Was it fair?

CASE 5.11

The Inside Tract: Dan Dorfman

Late in 1995 and early in 1996, reports about Dan Dorfman, a markets expert who then did commentary for CNBC, emerged in the business press regarding Mr. Dorfman's relationship with a stock trader and the possibility of insider trading. The reports included statements that Mr. Dorfman was under investigation by the Securities and Exchange Commission (SEC), a statement the SEC and Justice Department officials neither confirmed nor denied.

The reports alleged that Mr. Dorfman moved particular stocks for friends and then profited by trading in those stocks. After the business press reported the allegations,

[186] Id.

[187] *Noelle Knox, "Teen Settles Stock-Manipulation Case for $285,000,"* USA Today, *September 21, 2000, p. 1B.*

[188] *Gretchen Morgenson, "S.E.C. Says Teenager Had After-School Hobby: Online Stock Fraud,"* The New York Times, *September 21, 2000, pp. A1, C10.*

Money magazine terminated Mr. Dorfman but noted that the termination was because Mr. Dorfman was hired to increase subscriptions and those numbers had, in fact, not improved. CNBC's parent company hired a law firm to conduct an investigation into the allegations.[189]

Mr. Dorfman was famous for his saying, "I own three stocks—AT&T, Boeing, and Gannett—and I never write about them."[190]

On May 7, 1996, Mr. Dorfman suffered a mild stroke and his reports could not be aired on CNBC. On August 30, 1996, CNBC announced that its internal investigation was complete, that Mr. Dorfman had cooperated fully, and that the law firm could find no evidence of illegal activity. The law firm did note, however, that it did not have the power of subpoena available to the U.S. government and that it had not examined records beyond what was publicly available and what Mr. Dorfman could furnish. According to the law firm's analysis, Mr. Dorfman's relationship with the stock promoter did not include any illegal activity.[191]

CNBC developed new conflicts of interest guidelines for its analysts in 1998. Concerned about "pump and dump," the network felt clear rules and guidelines were needed.[192] "Pump and dump" is the practice of a Wall Street professional appearing on a CNBC business show and touting a particular stock as being a potential good buy. Often unbeknownst to the viewing audience, the analyst promoting a particular stock has a large holding in the stock. After promoting the stock and the resulting price increase, the analyst sells his or her stock at a substantial gain.

Under the new rules, analysts must disclose any trading they have done in the stock prior to touting it. Analysts may not purchase stock, appear on the air to promote it, and then sell it after the price has increased.

In 2000, Arthur Levitt, the chairman of the SEC, asked that the National Association of Securities Dealers (NASD) and the New York Stock Exchange work with the SEC to develop rules to require analysts and money managers to make disclosures about potential conflicts of interest.

Levitt's immediate concerns focused on radio and television commentators who recommend stocks or offer highly favorable information about stock without disclosing their holdings or recent purchases in the stock. Currently, analysts who furnish reports must make disclosures in their reports about their holdings.[193]

While CNBC, Dorfman's network, investigated and found no violation of the law, Levitt pointed to Dorfman as an example of nondisclosures by media market commentators.

[189] *Patrick M. Reilly, "*Money *Fires Dan Dorfman for Not Divulging Sources,"* The Wall Street Journal, *January 4, 1996, pp. B1, B6.*

[190] *Laurie P. Cohen and Amy Stevens, "Dan Dorfman's Woes Mount as Investigators Widen Criminal Probe,"* The Wall Street Journal, *February 16, 1996, pp. A1, A7.*

[191] *Michal Schroeder, "Losing* Money,*"* Business Week, *January 15, 1996, p. 40.*

[192] *AP Wire Reports, December 23 and 24, 1998.*

[193] *Noelle Knox, "TV Stock Analysts May Soon Need Disclaimer,"* USA Today, *December 8, 2000, p. 3B.*

Many broadcasters allege the restrictions would make for boring radio and television programs. They have also claimed that such restrictions run contrary to First Amendment protections.

Discussion Questions

1. What are the ethical issues in this scenario?
2. Are there any ethical breaches that you can see?
3. CNBC and *Money* were placed in difficult situations that many employers must confront. What happens when allegations are made against an employee or a contractor who works for your company? What steps should the employer take? The mere suspension of an employee, even with pay, can harm the employee's reputation. However, an employer, particularly one whose own reputation is tied to the work of the employee, is at issue and it is often not possible to simply wait for the government to take action, if such action is planned. In Mr. Dorfman's case, the dilemma of the employer was compounded because Mr. Dorfman's health prevented his continuing appearances. Did CNBC act responsibly? Could they have done anything differently? What can an employer do to protect both its reputation and that of its employee?
4. Can you apply the principles of the regulatory cycle to this case? Did the networks wait too long? Should they have taken voluntary action?

CASE 5.12
The Ethics of Derivatives

Generically called "derivatives," financial instruments from secondary lease obligation bonds (SLOBS) to swaps and hedging have captured financial news headlines since February 1994. Derivatives are securities that derive value from something else investors buy, such as stocks, bonds, foreign currencies, or commodities contracts. Derivatives have allowed corporations, financial firms, and government entities to hedge their exposure to interest rates—and to speculate on market changes. At one end are options, which allow a purchaser to buy or sell a fixed amount of an asset within a given period. They are traded on major exchanges and have been around for nearly a decade.

Other forms of derivatives, such as swaps, are traded over the counter. Interest-rate swaps, for example, allow one party to make payments on a fixed rate of interest in exchange for another party's payments based on a variable rate. Swaps may also derive their value from being tied to several indexes or financial assets.

Mortgage derivatives are securities created by pooling government-backed mortgages and then separating them into either just the interest portion or the principal; they are not contracts between two parties. Because these instruments are essentially bets on the pace at which homeowners will refinance their mortgages (thus influencing cash flow), they are tied directly to changes in interest rates. When the Federal Reserve raised rates in 1994, the market for mortgage derivatives disappeared, and they could be sold only at a loss.

From the risky and leveraged investment of a gamble on stock market prices going up or down to secondary mortgage pool investments, the range of derivative instruments is broad and complex. With these instruments, investors could substantially leverage their portfolios and, if correct in their judgment, reap huge returns. If they were wrong and substantially leveraged, however, the losses could bankrupt them.

The first forms of derivative investments appeared in 1986. Six years later, the total derivatives market was $12.1 trillion. European firms were among the earliest and heaviest investors in derivative instruments. Metallgesellschift, a large German industrial conglomerate, was heavily invested in 1992 and eventually took a $1 billion write-off. U.S. government agencies and several large U.S. corporations, including Procter & Gamble, Gibson Greetings, Mellon Bank, and Bankers Trust New York, made significant investments in derivatives in 1992. In Canada, the Bank of Montreal was heavily invested in mortgage derivatives.[194]

A variety of government entities and other organizations invested in derivatives via leveraged funds. Among these were Orange County, California; Charles County, Maryland; Cuyahoga County, Ohio; West Virginia; Florida; and the Shoshone Tribe. Odessa College in Texas was one of several colleges that invested in collaterized mortgage obligations.

The market estimate of total derivatives investments rose to $35 trillion in 1993. At the end of that year, however, losses from derivatives began to surface. Procter & Gamble announced that it would take a $157 million charge to cover its losses.[195] As a result of the Procter & Gamble losses, the Financial Accounting Standards Board (FASB) promulgated and eventually adopted stricter standards regarding the reporting of derivative investments and disclosure of such investments, their risks, and potential exposure in the management discussion and analysis. FASB, along with the Securities and Exchange Commission (SEC), sets financial reporting requirements for publicly traded companies.[196]

The most commonly asked question by shareholders at annual meetings during the spring of 1994 was, "What derivative exposure does this company have?" During 1994, losses due to derivative investments continued to mount. Table 1 illustrates losses by various investors.

By mid-1994, derivatives were referred to as the "D word," and the SEC demanded accelerated FASB action. Several class action lawsuits were filed against entities that had losses as well as their brokers, including:

Paine Webber	(Settled for $33 million)
Piper Jaffray	(Settled for $70 million)

[194] *Andrew Pollack, "First Boston to Pay Fine in Orange County Bond Offering,"* The New York Times, *January 30, 1998, pp. C1, C6;* see also *"Survey Reports on Derivative Usage,"* Deloitte & Touche Review, *May 13, 1996, p. 1.*

[195] *Susan Antilla, "P & G Sees Change on Derivatives,"* The New York Times, *April 13, 1994, pp. C1, C16.*

[196] *"The Sound of Pips Squeaking,"* The Economist, *November 23, 1996, p. 91.*

Table 1 *Losses by Various Investors*

entity	*loss*
Charles County	\$8.3 million (98 percent of its assets in collateralized mortgage obligations)
Cuyahoga County	\$137 million (leveraged its \$1.8 billion fund)
West Virginia	\$279 million
Florida	\$175 million
Metallgesellschift	\$1 billion
Askin Capital Management	\$2 billion (firm is liquidated)
Procter & Gamble	\$102 million
Gibson Greetings	\$23 million
Bankers Trust	\$130 million[197]

Bankers Trust	(Pending)
Gibson Greetings	(Settled for \$23 million)[198]

In November 1994, the SEC brought a fraud action against Bankers Trust. The commission focused on Bankers Trust because of its involvement with Gibson Greetings. The case was settled for \$10 million in fines.

In December 1994, Orange County, facing a \$1.5 billion loss, filed for bankruptcy—possibly the largest muncipal bankruptcy ever. School projects were put on hold, and the funds of 185 school districts, towns, and local agencies, including their employee pension funds, were put on hold.[199] As a result, the Commodity Futures Trading Commission launched a probe into the Orange County derivative portfolio and the actions of its treasurer, Robert Citron. Mr. Citron was sentenced to one year in prison in 1996 and fined \$100,000 following a guilty plea to several counts of fraud.[200]

On February 25, 1995, losses from derivatives also led to the downfall of Barings, a 233-year-old British bank that financed the Napoleonic Wars and the Louisiana Purchase.[201] Barings announced its collapse on February 25, 1995, due to the staggering loss of \$1.2 billion in derivatives trading by Nick Leeson, a 28-year-old employee in its Singapore offices.[202] Leeson had traded futures contracts pegged to the Nikkei Number 225, one of Japan's major indexes. He had been arbitraging and had bet that

[197] *Matt Murray and Paulette Thomas, "After the Fall: Fingers Point and Heads Roll,"* The Wall Street Journal, *December 23, 1994, pp. B1, B4.*

[198] *Saul Itansell, "Piper Jaffray Agrees to Pay \$70 Million,"* The New York Times, *February 16, 1995, p. C3.*

[199] *Pollack, "First Boston to Pay Fine in Orange County Bond Offering," pp. C1, C6;* see also *"Survey Reports on Derivative Usage," p. 1.*

[200] *Karen Donovan, "Mutual Funds Confront Lawsuits over Derivatives,"* National Law Journal, *November 7, 1994, pp. A1, A24;* see also *John Greenwald, "Derivatives Slump; Losers Go to Court,"* National Law Journal, *November 7, 1994, pp. A1, A24.*

[201] *"Britain's Barings PLC Bets on Derivatives—and the Cost Is Dear,"* The Wall Street Journal, *February 27, 1995, pp. A1, A6.*

[202] *David Craig, "Week's Hunt for Barings Trader Ends,"* USA Today, *March 3, 1995, pp. 1B, 2B.*

the Nikkei exchange would go up. Instead, Japan's economy (and the January 1995 earthquake) caused the index to plummet.

Following the Barings debacle, the SEC held a panel discussion on March 3–4, 1995, for securities lawyers that raised several key questions:

- Should brokers be held liable for failing to disclose derivative risk?
- Should brokers be required to explain investment vehicles to clients?
- Should companies be required to highlight their total derivative portfolio in their financial statements?
- Should boards of directors be held liable for setting inappropriate risk levels for investments?
- Should the SEC, in light of the FASB's failure to act, set standards for financial reporting?[203]

In a March 1995 report, an advisory group of six securities firms offered to voluntarily tighten their oversizing on customers' derivatives exposure. However, the report concluded that "derivatives transactions are predominantly arms length transactions" for which customers ultimately have the obligation to review for potential risks and should seek independent advice.[204]

But firms continue to rely on derivative financial investments with 49 percent of companies using them to manage cash flow volatility and 42 percent using them to manage the volatility of "accounting earnings."[205] Fifty-nine percent of all firms with assets of $250 million or more use derivatives.

Discussion Questions

1. Suppose that you were the treasurer and chief financial officer for Gibson Greetings in 1986. You learn of several derivative vehicles with a 15 percent rate of return through Bankers Trust. The risk on these investments is substantially greater than any Gibson has had before. However, the pension fund requires contributions this year, competition is very threatening from Hallmark's success with its Shoebox Greeting division, and Bankers Trust indicates Procter & Gamble and several municipalities are already heavily invested.[206] In making your decision:

   a. Determine who will be affected by your decision.
   b. Apply at least two appropriate ethical models to your investment dilemma and reach a conclusion about the ethics of this derivative investment by Gibson.

2. What drove Procter & Gamble, Orange County, and others to make risky derivative investments?

3. What motivated Leeson's decisions and the resulting exposure of Barings?

[203] *Karen Donovan, "SEC, Lawyers Spar over Derivatives Restrictions,"* National Law Journal, *March 20, 1995, pp. B1, B2.*

[204] *Kelly Holland, "Derivatives: Alive, but Oh So Boring,"* Business Week, *January 30, 1995, pp. 76–77.*

[205] *Elizabeth MacDonald, "FASB Moving Ahead on Rule on Derivatives,"* The Wall Street Journal, *July 17, 1997, p. A7.*

[206] *Steven Lipin, "Bankers Trust Say P&G Deal Wasn't Unique,"* The Wall Street Journal, *November 22, 1994, pp. C1, C20.*

4. Before his last "bet," Leeson had served Barings well, earning high returns on his investment decisions in the derivatives market.[207] Why didn't anyone at Barings question his highly leveraged portfolio?

5. In the business section of *The New York Times* for September 1, 1996, there is the story of two sisters, Olga Monetti and Fannie Monetti, who became victims of the derivative investment craze.[208]

   The Monetti sisters had saved for 40 years all that they were able to set aside from their jobs as a technician at a blood bank (Olga) and file clerk at Borden (Fannie). The sisters shopped for their clothing at thrift stores and refinished used furniture for their East Harlem apartment that they shared with their ill mother until she died in 1993.

   By 1991, the sisters had saved $1.2 million, noting that in one year they had earned $57,000 in interest. They had employed a conservative investment strategy, relying on certificates of deposit and Treasury bonds.

   In 1991, the Monetti sisters responded to an ad for high CD yields. At first, the company placing the ad, High Yield Management Securities, placed the sisters' funds in conservative bond investments because of their ages then of 57 and 64. Slowly, however, their funds were moved over into derivatives, particularly the high-yield but high-risk collateralized mortgage obligations (CMOs).

   The Monettis not only lost their $1.2 million, they lost an additional $1.3 million. A securities arbitration panel ruled that the Monettis did not have to pay the $1.3 million because the risk of the CMOs was not explained to them. The same panel also ordered the owner of High Yield, Philip Eitman, to pay the Monettis $1 million for his failure to disclose to them the risk associated with CMOs. The Monettis have not been able to collect the $1 million. High Yield has filed for bankruptcy, and Mr. Eitman, who says he also faces problems with the IRS, is struggling to avoid personal bankruptcy.

   The Monettis now struggle from month to month trying to meet expenses. Fannie has a social security check of $550 per month and a $45-per-month pension from her clerk job at Borden. Olga's take-home pay from her job is $520 per week. Olga, who is a polio survivor, requires special shoes that cost over $200. The sisters own the brownstone building in which their apartment is located and they rent the other two apartments, but maintenance expenses eat up their profits. A sale of the brownstone, because it is located in such a bad neighborhood, would bring only $100,000. Olga asks, "How can we live? I didn't think things like this could happen in America."

   How does personalizing harms help avoid poor ethical choices? Would you have made more disclosures to the Monetti sisters? Would you have placed their money in the CMO derivative? Are the Monetti sisters at the same level of sophistication as Procter & Gamble and Gibson Greetings who also lost money in derivative investments?

[207] *Paula Dwyer, et al., "The Lesson from Barings' Straits,"* Business Week, *March 13, 1995, pp. 30–32.*

[208] *Dan Colarusso, "Picking Up the Shattered Pieces of a Lifetime of Saving,"* The New York Times, *September 1, 1996, p. F3.*

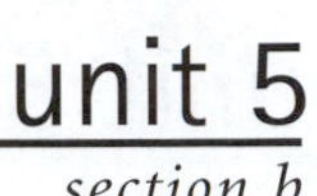

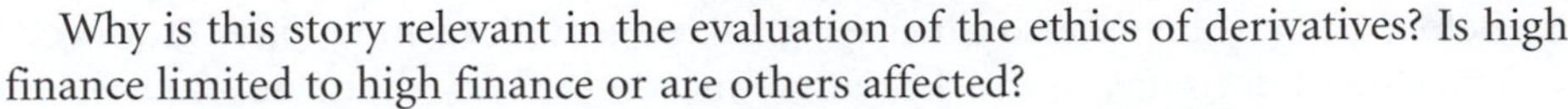
Why is this story relevant in the evaluation of the ethics of derivatives? Is high finance limited to high finance or are others affected?

CASE 5.13

Compensation-Fueled Dishonesty: Fraud to Get Results

Joseph Jett earned his Harvard master's degree in business administration in 1987.[209] Dismissed from his first post-degree job at CS First Boston, he then worked for Morgan Stanley but was laid off in the post-1980s Wall Street cutbacks. Despite his lack of experience in government securities, Jett was hired in 1991 by Kidder Peabody & Company to work in the government bonds section of its fixed-income department.

The fixed-income department was headed by Edward A. Cerullo, an exceptionally bright, hands-off manager who emphasized profits and was credited with turning Kidder around following the late-1980s insider trading scandals. Some fixed-income traders so feared telling Cerullo of losses that they underreported their profits at certain times so that they would have reserves to cover any future losses.

At the time of Cerullo's tenure and Jett's employment, Kidder Peabody was owned by General Electric (GE), which had purchased it in 1986 for $602 million. To establish Kidder as a Wall Street force, GE poured $1 billion into the firm and had begun to see a return only from 1991 to 1994. In 1992, GE had tried to sell Kidder to Smith Barney, Harris Upham & Company, but the sale fell through when Smith Barney learned of the extent of Kidder's mortgage-backed bond inventory.

Jett's initial performance in the bonds section was poor: he lost money. Fellow traders recalled Jett's first months on the job as demonstrating his lack of knowledge; some questioned whether Jett should have been hired at all. Even when Jett began earning profits, his reputation remained mediocre. "I don't think he knew the market. He made mistakes a rookie would make," said a former Kidder trader who worked in the 750-member fixed-income section with Jett.

Hugh Bush, a trader at Kidder, raised questions when he examined Jett's trades. In April 1992, Bush accused Jett of "mismarking" or misrecording trading positions, an illegal practice. Bush's allegations were never investigated, and he was fired within a month.

In 1991, Linda LaPrade sued Kidder, claiming that she was terminated as a vice president when she brought illegal trading to the attention of Cerullo. She also claimed she was told to increase allotments from government agency security issuers by "any means necessary."

[209] *Because of a balance on his tuition bill, he did not receive his degree until 1994. In June 1994, he paid the balance due on his tuition, and Harvard processed his degree.*

Also in 1991, the National Association of Securities Dealers (NASD) fined Kidder and Cerullo $5,000 for conduct by one of Kidder's bond traders, Ira Saferstein, who profited from a customer error.[210]

During this same period, Jett's profits bulged to 20 percent of the fixed-income group's total, and he was made head of the government bond department. Jett's profits, however, did not exist. Jett had taken advantage of an accounting loophole at Kidder that enabled him to earn a $9 million bonus for 1993 alone. The fictitious profits were posted through an accounting system that separated out the interest portion of the bond. Jett captured the profit on the "strip" (the interest portion of the bond) before it was reconstituted or turned back into the original bond. Kidder's system recognized profits on the date that the reconstituted bond was entered into the system. The result was that over two and one-half years, Jett generated $350 million in fictitious profits. When the scheme was uncovered by auditors in April 1994, GE had to take a $210 million write-off in its second quarter.

On April 17, 1994, Jett was fired, his bonus and accounts frozen, and the SEC began an investigation. Kidder hired Gary G. Lynch, a lawyer and former head of enforcement at the SEC, to conduct an inquiry into the losses and Jett's conduct.

As Lynch's inquiry progressed and the SEC stepped in, the casualties at Kidder began and continued in a steady stream:

- June 22, 1994: GE fired Kidder CEO Michael Carpenter.
- July 14, 1994: Kidder's brokerage chief, Michael Kechner, quit.
- July 22, 1994: Cerullo quit.
- August 4, 1994: Kidder fired three additional trading managers.

In December 1994, GE sold Kidder to Paine Webber for $670 million. The sale required GE to take a $917 million loss on the value of Kidder's assets and a $500 million write-off for the fourth quarter of 1994. GE's income dropped 48 percent for the quarter or about 45 cents per share. About half of Kidder Peabody's 5,000 employees would be laid off following completion of the deal.

A group of GE shareholders sued GE for the loss in share value resulting from the Kidder problems, the write-off, and the subsequent sale of Kidder for a loss.

Lynch determined that Jett acted alone: "The obvious motive for this effort was to achieve a degree of recognition and compensation that had previously eluded Jett in his professional career." Lynch added that the fraud was not detected because Jett's immediate supervisors did not understand the nature of his trading activities. Their failure to review trade tickets allowed Jett to perpetrate his fraud. Lynch concluded with what he called a simple message: "You have to understand how people are making money."

When the logistics of the fraud were explained, GE Chairman John F. Welch, Jr., said, "It's a pity that this ever happened. Jett could have made $2 to 3 million honestly."

Mr. Jett did file a $25 million libel suit against Kidder, Peabody, and its lawyers and officers. However, the papers were not served on any of the defendants perhaps because such litigation would permit unlimited discovery and questioning of Mr. Jett.

[210] *Cerullo said of the Saferstein incident, "The guy did something we told him not to. He did it again, and we fired him on the spot. He did the trade, and I got smacked."*

In early January 1996, the SEC filed civil administrative charges against Jett. Mr. Jett responded by saying, "I am completely innocent of these charges against me—I will not allow people to condemn me wrongly."

Edward Cerullo was charged with the failure to supervise. Mr. Cerullo settled and agreed to a one-year suspension as well as a fine of $50,000.

Mr. Jett decided to fight the charges and said, "Kidder and GE have taken my name and dragged it through the mud. They have robbed me of two of the most productive years of my life." Mr. Jett gave up his apartment and has lived with friends. Kidder permitted him to take $150,000 he had in his retirement account, and he has worked hauling furniture for $8 per hour. Mr. Jett says he gave $2 million of the money to his parents. In late 1996, a panel of NASD arbitrators agreed to release $1 million from Jett's brokerage account that had been frozen.

In a 1996 interview on CBS's *60 Minutes*, Gary Lynch was asked if there was any chance Mr. Jett was innocent. Mr. Lynch responded, "There's no chance." However, *Business Week* did produce an opinion piece on Joseph Jett and referred to the SEC case as "flimsy."

At Mr. Jett's June 1996 hearing, he testified, using his computer diary, that management knew about his bond-trading strategy. The alleged scheme was one of using government strips or securities that were created by peeling away and repackaging the interest payments on 30-year government bonds. One expert explained it as changing $1 into four quarters. There is a change in structure, but there are no revenues, and Mr. Jett was booking the changes as revenues.

Following Mr. Jett's hearing, the SEC filed a brief in the matter accusing Mr. Jett of introducing "bogus diary entries" from his computer. Mr. Jett had introduced 20 diary entries at his hearing to show management knowledge. However, only 5 of those entries matched entries retrieved from the master computer files of Kidder and obtained by the SEC. The matter remains pending.

Discussion Questions

1. An executive noted that Wall Street firms "have become victims of compensation schemes resulting in outrageously high salaries and bonuses. It brings out the worst in people who have any worst in them." Are compensation schemes responsible for poor ethical choices? Does a firm establish an ethical tone or culture with its compensation system? Should the jump in revenues from Jett's unit from 6% to 27% have triggered an investigation?
2. Cerullo earned an estimated $20 million in compensation during the time of Jett's alleged scam. In other words, he enjoyed increased compensation if Jett did well.

   Consider this rap song, "Requiem Rap at Kidder P Blow," that circulated around Kidder during its final pre-sale days:

   Big Boss and Joe went skiing in the snow:
   He said, Joe, what you're doing, don't wanna know;

But, keep on doing it, doing it though,
'Cause I am the Main Man at Kidder P Blow.
. . . Then one month Kidder P took a double blow;
Joe's profits were phony, the Man said so;
And the Fed jacked rates so the economy'd slow;
April was the cruelest month at Kidder P Blow.
. . . GE aimed all the blame at Ed Curello [sic]
He was the man who'd let the boys go.
To Joe and the V-Man he never said no.
'Twas the worst of times at Kidder P Blow.

Jett maintains his supervisors knew what he was doing, directed his trading, and used the profits to deflect scrutiny from Kidder's mortgage bond problems. Even if his supervisors did not know, did they not want to know? Is it an ethical violation to ignore signals?

3. What parts of the GE-Kidder culture and circumstances contributed to the "do what is necessary" ethical posture?
4. Why were Bush's and LaPrade's allegations so readily dismissed? Why were they fired?
5. Lynch's report concluded that the attitude in the Kidder bond department was "never question success," and that no one was willing to ask hard questions about Jett's ever-increasing profits. Were other employees enjoying the success too much? What ethical breaches did they commit by ignoring the implausibility of the success?
6. Lynch's report noted that some Kidder employees had questions about Jett's trading but "were reluctant or unsure how to report their concerns despite the existence of legal and compliance departments and an ombudsman." What could Kidder Peabody have done to eliminate such hesitancy?
7. List all the lives affected and harm resulting from Jett's conduct.

CASE 5.14

The Ethics of Bankruptcy

In 1980, there were 287,570 personal bankruptcies filed in the United States. In 1996, the number of personal bankruptcies topped one million for the first time in history. In 2001, the number of bankruptcies reached 1.5 million.[211] That number translates to a bankruptcy for 1 of every 100 households in the United States. The rate of bankruptcy filing in the United States for 1996 was eight times higher than the bankruptcy rate during the Great Depression.[212]

[211] *http://www.abiworld.org/research/yearreview*

[212] *Christine Dugas, "Credit Card Delinquencies Near Record,"* USA Today, *September 18, 1997, p. B1.*

The number one reason for bankruptcy declaration for the past three years was not loss of job or health problems or divorce.[213] Nearly 30 percent of all bankruptcy filings were attributed by the petitioner to simply being "overextended."[214] Over 70 percent of those filing for personal bankruptcy chose Chapter 7, or full bankruptcy, as opposed to Chapter 13 for a consumer debt adjustment plan.[215]

Most consumer debt is owed by those who earn between $50,000 and $100,000 a year. As one lender remarked, "These are people who could afford to save and buy later." (Consumer installment debt is at 85 percent of disposable income—an increase of 23 percent in the past decade.)[216]

Current laws are perhaps too permissive and make the declaration of bankruptcy very easy and very tempting. Changing the laws and requiring different standards could hamper investment, yet the average loss of $11,000 in debt write-off per bankruptcy costs each family in the United States $100 in higher prices as creditors try to cover the losses of bankruptcy.[217]

Bankruptcy declarations became a sore spot and a source of congressional hearings and proposed bankruptcy reforms in 1999, with legislation still pending as of March 2002. By 2001, the average amount of total debt for those consumers declaring bankruptcy was $82,852. The amount of debt that was not secured by collateral was $40,654 (includes credit card and medical debt). Other information about the average consumer bankruptcy declarant:

- Owes $2,528 in back child support
- Owes $38,760 on car loans and mortgage
- Has net income of $21,444
- Has total annual expenses of $24,324[218]

An issue that attracted Congressional attention was the homestead exemption in bankruptcy. Under this exemption, those who declare bankruptcy are able, under federal and state laws, to keep a portion or all of the equity in their home after emerging from bankruptcy. The examples that emerged during the hearings were that of corporate raider Paul A. Bilzerian being able to emerge from bankruptcy in Florida with his $5 million home because of Florida's rather generous homestead exemption. He had over $300 million in debts. Mr. Bilzerian served 20 months in federal prison following his conviction for securities crimes. Mr. Bilzerian graduated from Harvard Business School and was best known for his hostile takeover of Singer, the sewing machine company.[219]

Actor Burt Reynolds also emerged as an example because he was able to keep his $2.5 million home and estate, called Valhalla. After he declared bankruptcy in 1996, Mr. Reynolds had $10 million in debts.[220]

[213] *Damon Darlin, "The Newest American Entitlement,"* Forbes, *September 8, 1997, p. 113.*

[214] *Christine Dugas, "Non-Mortgage Debts Top Income for Millions,"* USA Today, *October 2, 1997, p. B1.*

[215] *Fred Waddell, "Easy Credit: A Wall Around the Poor,"* The New York Times, *February 15, 1998, p. BU12.*

[216] *Timothy L. O'Brien, "Giving Credit Where Debt is Due,"* The New York Times, *December 14, 1997, p. 14.*

[217] *Gregory Zuckerman, "Borrowing Levels Reach Record High,"* The Tribune, *July 9, 2000, pp. B1, B2.*

[218] *Peter T. Kilborn, "Mired in Debt and Seeking a Path Out,"* The New York Times, *April 1, 2001, pp. A1, A16.*

[219] *Philip Shenon, "Home Exemptions Snag Bankruptcy Bill,"* The New York Times, *April 6, 2001, pp. A1, A15.*

[220] Id.

Some experts have noted that the bankruptcy process is being used for strategic planning and a way to avoid contracts.[221] The following examples illustrate:

> TLC was an Atlanta rhythm, blues, and hip-hop band that performed at clubs in 1991. The three-woman group signed a recording contract with LaFace Records. The group's first album that LaFace produced—"Ooooooohhh . . . on the TLC Tip" in 1992—sold almost three million albums. The group's second album, "Crazysexycool," also produced by LaFace, sold five million albums through June 1996. The two albums together had six top-of-the-chart singles.
>
> LaFace had the right to renew TLC's contract in 1996 following renegotiation of the contract terms. Royalty rates in the industry for unknown groups, as TLC was in 1991, are generally 7 percent of the revenues for the first 500,000 albums, and 8 percent for sales on platinum albums (albums that sell over one million copies). The royalty rate increases to 9.5 percent for all sales on an eighth album.
>
> Established artists in the industry who renegotiate often have royalty rates of 13 percent, and artists with two platinum albums can command an even higher royalty.
>
> The three women in TLC, Tionne Watkins (T-Boz), Lisa Lopes (Left-Eye), and Romanda Thomas (Chili), declared bankruptcy in July 1995. All three listed debts that exceeded their assets, which included sums owed to creditors for their cars and to Zale's and The Limited for credit purchases. Lopes is being sued by Lloyd's of London, which claims Lopes owes it $1.3 million it paid on a policy held by her boyfriend on his home. Lopes has pleaded guilty to one count of arson in the destruction of the home but denies that she intended to destroy the house.
>
> Lopes has asked that the Lloyd's claim be discharged in her bankruptcy. All three members of TLC have asked that their contract with LaFace be discharged in bankruptcy because being bound to their old contract could impede their fresh financial starts.
>
> During 1996 the members of three music groups declared bankruptcy just before their contracts were due for renegotiation. One record company executive has noted that record company owners are frightened by the trend: "You invest all the money and time in making them stars. Then they leave for the bigger companies and a higher take on sales. It has all of us scared."[222]
>
> Pop singer Billy Joel also had a record contract with a small company during the initial stages of his career. When the company refused, during renegotiations, to increase his royalty rate, Joel did not produce another album during the period of the contract renewal option. Instead, he used a clause in the contract that limited him to night club and "piano bar" appearances in the event another album was not produced. For three years, Joel played small clubs and restaurants and did not produce an album. At the end of that period when his contract had expired, he negotiated a contract with Columbia. His first album with Columbia was "Piano Man," a multi-platinum album.[223]

[221] *Jeff Bailey and Scott Kilman, "Here's What's Driving Some Lenders Crazy: Borrowers Who Think,"* The Wall Street Journal, *February 20, 1998, p. A1.*

[222] *Laura M. Holson, "Music Stars Complain About Stringent Contracts,"* The New York Times, *September 6, 2001, pp. C1, C12.*

[223] *Reprinted from* Anderson's Business Law: The Regulatory Environment, *14th ed., 2001, p. 658.*

Discussion Questions

1. Do the three women meet the standards for declaring bankruptcy? Evaluate whether Lopes's Lloyd's claim should be discharged. Determine whether the record contract should be discharged.

2. Is declaring bankruptcy by the members of these musical groups legal? Is it ethical? Are the musicians using bankruptcy as a way to avoid contract obligations? Are the musicians using bankruptcy as a way to maximize their income?

3. Did Joel take an ethical route? Is his solution more ethical than bankruptcy?

4. Is there a presumption of good faith built into the bankruptcy code?

5. What about millionaires who declare bankruptcy and keep their homes? Is their conduct ethical?

5C

Conflicts between the Corporation's Ethical Code and Business Practices in Foreign Countries

Although we have a global market, we do not have global safety laws, ethical standards, or cultural customs. Businesses face many dilemmas as they decide whether to conform to the varying standards of their host nations or to attempt to operate with universal (global) standards.

CASE 5.15

Product Dumping

Once the Consumer Product Safety Commission prohibits the sale of a particular product in the United States, a manufacturer can no longer sell the product to U.S. wholesalers or retailers. However, the product can be sold in other countries that have not prohibited its sale. The same is true of other countries' sales to the United States. For example, Great Britain outlawed the sale of the prescription sleeping pill, Halcion, but sales of the drug continue in the United States.[224] The British medical community reached conclusions regarding the pill's safety that differed from the conclusions reached by the medical community and the Food and Drug Administration here. Some researchers who conducted studies on the drug in the United States simply concluded that stronger warning labels were needed.

The Consumer Product Safety Commission outlawed the sale of three-wheel all-terrain cycles in the United States in 1988.[225] While some manufacturers had already

[224] *"The Price of a Good Night's Sleep,"* The New York Times, *January 26, 1992, p. E9.*

[225] *"Outlawing a Three-Wheeler,"* Time, *January 11, 1988, p. 59.*

turned to four-wheel models, other manufacturers still had inventories of three-wheel cycles. Testimony on the cycles ranged from contentions that the vehicles themselves were safe but the drivers too young, too inexperienced, and more inclined to take risks (i.e., to "hot dog"). However, even after the three-wheel product was banned here, outlawed vehicles could still be sold outside the United States.

For many companies, chaos follows a product recall because inventory of the recalled product may be high. Often, firms must decide whether to "dump" the product in other countries or to take a write-off that could damage earnings, stock prices, and employment stability.

Discussion Questions

1. If you were a manufacturer holding a substantial inventory of a product that has been outlawed in the United States, would you have any ethical concerns about selling the product in countries that do not prohibit its sale?
2. Suppose the inventory write-down that you will be forced to take because of the regulatory obsolescence is material—nearly a 20 percent reduction in income will result. If you can sell the inventory in a foreign market, legally, there will be no write-down and no income reduction. A reduction of that magnitude would substantially lower share market price, which in turn would lead your large, institutional shareholders to demand explanations and possibly seek changes in your company's board of directors. In short, the write-down would set off a wave of events that would change the structure and stability of your firm. Do you now feel justified in selling the product legally in another country?
3. Is selling the product in another country simply a matter of believing one aspect of the evidence—that the product is safe?
4. Would you include any warnings with the product?

CASE 5.16
The Taboo of Women in Management

International management consulting firm Burns & McCallister is listed by *Working Mother* magazine as one of the top fifty firms in the United States for employment of working mothers and by *Working Woman* magazine as one of the top ten firms for women. The firm has earned this reputation for several reasons. First, nearly 50 percent of its partners are women. Second, it has a menu of employee benefits that includes such things as flex hours, sabbaticals, family leave, home-based work, and part-time partner-track positions.

However, Burns & McCallister recently has been the subject of a series of reports by both the *Los Angeles Times* and *The New York Times* that scrutinize its policy on female executives in certain nations. Burns & McCallister has learned, through fifty years of consulting, that certain countries in which it negotiates for contracts prohibit the use of women in the negotiation process. The cultures of many of these countries do not permit women to speak in a meeting of men. Consequently, Burns & McCallister has implemented a policy prohibiting women partners from being assigned these potential account negotiations and later the accounts themselves. Clerical help in the offices can be female, but any contact with the client must be through a male partner or account executive.

For example, Japan still has a two-track hiring system with only 3 percent of professional positions open to women.[226] The remainder of the women in the Japanese corporate workforce become office ladies who file, wear uniforms, and serve tea. Dentsu, Inc., a large Japanese ad firm, had a picture of the typical Dentsu "Working Girl" in its recruiting brochure. Surrounding the photo are comments primarily about her physical appearance: (1) Her breasts are "pretty large." (2) Her bottom is "rather soft."

In response to criticism regarding Burns & McCallister's posture, the head of the firm's New York office has explained:

> Look, we're about as progressive a firm as you'll find. But the reality of international business is that if we try to use women, we don't get the job. It's not a policy on all foreign accounts. We've just identified certain cultures in which women will not be able to successfully land or work on accounts. This restriction does not interfere with their career track. It does not apply in all countries.

The National Organization for Women (NOW) would like Burns & McCallister to apply to all its operations the standards that it employs in the United States. No restrictions are placed on women here, the organization argues, and other cultures should adapt to our standards; we should not change U.S. standards to adapt to their culture. NOW maintains that without such a posture, change can never come about.

Discussion Questions

1. Do you agree with Burns & McCallister's policy for certain cultures with regard to women partners?

2. Is Burns & McCallister doing anything that violates federal employment discrimination laws?

3. Given Burns & McCallister's record with regard to women, is the issue really relevant to women's advancement in the firm?

4. What if the cultures in which the prohibition of women applied traditionally bring in the highest dollar accounts? Would your opinion regarding the posture be different?

5. Do you agree with the position that change can never come about if Burns & McCallister does not take a stand?

6. Would Burns & McCallister be sacrificing revenues in changing its policies? Is this an appropriate sacrifice?

[226] *Ted Holden and Jennifer Wiener, "Revenge of the 'Office Ladies,'"* Business Week, *July 13, 1992, pp. 42–43.*

5d

Unauthorized Payments to Foreign Officials

What we would call a bribe and illegal activity in the United States may be culturally acceptable and necessary in another country. Could you participate in such a practice?

READING 5.17

The Ethics of Business in China and Business Ethics in China[227]

Marianne M. Jennings

I. Introduction

It isn't often that company officers examine an untapped market of nearly a billion consumers and then take a pass on having their company be the first-mover in that market. Yet more companies have made that decision than not with respect to doing business in China. Perhaps they see too much investment with too little returns for too long. Or perhaps they have reached a far more sophisticated conclusion about new markets in this global economy. That sophisticated conclusion comes from the realization that the presence of bribery and its resulting corruption in any country is a real risk.[228] Indeed, businesses have come to understand that the ethical issue in moving into a market fraught with bribery and corruption is not whether they would engage in bribery to do business in that country. The real ethical issue is whether you do business in the country at all.

[227] Corporate Finance Review *5(6): 42–45 (2001). Reprinted from Corporate Finance Review by RIA, 395 Hudson Street, New York, NY 10014.*

[228] The New York Times *noted in March 1999 that the number one complaint of the Chinese is "All this corruption." The report noted, "Yet corruption is now virtually built into the middle levels of China's vast authoritarian apparatus, under an ideology that has become a hollow shell while the new market economy swells around it." Seth Faison, "No. 1 Complaint of Chinese: All This Corruption,"* The New York Times, *March 11, 1999, p. A3.*

It cannot be easy for companies and their officers to remain committed to the principle of "we don't bribe" when new markets and opportunities are so extensive. However, the decision "we don't bribe" is not just one of principle. This is a decision grounded in economics and as companies and officers consider their strategic global moves, the internal moral wrestling match over entering markets should be brief for the moral and financial decisions on those markets and the issues of corruption and bribery are one and the same.

In the following sections are the reminders of why bribery and corruption, an ongoing problem in China, are such detrimental forces in economic and social progress in the untapped markets that await the advances global business can bring. Finally, there is a conclusion that provides direction to businesses in moving forward a global economy free from the self-imposed restraints of corruption.

II. Don't Lose Sight of the Bottom Line

It is nothing less than a fascinating exercise when teaching MBA students ethics to come to the point in the semester where we discuss what I have come to call the role of "stuff" in doing business. In China, it is referred to as "guanxi." In Mexico, it is called "mordida." "Stuff" is comprised of the gifts and perks we take and spread in the hope of landing a sale, closing a deal or doing business in a country. Businesses give away everything from Super Bowl tickets to lunches to embroidered logo shirts in the hope of gaining more business.

MBA students, experienced in the ways of business prior to returning to school, cite the benefits of stuff as follows: good will, loyalty, advertising and a host of other non-quantifiable benefits that accrue because of the gifts, token and otherwise, of business. However, what they cannot give to me in any of the cases we study or from their experiences is a formula correlation between the amount spent on "stuff" and increases in revenues. In other words, "stuff" is a business custom in the United States and the degree of "stuff" exchanged is often greater in other countries such as China, but there is little analytical evidence to show that the expense of "stuff" actually produces a return of the investment.

During a seminar for regional sales reps, I raised the issue of "stuff" with them and was met with understandable discomfort. The reason they were in Phoenix was to entertain potential buyers they were flying in for the Phoenix Open Golf Tournament. They explained the thousands of dollars they were spending on each potential client. I asked them how many clients they had gained when they had done the same thing last year for the Phoenix Open. Their response was, "None." In fact, one regional manager pointed out that the company executive he had flown in took the trip and then negotiated a deal with a competitor.

The panic of "this is the way it has always been done," or "everybody does this"[229] often overtakes the usual business analysis of, "How much is this costing me?" and "What will I get in return?"

[229] *Professor Henri-Claude de Bettignes has provided the following descriptions of bribery or "extensive stuff" in international business: "(1) Refusal to bribe is a Western hang-up. (2) Bribery is a parallel distribution system. Everyone does it. (3) It is the traditional way of doing business in this culture." Ron Berenbeim, "Cutting Off the Supply Side of Bribes,"* Vital Speeches of the Day, *Vol. LXV, April 15, 1999, p. 409.*

In forgetting to perform that simple financial analysis, companies also fail to recognize that those businesses that are contracting with them must also perform a similar analysis, "What do they propose for the cost?" "Is there someone who is cheaper?" "Is their service or product better?" In other words, "stuff" does not make accounting and revenue principles disappear. And decision-makers are always accountable for the purchasing contracts they make. "Stuff" is really a superficial fix for what should be the real foundation of a long-term business relationship: service; quality; reliability; promptness; and accuracy. In short, what keeps business is working long and hard at business, not "stuff."

The principles of business do not change across international boundary lines. The exchange of gifts may be customary in a country but should always be undertaken with the same quantitative analysis as other business expenditures: why am I spending this money? What do I expect in return? Over the long term, what will be the return on this expenditure?

Businesses too often retreat to the facile position that there can be no success in a country that has a culture in which gifts and even bribes are "the way business is done." They abandon not only sound decision-making tools in retreating to such a rationalization, but they shortchange their earnings and their shareholders as they adopt a quick-fix solution rather than a strategy of a long-term presence and continuing and stable returns.

III. Don't Forget the Need for Trust in Business

Free trade is not possible in an atmosphere of bribery, graft and corruption. In the 1996 Congressional hearings on international corruption, Robert S. Lieken testified, "reducing bribery, smuggling and kickbacks is part and parcel of free trade; anti-corruption is part and parcel of democracy. Today's decisive battles for free trade, development and democracy may well be fought on the terrain of corrupt practices."[230]

While urban legend holds that bribery is an inevitable part of international business, business transactions and the nature of doing business in any particular country are becoming more and more transparent.[231] Most countries are moving in the direction of full disclosure among their government officials, as in the case of Tanzania where the president now makes his assets public.[232] This slow but certain movement is the result of leaders in these countries being trained in U.S. universities and returning to their countries with the principles and requirements for free trade. Some countries even ban companies from doing business within their borders when they discover that the company has engaged in bribery.[233] *The Wall Street Journal* notes that there

[230] Hearings of the Senate Caucus on Int'l Narcotics Control & the Senate Finance Comm. Subcomm. On Int'l Crime, *104th Cong. (1996). Leiken is the president of New Moment, a nonprofit organization dedicated to fostering democracy internationally.*

[231] *Transparency International, a nonprofit devoted to creating international disclosure standards for business, has written, "major multi-nationals have not understood that the whole value system of dealing with developing countries is changing radically and rapidly . . . The colonial mind-set of 'bribery as usual' is coming under greater risk for bribers." See http://www.transparency.org.*

[232] *Michael A. Almond and Scott D. Syfert document a number of changes in countries' leaders in "Beyond Compliance: Corruption, Corporate Responsibility and Ethical Standards in the New Global Economy," 22* N.C. J. Int'l L. & Com. Reg. *389, 431 (1997).*

[233] *Mark J. Murphy, "International Bribery: An Example of an Unfair Trade Practice?" 21* Brooklyn J. Int'l L. *385, 391 (1995).*

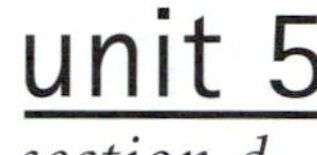

section d

are not more European scandals, there are simply "a more assertive judiciary, a more aggressive press, and a more inquisitive citizenry."[234]

There are significant costs associated with the presence of corruption. There is the political unrest caused by the prosecution and conviction of government officials engaged in bribery, but there is the resulting reluctance for businesses to initiate either new business or new contracts in a country where there is unrest and the stigma of corruption. There is also the impact of a market operating with prices being set artificially so that the few can command the fees they deem appropriate. Hong Kong has established its Independent Commission Against Corruption and its studies estimate the guanxi constitutes 3 to 5 percent of companies' operating costs or between $3 and $5 billion each year.[235] The list of cost reductions when bribery was eliminated includes: Russia where food prices dropped nearly 20 percent when vendors were protected from extortion by government officials; and Italy where freeway construction costs dropped 50 percent when government officials responsible for that contracting were indicted and convicted for bribery.

The final impact of corruption is on the perceptions of all those potential consumers in these untapped markets. The presence of bribery and corruption is more than just demoralizing; the presence of bribery deprives a market of its central characteristic of trust. Free markets are markets of honesty and independence, not dependence and a veil of secrecy. Hayek noted that the greatest impact of governmental actions that run contra to free market concepts is the psychological change or the alteration in the character of the people.[236] In China, a businessman noted that other businesspeople were paying to become their own regulators or even decision-makers on contracts they could award themselves when he noted, "An official job is like a piece of fruit. You pay the money and it is yours."[237] Such cynicism is not conducive to the entrepreneurial spirit needed for economic progress.

IV. What Business Is Doing About Corruption

The Conference Board's Working Group on Global Business Ethics is but one of many organizations working to halt corruption, particularly in China. Their proposal is one to "cut off the supply side of bribes."[238] In doing so, the group asks that its members make two firm commitments, the first to quality and the second to a resolve not to engage in bribery no matter how justified they may feel in taking such actions. The quality commitment is at the heart of business longevity and customer trust and represents a reaffirmation of Friedman's notion that ethical behavior leads to successful performance over the long term. Just U.S. business devotion to the theories of Deming's total quality management makes the first commitment relatively easy.

It is, however, the second area of commitment, which requires a pledge not to engage in bribery that the Conference Board emphasizes as it notes how easily firms can waver without such an absolute standard. An example illustrates the level of

[234] *Thomas Kamm et al., "Europe Can't Decide Whether Dirty Money In Politics Is a Problem,"* The New York Times, *January 9, 2000, p. A1.*

[235] *Karen Pennar, "The Destructive Cost of Greasing Palms,"* Business Week, *December 6, 1993, p. 133.*

[236] *F.A. Hayek,* The Road to Serfdom, *University of Chicago Press, 1994, p. xxxix.*

[237] *Faison, supra note 228.*

[238] *Berenbeim, "Cutting Off the Supply Side of Bribes," p. 408.*

justification or rationalization that can arise when utilitarianism rather than absolutism becomes a company's standard of conduct. Suppose that a foreign government is about to award a contract for the construction of a bridge in that country. A U.S. firm wishes to bid for the project but knows that the other firms' bids will be lower and that they will pay bribes to the government officials making the decision. The executives of the U.S. firm are also relatively confident that the firms engaged in bribery for the bridge contract will cut corners, provide a lower quality bridge, and perhaps sacrifice safety in the process. Those executives might feel comfortable, under a standard of utilitarianism, in engaging in bribery to get the contract because they would, after all, be saving lives by building a higher quality bridge.

The firm is rationalizing. It is impossible for that firm to draw knowledgeable conclusions on the other firms' quality levels. The firm is simply using its perceived superior quality to justify bribery. The firm has fallen victim to the "everyone else does it" syndrome. While the question seems to become gray as the issue of quality is factored in, it is important to understand that the market is capable of screening quality. For the country's future, the best solution is for the company to bid, not pay the bribes and then disclose the practices publicly. There is a cleansing process that immediately follows such a disclosure and the company with the winning bid may find itself banned from doing business. This cleansing, as noted above, is becoming more common because freedom from corruption is inextricably intertwined with economic progress.

The Conference Board solution is the correct one. It is incumbent upon businesses to eliminate the supply side of corruption so that in a true utilitarian sense those countries in which they choose to do business can have the benefits and growth of free trade in a transparent economy.

Discussion Questions

1. Why do companies pay bribes in other countries?
2. What are the short-term implications of bribes?
3. What are the long-term implications of bribes?
4. What impact do bribes have on economic systems?

CASE 5.18

The Adoption Agency and Señor Jose's Fees

Ninos and Ninas, Inc. is an adoption agency located in El Paso, Texas, that focuses on international adoptions. Most of the infants Ninos and Ninas places are from South American countries.

Couples, primarily from the United States, work with Ninos and Ninas to adopt children. The fee for Ninos and Ninas' work ranges from $15,000 to $20,000. Couples pay the fee willingly because of the agency's twenty-year history of excellent work and its extensive knowledge of adoption requirements in South American countries.

Joan and David Ryan have applied with Ninos and Ninas to adopt a child. Their U.S. certification is complete, and they have submitted their application along with a $10,000 deposit to Ninos and Ninas.

After their application is processed, the Ryans receive a notice from Esther Tomkin, Ninos and Ninas' director of adoption services, that a baby girl is now available. Ms. Tomkin instructs them that she will need an additional $5,000 as well as $5,000 in cash in unmarked bills in an envelope to be placed in a postal box located in El Paso. Ms. Tomkin's letter explains:

> You should bring the $5,000 with you when you come to El Paso to pick up your new daughter. Once you have paid the $5,000 to Ninos and Ninas and deposited the $5,000 in cash, you will have your little girl within 24 hours. You should be prepared to come to El Paso on April 10. The envelope with the cash should be marked for "Señor Jose."

Joan is concerned about the odd cash payment and phones Ms. Tomkin to discuss it. Ms. Tomkin assures Joan that "the payment is just the way adoption works in these countries. It is not a bribe; it is not a violation of the Foreign Corrupt Practices Act; it is simply a requirement to get the adoption paperwork through. Your adoption just can't get through the system without it. This is the way we've been doing business for twenty years." Joan asks, "Who is Señor Jose?" Ms. Tomkin responds, "He's just an official in the social agency who handles adoptions. He isn't even the judge who approves the adoption. Without this money, your little girl ends up a street child or malnourished in an orphanage."

Discussion Questions

1. Would the payment to Señor Jose violate U.S. laws? Does the international nature of the adoption agency's operations affect its operational standards?
2. Is the payment a bribe or a facilitating "grease" payment? Is there a difference? Does the fact that the payment is legal control the determination of whether it is ethical?
3. Does the benefit to the infant girl justify the method for accomplishing that benefit?
4. Would you go forward with the adoption?
5. Would you feel comfortable working for or adopting from Ninos and Ninas?

CASE 5.19

Salt Lake City, the Olympics, and Bribery

Officials in Salt Lake City had been trying to win the International Olympic Committee (IOC) nod for the Winter Olympics since 1966. For the IOC meeting in Rome at which the 1966 decision would be made, the Salt Lake City Olympic Committee raised $24,000 by selling Olympic pins for $1 each. Following a trip to

Rome, there was $10,305 left and a two-page audit documented all the expenses for the failed try.

Business and government leaders kept trying to win over the IOC, but continued to do so on a spartan budget. For example, in 1989 the Salt Lake leaders journeyed to Greece to meet with the IOC and noted that other cities were giving the IOC members jewelry and crystal vases. Atlanta had created "The Atlanta House" and had furniture shipped from Atlanta to create an authentic Southern home. Other cities had created rooms for breakfast and lunch buffets for the IOC members. That year, Salt Lake City leaders, concerned about their lack of gifts, had some letter openers flown in to give to the IOC members.

When Salt Lake City was trying for the 1998 Winter Games, they were told in a letter from the head of Ireland's Olympic Committee that some of the IOC members were selling their votes for $100,000 in exchange for a vote for Nagano, Japan (the site eventually chosen). One of the children of a member of the IOC approached Thomas Welch, the head of the Salt Lake City Olympic Committee, and said that he could help get Salt Lake City the votes in exchange for $35,000. Mr. Welch and the members of the Salt Lake City Olympic Committee (SLCOC) refused to pay the money, although many have said it was because they simply could not raise the $35,000 at the last minute. The SLCOC had simply paid for travel expenses for IOC members. For example, an audit of the 1991 expenses for the unsuccessful bid for the 1998 Winter Olympics revealed that Mr. David R. Johnson was reimbursed $2.73 for a receipt from a 7-11 convenience store near Utah's ski areas and an accompanying note that read, "juice for Prince Albert." Prince Albert of Monaco was an IOC member at the time and had traveled to Utah to view the sites for events. Prince Albert refused any special treatment, including limousines and any types of events or dinners in his honor. Such simplicity from a member of a royal family and also an IOC member perhaps also convinced the SLCOC members that the exchange of cash was unnecessary.

However, when SLCOC lost its bid to Nagano, despite its hopes that the issues of cash payments were not effective, its members began to talk openly about "what it took to win the Olympics" for their city. When the SLCOC began its planning in 1991 for its bid for the 2002 Winter Olympics, even the minutes from the meetings make it clear that committee members were single in purpose in doing all it took to get the Olympics. Mr. Johnson, a continuing and prominent member of the 2002 SLCOC, said, "Everything we had was about getting the bid. All our money was to get votes." Others have described the attitude of "doing whatever it takes" to get the Winter Olympics because the cause was a good one and it seemed that Salt Lake City was losing "for not playing the game," and "doing what everyone else was doing." There was an attitude of "if we don't do it, someone else will" and "this is the way it's always been done—we just didn't understand that."

Beginning in 1991, on the heels of their loss to Nagano, the SLCOC began its new style of garnering votes, particularly, as they thought through their strategy, the African votes. From 1991 through 1995, the SLCOC gave an estimated $1.2 million to members of the IOC or their families. Nearly $100,000 in scholarships went to children of members of the IOC. Other children of IOC members stopped by the SLCOC offices on a regular basis and picked up checks for themselves. Sibo Sibandze, son of an IOC member from Swaziland, picked up weekly checks from the SLCOC offices that ranged from $250 to $590.

A volunteer staff member described the situation on the payments and checks as follows:

> You knew these guys, they came in weekly. You saw them pick up their checks. You took them places. You didn't have to be a brain surgeon to know what was going on. It was always whispered, "Whose son is he? How much of a scholarship is he getting? How does that work?" People freaked out the first time they heard about it. Then it became second nature.[239]

Audits of the SLCOC's books from this time period reveal a dramatic drop-off in documentation for payments, with many never explained. There were a series of payments to Raouf Scally totaling $14,500 in $500 installments with a notation that Mr. Scally was a son of a member of the IOC. No one has ever been able to tie him to any IOC member and subsequent investigations have not determined who he is and what role he played in the SLCOC's successful bid.

An examination of the records also revealed that the members of the SLCOC had done their homework in terms of vulnerability. Some of the dossiers on IOC members made reference to those who had complained about financial difficulties, including issues of making their mortgage payments. While IOC members are prohibited from accepting gifts valued over $150, the following are documented benefits to IOC members from the SLCOC:

- Lawn equipment, $268
- Violin, $524
- Doorknobs, $673 (one of the IOC members, Jean-Claude Ganga, an IOC member from Congo Republic, was remodeling his home)
- Jean-Claude Ganga received more than $200,000 in cash and medical treatment
- Ganga's wife used a SLCOC member's credit card at Wal-Mart for various items and reached the maximum credit limit on the member's card
- Bathroom fixtures, $1,488 (the same)
- Draperies, $3,117 (the same)
- Dogs, $1,010
- Letterhead stationery for the nation of one of the IOC member's country, $6,934
- Super Bowl trip for Mr. Welch and IOC members Philip Coles of Australia and Willi Kaltschmitt of Guatemala, $19,991. These two IOC members never visited Salt Lake City.
- Two-week Park City condominium rental for a vacation for Agustin Arroyo, the ICO member from Ecuador, $10,000
- The daughter of Kim Un Yung, an IOC member from South Korea, was given a contract playing with the Utah Symphony
- English language training, $1,390
- Disneyland trip, $1,202
- Yellowstone trip, $926
- Ski lessons for a child, $414
- Furniture rental for a child, $250

Ernst & Young, the auditors for the SLCOC, uncovered most of the questionable items during a 1995 audit. The auditors' work papers indicate that they talked to SLCOC members about the scholarship programs, the amounts, and the purposes. These committee members deny that they were informed of these issues by the auditors.

[239] *Jo Thomas, Kirk Johnson, and Jere Longman, "From an Innocent Bid to Olympic Scandal,"* The New York Times, *March 11, 1999, pp. A1, A14, A15.*

However, the auditors did not uncover any evidence that any of the checks that were issued were unauthorized.

What happened following the audit and the eventual public disclosure of these payments was a complex tale of several individuals trying to have someone review what the SLCOC was doing. Mr. Ken Bullock, a member of the SLCOC Board of Trustees, talked with both Governor Michael O. Leavitt's staff and members of the Salt Lake City city council. In many cases, he was dismissed as being "a little out there." Friends said that Mr. Bullock was frustrated, bloodied, and bruised as he tried to bring the matters to someone's attention. One city council member did have a meeting with Rod Decker, a television reporter, about the scholarship issues on June 3, 1997. However, Mr. Decker accepted Mr. Johnson's explanation that children of members of the IOC had simply toured the University of Utah and that there were no scholarships. It was during this time that the law firm housing the records of the SLCOC meetings ordered the destruction of firm documents with no indication of who had given the order for their destruction. The destruction was accomplished at a time when the time frame for retention of the client's documents would not have provided for their destruction.

The story finally came to public light when a staff member from the SLCOC offices sent an anonymous letter reflecting the payment of scholarship monies to one of the children of an IOC member to a different television station from Mr. Decker's that did not run the story. On November 4, 1998, the first television story ran about possible scholarship and other payments to IOC members and their children. Both local and national news outlets descended on Salt Lake City to investigate the full extent of the payments. When a high-ranking member of the IOC used the word "bribes" in connection with the SLCOC bid, government agencies began investigations. Mr. Welch resigned from his $10,000-per-month job as head of the SLCOC, and Mitt Romney, former candidate for the U.S. Senate in Massachusetts, the owner of Staples, Inc., and candidate for Massachusetts governor in 2002, took over as head of SLCOC.

Once the news stories began, the following investigations and their outcomes resulted:

- Ethics Investigation by Gordon R. Hall, former chief justice of the Utah Supreme Court—issued a 300-page report in February 1999 that concluded no criminal activity but a host of ethical issues and violations of trust in the SLCOC's bid for the 2002 games; 24 members of the IOC are mentioned by name in the report as having received gifts and others items from the SLCOC.
- United States Olympic Committee investigation by George Mitchell (former U.S. Senator, ambassador to Ireland and head of the USOC Ethics Committee)—recommends processes, procedures, checks, and balances for future bids for games from the United States.
- U.S. Justice Department—investigation of SLCOC activities that resulted in indictments. David Simmons entered a guilty plea to charges of tax evasion after admitting that he set up a sham job for John Kim, the son of Yong Kim, an IOC member from Korea (in response to a request from Mr. Welch); John Kim is charged with lying to the FBI about his job and lying to obtain a green card. David Simmons was the head of Keystone Communications. He set up a job for John Kim that paid between $75,000 and $100,000; Keystone was then reimbursed by the SLCOC for the salary. The investigation was referred to the Reno Justice Department after the U.S. Attorney for Utah, Paul Warner, recused himself and his office from any SLCOC investigations and related matters. Justice Department investigators zeroed in on violations of the Foreign Corrupt Practices Act and tax fraud. Mr. Johnson and Mr. Welch were charged with RICO violations, bribery, and conspiracy in a grand jury in-

dictment handed down in July 2000. Both rejected plea bargain agreements from the Justice Department.[240] Their trial was scheduled to begin on July 16, 2001, however, the federal district judge dismissed the charges, noting that the state of Utah had declined to prosecute. The U.S. Attorney has filed an appeal of the dismissal.[241]

- IOC internal investigation—resulted in the expulsion of 6 IOC members; a reprimand to Phillip Coles of Australia, who also resigned his position as a member of the Sydney Olympics Board; and revisions in rules on choosing an Olympic site. A new code of ethics was also adopted. The final years of IOC President Juan Antonio Samaranch's tenure were rocky because of the SLCOC scandal. Many had called for his resignation, but he stayed until July 2001 when his tenure expired, promising ethics reform during those final years.
- Utah Attorney General—investigating possible criminal wrongdoing.
- U.S. Congress—conducted hearings on IOC reforms with a stern admonition to ICO members that there would be continuing oversight on the gifts aspects of the IOC's code of ethics and that reforms were not yet complete. Congressional budget committees also examined the award of federal funds to Utah and Salt Lake City for Olympics-related transit and highway improvements.

Salt Lake City was permitted to keep the 2002 Winter Olympics after the news of the "gifts" broke, but it had trouble with corporate sponsorships and raising funds during 1999–2000 because confidence in the games was so shaken.[242] It was not until the announcement in November 1999 that Gateway Computer would be a $20 million sponsor that the tide on fund-raising was turned.[243] VISA followed later in November.[244] Further, the Sydney Summer Olympics in 2000 experienced many sponsorship withdrawals because of the Salt Lake City bid scandal.[245] Although John Hancock Mutual Life Insurance Company criticized the IOC for the scandal[246] and initially indicated it would withdraw its support, it re-upped as a sponsor for $55 million.[247]

Discussion Questions

1. Tom Schaffer, the attorney for Mr. Welch, said that his client and Mr. Johnson did "what they had to do" to win a bid in a system that "stinks."[248] Are the flaws in a system a justification for the payments? Ken Bullock has noted, "The Games are an aphrodisiac, If you want something bad enough, you stretch the boundaries. The IOC allowed this sucking up."[249]

[240] *Vicki Michaelis, "Salt Lake Bid Leaders Spurn Deal,"* USA Today, *July 14, 2000, p. 1C.*

[241] *Patrick O'Driscoll, "U.S. Appeals in Olympics Bribery Case,"* USA Today, *January 24, 2002, p. 2A.*

[242] *For example, Johnson & Johnson withdrew its sponsorship. "Johnson & Johnson Decides Against Olympic Scholarship,"* Arizona Republic, *April 19, 1999, p. A5.*

[243] *Bruce Horovitz, "Gateway Logs On As Salt Lake Olympics Sponsor,"* USA Today, *November 3, 1999, p. 1B.*

[244] *Bruce Horovitz, "Visa Reviews Support for Olympic Games,"* USA Today, *November 12, 1999, p. 1B.*

[245] *A. Craig Copetas, "After Scandal, Local Sponsors Shun Olympics,"* The Wall Street Journal, *April 4, 2000, pp. B1, B4.*

[246] *Joseph B. Treaster, "Monitor of the Olympic Mettle,"* The New York Times, *March 28, 1999, p. BU2.*

[247] *Bruce Horovitz, "Reaching for Rings,"* USA Today, *March 16, 2000, p. 1B.*

[248] *Kirk Johnson, "E-Mail Trail Adds Details to U.S.O.C.'s Role,"* The New York Times, *February 10, 1999, pp. C1, C25.*

[249] *Nadya Labi, "The Olympics Turn into a Five-Ring Circus,"* Time, *January 11, 1999, p. 33.*

2. In one discussion of exchanges with IOC committee members, SLCOC members brought athletes from the Sudan to the United States for training as part of an exchange for Sudan members' votes. One person associated with the exchange has said, "In our minds, we distinguished the transactions in which Sudanese athletes were brought to the United States, apparently with some understanding that we would receive Sudanese votes, from an example in which an IOC member sells their vote. It's a different thing. A distinction needs to be made."[250] Do you agree? However, another e-mail exchange raises some concerns about the funding being taken from U.S. athletes. One U.S. Olympic Committee member (USOC) wrote, "Should I take financial support away from American athletes? Or does your budget cover these international political initiatives?" A response from another USOC member was, "You can take it away from the additional revenue we will ALL benefit from after having won the 2002 Games for SLC."[251] Was there harm in this benefit to the athletes?

   Dick Schultz, the executive director of the USOC, said of the e-mail exchanges that they were "unfortunate," and "People make flippant remarks on E-mails that aren't always accurate. It seems like it was handled appropriately. 'If you do this they'll vote for us'—I don't see that in any records we've turned up."[252] Do you think that the statement must be made expressly for exchanges for votes to take place?

3. Richard Pound, an IOC member and a lawyer from Montreal, was the lead investigator for the IOC report. His 24-page summary indicated, "inappropriate activities of certain members of the IOC did not commence with the candidacy of Salt Lake City." The report also notes, "It is clear the matter of gifts is going to be troublesome. In some cases, the value of the gifts was . . . not reasonably perceived as ordinary or routine."[253] How does one define appropriate gifts? What are ordinary and routine gifts? Does it make a difference that Salt Lake City was not the first site bidder to give these types of gifts?

4. When Pound issued his report and recommended a reprimand for Phil Coles, *USA Today* columnist Christine Brennan wrote the following:

   > This reminds me of the fabulous way the IOC handled a messy gift-taking situation involving member Phil Coles earlier this year. The IOC refused to use an independent investigator and instead let vice president Dick Pound handle the case. First Pound interrogated Coles, then he went to dinner with him. The two men, it turns out, are good friends. When the investigation was completed do you think the IOC expelled Coles? Heavens no.[254]

   Why does Brennan make this point?

5. Why do you think the expelled members were from third world nations (Togo, India, Mauritius, Nigeria, Mongolia, and Algeria)?

[250] Id.

[251] Id.

[252] Id.

[253] *A. Craig Copetas and Roger Thurow, "A Preliminary Report on Salt Lake Scandal Certain to Rile the IOC,"* The Wall Street Journal, *January 20, 1999, pp. A1, A8.*

[254] *Christine Brennan, "Some IOC Fixes Sound Like Trouble,"* USA Today, *December 16, 1999, p. 3C.*

6. One member of the SLCOC noted that a shopping trip to Wal-Mart was a "good value" and could not be corruption. Do you agree?

7. A lawyer representing the SLCOC in the Justice Department probe has stated, "There were a lot of things that were unethical, but that's a long way from being criminal."[255] Do you agree with her assessment?

8. Tom Welch sent a fax to his friends and copied reporters. The note contained the following language:

   > I am saddened and dismayed that so many feel the need to isolate responsibility for what—at the time—were cooperative decisions. Had our agreed course of action been questioned at the time by those to whom we reported, no doubt we would have been pleased to pursue other avenues. It is ironic that those who were so supportive of our efforts to secure the Games now feel the need to distance themselves.[256]

   Do you think others knew and abandoned him once the information was public?

9. A letter to the editor of the Salt Lake City paper, *The Deseret News*, read as follows:

   > Instead of pursuing legal proceedings, we should be erecting a statue of Tom Welch in Washington Square and put a canopy to keep the pigeons, vultures, the Chris Vancours and the Steve Paces off of him. It is people like Tom, with deep passions, who accomplish much and who almost single-handedly brought the Olympics to Salt Lake and Utah.
   >
   > There is a lot of truth in the adage, no good deed goes unpunished. I know to be politically correct we had to dump him but only because he played the age-old game of favor for favor, something everyone of us plays daily. Good luck, Tom and Dave. I wish I could be on the jury.[257]

   Is the writer correct? Was it a favor-for-favor game that all of us play every day?

Sources

"A Time of Turmoil," *USA Today*, December 8, 1999, p. 10C.

Caldwell, Christopher, "Pillars of Salt Lake," *National Review*, March 8, 1999, pp. 35–36.

Copetas, Craig, and Roger Thurow, "Closing Ceremony: The Olympics Say Farewell to Samaranch," *The Wall Street Journal*, August 12, 2001, pp. A1, A10.

Dodd, Mike, "10 More Are Cited for Misconduct," *USA Today*, February 10, 1999, p. 4C.

[255] *Laurie P. Cohen and David S. Cloud, "U.S. Probe Into Salt Lake Bid Scandal To Explore Possible Federal Violations,"* The Wall Street Journal, *February 18, 1999, p. A6.*

[256] *Kristen Moulton, "Welch Defends Actions in Olympics,"* LA Times.com, *http://www.latimes.com, Thursday, February 4, 1999.*

[257] The Deseret News, *June 24, 2001, http://www.desnews.com.*

Fatis, Stefan, "Olympic Broadcaster's IOC Ties Raise Questions," *The Wall Street Journal*, January 19, 1999, pp. B1, B6.

Longman, Jere, and Jo Thomas, "Report Details Lavish Spending in Salt Lake's Bid to Win Games," *The New York Times*, February 10, 1999, pp. A1, C25.

"Probe Won't Have Salt Lake Federal Prosecutor," *USA Today*, December 22, 1998, p. 3C.

Raboin, Sharon, and Kevin Johnson, "Salt Lake Fund-Raising Slowed," *USA Today*, January 14, 1999, p. 2C.

Titze, Maria, "Bid-Scandal Lawyers File Objection," *The Deseret News*, June 26, 2001, http://www.desnews.com.

5e

Workplace Safety

Certain safety issues continue to evolve. While given hazards await regulation, workers eventually will experience harm. How much responsibility does an employer have? Is an employer required to be proactive?

READING 5.20

The Regulatory Cycle

Marianne M. Jennings

Some years ago, when he was serving as the CEO for Motorola, before going on to become Kodak's CEO, George Fisher spoke to a group of our masters students from both engineering and business. One of the questions the students asked after he had given his thoughts on success in life and business was, "How do you become a leader in business?" His response was that those in business should take an evolving problem in their business units, their companies, their industries, or their communities and fix it before the problem was regulated or litigated. He assured the students that business people who voluntarily undertake self-correction are always ahead of the game.

There is a diagram I use to teach students this Fisher principle of leadership that shows how its best execution is found in focusing on ethics (see Figure 1).

Every area that is now the subject of regulation or litigation began at the left side of the scale, in the latency stage, with plenty of options for how to handle a gray area. For example, prior to the savings and loan crisis of the 1980s, appraisers were not regulated. The qualifications for an appraiser were limited and issues such as conflicts of interest were not controlled. In an area in which there are few legal guidelines, businesses have leeway in terms of their decisions. However, should those decisions violate ethical notions, then the courts and/or the legislatures will step in to legislate ethics. In the case of appraisers there are now complete federal and state regulations on qualifications, licensing, and issues of conflicts of interest.

The regulatory cycle moves, not by data, but by public perception. Public perception changes through examples and anecdotes. We are witnessing a regulatory cycle with regard to cell phone use in cars. On the list of causes of accidents, cell phones are

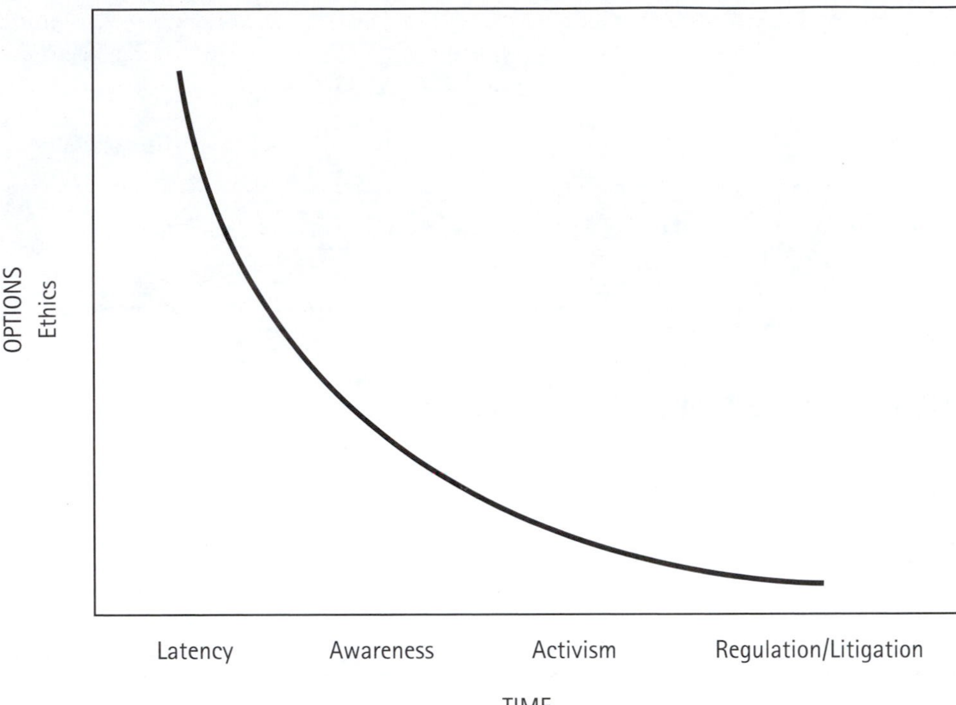

Figure 1
Leadership and Ethics: Making Choices before Liability

Source: Adapted from James Frierson's "Public Policy Forecasting: A New Approach," SAM Advanced Management Journal, *Spring 1985, pp. 18–23.*

at the very bottom with eating, reaching, and talking to another passenger being more frequent causes of accidents than cell phone use. Nonetheless, New York and other states have already moved to regulate cell phone use by drivers. We were living in an area untouched by regulation. We could use our cell phones when and how we wanted. However, there were safety issues, in terms of distraction, associated with the use of cell phones while driving. We could have voluntarily abstained but were unwilling to exercise that self-restraint. The result is that the law will do it for us both through attributing accident liability to us when we have an accident while using cell phones and through legislation that will permit tickets for using them while driving.

The ethical issue we are trying to solve with such regulation is whether drivers were behaving in a fashion that would be comfortable for them if other drivers behaved in the same way. In other words, would we want to be on the same road with us when we are trying to do cell phone business and drive at the same time? Probably not, but we could not voluntarily constrain ourselves and regulation stepped in to mandate such constraints.

There are businesses that do seize the moment. There is little question that the electric utility industry would look a great deal different today if it had not handled the issue of EMF (electromagnetic fields) as effectively and openly as it did.

During the late 1970s, a scientist released a study showing that children in the Denver area who lived near transmission wires and poles were more likely to develop leukemia. Whether the study was correct or had the wrong causation was impossible to know. The electric utility industry was under no legal obligation to change anything in terms of its transmission wires and their location. Nor were they obligated to the public to research the issue or even disclose the research. Nonetheless, the industry was very aggressive and included information in customer bills about EMF: what it is, how to measure, and how to obtain help on evaluating your risk and exposure. At the same time, the utilities sponsored research on the issue to determine whether the studies were accurate.

The information in the study might have been true or false, but leaders in the industry were not going to allow the issue to be shaped by others; they took the initiative to manage an issue from an ethical perspective. If the study conclusion was correct, then the utilities had to take action to stop any further injury to those living near power lines. However, if the study conclusion was incorrect, the utilities had an issue to manage and a study to refute.

The results of that initiative on the part of the utilities were that the public was informed, the studies were conducted, and we now have data from all types of studies. The original study conclusion was correct in the sense that there were pockets of childhood leukemia, but the pockets were better explained by socioeconomic factors and not the presence of power lines. In fact, the studies seem to show that there is no connection between cancer rates and proximity to EMF. Without these voluntary steps on the part of the utilities, I am convinced that utilities today would be managing a crisis similar to the asbestos litigation and regulation.

Those in the asbestos industry were selling an effective and unregulated product. They also had information about negative health effects from exposure to asbestos. Those effects were documented in board meeting minutes as early as 1933. However, those in the asbestos industry declined to take any steps with regard to those health studies. So long as the law permitted asbestos, they would sell it. In fact, they even tried to conceal the studies. By 1976, the industry was experiencing litigation that forced many of them into bankruptcy because the public was driving the issue, not the companies that had neglected to acknowledge and take action when they had options and opportunities. The demise of their product was managed for them by crippling litigation.

No one required action on the part of the utilities, but they made their decision from an ethical perspective. The result is that they did not see the cycle evolve to the point where they had no choices in terms of wire placement and had tremendous liability exposure because of public perception regarding EMF.

There are ethical issues that are now in the latency stage—that stage where the public is not aware of a problem and no one is filing suit or demanding regulation. Leaders take voluntary steps while there are options and emerge not only ahead in terms of financial performance, but also as individuals with foresight who recognize issues and solve them before there is any harm.

Discussion Questions

1. Name several issues you can think of in the latency stage.

2. What types of voluntary actions can businesses take?
3. What happens with regulation and litigation?

CASE 5.21

Electromagnetic Fields: Exposure for Workers and Customers

EMFs Are Discovered

Technology has brought us the phenomenon of electromagnetic fields (EMFs)—magnetic fields that result from electrical current. These fields can be found around transmission lines, home appliances, and video display terminals for computers. Wherever there is electric power, there are electric and magnetic fields that result from the charge in the electric power system. The amount of the charge produces the electric field, and the motion of the charge produces the magnetic field. Together, these two types of fields are often called an electromagnetic field (EMF).[258] Much has been written recently about the health hazards of electromagnetic fields, but the controversy has in fact been developing for over forty years.

In 1950, following its first study of electromagnetic fields, the U.S. Public Health Service reported that workers who were exposed to alternating electromagnetic fields developed cancer at a rate significantly higher than that of the population as a whole. Following this first study, public concerns about EMFs arose as utilities turned more and more to extra high voltage (EHV) transmission lines to handle increases in electrical demand. The public first noticed EHV lines as nuisances; the lines impaired TV and radio reception.

During the 1960s, Dr. Robert O. Becker found, in experiments conducted with salamanders, that the electric current associated with the animals' nervous systems triggered their regenerative process. Later Dr. Becker, working with Dr. Howard Friedman, discovered that exposing human volunteers to pulsed magnetic fields of similar frequency and considerably greater strength than those associated with magnetic storms significantly reduced the volunteers' ability to react to the appearance of light.

While EMF research continued, U.S. military projects spurred the first public involvement in the EMF issue. A Navy and GTE Sylvania project for an extra low-frequency (ELF) test facility in Wisconsin (called Project Sanguine) met with powerful objections in 1968 from environmental groups. Neighbors of the Navy's test facility at Clam Lake reported that they were receiving electrical shocks when they turned on water faucets.[259] Environmentalists claimed that alternating magnetic fields generated by the ELF antennas could produce dangerously high voltages in power and tele-

[258] *"Biological Effects of Power Frequency Electric and Magnetic Fields," Congressional Background Paper, Office of Technology Assessment, 1989.*

[259] *Paul Brodeur, "Annals of Radiation: The Hazards of Electromagnetic Fields,"* New Yorker, *June 12 1989, pp. 51–58, 62.*

phone lines.[260] The Navy responded to the objections in an environmental impact statement by demonstrating that household appliances give off stronger magnetic fields than the ELF facility.

Concerns about EMF were initially minimal for two reasons. First, no transfer of energy occurs, as in X-rays where chemical bonds are broken or microwaves where tissue is heated. Second, all cells in the body have natural electric fields that are at least one hundred times more intense than any induced by exposure to common power-frequency fields.[261]

Dr. Becker strongly urged the Institute of Electrical and Electronic Engineers at its summer 1972 meeting to begin a program to study human exposure to electromagnetic fields. In 1973, Dr. Becker was asked to serve on the Navy's Bureau of Medicine and Surgery to review the Navy's research on the biological and ecological effects of ELF radiation. Though Dr. Becker and other members of the advisory committee recommended that the Navy further study the effects of Project Sanguine on human beings and animals, the Navy proceeded with the project. The advisory committee's warnings were never made public.[262]

Power Line Placement Becomes an Issue

During the time of the initial EMF research and the military controversies, the siting of power lines became an issue as the public became more aware of EMF. In 1973, the Power Authority of the State of New York (PASNY) was considering the construction and placement of a 765-kilovolt power line in upstate New York. Dr. Becker wrote to the PASNY and urged it to delay its decision on placement until the Project Sanguine experiments were completed. The Public Service Commission of New York (PSC) began hearings on the 765-kilovolt line in 1973.

The hearings were long and complicated, with utility experts testifying that the line's placement would present no biological hazard to citizens. Andrew Marino, a colleague of Dr. Becker, testified about his work in exposing rats to sixty-hertz ELF electric fields. The exposed rats gained less weight, drank less water, and showed altered levels of blood proteins and enzymes compared to control rats. After Dr. Marino testified that ELF radiation could biologically affect humans, the utilities involved requested and received a postponement of the PSC hearings for a year. The hearings resumed in late 1975, and after pressure from Governor Hugh Carey, the PSC authorized construction of the line in 1976 but left open the issue of the required right-of-way width.

Both Drs. Becker and Marino were strongly attacked following their testimony at the PSC hearing. The chair of the National Academy of Sciences Committee told the *Saturday Review*:

> The judges threw out the case with prejudice. They ruled that Marino's not a believable witness, that he's evasive and deceitful. Here we were, being attacked by people who ultimately were thrown out of a court of justice in that way. They've all been thrown out. These guys are all a bunch of quacks.[263]

[260] Id.

[261] *"Biological Effects of Power Frequency Electric and Magnetic Fields," p. 1.*

[262] *Brodeur, "Annals of Radiation," p. 67.*

[263] Id., *p. 76.*

At the same time, politically based environmental opposition drove Project Sanguine from Wisconsin. The Navy's advisory committee report with Dr. Becker's recommendation to study the effects of Project Sanguine on residents near Clam Lake finally was made public after Senator Gaylord Nelson of Wisconsin received a copy of it. In a press release, Senator Nelson accused the Navy of suppressing evidence and failing to follow through on the effects of radiation.[264]

The Werthemeier Seminal Study on EMFs

In the spring of 1974, epidemiologist Nancy Werthemeier began to study children who had died from leukemia in the Denver area. The results suggested a connection between the proximity of the children's homes to transmission lines and the incidence of leukemia. The studies, published in the *American Journal of Epidemiology*, concluded that the cancer rate of children from homes located near high-current configurations (HCC) was two to three times the normal rate of cancer. That is, if one child in a thousand gets cancer in the general population, two to three children living near HCCs would be expected to get it.[265] The homes affected included those that were less than:

1. Forty meters from large-gauge primary wires or arrays of six or more thin primary wires;
2. Twenty meters from an array of thirty-five thin primary wires or high-tension (50,230-kilovolt) wires; and
3. Fifteen meters from 240-volt wires.[266]

Dr. David Savitz repeated a Werthemeier-type study in Denver and released his results in 1986. Dr. Savitz agreed with the Werthemeier conclusion that exposure to EMF may increase the risk of developing cancer in children. However, Dr. Savitz also suggested that simple reconfiguration of the wires on transmission lines could reduce that risk substantially.

Cape Cod's PAVE PAWS

In 1976, the Air Force proposed installing a PAVE PAWS radar facility at Cape Cod, Massachusetts. No environmental impact statement was prepared, and installation began with no public input. PAVE PAWS is an acronym for Precision Acquisition of Vehicle Entry Phased Array Warning System. PAVE PAWS differs from regular radar in that instead of a rotating antenna, it has solid-state components that are controlled by computer and steered electronically; it emits ELF radiation. PAVE PAWS was used to detect sea-launched ballistic missiles.[267] The Air Force issued a 250-page report on environmental issues surrounding ELF that mentioned PAVE PAWS might cause cardiac pacemakers to skip a beat. However, construction of the project was approved and work began.

As construction began on the PAVE PAWS facility, local residents sought help from their congressman, Gerry E. Studds, who asked the Air Force for the research sup-

[264] Id., *p. 63.*

[265] *Nancy Werthemier and Ed Leeper, "Electrical Wiring Configuration and Childhood Cancer,"* American Journal of Epidemiology *109, 1979, p. 273.*

[266] Id., *p. 277.*

[267] *Paul Brodeur, "Annals of Radiation: The Hazards of Electromagnetic Fields Part II,"* New Yorker, *June 19, 1989, p. 47.*

porting its conclusion that PAVE PAWS presented no long-term danger to human health. At a town meeting, an Air Force official told residents that he could not guarantee that they would be safe from the effects of PAVE PAWS radiation.[268]

Following these public meetings, the Cape Cod Environmental Coalition sued the Air Force for violating the National Environmental Policy Act by not issuing an environmental impact statement (EIS) before constructing PAVE PAWS. As a result of the suit, the Air Force agreed to study the radiation from facility towers and do an EIS.

In January 1980, Dr. Adey denounced the Air Force for its unwillingness to study PAVE PAWS and its effects on residents before building the towers. Reports of Dr. Adey's denunciation appeared in newspapers across the country.

At about the same time that the issue of ELF impact was gaining national momentum, the New York PSC issued its final decision on the 765-kilovolt line. The PSC reached the conclusion that ELF fields could have effects on humans, yet still authorized the line provided the right of way was widened to 350 feet.

Corroboration of Werthemeier's Work

Scientific studies about ELF and EMF continued. Dr. Adey released the results of his studies that showed weak ELF fields could alter the flow of calcium from brain cells and thereby alter the chemistry of the brain. Dr. Adey had used brain tissue from chicks in his studies and had also observed the behaviors of monkeys and cats. In 1976 and 1979, Carl F. Blackman, an Environmental Protection Agency (EPA) scientist, duplicated Dr. Adey's work and reached the same conclusions.[269]

In June 1982, a preliminary report of a Swedish study of childhood leukemia by Dr. Lennart Tomenius corroborated Werthemeier's results. Also in 1982, Drs. Werthemeier and Leeper published the results of their adult cancer study that indicated a correlation between transmission lines and the incidence of cancer in adults. At nearly the same time, Dr. Samuel Milham's study correlating leukemia to occupational exposure to electric and magnetic fields was published in *The New England Journal of Medicine.* Later that year, studies from the University of Southern California School of Medicine confirmed Dr. Milham's findings.[270]

Late in 1982, an article in the *Cape Cod Times* about the possible health effects of PAVE PAWS revealed that Arthur Guy was conducting a study for the Air Force of the long-term effects of low-level microwave radiation. The article entitled "PAVE PAWS: Where Has the Controversy Gone?" discussed the studies to date and questioned the Air Force figures.

In 1983, Drs. Adey and Daniel B. Lyle published the results of their further studies in *Bioelectromagnetics.* They concluded that a PAVE PAWS carrier frequency could significantly suppress the ability of cultured T-lymphocyte cells in mice to kill cultured cancer cells.

At the same time, the first studies of electrical workers appeared when Michael McDowell released the results of his studies that showed an increased risk of leukemia

[268] Id., *p. 48.*

[269] Id., *p. 47.*

[270] Id.

among workers in all electrical occupations. A 1984 study of white males in Maryland who had died of brain tumors revealed that a significantly higher than expected number had been employed in electrical occupations. Leading electronics and communications firms formed the Electromagnetic Energy Policy Alliance in 1984 to downplay the hazards of radiation. That same year, the Illinois Institute of Technology Research prepared a report for the Navy that showed that the strength of magnetic fields from household appliances dropped off so quickly with distance that such devices could not be considered major sources of indoor exposure.

In 1985, Dr. Guy released the results of his study for the Air Force, which found higher incidences of cancer in rats exposed to microwave radiation. A study done by Stanislaw Szmigielski and published that same year indicated that Polish military personnel who worked with or near radiation-emitting devices were more than three times as likely to develop cancer as unexposed personnel.

Houston Lighting Case and Public Knowledge of EMF

The first court case involving power lines was brought by Houston Lighting & Power Company in 1985 against the Klein Independent School District for the district's refusal to grant right-of-way access for the construction of power lines. The jury found for the school district and awarded compensatory and punitive damages. An appellate court later reversed the punitive damages but upheld the right of the school district to refuse the right-of-way on the grounds that the electromagnetic fields of the lines presented potential health hazards.

Following the Houston case, studies on EMF and health hazards were conducted and reported in a nearly continuous stream. In 1986, Drs. Werthemeier and Leeper released another study that demonstrated a direct connection between fetal development and the use of electric blankets and water beds. Electromagnetic fields from the water bed heaters and the blankets sent pulses that resulted in a significantly higher rate of defects in exposed fetuses. Also in 1986, the utility-funded Electric Power Research Institute (EPRI) released results of a study that indicated lower birth weights and a significant increase in the number of birth defects among swine exposed to electromagnetic radiation.

As these study results were being released, the impact of operating projects was assessable based on epidemiological studies. In March 1986, the Massachusetts Department of Health reported that women living near the Cape Cod PAVE PAWS facility had a significantly higher rate of cancer than the general population.

By 1987, Congress and state legislatures and agencies began to conduct both generic and specific-issue hearings on the placement of power lines. With all the public attention, the issue of overhead power lines near property became a discussion topic in seminars for real estate developers and agents.

The first lawsuits alleging declines in property value because of power line location and public fear began in 1988, when New York landowners sued the New York Power Authority alleging that the 345-kilovolt line, the subject of the landmark hearings in the 1970s, created a "cancer corridor" and had destroyed the market value of their properties.

The Follow-Up Studies

Studies continued to indicate the dangers of EMF. A study of Texas utility workers showed that they had a cancer rate thirteen times greater than that of workers who were not exposed to electromagnetic fields. A later study by the University of Southern California established that electrical workers with ten years on the job had a higher risk for certain forms of brain tumors than those with five years' experience. By 1990, many counties had approved measures limiting construction of power lines. School boards, following the lead of the Houston case, closed off buildings near power lines to protect their children.[271]

A Congressional Office of Technology Assessment report on EMF concluded: "The emerging evidence no longer allows one to categorically assert that there are no risks."[272] Department of Energy researchers noted, "There is clearly cause for concern but not for alarm."[273] Dr. David Carpenter, dean of the school of public health at the State University of New York, Albany observed, "This is really harming people. In my judgment the present state of affairs is like the correlation between smoking and lung cancer 30 years ago."[274]

Utilities, through EPRI, have quadrupled spending on EMF research since 1986. But public concern continues to build. Some environmental consultants predict that EMF will become the biggest environmental challenge electric utilities face.

Cyrus Noe, editor of *Clearing Up*, a utility newsletter, says that electricity is a necessity of modern life and "no one is going to say that we have to turn off the lights. But utilities cannot simply gin up a plan, award a bunch of contracts and spend the EMF dilemma away. We just don't know the answers."[275]

A 1993 study conducted by Dr. David Savitz, reported in *Epidemiology* and based on his examination of 36,221 Southern California Edison workers, concluded there was no evidence of increased levels of leukemia, brain cancer, or lymphoma from EMF exposure. Savitz commented on the study's credibility and indicated that workplace EMF exposure probably could not be linked to cancer. However, he noted that further research is needed on childhood exposure to EMF and the incidence of leukemia.

In 1995, the *American Journal of Epidemiology* reported the largest study of utility workers to date. The EPRI-funded study looked at 138,905 men who worked for power companies between 1950 and 1986, including 20,733 who had died. It was the first study to take actual measurements of exposure levels.

Overall, the workers' death risk was lower than that of the general population. However, the brain cancer risk was 50 percent higher for men who worked more than five years as a lineman or electrician. Further, those who were exposed to the highest levels of EMFs had more than double the risk of brain cancer. The study found that

[271] *David Kirkpatrick, "Can Power Lines Give You Cancer?"* Fortune, *December 31, 1990, pp. 80–85.*

[272] Id.

[273] Id.

[274] Id.

[275] *Keith Schneider, "Electricity and Cancer? The Mystery Increases,"* The New York Times, *February 3, 1991, p. E3.*

brain cancer is so rare that electrocution and work accidents should be the focus of safety measures. Further, it found no association between EMF exposure and leukemia.

Where EMF Stands Today

In 1996, the National Research Council (NRC) issued its report on EMF after examining 500 studies over 17 years. The NRC study was sponsored by the U.S. Department of Energy. The NRC is a private, nonprofit institution that provides research and technological advice to Congress. The NRC issued the following observations about the Werthemeier and Savitz studies:

> The weak link shown between proximity to power lines and childhood leukemia may be the result of factors other than magnetic fields that are common to houses with the types of external wiring identified with the disease. These include: a home's proximity to high traffic density, local air quality, and construction features of older homes that fall into this category.[276]

The NRC report also concluded that only at levels between 1,000 and 100,000 times stronger than residential fields do cells show reaction to EMF exposure, and there is no evidence that such reactions produce adverse health effects.[277] Finally, the NRC review concluded that even high exposure to EMF does not affect the DNA of the cell, it does not act as a carcinogen, and also does not affect reproduction, development, or behavior in animals.

Several recommendations for future research were offered by the NRC:

1. Further research on occupational exposure because its efforts focused on low-frequency electric and magnetic fields in homes; and
2. Determining the reason(s) for the small increase in childhood leukemia (rare) among children in homes near power lines.[278]

In 1997, the National Cancer Institute reported its findings on children living near high voltage power lines and cancer in *The New England Journal of Medicine.* The study's authors concluded "that exposure to electromagnetic fields does not increase a child's risk of leukemia" after reviewing the health records and EMF levels in the homes of 629 children with leukemia and 619 healthy children in a nine-state area. The study found that children without cancer were exposed to the same levels of EMF energy as those with cancer.[279]

Lawsuits against utilities began with the Houston case and have continued. In one action over the leukemia death of a child whose home was near a transformer, the jury found for the utility. Still pending are economic-loss lawsuits in which homeowners are seeking recovery for property value losses due to their home's location next to transformers or wires and public fears about such proximity and EMF. The Office of

[276] *NRC Report on EMF (1996), p. ii (Executive summary).*

[277] *In fact, several studies showed that the exposure helped by speeding up the healing process after a bone is broken.* National Research Council News, *October 31, 1996, p. 2 as excerpted from* Possible Health Effects of Exposure to Residential Electric and Magnetic Fields, *National Academy Press, 1996.*

[278] Id.

[279] *Steve Sternberg, "Power Lines Not a Cancer Risk for Kids,"* USA Today, *July 3–6, 1997, p. 1A.*

Technology and Assessment estimates that the cost of EMF litigation is between $1 billion and $3 billion per year. To date, no utility has lost a case in which there has been health-related litigation. However, utilities have settled a number of cases brought by property owners for the decline in value of their homes or the so-called psychological impact on property values. Those suits are expected to dwindle as utilities engage in the process of "prudent placement," which is the placement of power lines in areas away from private landowners and residences.

Discussion Questions

1. Does a clear causal connection exist between EMFs and cancer?
2. What companies should be concerned about liability for exposure to EMFs?
3. What regulations do you foresee being enacted to address the EMF issue?
4. What problems do you see for owners of land located near power lines?
5. If you were a human resources officer in an electric utility, what, if any, action would you take to protect your company's workers?
6. If you were a manufacturer or seller of electric blankets or water beds, would you warn purchasers of your products about the possible dangers of EMFs?
7. Should electric utilities make any workplace changes for safety because of EMFs?
8. Should electric utilities reconfigure wiring to minimize EMF exposure of residents near power lines?

CASE 5.22

Johns-Manville and the Asbestos Exposure

While the public gained much of its knowledge regarding the dangers of asbestos after the litigation against asbestos manufacturers began, that body of knowledge had been building for some time. Retracing the historical, scientific, medical, legislative, and litigation events that led to the bankruptcy of Johns-Manville offers insight into the steady progression of this business crisis.

Early History of Asbestos

Asbestos is a gray-white fibrous mineral that is heat-resistant and possesses great strength. It was mined in Canada and South Africa and processed at plants throughout the world. The largest processors were Johns-Manville, Raybestos-Manhattan, Pittsburgh-Corning, Owens-Corning, GAF, UNR, AMATEX, Owens-Illinois, Nicolet, Celotex, Eagle-Picher, Keene, Fibreboard, Standard Asbestos, and Armstrong Cork. The qualities of asbestos made it seem unique and irreplaceable. At the height of its use in the United States, it could be found in everything from hair dryers to potholders to brake drums.

unit 5
section e

As early as 1 A.D., Strabo and Pliny the Elder mentioned a sickness of the lungs in slaves who wove asbestos into cloth. Hippocrates (460–377 B.C.) described silicosis in a metal digger and noted that the man "breathes with great difficulty." Marco Polo even learned of the "mineral in the mountain" that contained threads like those of wool. Autopsies performed on stonecutters in 1672 by Ijsbrand van Diemerbroech, a professor of medicine at the University of Utrecht in the Netherlands, revealed that the vesicles of their lungs were so clogged with fine dust that dissecting them was like cutting through sand. In 1700, Bernardino Ramazzini, a professor of medicine at the University of Padua, suggested that stonecutters perform their work with their backs to the wind, so as to avoid inhaling.

In the late eighteenth century, western technology began to utilize the properties of asbestos. The material came to be used as an insulator for boilers, steampipes, turbines, ovens, kilns, and other high-temperature equipment. In England in 1819, workers who ground dry stones suffered such a high rate of silicosis (called "grinders asthma") that it was proposed that criminals be used for the task.[280]

The Connection between Industrial Dust and Lung Disease

The problem of lung-dust infestation came to light in the United States in 1887 when an autopsy was performed on a stove-foundry worker from Poughkeepsie, New York, whose lungs showed the presence of silicosis. In 1898, when Henry Ward Johns, the founder of H. W. Johns Manufacturing (the forerunner of Johns-Manville), died, his death certificate listed the cause of death as "dust phthisis pneumonia," or what appeared to be a description of asbestosis.

Dr. Montague Murray, a London physician, established the first connection between asbestos-textile factory work and severe pulmonary fibrosis. During the course of an autopsy in 1900, Dr. Murray found spicules of asbestos in the lungs of a 33-year-old man who had died from the disease.

After Dr. Murray made his finding, other physicians reported connections between asbestos workers' occupations and their deaths by lung disease. By 1918, the U.S. government had become involved in the health issues surrounding asbestos workers, and the Bureau of Labor Statistics published a report by statistician Frederick L. Hoffman that established that asbestos workers had an unusually high death rate at an unusually early age. The report noted, moreover, that many American and Canadian insurance companies were no longer issuing policies to asbestos workers because of the "health-injurious conditions" assumed to exist in the asbestos industry.

The first asbestosis death described in medical literature appeared in the *British Medical Journal* in 1924 in an article by Dr. W. E. Cooke, who named the disease asbestosis. Shortly after, state governments began to note workers' compensation claims being filed by asbestos workers. As early as 1928, Johns-Manville sponsored studies by Dr. Leroy U. Gardner, who produced asbestosis in test animals by allowing them to inhale asbestos fibers. These studies, which were not released, were uncovered during litigation in 1971.

[280] *Most of the material in the historical section of the case, while corroborated in later litigation, was taken from what remains the authoritative work in this field: Paul Brodeur, "The Asbestos Industry on Trial,"* New Yorker. *Mr. Brodeur's four-part series appeared in the issues of June 10, 1985, p. 64; June 17, 1985, p. 69; June 24, 1985; and July 1, 1985. The historical discussion here draws only on the June 10 and June 17 pieces.*

The Medical Inspector of Factories for the British Home Office conducted an epidemiological study of asbestos workers in 1928 that showed, among other things, an 81 percent rate of fibrosis in workers who had been in the industry twenty years or more. Based on the study findings, Parliament in 1931 enacted legislation designed to provide protection for asbestos workers. Subsequently, Dr. Anthony Lanza found, in a study he conducted for Metropolitan Life Insurance, that 106 of 126 X-rayed asbestos workers had already developed asbestosis.

During this period of medical discovery in the asbestos industry, so-called "silicosis suits" began to appear around the country. Damages in these suits, which were brought by workers who alleged harmful exposure to silica dust and resulting lung problems, totaled $300 million by 1934. Alarmed by the increasing numbers of suits, several insurance companies recommended that silicosis and other pulmonary dust diseases be taken out of the courts and covered under workers' compensation.

Johns-Manville's Initial Approach to Liability

It was also during this period of medical discovery and silicosis suits that Johns-Manville experienced its first asbestos litigation. In 1933, the board of directors of Johns-Manville directed the company's CEO and president to settle asbestosis lawsuits that had been brought against Johns-Manville in New Jersey courts by Samuel Greenstone, an attorney, on behalf of eleven workers. The company made a $30,000 settlement payment in exchange for Greenstone's promise that he would not "directly or indirectly participate in the bringing of new actions against the Corporation."[281] The settlement terms, documented in the board's minutes, were not revealed until discovery during litigation some forty-five years later. They read as follows:

> The President advised the meeting that Messrs. Hobart & Minard of Newark had been approached by the attorney for the plaintiffs in the eleven pending "asbestosis" cases with an offer to settle all the cases upon a much lower basis than had ever been previously discussed. He further stated that our general counsel, Messrs. Davis Polk Wardell Gardiner & Reed, as well as Messrs. Hobart & Minard, had recommended that we settle for approximately $30,000 provided written assurances were obtained from the attorney for the various plaintiffs that he would not directly or indirectly participate in the bringing of new actions against the corporation.[282]

Johns-Manville was then the largest producer of asbestos in the United States. The company also sold asbestos to many other firms for use in other products. Manville had great liability exposure not only through its own sales, but through its sales to other companies, and eventually, to third-party buyers.

When Dr. Lanza was to submit his X-ray study results to the U.S. Public Health Service, George S. Hobart, a Johns-Manville attorney, and Vandiver Brown, a corporate attorney for Johns-Manville, asked him to soften the description of asbestosis in his report. Hobart remarked:

> It is only within a comparatively recent time that asbestosis has been recognized by the medical and scientific professions as a disease. One of our principal defenses in actions against the company on the common law theory of negligence has been that the

[281] Id.

[282] Id.

> scientific and medical knowledge has been insufficient until a very recent period to place upon the owners of plants or factories the burden of taking special precautions against the possible onset of the disease to their employees.[283]

Brown added the following when he forwarded Hobart's remarks to Dr. Lanza:

> I am sure that you understand fully that no one in our organization is suggesting for a moment that you alter by one jot or tittle any scientific facts or inevitable conclusions revealed or justified by your preliminary survey. All we ask is that all of the favorable aspects of the survey be included and that none of the unfavorable be unintentionally pictured in darker tones than the circumstances justify. I feel confident we can depend upon you . . . to give us this "break" and mine and Mr. Hobart's suggestions are presented in this spirit.[284]

By 1935, asbestosis was widely discussed at medical meetings, and research into the disease was ongoing. During that year, Vandiver Brown wrote to Sumner Simpson, the president of Raybestos-Manhattan. Through a series of letters, both agreed that asbestosis should not be mentioned in industry trade journals. Raybestos-Manhattan did join, however, with other asbestos product manufacturers in sponsoring long-range research programs on the biological effects of asbestos. On October 1, 1935, Sumner Simpson wrote the following in a letter to Vandiver Brown about possible publication of survey results in *Asbestos*, a trade magazine:

> As I see it personally, we would be just as well off to say nothing about [asbestosis] until our survey is complete. I think the less said about asbestos, the better off we are, but at the same time, we cannot lose track of the fact that there have been a number of articles on asbestos dust control and asbestosis in the British trade magazines. The magazine *Asbestos* is in business to publish articles affecting the trade and they have been very decent about not re-printing the English articles.[285]

Vandiver Brown replied to Simpson's letter as follows:

> I quite agree with you that our interests are best served by having asbestosis receive a minimum of publicity.[286]

Widespread Medical Evidence of Asbestosis and Asbestos As a Carcinogen

Eventually, medical research identified two major diseases that could result from exposure to asbestos dust. The first, the focus of the research, was asbestosis, which is a scarring of the lung tissue. Asbestosis does not appear immediately and may not manifest itself for ten to thirty years after initial exposure. During this time, the inhaler will appear healthy and normal and will experience no symptoms of the disease. However, inhaled asbestos fibers that remain in the lungs cause a tissue reaction that is progressive and, apparently, irreversible. The result is a slow buildup of problems, such as breathing difficulties that eventually become severe enough to make any physical exertion impossible. The second disease, mesothelioma, is a malignant and extremely painful cancer of the chest lining. This cancer has been associated only with asbestos

[283] Id., *p. 63.*

[284] Id.

[285] Id.

[286] Id.

exposure; it usually is fatal within one year after symptoms appear. Like asbestosis, this disease may not appear for twenty years after initial exposure to asbestos. For example, the mother of an asbestos worker, whose only exposure to asbestos came through washing his factory clothes in the 1960s, died of mesothelioma in 1983.

In 1936, Vandiver Brown and Sumner Simpson informed Dr. Leroy Gardner of their willingness to fund his asbestosis research, but a condition of the funding was a "bargain of silence." Gardner would be unable to publish the results of his work. In 1977, attorney Karl Asch discovered the agreement and the results of Gardner's work, which indicated a connection between exposure to asbestos and pulmonary dust disease. Asch used the so-called "Sumner Simpson papers" as a smoking gun to show that Raybestos-Manhattan not only knew of the disease dangers but attempted to suppress the information.

The U.S. Public Health Service recommended in 1938 an average dust level of five million particles per cubic foot to be the acceptable level of exposure for American asbestos workers. However, research into asbestosis continued to produce hundreds of medical journal articles on the disease. Theories regarding appropriate levels of exposure conflicted with each other; some research suggested that no level was appropriate.

In 1948, Dr. Kenneth Smith, the medical director for Canadian Johns-Manville, conducted an industrial hygiene survey of 708 men working at an asbestos plant in Quebec and discovered that only four of them had X-rays that showed normal, healthy lungs. The findings, which at the time were neither published nor revealed to the workers, first became public in 1976, when litigation discovery revealed the study and its results.

Because of the mounting research findings, some workers began wearing respirators to block their inhalation of asbestos dust. Finally, in the early 1950s, the information on asbestosis and asbestosis research made its way into the popular press. In 1952, the January issue of *Search*, a monthly journal of the California Tuberculosis Association, printed a picture of Johns-Manville's Lompac, California, plant with a caption that read, "Death by Dust." The articles in the journal described poor working conditions at the plant. In that same year, a week-long symposium on the subject of asbestos-related lung cancer was held, but its results were never published and, again, were discovered only during later litigation.

By 1955, unions for asbestos workers and miners had begun to raise the issue of asbestosis. Also at this time, the general counsel for the Quebec Asbestos Mining Association (Johns-Manville was a leading member of this trade group) warned the association's members that asbestos exposure posed a serious health problem for the industry.

Shortly thereafter, Johns-Manville experienced an unprecedented third-party lawsuit for negligence and breach of warranty brought by Frederick LeGrand, a New Jersey asbestos insulator who had developed asbestosis. Another New Jersey insulator filed a similar suit in 1961. These suits were the beginning of the third-party liability suits that Manville would experience over the next thirty years.

Product purchasers, installers, ship builders, and even those who occupied buildings insulated with asbestos would file suits against Manville as the ultimate supplier and responsible party for the lung disease not limited to actual asbestos purchasers and users.

The Beginning of the End: Manville's Litigation Crisis

In 1966, attorney Ward Stephenson filed suit against eleven asbestos manufacturers on behalf of his client, Claude Tomplait, an insulator who had developed asbestosis. This was Stephenson's first third-party liability case; it would not be his last. Stephenson also litigated on behalf of Clarence Borel, another insulator who sued several asbestos manufacturers. The trial court found for Borel and more significantly, its verdict was upheld by the Fifth Circuit Court of Appeals. The appellate decision triggered 25,000 third-party asbestos lawsuits that would be brought against asbestos manufacturers over the next decade. The 1973 *Borel*[287] decision marked the beginning of the end for the asbestos industry. Between 1974 and 1988, asbestos litigation increased tenfold.

At this time, Congress had just created OSHA, and numerous recommendations for lowering the exposure levels of asbestos workers were being made. Raybestos-Manhattan shut down its New Jersey plant in 1973, and Pittsburgh-Corning, facing multimillion-dollar claims, shut down its Tyler, Texas, asbestos plant in 1974.

The 1974 annual report for Raybestos-Manhattan included the following language:

> For many years it has been known that prolonged inhalation of asbestos dust by factory workers could lead to disease. As early as 1930, Raybestos-Manhattan commissioned the Metropolitan Life Insurance Company to survey all of its factories and to make recommendations for the elimination of conditions which might present health hazards. Following presentations of the reports and recommendations, extensive long-range engineering programs were instituted at all plants to develop effective dust control systems.

In addition to pioneering in the design of engineering controls, Raybestos-Manhattan joined with other asbestos products manufacturers in the mid-1930s in funding long-range research programs on the biological effects of asbestos.

Because of the long latent period of asbestos-related disease, the disease being found today among some industry employees is a result of conditions existing decades ago when little was known about the health effects of asbestos or proper means of control.[288]

In 1976, 159 cases had been filed against Johns-Manville; in 1978, 792 suits were filed; and by 1982, suits were being filed at a rate of 6,000 per year. Manville settled asbestos-related suits for an average of $21,000, but by 1982 this settlement amount doubled.

Attempted Legislative Remedies for the Asbestos Litigation Crisis

The first federal legislation designed to aid asbestos manufacturers was introduced in 1977 by Representative Milicent Fenwick, a New Jersey Republican whose district included the town of Manville. The proposed Asbestos Health Hazards Compensation Act would have prohibited workers from bringing third-party negligence or product liability suits against the asbestos industry, the tobacco industry, or the federal government. Victims, instead, would receive compensation from a federally administered cen-

[287] Borel v. Fibreboard Paper Products Corp., *493 F.2d 1076 (5th Cir. 1973).*

[288] *Paul Brodeur, "The Asbestos Industry on Trial,"* New Yorker, *June 17, 1985, p. 69.*

tral fund. The federal government would pay claims accruing before 1980; claims arising after that time would be paid out of mandatory contributions from the government and from the asbestos and tobacco industries. Under the plan, the maximum payment for a totally disabled asbestosis victim would be $500 per month ($1,000 if he had a wife and two children). The bill met with anger and criticism in the House and was labeled as an attempted federal government bail-out for the asbestos industry.

A second bill was introduced in 1980 by Senator Gary Hart of Colorado. Johns-Manville had moved its headquarters from New York to Denver in 1972. Later, John McKinney, Manville's CEO and chairman, would reveal in testimony that the Manville PAC had contributed to Senator Hart's campaigns. Hart's bill was also called the Asbestos Health Hazards Compensation Act, and it too would have eliminated tort claims by victims; unlike Fenwick's proposal, however, Hart's bill would have left compensation solely to the state worker compensation systems. The bill also would have eliminated punitive damages and still require plaintiffs to prove negligence claims. Congress labeled the bill a "Manville bail-out," and rejected it in 1980 as well as in all later sessions.

Manville's Chapter 11 Resolution

With a congressional bail-out no longer a possibility, asbestos manufacturers faced mounting litigation on their own. Ultimately, it was an accounting rule, FASB-5, that led Manville into Chapter 11. Coopers & Lybrand had taken the position in the previous eight SEC filings that, under FASB-5, it could not reliably estimate the costs of disposition of the suits and therefore need not make any disclosures about them before certifying the financial statements. However, before the ninth SEC filing, Litigation Analysis Group (LAG), a litigation consultant for Manville's cases, gave Manville an estimate that the cost of disposition of all future suits would be 1 billion, 900 million dollars. With this expert opinion in place, Coopers & Lybrand could no longer take its "no estimate possible" position under FASB-5. When Coopers & Lybrand refused to sign off on the financial statements needed for the SEC filing without a disclosure of the litigation liability, Manville dismissed them and hired Price Waterhouse. But, after reviewing the LAG report, Price Waterhouse reached the same conclusion and refused to certify the financial statements without a disclosure on the litigation. Unable to issue financial statements, Manville filed for Chapter 11 bankruptcy protection on August 26, 1982.

The Committee of Asbestos-Related Litigants was then formed to contest the Manville bankruptcy. The committee filed a motion to dismiss the bankruptcy in November of 1982 on the grounds that Manville had filed the Chapter 11 proceedings in bad faith. The committee also had the Senate Judiciary Committee convene a hearing on November 10, 1982, to investigate whether it was proper for a solvent company to file for reorganization under the federal Bankruptcy Code. Despite the significant testimony presented during the hearing, the committee declined to make changes in the Bankruptcy Code.

The big problem in the Manville Chapter 11 proceedings was the disposition of all the actual and pending suits against the company. The issue involved dealing with Manville, its insurers, and the lawyers for the litigants. The bankruptcy proceedings continued through 1989, when Manville and others agreed to the Manville Personal Injury Settlement Trust. Under the agreement, Manville was required to give $2.5

billion in assets (mostly stock) to the trust. Manville was also required, beginning in 1991, to pay annually to the trust $75 million and 20 percent of its annual net income.[289] So far, 152,000 claims have been filed and 3,000 more are expected. The average settlement has been $42,000. The approval for paying claims came in December 1994, and the resulting payment settlement gives claimants ten cents on the dollar. Also, $55.7 million of the trust funds were awarded to co-defendants who had paid Manville's share of the liability while the trust payments were in litigation.[290]

In 1976, asbestos sales accounted for 31 percent of Manville's business, or $1.6 billion. Today, 42 percent, or $2.2 billion, of the company's sales comes from fiberglass insulation. However, Manville admits to lost customers and a stock price that seems to keep dropping.

Some aspects of the asbestos saga remain unresolved. For example, the cleanup of asbestos in Chicago school districts has had an estimated cost of $500 million, and the Illinois Supreme Court has ruled that the school districts can proceed to recover property damages from asbestos manufacturers. The EPA, in turn, has begun issuing complaints against school districts that do not act quickly enough to replace asbestos insulation; those districts that fail to clean up their asbestos problems face a $25,000 fine.[291]

Today, asbestos liability continues for other manufacturers. In mid-1992, after a two-year jury trial, six other companies were found negligent in installing, manufacturing, or supplying asbestos. The case involved 8,555 plaintiffs, whose damages will be determined in separate proceedings. Many cases are still not settled. Two-hundred thousand pending claims remain.[292] Twenty former asbestos manufacturers have settled potential future claims for $1 billion. In early 1995, OSHA issued new regulations requiring employer disclosure of the presence of asbestos in the workplace. The impact of exposure remains an issue for regulators as well as a potential source of liability. In 2000, Merrill Lynch estimated outstanding liability to be between $20 and $30 billion.[293]

The issues of asbestos abatement and removal continue to result in litigation and costs as schools, businesses, and government office buildings are remodeled and repaired. In 2001, new litigation emerged against W.R. Grace because of allegations that its claimed asbestos-free product, Mondcote, contained asbestos.[294] Special approval and procedures are necessary before these buildings can be modified or repaired. Further, the additional exposure issues that arise because these buildings and their as-

[289] *"Manville Trust Gets Clearance to Begin Asbestos Payments,"* The Wall Street Journal, *December 16, 1994, p. B3.*

[290] *Marj Charlier, "Manville Trust, Victims' Lawyers Plan Payment Pact,"* The Wall Street Journal, *November 19, 1990, p. B5.*

[291] *Barnaby Feder, "Asbestos: The Saga Drags On,"* The New York Times, *April 2, 1989, pp. 1, 11.*

[292] *Gregory Zuckerman, "Specter of Costly Asbestos Litigation Haunts Companies,"* The Wall Street Journal, *December 27, 2000, pp. C1, C15.*

[293] Id.

[294] *Michael Moss and Adrianne Appel, "Company's Silence Countered Safety Fears About Asbestos,"* The New York Times, *July 9, 2001, pp. A1, A10.*

bestos insulation are now disrupted and there is a release of fibers create new liability issues.

Discussion Questions

1. Suppose that you had been attorney Samuel Greenstone. Would you have agreed to no further lawsuits in exchange for the Manville settlement?
2. Suppose that you had been Dr. Anthony Lanza. Would you have taken any action with respect to the actions of George Hobart and Vandiver Brown?
3. Was Sumner Simpson morally responsible for the deaths of asbestos workers?
4. If you had been Dr. Leroy Gardner, would you have accepted Manville's funding under the conditions required?
5. Should Dr. Kenneth Smith have disclosed the findings in his X-ray study to the workers involved?
6. Could Johns-Manville have taken alternative steps that would have prevented the injuries?
7. Was asbestos a needed commodity?
8. Was Johns-Manville rewarded for ignoring the asbestos problem for so long? Should Manville (as it exists today) be required to liquidate its assets to pay all the claims?

Sources

"A Big Win for Asbestos Workers," *Time*, July 27, 1992, p. 17.

"Asbestos Defendants Must Pay Punitive Damages," *The Wall Street Journal*, July 31, 1992, p. B6.

Lambert, Wade, and Ellen Joan Pollock, "Manville to Add Funds to Asbestos Trust," *The Wall Street Journal*, September 10, 1990, p. B11.

Lambert, Wade, and Ellen Joan Pollock, "Owen-Illinois's Insurers Receive Setback in Asbestos Case Ruling," *The Wall Street Journal*, April 10, 1990, p. B11.

Moses, Jonathan M., "Former Asbestos Makers, 2 Law Firms Map $1 Billion Pact to Curb Litigation," *The Wall Street Journal*, January 18, 1993, p. A14.

Oberkfell, Sandra L., "New OSHA Regulations Significantly Increase the Obligation of Building and Facility Owners to Protect Employees and Other Workers from Asbestos Hazards," *National Law Journal*, January 30, 1995, p. B5.

Sanchez, Sandra, "Asbestos Firms Ruled Negligent," *USA Today*, July 14, 1992, p. 1A.

Whitaker, Leslie, "Monster in the Closet," *Time*, February 6, 1989, p. 53.

Wingo v. Celotex Corp., 834 F.2d 375 (4th Cir. 1987).

CASE 5.23

Domino's Pizza Delivers

Thomas S. Monaghan invented today's pizza delivery system when, in 1960, he opened the first Domino's in Ypsilanti, Michigan. By 1993, the company had grown to 5,300 U.S. franchises. Part of Domino's success was due to its 30-minute guarantee: the pizza is delivered in 30 minutes, or it's free.[295]

Domino's fleet of drivers across the United States ranges from 75,000 to 80,000. Because of the time pressure, some drivers were speeding and breaking the law. In 1990, 20 traffic fatalities in the United States involved Domino's drivers.

In 1985, Frank Kranack and his wife, Mary Jean, were struck by a Domino's delivery car while driving in their station wagon just outside a suburban Pittsburgh Domino's store. Frank suffered whiplash, and Mary Jean had neck and back injuries plus permanent disability in her right arm, the area of her body nearest the impact. When the accident occurred, the manager of the Domino's store rushed out to the wreckage and told the driver, "Let's get this pizza on the road." The Kranacks filed suit seeking damages and a halt to the Domino's 30-minute policy.[296]

In 1991, Domino's changed the on-time policy to a $3 refund if delivery is late to curb fraud by college students who gave incorrect directions to slow their deliveries.

In December 1992, a St. Louis jury awarded $78 million to Jean Kinder, who had been hit by an 18-year-old Domino's delivery driver in 1989. Within one week of that award, Domino's dropped its 30-minute guarantee. Monaghan noted:

> I believe we are the safest delivery company in the world. But there continues to be a perception that the guarantee is unsafe.[297]

Some franchisees had already abandoned the 30-minute guarantee. A marketing strategist commented on the decision:

> The critical issue to them is still home delivery. It's their franchise. Abandoning a time limit isn't necessarily "mortally wounding" if they can come up with another way of talking about how terrific they deliver to the home.[298]

Discussion Questions

1. Even with monitoring, screening, and training of its drivers, could Domino's guarantee that all of them would drive safely? Was the risk too great?

[295] *Michael Clements, "Domino's Detours 30-Minute Guarantee,"* USA Today, *December 22, 1993, p. 1A.*

[296] *Peter Mattiace, "Suit Asks Domino's Pizza Be Pulled From Fast Lane,"* Arizona Republic, *December 1, 1990, pp. A1, A7.*

[297] *Krystal Miller and Richard Gibson, "Domino's Stops Promising Pizza in 30 Minutes,"* The Wall Street Journal, *December 22, 1993, pp. B1, B3.*

[298] *Clements, "Domino's Detours 30-Minute Guarantee," p. 1A.*

2. Was the public perception of safety issues hurting Domino's more than the 30-minute guarantee helped it?
3. Did the $78 million jury verdict punish Domino's for its focus on the 30-minute delivery time?
4. Would you have made the same decision as Domino's?
5. How would you characterize the ethics of the college students who purposely gave incorrect directions to get their pizzas free?

CASE 5.24

Cell Phones

The ubiquitous cell phone has come to be a lightening rod for all manner of criticism. There are now 120 million cell phone subscribers in the United States, a figure that has increased 20 times since 1990. The annoyances range from users talking too loudly to the interruption of cell phones ringing in restaurants, during concerts, and in the middle of meetings and speeches.

Jacqueline Whitmore, an expert on business manners, has been teaching the etiquette of cell phones, which includes the following rules:

1. If you must talk on the cell phone while using the restroom, wait until the conversation has ended to flush.
2. Turn cell phones off at weddings, funerals, church services, and movies. An alternative is to switch the phone to vibrate rather than ring.
3. Respect rules established for cell phones such as Amtrak's quiet car (cars designated on their trains as being free from cell phone conversation) and at opera houses in Europe where cell phones must be checked in the cloakroom.
4. Use an appropriate level of voice. Avoid "cell phone voice," which is a tendency to talk louder than normal because of surrounding activity and noise.
5. Don't discuss personal matters on a cell phone while in public.
6. It may be easier to move away than to ask the person to stop talking on a cell phone.[299]

However, these daily annoyances and frustrations with cell phones have come to a head on an issue of safety related to cell phone use. Several accidents also brought the issue to the forefront in 2000. Jason Jones, a 19-year-old midshipman at the United States Naval Academy, was charged with vehicular manslaughter in November 1999 when he veered off the highway and ran into John and Carole Hall, who were in their car which was parked alongside the road. Mr. and Mrs. Hall were both killed instantly. Jones was charged with manslaughter because prosecutors alleged that he was driving at speeds ranging from 80 to 105 miles per hour while talking on the cell phone. Jones did not deny using the cell phone, but indicated he was not speeding.

[299] *Deborah Sharp, "Cellphones Reveal Screaming Lack of Courtesy,"* USA Today, *September 4, 2001, p. 4A.*

The jury refused to convict him of manslaughter but did find him guilty of reckless driving.

Also during 2000, several studies were published indicating the risks associated with cell phone usage while driving. Prior to this time there had been only the study published in *The New England Journal of Medicine* that concluded a driver using a cell phone is four times as likely to be involved in an accident. According to the study, the accident rate for cell phone users while driving is higher than that for those who drive while above the legal limit for intoxication.[300] Dr. Frances Bent co-authored one study that indicated the laws for reckless driving do not carry sufficiently severe penalties for the level of distraction and carelessness resulting from cell phone use while driving. "There are no appropriate penalties for the tragedies that can result from using a cellphone while driving. Many people are in denial that the distraction they are suffering while talking on a cellphone is dangerous. Drunks drive for a long time too—until the day they get in a crash."[301] A study by the Center for Urban Transportation at the University of South Florida indicates that cell phone use during driving increases the accident rate anywhere from 34 to 300 percent.

Statistically, cell phone usage is not the most common cause of driver distraction, as noted below.

what distracts drivers	
Something outside the vehicle	29.4%
Adjusting the radio	11.4%
Other occupants of vehicles	10.9%
A moving object in the car	4.3%
Other device or object	2.9%
Adjusting vehicle climate	2.9%
Eating, drinking	1.7%
Using cell phone	1.5%
Smoking	0.9%[302]

During 2001, there were 43 states that had some form of legislation proposed to prohibit or limit the use of cell phones while driving. Most of the legislation died in legislative committees because of the powerful lobbying by cell phone companies and also because legislators themselves are dependent upon cell phone usage in their cars. The Cellular Telecommunications Industry Association supports strict enforcement of existing laws for reckless driving as applied to cell phone use while driving, but it does not support legislative bans on their use while driving. However, New Jersey has legislation that prohibits those who are driving with learner's permits from using the cell phone. Massachusetts prohibits bus drivers from using cell phones while on duty unless there is an emergency. On the other hand, Oregon and Oklahoma passed laws that prohibits cities and towns from passing ordinances that prohibit cell phone use while

[300] *Jeffrey Ball, "Safety Risk of Letting Drivers Use Cell Phones to Get Federal Scrutiny,"* The Wall Street Journal, *July 14, 2000, pp. B1, B4.*

[301] *Jessie Halladay, "Driver Wins Cellphone-Crash Verdict,"* USA Today, *December 7, 2000, p. 10A.*

[302] *Gregory L. White and Andrea Peterson, "Cell Phone Firms Make Adjustments,"* The Wall Street Journal, *July 4, 2001, p. B1.*

driving.[303] Italy and Japan prohibit cell phone use in cars unless the driver is using hands-free technology.[304]

The drive for banning cell phones while driving is largely spearheaded by Patricia Pena, a mother whose 2-year-old daughter was killed when a driver talking on a cell phone ran a stop sign and hit the Pena vehicle. Mrs. Pena began the "Advocates for Cell Phone Safety," a group that has been lobbying for laws limiting cell phone use while driving.

New York became the first state to pass restrictions on cell phone use in cars. Except for emergencies, and effective December 1, 2001, New York drivers are not permitted to use a cell phone with it next to their ears. Dialing a phone that is in a cradle or attached to a headset will be legal. Following the passage of the New York law, similar bills were introduced in 35 other states, even in those states that had declined to act on some form of legislation on driving and cell phones earlier in the year.

In response to the growing legislative trend, cellular phone companies are scrambling to develop technology to permit continued use of cell phones even when regulations are imposed. The companies fear a decline in business of the $53 billion per year cell phone industry sales. They are developing voice dialing and other hands-free technology for cell phone users. For a New York-type statute, cell phone users need only use a headset; Sprint in New York is already offering customers such a headset at a discount. Sprint also offers voice command dialing for an extra $10 per month and about 10 percent of its customers have signed on for the technology.

In addition, automakers are working to develop in-auto systems with phone companies. Ford has a joint venture with one cellular phone company in an attempt to develop a cell phone system that will meet the most stringent forms of proposed cell phone legislation.

There is one additional issue that cell phone manufacturers continue to face—a health issue related to the use of cell phones. The other controversy is whether the cell phones cause cancer.

Some studies conclude that they do not, but the Wireless Technology Research program, a program funded by the cellular phone industry, has concluded that there are enough questions about their safety that no one should assure users that the phones are absolutely safe.[305]

The FDA's Center for Devices and Radiological Health has concluded that there are no adverse health effects from cell phones and that no additional warnings are needed. Following a lawsuit filed by a cell phone user in 1993 in which the allegation was made that the cell phone caused his cancer, the industry placed $27 million into a blind trust for research projects supported by the funding. The Wireless Technology Research program was one of the beneficiaries of the trust.[306]

[303] *Same Howe Verhovek, "Drive Talking: Cell Phone Debate Set to Heat Up,"* The New York Times, *September 2, 2001, p. A14.*

[304] *Ball, "Safety Risk of Letting Drivers Use Cell Phones to Get Federal Scrutiny," pp. B1, B4.*

[305] *John Tuohy, "Cell Phone Researcher's Call: Be Cautious,"* USA Today, *August 1, 2000, p. 1D.*

[306] *Review the findings on cell phone safety at http://www.medscape.com.*

Two additional studies, one by the National Cancer Institute, indicate that cell phone users are no more likely to develop benign tumors or malignant brain cancers. The studies, published in *The New England Journal of Medicine* and *Journal of the American Medical Association* indicate that exposure to radiofrequency (RF) through use of the phones is safe.

The researchers conducting the study indicated that cell phone use at the time of the studies was not as extensive or widespread and that those involved in the study had used the cell phones for only three years. Their advice is to repeat the studies in a few years to determine whether there might be some long-term impact from cell phone use. Dr. Mark Malkin, the author of the second study by the American Health Foundation, says that he does indeed use a cell phone.[307]

There are suits pending by cell phone users who allege that the phones do indeed cause brain cancer.

Discussion Questions

1. If you were a cell phone manufacturer, would you take any steps to change your product?
2. Would you participate in the political and legislative processes and what position would you take?
3. Should the cell phone manufacturers undertake a vehicle safety campaign?
4. Why do you think the cell phone manufacturers' association opposes cell phone use restrictions? Do you think it will hamper sales? Do they believe so?
5. Is it ethical to use a cell phone while driving?

[307] *Gina Rolata, "Cell Phone Studies See No Link to Brain Cancer,"* The New York Times, *December 20, 2000, pp. A1, A21.*

5f

Plant Closures and Downsizing

Economic downturns, intense competition, and the need to cut costs often force employers to close facilities and lay off workers. What obligations do businesses have to their employees? To the communities where their facilities are located? The dilemma of employer loyalty and shareholder profit is a difficult one to resolve.

CASE 5.25

Aaron Feuerstein and Malden Mills[308]

Aaron Feuerstein is the chief executive officer and chairman of the board of Malden Mills, a 93-year-old privately-held company that manufactures Polartec and is located in Mathuen, Massachusetts. Polartec is a fabric made from recycled plastic that stays dry and provides warmth. It is used in everything from ski parkas to blankets by companies such as L.L. Bean, Patagonia, Lands' End, and Eddie Bauer. Malden employs 2,400 locals and Mr. Feuerstein and his family have steadfastly refused to move production overseas. Their labor costs are the highest in the industry—an average of $12.50 per hour.

On December 11, 1995, a boiler explosion at Malden Mills resulted in a fire that injured 27 people and destroyed three of the buildings at Malden Mills' factory site. With only one building left in functioning order, many employees assumed they would be laid off temporarily. Other employees worried that Mr. Feuerstein, then 70 years old, would simply take the insurance money and retire. Mr. Feuerstein could have retired with about $300 million in insurance proceeds from the fire. Malden Mills is the largest employer in what is one of Massachusetts' poorest towns.

Instead, Mr. Feuerstein announced on December 14, 1995, that he would pay the employees their salaries for at least thirty days. He continued that promise for six months, when 90 percent of the employees were back to work. The cost of covering

[308] *Adapted from Marianne M. Jennings, "Aaron Feuerstein–An Odd CEO,"* Business: Its Legal, Ethical and Global Environment, *6th ed., 2002, pp. 767–768.*

the wages was approximately $25 million to the company. During that time, Malden ran its Polartec through its one working facility as it began and completed the reconstruction of the plant, at a cost of $430 million. Interestingly, production output during this time was nine times what it had been before the fire. One worker noted, "I owe him everything. I'm paying him back."[309] After the fire and Feuerstein's announcement, customers pledged their support with one customer, Dakotah, sending in $30,000 to help. Within the first month following the fire, $1,000,000 in donations were received.[310]

Malden Mills was rededicated in September 1997 with new buildings and technology. About 10 percent of the 2,400 employees were displaced by the upgraded facilities and equipment, but Feuerstein created a job training and placement center on site in order to ease these employees' transition.

By the end of 2001, six years after the fire, Malden Mills had debts of $140 million and was teetering near bankruptcy. However, Malden Mills has been through bankruptcy before, in the 1980s, and emerged very strongly with its then new product, Polartec, developed through the company's R&D program.

Some have suggested that Mr. Feuerstein's generosity during that time is responsible for the present financial crisis. However, the fire destroyed the company's furniture upholstery division and customers were impatient at that time. They were not inclined to wait for production to ramp up, and Malden Mills lost most of those customers. It closed the upholstery division in 1996.

Also, there was the threat of inexpensive fleece from the Asian markets that was ignored largely because of the plant rebuilding and the efforts focused there. Finally, in 2000, the company had a shakeup in its marketing team just as it was launching its electric fabrics—fabrics with heatable wires that are powered by batteries embedded in the fleece.

Once again, however, the goodwill from 1995 remains. Residents of the town have been sending in checks to help the company, some as small as $10. There is an Internet campaign begun by town residents to "Buy Fleece." The campaign is enjoying some success as Patagonia, Lands' End, and L.L. Bean report increased demand. In addition, the U.S. military has placed large orders for fleece jackets for soldiers now fighting in Operation Enduring Freedom in Afghanistan.

Senators Ted Kennedy and John Kerry have been lobbying GE not to involuntarily petition Malden Mills into bankruptcy. GE Capital holds one-fourth of Malden Mills' debts. Its other creditors include Finova Capital, SAI Investment, Pilgrim Investment, LaSalle Bank, and PNC Bank.

The union, about to begin contract negotiations, has spoken through its leader, "We're ready to make sacrifices for a little while. Whatever he asks us to do to keep the place going."[311]

[309] *"Malden Mills,"* Dateline NBC, *August 9, 1996.*

[310] *Steve Wulf, "The Glow From a Fire,"* Time, *January 8, 1996, p. 49.*

[311] *Lynnley Browning, "Fire Could Not Stop a Mill, but Debts May,"* The New York Times, *November 28, 2001, pp. C1, C5.*

As for Mr. Feuerstein, his view is simple, "There are times in business when you don't think of the financial consequences, but of the human consequences. There is no doubt this company will survive."[312]

Discussion Questions

1. Mr. Feuerstein has stated, "I don't deserve credit. Corporate America has made it so that when you behave the way I did, it's abnormal." Is he right? Was he right in continuing the salaries?
2. What impact would a closure of Malden Mills have had on Mathuen?
3. Does the fact that Malden Mills is privately held make a difference in Feuerstein's flexibility?
4. Did Mr. Feuerstein focus too much on benevolence and not enough on business? Is he relying only on goodwill to survive and did he neglect the basics of strategy, marketing, and addressing the competition?

CASE 5.26

GM Plant Closings and Efforts at Outplacement

Bleeding from losses of $4.45 billion for 1991, General Motors (GM) announced on February 24, 1992, that it would close twenty-one plants over the next few years, with twelve to be shut down in 1992, affecting over 16,300 workers.[313]

GM is the nation's largest manufacturer, and the $4.45 billion loss was the largest ever in American corporate history.[314] Robert C. Stempel, then-GM chairman, said the United States was in an unusually deep automotive slump: "The rate of change during the past year was unprecedented. And no one was immune to the extraordinary events which affected our lives and the way in which we do business."[315]

More than 3,400 workers at GM's North Tarrytown, New York, plant were to be laid off by 1995. The plant manufactured GM mini-vans: the Chevrolet Lumina, the Pontiac Trans Sports, and the Oldsmobile Silhouette. The mini-van, originally designed in the United States, was executed by GM with a wide stance and a sloping, futuristic nose. From 150,000 to 200,000 of the vans were expected to be sold annually, but sales reached only 100,000 per year—one-half of the Tarrytown plant's capacity.[316] Dealers

[312] Id., *p. C1.*

[313] *James B. Treece, "The Plants That GM Will Probably Padlock,"* Business Week, *December 14, 1992, pp. 34–35.*

[314] *Doron P. Levin, "Court Backs G.M. on Plant Closing,"* The New York Times, *August 5, 1993, p. C4.*

[315] *Doron P. Levin, "GM Picks 21 Plants to Be Shut as It Reports a Record U.S. Loss,"* The New York Times, *February 25, 1992, p. A1.*

[316] *Adam Bryant, "Swinging the G.M. Ax: Which Plants Are Next?"* The New York Times, *November 10, 1992, p. C1.*

maintained the shape of the van was too avant-garde for significant sales. "It looks like a Dustbuster," noted a GM manager anonymously.[317]

GM executives acknowledged that building one model per plant was a sloppy and expensive way to do business.[318]

The Tarrytown UAW local had negotiated with GM in 1987 to bring the mini-van production to the plant. The union members voted to accept innovative and cooperative work rules to replace expensive practices under the old contract. Also, state and local governments contributed job training funds, gave tax breaks, and began reconstructing railroad bridges to win the mini-van production plant.[319]

Dan Luria, automotive analyst for the Industrial Technology Institute, a nonprofit institute in Ann Arbor, Michigan, said "The workers did all the right things to get the mini-van but GM was just too optimistic about how many it could sell."[320]

In his speech announcing the closures, Stempel said, "We are asking you to help remake the world's largest automobile company. We can't wait."[321]

Tarrytown was only the beginning of the GM closures. In February 1993, GM announced the closure of 21 plants, with resulting layoffs of 16,300 workers. Another closure was the Willow Run plant in Ypsilanti Township, Michigan, a loss of 2,200 jobs. However, Ypsilanti Township and Washtenaw County filed suit challenging the closure because GM had promised to build cars at Willow Run through the late 1990s in exchange for tax abatements.[322] The suit alleged $13.5 million was owed in back taxes by GM for reneging on its promise to operate the plant. The suit was settled in 1994 with GM agreeing to pay half the abated taxes.[323]

Discussion Questions

1. When unions and governments provide financial assistance in exchange for promises from a manufacturer to locate a plant in a particular area, should the plant owner have an obligation to continue operations?
2. Did GM just make a business decision to stop losses?
3. Should workers and governments absorb the cost of business risks, such as a poor-selling mini-van?
4. Did GM renege on its promise to Ypsilanti Township and Washtenaw County? Should business setbacks excuse plant closures? Should tax abatements be repaid?

[317] *Doron P. Levin, "Vehicle's Design Dooms Van Plant,"* The New York Times, *February 26, 1992, p. C4.*

[318] *David Woodruff and Zachary Schiller, "Smart Step for a Wobbly Giant,"* Business Week, *December 7, 1992, p. 38.*

[319] *Arthur S. Hayes, "Concerns Find It Harder to Leave Town after Receiving Tax Breaks,"* The Wall Street Journal, *March 1, 1993, p. B10.*

[320] *Levin, "Vehicle's Design Dooms Van Plant," p. C4.*

[321] *William McWhirter, "Major Overhaul,"* Time, *December 30, 1991, p. 56.*

[322] *Doron P. Levin, "Judge Blocks Plan by G.M. to Close a Plant in Michigan,"* The New York Times, *February 10, 1993, pp. C1, C5.*

[323] *James Bennet, "G.M. Settles Suit over Plant Closing,"* The New York Times, *April 15, 1994, p. C3.*

5g

Environmental Issues

The quality of the environment has become a personal issue. Many consumers base their buying decisions on the commitment of manufacturers and other businesses to protect the environment. The environment has become a stakeholder in business operations.

CASE 5.27

Herman Miller and Its Rain Forest Chairs

In March 1990, Bill Foley, research manager for Herman Miller, Inc., began a routine evaluation of new woods to use in the firm's signature piece—the $2,277 Eames chair. The Eames chair is a distinctive office chair with a rosewood exterior finish and a leather seat.

At that time, the chair was made of two species of trees: rosewood and Honduran mahogany. Foley realized that Miller's use of the tropical hardwoods was helping destroy rain forests. Foley banned the use of the woods in the chairs once existing supplies were exhausted. The Eames chair would no longer have its traditional rosewood finish.

Foley's decision prompted former CEO Richard H. Ruch to react: "That's going to kill that [chair]."[324] Effects on sales could not be quantified.

Herman Miller, based in Zeeland, Michigan, and founded in 1923 by D. J. DePree, a devout Baptist, manufactures office furniture and partitions. The corporation follows a participatory-management tradition and takes environmentally friendly actions. The vice president of the Michigan Audubon Society noted that Miller has cut the trash it hauls to landfills by 90 percent since 1982: "Herman Miller has been doing a super job."[325]

Herman Miller built an $11 million waste-to-energy heating and cooling plant. The plant saves $750,000 per year in fuel and landfill costs. In 1991, the company

[324] *David Woodruff, "Herman Miller: How Green Is My Factory?"* Business Week, *September 16, 1991, pp. 54–55.*
[325] Id.

found a buyer for the 800,000 pounds of scrap fabric it had been dumping in landfills. A North Carolina firm shreds it for insulation for automobile roof linings and dashboards. Selling the scrap fabric saves Miller $50,000 per year in dumping fees.

Herman Miller employees once used 800,000 styrofoam cups a year. But in 1991, the company passed out 5,000 mugs to its employees and banished styrofoam. The mugs carry the following admonition: "On spaceship earth there are no passengers . . . only crew." Styrofoam in packaging was also reduced 70 percent for a cost savings of $1.4 million.

Herman Miller also spent $800,000 for two incinerators that burn 98 percent of the toxic solvents that escape from booths where wood is stained and varnished. These furnaces exceeded the 1990 Clean Air Act requirements. It was likely that the incinerators would be obsolete within three years, when nontoxic products became available for staining and finishing wood, but having the furnaces was "ethically correct," former CEO Ruch said in response to questions from the board of directors.[326]

Herman Miller keeps pursuing environmentally safe processes, including finding a use for its sawdust by-product. However, for the fiscal year ended May 31, 1991, its net profit had fallen 70 percent from 1990 to $14 million on total sales of $878 million.

In 1992, Herman Miller's board hired J. Kermit Campbell as CEO. Mr. Campbell continued in the Ruch tradition and wrote essays for employees on risk-taking and for managers on "staying out of the way." From 1992–1995, sales growth at Herman Miller was explosive, but as one analyst described it, "expenses exploded." Despite sales growth during this time, profits dropped 89 percent to a mere $4.3 million.

Miller's board, concerned about Campbell's lack of expedience, announced Campbell's resignation, and began an aggressive program of downsizing. Between May and July, 1995, 130 jobs were eliminated. Also in 1995, sales dropped from $879 to $804 million. The board promoted Michael Volkema, then 39 and head of Miller's file cabinet division, to CEO.[327]

Volkema refocused Herman Miller's name with a line of well-made, lower-priced office furniture using a strategy and division called SQA (Simple, Quick, and Affordable). The dealers for SQA work with customers to configure office furniture plans and Miller ships in less than two weeks all the pieces ordered.

Revenues in 1997 were $200 million with record earnings of $78 million. In 1998, Miller acquired dealerships around the country and downsized from its then 1,500 employees.[328]

Volkema notes that staying too long with an "outdated strategy and marketing" nearly cost the company. By 1999, Herman Miller was giving Steelcase, the country's number one office furniture manufacturer, stiff competition with its Aeron chair. The Aeron chair, which comes in hundreds of versions, has lumbar adjustments, varying types of arms, different upholstery colors, and a mesh back. Its price is $765 to $1,190, and it is said to be capitalizing on its "Austin Powers-like" look. The chair has thirty-

[326] Id.

[327] *Susan Chandler, "An Empty Chair at Herman Miller,"* Business Week, *July 24, 1996, p. 44.*

[328] *Bruce Upjohn, "A Touch of Schizophrenia,"* Forbes, *July 7, 1997, pp. 57–59.*

five patents and is the result of $35 million in R&D expenditures and cooperation with researchers at Michigan State, the University of Vermont, and Cornell who specialize in ergonomics. The seat features a sort of spine imprimatur. That is, the chair almost conforms to its user's spine.[329]

Discussion Questions

1. Evaluate Foley's decision on changing the Eames chair woods. Consider the moral standards at issue for various stakeholders.
2. Is it troublesome that Miller's profits were off when Foley made the decision?
3. Is Herman Miller bluffing with "green marketing"? Would Albert Carr support Herman Miller's actions for different reasons?
4. Why would Herman Miller decide to buy equipment that exceeded the 1990 Clean Air Act standards when it would not be needed in three years?
5. Would you be less comfortable with Herman Miller's environmental decisions if it advertised them?
6. Has Herman Miller changed its focus? Why? Was the change in focus a chance to compete more effectively?

CASE 5.28

Exxon and Alaska

On March 24, 1989, the Exxon *Valdez* ran aground on Bligh Reef, south of Valdez, Alaska, and spilled nearly 11 million gallons of oil into Prince William Sound. The captain of the tanker was Joseph Hazelwood.

Hazelwood had a history of drinking problems and had lost his New York driver's license after two drunken-driving convictions. In 1985, with the knowledge of Exxon officials, Hazelwood joined a twenty-eight-day alcohol rehabilitation program. Almost a week after the Prince William Sound accident, Exxon revealed that Hazelwood's blood-alcohol reading was 0.061 in a test taken ten and one-half hours after the spill occurred—a level that would indicate intoxication. Exxon also announced it had fired Hazelwood.

The magnitude of the spill seemed almost incomprehensible. U.S. Interior Secretary Manual Lujan called the spill the oil industry's "Three Mile Island." After ten days, the spill covered 1,000 square miles and leaked out of Prince William Sound onto beaches along the Gulf of Alaska and Cook Inlet. A cleanup army of 12,000 was sent in with hot water and oil-eating microbes. The workers found more than 1,000 dead otters, 34,400 dead sea birds, and 151 bald eagles that had died from eating the oil-contaminated remains of sea birds.

[329] *Terril Yue Jones, "Sit on It,"* Forbes, *July 5, 1999, pp. 53–54.*

By September 15, Exxon pulled out of the cleanup efforts after having spent $2 billion but recovering only 5 to 9 percent of the oil spilled. Alaskan officials said about 20 to 40 percent of the oil evaporated. This meant that 50 to 75 percent of the oil was either on the ocean floor or the beaches.

Hazelwood was indicted by the state of Alaska on several charges, including criminal mischief, operating a watercraft while intoxicated, reckless endangerment, and negligent discharge of oil. He was found innocent of all charges except the negligent discharge of oil, fined $50,000, and required to spend 1,000 hours helping with the cleanup of the beaches. Exxon paid Hazelwood's legal fees. Hazelwood now works as a maritime consultant for a New York City law firm and still holds a valid sea license.

When the *Valdez* was being repaired, shipworkers observed that Hazelwood and his crew had kept the tanker from sinking by quickly sealing off the hatches to the ship's tank, thus making a bubble that helped stabilize the ship. Citing incredible seamanship, the workers noted that an 11-million-gallon spill was preferable to a 60 million one—the tanker's load.

Following the spill, critics of Exxon maintained that the company's huge personnel cutbacks during the 1980s affected the safety and maintenance levels aboard its tankers. Later hearings revealed that the crew of the *Valdez* was overburdened with demands for speed and efficiency. The crew worked ten- to twelve-hour days and often had their sleep interrupted. Lookouts frequently were not properly posted, and junior officers were permitted to control the bridge without the required supervision. Robert LeResche, oil-spill coordinator for Alaska, said, "It wasn't Captain Ahab on the bridge. It was Larry and Curly in the Exxon boardroom."[330] In response to critics, Exxon's CEO Lawrence Rawl stated:

> And we say, "We're sorry, and we're doing all we can." There were 30 million birds that went through the sound last summer, and only 30,000 carcasses have been recovered. Just look at how many ducks were killed in the Mississippi Delta in one hunting day in December! People have come up to me and said, "This is worse than Bhopal." I say, "Hell, Bhopal killed more than 3,000 people and injured 200,000 others!" Then they say, "Well, if you leave the people out, it was worse than Bhopal."[331]

On January 1, 1990, a second Exxon oil spill occurred when a pipeline under the Arthur Kill waterway between Staten Island and New Jersey burst and spilled 567,000 gallons of heating oil. New York and New Jersey officials criticized Exxon, citing shoddy equipment and poor maintenance. It was six hours after an alarm from the pipeline safety system went off before Exxon workers shut down the pipeline. Albert Appleton, New York City commissioner on the environment, said, "Exxon has a corporate philosophy that the environment is some kind of nuisance problem and a distraction from the real business of moving oil around."[332]

Late in February 1990, Exxon was indicted on federal felony charges of violating maritime safety and antipollution laws in the *Valdez* spill. The charges were brought

[330] *Jay Mathews, "Problems Preceded Oil Spill,"* Washington Post, *May 18, 1989, pp. A1, A18.*

[331] *Chris Welles, "Exxon's Future: What Has Larry Rawl Wrought?"* Business Week, *April 2, 1990, pp. 72–76.*

[332] *Barbara Rudolph, "Exxon's Attitude Problem,"* Time, *January 22, 1990, p. 51.*

after Exxon and the Justice Department failed to reach a settlement. The oil company also faced state criminal charges. Alaska and the Justice Department also brought civil suits against Exxon for the costs of cleaning up the spill. Approximately 150 other civil suits were filed by fishing and tour boat operators whose incomes were eliminated by the spill. At the time of the federal indictment, Exxon had paid out $180 million to 13,000 fishermen and other claimants.

By May 1990, Exxon had renewed its cleanup efforts at targeted sites with 110 employees. Twice during 1991, Exxon reached a plea agreement with the federal government and the state on the criminal charges. After Alaska disagreed with the terms of the first, a second agreement was reached in which Exxon consented to plead guilty to three misdemeanors and pay a $1.15 billion fine. The civil litigation was settled when Exxon agreed to pay $900 million to both Alaska and the federal government over ten years.

The plea agreement with the governments did not address the civil suits pending against Exxon. At the end of 1991, an Alaska jury awarded sixteen fishers more than $2.5 million in damages and established a payout formula for similar plaintiffs in future litigation against Exxon. As of September 1994, Exxon had spent $2 billion to clean up shores in Alaska.

Exxon has had a stream of payouts since 1991—a total of $3.4 billion of its $5.7 billion in profits for that period. Payouts included:

- $20 million to 3,500 native Alaskans for damages to their villages;
- $287 million to 10,000 fishers;
- $1.5 billion for damages to wildlife; and
- $9.7 million for damages to Native American land.

In September 1994, a federal jury awarded an additional $5 billion in punitive damages against Exxon for the suits filed since 1991. The original verdict of Exxon's recklessness and the resulting damage awards were made by a jury following a trial that ended in 1994. The damage award was the largest in history at that time.

Exxon appealed the verdict to the 9th Circuit. Exxon's stock fell two and five-eighths points following the verdict.

In 1996, during a court review of the distribution of an award in an Alaskan case, a *Wall Street Journal* article revealed that Exxon had reached secret agreements with fish processors that would require them to refund the punitive damages awarded by juries. Apparently, some type of high/low settlement was reached with the plaintiffs prior to trial, but the jury trial proceeded without disclosure of the settlement and potential refund by the plaintiffs.

U.S. District Judge H. Russel Holland learned of the refund requirements and called the agreements an "astonishing ruse" to "mislead" the jury. Judge Holland set aside the agreements and allowed punitive damages to stand.

By November 1, 1996, Exxon had settled all of the *Valdez* cases and settled with its insurers for its claims. Exxon recovered $780 million of its $2.5 billion in costs, including attorney fees. Exxon had been in litigation with its insurers over coverage. Eugene Anderson, a lawyer who represents corporations in insurance actions, noted that insurance companies virtually always deny all large claims because "they pay lawyers much less each year in these cases than they earn in interest."[333]

In November 2001, the U.S. Court of Appeals for the 9th Circuit ruled that the $5 billion verdict in the Exxon *Valdez* case for punitive damages was excessive. The case was remanded to the federal district court for a redetermination of that damage figure.[334]

Exxon has publicly admitted responsibility for the spill and has paid in excess of $3 billion to clean up the area along the Alaska coastline that has been a prime fishing area and an economic base for people of the area.[335]

The $287 million verdict for the fishermen, awarded as compensatory damages for the loss of their fishing rights during the cleanup, was upheld by the 9th Circuit.

Congress passed the Oil Spill Act in response to the *Valdez* disaster as well as other provisions that effectively preclude the *Valdez* from ever entering Prince William Sound again.[336]

Discussion Questions

1. Evaluate Exxon's "attitude" with regard to the spill.
2. Why did the company cut back on staff and maintenance expenditures?
3. Was Hazelwood morally responsible for the spill?
4. Was Exxon management morally responsible for the spill?
5. What changes in Exxon's ethical environment would you make?
6. Would Exxon make the same decisions about Hazelwood and cost-cutting given the costs of the spill?
7. Evaluate the ethics in Exxon's secret deal on punitive damages.
8. Evaluate the ethics of the insurers in denying large claims in order to earn the interest while litigation over the claim is pending.
9. Why do you think the court held that the punitive damage verdict was excessive? Is there another social issue regarding litigation here?

Sources

Dietrich, Bill, "Is Oil-Spill Skipper a Fall Guy?" *Arizona Republic*, January 28, 1990, p. A2.

333 *Joseph B. Treaster, "With Insurers' Payment, Exxon Says Valdez Case Is Ended,"* The New York Times, *November 1, 1996, p. C3.*

334 In re Exxon, *270 F.3d 1215 (9th Cir. 2001).*

335 *"$5 B Exxon Verdict Is Tossed Out,"* National Law Journal, *November 19, 2001–November 26, 2001, p. A6.* See also *http://www.exxon.com.*

336 *33 U.S.C. §2732 (2001).*

"Exxon Labeled No. 1 in Bungling a Crisis," *Arizona Republic*, March 24, 1990, p. A8.

"Exxon, Lloyd's Agree to Valdez Settlement," *The Wall Street Journal*, November 1, 1996, p. B2.

"Exxon Stops the Flow," *Time*, March 25, 1992, p. 51.

"Exxon to Pay $1.1 Billion in Spill," *Arizona Republic*, March 13, 1991, p. A3.

Foster, David, "Oily Legacy," *Mesa Tribune*, March 18, 1990, p. D1.

Galen, Michele, and Vicky Cahan, "Getting Ready for Exxon vs. Practically Everybody," *Business Week*, September 25, 1989, pp. 190–192.

Galen, Michele, and Vicky Cahan, "The Legal Reef Ahead for Exxon," *Business Week*, March 12, 1990, p. 39.

Hayes, Arthur S., and Milo Geyelin, "Oil Spill Trial Yields $2.5 Million," *The Wall Street Journal*, September 11, 1991, p. B2.

Kangmine, Linda, and Carol Castaneda, "For Alaska, Tide Has Changed," *USA Today*, June 14, 1994, p. 3A.

"Like Punch in Gut: Exxon Skipper Talks," *Arizona Republic*, March 25, 1990, pp. A1, A12.

McCoy, Charles, "Exxon Reaches $1.15 Billion Spill Pact That Resembles Earlier Failed Accord," *The Wall Street Journal*, October 1, 1991, p. A3.

McCoy, Charles, and Peter Fritsch, "Legal Experts Surprised by Exxon Deals With Fish Processors in Valdez Case," *The Wall Street Journal*, June 14, 1996, p. B5.

Marshall, Steve, "Jury Rules Exxon Must Pay $287 Million to Alaska Fishermen," *USA Today*, August 12, 1994, p. 3A.

"Native Americans Awarded $9.7 Million from Exxon," *National Law Journal*, October 10, 1994, p. A19.

"Nice Work, Joe," *Time*, December 4, 1989, p. 48.

"Paying up for the Exxon Valdez," *Time*, August 8, 1994, p. 18.

Rempel, William C., "Exxon Captain Acquitted," *Arizona Republic*, March 23, 1990, p. A1.

Rubin, Julia, "Exxon Submits Final Oil-Spill Cleanup Plan," *Burlington Vermont Free Press*, April 28, 1990, p. 2A.

Satchell, Michael, and Betsy Carpenter, "A Disaster That Wasn't," *U.S. News & World Report*, September 18, 1989, pp. 60–69.

Schneider, Keith, "Jury Finds Exxon Acted Recklessly in Valdez Oil Spill," *The New York Times*, June 14, 1994, pp. A1, A8.

Schneider, Keith, "$20 Million Settlement in Exxon Case," *The New York Times*, July 26, 1994, p. A8.

Solomon, Caleb, "Exxon Attacks Scientific Views of Valdez Spill," *The Wall Street Journal*, April 15, 1993, pp. B1, B10.

Solomon, Caleb, "Exxon's Real Problem: Many of Its Oil Fields Are Old and Declining," *The Wall Street Journal*, September 19, 1994, pp. A1, A6.

Solomon, Caleb, "Jury to Weigh Exxon's Actions in Spill," *The Wall Street Journal*, June 7, 1994, p. B5.

Sullivan, Allanna, "Exxon Begins Final Defense in Valdez Spill," *The Wall Street Journal*, May 2, 1994, pp. B1, B3.

Sullivan, Allanna, and Arthur S. Hayes, "Exxon's Plea Bargaining," *The Wall Street Journal*, February 21, 1990, p. B8.

Tyson, Rae, "Valdez Cleanup Is Skin Deep," *USA Today*, March 22, 1994, p. 3A.

CASE 5.29

The Death of the Great Disposable Diaper Debate

In the late 1980s, environmentalists raised concerns about the disposal of diapers in municipal landfills, space for which is scarce and becoming more so. The average child uses 7,800 diapers in the first 130 weeks of life.

The debate over disposable diapers was complex. Disposable diapers account for just 2 percent of municipal solid waste. The time required for plastic to break down is 200 to 500 years. Eighteen billion disposable diapers go into landfills each year. An Arthur D. Little study comparing the environmental impact of cloth and disposable diapers over the products' lifetimes found cloth diapers consume more energy and water than disposables. Cloth diapers also cost more (not counting diaper-service fees) and create more air and water pollution through washing. Critics point out that the study was commissioned by Procter & Gamble, the largest maker of disposable diapers, with 50 percent of the market. However, the study was a sophisticated "life-cycle analysis" that used elaborate computer models, and Arthur D. Little is considered an eminent research firm.[337]

In surveys in the early 1990s, four of five American parents preferred disposables. Most hospital staffs and day care centers favor using disposables even though many personally use cloth diapers. Switching from disposable to cloth diapers costs about 2.5 percent more. The disposability of the diapers was also improving with companies devoting significant R&D dollars to reducing the time for biodegradation. Procter & Gamble created advanced techniques for industrial composting of solid waste and spent $20 million to develop diapers that break down into humus.[338]

Environmentalists, however, were quite successful in obtaining regulation of disposables. Twenty states considered taxes or complete bans on disposables. Nebraska

[337] *Arthur Little declared bankruptcy in January 2002. Jonathan D. Glater, "Arthur D. Little Plans Bankruptcy Filing,"* The New York Times, *February 6, 2002, p. C4.*

[338] *Zachary Schiller, "Turning Pampers Into Plant Food?"* Business Week, *October 22, 1990, p. 38.*

banned nondegradable disposables, with a law that took effect in October 1993. Maine required day-care centers to accept children who wear cloth diapers. New York considered requiring that new mothers be given information explaining the environmental threat of disposables. In 1990, the Wisconsin legislature barely defeated a measure to tax disposables.

Alternatives to disposables were being developed. R Med International distributes Tender Care, a disposable diaper that degrades in two to five years because its outer lining is made of cornstarch. However, the price of these diapers was substantially higher than that of other disposables and made mass market appeal impossible.

The great disposable diaper debate peaked on Earth Day in 1990. After the Little study appeared, parents' guilt about rain forests and landfills was relieved and by 1997, 80 percent of all babies were wearing disposables. Many attribute the change in attitude as well as the halt in legislative and regulatory action to Procter & Gamble's effective public relations using the Little study results. Also, Allen Hershkowitz, a senior scientist at the Natural Resources Defense Council, said, "The pediatric dermatology clearly seemed to favor disposables, while the environmental issues were murky." Environmentalists referred to Mr. Hershkowitz as "the skipper of the Exxon Valdez."[339]

During the 1990s, all disposable diaper manufacturers were able to develop materials that were much thinner and lighter than their predecessors. Not only were the diapers decomposing faster, they took up less room in the landfills.

By 1997, the National Association of Diaper Services (NADS) reported its membership at an all-time low, with closings of cloth diaper services even in ecologically conscious Boston. There are no diaper services located in any of New York City's five boroughs. Their current marketing campaign emphasizes a two-year guarantee for potty-training with diapers free after that. Babies, the NADS says, can't feel the wetness in disposables.

The Internet has created a new submarket for cloth diapers because the network of parents who prefer cloth diapers is so easily connected. The two national companies remain Mother-ease of New York and Kooshies Baby Products of Ontario, Canada, but there are several small companies, including Darla's Place, based in Imlay City, Michigan. Founded by Darla Sowders because of her frustration with the national brands, the company uses at-home mothers to sew its product, which captures the "brown market," or the market for used diapers. The diapers are sewn a certain way that customers say prevents leaks. The brand is regarded as the champagne of diapers and sells at a premium above other diapers in the submarket. Despite this activity, Kimberly-Clark indicates there is no change in the demand for cloth diapers nor any reduction in the use of disposables.[340] P&G reports sagging diaper sales and is competing with a new premium brand marketed as an item of clothing.[341]

[339] *Kathleen Deveny, "States Mull Rash of Diaper Regulations,"* The Wall Street Journal, *June 15, 1990, p. B1.*

[340] *Lisa Moricoli Latham, "The Diaper Rush of 1999: Cloth Makes a Comeback on the Net,"* The New York Times, *September 19, 1999, p. BU6.*

[341] *Emily Nelson, "Diaper Sales Sagging, P&G Thinks Young to Reposition Pampers,"* The Wall Street Journal, *December 27, 2001, pp. A1, A2.*

unit 5

section g

Discussion Questions

1. Did Arthur D. Little have a conflict of interest with Procter & Gamble's sponsorship of its work?
2. Would it be a breach of duty to the hospital's patients and shareholders to adopt a position (that is, using cloth diapers) that increases costs?
3. Do people ignore environmental issues for the sake of convenience? Do your arguments depend on whether you must change diapers?
4. What lessons are learned from this case for applicability in other industries?
5. Did environmentalists exaggerate?

5h

Purchasing: Conflicts and Bribery

Purchasing agents hold powerful positions. They make the choices to award business to other companies. Often, contractors employ tools of influence to gain favor. When are such tools unethical? Can an agent accept gifts for the award of business?

CASE 5.30

JCPenney and Its Wealthy Buyer

Purchasing agent Jim G. Locklear began his career as a retail buyer with Federated Department Stores in Dallas, where he became known for his eye for fashion and ability to negotiate low prices. After ten years with Federated, he went to work for Jordan Marsh in Boston in 1987 with an annual salary of $96,000. But three months later, Locklear quit that job to take a position as a housewares buyer with JCPenney so he could return to Dallas. His salary was $56,000 per year, he was 38 years old, he owed support payments totaling $900 per month for four children from four marriages, and the bank was threatening to foreclose on his $500,000 mortgage.[342]

Locklear was a good performer for Penney. His products sold well, and he was responsible for the very successful JCPenney Home Collection, a color-coordinated line of dinnerware, flatware, and glasses that was eventually copied by most other tabletop retailers. Locklear took sales of Penney's tabletop line from $25 million to $45 million per year and was named the company's "Buyer of the Year" several times.

However, Locklear was taking payments from Penney's vendors directly and through front companies. Some paid him for information about bids or to obtain contracts, while others paid what they believed to be advertising fees to various companies that were fronts owned by Locklear. Between 1987 and 1992, Locklear took in $1.5 million in "fees" from Penney's vendors.

[342] *Andrea Gerlin, "How a Penney Buyer Made Up to $1.5 Million on Vendors' Kickbacks,"* The Wall Street Journal, *February 7, 1995, pp. A1, A18.*

Penney hired an investigator in 1989 to look into Locklear's activities, but the investigator uncovered only Mr. Locklear's personal financial difficulties.

During his time as a buyer, Locklear was able to afford a country club membership, resort vacations, luxury vehicles, and large securities accounts. While his lifestyle was known to those who worked with him, no questions were asked again until 1992, when Penney received an anonymous letter about Locklear and his relationship with a Dallas manufacturer's representative. Penney investigated and uncovered sufficient evidence of payments to file a civil suit to recover those payments and referred the case to the U.S. attorney in Dallas for criminal prosecution.

Mr. Locklear was charged by the U.S. attorney with mail and wire fraud. Mr. Locklear entered a guilty plea and provided information to the U.S. attorney on suppliers, agents, and manufacturers' reps who had paid him "fees." Mr. Locklear was sentenced to eighteen months in prison and fined $50,000. Penney won a $789,000 judgment against him and Mr. Locklear's assets have been attached for collection purposes.[343]

Discussion Questions

1. What ethical violations did Locklear commit?
2. Was anyone really harmed by Locklear's conduct? List the stakeholders who were affected.
3. Given Locklear's lifestyle, why did it take so long for Penney to take action? Do you see any red flags in the facts given?
4. A vendor who paid Locklear $25,000 in exchange for a Penney order stated, "It was either pay it or go out of business." Evaluate the ethics of this seller.
5. Do you agree that both the buyer and the seller are guilty in commercial bribery cases? Is the purchasing agent "more" wrong?
6. Many companies provide guidelines for their purchasing agents on accepting gifts, samples, and favors. For example, under Wal-Mart's "no coffee" policy, its buyers cannot accept even a cup of coffee from a vendor. Any samples or models must be returned to vendors once a sales demonstration is complete. Other companies allow buyers to accept items of minimal value. Still others place a specific dollar limit on the value, such as $25. What problems do you see with any of these policies? What advantages do you see?
7. Describe the problems that can result when buyers accept gifts from vendors and manufacturer's representatives.
8. Mr. Locklear said at his sentencing, "I became captive to greed. Once it was discovered, I felt tremendous relief." Mr. Locklear's pastor said Locklear coached little league and added, "Our country needs more role models like Jim Locklear."[344] Evaluate these two quotes from an ethical perspective.

[343] *Andrea Gerlin, "J. C. Penney Ex-Employee Sentenced to Jail,"* The Wall Street Journal, *August 28, 1995, p. A9.*

[344] Id.

CASE 5.31

Cars for Cars: Honda Executives' Allocation System

From 1978 through early 1992, the amazing popularity of Honda cars, including its luxury car Acura, created excessive demand for both the cars and the franchises (dealerships). Dealers were able to sell the vehicles at thousands of dollars above the sticker price, virtually guaranteeing high profits. This intense demand and resulting guaranteed success led to American Honda Motor Co. executives getting cash and gifts from dealers and potential dealers in exchange for auto delivery allocations and the award of franchises. One man who was eventually awarded a dealership presented a Honda executive with a Mercedes-Benz. Some Honda executives accepted cash payments of up to $1 million in exchange for a franchise. Others received such gifts as swimming pools, paintings (one worth $50,000), Rolex watches, and laser karaoke machines.[345]

Honda officials in Japan were unaware of this activity by American Honda executives. Meanwhile, one person, Joseph R. Hendrick, was awarded twenty-eight dealerships during this time. An assistant U.S. attorney in New Hampshire, Michael J. Conolly, presented evidence in court that Hendrick sent payments to Stanley James Cardiges, senior vice president of sales for Honda America. Cardiges and sixteen other Honda executives pleaded guilty to federal charges of racketeering, mail fraud, and conspiracy to commit mail fraud and have forfeited $10 million to the U.S. government. Two other Honda executives were found guilty of accepting more than $15 million in kickbacks from auto dealers that were the basis of federal fraud charges in a scheme that involved dealers in thirty states.[346] In the trial of these two executives, Cardiges testified that the practice of accepting gifts was widespread in the executive suite.[347]

The total of former Honda executives and employees to plead guilty or be convicted reached twenty in 1995. Cardiges was sentenced to five years and fined $364,000.[348]

In 1996, a federal judge ruled that Honda dealers who claimed injury from the company-wide bribery scheme could file suit against Honda for racketeering and antitrust violations. The judge also ruled that high-ranking Honda Japanese executives could be named in the suit.[349]

The dealers who have brought suit claim that they lost millions in business because they refused to pay bribes and were not given car allocations at a time when Hondas could be sold at thousands above the sticker price. Honda settled the suit for $316 million in 1998.[350]

345 *James Bennet, "Corruption Called Broad in Honda Case,"* The New York Times, *April 4, 1995, pp. C1, C6.*

346 *"Honda Sentence,"* USA Today, *August 28, 1995, p. 1B.*

347 *"A Big Honda Dealer Is Indicted in Federal Bribery Case,"* The New York Times, *December 5, 1996, p. C4.*

348 *James Bennet, "Guilty Plea in Honda Bribery Case,"* The New York Times, *February 8, 1995, pp. C1, C8.*

349 *"Dealers Given Right to Sue Honda Over Bribery Scheme,"* Arizona Republic, *August 31, 1996, p. A8.*

350 *"Honda Dealers Said to Settle Suit,"* The New York Times, *July 29, 1998, p. C1.*

Throughout the country, indictments of dealers who paid bribes to the American Honda executives resulted in charges and convictions for conspiracy, money laundering, and mail fraud. Mr. Hendrick was indicted on thirteen counts of money laundering, one count of conspiracy, and one count of mail fraud. Mr. Hendrick's brother, John, was also indicted. Mr. Hendrick stated that he gave Mr. Cardiges gifts, but called them gifts to a friend, not for influence.[351] Mr. Hendrick entered a guilty plea to mail fraud.[352]

Discussion Questions

1. What type of atmosphere did Honda America have to have for this scheme to go on for so long?
2. To whom did the money and goods paid to the executives actually belong? Were the Honda executives collecting economic rents that belonged to Honda because of the high demand for its cars?
3. Why does it matter that these executives enjoyed some extra money from Honda's success? Are these economic rents that belong to Honda?
4. If you were an executive, how would you confront your fellow officers about such payments and your unwillingness to accept them? Could you lose your job for taking such a position?
5. A defense lawyer in the trial of two executives said that Honda's top management "turned a blind eye to the kick backs and that bribe-taking was implicit, though unofficial, company policy, and therefore did not constitute a crime."[353] Evaluate his statement.

CASE 5.32

Ford, Firestone, and the Rolling Explorer

Firestone ATX, ATX II, and Wilderness tires came under fire in the media because of complaints about the failure of those tires being linked to so many accidents. In May 2000, following a report by a Houston television station on a correlation between the tires and accidents in that area, the National Highway Traffic Safety Administration (NHTSA) received a flurry of complaints about the tires.

The treads on the approximately 48 million tires, found on many trucks and SUVs and used mostly on Ford Explorers, seem to suddenly separate, although no one yet understands why. One theory is heat and poor tire maintenance. A former Firestone tire engineer, however, theorizes that these particular tires lack nylon caps between

[351] *"Honda Execs Guilty in Bribery Scheme,"* USA Today, *June 2, 1995, p. 1B.*

[352] *"Auto Dealer Pleads Guilty in Honda Bribery Inquiry,"* The New York Times, *August 15, 1997, p. C1.*

[353] *Bennet, "Corruption Called Broad in Honda Case," pp. C1, C6.*

their steel belts and the rubber to keep the belts from sawing through the tread. Such caps are common in other tires and cost about $1.

There are currently 100 lawsuits pending around the country that involve accidents resulting from the tires separating. Records for the agency reveal that it has four deaths documented as well as 193 accidents from the tires. Reports of tread failure have been documented at speeds of 20 mph and the vehicle appearing most often in the reported crashes is the Ford Explorer. Many of the tire failures have occurred in vehicles with less than 2,000 odometer miles.

The NHTSA has known of the Firestone tire issues for at least ten years. At least six other nations have issued product recall notices on the tires. Ford has replaced tires in Venezuela, Ecuador, Thailand, Malaysia, Colombia, and Saudi Arabia. Ford referred to the replacements in those nations as a "customer satisfaction issue."[354]

As the Ford/Firestone tire issue continued to evolve with both civil litigation and an investigation by the federal government, depositions of top executives in the companies were made public. Those depositions revealed some inconsistencies with some of the public statements by Bridgestone/Firestone.

For example, Bridgestone/Firestone issued public statements that it was not aware of peeling issues with the tires used on the Ford Explorer. However, a deposition of Firestone's chief of quality revealed that he believed he discussed the issue of the tires with the company's CEO in 1999, a full year before the issue became public with the resulting recall. David Laubie, who retired from the company in May 2000, said that he handled consumer claims and quality control issues for the company and had received complaints which he passed along to the CEO in memo form as well as in their regular meetings.

In testimony before Congress in September 2000, Firestone's executive vice president, Gary Crigger, testified that the company only became aware of the problem in July or August of 2000.

Firestone then began to raise the issue of whether Ford put proper tire pressure instructions with the Ford Explorer. Firestone maintained that Ford's recommendation of an unusually low tire pressure, 26 pounds per square inch, caused the sidewalls to flex and get hot, which then weakened the tires. However, both the depositions of Mr. Laubie and the current quality control chief of Firestone indicate that no one from Firestone ever discussed the low tire pressure issue with anyone at Ford.[355]

Bridgestone/Firestone, Inc. issued a recall of its defective tires in August 2000, for a recall totaling 6.5 million tires, the largest ever in the United States. The recall applied to tires on the Ford Explorer and Mercury Mountaineer sport utility vehicles that involved Firestone/Bridgestone's 15-inch ATX tires and 15-inch Wilderness AT tires. Those tires had been tied specifically to Firestone's Decatur, Illinois, plant.

[354] *James R. Healey and Sara Nathan, "More Deaths Linked to Tires,"* USA Today, *August 2, 2000, p. 1A; James R. Healey and Sara Nathan, "Officials Have Known SUV Tire Suspicions for Decade,"* USA Today, *August 2, 2000, p. 1B.*

[355] *James R. Healey and Sara Nathan, " Depositions in Tire Lawsuits Don't Match Company's Lines,"* USA Today, *December 11, 2000, p. 3B.*

However, the company simply did not have the inventory to replace all the tires at one time and many drivers and car owners were required to wait. The company ramped up production to 500,000 per month but, even at that rate, the replacements were not done within one year. Bridgestone/Firestone also instructed its dealers that it could offer customers any of ten acceptable substitutes for the tires, including tires from other manufacturers who would be reimbursed by the Bridgestone/Firestone dealers.[356]

Ford, after performing its own analysis of its data, including warranty claims, issued its recall because of fears that the problem was more widespread. Ford said that there was "a higher than acceptable rate of defect."

Concerned about the slow rate of replacement, and being the auto manufacturer most affected by the tire issue, Ford announced that it would replace the tires for buyers of its Ford Explorer. The recall involved about 13,000,000 tires. The result of the announced Ford recall was that Firestone ended its 95-year contractual relationship with Ford. There were acrimonious exchanges between the companies about responsibility, liability, and who told what to whom. The announcement from Bridgestone/Firestone, as it appeared on its Web site, was as follows:

Bridgestone/Firestone, Inc. Ends Ford Tire Business in the Americas[357]

NASHVILLE, Tenn. (May 21, 2001)—Bridgestone/Firestone, Inc. today announced it is terminating its almost 100-year business relationship of supplying tires to the Ford Motor Company.

"Business relationships, like personal ones, are built upon trust and mutual respect. We have come to the conclusion that we can no longer supply tires to Ford since the basic foundation of our relationship has been seriously eroded," said John T. Lampe, chairman, CEO and president of Bridgestone/Firestone, Inc. "This is not a decision we make lightly after almost 100 years of history. But, we must look to the future and the best interests of our company, our employees and our other customers."

Lampe informed Ford of the decision during an early morning meeting at Firestone headquarters in Nashville, Tenn. attended by Carlos Mazzorin, Ford Group Vice President of Global Purchasing, and in a letter sent to Ford Motor Company CEO Jacques Nasser.

"Our analysis suggests that there is a significant safety concern with a substantial segment of Ford Explorers. We have told Ford of our concerns. They have steadfastly refused to acknowledge those concerns. We have always said that in order to insure the safety of the driving public, it is crucial that there be a true sharing of information concerning the vehicle as well as the tires. Ford simply is not willing to do that," Lampe said. "We believe they are attempting to divert scrutiny of their vehicle by casting doubt on the quality of Firestone tires. The tires are safe, and as we have said before, when we have a problem, we will acknowledge that problem and fix it. We expect Ford to do the same."

[356] *Norihiko Shirouzu and Timothy Aeppel, "Firestone Says It Acted to Improve Problem Tires,"* The Wall Street Journal, *August 18, 2000, p. A3; David Kiley, "Ford Chief Wants to Speed Tire Recall,"* USA Today, *August 17, 2000, p. 1A.*

[357] *http://www.ford.com*

Bridgestone/Firestone Inc. will honor the terms of its existing agreements but will enter into no new tire sales agreements in the Americas with Ford beginning today. A copy of the letter (pdf) sent from Mr. Lampe to Mr. Nasser is included with this release.

The CEOs of the two companies exchanged letters regarding their respective decisions. Jacques Nasser, the CEO of Ford, wrote to Firestone's CEO, John Lampe, "We are deeply disappointed that upon hearing and seeing this analysis of Firestone Wilderness AT tires, Firestone decided not to work together for the safety of our shared customers."

John Lampe's letter included the following, "Our analysis suggests that there are significant safety issues with a substantial segment of Ford Explorers. We have made your staff aware of our concerns. They have steadfastly refused to acknowledge those issues." The letter can be found at: http://mirror.bridgestone-firestone.com/homeimgs/Ford-Nasser.pdf Firestone also responded with the following press release after Ford's announcement:

Statement by John Lampe, Chairman, CEO and President Bridgestone/Firestone, Inc.[358]

NASHVILLE, Tenn. (May 22, 2001)—No one cares more about the safety of the people who travel on our tires than we do. Our tires are safe. When we have a problem, we admit it and we fix it. We've proven that.

The real issue here is the safety of the Explorer. Ford refused to look at issues surrounding the Explorer in August. Ford failed to do that today.

We stand by our tires and look forward to the opportunity to show Congress, NHTSA and the American public why our tires are safe and that there are significant safety concerns with the Ford Explorer.

Firestone also requested that the federal government conduct an investigation and released the following statement:

Firestone Requests NHTSA Investigation into Ford Explorer Safety[359]

NASHVILLE, Tenn. (May 31, 2001)—Citing the findings of a well-respected vehicle expert, Bridgestone/Firestone, Inc. President and CEO John T. Lampe today requested that the National Highway Traffic Safety Administration (NHTSA) begin an investigation into the safety of certain models of the Ford Explorer.

The company said its analysis clearly shows that a substantial segment of Ford Explorers are "defectively designed," putting the driver and the passengers at increased risk during routine, foreseeable highway driving maneuvers following events such as a tread separation. According to Lampe, "The company today presented the NHTSA with a testing analysis of certain Explorers that shows there is a serious safety issue with the vehicle. As a result, the company is asking the agency to begin an investigation into this potential safety defect."

Dr. Dennis A. Guenther, Professor of Mechanical Engineering at The Ohio State University, conducted the study cited by Lampe. Dr. Guenther's study shows that in

[358] *Courtesy: Bridgestone/Firestone Americas Holding, Inc.*

[359] Id.

most circumstances, certain models of the Explorer will experience an "oversteer" condition following a tread separation on a rear tire, a clearly foreseeable event.

The Firestone report released today on Dr. Dennis Guenther's study quotes the professor saying: "An oversteer vehicle is not safe at highway speeds in the hands of an average driver. This must be regarded as a highway safety defect within the meaning of NHTSA's charter."

Based on his initial findings, Dr. Guenther has concluded that the Explorer as tested is defectively designed in that it has an inadequate margin of control to permit control by average drivers in the foreseeable event of tread separation during normal highway driving in most load and turning circumstances. This makes the Explorer's handling imprecise and unpredictable in foreseeable circumstances, such as tread separation where precise and predictable handling is essential to safe vehicle control.

As noted by Dr. Guenther, the engineering literature proves that a tread separation does not ordinarily cause a vehicle to lose control.

Commenting on the issue of foreseeable circumstances, Lampe said, "All tires can and some do fail. That's why vehicles carry a spare tire. When tires fail, either from a tread separation or a road hazard or other causes, drivers should be able to pull over, not rollover. The Explorer does not appear to give the driver that margin of safety to make it to the side of the road and change the tire."

Dr. Guenther's investigation has found that:

- The Explorer as designed has a significantly lower amount of understeer than other SUV's. In fact, the Explorers that were tested had less than half the amount of understeer as the Jeep Cherokee and Chevrolet Blazer. "Understeer" is a cornering situation where the front of a vehicle turns less sharply than the driver intends. (Virtually all passenger vehicles are designed for understeer rather than for oversteer so the vehicle can be easily controlled by the average driver. Car designers can increase or decrease the amount of understeer in a vehicle by many different means—by adjusting spring rates, shock absorber stiffness, frame stiffness, roll damping, tire properties, tire pressure weight distribution, and other component functions.) Understeer is compensated for by the addition of more steering input.
- The Explorer loses much of what understeer it has when it is loaded to the vehicle design limit while the Cherokee and the Blazer do not.
- Following a tread separation on a rear tire, the Explorer loses its small amount of understeer. This results in an oversteer condition. A vehicle with an oversteer situation is generally not controllable by most drivers, particularly at highway speeds. "Oversteer" is a cornering condition where the front of the vehicle turns more sharply than the driver intends during a turn while the rear of the vehicle skids around. For example, if a vehicle is in a turn and an oversteering condition exists, the driver may have the impression that the rear end of the vehicle is swinging out. A vehicle with an oversteer condition is increasingly difficult to control as speed increases.

The tests performed by Dr. Guenther were standard vehicle dynamics test procedures. The vehicles tested were 1996 Ford Explorer 4-door 4X2, 2000 Ford Explorer 4-door 4X2, 2001 Jeep Cherokee 4-door 4X2, and 1996 Chevrolet Blazer 4-door 4X2. The tests were performed over the last month at the Transportation Research Center, the same facility that the NHTSA uses for a variety of vehicles tests.

Dr. Guenther's analysis will be continuing and Firestone has committed to providing the NHTSA and Congress with updates as additional information from the ongoing study becomes available.

"Firestone's priority has and will continue to be the safety of our customers. We will continue to provide information to the NHTSA, the Congress and the public concerning the vehicle and the tire," said Lampe. "As I have said many times in the past, it is critically important to look at the tire and the vehicle as an integrated system. What affects one, affects the other."

A copy of the letter sent to NHTSA Acting Administrator L. Robert Shelton is attached along with Firestone's report and Dr. Guenther's analysis. Firestone has also sent a copy of its report addressing Dr. Guenther's analysis to the Ford Motor Company. In addition, a copy of Firestone's report on Dr. Guenther's analysis is available through Firestone's media hotline, 877-201-2373

Firestone also released a statement from General Motors which reaffirmed its support for Firestone products:

GM Reaffirms Commitment to Bridgestone/Firestone Products[360]

NASHVILLE, Tenn. (May 24, 2001)—Contrary to published reports circulating today, General Motors and Bridgestone/Firestone are continuing their long-standing relationship. GM currently purchases and intends to continue to purchase both Firestone and Bridgestone brand tires from Bridgestone/Firestone.

Said William J. Kemp, Executive Director of Safety Communications for GM, "Bridgestone/Firestone is a valued supplier and we are proud to offer both the Firestone and the Bridgestone brands as original equipment tires on our vehicles. These tires perform, and have always performed, in a safe and outstanding manner for us and our customers."

"We are very gratified by the support and confidence shown by GM in our company and our products," said Christine Karbowiak, VP Public Affairs for Bridgestone/Firestone. "We are proud to be the recipient of the prestigious 'GM Supplier of the Year' award for six straight years, including the award presented this past April. We look forward to many years of a mutually beneficial relationship with GM."

Ford posted the following press release on its Explorers.[361]

Myths & Facts About the Explorer

Myth: SUVs are unsafe because they roll over. SUV owners would be better off driving cars.

Fact: That's false. Advances in safety technology have made all types of passenger vehicles safer than the vehicles on the road a generation ago. And Ford's analysis of federal and state government safety data shows that, overall, SUVs are even safer than

[360] *http://www.gm.com*

[361] *http://www.ford.com*

passenger cars. That's because SUVs are involved in fewer accidents—SUV drivers often have better lines of sight and SUVs are more visible to other drivers. Also, SUV occupants are often better protected when they are involved in collisions.

Although SUVs are involved in more rollover crashes than passenger cars, there is a greater risk of fatality in a passenger car in frontal, side and rear impacts. As a result, SUVs are safer overall.

SUVs do handle differently. That is a key reason that the different handling characteristics are printed on a label appearing on the visor of every SUV all automakers build.

Leading edge safety technology available later this year on the 2002 Ford Explorer—including AdvanceTrac™ electronic stability control and Ford's new Safety Canopy™—will further reduce the risk of a rollover and serious injury or death if a rollover accident occurs. But a buckled safety belt is still the best and primary line of defense for any adult occupant in a serious accident. Children should of course be in the proper restraint system (child seat, booster seat, etc.) until they are large enough to use adult safety belts.

Myth: The Ford Explorer is more prone to roll over than other SUVs.

Fact: Not true. Ford's analysis of safety data from the U.S. Department of Transportation confirms that over the past 10 years Explorer consistently ranks among the safest vehicles in its class. The fatality rate for passenger cars is 1.5 per 100 million miles of vehicle travel. The rate for compact SUVs is lower—1.3. And the Explorer is even lower at 1.1.

Focusing on rollover accidents alone, the Explorer is safer than competitive SUVs. Ford analysis of government safety data reveals that the Explorer line is involved in 19 percent fewer fatal rollovers than other similar SUVs. And, state safety data, which covers fatal and non-fatal rollovers, show that Explorers are involved in 16 percent fewer rollovers than competitive SUVs.

Myth: Ford launched this tire replacement effort to shift blame away from the Explorer. Something is wrong with the Explorer, but Ford wants people to think it's just a tire issue.

Fact: Not true. Ford Motor Company is replacing these tires because its number one priority is to ensure the safety of our customers and their families. Ford's concern is the Wilderness AT tire. The facts are as follows:

First, Ford fitted both Firestone tires and Goodyear tires on Explorers beginning in 1995 and through the 1997 model year. And the difference in performance is dramatic. For the roughly 3 million Firestone tires equipped on about 500,000 Explorers, Firestone's own claims database shows that there have been *1,183* claims of tread separation. For the 3 million Goodyear tires on another 500,000 Explorers (that have traveled more than 25 *billion* miles), there have been only *two* minor claims of tread separation according to claims information supplied by Goodyear. The performance on the Firestone AT tires on Explorer is 600 times worse than Goodyear tires on Explorer. *This remains the only apples-to-apples comparison in this issue.* If the vehicle was the issue, or at the very least a contributing factor, the tread separations between the

Firestone and Goodyear tires would be in the same ballpark. They are not even close. That's why Ford is replacing the Firestone Wilderness AT tires.

Second, when Ford engineers tested the Wilderness AT tires over the past nine months, they found that the tires were more sensitive to stresses and consistently failed at higher rates, at lower speeds and lighter loads than other tires tested, including the Goodyear tires used on Explorer.

Third, the failure rates of Firestone Wilderness AT tires differ dramatically based on the plant in which they were made. If the vehicle were the cause of these separations, the tire plant location would not make a difference in rate of tread separations reported.

Finally, Firestone CEO John Lampe testified last year before Congress under oath and said the following: "We made some bad tires and we take full responsibility for those." When a Senator asked, "Are bad tires equated to be tires that have defects of some kind," Mr. Lampe responded, "Yes, sir."

Myth: The Firestone tires performed far better on the Ranger than the Explorer. That's proof that the Explorer is part of the reason for these tire failures.

Fact: The tires have performed better on Ranger, however the Firestone tread separation claims on Ranger are still higher than average. And, importantly, the Firestone tread separation claims on Ranger are higher than Goodyear claims on Explorer.

In the June 11, 2001-dated issue of Business Week, Brian O'Neill, president of the Insurance Institute for Highway Safety, was asked about the Explorer-Ranger comparison. He said, "It's an apples-to-oranges comparison that has no validity in my opinion."

Ford agrees with Mr. O'Neill. Tires used on any SUV perform differently compared with tires installed on a pickup. The two vehicles are used differently. SUVs typically weigh more, and frequently are more heavily loaded, putting more stress on the tires. A sensitive tire, like we have discovered with the Wilderness AT, will not perform as well under these conditions.

Nevertheless, the larger-than-average numbers of tread separation claims for Firestone tires on Rangers *are* proof—proof that these tires should be replaced. This is why Wilderness AT tires on Ranger are part of Ford's replacement campaign.

Myth: Even if the Explorer does not cause the tread separation, it certainly is more likely to roll over as a result of the tread separation.

Fact: Not true. Ford has conducted many tests comparing Explorer with competitive SUVs and we have shared our findings with the National Highway Traffic Safety Administration. By inducing a tread separation at speeds approaching 70 mph on Explorer and competitive vehicles, with various load conditions, the Explorer's performance before, during and after a tread separation was found to be typical of other SUVs. This exhaustive study was shared with NHTSA *and* Firestone in March 2001.

The real-world accident experience shows when a Firestone tire separated on an Explorer, a rollover accident occurred on average less than 7 percent of the time. This information is based on Firestone's own claims data. Government data show Explorer and competitive SUVs have similar rollover experience in tire-related accidents. Unfortunately, Firestone tires on Explorer have separated with far greater frequency than tires on other SUVs and, of course, Goodyear tires on Explorer. *The two known Goodyear tire separations, out of about 3 million Goodyear tires in service on Explorers over the last six years, did not result in any accidents, rollovers or injuries.*

Myth: Safetyforum says that when tires fail on Explorers the results are four times more likely to produce catastrophic rollover than when they fail on other SUVs.

Fact: Ford's analysis of government data show that the Explorer has a considerably better safety record than other SUVs both in terms of fatal crashes and fatal rollover crashes. Safetyforum is misinterpreting data by using unverified reports for a variety of manufacturers. It's also misleading because it compares the Explorer to all light trucks and not just competitive SUVs.

Ford and the U.S. government use tire makers' claims data, not this collection of unverified reports. Even Safetyforum, which is a plaintiff's attorney resource organization, says they do not take into account the tire model in their analysis. The fact is that Ford's testing shows Explorers perform like other SUVs before, during and after a tire tread separation, and real world safety data show that Explorer is among the safest vehicles on the road year after year.

Myth: Internal memos show that Ford knew about the instability of the Explorer years ago and did nothing.

Fact: That's just plain wrong. The Explorer team sought to develop a safe vehicle, recognizing that safety performance among the leaders in its class would help it to become the sales leader. And that's just what they accomplished—over the past 10 years Explorer consistently has ranked among the safest vehicles in its class based on Ford's analysis of the Federal government's real world database of crash statistics. And Explorer has been the best-selling SUV in the world each year.

Memos from engineers working on the original Explorer show them working hard to make it a safety leader, and sweating over small changes necessary for prototype vehicles to pass Ford's stringent internal safety tests that ensure safe, predictable vehicle responses in severe "limit handling" maneuvers. And yes, from time to time, they debated among themselves in their search for the optimum solutions. That is what our engineers get paid to do. If any version of those prototypes didn't pass every stringent test, changes were made until they did. That's exactly why prototypes are built. By the time the first Explorer was driven by the first customer on a real road, the vehicle had passed all of Ford's internal safety tests.

Myth: Ford has spent a lot of time looking at tires as the root cause of the problem and has done little to evaluate Explorer handling due to tire separation and rollover. It seems odd that Ford has relied solely on government data for its analysis.

Fact: While important, government data is not the only part of the evaluation of the Explorer. On March 28 and 29, 2001, Ford presented NHTSA with an exhaustive analysis of Explorer. (This technical analysis is available from NHTSA.) The analysis included stringent on-road and computer-aided testing of the Explorer and comparative SUVs in its class. The analysis dissected the performance of every major component of the

Explorer that has anything to do with ride and handling, including emergency handling maneuvers and tread separation of the tires. Contrary to recent Firestone charges, it is a fact that Firestone received this thorough analysis from Ford on March 30, 2001.

The conclusion: Before, during and after a tread separation the Explorer controllability is typical of comparative SUVs. Bring in the government's data and these conclusions are consistent in the real world where analysis of statistics from the U.S. Department of Transportation shows that over the past 10 years Explorer consistently ranks among the safest vehicles in its class. The fatality rate for passenger cars is 1.5 per 100 million miles of vehicle travel. The rate for compact SUVs is lower—1.3. And the Explorer is even lower at 1.1. Likewise, focusing solely on rollover accidents, the Explorer is safer than its competition. Government figures reveal that Explorers are involved in 19 percent fewer fatal rollovers than other competitive SUVs. The same is true for single-vehicle rollover accidents—Explorer is safer than other similar-sized SUVs.

Myths & Facts About the Firestone Tires

Myth: Explorer's 26 psi recommended tire pressure is too low. That's why the tires failed.

Fact: Not true. The 2.9 million Goodyear tires performing at world-class levels on Ford Explorers convincingly disprove this myth. The recommended tire pressure for the Goodyear tires also was and, importantly, still is 26 psi. Yet the Goodyear tires are not showing the same tread separation problems. If tire pressure were really the issue, why isn't it an issue for the Goodyear tires? In addition, the extensive analysis by Ford and Firestone's independent experts show that inflation pressure generally does not cause tread separations on robust tires unless the tire is operated substantially below 26 psi.

Incidentally, the 16-inch Wilderness AT tires in the replacement program have a recommended pressure of 30 psi. Ford's analysis of Firestone's latest claims data (May 2001) showed increasing failure rates for the 16-inch tires similar to the failure rates of the 15-inch tires made in the same plant.

Myth: Ford told Firestone to decrease tire pressure to 26 psi so the vehicle could pass Ford's handling exercises and/or reduce the center of gravity. That increased the heat of the tire and caused these tread separations.

Fact: Not true. Working with Firestone, Ford engineers selected the recommended tire pressure for Explorer to optimize numerous vehicle and tire characteristics including ride quality and handling. The tire pressure selected—26 psi—is not unusual. Dozens of other competitive light trucks, SUVs, and passenger cars run on similar sized (15-inch) tires specified at 26 psi. Ford did not recommend 26 psi to lower the Explorer's center of gravity, since tire pressure has nothing to do with a vehicle's center of gravity. A 4 psi decrease (30 psi to 26 psi) lowers the center of gravity by 90 thousands of an inch (about the thickness of a nickel).

As was said earlier, the 16-inch Wilderness AT tires in the replacement program have a recommended pressure of 30 psi. Ford's analysis of Firestone's latest claims data (May 2001) showed increasing failure rates for the 16-inch tires similar to the failure rates of the 15-inch tires made in the same plant.

Myth: Firestone never agreed with Ford's recommended 26 psi tire pressure.

Fact: Firestone consistently supported Ford's recommended inflation pressure, at least until NHTSA opened its investigation in May 2000. In fact, Firestone delivered tires and paid warranty claims on those tires, year after year, under the 26 psi specification. In addition, the catalogs that Firestone issued to its dealers and customers from 1993 through 2000 state that Firestone, not just Ford, recommended 26 psi on the 15-inch tires. Furthermore, Firestone CEO Masatoshi Ono, told the Wall Street Journal on August 18, 2000, that "we do not believe Ford's recommendation of 26 psi [pounds per square inch] for our tires was a mistake." Firestone approved the 26 psi recommendation in December 1989, prior to Explorer production. Goodyear also concurred in the recommendation when Ford bought Goodyear tires for Explorer.

Myth: Tires cannot tell where they have been placed on a vehicle. Yet most of the Firestone tread separations on Explorer occurred on the left rear tire. That's a sign it's the vehicle that is causing this.

Fact: False. Firestone claim data shows the same pattern for nearly all trucks and SUVs. It's consistent for GM and Daimler-Chrysler vehicles as well as Ford vehicles—the rear tires have more tread separation claims for property damage or injury than the front tires and the left rear tire tread separation claims outnumber the right rear tire tread separation claims.

Myth: Ford knew, or should have known, last summer that the recall should have been wider and are only now reluctantly replacing all the Wilderness AT tires.

Fact: Not true. Ford didn't have all the information last summer that it has today. Last summer, Ford's review of the Firestone claims data showed alarming failure rates for Firestone 15-inch ATX and Decatur-built 15-inch Wilderness AT tires. And so Ford urged Firestone to recall those tires. The Firestone claims data available to Ford *at the time* showed other Firestone Wilderness AT tires performing at world-class levels with no crashes, no rollovers, no injuries and no fatalities.

Since last August, Ford has invested nearly 100,000 people-hours studying tires, testing tires on rigs, pouring over field analysis and conducting tire design case studies. Then, after repeated requests, Ford obtained on May 11, 2001, additional claims data from Firestone—another piece of the puzzle that confirmed Ford's research and analysis. That data showed significantly increasing failure rates for some Wilderness AT tires and raised serious questions about the long-term durability of all of the non-recalled Wilderness AT tires. Once it obtained this information, Ford did not wait and took this preventive action to protect its customers.

Myth: Ford replaced the 16-inch Wilderness ATs overseas more than a year ago. That's proof Ford knew about the problem before last summer.

Fact: False. Ford had not, in fact, found the same failure pattern in the U.S. as it had in the overseas locations where unique usage and environmental conditions existed. Nor did Ford see the same failure pattern in the U.S. that it saw overseas. However, more recently we have seen warning signs in the U.S. that led Ford to take this action as a precautionary measure.

Myth: Ford should not have accepted "C" temperature-rated tires from Firestone. They are only tested to 85 mph.

Fact: The Firestone Wilderness AT tires are, in fact, certified to 112 mph at full vehicle loads.

The confusion is that there are two different tests used to rate tire characteristics. One test, for temperature rating, is run on a test drum with huge loads placed on the tire—far greater than the tires experience in the real world even when the vehicle is fully loaded. The 85-mph threshold a tire must pass on the test drum to be certified actually translates to speeds significantly higher in on-road usage by our customers.

A "C" temperature-rated tire is an appropriate tire for a vehicle if the tire is well manufactured and meets the performance criteria set by the automaker. Tires certified with a "C" temperature label have passed a stringent government standard, and are therefore determined to be fully acceptable. In fact, there are millions of "C" tires on some GM, Toyota and Nissan SUVs and light trucks and these tires appear to have performed well.

There is a separate test that certifies tires for a speed rating. This test is run at higher speeds and full vehicle loads. All Wilderness AT tires are speed rated "S" and are certified to 112 mph, substantially higher than the top speed of an Explorer.

Myth: The other companies are not replacing Firestone Wilderness AT tires on their vehicles. That means the tires are fine.

Fact: That is a decision that the other automakers have to make. Ford conducted extensive vehicle and tire testing, analyzed Firestone field data and discussed findings with NHTSA. Ford concluded that there was a growing risk of additional tire failures in the future and decided to replace all Wilderness AT tires on Ford vehicles as a precautionary measure.

Other auto companies may be using different types of Firestone Wilderness tires having different specifications. It is interesting to note that days after supporting their use of Firestone tires, some of these manufacturers acknowledged that they are replacing Firestone tires on future vehicle production.

Myths & Facts About Actions in Venezuela

Myth: The Explorer is still rolling over at high rates in Venezuela. And they now have Goodyear tires. That's more proof that it's not the tire.

Fact: Absolutely false. For one thing, there has been no attempt to make any connection between these accident reports and tire failures. For another, many of these reports of "Explorer rollovers" have actually been other vehicles misreported as Ford Explorers. Other accidents mentioned include an Explorer in heavy traffic that was rear-ended by a large truck and then sandwiched between two heavy vehicles. The vehicle did not roll over, it was not in any way a tire-related incident and, thankfully, the occupants walked away with only scratches. No one, including Firestone, should make claims or allegations based on this data that is, at best, clearly flawed.

Newly obtained data from the Venezuelan transportation authority, SETRA, show that most SUV accidents in Venezuela involve vehicles other than Explorers. In the period 2000 to 2001, there were 701 accidents reported involving SUVs, but only 9 percent involved Explorers.

This data involves both fatal and non-fatal accidents in ten Venezuelan states. Two other competitors' SUVs had more fatal accidents than Explorers in Venezuela. The data was gathered and analyzed from traffic reports in the SETRA records.

The fact is Explorer, in addition to being a very popular SUV in Venezuela, has one of the safest records of any SUV in the country. Explorer's safety record in Venezuela is consistent with its performance in the U.S. where the DOT accident data confirms that Explorer is among the safest vehicles in its class.

Myth: Venezuela may ban the sale of Explorer and that's more proof that it is a dangerous vehicle.

Fact: The misinformed accusations by one Venezuelan investigator, acting on the flawed data mentioned above, does not change the fact that Explorer is a safe vehicle. The investigator has failed to substantiate any of his theories, which do not withstand any serious technical review. The Venezuelan National Assembly established an independent Technical Commission to review the investigator's allegations. Ford has been working closely with the Technical Commission and has shared its testing and analysis with them. This data and analysis disproves the investigator's allegations, including suggestions that electromagnetic interference or aerodynamic turbulence were causing vehicle rollovers.

We would expect the Venezuelan governmental agencies to act responsibly, not on a misrepresentation of hearsay.

Discussion Questions

1. Do you think it will ever be clear what happened here?
2. Who do you think will bear liability for the accidents and injuries that have resulted?
3. What conflict existed between the parties? Do you think the 95-year relationship affected the ability of both parties to see the evolving issues with the tires and the Explorer?
4. Can relationships be too long and too comfortable for the parties to confront each other?
5. What would have made the departure less acrimonious?

Sources

Bradsher, Keith, "Firestone to Stop Sales to Ford Saying It Was Used as a Scapegoat," *The New York Times*, May 22, 2001, pp. A1, C4.

Bridgestone/Firestone Web site: http://www.bridgestone-firestone.com

Kiley, David, "Ford to Replace up to 13 Million Firestone Tires," *USA Today*, May 22, 2001, p. 1A.

"Firestone Quits as Tire Supplier to Ford," *The Wall Street Journal*, May 22, 2001, pp. A3, A12.

Firestone's Web site: http://www.firestone.com

Ford's Web site: http://www.ford.com

unit 6

Business and Its Competition

A business's relations with its competitors are evidenced in its advertising, product similarity, and pricing. The heat of competition often creates dilemmas on what to say in ads or how similar to make a product.

6a

Advertising Content

Ads sell products. But how much can the truth be stretched? Are ads ever irresponsible by encouraging harmful behavior?

CASE 6.1

Joe Camel: The Cartoon Character Who Sold Cigarettes and Nearly Felled an Industry

Old Joe Camel, originally a member of a circus that passed through Winston-Salem, North Carolina, each year, was adopted by R.J. Reynolds (RJR) marketers in 1913 as the symbol for a brand being changed from "Red Kamel" to "Camel." In the late 1980s, RJR revived Old Joe with a new look in the form of a cartoon. He became the camel with a "Top Gun" flier jacket, sunglasses, a smirk, and a lot of appeal to young people.

In December 1991, the *Journal of the American Medical Association (JAMA)* published three surveys that found that the cartoon character Joe Camel reached children very effectively. Of children between the ages of 3 and 6 who were surveyed, 51.1 percent recognized Joe Camel as being associated with Camel cigarettes.[1] The 6-year-olds were as familiar with Joe Camel as they were with the Mickey Mouse logo for the Disney Channel. The surveys also established that 97.7 percent of students between the ages of 12 and 19 have seen Old Joe and 58 percent thought the ads he was used in were cool. Camel was identified by 33 percent of the students who smoke as their favorite brand.[2]

Before the survey results appeared in *JAMA*, the American Cancer Society, the American Heart Association, and the American Lung Association had petitioned the FTC to ban the ads as "one of the most egregious examples in recent history of tobacco advertising that targets children."[3]

[1] *Kathleen Deveny, "Joe Camel Ads Reach Children, Research Finds,"* The Wall Street Journal, *December 11, 1991, p. B1.*

[2] *Walecia Konrad, "I'd Toddle a Mile for a Camel,"* Business Week, *December 23, 1991, p. 34. While the studies and their methodology have been questioned, their impact was made before the challenges and questions were raised.*

[3] *Deveny, "Joe Camel Ads Reach Children," p. B1.*

In 1990, Camel shipments rose 11.3 percent. Joe Camel helped RJR take its Camel cigarettes from 2.7 to 3.1 percent of the market.[4]

Michael Pertschuk, former FTC head co-director of the Advocacy Institute, an antismoking group, said, "These are the first studies to give us hard evidence, proving what everybody already knows is true: These ads target kids. I think this will add impetus to the movement to further limit tobacco advertising.[5] Joe Tye, founder of Stop Teenage Addictions to Tobacco, stated, "There is a growing body of evidence that teen smoking is increasing. And it's 100 percent related to Camel."[6]

A researcher who worked on the December 1991 *JAMA* study, Dr. Joseph R. DiFranza, stated, "We're hoping this information leads to a complete ban of cigarette advertising."[7] Dr. John Richards summarized the study as follows, "The fact is that the ad is reaching kids, and it is changing their behavior."[8]

RJR spokesman David Fishel responded to the allegations with sales evidence: "We can track 98 percent of Camel sales; and they're not going to youngsters. It's simply not in our best interest for young people to smoke, because that opens the door for the government to interfere with our product."[9] At the time the survey results were published, RJR, along with other manufacturers and the Tobacco Institute, began a multimillion-dollar campaign with billboards and bumper stickers to discourage children from smoking but announced it had no intention of abandoning Joe Camel. The Tobacco Institute publishes a free popular pamphlet called "Tobacco: Helping Youth Say No."

Former U.S. Surgeon General Antonia Novello was very vocal in her desire to change alcohol and cigarette advertising. In March 1992, she called for the withdrawal of the Joe Camel ad campaign: "In years past, R.J. Reynolds would have us walk a mile for a Camel. Today it's time that we invite old Joe Camel himself to take a hike."[10] The AMA's executive vice president, Dr. James S. Todd, concurred:

> This is an industry that kills 400,000 per year, and they have got to pick up new customers. We believe the company is directing its ads to the children who are 3, 6 and 9 years old.[11]

Cigarette sales are, in fact, declining 3 percent per year in the United States.

The average Camel smoker is 35 years old, responded an RJR spokeswoman: "Just because children can identify our logo doesn't mean they will use our product."[12] Since the introduction of Joe Camel, however, Camel's share of the under-eighteen market has climbed to 33 percent from 5 percent. Among 18- to 25-year-olds, Camel's market share has climbed to 7.9 percent from 4.4 percent.

[4] *Konrad, "I'd Toddle a Mile for a Camel," p. 34.*

[5] *Deveny, "Joe Camel Ads Reach Children," p. B6.*

[6] *Laura Bird, "Joe Smooth for President,"* Adweek's Marketing Week, *May 20, 1991, p. 21.*

[7] *Konrad, "I'd Toddle a Mile for a Camel," p. 34.*

[8] *"Camels for Kids,"* Time, *December 23, 1991, p. 52.*

[9] Id.

[10] *William Chesire, "Don't Shoot: It's Only Joe Camel,"* Arizona Republic, *March 15, 1992, p. C1.*

[11] Id.

[12] *Konrad, "I'd Toddle a Mile for a Camel," p. 34.*

The Centers for Disease Control reported in March 1992 that smokers between the ages of 12 and 18 prefer Marlboro, Newport, or Camel cigarettes, the three brands with the most extensive advertising.[13]

Teenagers throughout the country were wearing Joe Camel T-shirts. Brown & Williamson, the producer of Kool cigarettes, began testing a cartoon character for its ads, a penguin wearing sunglasses and Day-Glo sneakers. Company spokesman Joseph Helewicz stated that the ads are geared to smokers between 21 and 35 years old. Helewicz added that cartoon advertisements for adults are not new and cited the Pillsbury Doughboy and the Pink Panther as effective advertising images.

In mid-1992, then-Surgeon General Novello, along with the American Medical Association, began a campaign called "Dump the Hump" to pressure the tobacco industry to stop ad campaigns that teach kids to smoke. In 1993, the FTC staff recommended a ban on the Joe Camel ads. In 1994, then-Surgeon General Joycelyn Elders blamed the tobacco industry's $4 billion in ads for increased smoking rates among teens. RJR's tobacco division chief, James W. Johnston, responded, "I'll be damned if I'll pull the ads."[14] RJR put together a team of lawyers and others it referred to as in-house censors to control Joe's influence. A campaign to have Joe wear a bandana was nixed, as was one for a punker Joe with pink hair.[15]

In 1994, RJR CEO James Johnston testified before a Congressional panel on the Joe Camel controversy and stated, "We do not market to children and will not," and added, "We do not survey anyone under the age of 18."[16]

As health issues related to smokers continued to expand, along with product liability litigation and state attorneys' general pursuit of compensation for their states' health system costs of smokers, more information about the Joe Camel campaign was discovered. Lawyers in a California suit against RJR discovered charts from a presentation at a September 30, 1974 Hilton Head, South Carolina, retreat of RJR top executives and board.[17] The charts offered the following information:

company	*brand*	*share of 14–24-year-old market*
Philip Morris	Marlboro	33%
Brown & Williamson	Kool	17%
Reynolds	Winston	14%
Reynolds	Salem	9%[18]

RJR's then-vice president of marketing, C.A. Tucker, said, "As this 14–24 age group matures, they will account for a key share of total cigarette volume for at least the next 25 years."[19] The meeting then produced a plan for increasing RJR's presence among

[13] *"Selling Death,"* Mesa Tribune, *March 16, 1992, p. A8.*

[14] *Anna White, "Joe Camel's World Tour,"* The New York Times, *April 23, 1997, p. A21.*

[15] *Melanie Wells and Chris Woodyard, "FTC Says Joe Camel Tobacco Icon Targeted Young,"* USA Today, *May 29, 1991, p. 1A.*

[16] *Milo Geyelin, "Reynolds Aimed Specifically to Lure Young Smokers Years Ago, Data Suggest,"* The Wall Street Journal, *January 15, 1998, p. A4.*

[17] *Doug Levy and Melanie Wells, "Papers: RJR Did Court Teens,"* USA Today, *January 15, 1998, pp. 1A, 1B.*

[18] *Eben Shapiro, "FTC Staff Recommends Ban of Joe Camel Campaign,"* The Wall Street Journal, *August 11, 1994, pp. B1, B8.*

[19] *Bruce Horovitz and Doug Levy, "Tobacco Firms Try to Sow Seeds of Self-Regulation,"* USA Today, *May 16, 1996, pp. 1B, 2B.*

the under-35 age group which included sponsoring NASCAR auto racing. Another memo described plans to study "the demographics and smoking behavior of 14-to-17 year olds."[20]

Internal documents about targeting young people were damaging. A 1981 RJR internal memo on marketing surveys cautioned research personnel to tally underage smokers as "age 18."[21] A 1981 Philip Morris internal document indicated information about smoking habits in children as young as 15 was important because "today's teenager is tomorrow's potential regular customer."[22] Other Philip Morris documents from the 1980s expressed concerns that Marlboro sales would soon decline because teenage smoking rates were falling.[23]

A 1987 marketing survey in France and Canada by RJR before it launched the Joe Camel campaign showed that the cartoon image with its fun and humor attracted attention. One 1987 internal document uses the phrase "young adult smokers"[24] and notes a target campaign to the competition's "male Marlboro smokers ages 13–24."[25]

A 1997 survey of 534 teens by *USA Today* revealed the following:

ad	*have seen ad*	*liked ad*
Joe Camel	95%	65%
Marlboro Man	94%	44%[26]
Budweiser Frogs	99%	92%

Marlboro was the brand smoked by most teens in the survey. The survey found 28 percent of teens between the ages of 13 and 18 smoke—an increase of 4 percent since 1991.[27] In 1987, Camels were the cigarette of choice for 3 percent of teenagers when Joe Camel debuted. By 1993, the figure had climbed to 16 percent.[28]

In early 1990, the Federal Trade Commission (FTC) began an investigation of RJR and its Joe Camel ads to determine whether underage smokers were illegally targeted by the ten-year Joe Camel Campaign.[29] The FTC had dismissed a complaint in 1994, but did not have the benefits of the newly-discovered internal memos.[30]

By late 1997, RJR began phasing out Joe Camel.[31] New Camel ads feature men and women in their 20s, with a healthy look, in clubs and swimming pools with just a dromedary logo somewhere in the ad. Joe continued as a youth icon. A "Save Joe Camel" Web site developed and Joe Camel paraphernalia brought top dollar. A Joe

[20] *Bruce Ingersoll, "Joe Camel Ads Illegally Target Kids, FTC Says,"* The Wall Street Journal, *May 29, 1997, pp. B1, B8.*

[21] *Suein L. Hwang, Timothy Noah, and Laurie McGinley, "Philip Morris Has Its Own Youth-Smoking Plan,"* The Wall Street Journal, *May 16, 1996, pp. B1, B4.*

[22] *Geyelin, "Reynolds Aimed Specifically to Lure Young Smokers Years Ago," p. A4.*

[23] *Barry Meier, "Tobacco Executives Wax Penitent Before House Panel in Hopes of Preserving Accord,"* The New York Times, *January 30, 1998, p. A15.*

[24] *Wells and Woodyard, "FTC Says Joe Camel Tobacco Icon Targeted Young," p. 1A.*

[25] Id.

[26] *"Joe Camel Shills to Kids,"* USA Today, *June 2, 1997, p. 12A.*

[27] Id.

[28] *Alan Kline, "Joe Camel is One Species the Government Wants Extinct,"* Washington Times, *June 8, 1997, p. 10.*

[29] *Doug Levy, "Blowing Smoke?"* USA Today, *January 15, 1998, pp. 1B, 2B.*

[30] *Shapiro, "FTC Staff Recommends Ban of Joe Camel Campaign," pp. B1, B8.*

[31] *"Smokin' Joe Camel Near His Last Gasp,"* Time, *June 9, 1997, p. 47.*

Camel shower curtain sold for $200. RJR also vowed not to feature the Joe Camel character on non-tobacco items such as T-shirts. The cost of the abandonment was estimated at $250 million.[32]

Philip Morris proposed its own plan to halt youth smoking in 1996, which includes no vending machine ads, no billboard ads, no tobacco ads in magazines with 15 percent or more of youth subscribers, and limits on sponsorships to events (rodeos, motor sports) where 75 percent or more of attendees are adults.[33, 34]

It was also in 1997 that the combined pressure from Congress, the state attorneys general, and ongoing class action suits produced what came to be known as "the tobacco settlement." The tobacco settlement in all of its various forms bars outdoor advertising, the use of human images (Marlboro man) and cartoon characters, and vending-machine sales. This portion of the settlement was advocated by those who were concerned that teenagers and their attraction to cigarettes via these ads and their availability in machines.[35]

While the governmental suits were settled, those suits focused simply on reimbursement for government programs costs in treating smokers for their health issues related to smoking. The private litigation has not ended. A Florida jury, after finding tobacco companies guilty of fraud and conspiracy, issued a damage award of $144 billion against several companies. The bulk of the award was punitive damages. The total losses to date are as follows:

$144 billion—verdict in Florida class action suit

$40 billion—settlement of Florida, Texas, and Minnesota suits

$206 billion—settlement of suits by 46 states and 5 territories

$3.4 billion—settlement of Mississippi Medicaid suit

The Florida judgment would be allocated among the tobacco companies as follows:

Phillip Morris—50%, or $73.96 billion

Lorillard—10%, or $16.25 billion

Brown & Williamson—13%, or $17.59 billion

R.J. Reynolds—24%, or $36.28 billion

The annual sales of the companies are as follows:

Phillip Morris—$19.6 billion

R.J. Reynolds—$7.5 billion

Brown & Williamson—not available

Lorillard—$4.0 billion

Liggett—$423 million[36]

[32] *Maria Mallory, "That's One Angry Camel,"* Business Week, *March 7, 1994, pp. 94, 95.*

[33] *Horovitz and Levy, "Tobacco Firms Try to Sow Seeds of Self-Regulation," pp. 1B, 2B.*

[34] *Gary Rausch, "Tobacco Firms Unite to Curb Teen Smoking,"* Mesa Tribune, *June 24, 1991, pp. B1, B6.*

[35] *Meier, "Tobacco Executives Wax Penitent Before House Panel," p. A15.*

[36] *Rick Bragg and Sarah Kershaw, "Juror Says a 'Sense of Mission' Led to Huge Tobacco Damages,"* The New York Times, *July 16, 2000, pp. A1, A16.*

Discussion Questions

1. Suppose you were the executive in charge of marketing for R.J. Reynolds. Would you have recommended an alternative to the Joe Camel character? What if RJR insisted on the Joe Camel ad?
2. Suppose you work with a pension fund that has a large investment in RJR. Would you consider selling your RJR holdings?
3. Do you agree with the statement that identification of the logo does not equate with smoking or with smoking Camels? Do regulators agree? Did the Joe Camel ads generate market growth?
4. What effect will RJR's voluntary action have on the regulatory trend?
5. Anti-tobacco activist Alan Blum said, "This business of saying 'Oh, my God, they went after kids' is ex post facto rationalization for not having done anything. It's not as if we on the do-good side didn't know that." Is he right?

Sources

Beatty, Sally Goll, "Marlboro's Billboard Man May Soon Ride Into the Sunset," *The Wall Street Journal*, July 1, 1997, pp. B1, B6.

Boot, Max, "Turning a Camel Into a Scapegoat," *The Wall Street Journal*, June 4, 1997, p. A19.

Burger, Katrina, "Joe Cashes In," *Forbes*, August 11, 1997, p. 39.

Dagnoli, Judann, "RJR Aims New Ads at Young Smokers," *Advertising Age*, July 11, 1988, pp. 2–3.

Horovitz, Bruce, and Melanie Wells, "How Ad Images Shape Habits," *USA Today*, January 31–February 2, 1997, pp. 1A, 2A.

Lippert, Barbara, "Camel's Old Joe Poses the Question: What Is Sexy?" *Adweek's Marketing Week*, October 3, 1988, p. 55.

"March against Smoking Joe," *Arizona Republic*, June 22, 1992, p. A3.

Martinez, Barbara, "Antismoking Ads Aim to Gross Out Teens," *The Wall Street Journal*, March 31, 1997, pp. B1, B5.

CASE 6.2

Alcohol Advertising: The College Focus

The mix is unquestionably there. Alcohol ads mix youth, fun, and enticing activities like scuba diving and skiing. Anheuser-Busch's Bud Light ads have Spuds MacKenzie, the "Party Animal" dog. Stroh's has its Swedish Bikini Team. Beer companies sponsor large promotions of their products on the beaches during college spring break.[37]

In 1991, then-U.S. Surgeon General Antonia Novello asked the industry to voluntarily cut ads that attract minors. Novello stated, "I must call for industry's voluntary elimination of the types of alcohol advertising that appeal to youth on the bases of certain life-style appeals, sexual appeals, sports appeal, or risky activities, as well as advertising with the more blatant youth appeals of cartoon characters and youth slang."[38] A 1991 survey revealed that 10.6 million of the 20.7 million students in grades seven through twelve had had at least one drink in the last year.[39] Of the drinking group, 8 million drank weekly, 5.4 million had drinking binges, and one-half million had five or more drinks in a row at least once a week.[40]

Industry officials maintain that they are very active in and financially supportive of programs for alcohol-use education, including Mothers against Drunk Driving.

Anheuser-Busch spends $20 million of its $260 million ad budget on a campaign that features the slogan "Know when to say when." Miller Brewing Company runs a thirty-second television ad with the slogan "Think when you drink" as part of the $8 million per year it spends to promote responsible drinking.

During spring breaks in 1991 and 1992, Miller and Anheuser-Busch did not use their multistory inflatable beer cans on popular beaches in Florida, Texas, and Mexico. In Daytona Beach, Florida, Miller put billboards along the highways with the slogan "Good beer is properly aged. You should be too." Miller's manager for alcohol and consumer issues, John Shafer, explained, "It's just good business sense to make sure we're on the right side of these issues."[41]

Patricia Taylor, a director at the Center for Science in the Public Interest, responded to the efforts by saying: "The beer companies are spending hundreds of millions every year to present a very positive image of drinking. That overwhelms all attempts to talk about the other side of the issue."[42]

Novello ordered new studies of the link between alcohol advertising and underage drinking. She also urged the industry to drop advertising meant to appeal to young people.[43] Anheuser-Busch created a campaign with ads in trade magazines and posters for stores to remind retailers not to sell beer to underage buyers. Novello responded, "These ads may be a stronger influence on students than they realize."[44]

Late in 1996, Anheuser-Busch announced that it would stop advertising its beer on MTV. Anheuser-Busch spent $534 million on advertising in 1995, with MTV spending equaling $2 million of that total budget. However, television is known as the best

[37] *The industry promoted products with multi-story inflatable beer cans. Jeffrey Zbar, "Spring Break, Inflatable Beer Bottles Gone but Other Marketers Move In,"* Advertising Age, *April 1, 1991, p. 16.*

[38] *Hilary Sout, "Surgeon General Wants to Age Alcohol Ads,"* The Wall Street Journal, *November 5, 1991, p. B1.*

[39] *Julia Flynn Siler, "It Isn't Miller Time Yet, and This Bud's Not for You,"* Business Week, *June 24, 1991, p. 52.*

[40] Id.

[41] Id.

[42] Id.

[43] *Stuart Elliott, "A Rising Tide of Rhetoric over Warnings on Alcohol,"* The New York Times, *April 2, 1991, p. D18.*

[44] Id.

method for reaching Generation X buyers. The ads were shifted to VH1. Coors has never advertised on MTV, stating "we don't like to walk the fine line." Miller Brewing Company continues its MTV ads.

In 1998, the American Academy of Pediatrics and the American Public Health Association joined together to launch a campaign to ask Anheuser-Busch to stop using frogs, lizards, and other amphibians in its ads. The posters for these two groups trace beer ads from Spuds MacKenzie to Frank and Louis, the lizards, and ask, "Fed up with beer ads that look like cartoons?" The posters liken the animals to Joe Camel. The two groups also ran a presentation to shareholders at Anheuser-Busch's 1998 annual meeting. They were joined by Mothers Against Drunk Driving, the Marin Institute, and the Center on Alcohol Advertising.

Anheuser-Busch issued a response to the campaign noting that drunk-driving fatalities involving teens and underage drinking have both declined since 1982, and that Anheuser-Busch has spent $200 million since that time on education programs designed to halt underage drinking. Also, Anheuser-Busch did voluntarily abandon, in 1997, the frogs that refrained "Bud-weis-er."

Discussion Questions

1. Suppose you were an officer of a brewery whose advertising campaign targets young adults (18–21). Would you change the campaign?
2. Wouldn't your ads appeal to various groups regardless of their focus?
3. Would it be censorship for the government to control the content of your ads?
4. Are campaigns on responsible drinking sufficient?
5. Do beer companies' ads attempt to encourage underage people to drink?

Sources

Balu, Rekha, "Anheuser-Busch Amphibian Ads Called Cold-Blooded by Doctors," *The Wall Street Journal*, April 10, 1998, p. B6.

Buck, Rinker, "Ode to Miller Beer," *Adweek's Marketing Week*, May 27, 1991, p. 16.

Colford, Steven W., "FTC May Crash Beer Promos' Campus Party," *Advertising Age*, March 25, 1991, pp. 3–4.

Horovitz, Bruce, "Brewer to Stop Ads on MTV," *USA Today*, December 23, 1996, p. 1A.

Wells, Melanie, "Budweiser Frogs Will be Put Out to Pasture," *USA Today*, January 14, 1997, pp. 1B, 8B.

Yang, Catherine, and Stan Crock, "The Spirited Brawl Ahead Over Liquor Ads on TV," *Business Week*, December 16, 1996, p. 47.

CASE 6.3

The Obligation to Screen? The Obligation to Reject—*Soldier of Fortune* Classifieds[45]

Soldier of Fortune (SOF) is a national magazine focused on guns and military clothing and aimed at "professional adventurers." In its large classified advertising section, individuals and companies offer guns, gun-related products, gun and equipment repairs, employment opportunities, and personal services.

Some of the classified ads printed between 1975, the magazine's debut, and 1984 offered services under such titles as "Mercenary for Hire," "Bounty Hunter," "High-Risk Contracts," "Dirty Work," "Mechanic," and "Do Anything, Anywhere at the Right Price." During this period, *SOF* ran 2,000 classified ads, about three dozen of which had titles like these.

Various media, including the Associated Press, United Press International, *Rocky Mountain News, Denver Post, Time,* and *Newsweek,* reported links between *SOF* classified ads and crimes or criminal plots. These connections were made directly to five specific *SOF* ads and alleged with four others. Law enforcement officials contacted *SOF* staffers in investigating two crimes linked to personal service ads in the magazine.

Nature of *SOF* Ads

Dr. Park Dietz, a forensic psychiatrist, concluded from his study of the ads that the average *SOF* subscriber—a male who owns camouflage clothing and more than one gun—would understand some phrases in *SOF's* classified ads as solicitations for illegal activity given the ads' context. At that time, *SOF* contained display ads for semiautomatic rifles and books with titles such as *How to Kill,* along with articles on "Harassing the Bear, New Afghan Tactics Stall Soviet Victory," "Pipestone Canyon, Summertime in 'Nam and the Dyin' Was Easy," and "Night Raiders on Russia's Border."

Dietz suggested that the *SOF* personal service ads carry the connotation of criminal activity because of the nature of the magazine. He noted that the same ads would not carry that connotation if they appeared in *Esquire* or *Vanity Fair.*

The Hearn Ad

In September, October, and November of 1984, *SOF* ran the following ad:

> EX-MARINES-67–69 'Nam Vets, Ex-DI, weapons specialist—jungle warfare, pilot, M.E., high risk assignments, U.S. or overseas. [Phone number]

"Ex-DI" means ex-drill instructor; "M.E." means multiengine planes; and "high risk assignments" means work as a bodyguard or security specialist.

The ad was placed by John Wayne Hearn, who said he wanted to recruit Vietnam veterans for work as bodyguards and security men for executives. Hearn's partner said they also hoped to train troops for South American countries. Hearn said he did not

[45] *Adapted from M. Jennings,* Legal Environment of Business, *2d ed., PWS Kent, Boston, 1991, pp. 229–231.*

place the ad with an intent to solicit criminal employment but that 90 percent of the responses to the ad sought his participation in illegal activities, such as beatings, kidnappings, jailbreaks, bombings, and murders. His only lawful inquiry was from a Lebanese oil conglomerate seeking bodyguards; Hearn received a commission to place seven men with it.

Robert Black contacted Hearn through the *SOF* ad. Between 1982 and 1984, Black had asked at least four friends or coworkers in Bryan, Texas, to kill his wife, Sandra Black, or help him kill her. Initially, Black discussed bodyguard work with Hearn, then their conversations focused on Black's gun collection. In October 1984, Hearn traveled to Texas from his Atlanta home to see Black's collection. During the visit, Black told Hearn his plans for murdering his wife. After Hearn returned to Atlanta, Black repeatedly called him. In a conversation with Debbie Bannister, Hearn's girlfriend, Black offered Hearn $10,000 to kill Black's wife. Bannister then communicated the offer to Hearn.

Hearn had no previous criminal record, but on January 6, 1985, he killed Bannister's sister. On February 2, he murdered Bannister's husband, and nineteen days later, he killed Sandra Black. He was convicted of the murders and sentenced to concurrent life terms.

The Victims' Suit against *SOF*

Sandra Black's mother, Marjorie Eimann, and her son, Gary Wayne Black, sued *SOF* for negligence in publishing Hearn's ad. The trial court awarded Eimann and Black $9.4 million in damages.

An appellate court reversed the decision, saying:

> Given the pervasiveness of advertising in our society and the important role it plays, we decline to impose on publishers the obligation to reject all ambiguous advertisements for products or services that might pose a threat of harm. The burden on a publisher to avoid liability from suits of this type is too great.[46]

Other Cases of Ad Liability

SOF was sued again over a classified ad after Douglas Norwood was ambushed, assaulted, shot, and finally killed by a car bomb late in 1985. Each of his assailants had been hired through the following *SOF* ads:

> GUN FOR HIRE: 37-year-old professional mercenary desires jobs. Vietnam Veteran. Discreet and very private. Bodyguard, courier, and other special skills. All jobs considered. [Phone number]

> GUN FOR HIRE: Nam sniper instructor. SWAT. Pistol, rifle, security specialist, bodyguard, courier plus. All jobs considered. Privacy guaranteed. Mike [Phone number].[47]

The case was settled out of court in 1987.

In another case, Richard Braun was shot and killed outside his Atlanta home by an experienced mercenary, Richard Savage, who had been hired by Braun's business associate, Bruce Gastwirth, through an ad in *Soldier of Fortune.* Savage's ad began with

[46] Eimann v. Soldier of Fortune Magazine, Inc., *880 F.2d 830 (5th Cir. 1989),* cert. denied, *493 U.S. 1024 (1990).*

[47] Norwood v. Soldier of Fortune Magazine, *651 F.Supp 1397 (W.D. Anc. 1987).*

the words "Gun for Hire." Braun's sons sued the magazine and were awarded $4.3 million. The amount was later reduced in a settlement of the case.[48]

The Association of Newspaper Classified Advertising Managers, Inc. (ANCAM) has the following policy:

> Advertisements containing statements that injure the health of readers, directly or indirectly, are not acceptable.

Another ANCAM section provides:

> Any advertisement fostering the evasion or violation of any law or making a direct or indirect offer of any article or service that violates a city, state or federal statute is unacceptable.[49]

Discussion Questions

1. Assume that you are *SOF's* new director of display and classified advertising. You know *SOF* was relieved of any liability for Sandra Black's death, so it is not obligated to check or reject ads. Your conscience, however, remains troubled as you review ads with such language as "high-risk assignment" and "bounty hunter." As you think about the Black case, you rationalize that Hearn was on a murder spree and Black was simply a victim of his sudden violence. On the other hand, Hearn would never have known Black if his classified ad had not brought a call from Robert Black. Further, only five to ten ads of over a total of 2,000 classifieds have resulted in crimes or criminal plots. You discuss this dilemma over lunch with your senior staff member, who responds: "Yes, but we could have prevented those crimes by not running the ads."

   Screening the ads will take time, private detectives, and an assumption of liability the law does not require you to make. Will you change *SOF's* ad policy? Will you conduct ad background checks?
2. Does this dilemma present conflicting moral standards?
3. To whom do you owe your loyalty in making your decision?
4. Should *SOF* feel morally responsible for Sandra Black's death?
5. Is the appellate court's decision not to impose liability on *SOF* an application of utilitarianism?
6. Should the decision on advertising policy be different following Sandra Black's murder?
7. William L. Prosser, a legal scholar, has stated, "Nearly all human acts . . . carry some recognizable possibility of harm to another." Why do we allow recovery for some of those harmful acts and not others?
8. *Soldier of Fortune* stopped accepting personal service ads in 1986. Is that an appropriate and ethical resolution?

[48] *"Military Magazine Gets Jury Judgment Reduced,"* The Wall Street Journal, *March 1, 1993, p. B3.*

[49] *Don Tomlinson, "Choosing Social Responsibility Over Law: The* Soldier of Fortune *Classified Advertising Cases,"* Business & Professional Ethics Journal *9, 1990, pp. 79–96.*

CASE 6.4

Aggressive Marketing of Prescription Drugs: Forms of Direct Sales

A national television advertising campaign began in April 1993 (during CBS-TV's "60 Minutes") on the signs of clinical depression and the importance of obtaining help. Ads on the same topic appeared in *The New York Times* and *Parade* magazine. The campaign was run by the National Mental Health Association, but the $3 to $4 million cost of the campaign was paid by Eli Lilly & Company, the manufacturer of Prozac, the top-selling antidepressant drug in the world. Lilly also gave the mental health association a $500,000 grant to help identify people who are suffering from depression and need treatment.[50]

The ads did not mention Prozac, but they did note Eli Lilly's financing. An Eli Lilly spokesman said, "It isn't a campaign to promote Prozac. It's a campaign to promote awareness."[51] Dr. Sidney Wolfe, head of the Public Citizen Health Research Group, disagreed:

> The money is given to try to curry favor with groups so they don't resist or oppose things happening with a drug. Or they become *de facto* advocates for a drug. If Lilly is doing this out of the goodness of its heart, why does it have to have its name there? They don't want to be anonymous and that's what the problem is.[52]

In defense of its donation and the ads, Lilly responded that "These programs save lives and aren't promoting any one specific product." The mental health association said, "We are working in partnership with corporate America to disseminate messages of hope and help to the American people." [53]

Other companies go beyond the "infomercial" approach of Eli Lilly and market their prescription products directly to consumers. For example, Genentech, Inc., has so successfully marketed its growth hormone (protropin/hutropin) for children that the drug is sold to 14,000 patients in the United States—twice the number estimated to have the medical condition that would warrant its use. Genentech's top sales executive was indicted on charges of bribing a Minneapolis physician to prescribe the growth hormone more often. A total of $224,000 was funneled to the physician in the form of research grants and consulting fees.[54]

Genentech sales employees have entered restricted patient areas and scattered literature among patients on Genentech's products. Further, Genentech pays doctors and nurses to contribute information to its registry on patients that describes illnesses

[50] *Joseph Weber and John Carey, "Drug Ads: A Prescription for Controversy,"* Business Week, *January 18, 1993, pp. 58, 60.*

[51] *Elyse Tanouye, "Critics See Self-Interest in Lilly's Funding of Ads Telling the Depressed to Get Help,"* The Wall Street Journal, *April 15, 1993, pp. B1, B6.*

[52] Id.

[53] *Ralph T. King, Jr., "In Marketing of Drugs, Genentech Tests Limits of What Is Acceptable,"* The Wall Street Journal, *January 10, 1995, pp. A1, A14.*

[54] Id.

and how they were treated; the registry is limited to patients who have been treated with Genentech drugs.[55]

Upjohn, the manufacturer of the antibaldness drug Rogaine, offers "free, private hair-loss consultation" with a doctor in its ads. Generally, the doctor produces a Rogaine prescription. Schering-Plough handed out $5 coupons for its antihistamine, Claritin, which customers could redeem by having their doctors prescribe the drug.[56]

The Food and Drug Administration (FDA) has been policing excessive advertising claims with fines and injunctions. However, in 1993, pharmaceutical companies spent over $200 million on ads in everything from the *New Yorker* to *Popular Mechanics*.[57] Edwin P. Maynard, past president of the American College of Physicians and former chairman of its ethics committee, said of the manufacturers: "They are taking the route of advertising directly to this vulnerable population."[58] From 1996 to 1997, ad spending by pharmaceuticals for their prescription drugs increased 90 percent.[59] In 1998, the increase was expected to be up 60 percent to $1.6 billion per year.

In 1997, the FDA liberalized its policy on direct advertising and issued new regulations permitting companies to advertise specific products without the scrolling addendum of warnings and side effects. The FDA established as its goal "realistic standards" for the companies as well as a desire to promote greater consumer awareness of prescription drugs.[60]

Discussion Questions

1. Does it matter that Eli Lilly enjoys increased sales as a result of the campaign?
2. Does a pharmaceutical company suppress opposition by making these donations?
3. Do nonprofit organizations compromise their independence by accepting funding from pharmaceutical manufacturers?
4. Do users of prescription drugs require more information than ads in the popular media can convey?
5. Are pharmaceutical firms appealing to a vulnerable population?
6. Do the ads create conflicts between physicians and patients?
7. What do you think will occur in ads for these prescription drugs? Could all parties, both physicians and patients, benefit from more information?

55 Id.

56 *Yumiko Ono, "Prescription Drug Makers Heighten Hard-Sell Tactics,"* The Wall Street Journal, *August 29, 1994, pp. B1, B4.*

57 *Holman W. Jenkins, Jr. "Is Advertising the New Wonder Drug?"* The Wall Street Journal, *March 25, 1998, p. A23.*

58 *Rose Gutfeld, "FDA Attacks Drug Makers' Ads to Doctors,"* The Wall Street Journal, *August 3, 1993, pp. B1, B6.*

59 *Ono, "Prescription Drug Makers Heighten Hard-Sell Tactics," pp. B1, B4.*

60 *Bruce Ingersoll and Yumiko Ono, "FDA to Clear Way for Blitz of TV Drug Ads,"* The Wall Street Journal, *August 8, 1997, p. B1.*

CASE 6.5

Hollywood Ads

Actress Demi Moore starred in the 1995 movie entitled *The Scarlet Letter*, which was based on Nathaniel Hawthorne's book of the same name. Hollywood Pictures ran the following quote from a *Time* magazine review: "'Scarlet Letter' Gets What It Always Needed: Demi Moore." The actual review by *Time* magazine read: "Stuffy old *Scarlet Letter* gets what it always needed: Demi Moore and a happier ending." A *Time* spokesman noted that the statement was clearly ironic. In the same review, the *Time* critic, Richard Corliss, referred to the movie as "revisionist slog" and gave it an "F."

An ad for the 1995 movie *Seven* quoted *Entertainment Weekly* as calling it a "masterpiece." The actual review read, "The credits sequence . . . is a small masterpiece of dementia."

A movie industry observer stated in response to these examples, "The practice of fudging critics' quotes [in ads] is common." However, there is more than simple "fudging." Ads for the movie *Thirteen Days* included the descriptive phrases "by-the-numbers recreation" and "close to perfect" in order to reflect what producers touted as the strength of the film—its historical accuracy. But the ads also included pictures of the Spruance-class destroyer and F-15 jet fighters. Neither of these defense systems was available in 1962, the time of the movie, which is a depiction of the 13-day Cuban missile crisis during the Kennedy administration. These systems were not developed until the 1970s.

The movie studios pulled the ads after they had run for one weekend. They also pulled those ads that showed the movie's star, Kevin Costner, walking with the actors who played John and Robert Kennedy because that scene was not a part of the movie.

In 2001, ads by Sony Studios has theater critic David Manning proclaiming that *The Animal*, starring Rob Schneider and ex-"Survivor" Colleen Haskell, was "another winner." Mr. Manning also gave a favorable review of Sony's *A Knight's Tale*. However, David Manning is fictitious. He is a critic created out of whole cloth by young marketing staff members at Sony.[61]

Discussion Questions

1. Is the practice of fudging quotes ethical? Should Hollywood Pictures have pulled the *Scarlet Letter* ads?

2. Is the practice of making up critics to provide quotes on movies ethical?

[61] *"Ads for Missile Crisis Movie Are Pulled Because of Errors,"* The New York Times, *January 13, 2001, p. A8.*

6b

Appropriation of Others' Ideas

When does an idea belong to someone else? Laws on patents and copyrights afford protection in some cases, but other situations are too close to call—or are they?

CASE 6.6

Ragu Thick and Zesty

Ragu Foods, Inc., has been the leading seller of prepared spaghetti sauce in the United States since 1972. By 1973, Ragu held over 60 percent of the market. Late in that year, Hunt-Wesson Foods, Inc., decided to enter the market with "Prima Salsa" spaghetti sauce. After extensive marketing and taste studies, Hunt's introduced its sauce in 1976 using the slogan "Extra Thick and Zesty."

Just before Hunt's launched "Prima Salsa," Ragu introduced a new sauce called "Ragu Extra Thick and Zesty." Ragu's advertising campaign used a photo similar to Hunt's of a ladle of sauce being poured over noodles. Ragu's sauce was thickened with starch, whereas Hunt's used a longer cooking process. The label on the Ragu sauce did not make this distinction clear.

Hunt's executives claimed the introduction of the Ragu sauce appropriated all their work and research and created product confusion in consumers' minds.[62]

Ragu maintained that its product was simply a response to competition and good business strategy. Hunt's claimed there can be no competition because of Ragu's domination of the market, which was 65 percent in 1975. Hunt's felt Ragu's methods were unfair.

In 1990, Ragu introduced a sauce called "Ragu Fresh Italian." The Food and Drug Administration (FDA) cited Ragu for six violations of federal labeling law that centered on the word *fresh*. FDA regulations prohibit the use of "fresh" if chemical or heat

[62] *"Critics Take Apart Label of Ragu a Word at a Time,"* Arizona Republic, *May 2, 1990, p. A7.*

processing is used. Ragu acknowledged using heat processing but maintained "fresh" is part of a trademark, not a description.[63]

In 1993, Campbell Soup introduced its Prego sauce with comparison ads that depicted Ragu as runny. Ragu sued Campbell for these "misleading ads" since Campbell did not use Ragu's Thick & Chunky sauce to compare.[64]

At the end of 1993, Ragu sauces had 36.2 percent of this $1.1 billion market (down from 50 percent in 1992), while Prego had 26.3 percent (up from 20 percent).

Discussion Questions

1. Was Ragu just an aggressive competitor, or did it appropriate ideas or mislead?
2. Are any moral standards violated by Ragu's conduct in these campaigns?
3. Would you feel comfortable with the "Prima Salsa" name if you were a marketing executive with Ragu? Or with the use of the term "fresh"?
4. Is product confusion a fair method of competition?
5. Aren't companies free to meet the market with their product lines?

CASE 6.7

The Little Intermittent Windshield Wiper and Its Little Inventor

Robert W. Kearns obtained a patent for his first intermittent car windshield wiper system in 1967. During the 1970s, intermittent wiper systems began appearing on the cars of major U.S. and Japanese automakers. Kearns received no money for the use of these systems. The automakers maintained that the idea was an obvious one and it was only a matter of time before their engineers developed the same type of system. They also claimed that their systems differed from Kearns's in design and function.

Kearns filed suit against Ford, General Motors, Chrysler, Fiat, Toyota, and other Japanese auto manufacturers. He had planned to open his own firm to supply the intermittent windshield wiper systems to all automakers but was unable to do so after the companies manufactured the systems in-house. Dr. Kearns represented himself in the cases that ran through 1995 until final resolution or settlement.

In November 1990, Kearns settled his case with Ford Motor Company for $10.2 million, which amounted to 30 cents per car Ford sold with the intermittent wiper systems. In June 1992, a jury awarded Kearns $11.3 million in damages from Chrysler, or about 90 cents per car, for Chrysler's infringement of Kearns's patent. Chrysler had

[63] Hunt-Wesson Foods, Inc. v. Ragu Foods, Inc., *627 F.2d 919 (9th Cir. 1980).*

[64] *Jack Rejtman, "Spaghetti Sauce Spat between Prego, Ragu Is Set to Thicken,"* The Wall Street Journal, *August 4, 1993, p. B5.*

sold 12,564,107 vehicles with the device. Kearns had originally asked for damages ranging from $3 to $30 per car, or $37.7 to $377 million, based on the treble damage provisions of the patent infringement laws.[65]

Kearns still has suits pending against the other car companies. He spent $4 million in legal fees in the Ford case and expects to spend $5.5 million on the case against Chrysler. Chrysler announced it will appeal the "unreasonable and excessive" verdict, however, the appeal was dismissed.[66]

Kearns said his success should be an inspiration for other inventors because it proves they can win against large corporations that have used others' ideas without reimbursement.

Discussion Questions

1. Is it ethical to use an idea based on the risk analysis that the owner of that idea simply cannot afford to litigate the matter?
2. Why was the intermittent wiper system so important to the automakers?
3. Could Kearns have done anything further to protect himself?
4. If you were an executive with one of the companies still in litigation with Kearns, would you settle the case? Why or why not?

CASE 6.8

V-A-N-N-A: It Belongs to Me

Samsung Electronics ran an advertising campaign that had a letter-turning blonde robot dressed in a red evening dress, complete with diamond bracelet and necklace. The ad was a takeoff on Vanna White's role of turning letters for contestants on television's "Wheel of Fortune." White filed suit alleging that Samsung's use of the "Robo Vanna" was an appropriation of her image and a taking of her creative output. Samsung maintained there was no appropriation because the ads were a takeoff on "Wheel of Fortune." The court found for Ms. White.[67]

Discussion Questions

1. Has something been taken without compensation in this case?
2. Is Samsung taking advantage of "Wheel of Fortune" and Vanna White?

[65] Kearns v. Ford Motor Co., *726 F.Supp 159 (E.D. Mich. 1989); see also "Chrysler Told to Pay Inventor $11.3 Million,"* The New York Times, *June 12, 1992, p. C3.*

[66] Kearns v. Chrysler Motor Corp., *62 F.3d 1430 (C.A.F.C. 1995),* cert. denied, *516 U.S. 989 (1995).*

[67] White v. Samsung Elect. Am., Inc., *971 F.2d 1395 (9th Cir. 1992).*

3. One advertising law expert has stated, "I wish these people would take a joke." Is the takeoff satire or appropriation?[68]

4. Should Samsung have sought permission to run its ads?

CASE 6.9

Copyrights, Songs, and Charity

Children at camps around the country in the summer of 1996 were not able to dance the "Macarena" except in utter silence. Their usual oldies dances were halted in 1996. The American Society of Composers, Authors & Publishers (ASCAP) notified camps and the organizations that sponsor camps (such as the Boy Scouts of America and the Girls Scouts USA) that they would be required to pay the licensing fees if they used any of the 4,000,000 copyrighted songs written or published by any of the 68,000 members of ASCAP.

The fees for use of the songs have exceeded the budgets of many of the camps. One camp that operates only during the day charges its campers $44 per week. ASCAP wanted $591 for the season for the camp's use of songs such as "Edelweiss" (from "The Sound of Music") and "This Land is Your Land." ASCAP demanded fees for even singing the songs around the campfire. ASCAP's letters to the camps reminded the directors of the possible penalties of $5,000 and up to six days in jail and threatened lawsuits for any infringement of the rights of ASCAP members. Luckily, "Kumbaya" is not owned by an ASCAP member.

Several camp directors wrote and asked for a special program that would allow the camps a discount for the use of the songs. Many of the camps are not run as for-profit businesses but rather include camps such as those for children with cancer and AIDS.

The issue of public use of popular songs surfaced after the September 11, 2001, attacks when Congress stood on the steps of the Capitol on the evening of September 11, 2001, and sang, "God Bless America." It was a spontaneous moment and from that time, the song became an integral part of all public functions, including the seventh inning stretch during the World Series.

Irving Berlin wrote "God Bless America" in 1940. When he did, he pledged all the royalties from the song to benefit youth organizations in the United States, specifically the Girl Scouts and Boy Scouts.

Each time there is a performance of the song, royalties are paid to the trust fund Berlin established for the administration of the royalties for the Scouts. Since that time, just the groups in New York City have received over $6,000,000 from song performances. The annual income from "God Bless America" public performances has been about $200,000. However, the song has become a sort of second national anthem since the time of the World Trade Center attacks and the predictions are that the royalties from public performances will generate triple that income for this year.

[68] *"Do You Vanna Dance with Lawyer?"* Business Week, *October 18, 1993, p. 8.*

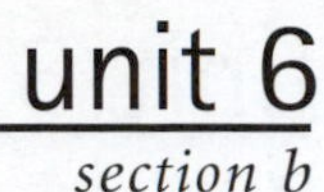

Mr. Berlin died in 1989 at the age of 101 and his daughter, Mrs. Linda Emmett, administers the trust fund. Mrs. Emmett, who shares her father's commitment to the children of the United States, says that nothing would have pleased her father more than the song's newfound popularity and the resulting benefits to the Scouts.[69]

Discussion Questions

1. Why does ASCAP work so diligently to enforce its rights and collect the fees for its members' songs?
2. What risks does ASCAP run if the camps continue to use the songs without payment of the licensing fees?
3. What ethical and social responsibility issues do you see with respect to those camps that are strictly nonprofit operations?
4. Can you think of a compromise that would protect ASCAP members' rights but still offer the camps a reasonable chance to use the songs?
5. What would you do if you were an ASCAP member and owned the rights to a song a camp wished to use? Do you think Mr. Berlin's trust has the correct approach? Could his trust not simply donate the use of the song? What problems do you see with that practice?

[69] *William Glaberson, "Irving Berlin Gave the Scouts a Gift of Song,"* The New York Times, *October 14, 2001, p. A21.*

6C

Pricing

What price is fair? Is a fair price always the most customers are willing to pay? Should businesses give special discounts to nonprofit buyers?

CASE 6.10

Salomon Brothers and Bond Pricing

Before the summer of 1991, Salomon Brothers, an investment banking firm founded in 1911, was the most powerful dealer on Wall Street in the $2.3 trillion U.S. government bond market.

Bond market regulations prohibit any firm from acquiring more than 35 percent of the Treasury notes and bonds at government auctions. This "35 percent rule," as it is known, exists to prevent one firm from buying enough of the market to unilaterally dictate the prices of the instruments.

On August 9, 1991, Salomon announced it was suspending two managing directors, Paul Mozer and Thomas Murphy, along with two other employees, for violations of the 35 percent rule. Mozer had been so publicly critical of the 35 percent rule that it was often referred to as "the Mozer rule."

The suspension led to the discovery of several other problems involving the rule. In December 1990, Salomon bought 35 percent of an $8.5 billion four-year-note Treasury auction item and also submitted, through a customer, another $1 billion bid on the same notes. The $1 billion was really for Salomon, which ended up with 46 percent of the offering. Salomon had placed a "squeeze" on the market; huge distortions in supply caused by Salomon forced the payment of high prices.

In February 1991, Mozer had a customer, Mercury Asset Management, a branch of S. G. Warburg, place a $1 billion order for thirty-year Treasury bonds. Mozer meant the order to be bogus to surprise a new trader at Salomon Brothers. However, the deal went through and was booked to Salomon. Rigged bids were discovered in three Treasury auctions during 1991.

At the Treasury auction on May 22, 1991, Salomon Brothers bought nearly 90 percent of the two-year-note instruments valued at $12.26 billion through hedge funds, or large partnerships. Prices for the instruments skyrocketed as a result. Salomon denied there was any collusion with the hedge funds, but a government investigation was launched.

The result of Salomon's cornering of the Treasury market was that small bond-trading houses and commercial banks experienced substantial losses—$100 million from the May auction alone. A Texas Christian University MBA graduate, Michael Irelan, was fired from Boatmen's National Bank in St. Louis when he lost $400,000 in the Salomon May "squeeze." "I liked my job and believe I had become a good, sound trader," Irelan said. "But now, who knows if I will be able to do this again."[70]

Hickey Securities, Inc., lost several million dollars in the May "squeeze," and its investors defected, causing its assets to fall from $100 to $30 million in four months.

Richard Breeden, chairman of the SEC, said that there were not just a few bad apples in the Treasury market but the structure of the market was wrong. "It's very important that we . . . take a cold, hard look at: Do the intermediaries, the people who stand behind the Treasury and the ultimate purchasers of these bonds, have too much power?"[71] For some time, primary dealers like Salomon had been advising the Treasury on how to run the market. The dealers could corner the market as follows:

1. The firm puts in a bid for its maximum 35 percent share of the government bonds being auctioned. To ensure that the bid is accepted, it is made slightly above the going price of the bonds already being quoted in the "when-issued" market.
2. The firm simultaneously puts in a bid, at a similarly high price, for more bonds on behalf of its major customers.
3. The bids are accepted by the Treasury Department.
4. In a prearranged transaction, the firm purchases at cost the bonds it bought on behalf of its customers. When the firm has enough bonds to control the supply, it has cornered the market.
5. When other bond dealers want to buy the bonds, perhaps to cover short positions (bonds they sold that they did not own), the firm can name its price.[72]

Up until the trading scandal broke, Salomon had the top profits of all the Wall Street firms: $451 million for the first half of 1991. After the scandal broke, Salomon's stock went from $36 per share in August to $23 per share by the end of September, a 30 percent drop.

Clients of Salomon began looking elsewhere. By mid-September, Maryland's $13 billion state pension fund was talking with Goldman Sachs and other firms. Salomon sold $40 billion in securities between May 1991 and September 1991, reducing its assets to $105 billion.

Salomon's accounting reserves for litigation by Treasury investors, Salomon shareholders, and competitors were estimated at $1 billion, or one-third of Salomon's net worth. Salomon took a conservative $200 million reserve in October, with the resulting reduction in earnings in what was otherwise a banner year.

[70] *Constance Mitchell, "Salomon's 'Squeeze' in May Auction Left Many Players Reeling,"* The Wall Street Journal, *October 31, 1991, p. A10.*

[71] *David Wessel, "Treasury and the Fed Have Long Caved in to 'Primary Dealer,'"* The Wall Street Journal, *September 25, 1991, p. A7.*

[72] *Gary Weiss, et al., "The Salomon Shocker: How Bad Will It Get?"* Business Week, *August 26, 1991, pp. 54–57.*

Warren E. Buffett, whose firm owned $700 million in Salomon convertible shares, was named interim chairman of the dealer in August 1991. He went before the House Subcommittee on Telecommunications and Finance and confirmed misdeeds by the firm. His testimony indicated Salomon had $10.6 billion, or 94 percent, of the May 1991 Treasury-note auction. Buffett's steps were viewed favorably by prosecutors. "The unquestionably substantial steps taken by Salomon inevitably reduce the government's need to punish," commented Bruce Baird, the prosecutor in the Drexel Burnham Lambert, Inc., junk bond case.[73]

In May 1992, Salomon settled with the SEC for a $290 million penalty and a two-month suspension from trading.[74] Drexel Burnham Lambert had paid $600 million in penalties in 1989 for its junk bond activities. Former Treasury secretary William E. Simon, commenting on Salomon's fine, stated, "It's an absolutely startling number. If I understood the infractions, this is an extremely severe penalty against the firm and will most certainly send a message to Wall Street that infractions are going to be dealt with in very harsh ways."[75] No criminal charges were brought against the firm, but four former senior officials were charged with violations of securities laws in Treasury auctions during the 1989–1991 period. Their settlement with the SEC included "six-figure" fines and varying-length prohibitions on securities brokerage employment.

One who settled his case with the SEC is John H. Gutfreund, the former chairman of Salomon. He resigned his 38-year tenure with Salomon when the scandal erupted. His limousine, palatial office, and attentive subordinates are gone. He now has a modest, three-room office and a part-time secretary. He is shunned by many friends and colleagues. He has paid a $100,000 fine to the SEC and agreed to a permanent prohibition on becoming a chairman or chief executive of a securities firm. Mrs. Gutfreund says his activities have been curtailed, and she finds it "so sad to see him stymied." Gutfreund notes that his role at Salomon was "not a small mistake, in retrospect."

In early 1993, Salomon Brothers settled claims with thirty-nine states on the bond trading. As part of the settlement, Salomon agreed to pay $4 million, with half of the settlement going to a special fund to fight fraud and abuse in the brokerage industry.

Most civil suits by investors against Salomon in federal court and arbitration have been settled.

While Congress is considering restructuring the auction market, the Treasury has changed how the auction operates; it now requires verification of large bids and actual receipt of bonds.

Two years after the SEC settlement, Salomon continued to struggle to regain its reputation. It remained on Standard & Poor's credit watch. In the last quarter of 1992, Salomon's profits were down 93 percent. For the year, its profits had plummeted 74 percent. Its underwritings, once number one, placed it fourth among the Wall Street brokerage houses; it held less than 10 percent of the market. Perhaps its greatest loss was that of executive talent. One senior officer observed, "We lost good people we

[73] *Michael Galen, "Salomon: Honesty Is the Gutsiest Policy,"* Business Week, *September 16, 1991, p. 100.*

[74] *One hundred million dollars of the fine was tax-deductible. "Salomon Gets Break on Its Fine,"* USA Today, *September 30, 1992, p. 1B.*

[75] *Michael Siconolfi, Laurie P. Cohen, and Kevin G. Salwen, "Salomon Is Breathing Easier after Accepting Huge Fine in Scandal,"* The Wall Street Journal, *May 21, 1992, p. A1.*

didn't want to lose. Those good people had experience, relationships and experience in the business. And those things are not going to be rebuilt in a day even if you hire somebody good from the outside."[76]

From 1992 to 1994, Salomon's return on equity was less than the other Wall Street trading firms. By the end of 1994, Salomon had slipped to seventh place among the Wall Street firms in terms of numbers of debt and equity offering. Losses in 1994 totaled $399 million, and the problems of the firm, from trading losses to accounting snafus to potential rating downgrades, continued to mount.

In 1995, Salomon's earnings level did recover somewhat in the third quarter, but in 1996, its earnings dropped by 60 percent by the third quarter. Warren Buffett has described this investment in Salomon of nearly nine years as just a "scratch single."[77]

Salomon merged with Smith Barney in 1997 to become Salomon Smith Barney and has enjoyed the resulting benefits of being a subsidiary of the Citigroup conglomerate.[78]

Discussion Questions

1. Was Salomon's conduct harmful to others?
2. What factors contributed to Salomon's illegal activity?
3. Was the SEC penalty sufficient?
4. Why didn't someone disclose Salomon's practices before the congressional hearings resulted?
5. Can people like Michael Irelan ever be adequately compensated for the losses they suffered through Salomon's actions?
6. In mid-1992, Salomon named Charles Williams, a well-known Wall Street troubleshooter, as its chief of fixed-income compliance. Salomon was said to want "suspenders on top of belts" in its compliance units. Williams reportedly received a $200,000 pay package. Is this the cost of ethics or the price of ethical violations?
7. When Warren Buffett took over temporarily as chairman of Salomon, he made the following statement:

   Contemplating any business act, an employee should ask himself whether he would be willing to see it immediately described by an informed and critical reporter on the front page of his local paper, there to be read by his spouse, children and friends. At Salomon we simply want no part of any activities that pass legal tests but that we, as citizens, would find offensive.[79]

[76] *Michael Siconolfi, "Scandal at Salomon Leaves Its Mark on the Bottom Line,"* The Wall Street Journal, *February 7, 1992, p. C1.*

[77] *Gary Weiss, et al., "How Bad Will It Get?"* Business Week, *October 7, 1991, pp. 122–124.*

[78] *See http://www.salomonsmithbarney.com/abt*

[79] *Gary Weiss, "Behind the Happy Talk at Salomon,"* Business Week, *November 11, 1991, pp. 150–152; see also Carol Loomis, "Warren Buffett's Wild Ride at Salomon,"* Fortune, *October 27, 1991, pp. 114–132.*

Is this a good ethical test for business conduct?

8. Would Gutfreund make the same choices today, given his post-Salomon circumstances?

Sources

Baumohl, Bernard, "Swaggering into Trouble," *Time*, August 26, 1991, p. 41.

Laurie P. Cohen, "Ex-Salomon Trader Supplied Information to Prosecutors," *The Wall Street Journal*, May 28, 1992, p. C1.

Laurie P. Cohen, "Gone From Salomon 16 Months, Gutfreund Finds Life Frustrating," *The Wall Street Journal*, December 4, 1992, pp. A1, A4.

Eichenwald, Kurt, "Former Top Salomon Officers Settle Bid Case," *The New York Times*, December 4, 1992, p. C1.

Eichenwald, Kurt, "Outside Lawyer Appointed General Counsel at Salomon," *The New York Times*, September 2, 1992, p. C3.

Eichenwald, Kurt, "Salomon Still Struggling to Diversify Its Business," *The New York Times*, September 8, 1992, pp. C1, C4.

Eichenwald, Kurt, "Two Sued by SEC in Bidding Scandal at Salomon Bros.," *The New York Times*, December 3, 1992, pp. C1, C2.

Gilpin, Kenneth N., "Salomon Profit Drops 93% in Quarter," *The New York Times*, October 23, 1992, p. C1.

Gilpin, Kenneth N., "Salomon Reports Surprising Earnings Drop of Nearly 60%," *The New York Times*, October 23, 1996, p. C5.

Hertzberg, Daniel, and Laurie P. Cohen, "Scandal Is Fading Away for Salomon, but Not for Trader Paul Mozer," *The Wall Street Journal*, August 7, 1992, p. A1.

Labaton, Steven, "Wall Street Opposing Bond Rules," *The New York Times*, June 1, 1991, p. C1.

McNamee, Mike, "The Judgment of Salomon: An Anticlimax," *Business Week*, June 1, 1992, p. 106.

Moses, Jonathan M., "Ruling Leaves Salomon Scandal Claims on Two Fronts," *The Wall Street Journal*, December 17, 1992, p. B10.

Power, William, "Salomon's Big Loss Could Well Become Goldman Sach's Gain," *The Wall Street Journal*, September 10, 1991, pp. A1, A8.

"The Salomon Scandal in Bondage," *The Economist*, September 14, 1991, pp. 92–93.

"Salomon: The SEC Points Its Finger," *Business Week*, December 14, 1992, p. 46.

"Salomon Settlement," *USA Today*, January 7, 1993, p. 1D.

Salwen, Kevin G., "Salomon's Dealer Role Is Supported," *The Wall Street Journal*, September 27, 1991, pp. C1, C17.

Salwen, Kevin G., "House Panel Seeks to Amend Securities Bill," *The Wall Street Journal*, August 7, 1992, p. A5.

Salwen, Kevin G., and John Connor, "SEC Mulls Penalties for Street," *The Wall Street Journal*, October 2, 1991, p. C1.

Salwen, Kevin G., and Tom Herman, "Freddie Mac Fines Firms for Inflated Orders," *The Wall Street Journal*, October 4, 1991, p. C1.

Salwen, Kevin G., and Jonathan M. Moses, "SEC Sues Ex-Trader at Salomon," *The Wall Street Journal*, December 3, 1992, p. C1.

Siconolfi, Michael, "Salomon Names Charles Williams a Compliance Chief," *The Wall Street Journal*, June 16, 1992, p. B14.

Spiro, Leah Nathans, "The Bomb Shelter Salomon Built," *Business Week*, September 9, 1991, pp. 78–80.

Spiro, Leah Nathans, "Turmoil at Salomon," *Business Week*, May 1, 1995, pp. 144–154.

"The Judgment of Salomon," *The Economist*, September 21, 1996, pp. 75–76.

Weiss, Gary, "Clearing the Wreckage," *Business Week*, September 2, 1991, pp. 66–68.

CASE 6.11

Archer Daniels Midland: A Giant in Grain

When the Justice Department raided the offices of Archer Daniels Midland (ADM) on June 26, 1995, to search for records related to its investigation of ADM and its competitors for possible violations of federal antitrust laws, an employee in a photo store in Decatur, Illinois (the home of ADM) said, "ADM will probably get a slap on the wrist and that will be the end of it. If I got caught doing that, I'd go to jail. It is scary to think of a company being that powerful."[80]

Between that June day and October 20, 1995, ADM's stock price fell 6.5 percent. ADM, a grain-processing company, was eventually charged with price fixing for two corn-derived products: lysine, a feed supplement for cattle; and citric acid. The Justice Department was tipped off to the ADM conduct in 1992 by an ADM executive, Mark E. Whitacre. Whitacre continued to work for ADM while serving as a government informant. Mr. Whitacre's undercover work resulted in guilty pleas by three Asian companies in 1995. It was revealed during evidentiary hearings that Mr. Whiteacre "selectively recorded" the conversations. Whitacre eventually agreed to plead guilty to two felonies in August 1995. The felonies were evasion of income tax and failure to disclose compensation to shareholders. When Mr. Whitacre's role with federal investigators was disclosed, ADM charged that the conspiracy was Whitacre's doing and that he had embezzled the gains from the conspiracy from ADM.

[80] *Kurt Eichenwald, "Archer Daniels Midland to Pay a $100 Million Fine in Pricing Case,"* The New York Times, *October 15, 1996, pp. A1, C3.*

On Wednesday, October 16, 1996, ADM pleaded guilty to charges that it had fixed prices. As part of the plea agreement, ADM agreed to pay $100 million in fines and to cooperate with the government in its continuing investigation. Outraged shareholders staged a revolt at the October 17, 1996, shareholder meeting. James E. Burton, chief executive officer of the California Public Employees Retirement System, stated, "The $100 million fine is shareholder assets that are being squandered to pay for criminal activity that never should have occurred. Where was the board of directors?"[81]

Two days after the board meeting, the ADM board accepted the resignation of Michael D. Andreas, the vice chairman of ADM and son of ADM's chairman, and Terrance Wilson, the head of ADM's corn-processing division. ADM board member Brian Mulroney, the former Prime Minister of Canada, stated upon departure from the meeting, "They no longer work here."[82]

On December 3, 1996, three officers of ADM were indicted for conspiracy in fixing prices on lysine, including Terrance Wilson and Michael Andreas. Two Japanese executives were also indicted on conspiracy charges. The executives were found guilty of price fixing in 1998.[83] They were sentenced in 1999 to between 20 months and 2.5 years with fines of $350,000 each.[84]

Discussion Questions

1. What criminal violations do you think occurred? What ethical violations occurred?
2. Do you agree with Mr. Burton's statement?
3. Who is responsible for the conduct that led to the guilty plea? Was it best for ADM to plead guilty?
4. What do you think of Mr. Whitacre's undercover work? Would you have done the same thing and worked for the government?
5. Do you agree with the photo employee's statement? Did ADM get just a slap on the wrist? Visit http://www.admworld.com for an update on ADM's policies.

Sources

Armstrong, Larry, "All Roads Lead to ADM," *Business Week*, September 23, 1996, pp. 42–43.

Burton, Thomas M., "Former ADM Executive Mark Whitacre Pleads Guilty to Embezzling $9 Million," *The Wall Street Journal*, October 13, 1997, p. B12.

[81] *"ADM Still Doesn't Get It,"* Fortune, *November 11, 1996, pp. 30–31.*

[82] *Kurt Eichenwald, "2 Executives Step Down at Archer Daniels,"* The New York Times, *October 18, 1996, pp. C1, C4.*

[83] *Kurt Eichenwald, "Former Archer Daniels Executives Are Found Guilty of Price Fixing,"* The New York Times, *September 18, 1998, p. C1.*

[84] *Kurt Eichenwald, "Three Sentenced in Archer Daniels Midland Case,"* The New York Times, *July 10, 1999, pp. B1, B14.*

Eichenwald, Kurt, "Informant Said to Agree to Plea Deal," *The New York Times*, September 27, 1995, pp. C1, C3.

Eichenwald, Kurt, "Judge Lets Archer Tapes Be Admitted," *The New York Times*, April 17, 1998, p. C6.

Kilman, Scott, "Ajinomoto Pleads Guilty to Conspiring With ADM, Others to Fix Lysine Price," *The Wall Street Journal*, November 15, 1996, p. A18.

CASE 6.12

Sotheby's and Christie's: The No-Auction Prices

Christie's International and Sotheby's—international auction houses for art and estate items and known for their handling of the estates and property of the rich and famous such as the estate of Jaqueline Kennedy Onassis, the gowns of Diana, Princess of Wales, and the effects of Marilyn Monroe—became the subject of a price fixing investigation by the Federal Trade Commission and Justice Department. Together, the two firms controlled 95 percent of the international auction market.

The allegations of price fixing have their origins in "conscious parallelism." That is, the two federal agencies were investigating why the two auction houses raised their commissions in lock step over the years with virtually no price competition in auction commissions.

The drama surrounding the Christie's and Sotheby's antitrust investigation and now trial has captured the interest of all levels of society in New York City and elsewhere.

In December 1999, Christopher M. Davidge, the CEO of Christie's, was terminated. Upset about what he called his "paltry" severance package and others say was his concern that he might have been set up to take the blame for any antitrust charges, Davidge demanded all of his business records from Christie's. He took everything from his files, including handwritten notes he had sent to Christie's CEO, Diana (Dede) Brooks. Also implicated in his files were then-chairman of Sotheby's, A. Alfred Taubman.

Mr. Davidge had initially denied, when questioned by the Justice Department, that he had any inappropriate communications with Sotheby's and Ms. Brooks. However, Mr. Davidge's former assistant, Irmgrad Pickering, told the Justice Department that she believed Mr. Davidge and Ms. Brooks had held meetings.

He turned the records over to his lawyer who, in turn, turned them over to the Justice Department. The records have been described as establishing "classic cartel behavior—price fixing pure and simple" between Christie's and Sotheby's.[85] The correspondence in his files was between him and Diana Brooks, CEO of Sotheby's. The correspondence reflects a pattern of the two auction houses matching their commission rates. For example, in March 1995, Christie's announced it was increasing its sell-

[85] *Shawn Tully, "A House Divided,"* Fortune, *December 18, 2000, pp. 264–275.*

ers' fees from a flat rate to a sliding scale ranging from 2 to 20 percent. Sotheby's made an announcement of the same change in sellers' rates one month later.[86]

Soon after Christie's became aware of the documents and correspondence in the hands of the Justice Department, it announced its cooperation with the federal government and was given amnesty. At the same time, Christie's announced that it was raising its buyer's commission from 17.5 to 18 percent (for buyers spending up to $80,000 and 10 percent for buyers above that amount) and charging its sellers less, taking its commission for sales down 1 to 5 percent and as low as 1.25 percent for amounts greater than $1,000.[87]

Both changes placed Sotheby's, Christie's prime competitor, in the position of charging higher commissions. The disparity in commission was the first time there was any difference in the competitors' prices in over a decade.

Mr. Taubman denied any involvement in the price fixing and offered a lie detector test conducted by a former FBI agent to establish that he did not know of the arrangements and communications between Ms. Brooks and Mr. Davidge. The two key questions in the polygraph exam, which Mr. Taubman passed, were:

> Did you tell Dede Brooks to try and reach an agreement with Davidge regarding amounts to be charged to buyers or sellers?
>
> Did Dede Brooks ever tell you that she had reached an agreement with Davidge about amounts to be charged to buyers and sellers?[88]

Mr. Taubman's answers of "no" to each of these questions were found to be truthful by the examiner for the polygraph. The test was conducted without any law enforcement agents present.

At nearly the same time, Christie's agreed to pay a $256 million, one-half of a $512 million civil suit brought against the company, and settled a shareholder lawsuit for $30 million. Sotheby's also agreed to pay its $256 million share of the suit amount to settle civil claims. Mr. Taubman agreed to be responsible for paying $156 million of that corporate obligation. Representing the plaintiffs in the antitrust suit against the two auction houses was David Boies, the lawyer who represented Al Gore in the 2000 presidential election litigation, Shawn Fanning and Napster in their copyright litigation, and the federal government in the Microsoft antitrust case.

Davidge got immunity in exchange for his cooperation. Ms. Brooks entered a guilty plea on October 5, 2000, and declined all of her stock options. Her friends say she refused the options so as to put the case behind her. Others say she declined them so that she would not be held responsible for any of the costs the company incurred related to the antitrust activities. In exchange for favorable sentencing (she is hoping to get a substantial reduction of the possible three years as well as in the fine), Ms. Brooks, Mr. Taubman's one-time protégé, turned state's evidence and cooperated with the Justice Department in its investigation.

[86] *Douglas Frantz, with Carol Vogel and Ralph Blumenthal, "Files of Ex-Christie's Chief Fuel Inquiry Into Art Auction,"* The New York Times, *October 8, 2000, pp. A1, A28.*

[87] *Alexandria Peers and Ann Davis, "Christie's Overhauls Commissions,"* The Wall Street Journal, *February 8, 2000, pp. A3, A10.*

[88] *Frantz, Vogel, and Blumenthal, "Files of Ex-Christie's Chief," pp. A1, A28.*

In May 2001, four years after the investigation began, the Justice Department announced the indictment of Mr. Taubman as well as his counterpart at Christie's, Sir Anthony Tennant. The indictment charges price fixing over a six-year period involving over 13,000 customers. Mr. Taubman requested a separate trial from his British counterpart and his trial began in New York in November 2001.

Seven days into the trial Diana D. Brooks, who worked for Sotheby's for more than twenty years, testified that Mr. Taubman had twelve meetings with Sir Anthony from 1993 through 1996, at which Mr. Taubman told her he had indicated that the two houses were killing each other and that they needed to take action. Mr. Taubman had reached a general agreement with Sir Anthony and gave Mrs. Brooks a list of issues on which they had general agreement and told her to work out the details with Mr. Davidge.

Mrs. Brooks did meet with Mr. Davidge on a number of occasions. She described in some detail their meetings at which they agreed mutually, sometimes simply in the back seat of her car after she picked him up at the airport, when they would raise prices and by how much. She testified that Mr. Taubman congratulated her when she advised him that she had completed the details and reached an agreement.

However, when the agreement collapsed, she refused to meet with Mr. Taubman unless Sotheby's lawyer was present. She testified that Mr. Taubman told her two things at that time (January 2000), "Just don't act like a girl," and "You'll look good in stripes."[89]

Mr. Davidge followed Mrs. Brooks to the witness stand at the trial and largely corroborated her testimony. Mr. Davidge also testified that Sir Anthony Tennant gave him a memo that outlined the agreement he had reached with Mr. Taubman to change the way the auction houses did business.[90]

Some have called the trial a "he said, she said" battle.[91]

Both Christie's and Davidge are immune from prosecution for antitrust violations because of their cooperation.

Following the settlements by the companies, Sotheby's, a 256-year-old company, hired Michael I. Sovern, the former president of Columbia University, as chairman of the board.

Sotheby's stock suffered during the time of the daily disclosures about the investigations, the evidence, and the resulting litigation. At the beginning of the investigation, Sotheby's stock was trading in March 1999 at $42 per share. By March 2000, it was down to $15 per share. In November 2001, as the trial unfolded, the share price was $16.24.

[89] *Ralph Blumenthal and Carol Vogel, "Chief Witness Accuses Former Boss at Sotheby's,"* The New York Times, *November 20, 2001, pp. A1, A16.*

[90] *Kathryn Kranhold, "Former Christie's CEO Testifies on Key Memo in Taubman Trial,"* The Wall Street Journal, *November 15, 2001, p. B2.*

[91] *Kathryn Kranhold, "Likely Evidence at Taubman Trial Boils Down to 'He Said, She Said,'"* The Wall Street Journal, *November 8, 2001, pp. B1, B12.*

Discussion Questions

1. Why do we worry that two auction houses were agreeing on increases in their commission rates?
2. What do you think of Mr. Davidge's ethics? Did his intent to sue Christie's for terminating him turn out to provide Christie's with a break in the antitrust case?
3. What do you think of Mrs. Brooks providing evidence on her former mentor?
4. Who is harmed if the two auction houses agree on their commissions and follow common business practices?
5. The two auction houses, by the testimony of Mrs. Brooks and Mr. Davidge, also shared client lists. Is there a problem with this practice?
6. Do you think the shareholders were served well by the conduct of Sotheby's and Christie's?

6d

Competitors, the Playing Field, and Competition

When is it a fair fight? When has competition moved into the illegal and unethical?

CASE 6.13

Slotting: Facilitation, Costs, or Bribery[92]

Finding "Bearwiches" on the cookie shelf in your grocery store will be a daunting task. Locating some "Frookies," a new line of fat-free, sugarless cookies, will take you on a journey through various aisles in the store, and you may find them at knee level in the health foods section. You can find packaged Lee's Ice Cream from Baltimore in Saudi Arabia and South Korea, but it will not be found on the grocery store shelves in Baltimore. The difficulty with finding these items is not that they are not good products. The manufacturers of these products cannot afford to buy shelf space. The shelf space in grocery stores is not awarded on the basis of consumer demand for Bearwiches or Frookies. Shelf space in grocery stores is awarded on the basis of the manufacturer's willingness to pay "slotting" fees. If manufacturers pay, they are given a space on the grocer's shelf. If the slotting fees are not paid, the product is not sold by the grocer.

Slotting fees are fees manufacturers pay to retailers in order to obtain retail shelf space.[93] The practice has been common in the retail grocery industry since 1987. The origins of slotting fees are unclear with different parties in the food chain offering various explanations. Retailers claim slotting was started by manufacturers with the fees paid to retailers as an inducement to secure shelf space. Another theory of origin offered by retailers is that manufacturers use slotting fees to curtail market entrants. If a manufacturer buys more space with additional fees, the market can be controlled by

[92] *Adapted from Robert J. Aalberts and Marianne M. Jennings, "The Ethics of Slotting: Is This Bribery, Facilitation, Marketing or Just Plain Compensation?" 20* Journal of Business Ethics *207–215 (1999). Reprinted with kind permission of Kluwer Academic Publishers.*

[93] *"Slotting fees" actually pertain to obtaining space in the grocer's warehouse. "Shelf fees," which are fees for placement on the shelf are also charged by some grocery retailers.*

existing manufacturers. Manufacturers claim slotting was started by retail grocers as a means of covering the bookkeeping and warehousing costs of the introduction of a new product. However, two things are clear. First, the practice of affiliated fees for sale has expanded to other industries. The retail book industry, particularly the large chains, now demands fees from publishers for shelf slots and displays for their books. In malls, developers/landlords now demand sums as large as $50,000 from tenants or prospective tenants before a lease can be negotiated or renegotiated. These fees for a position in the mall are referred to as "key money" or "negative allowances." In certain areas, home builders are demanding "access fees" or "marketing premiums" from appliance makers and other residential construction suppliers for use of their products in the builders' developments. In the computer software industry, the packaging of software programs with computers ensures sales and requires a fee. Even the display of programs in electronic stores is subject to a fee. The second clearly evolving trend in affiliated fees is that the practice is inconsistent and the purposes of the fees are unknown. Fees differ from manufacturer to manufacturer, from product to product, and from retailer to retailer.

How Slotting Works

Food manufacturers produce over 10,000 new products each year. However, store shelf space remains fixed. Because profit margins at grocery stores hover at very narrow levels of only 1 to 2 percent of sales,[94] additional shelf space would not increase profits nor produce guaranteed returns from the new products displayed there. Additionally, grocers must assume the risk of allocating shelf space to a new product that would not sell at a level sufficient to provide even the narrow margins. Retail grocers must absorb the cost of warehousing the product, accounting for it in inventory, barcoding it, and eventually stocking the shelves with it.[95] In many cases, particularly where the manufacturer is a small company, there has been little or no advertising of the product and the retail grocer must also incur the cost of advertising the product in some way or offer in-store coupons to entice customer purchases. To the retail grocer, the introduction of a new product and the allocation of precious shelf space is a high-cost risk. There are no guarantees that a new product will garner sales, and there is the downside of the loss of revenue from whatever product is displaced by the new product. To retail grocers, a slotting fee is a means of insulation from the risk of new product introduction and a means of advance recoupment of costs.

Within some retail grocery chains, slotting fees represent the net profits for the organization. Similar to the rental car industry in which earnings come from renters' fees for insurance, car seats, and additional driver coverage, some retail grocers' profits come not from the sales of food but from the fees manufacturers pay for access.

The level and nature of slotting fees vary significantly. Some retailers have a flat fee of $5,000 per product for introduction. Other retailers have a graduated fee schedule tied to the shelf space location. Eye-level slots cost more than the knee or ground level slots. The prime spaces at the ends of grocery aisles bring premium slotting fees since

[94] *Costs in the retail grocery industry are relatively fixed and cannot be readily reduced. Union wages and other unmanageable cost elements preclude effective efforts at increasing profit margins. Further, competition from the "club" stores (Costs, Sam's Club, Price Club) is intense.*

[95] *The cost of shelving is that of the labor and materials involved in simply changing the shelf sign. Shelf fees are typically a minimal amount such as $50.*

those spaces virtually ensure customer attention.[96] Other stores require that a "kill fee" be paid when a product does not sell. One supermarket chain requires $500 just for a manufacturer to make an appointment to present a new product. Some retailers will not accept a new product even with a slotting fee. Small businesses often incur the cost of product development only to be unable to place the product with grocery stores.

Some stores charge a slotting fee, an additional fee if the product is new, and a "failure fee" on new products to cover the losses if the product fails to sell. A new fee, called the "staying fee," has also developed. A staying fee is an annual rent fee that prevents the retailer from giving a manufacturer's product slot to someone else. Some manufacturers offer to buy out the product in existing space in order to make room for their product. A 1988 survey found that 70 percent of all grocery retailers charge slotting fees, with one retail store disclosing that its $15-per-store per-product slotting fees bring in an additional $50 million in revenue each year.[97] Examples of various slotting fees paid and documented are found in Table 1. The most typical slotting fee for a new product to be placed with a grocery retailer was $10,000. Slotting fees do not typically come down over time, even if the product sells well. At the retail level for CD-ROM sales, the producers pay a 20 percent fee per shipment, regardless of whether their product is in demand.

The Legal Issues Surrounding Slotting

The chairman of the board of a small food manufacturer in Ohio wrote to his Congressman and described slotting fees in this way: "This is nothing but a device to extort money from packers and squeeze all the independent and smaller processors off the shelves and out of business. We believe this is the most flagrant restraint of trade device yet conceived."[98] The Senate Small Business Committee's investigation included a report on an interview with one small manufacturer who said, "I know for a fact that my competition is paying the lease on the buyer's BMW."[99] It is possible that a slotting fee might fall under the legally prohibited conduct of commercial bribery. However, for a successful prosecution for payment of a bribe, the conduct required must be that in which funds are paid by a seller to a buyer solely for the purpose of acquiring a contract or business opportunity (in the case of slotting, a space on the shelf). As noted earlier, however, the reality is that there are costs associated with awarding an item shelf space. If the funds are simply received by the retailer and used for general operating expenses which include advertising, bookkeeping, and warehousing, then the notion that a slotting fee is commercial bribery does not fit within the actus reus, or the required conduct, for criminal prosecution.[100]

Regardless of legalities, the use of slotting fees creates an atmosphere of confusion. It is unclear how slotting payments are made and where the payments are reported.

[96] *Referred to as "prime real estate" in the industry, slotting fees follow a graduated schedule for the locations. Amounts vary according to aisle space. Bread slotting fees are $500–$1,000 per bread-type. Ice cream, with one small segment in frozen foods brings $25,000 per flavor.*

[97] *No convenience store chains charge slotting fees. However, convenience stores do not warehouse inventory. Manufacturers deliver directly to the convenience stores (Gibson).*

[98] Slotting: Fair for Small Business and Consumers? *Hearing before the Committee on Small Business, United States Senate, 106th Congress, 1999.*

[99] *Roger K. Lowe, "Stores Demanding Pay to Display Products on Shelves, Panel Told,"* Columbus Dispatch, *September 15, 1999, p. 1H.*

[100] *Again, it is important to note that a retailer may also charge an "advertising fee."*

payer	amount	terms	payee
Truzzolino Pizza Roll	$25,000	Chain-wide	Safeway
Old Capital Microwave Popcorn	$86,000	Chain-wide for $172,000	Shoprite stores
United Brands	$375,000	Frozen fruit juice bar	New York City area stores
Apple & Eve	$150,000	Fruit punch product	Limited stores in Northeast
Frookies	50¢ per box (Increased price from $1.79 to $2.29)	Sugar-free cookies	100 stores various
Frito-Lay	$100,000	New product	Each grocery store chain
Lee's Ice Cream	$25,000 per flavor	Ice cream	Each grocery
Bread	$1,500 per store per bread	Chain-wide cost is $100,000	Chains
General/manufacturers/producers	$15,000–$30,000 per SKU (item)	New products—chain-wide	Chains

Table 1
Slotting Fees: Amounts and Terms[101]

Many small business owners report that the payments they make to grocery retailers must be made in cash. Some owners report that payments are made in cash to both the chain and to individual store managers. The atmospheric result is that there are large amounts of cash changing hands among sellers, managers, and purchasers. The former CEO of Harvest Foods, a food retailer in the South, has been indicted on charges of bribery and other related offenses for the alleged receipt of hundreds of thousands of dollars in cash for slotting fees.

Because slotting fees are non-uniform and even non-universal, it is impossible to understand how the fee structure works, how much the fees should be, and whether the fees are actually related to the costs incurred by retailers in getting a new product to the shelf. The secretive and inconsistent nature of slotting fees and their payment in cash creates an atmosphere similar to that in drug trade.[102] Market entry rights are

[101] *Updated from Robert J. Aalberts and Marianne M. Jennings, "The Ethics of Slotting: Is This Bribery, Facilitation, Marketing or Just Plain Compensation?" 20* Journal of Business Ethics, *1999, pp. 207–215. A 1997 survey indicates the following:*

Usual slotting fees:

Retailers	*Varies from free to $20,000 per SKU (product)*
Wholesalers	*$500–$10,000 per SKU*
Manufacturers	*$500–$10,000 per SKU*

The figures in the chart were updated through May 2001.

[102] *The authors could find only three manufacturers willing to discuss their personal experiences with slotting fees or industry practices. Retribution (i.e., denial of retail access) was cited as the reason for their reluctance. These three manufacturers spoke on condition of anonymity. Two other manufacturers, Richard Worth (Frookies) and Scott Garfield (Lee's Ice Cream) have been public in their discussion of slotting fees. Grocery retailers referred all questions to legal counsel or corporate officers who declined to be interviewed.*

unclear, fees change, not everyone is permitted to buy into the system, and the use and declaration of revenues is unknown. In at least four reports on the practice of slotting fees, parties on both sides referred to slotting as the grocery industry's "dirty little secret:" Cost recoupment, the public airing of the fees, and public accounting disclosures are non-existent for slotting fees. The secrecy of the fees and the industry's unwillingness to discuss or disclose them is problematic for manufacturers.

From the cost figures offered in Table 1, it is safe to conclude that slotting fees could make market entry prohibitive for many small companies. In some instances, fees have gone beyond the initial slotting costs, with some grocery chains now demanding up to $40,000 per year for a company to maintain just a square foot of retail space for its product. Even some of the larger companies have difficulty competing because of the large fees. Frito-Lay recently purchased Anheuser Busch's Eagle Snacks after Anheuser had spent over $500 million trying to increase its 17 percent market share. Frito-Lay now holds 55 percent of the snack market and pays the largest slotting fees in the grocery industry. Borden ended its foray into the snack market in 1995, and barely survived before it did so. Nearly 30 regional snack companies have gone out of business in the last three years. A vice president of Clover Club Foods, a Utah-based snack company, believes Frito-Lay's goal is to be the only salted-snack food company in the country. The Independent Baker's Association has described the current situation with slotting fees as being "out of control."

The following questions and results reflect the attitudes of those in the retail food business toward slotting:

Slotting allowances are a way of penalizing manufacturers for inadequate market tests.	52% of retailers, 72% of wholesalers, and 77% of manufacturers said they disagreed or disagreed strongly
If a supplier can demonstrate adequate market testing of a new product, slotting fees should not be charged.	54% of retailers, 50% of wholesalers, and 0% of manufacturers said they disagreed or disagreed strongly
Slotting fees hamper a retailer's ability to maximize the effectiveness of his product assortment.	58% of retailers, 54% of wholesalers, and 94% of manufacturers agreed strongly or agreed somewhat[103]

A 1997 survey by *Supermarket Business* found the following:

At present, some slotting fees are an "under the table" form of payment.	83% of retailers, 85% of wholesalers, and 79% of manufacturers strongly agreed or agreed somewhat with the statement

Discussion Questions

1. Are slotting fees a means of allocating risk?
2. What possible employee temptations exist?
3. Would a schedule of fees help?

[103] *Adapted from Robert Aalberts, Marianne Jennings, and Stephen Happel, "The Economics, Legalities and Ethics of Slotting Fees,"* Journal of Law and Commerce, *forthcoming.*

4. Are slotting fees ethical?
5. Are the perceptions of the industry participants a reflection of their questions about the ethics of slotting?

CASE 6.14

Mr. Gates: Genius and Fierce Competitor

The profit for Microsoft Corporation was $3.5 billion for fiscal 1997. Founder Bill Gates was able to capture approximately 90 percent of the personal computer (PC) market. While many argue Mr. Gates' market share is primarily the result of building a better mouse trap, Compaq Computer Co. sees Microsoft's market conquest slightly differently. In the spring of 1996, Compaq notified Microsoft that it intended to replace Microsoft's Internet access program, Explorer, with Microsoft's chief competitor's program, Netscape.

Shortly after the notification, Compaq was notified by Microsoft that its Windows 95 licensing agreement was terminated. A follow-up letter offered restoration of licensing if Compaq restored the Explorer program to its Presarios within 60 days. Compaq did so and got the licensing back.

The U.S. Justice Department brought an action seeking to hold Microsoft in contempt for violating an earlier order on "coercion by a dominant company in a way that distorts competition."[104] The 1995 order prohibited Microsoft from tying the sale of one product to the sale of another, as was proposed to Compaq.

Microsoft maintains Explorer is part of an integrated product that they can force buyers to take. However, Netscape maintains that Explorer is produced, advertised, and sold separately as a stand-alone product.

A judge issued a $1 million per day fine after a hearing on the alleged violation of tying by Microsoft. A second hearing produced an order precluding Microsoft from forcing PC makers to install Explorer.

Microsoft continued its sales practices, pointing to language in the consent decree that reads Microsoft "shall not be construed to prohibit Microsoft from developing integrated products." Microsoft endured the fines until January 1998, when Microsoft agreed to a settlement under which it will not require PC makers to take Explorer. Shortly after the settlement, the Justice Department announced a new antitrust investigation based on allegations of collusion.

Microsoft was concerned about its strategic position with respect to the Internet, a global electronic network consisting of smaller interconnected networks, which allows millions of computers to exchange information over telephone wires, dedicated data cables, and wireless links.

The United States Justice Department had an ongoing inquiry into the market shares and practices of Microsoft and twenty-three state attorneys general were also

[104] *http://www.justice.gov. See complaint.*

looking into the company's practices. The concerns of the Justice Department and attorneys general include:

1. Microsoft's position in the market as a monopolist (90 percent market share for operating systems).
2. Microsoft's barriers to entry for other operating systems and Web browsers. Microsoft has refused to sell its software operating system to computer companies that installed Microsoft's competitive browser, Netscape, which was gaining popularity as Microsoft's Explorer struggled.
3. Microsoft worked to inhibit the efforts of Netscape with its browser by first trying to acquire Netscape and then working to "cut off [its] air supply" by retarding Sun Corporation's development and implementation of the Java program. When Microsoft altered the portions of Sun's Java program that allowed it to work without Windows, Sun notified Microsoft that such was a violation of its licensing agreement. Microsoft's response was, "Sue us." Sun sued Microsoft one week before the Justice Department brought its suit against Microsoft. Sun's suit then ran parallel with the Justice Department's.

In issuing a three-part opinion, Judge Thomas Penfield Jackson of the district court found that Microsoft had violated the antitrust laws and ordered a remedy of breaking up the company. Microsoft appealed the decision. The federal appeals court upheld the finding that Microsoft violated the antitrust laws but remanded the case for a new remedy. While the remedy retrial was pending, Microsoft and the Justice Department settled the case with Microsoft agreeing to contribute $800 million in software to schools around the country.[105] State antitrust litigation is still pending.

Discussion Questions

1. Is Microsoft just competing? Would you call them a fair competitor?

2. Is there anything unethical about tying product sales?

3. What free market issues exist here?

4. Do you think that Microsoft will behave differently following the court case?

5. Does the settlement provide for sufficient damages?

Sources

Bank, David, and John R. Wilke, "Microsoft and Justice End a Skirmish, Yet War Could Escalate," *The Wall Street Journal*, January 23, 1998, pp. A1, A6.

Krantz, Michael, "Will Reno Brake Windows?" *Time*, November 3, 1997, pp. 76–78.

Lohr, Steve, "Court Is Not Where They'd Like to Go Today," *The New York Times*, January 18, 1998, p. WK5.

Wilke, John R., "Microsoft Subject of New Antitrust Probe," *The Wall Street Journal*, April 24, 1998, p. A2.

[105] U.S. v. Microsoft, *253 F.3d 34 (C.A. D.C. 2001).*

6e

Business and Its Shareholders

Businesses also compete for shareholders. With so many possible investments and companies to choose from, what affects shareholders' decisions to invest and what rights do they have once they have made an investment in a company? Should shareholders have the right to control the amount paid to executives and the conduct of the company in which they have an ownership interest?

CASE 6.15

Executive Compensation

Pay levels for executives have been increasing rapidly since 1980. Sibson & Company data show that between 1980 and 1990, the average cash compensation for CEOs grew over 160 percent.[106] At the same time, the average hourly wage paid to nonsupervisory manufacturing employees did not keep pace with inflation. CEOs in United States-based companies earn 363 times more than the average employee, while Japanese CEOs earn only 16 times more.[107] Since 1990, the pay levels have more than doubled when stock options are included.

Graef Crystal conducts an annual study of CEO pay packages with an analysis of 850 CEOs of publicly-traded companies. Crystal provides the data for the best CEO performers, in terms of stock and company performance, as well as the worst performers. The 2001 study includes the following conclusions:

- The most over-compensated CEO in America is Linda Wachner, CEO of Warnaco Group. From 1991 to 1998, shares of Warnaco gave investors a total return of 10.4 percent, as compared to the 21 percent for the S&P 500. Yet during 1998, Wachner was compensated as follows:

[106] *Jeffrey Birnbaum, "From Quayle to Clinton, Politicians Are Pouncing on the Hot Issue of Top Executives' Hefty Salaries,"* The Wall Street Journal, *January 15, 1991, p. A16.*

[107] *Jill Abramson and Christopher J. Chipello, "High Pay of CEOs Traveling with Bush Touches a Nerve in Asia,"* The Wall Street Journal, *December 30, 1991, p. A1.*

$2.7 million	Salary
$6.0 million	Bonus
$6.5 million	Restricted stock
$73.5 million	Options
$75.6 million	Gain from exercised options

- Other CEOs on the worst performer list include Sanford Weill and John Reed, the co-CEOs for Citigroup (the merger of Citibank and Travelers), who were each paid $176 million even though there was a 2 percent drop of Citigroup's share price in 1998.

The "compensation heroes," as Crystal calls them, or those CEOs delivering the most for their salaries, are:

- Bernard Marcus and Arthur Blank—Home Depot, who each had pay of $3 million but who delivered an average annual return of 45 percent.
- Herb Kelleher—Southwest Airlines, who was paid only $674,000 despite the fact that Southwest's stock was up 38.4 percent in 2000.

Crystal presents his report to the Council of Institutional Investors, a group of portfolio managers with over $1 trillion in assets. Members of this group use the list as a starting point in making decisions as to where and when to invest their funds.

Michael S. Kesner, National Director of Compensation and Benefits Consulting for Arthur Andersen Company, notes:

> With restructuring, cost-cutting, and consolidation the order of the day, the actual impact of, say, a $5 million CEO pay package on the bottom line of a $2 billion sales company is not clearly the issue. People are now saying, to paraphrase the sound advice of late Illinois Senator Everett Dirksen, "Hey, a percent of a billion here and a percent of a billion there adds up to real money." In light of widespread plant closings, layoffs, and long lines of unemployed workers seeking limited jobs, "pay for performance" has simply taken a backseat to what the general public considers "fair."[108]

Warren Buffett, the chief executive officer of Berkshire Hathaway, disclosed that his salary of $100,000 remained the same in 1998 but that his fees for being a director fell about 11 percent to $176,600. Some of the salary and fees are taken in cash and some in equity securities.

Mr. Buffett does not use a compensation committee or consultant to determine the salaries of his officers. He alone makes the recommendations to the board on what he believes the officers should be paid. Prior to the imposition of SEC requirements, the proxy materials for Berkshire Hathaway do not include any information on how salaries are determined or whether they are competitive.

Berkshire Hathaway permits bonuses for officers but none have been paid in a number of years. The highest paid officer for Berkshire Hathaway, earned more than Mr. Buffett, and was paid $412,500 in 2001 with $31,500 additional compensation from subsidiaries.[109]

[108] *Gary Strauss, "Study: Some CEO Salaries Don't Compete,"* USA Today, *September 28, 1999, p. 3B.*

[109] *Form 14 found in the SEC filings for the company under edgar at: http://www.sec.gov/edgar/searchedgar/webusers.htm*

The latest CEO compensation figures follow (these figures appeared in 2001 reflecting the compensation paid in 2000).

name	company	compensation
Sanford Weill	Citigroup, Inc.	$224.4 million
John T. Chambers	Cisco Systems, Inc.	$157.3 million
Kenneth L. Lay	Enron Corp.	$140.4 million
L. Dennis Kozlowski	Tyco International	$125.3 million
John F. Welch	General Electric Co.	$122.5 million
Joseph P. Nacchio	Qwest Communications	$96.6 million
W.J. Sanders III	Advanced Micro Devices	$92.4 million[110]

The levels of CEO compensation have outraged large institutional investors and small shareholders. Shareholder proposals calling for reform in the setting of executive pay were submitted at the 1997 annual meetings of forty-three companies. The New York City Employees Retirement System, for example, proposed through its 259,328 shares of Reebok that executive compensation be established by an independent panel. Said Elizabeth Holztman, a trustee of the New York system, "It is unconscionable to have sky-high executive compensation that is not related to long-term corporate performance."[111]

The California Public Employee Retirement System (Calpers) released a list of executives and their pay in twelve high-profile companies for 1991 in an attempt to pressure management of the firms into reform. Calpers had tried to negotiate privately with the firms but was rebuffed in some cases. Calpers spokesman Richard H. Koppes stated "This year, the kinder and gentler approach doesn't seem to be working. That's why we released the names."[112]

Some shareholders have pointed to conflicts of interest in board compensation committees: CEOs from other firms are members of the board, and lawyers whose firms furnish the bulk of the company's legal services sit on the committee that determines the compensation of the CEO—the same person who hires the law firm. Management consultant Graef Crystal explained, "It's a cozy you-scratch-my-back-I'll-scratch-yours arrangement. If you're a CEO, you don't want Mother Teresa or the Sisters of Charity on your compensation committee."[113]

Stanley C. Gault, chairman of Goodyear Tire & Rubber Company, has joined with the shareholders in their complaints: "The American public is tired of seeing executives make many, many millions of dollars a year when the stock price goes down, the dividends are cut, and the book value is reduced."[114] Some executives have initiated reform in their compensation system out of fear of new federal regulations. On the other hand, others, such as the late Roberto C. Goizueta of Coca-Cola, continue to defend their compensation: "Our stock outperformed the other twenty-nine stocks in the Dow industrial average in the past decade. The end result has been the creation of $50

[110] *From* Business: Its Legal, Ethical and Global Environment, *6th Ed., by Marianne M. Jennings, p. 46. Copyright © 2003. Reprinted with permission of South-Western, a division of Thomson Learning.*

[111] *"Reebok Comes under Fire for Executive Pay,"* The Wall Street Journal, *March 21, 1991, p. G1.*

[112] Id.

[113] *Thomas McCarroll, "The Shareholders Strike Back,"* Time, *May 4, 1992, pp. 46–47.*

[114] *John Byrne, Dean Foust, and Lois Therriem, "Executive Pay,"* Business Week, *March 30, 1992, p. 52.*

billion of additional wealth for the share owners of our company in the same time period."[115] Goizueta's defense of his compensation at the annual shareholders' meeting met with applause.

Ben & Jerry's Homemade, Inc., the Vermont ice cream manufacturer, once limited its CEO pay to seven times the average worker's salary. Herman Miller, a Fortune 500 company, limits its CEO's pay—salary and bonus—to twenty times the average employee paycheck, which was $28,000 in 1991. The average CEO compensation in the other Fortune 500 companies is 117 times the salary of the average worker. Max DePress, a member of Herman Miller's founding family and chairman of the company's board, said, "People have to think about the common good. Our CEO and senior officers make good competitive salaries when the performance is there."[116] Miller's nonunionized plant workers support the plan, he said: "This is a fair and equitable way to pay. . . . If they tried to revoke it, people would speak out."[117]

James O'Toole, executive director of the leadership institute at the University of Southern California, said the Herman Miller plan should be the model others follow, "instead of the bad examples of the 1980s. The purpose of the corporation is much broader than meeting the needs of stock speculators or the power needs of top managers."[118]

In 1992, Congress limited the ability of companies to deduct CEO compensation from their taxes as a means of controlling increases. The bill puts an upper limit of $1,000,000 on such tax deductions. At the same time, the SEC passed new rules and formats for disclosing of executive compensation in annual proxy materials. Boards have also begun to act on the issue. Compensation committees comprised only of outside directors exist at 80 percent of the institutions surveyed by Dow Jones. These committees are hiring independent consultants to advise them on compensation issues.

A new question that arises is whether the additional perks provided to executives are counted as part of the compensation package for tax purposes or reflected in the total benefits paid reports to shareholders. The types of perks many CEOs enjoy (in order of the number of corporations offering them) are:

- Annual physical
- Company car
- Financial planning
- Car phone
- Car allowance
- Tax planning/tax return preparation
- Country club membership
- First class air travel
- Company airplane usage
- Health club membership
- Luncheon club membership

[115] *Jerry Schwartz, "Coke's Chairman Defends $86 Million Pay and Bonus,"* The New York Times, *April 16, 1992, p. C1.*

[116] *Jacqueline Mitchell, "Herman Miller Links Worker-CEO Pay,"* The Wall Street Journal, *May 7, 1992, p. B1.*

[117] Id.

[118] Id.

- Legal counseling
- No/low interest loans

That last category has seen increasing attention because of the amounts involved. The relatively new practice of corporations loaning money to executives for their mortgages and other purposes is getting shareholder attention. Wells Fargo gave its CEO an interest-free $1 million loan to cover the down payment on his home. His total compensation package without the loan was $6.8 million.[119] Also, when those executives depart, these loans are often forgiven. For example, Mattel Corporation forgave Jill Barhad's debt when she left the company at a time when its performance was suffering dramatically.

There appears to be no limit to the types of perks executives receive. For example, Vince McMahon, head of WWF, receives up to $50,000 per year for cleaning expenses. Macy's, Bloomingdale's, and other department stores offer up to 38 percent discounts to their executives. Avon's Andrea Jung had a $19,000 security system installed in her home at company expense.

Discussion Questions

1. So long as a company is performing and providing a return to investors and growth in the value of their investment, should executive compensation be an issue?
2. The compensation of executives is largely a deductible business expense. Are U.S. taxpayers subsidizing the large CEO salaries?
3. Should CEO pay be tied to workers' compensation?
4. Should CEO pay be tied to company performance?
5. Who should establish executive pay rates?
6. Should institutional investors and other shareholders have input on executive compensation?
7. Do directors who work for the company as consultants or lawyers have conflicts of interest in setting executive compensation?
8. Would government regulation of executive pay interfere with the free enterprise system?
9. How can executive compensation have an impact on company performance as well as share performance? How do you think Milton Friedman would react to controls on levels of compensation? How do you think he would react to this type of compensation program?
10. Do you see any additional conflicts issues with the perks? Do you see any issues that are prevented because executives are given these perks?

[119] *Gary Strauss, "Many Execs Pocket Perks Aplenty,"* USA Today, *May 1, 2001, p. 1B.*

CASE 6.16

Shareholder Proposals and Corporate Governance

Shareholders can submit proposals to be included in proxy solicitation materials. If the company does not oppose what is being proposed, the proposition is included as part of the proxy materials. If management is opposed, the proposing shareholder has the right of a 200-word statement on the proposal in the materials. These proposals are not permitted along with their 200-word statements unless they propose conduct that is legal and related to business operations, as opposed to social, moral, religious, and political views. During the Vietnam era, many shareholders wanted to include proposals in proxy materials for companies that were war suppliers. Their proposals centered around the political opposition to the war and not the business practices of the company.

The proposals have become an area of contention among and between management, the Securities and Exchange Commission (SEC), and shareholders because of the difficulty in defining what constitutes a business issue and what is a political issue. Shareholders argue that the company's position on social issues can be costly in terms of customer boycotts and PR backlash.

For example, Iroquois Brands, Ltd., a food company that imports French foie gras, a pâté made from the enlarged livers of force-fed geese, faced shareholder litigation over this French practice in raising the geese. The practice involves funneling corn down the geese's throats and gagging them with rubber bands to keep them from regurgitating. A shareholder asked to have a proposal included in the proxy materials that proposes that the company study the practice as an unethical business practice (cruelty to animals).[120]

Another example involved Steve Hindi, an animal rights activist who owns $5,000 in Pepsi stock. He discovered that Pepsi advertises in bull rings in Spain and Mexico and has attended annual shareholder meetings and put forward shareholder proposals to have the company halt the practice.

His proposal has not yet passed, but he has started a Web site (http://www.pepsibloodbath.com) to increase pressure on the company.

Pepsi has withdrawn from bullfighting ads in Mexico, but continues with them in Spain. Mr. Hindi continues his quest.[121]

The *Corporate Social Issues Reporter* has provided a tally of the types of shareholder proposals included in the proxies for publicly held companies during the 1999 annual meeting season. The tally is as follows:

Environmental measures	33
Environmental standards compliance (Such as CERES environmental principles)	10
Board diversity	7

[120] Lovenheim v. Iroquois Brands, Ltd., *618 F.Supp. 554 (D.C. 1985).*

[121] *Constance L. Hays, "A PepsiCo Shareholder Meeting and a Very Unhappy Shareholder,"* The New York Times, *April 22, 2000, pp. B1, B4.*

The average shareholder support for the measures was 15 percent of all voting shares. None of the proposals was passed at the shareholder meetings. At Cypress Semiconductor, 42 percent of the shareholders voted in favor of increasing board diversity. However, there were several companies where shareholders dropped proposals after management agreed to comply with the demands in the proposal. For example, Paychex agreed to seek out more women and minorities for its board and the Calvert Group dropped its diversity proxy proposal. McDonald's agreed to ban workplace discrimination based on sexual orientation.

In 1998, Unocal pulled out of Afghanistan following a shareholder proposal relating to human rights issues there. The proposal was withdrawn because Unocal had withdrawn from doing business there.

The *National Law Journal* reports shareholder activism is on the increase. In 1971, a proposal by GM shareholders, including the Episcopal Church, to halt GM business in South Africa barely got 2 percent of the votes cast at the annual meeting. However, some activists have been successful in recent years with their shareholder proposals. For example:

- A Home Depot shareholder proposal to phase out sales of lumber from old forests passed and is in effect;
- A GE shareholder proposal for the company to clean up the Housatonic River in Massachusetts also passed and the company spent nearly $250 million doing so; and
- RJR split its food division from its tobacco division in response to shareholder activism.

The shareholder proposals for 2000 focused on opposition to genetically engineered food and Northern Ireland employment policies. Generic types of shareholder proposals include staggered terms for directors, independent board members, human rights issues, and diversity in boards and the company.[122]

Corporate secretaries who handle proposals and shareholders have their own organization. Their Web site (http://www.ascs.org) includes information on shareholder proposals and shareholder activism.

Institutional investors can also be very active in shareholder proposals and the California Public Employee Retirement Service is one of the country's most active institutional shareholders. (See http://www.calpers-governance.org.)

Discussion Questions

1. Are shareholder proposals an effective means for getting corporations to take action?
2. Are shareholders who bring these proposals acting as advocates for various stakeholders?
3. Are shareholders a means of encouraging social responsibility?
4. Are these proposals always in the best interest of the shareholders? Why do you think management opposes almost all shareholder proposals?

[122] *Richard H. Koppes, "Future Governance and Activism Trends,"* National Law Journal, *July 3, 2000, pp. B1, B14.*

unit 7

Business and Its Product

"A bad reputation is like a hangover. It takes a while to get rid of and it makes everything else hurt."

James Preston
Former CEO, Avon

Quality, safety, service, and social responsibility—customers want these elements in a product and a company. Does the profit motive interfere with these traits?

7a

Contract Relations

The law of contracts is detailed, but ethical discussions center on the fairness of treatment and the balance of the agreement.

CASE 7.1

Intel and Pentium: What to Do When the Chips Are Down

A joke about Intel's Pentium chip (source unknown) circulated on the Internet:

Top Ten Reasons to Buy a Pentium-Equipped Computer

10. Your current computer is too accurate.
9. You want to get into the *Guinness Book of World Records* as "owner of most expensive paperweight."
8. Math errors add zest to life.
7. You need an alibi for the IRS.
6. You want to see what all the fuss is about.
5. You've always wondered what it would be like to be a plaintiff.
4. The "Intel Inside" logo matches your decor perfectly.
3. You no longer have to worry about CPU overheating.
2. You got a great deal from the Jet Propulsion Laboratory.

And, the number one reason to buy a Pentium-equipped computer: It'll probably work.[1]

Intel, which makes components used in 80 percent of all personal computers sold, introduced the powerful Pentium chip in 1993. The firm spent $1 billion developing the chip, while the cost of producing it was estimated to be between $50 and $150 each. Intel shipped 4 million of the chips to computer manufacturers, including IBM.

In July 1994, Intel discovered a flaw in the "floating-point unit" of the chip, which is the section that completes complex calculations quickly.[2]

[1] *From memo furnished to author by Intel employee at that time.*

[2] *Evan Ramstad, "Pentium: a Cautionary Tale,"* Arizona Republic, *December 21, 1994, p. C1.*

The flaw caused errors in division calculations involving numbers with more than eight digits to the right of the decimal, such as in this type of equation:

$$\frac{4,195,835}{3,145,727} \times 3,145,727 = 4,195,835^3$$

Pentium-equipped computers computed the answer, in error, as 4,195,579. Before introducing the Pentium chip, Intel ran 1 trillion tests on it. The company calculated that the Pentium chip would produce an error once every 27,000 years, making the chance of an average user getting an error one in 9 billion.

In November, Thomas Nicely, a mathematician at Lynchburg College in Virginia, discovered the Pentium flaw. On Thanksgiving Day 1994, Intel publicly acknowledged the flaw in the Pentium chip, and the next day, its stock fell from 65 1/8 to 63 7/8. Intel stated that the problem had been corrected but flawed chips were still being shipped because a three-month production schedule was just ending. The firm initially offered to replace the chips but only for users who ran complicated calculations as part of their jobs. The replacement offer carried numerous conditions.[4]

On December 12, 1994, IBM announced that it would stop all shipments of its personal computers because its own tests indicated that Intel had underrepresented the extent of the Pentium flaw.[5] IBM's tests concluded that computer users working on spreadsheets for as little as fifteen minutes per day could produce a mistake every twenty-four days. Intel's CEO Andrew Grove called IBM's reaction "unwarranted." No other computer manufacturer adopted IBM's position. IBM's chief of its personal computing division, G. Richard Thoman, emphasized that IBM had little choice: "It is absolutely critical for this industry to grow, that people trust that our products work right."[6] Following the IBM announcement, Intel's stock price dropped 6.5 percent, and trading had to be halted temporarily.

On December 20, 1994, Grove announced that Intel would replace all Pentium chips:

> We were dealing with a consumer community that was upset with us. That they were upset with us—it has finally dawned on us—is because we were telling them what's good for them. . . . I think we insulted them.[7]

Replacing the chips could have cost up to $360 million. Intel offered to send owners a new chip that they could install or to have service firms replace chips for customers who were uncomfortable doing it themselves.

Robert Sombric, the data processing manager for the city of Portsmouth, New Hampshire, found Intel's decision to continue selling flawed chips for months inexcusable: "I treat the city's money just as if it were my own. And I'm telling you:

[3] *Janice Castro, "When the Chips Are Down,"* Time, *December 26, 1994, p. 126.*

[4] *James Overstreet, "Pentium Jokes Fly, but Sales Stay Strong,"* USA Today, *December 7, 1994, p. 1B.*

[5] *Ira Sager and Robert D. Hof, "Bare Knuckles at Big Blue,"* Business Week, *December 26, 1994, pp. 60–62.*

[6] *Bart Ziegler and Don Clark, "Computer Giants' War over Flaw in Pentium Jolts the PC Industry,"* The Wall Street Journal, *December 13, 1994, pp. A1, A11.*

[7] *Jim Carlton and Stephen Kreider Yoder, "Humble Pie: Intel to Replace Its Pentium Chips,"* The Wall Street Journal, *December 21, 1994, pp. B1, B9.*

I wouldn't buy one of these things right now until we really know the truth about it."[8, 9]

Following the replacement announcement, Intel's stock rose $3.44 to $61.25. One market strategist praised the replacement program: "It's about time. It's very clear they were fighting a losing battle, both in public relations as well as user confidence."[10,11,12]

Grove responded that Intel's delay in offering replacements was based on concerns about precedent. "If we live by an uncompromising standard that demands perfection, it will be bad for everybody,"[13] he said. He also acknowledged that Intel had agreed to sell the flawed Pentium chips to a jewelry manufacturer.[14]

By December 16, 1994, ten lawsuits in three states involving eighteen law firms had been filed against Intel for the faulty chips. While the suits progressed, replacement demands were minimal. Intel's internal employee newsletter had an April 1, 1995 edition that spoofed the infamous chip.[15] A form required customers with Pentium chips to submit a 5,000-word essay on "Why My Pentium Should Be Replaced."

In 1997, Intel launched two new products: Pentium Pro and Pentium II. A new potential bug, again affecting only intensive engineering and scientific mathematical operations, was uncovered. Intel, however, published the list of bugs with technical information and remedies for both of the new processors. One analyst commented on the new approach, "They have learned a lot since then. You can't approach the consumer market with an engineering mindset."[16]

In September 1997, the Federal Trade Commission (FTC) began a broad antitrust inquiry into Intel and whether its practices constituted monopolization. One practice alleged was tying new products to customers' exclusive purchase of existing products. Another practice alleged was "disciplining" customers who cross over to other chip suppliers by cutting off their Intel supply.[17]

Discussion Questions

1. Should Intel have disclosed the flaw in the Pentium chip when it first discovered it in July 1994?
2. Should Intel have issued an immediate recall?
3. Was it ethical to offer limited replacement of the chip?

[8] *Jim Carlton and Scott McCartney, "Corporations Await More Information; Will Consumers Balk?"* The Wall Street Journal, *December 14, 1994, pp. B1, B5.*

[9] *Stephen Kreider Yoder, "The Pentium Proposition: To Buy or Not to Buy,"* The Wall Street Journal, *December 14, 1994, p. B1.*

[10] *Carlton and Kreider Yoder, "Humble Pie: Intel to Replace Its Pentium Chips," pp. B1, B9.*

[11] *"Intel Eats Crow, Replaces Pentiums,"* Mesa Tribune, *December 21, 1994, p. F1.*

[12] *Catalina Ortiz, "Intel to Replace Flawed Pentium Chips,"* Arizona Republic, *December 21, 1994, pp. A1, A8.*

[13] *Ziegler and Clark, "Computer Giants' War over Flaw in Pentium Jolts the PC Industry," pp. A1, A11.*

[14] *Otis Port, "A Chip on Your Shoulder—or Your Cuffs,"* Business Week, *January 23, 1995, p. 8.*

[15] *Richard B. Schmitt, "Flurry of Lawsuits Filed against Intel over Pentium Flaw,"* The Wall Street Journal, *December 16, 1994, p. B3.*

[16] *James Kim, "Intel Proactive With Potential Buy,"* USA Today, *May 6, 1997, p. 1B.*

[17] *"Intel's PC Dominance Draws Scrutiny,"* The Wall Street Journal, *September 25, 1997, p. A3.*

4. Discuss the long-term damage to Intel.
5. Assume that you are an Intel manager invited to the 1994 post-Thanksgiving meeting on how to respond to the public revelation of the flawed chips. You believe the failure to offer replacements will damage the company over the long term. Further, you feel strongly that providing a replacement is a balanced and ethical thing to do. However, CEO Grove disagrees. How would you persuade him to offer replacements to all purchasers?
6. If you could not persuade Grove to replace the chips, would you stay at the company?
7. Has the Pentium incident caused long-term damage to the computer industry?
8. Consider the following analysis (from "Intel Eats Crow, Replaces Pentium," *Mesa Tribune*, December 21, 1994, p. F1):

   Regarding your article "Bare Knuckles at Big Blue" (News: Analysis & Commentary, Dec. 26), future generations of business school students will study Intel Corp.'s response to the problems with the Pentium chip as a classic case study in how to transform a technical problem into a public-relations nightmare.

   Intel's five-point plan consisted of:

   1) Initially deny that the problem exists;
   2) When irrefutable evidence is presented that the problem exists, downplay its significance;
   3) Agree to only replace items for people who can demonstrate extreme hardship;
   4) Continue running your current ad campaign extolling the virtues of the product as if nothing has happened;
   5) Count the short-term profits.[18]

   List other companies discussed in this book or in other readings that followed this same five-point pattern.
9. Do you think Intel's dominance is due exclusively to innovation and quality?

CASE 7.2

Hidden Car Rental Fees

During the 1980s, there were six major players in the global rental car market:

share	*(in billions)*
Hertz	$4.0
Avis	3.2
Budget	2.5
National	2.5
Alamo	0.6
Dollar	0.5
Other	2.5[19]

[18] *"Intel Eats Crow, Replaces Pentiums," p. F1.*

[19] *Matthew L. Wald, "Hertz to New York: Pay More,"* The New York Times, *January 19, 1992, p. F10.*

Customers are often perplexed by the variety of rates and additional charges they face when they go to rent a car. All the national firms have daily, weekend, and weekly rates. Some firms offer unlimited free mileage, while others offer 100 free miles with a charge for each additional mile.[20]

Extra charges may be made for a second driver, a child seat, remote dropoff, and insurance, including collision/damage waiver (CDW), liability, personal effects, and personal accident coverage. A National Car Rental customer in Boston who paid nine dollars a day on top of the sixty-dollar-per-day rental fee in 1987 said, "It's expensive, but I figure you get in a crack-up and you're going to get nailed if you don't have it."[21]

In 1988, regulatory and legislative bodies began taking on car rental practices.[22] Some states took the position that rental car agents should be licensed as insurance agents. In August 1988, a U.S. district court in New York ordered Hertz Corporation to refund $13 million to customers after the company pleaded guilty to criminal charges in connection with overcharging customers to repair vehicles that had been damaged but for which there was no CDW.[23]

On September 4, 1988, the National Association of Attorneys General appointed a task force headed by Kansas Attorney General Bob Stephan to study deceptive and unfair practices in the car rental industry.[24]

In August 1988, the Federal Trade Commission (FTC) cited both large and small companies for using deceptive practices in advertising. Clinton Krislov, a Chicago lawyer who represented consumers in class action lawsuits against rental agencies in Chicago and Des Moines, observed:

> This is sort of like trying to judge an ugly contest among frogs. There are, I suppose, some pockets of honesty in this business, but. . . .[25]

The FTC also proposed a regulation that would require the use of a standard rental contract and disclosure in all ads of full rental charges, including those for gas, collision protection, and repairs. The regulation would also limit charges for collisions and theft to $100.[26]

Some renters who refused CDW had been told no cars were available. Others had $1,000 to $3,000 frozen on their credit cards because they did not take CDW.[27]

In 1989, several states considered legislation to ban CDWs. California passed a law that limited the waiver fee to nine dollars per day and required disclosure to the customer about its purposes (including disclosure in ads). New York and Illinois limited charges for car damage to $100 and $200, respectively, which effectively eliminated the need for most renters to buy CDW.

[20] *Michael Katz, "FTC Forces Car Rental Firms to Reveal All,"* The Wall Street Journal, *August 14, 1992, pp. B1, B2.*

[21] *Corie Brown, "Cracking Down on a Costly Car-Rental Option,"* Business Week, *November 30, 1987, p. 135.*

[22] *Jonathan Dahl and Christopher Winans, "States, Car-Rental Firms Collide over Damage Waivers,"* The Wall Street Journal, *August 14, 1989, p. B1.*

[23] *Wald, "Hertz to New York," p. F10.*

[24] *David Jones, "Illinois Moves to Ban Rental Car Waivers,"* National Underwriter, *July 11, 1988, pp. 3, 79.*

[25] *Alex Taylor, III, "Why Car Rentals Drive You Nuts,"* Fortune, *August 31, 1987, p. 74.*

[26] *Earl Golz, "Hidden Auto Rental Charges, Fees Can Take You for a Ride,"* Mesa Tribune, *February 21, 1989, p. D1.*

[27] *Taylor, "Why Car Rentals Drive You Nuts," p. 74.*

CDW is the money-maker for the smaller rental agencies, which offer lower base rental rates and make their profits through extras such as CDW. These companies maintain that without CDW, which 90 percent of their customers take, they could not compete or survive, and prices would have to go up. Indeed, by 1992, prices at all car rental companies had risen an average of 12 percent.[28]

In 1992, the FTC charged Dollar Rent-A-Car Systems, Inc., and Value Rent-A-Car, Inc., with failure to fully disclose information on charges to customers. Both Dollar and Value settled with the FTC in 1993 by agreeing to disclose more information in their ads.[29]

Under greater scrutiny and regulatory supervision, the companies began implementing new strategies to increase earnings. For example, companies either refuse to rent to or levy a surcharge of ten to fifteen dollars a day on drivers between the ages of 21 and 25.[30, 31, 32] National screens potential renters in New York City and Florida for driving-while-intoxicated (DWI) convictions or suspended or revoked licenses. Some firms charge an additional twenty-five dollars for more than one driver and have raised dropoff and refueling fees.[33, 34, 35, 36]

In 1995, Avis and Hertz reinstated mileage charges for certain renters in certain areas in an attempt to recoup costs that doubled from 1992–1995 after manufacturers refused to buy back the rental cars.[37] In 1997, Budget began charging $30–$100 for no-shows on their reservations.[38] A ban on under-age 25 drivers is in effect in the industry, with the exception of New York where a judge has ruled such age-based distinctions to be a form of discrimination.[39, 40]

The industry underwent a period of restructuring with Dollar and Thrifty combining into one publicly-held company, Dollar Thrifty. National and Alamo are now owned by Republic Industries.

In 1996, Enterprise Rent-A-Car became the nation's largest rental car company, focusing not on airports, but on small towns and the need for rentals when the family car is in the shop. Enterprise holds 20 percent of the $15 billion U.S. market.[41] The

[28] *James S. Hirsch, "Rental Car Firms Jack up Their Prices,"* The Wall Street Journal, *November 4, 1992, pp. B1, B13.*

[29] *Katz, "FTC Forces Car Rental Firms to Reveal All," pp. B1, B2.*

[30] *Susan Brink, Edward C. Baig, Steven D. Kaye, and Margaret Mannix, "A Pox on Young Drivers,"* U.S. News & World Report, *March 29, 1993, p. 63.*

[31] *James S. Hirsch, "Auto Renters Hit the Brakes on Under-25s,"* The Wall Street Journal, *March 16, 1993, p. B1.*

[32] *Lisa Miller, "Young Drivers Can Rent Cars, New York Rules,"* The Wall Street Journal, *March 28, 1997, pp. B1, B2.*

[33] *"Car-Rental Firms Make Extra Drivers Costly,"* The Wall Street Journal, *November 10, 1992, p. B1.*

[34] *Jonathan Dahl, "Rental Counters Reject Drivers without Good Records,"* The Wall Street Journal, *October 23, 1992, p. B1.*

[35] *James S. Hirsch, "'Do-Not-Rent' Lists Tag Bad Drivers,"* The Wall Street Journal, *September 15, 1993, p. B1.*

[36] *Matthew L. Wald, "Car-Rental Computers Rejecting High-Risk Drivers,"* The New York Times, *September 9, 1993, pp. A1, A9.*

[37] *Lisa Miller, "Car Rental Industry Promises That Things Will Improve. Really,"* The Wall Street Journal, *July 17, 1997, pp. A1, A8.*

[38] *Donna Rosato, "Budget Rent-A-Car to Charge No-Shows,"* USA Today, *July 3, 1997, p. 1B.*

[39] *Miller, "Young Drivers Can Rent Cars, New York Rules," pp. B1, B2.*

[40] *Noelle Knox, "Cars Available! But With More Strings Attached,"* The New York Times, *January 11, 1998, p. BU6.*

[41] *Brian O'Reilly, "The Rent-A-Car Jocks Who Made Enterprise #1,"* Fortune, *October 28, 1996, pp. 126–128.*

price of an Enterprise rental is 30 percent below Avis or Hertz, and most of the company's fees are paid by warranty policies or insurance coverage (in the case of an accident).[42]

Discussion Questions

1. Assume you are the public affairs vice president for one of the top six rental car companies. Would you change any of your policies with respect to CDW?
2. Would you change your advertising to disclose CDW charges?
3. Would you instruct your counter agents to explain that the CDW coverage may be duplicative?
4. Would you change any of the other extra charges typical in the industry (that is, would you revamp your pricing policy)? Would such a change hurt or help your ability to compete?
5. Do you see practices in this industry that regulators may tackle in the future? Would you voluntarily change any of these practices?
6. Is it significant that Enterprise, with its different charges, captured the market?

Sources

Bryant, Adam, "GM Agrees to Sell Car Rental Unit," *The New York Times*, April 5, 1995, pp. C1, C2.

Jacobson, Gianna, "Enterprise's Unconventional Path," *The New York Times*, January 23, 1997, pp. C1, C6.

CASE 7.3

Thinning Diet Industry

Oprah Winfrey started a diet craze when she appeared on her television show in 1988 in her size-ten Calvin Klein jeans and boasted of losing sixty-seven pounds by using Sandoz Nutrition Corporation's Optifast Program. The preventive medicine center at Philadelphia's Graduate Hospital got 500 calls about Optifast the day of Oprah's announcement. Since then, the diet industry has grown 15 percent per year with total annual revenues topping $3 billion. The major competitors in 1992, at the height of the diet market were:

[42] *Matthew L. Wald, "Hertz Ends 'Drop Charges' on One-Way Rentals,"* The New York Times, *October 15, 1992, pp. C1, C10.*

Weight Watchers International	$1.3 billion
Nutri/System, Inc.	$764 million
Diet Center, Inc.	$275 million
Thompson Medical Company (Slim-Fast)	$260 million
Sandoz Nutrition (Optifast)	$120 million[43]

Diet programs are sold through celebrity endorsements and before-and-after ads. Lynn Redgrave has represented Weight Watchers, Susan Saint James has appeared for Diet Center, and Christina Ferrara, Tommy Lasorda, Kathie Lee Gifford, and others have endorsed Slim-Fast and Ultra Slim-Fast. Nutri/System has relied on radio disc jockeys to use its programs and then tell listeners about their weight losses.

The CEO of Weight Watchers likened the diet craze to the excesses of the 1980s on Wall Street: everything is more and more extreme.[44] By mid-year 1990, Representative Ron Wyden of Oregon, chair of the House Small Business Subcommittee, asked industry representatives to explain their hard-sell tactics. Wyden's hearings revealed that fully 90 percent of those who lose weight rapidly on the quick-loss programs regain the lost weight and often more within two years. Wyden asked why employees of these programs were referred to as weight loss specialists when in fact they had no expertise and were really sales personnel. Weight Watchers CEO Charles Berger testified:

> Without touching on the issue of greed, some companies in our field have over-promised quick weight loss. And the promises have grown increasingly excessive.[45]

Just before the House hearings, nineteen women sued Nutri/System and Jenny Craig, Inc., in Dade County (Miami), Florida, for gallbladder damage allegedly caused by the programs' diets. Seventeen of the women had had their gallbladders removed after participating in the Nutri/System program, even though they had no previous diagnosis of gallbladder difficulties.

In response to the suits and in the hearings, Nutri/System stated that obese people are vulnerable to a variety of ailments, including gallbladder disease. The company labeled the suits "without merit" and "a carefully orchestrated" campaign by the lawyers for the nineteen women.

Nutri/System was forced into Chapter 11 bankruptcy but emerged in 1993 under new ownership and a new weight loss philosophy that included encouraging the use of exercise equipment in its facilities.

A marketing consultant has observed about the diet industry:

> There is such a market for faddish nutritional services that even if you lose some customers you'll get new ones. To some extent in this industry, a lot more depends on how good your marketing is than your product.[46]

[43] *Kathleen Deveny, "Blame It on Dashed Hopes (and Oprah): Disillusioned Dieters Shun Liquid Meals,"* The Wall Street Journal, *October 13, 1992, pp. B1, B11.*

[44] *Julie Johnson, "Bringing Sanity to the Diet Craze,"* Time, *May 21, 1990, p. 74.*

[45] Id.

[46] *Alix Freedman and Udayan Gupta, "Lawsuits May Trim Diet Firms,"* The Wall Street Journal, *March 23, 1990, p. B1.*

In 1991, the Federal Trade Commission (FTC) charged Optifast 70, Medifast 70, and Ultrafast with making marketing claims that were deceptive and "unsubstantiated hype."[47] The agency called the statement "you'll have all you need to control your weight for the rest of your life" unsubstantiated.[48] The FTC also announced it was investigating other diet programs. Representative Wyden said the FTC's complaints against the three companies were only "the tail of the elephant; the real test is whether these standards will be applied throughout the industry."[49]

By mid-1992, the FTC completed its investigation of misleading advertising by more than a dozen diet chains and promulgated guidelines for such advertising.[50] Before-and-after testimonials must include pictures of typical clients, not just the most successful ones, and claims of keeping the weight off must be documented. The FTC's guidelines were the result of the National Institutes of Health's findings that virtually all dieters regain two-thirds of their weight within a year and all of it within five years.[51]

As the FTC was promulgating these rules, the Food and Drug Administration announced that it would decide whether phenylpropanolamine, an amphetamine-like stimulant, could continue to be used in appetite-suppressant products, such as Acutrim and Dexatrim. Further, lawsuits based in product liability on the inherent dangers of these diet pills (including wrongful death actions) are pending around the country.[52]

Meanwhile, Oprah Winfrey announced that she would never again use a liquid diet, and an Alabama jury awarded $15 million to the mother of a 23-year-old bride-to-be who died of heart failure after losing twenty-one pounds in six weeks under the supervision of the Physicians' Weight Loss Center.

Several sociological issues surround weight loss. Susie Orbach, author of *Fat Is a Feminist Issue*, observes that 50 million Americans begin diets every year: "When I started working in this field 22 years ago, eating problems affected a limited group, women in their 30s and 40s. Now, we know from studies that girls of 9 and women of 60 are all obsessed with the way they look."[53]

The top two companies in the diet industry—Jenny Craig and Weight Watchers—were cited by the FTC in October 1993 for falsely advertising the success of their programs.[54] Three other companies (Diet Center, Nutri/System, and Physicians' Weight Loss Centers of America) settled with the FTC by agreeing to (1) not misrepresent program performance in ads, (2) gather and make available supporting data, and (3)

[47] *Jeanne Saddler, "Three Diet Firms Settle False Ad Case; Two Others Vow to Fight FTC Charges,"* The Wall Street Journal, *October 1, 1993, p. B8.*

[48] *Molly O'Neill, "Five Diet Companies Ask U.S. for Uniform Rules on Ads,"* The New York Times, *August 25, 1992, pp. C1, C2.*

[49] *Jeanne Saddler, "FTC Targets Thin Claims of Liquid Diets,"* The Wall Street Journal, *October 17, 1991, pp. B1, B6.*

[50] *Mike Snider, "FTC Weighs Claims of Diet Program Ads,"* USA Today, *March 26, 1993, p. 1D.*

[51] *Mike Snider, "FTC Cites Diet Firms for False Claims,"* USA Today, *October 1, 1993, p. 1D.*

[52] *Joseph Weber, "The Diet Business Takes It on the Chin,"* Business Week, *April 16, 1990, pp. 86–87.*

[53] *Larry Armstrong and Maria Mallory, "The Diet Business Starts Sweating,"* Business Week, *June 22, 1992, pp. 32–33.*

[54] *Amy Barrett, "How Can Jenny Craig Keep on Gaining?"* Business Week, *April 12, 1993, pp. 52–53.*

include disclosures that most weight loss is temporary and say whether a testimonial is typical or not.[55]

The New York City Department of Consumer Affairs was the first in the nation to issue "truth-in-dieting" regulations for diet centers, violations of which carry a $500 fine:

1. Centers must post a prominent Weight-Loss Consumer Bill of Rights sign in every room where a sales presentation is made. The sign informs consumers there may be serious health problems associated with rapid weight loss and that only lifestyle changes, such as healthy eating and exercise, promote permanent weight loss.
2. All centers must also give every potential client a palm-size Consumer Bill of Rights card.
3. All centers must inform potential clients of hidden costs of products or laboratory tests that may be part of the program.
4. All centers must tell dieters the expected duration of the program.

The FTC actions against false advertising led to a 15 percent reduction in diet industry revenues in 1994.[56, 57]

In 1997, just as the industry was recovering, the American Society of Bariatric Physicians released a list of its concerns about the industry's usage of obesity drugs such as Redux and fen-Phen along with promises of permanent weight loss.[58] The presence of the new prescription obesity drugs produced new weight-loss clinics focusing entirely on the pills and prescriptions, with a total of 18 million monthly prescriptions in 1996 given, in many cases, not to the clinically obese but to those seeking to lose five to ten pounds.[59, 60]

A 1997 study found the presence of heart valve damage among users of fen-Phen and the FDA withdrew the diet drugs from the market.[61] Those who had been using the diet drugs began litigation. By 2000, American Home Products had agreed to a $4.8 billion settlement with 11,000 class action litigants.[62] Since the time of the FDA ban on the drugs, those companies with alternative diet drugs without as much risk have had a difficult time selling even prescription drugs. Anti-obesity drugs sales reached almost $500 million in 1996, but by 1998 had fallen to $28.8 million, a level at which they remain.[63] There are still cases pending involving those who did not settle with the class as part of the nationwide litigation. For example, a jury awarded Gloria Lopez, a cafeteria supervisor who took Pondimin, the fenfluramine portion of

55 *Keith L. Alexander, "A Health Kick at Weight Watchers,"* Business Week, *January 16, 1995, p. 36.*

56 *Weber, "The Diet Business Takes It on the Chin," pp. 86–87.*

57 *Ellen Neuborne, "Weight-Loss Programs Going Hungry,"* USA Today, *July 28, 1994, pp. 1C, 2C.*

58 *Laura Johannes, "New Diet-Drug Data Spark More Controversy,"* The Wall Street Journal, *October 1, 1997, pp. B1, B12.*

59 *Robert Langreth and Laura Johannes, "Redux Diet Pill Receives a Boost in New Study,"* The Wall Street Journal, *April 1, 1998, pp. B1, B4.*

60 *Gina Kolata, "Companies Recall 2 Top Diet Drugs at F.D.A.'s Urging,"* The Wall Street Journal, *September 16, 1997, p. A1.*

61 *Jeanne Saddler, "Diet Firms' Weight-Loss Claims Are Being Investigated by FTC,"* The Wall Street Journal, *March 26, 1993, pp. B1, B5.*

62 *Steve Sternberg, "Lawsuits: Drug Development's Big Side Effect,"* USA Today, *January 12, 2000, p. 10D.*

63 *Dana Canedy, "Predecessors' Woes Make Diet Drug a Tough Sell,"* The New York Times, *April 11, 1998, p. B1.*

fen-Phen, for five months and lost ten pounds, $54 million because her aortic valve was damaged and will eventually require replacement.[64]

Diet centers relying on the two drugs have also been named in the litigation and many, based solely on the prescription approach, have closed.[65, 66] Customers who have become plaintiffs are complaining about the lack of warnings given to them by these diet centers.

In early 1998, a study of 1,072 people, sponsored by the parent company of the manufacturers of Redux and Pondimin, found only a 6.5 to 7.3 percent rate of heart valve problems in patients who took the drugs, as opposed to a 4.5 percent rate in patients who took the dummy pill. A cardiologist labeled the difference in rates "not statistically significant." However, the FDA ban remained and the litigation continued.[67]

New products for weight reduction, speeding up the metabolism, and appetite suppression continue to come to market. Metabolife International, Inc., ran an aggressive Web-based campaign to counter negative media reports about side effects for its Metabolife dietary supplement that the company says speeds up metabolism and reduces the appetite.[68]

Discussion Questions

1. Assume that you get a part-time job as a "weight counselor" with a quick-weight-loss program. Would you have any ethical constraints in performing your job?
2. Don't people just want to lose weight quickly? What if you told them they would gain it back and face health risks but they decided to go forward anyway? Would you and your product be adhering to a proper moral standard of full disclosure and freedom of choice?
3. Does the diet industry make money from temporary motivation? Or does the diet industry only provide temporary motivation?
4. Are the weight-loss ads misleading?
5. Weight Watchers, which posted a $50 million loss in 1994, has begun a new program emphasizing health foods, heart disease prevention, and exercise. Will this type of program avoid the ethical issues of rapid-weight-loss programs?
6. Given the Redux and fen-Phen problems, what can be safely concluded about the diet industry? What would be an ethical approach to running a weight-loss clinic?
7. Do you think there is a conflict with the 1998 study's sponsorship? What precautions should those professors conducting the study take?

[64] *Margaret Cronin Fisk, "Fen-Phen Jury Awards $56 Million,"* National Law Journal, *April 23, 2001, p. A10.*

[65] *"A Bill of Rights for Dieters,"* Shape, *November 1993, p. 30.*

[66] *Freedman and Gupta, "Lawsuits May Trim Diet Firms," pp. B1, B2.*

[67] *Kolata, "Companies Recall 2 Top Diet Drugs at F.D.A.'s Urging," p. A1.*

[68] *Bruce Orwall, "Diet-Pill Maker Battles a Report Before It Airs,"* The Wall Street Journal, *October 6, 1999, pp. B1, B4.*

Sources

Hellmich, Nanci, "Heart Valve Damage Prompts Withdrawal," *USA Today*, September 16, 1997, p. 1A.

Hellmich, Nanci, "Withdrawal of Drugs Leaves Dieters in Quandary," *USA Today*, September 22, 1997, p. 6D.

Hilts, Philip J., "Medicine Remains as Much Art as Science," *The New York Times*, September 21, 1997, p. WK5.

Janofsky, Michael, "Hearing for Franchisees in Nutri/System Buyout," *The New York Times*, May 11, 1993, p. C6.

Johannes, Laura, and Steve Secklow, "Heart-Valve Problem That Felled Diet Pills Had Arisen Previously," *The Wall Street Journal*, December 11, 1997, p. A1.

Schroder, Michael, "The Diet Business Is Getting a Lot Skinnier," *Business Week*, June 24, 1991, pp. 132–134.

Sternberg, Steve, "Study: No Heart Damage From Diet Drug," *USA Today*, April 1, 1998, p. 1A.

CASE 7.4

Sears and High-Cost Auto Repairs

In 1991, the California Department of Consumer Affairs began investigating Sears Auto Repair Centers. Sears' automotive unit, with 850 repair shops nationwide, generated 9 percent of the merchandise group's $19.4 billion in revenues. It was one of the fastest-growing and most profitable divisions of Sears over the previous two years.

In the California investigation, agents posed as customers at thirty-three of the seventy-two Sears automotive repair shops located from Los Angeles to Sacramento. They found that they were overcharged 90 percent of the time by an average of $223. In the first phase of the investigation, the agents took thirty-eight cars with worn-out brakes but no other mechanical problems to twenty-seven Sears shops between December 1990 and December 1991. In thirty-four of the cases, the agents were told that their cars needed additional work. At the Sears shop in Concord, a San Francisco suburb, the agent was overcharged $585 to replace the front brake pads, front and rear springs, and control-arm bushings. Sears advertised brake jobs at prices of $48 and $58.[69]

In the second phase of the investigation, Sears was notified of the investigation and ten shops were targeted. In seven of those cases, the agents were overcharged. No springs and shocks were sold in these cases, but the average overcharge was $100 per agent.

[69] *James R. Healey, "Shops under Pressure to Boost Profits,"* USA Today, *July 14, 1992, p. 1A.*

Up until 1990, Sears had paid its repair center service advisors by the hour rather than by the amount of work.[70] But in February 1990, Sears instituted an incentive compensation policy under which employees were paid based on the amount of repairs customers authorized.[71] Service advisors also had to meet sales quotas on specific auto parts; those who did not meet the quotas often had their hours reduced or were assigned to work in other departments in the Sears stores. California regulators said the number of consumer complaints they received about Sears shops increased dramatically after the commission structure was implemented.

The California Department of Consumer Affairs charged all seventy-two Sears automotive shops in the state with fraud, false advertising, and failure to clearly state parts and labor on invoices.

Jim Conran, the director of the consumer affairs department, stated:

> This is a flagrant breach of the trust and confidence the people of California have placed in Sears for generations. Sears has used trust as a marketing tool, and we don't believe they've lived up to that trust. The violation of the faith that was placed in Sears cannot be allowed to continue, and for past violations of law, a penalty must be paid.[72]

Dick Schenkkan, a San Francisco lawyer representing Sears, charged that Conran issued the complaint in response to bipartisan legislative efforts to cut his agency's funding because of a state budget crunch and claimed, "He is garnering as much publicity as he can as quickly as he can. If you wanted to embark on a massive publicity campaign to demonstrate how aggressive you are and how much need there is for your services in the state, what better target than a big, respected business that would guarantee massive press coverage?"[73]

Richard Kessel, the executive director of the New York State Consumer Protection Board, stated that he also had "some real problems" with Sears' policy of paying people by commission. "If that's the policy," Kessel said, "that in my mind could certainly lead to abuses in car repairs."[74]

Immediately following the issuing of the California complaint, Sears said that the state's investigation was "very seriously flawed and simply does not support the allegations. The service we recommend and the work we perform are in accordance with the highest industry standards."[75]

It then ran the the following ad:

> With over two million automotive customers serviced last year in California alone, mistakes may have occurred. However, Sears wants you to know that we would never intentionally violate the trust customers have shown in our company for 105 years.

[70] *Gregory A. Patterson, "Distressed Shoppers, Disaffected Workers Prompt Stores to Alter Sales Commissions,"* The Wall Street Journal, *July 1, 1992, pp. B1, B4.*

[71] *James R. Healey, "Sears Auto Cuts Commissions,"* USA Today, *June 23, 1992, p. 2B.*

[72] *Lawrence M. Fisher, "Accusation of Fraud at Sears,"* The New York Times, *June 12, 1992, pp. C2, C12.*

[73] Id.

[74] Id.

[75] *Tung Yin, "Sears Is Accused of Billing Fraud at Auto Centers,"* The Wall Street Journal, *June 12, 1992, p. B1.*

Ten days after the complaint was announced, the chairman of Sears, Edward A. Brennan, announced that Sears was eliminating the commission-based pay structure for employees who propose auto repairs.[76] He conceded that the pay structure may have created an environment in which mistakes were made because of rigid attention to goals. Brennan announced the compensation system would be replaced with one in which customer satisfaction would now be the primary factor in determining service personnel rewards, shifting the emphasis away from quantity to quality. An outside firm would be hired to conduct unannounced shopping audits of Sears auto centers to be certain the hard sells were eliminated. Further, Brennan said, the sales quotas on parts would be discontinued. While he did not admit to any scheme to recommend unnecessary repairs, he emphasized that the system encouraged mistakes and he accepted full responsibility for the policies. "The buck stops with me," he said.[77]

Sears auto repair customers filed class action lawsuits in California, and a New Jersey undercover investigation produced similar findings of overcharging. New Jersey officials found that 100 percent of the Sears stores in its investigation recommended unneeded work compared to 16 percent of stores not owned by Sears.[78] On June 25, 1992, Sears ran a full-page ad in all major newspapers throughout the country. The ad, a letter signed by Brennan, had the following text:

An Open Letter to Sears Customers:

You may have heard recent allegations that some Sears Auto Centers in California and New Jersey have sold customers parts and services they didn't need. We take such charges very seriously, because they strike at the core of our company—our reputation for trust and integrity.

We are confident that our Auto Center customers' satisfaction rate is among the highest in the industry. But after an extensive review, we have concluded that our incentive compensation and goal-setting program inadvertently created an environment in which mistakes have occurred. We are moving quickly and aggressively to eliminate that environment.

To guard against such things happening in the future, we're taking significant action:

We have eliminated incentive compensation and goal-setting systems for automotive service advisors—the folks who diagnose problems and recommend repairs to you. We have replaced these practices with a new non-commission program designed to achieve even higher levels of customer satisfaction. Rewards will now be based on customer satisfaction.

We're augmenting our own quality control efforts by retaining an independent organization to conduct ongoing, unannounced "shopping audits" of our automotive services to ensure that company policies are being met.

We have written to all state attorneys general, inviting them to compare our auto repair standards and practices with those of their states in order to determine whether differences exist.

And we are helping to organize and fund a joint industry-consumer-government effort to review current auto repair practices and recommend uniform industry standards.

[76] *Lawrence M. Fisher, "Sears' Auto Centers to Halt Commissions,"* The New York Times, *June 23, 1992, p. C1.*

[77] *Gregory A. Patterson, "Sears' Brennan Accepts Blame for Auto Flap,"* The Wall Street Journal, *June 23, 1992, p. B1.*

[78] *Jennifer Steinhauer, "Time to Call a Sears Repairman,"* The New York Times, *January 15, 1998, pp. B1, B2.*

We're taking these actions so you'll continue to come to Sears with complete confidence. However, one thing we will never change is our commitment to customer safety. Our policy of preventive maintenance—recommending replacement of worn parts before they fail—has been criticized by the California Bureau of Automotive Repair as constituting unneeded repairs. We don't see it that way. We recommend preventive maintenance because that's what our customers want, and because it makes for safer cars on the road. In fact, 75 percent of the consumers we talked to in a nationwide survey last weekend told us that auto repair centers should recommend replacement parts for preventive maintenance. As always, no work will ever be performed without your approval.

We understand that when your car needs service, you look for, above all, someone you can trust. And when trust is at stake, you can't merely react, we must overreact.

We at Sears are totally committed to maintaining your confidence. You have my word on it.

Ed Brennan
Chairman and Chief Executive Officer
Sears, Roebuck and Co.[79]

On September 2, 1992, Sears agreed to pay $8 million to resolve the consumer affairs agency claims on overcharging in California. The $8 million included reimbursement costs, new employee training, and coupons for discounts at the service center. Another $15 million in fines was paid in 41 other states to settle class action suits.[80, 81]

In December 1992, Sears fired John T. Lundegard, the director of its automotive operations. Sears indicated that Lundegard's termination was not related to the controversy surrounding the auto centers.

Sears recorded a net loss of $3.9 billion despite $52.3 billion in sales in 1992—the worst performance ever by the retailer in its 108-year history and its first loss since 1933. Its Allstate Insurance division was reeling from damage claims for Hurricane Andrew in the Gulf Coast and Hurricane Iniki in Hawaii ($1.25 billion). Auto center revenue dropped $80 million in the last quarter of 1992, and Sears paid out a total of $27 million to settle state overcharging claims. Moody's downgraded Sears debt following the loss announcement.

In 1994, Sears partially reinstated its sales-incentive practices in its auto centers. Service advisors must earn at least 40 percent of their total pay in commissions on the sale and installation of tires, batteries, shock absorbers, and struts. Not included on commission scales are brakes and front-end alignments (the core of the 1992 problems). Earnings in auto centers have not yet returned to pre-1992 levels.

Discussion Questions

1. What temptations did the employee compensation system present?

[79] *"Open Letter,"* Arizona Republic, *June 25, 1992, p. A9.*

[80] *Barnaby J. Feder, "Sears Post First Loss Since 1933,"* The New York Times, *October 23, 1992, p. C1.*

[81] *"Sears Gets Handed a Huge Repair Bill,"* Business Week, *September 14, 1992, p. 38.*

2. If you had been a service advisor, would you have felt comfortable recommending repairs that were not immediately necessary but would be eventually?
3. What will the complaints cost Sears, regardless of their eventual disposition?
4. Did Brennan acknowledge moral responsibility for the overcharges?
5. Does it matter whether the overcharges were intentional or part of business incentives?
6. A public relations expert has said of the Sears debacle: "Don't make the Sears mistake. When responding to a crisis, tell the public what happened and why. Apologize with no crossed fingers. Then say what you're going to do to make sure it doesn't happen again."[82] What are the ethical standards in this public relations formula?
7. What will be the likely results of the incentive reinstatement?
8. There are some who have expressed concerns about the ethical culture at Sears. While incentive systems may have created the auto center fraud problems, consider the following dilemmas involving Sears since the time of its auto center fraud cases:

   - Montgomery Ward obtained an order from a federal court prohibiting Sears from hiring employees away from Wards as it works its way through Chapter 11 bankruptcy. The order was based on an e-mail sent from Sears' regional vice president, Mary Conway, in which Sears managers are instructed to "be predatory" about hiring away Montgomery Ward managers.
   - A class action civil suit was filed in Atlanta against Sears by consumers who allege that Sears sold them used batteries as new. One of the plaintiffs in the suit alleges that an investigator purchased one hundred "new" batteries from Sears in 1995 (in thirty-two states) and that seventy-eight of them showed signs of previous usage. A Sears internal auto-center document explains that the high allowances the centers must give customers on returns of batteries cuts into profits and induces the sale of used batteries to compensate. (Sears denies the allegation and attributes it to disgruntled former employees and not understanding that a nick does not necessarily mean a battery is used.)[83]
   - Sears admitted to "flawed legal judgment" when it made repayment agreements with its credit card customers who were already in bankruptcy, a practice in violation of creditors' rights and priorities. Sears agreed to refund the amounts collected from the 2,700 customers who were put into the program. Sears warned the refunds could have a "material effect" on earnings. The announcement caused a price of stock drop of 3 7/8. Sears included the following notice to its credit card customers:

   NOTICE: If you previously filed for personal bankruptcy under Chapter 7 and entered into a reaffirmation agreement with Sears, you may be a member of a Settlement Class in a proposed class action settlement. For information, please call 1-800-529-4500. There are deadlines as early as October 8, 1997 applicable to the settlement.

[82] *Nat B. Read, "Sears PR Debacle Shows How Not to Handle a Crisis,"* The Wall Street Journal, *January 11, 1993, p. A14.*

[83] *There were questions and investigations surrounding Exide Corporation, Sears battery supplier. The questions related to the quality of the batteries and Exide at one point announced that its expected to face criminal indictment for certain of its business practices. Keith Bradsher, "Exide Says Indictment Is Likely Over Its Car Battery Sales to Sears,"* The New York Times, *January 11, 2001, pp. B1, B7.*

Sears entered a guilty plea to criminal fraud charges in connection with the bankruptcy issues and agreed to pay a $60 million fine, the largest in the history of bankruptcy fraud cases.[84] The company also settled with the fifty state attorneys general, which included $40 million in state fines, $12 million for state shareholder suits, and a write-off of the $126 million owed by the cardholders involved which was forgiven as part of the settlement.[85]

Sears also settled the class action suit on the bankruptcy issue by agreeing to pay $36 million in cash and issuing $118 million in coupons to those cardholders affected by its conduct with regard to bankruptcy customers. Sears did not admit any wrongdoing as part of the settlement but indicated the action was taken "to avoid the litigation."[86] Sears spent $56 million in legal and administrative costs in handling the bankruptcy cases.

Sears has been struggling to find its market niche for some time. In 2001, it was forced to close eighty-nine stores as it watched its competitor, Montgomery Wards, close its doors for good.[87]

Discussion Questions

1. What do you believe creates Sears' culture? Sears' stock price and earnings fell.

2. What lesson is there in these consequences?

3. Compute the total costs of the bankruptcy cases to Sears.

Sources

Berner, Robert, "Sears Faces Controversy Over Car Batteries," *The Wall Street Journal*, August 26, 1997, p. B2.

Berner, Robert, and JoAnn S. Lublin, "Sears Is Told It Can't Shop for Ward Brass," *The Wall Street Journal*, August 13, 1997, pp. B1, B6.

Conlin, Michelle, "Sears: The Turnaround Is For Real," *Forbes*, December 15, 1997.

Flynn, Julia, Christina Del Valle, and Russell Mitchell, "Did Sears Take Other Customers for a Ride?" *Business Week*, August 3, 1992, pp. 24–25.

Fuchsberg, Gilbert, "Sears Reinstates Sales Incentives in Some Centers," *The Wall Street Journal*, March 7, 1994, p. B1.

Miller, James, "Sears Roebuck Expects Loss in Third Period," *The Wall Street Journal*, September 8, 1992, p. A3.

[84] *Joseph B. Cahill, "Sears Agrees to Plead Guilty to Charges of Criminal Fraud in Credit-Card Case,"* The Wall Street Journal, *February 10, 1999, p. B2.*

[85] Id.

[86] *Leslie Kaufman, "Sears Settles Suit on Raising of Its Credit Card Rates,"* The New York Times, *March 11, 1999, p. C2.*

[87] *Amy Merrick, "Sears to Shut 89 Stores and Report Big Changes,"* The Wall Street Journal, *January 5, 2001, p. A4.*

Patterson, Gregory A., "Sears Debt of $11 Billion Is Downgraded," *The Wall Street Journal*, December 11, 1992, p. A3.

"Sears Roebuck Fires Head of Its Auto Unit," *The Wall Street Journal*, December 21, 1992, p. B6.

Stevenson, Richard W., "Sears' Crisis: How Did It Do?" *The New York Times*, June 17, 1992, p. C1.

Woodyard, Chris, "Sears to Refund Millions to Bankrupt Customers," *USA Today*, April 11–13, 1997, p. 1A.

CASE 7.5

Magazine Contests: The Disclosure of Odds

Investigations of American Family Publishers and Publishers Clearing House centered around the mailings sent by the companies that included the term "finalist" on the envelope and whether the materials stated clearly enough that "no purchase is required." The "finalist" notification is mailed with subscription information for the purchase of subscriptions to magazines. Most people (99 percent) who send in their entries do order magazines.

Twenty-four states investigated Publishers Clearing House and American Family Publishers in twenty-one states. The Florida Attorney General filed suit against Publishers Clearing House as well as Ed McMahon and Dick Clark, their celebrity spokespersons, for deceptive practices.

One mailing from American Family Publishers includes the following:[88]

> So please accept our invitation as soon as you receive it. Once you do, you'll experience the thrill of winning—and that's guaranteed.

The investigation in the various states revealed that many senior citizens were subscribing to between twenty and thirty magazines with the hope of collecting prizes they believed were theirs. Some of the language used in the 200 million mailings included the following:

> John Doe, it's down to a 2 person race for $11,000,000—you and one other person in—(state's name placed here) were issued one of two winning numbers.
>
> We have reserved an $11,000,000 sum in your name.
>
> Are you willing to risk letting your alternative take it all?

These statements were in bold while disclaimers establishing that the win was not all that certain were in fine print. The language in bold caused many to buy yet another subscription with the hope of winning.

American Family Publishers (the company with the mailings that read "YOU MAY ALREADY BE A WINNER" on the outside of the envelope) agreed to pay $1.25

[88] *Tom Loury, "Settlement Won't End American Family Woes,"* USA Today, *March 20, 1998, pp. 1B, 2B.*

million to settle allegations in thirty-two states plus the District of Columbia regarding deceptive sales practices. Lawsuits against Dick Clark and Ed McMahon, the spokesmen for the company, were settled.

The settlement requires American Family to establish a toll-free telephone number for information requests as well as a Web site. Consumers must also be given information about getting off American Family mailing lists. Finally, American Family must stop using two mail addresses for the entries. Those who were simply entering the contest were instructed to use one address, while those who were subscribing and entering were told to send their envelope to another address. The two-address system led many to believe that an accompanying subscription was a key in collecting the prize described in the bold print.

Discussion Questions

1. Do you think there was deception in any of the practices?
2. What is the role of regulators in this situation?
3. Have the companies taken advantage of potential customers?

CASE 7.6

McDonald's and the Disappearing Dodge Viper Game Pieces

Jerome P. Jacobson was the marketing mastermind who managed McDonald's customer games such as Monopoly and Who Wants to Be a Millionaire. Though not an employee of McDonald's, Mr. Jacobson was a principal at Simon Marketing, which made and handled the distribution of the game materials and pieces.

Being in a position of security and trust, Mr. Jacobson was able to skim off winning game pieces before they were distributed to McDonald's and then to the customers. Beginning in 1995, Mr. Jacobson, or "Uncle Jerry," as he was known, operated a ring of at least eight people who conspired to take the trips, cars, and large prizes McDonald's games offered. They are alleged to have netted $13 million from obtaining the winning game pieces.

The FBI uncovered the prize network when it began working on an anonymous tip from someone who indicated that "Uncle Jerry" might be fixing the McDonald's games. The FBI tracked closely those who were claiming the prizes and then set up a series of wiretaps that eventually led to the disclosure of the ring. The agents were able to follow members of the ring to their clandestine meetings, one of which was held in, ironically, Fair Play, South Carolina.[89] In some of the wiretaps the agents listened as

[89] *David Stout, "8 Charged with Rigging McDonald's Promotional Games,"* The New York Times, *August 22, 2001, p. A14.*

the participants argued over how to split the proceeds. In other meetings they simply discussed ways to push McDonald's to pay their prizes more quickly.[90] With McDonald's cooperation in providing the names of winners for all their contests, the FBI was able to uncover the network of Uncle Jerry. McDonald's cooperated with the FBI in what would eventually become a sting operation.

What the FBI uncovered with this information and cooperation was a complex organizational structure headed by Uncle Jerry, who was based out of Lawrenceville, Georgia. Jacobson would embezzle the game pieces and then sell them to individuals around the country. These individuals would become recruiters who would ask friends and relatives to buy pieces and claim the prizes. Some of these individuals actually mortgaged their homes in order to be able to buy the winning pieces from the recruiters. When they claimed their prizes, and they were mostly the big prizes such as a Dodge Viper and the millionaire tickets, they would pay a portion to the recruiters. The recruiters would then give a portion of their proceeds to Uncle Jerry. No one is certain where the informant fits in the organization, but he was able to supply the FBI with several names of those who were eventually arrested.

In order to right the wrong to its customers, McDonald's ran a $10 million prize giveaway weekend over the Labor Day weekend from August 30 through September 2, 2001.[91] McDonald's ended its contract with Simon Marketing at the same time. It was a 25-year relationship and McDonald's was responsible for 77 percent of Simon's revenues.[92]

Discussion Questions

1. Although an accounting firm was hired to supervise Jacobson and his distribution, apparently Jacobson operated without any checks. What does this factor and the case teach about internal controls?
2. What is the significance of the informant's work and tip?
3. When the FBI approached McDonald's, it knew that its games and image would be tarnished. Why do you think McDonald's cooperated?
4. Why did McDonald's run the $10 million Labor Day weekend game?
5. Mr. Jacobson met some of his recruiters when he worked as a police officer. Do you think their skills in law enforcement helped them evade authorities and detection for as long as they did?

[90] *Gary Fields and Shirley Leung, "Eight People Arrested, Charged with Bilking McDonald's Contests,"* The Wall Street Journal, *August 22, 2001, pp. A3, A8.*

[91] *Bruce Horovitz, "Games Scandal Tarnishes Golden Arches,"* USA Today, *August 22, 2001, p. 1B.*

[92] *Gary Strauss, "Informant Key to Unlocking Scam Behind the Golden Arches,"* USA Today, *August 24, 2001, pp. 1B, 2B.*

7b

Product Safety

Only a manufacturer knows the results of its safety tests on a product. Only the manufacturer can correct defects or recall dangerous products. The decision to act on safety tests or recall a product is costly. The only "earnings" on recalls are the preservation of the company's reputation.

CASE 7.7

Tylenol: The Product and Its Packaging Safety

In 1982, 23-year-old Diane Elsroth died after taking a Tylenol capsule laced with cyanide. Within five days of her death, seven more people died from taking tainted Tylenol purchased from stores in the Chicago area.

Tylenol generated $525 million per year for McNeil Consumer Products, Inc., a subsidiary of Johnson & Johnson. The capsule form of the pain reliever represented 30 percent of Tylenol sales. McNeil's marketing studies indicated that consumers found the capsules easy to swallow and believed, without substantiation, that Tylenol in capsule form worked faster than Tylenol tablets.

The capsules' design, however, meant they could be taken apart, tainted, and then restored to the packaging without evidence of tampering. After the Chicago poisonings, which were never solved, McNeil and Johnson & Johnson executives were told at a meeting that processes for sealing the capsules had been greatly improved, but no one could give the assurance that they were tamperproof.

The executives realized that abandoning the capsule would give their competitors, Bristol-Myers (Excedrin) and American Home Products (Anacin), a market advantage, plus the cost would be $150 million just for 1982. Jim Burke, CEO of Johnson & Johnson, told the others that without a tamper-proof package for the capsules, they would risk the survival of not only Tylenol but Johnson & Johnson. The executives decided to abandon the capsule.

Frank Young, a Food and Drug Administration commissioner, stated at the time, "This is a matter of Johnson & Johnson's own business judgment, and represents a responsible action under tough circumstances."[93]

Johnson & Johnson quickly developed "caplets"—tablets in the shape of a capsule—then offered consumers a coupon for a bottle of the new caplets if they turned in their capsules. Within five days of the announcement of the capsule recall and caplets offer, 200,000 consumers had responded. Johnson & Johnson had eliminated a key product in its line—one that customers clearly preferred—in the interest of safety. Otto Lerbinger of Boston University's College of Communication cited Johnson & Johnson as a "model of corporate social responsibility for its actions."[94]

President Ronald Reagan, addressing a group of business executives, said, "Jim Burke, of Johnson & Johnson, you have our deepest admiration. In recent days you have lived up to the very highest ideals of corporate responsibility and grace under pressure."[95]

Within one year of the Tylenol poisonings, Johnson & Johnson regained its 40 percent market share for Tylenol. While many attribute the regain of market share to tamper-proof packaging, the other companies had moved to that form as well. However, it is interesting to note that McNeil was able to have its new product and packaging on the shelves within weeks of the fatal incidents. There had been some preparation for the change prior to the fatalities, but the tragedy was the motivation for the change to safer packaging and product forms.

McNeil continues to enjoy the goodwill from the rapid response to the poisonings. Even as new issues with Tylenol have developed, McNeil seems to be given the benefit of the doubt because of the goodwill and reputational capital it purchased with the capsule recalls.[96]

On December 21, 1994, the *Journal of the American Medical Association* published the results of a five-and-one-half-year study showing that moderate overdoses of acetaminophen (known most widely by the brand name Tylenol) led to liver damage in ten patients.[97,98] The damage occurred even in patients who did not drink and was most pronounced in those who did drink or had not been eating. Further, the study by Dr. David Whitcomb at the University of Pittsburgh medical school found that taking one pill of acetaminophen per day for a year may double the risk of kidney failure.[99]

The American Association of Poison Control Centers for 1996 shows 31,511 cases of inappropriate exposure to pediatric acetaminophen products.[100] There were minor

93 *"Drug Firm Pulls All Its Capsules off the Market,"* Arizona Republic, *February 18, 1986, p. A2.*

94 *Pat Guy and Clifford Glickman, "J & J Uses Candor in Crisis,"* USA Today, *February 12, 1986, p. 2B.*

95 *"The Tylenol Rescue,"* Newsweek, *March 3, 1986, p. 52.*

96 *"Legacy of Tampering,"* Arizona Republic, *September 29, 1992, p. A1.*

97 *"Acetaminophen Overdoses Linked to Liver Damage,"* Mesa Tribune, *December 21, 1994, p. A12.*

98 *Doug Levy, "Acetaminophen Overuse Can Lead to Liver Damage,"* USA Today, *December 22, 1994, p. 1D.*

99 *"Second Tylenol Study Links Heavy Use to Kidney Risk,"* Arizona Republic, *December 22, 1994, p. A6.*

100 *Thomas Easton and Stephan Herrera, "J & J's Dirty Little Secret,"* Forbes, *January 12, 1998, pp. 42–44.*

effects in 631 children and life-threatening permanent effects in six. Adult deaths from overexposure are put at 100, more than cocaine deaths (hospital statistics are not included).

Tylenol is a stunning source of revenue for McNeil and Johnson & Johnson, with revenue of $1.3 billion per year. In 1993, acetaminophen accounted for 48 percent of the total $2.9 billion in sales of all over-the-counter drugs. Tylenol made up 70 percent of all acetaminophen sales. Advil's total sales, the next in amount, trailed at less than $400,000,000.

Plaintiffs, who claim they are victims of overdose and the lack of effective warnings, have not been successful against Johnson & Johnson.[101] The product labels before current modification read "Gentle on an infant's stomach," and Tylenol's ad slogan was, "Nothing's safer."

Patients combining Tylenol with alcohol have produced 200 cases of liver damage in the past twenty years with fatality in 20 percent of those cases. The level of alcohol among these cases was multiple drinks every day.

In 1997, Tylenol added a new label to its infant Tylenol, "Taking more than the recommended dose . . . could cause serious health risks," because of liver damage in children.[102]

Discussion Questions

1. Was the risk small that there would be other poisonings of Tylenol capsules?
2. Were the shareholders' interests ignored in the decision to take a $150 million dollar write-off and a possible loss of $525 million in annual sales by abandoning the capsules?
3. Suppose that you were a Tylenol competitor. Would you have continued selling your capsules?
4. Was Burke's action a long-term decision? Did it take into account the interests of all stakeholders?
5. What financial arguments could be made against the decision to abandon the capsule?
6. Were the risks appropriately balanced in this case?
7. Following the poisonings, the federal government developed packaging regulations for nonprescription drugs. Should manufacturers have developed the tamper-proof packaging on their own?
8. General Robert Wood Johnson, the CEO of Johnson & Johnson from 1932 to 1963, wrote a credo for his company that states the company's first responsibility

[101] *Deborah Sharp, "Alcohol-Tylenol Death Goes to Trial in Florida,"* USA Today, *March 24, 1997, p. 3A.*

[102] *Richard Cole, "Tylenol Agrees to Warning on Labels of Risk to Children,"* Arizona Republic, *October 19, 1997, p. A5.*

is to the people who use its products and services; the second responsibility is to its employees; the third to the community and its environment; and the fourth to the stockholders.[103] Johnson and his successors have believed that if the credo's first three responsibilities are met, the stockholders will be well served. Does Johnson & Johnson follow its credo?

9. If you were a manufacturer of acetaminophen, how would you respond to the study results published in 1994? What action would you take?

10. How would you handle the resulting litigation?

11. Did the warning take too long?

CASE 7.8

Ford and Its Pinto

The Pinto's Development

In 1968, Ford began designing a subcompact automobile that ultimately became the Pinto. Lee Iacocca, then a Ford vice president, conceived the project and was its moving force. Ford's objective was to build a car weighing 2,000 pounds or less to sell for no more than $2,000. At that time, prices for gasoline were increasing, and the American auto industry was losing competitive ground to the small vehicles of Japanese and German manufacturers.

Ordinarily, automakers conduct marketing surveys and preliminary engineering before styling a new line. With the Pinto, however, styling dictated engineering design to a greater degree than usual because it was a rush project. Among the decisions dictated by styling was the placement of the fuel tank. The preferred practice in Europe and Japan was to locate the gas tank over the rear axle in subcompacts because a small vehicle has less "crush space" between the rear axle and the bumper than larger cars.[104] The Pinto's styling, however, required the tank to be placed behind the rear axle, leaving only nine to ten inches of "crush space"—far less than in any other American automobile or Ford overseas subcompact. In addition, the Pinto's bumper was little more than a chrome strip, less substantial than the bumper of any other American car produced then or later. The Pinto's rear structure also lacked reinforcing longitudinal side members, known as "hat sections," and horizontal cross members running between them, such as were found in cars of larger unitized construction and in all automobiles produced by Ford's overseas operations. The absence of the reinforcing members rendered the Pinto less crush-resistant than other vehicles. Finally, the Pinto's differential housing had an exposed flange and bolt heads. These protrusions were sufficient to puncture a gas tank driven forward against the differential by a rear impact.[105]

Pinto prototypes were built and tested. Mechanical prototypes duplicated mechanical features of the design but not its appearance, while engineering prototypes

[103] Brief History of Johnson & Johnson, *1992 (company pamphlet).*

[104] *Rachel Dardis and Claudia Zent, "The Economics of the Pinto Recall,"* Journal of Consumer Affairs, *Winter 1982, pp. 261–277.*

[105] Id.

were true duplicates of the design car. Ford tested these prototypes, as well as two production Pintos, to determine the integrity of the fuel system in rear-end accidents. It also tested to see if the Pinto would meet a proposed federal regulation requiring all automobiles manufactured in 1972 to be able to withstand a twenty-mile-per-hour fixed-barrier impact and those made after January 1, 1973, to withstand a thirty-mile-per-hour fixed-barrier impact without significant fuel spillage.[106]

The crash tests revealed that the Pinto's fuel system as designed could not meet the proposed twenty-mile-per-hour standard. When mechanical prototypes were struck from the rear with a moving barrier at twenty-one miles per hour, the fuel tanks were driven forward and punctured, causing fuel leakage in excess of the standard prescribed by the proposed regulation. A production Pinto crashed at twenty-one miles per hour into a fixed barrier resulted in the fuel neck being torn from the gas tank and the tank being punctured by a bolt head on the differential housing. In at least one test, spilled fuel entered the driver's compartment through gaps resulting from the separation of the seams joining the rear wheel wells to the floor pan. The seam separation was caused by the lack of reinforcement in the rear structure and insufficient welds of the wheel wells to the floor pan.

Ford tested other vehicles, including modified or reinforced mechanical Pinto prototypes, that proved safe at speeds at which the Pinto failed. Vehicles in which rubber bladders had been installed in the tank and were then crashed into fixed barriers at twenty-one miles per hour had no leakage from punctures in the gas tank. Vehicles with fuel tanks installed above rather than behind the rear axle passed the fuel system integrity test at thirty-one miles per hour against a fixed barrier. A Pinto with two longitudinal hat sections added to firm up the rear structure passed a twenty-mile-per-hour fixed-barrier test with no fuel leakage.[107]

When a prototype failed the fuel system integrity test, the standard of care in the industry was to redesign and retest it. The vulnerability of the production Pinto's fuel tank at speeds of twenty and thirty miles per hour in fixed-barrier tests could have been remedied inexpensively, but Ford produced and sold the Pinto without doing anything to fix the defects. Among the design changes that could have been made were side and cross members at $2.40 and $1.80 per car, respectively; a shock-absorbent "flak suit" to protect the tank at $4; a tank within a tank and placement of the tank over the axle at $5.08 to $5.79; a nylon bladder within the tank at $5.25 to $8; placement of the tank over the axle surrounded with a protective barrier at $9.59 per car; imposition of a protective shield between the differential housing and the tank at $2.35; improvement and reinforcement of the bumper at $2.60; and addition of eight inches of crush space at a cost of $6.40. Equipping the car with a reinforced rear structure, smooth axle, improved bumper, and additional crush space at a total of $15.30 would have made the fuel tank safe when hit from the rear by a vehicle the size of a Ford Galaxie. If, in addition, a bladder or tank within a tank had been used or if the tank had been protected with a shield, the tank would have been safe in a rear-end collision of forty to forty-five miles per hour. If the tank had been located over the rear axle, it would have been safe in a rear impact at fifty miles per hour or more.[108]

[106] Id.

[107] Id.

[108] Id.

The feasibility study for the Pinto was conducted under the supervision of Robert Alexander, vice president of car engineering. Ford's Product Planning Committee, whose members included Lee Iacocca, Alexander, and Harold MacDonald, Ford's group vice president of car engineering, approved the Pinto's concept and made the decision to go forward with the project. During the course of the project, regular product review meetings were held that were chaired by MacDonald and attended by Alexander. As the Pinto approached actual production, the engineers responsible for the components of the project "signed off" to their immediate supervisors, who in turn "signed off" to their superiors, and so on up the chain of command until the entire project was approved for release by Alexander, MacDonald, and ultimately, Iacocca. The Pinto crash tests results were known to these decision makers when they decided to go forward with production.

Analysis of the Gas Tank Issues

Harley Copp, a former Ford engineer and executive in charge of the crash testing program, testified that when the highest level of Ford's management decided to produce the Pinto, they knew that the gas tank was vulnerable to puncture and rupture at low rear-impact speeds, which created a significant risk of death or injury from fire, and that the problem could be fixed for a nominal cost. He testified that management's decision was based on the cost savings that Ford would incur from omitting or delaying implementing the remedies.

Other evidence corroborated Copp's testimony. At an April 1971 product review meeting chaired by MacDonald, a report by Ford engineers on the financial impact of a proposed federal standard on fuel system integrity and the cost savings that would accrue from deferring even minimal "fixes" of the Pinto was discussed. It is reasonable to infer that the report was prepared for and known to Ford officials in policy-making positions.

Finally, Copp testified to having conversations in late 1968 or early 1969 with the chief assistant research engineer in charge of cost-weight evaluation of the Pinto and later with the chief chassis engineer in charge of crash testing the early prototype. In these conversations, both men expressed concern to Copp about the integrity of the Pinto's fuel system and complained about management's unwillingness to deviate from the design if the change would cost money. Tables 1 and 2 show the estimated costs of design modification.

Table 1
Costs of the 1970 Potential Design Modification Strategy: Low Estimate[109]

calendar year	*sales (1,000)*	*estimated unit cost ($)*	*estimated total cost ($ million)*	*present value of estimated costs in 1970 ($ million)*
1970	76	8.00	.608	.608
1971	328	8.00	2.624	2.385
1972	287	8.00	2.296	1.897
1973	268	8.00	2.144	1.611
1974	192	8.00	1.536	1.049
1975	170	8.00	1.360	.844
1976	106	8.00	.848	.479
		Total		8.873

[109] Automotive News, *Almanac Issues for 1971–1979 (Detroit: Slocum Publishing Company, 1971, and Marketing Services, 1972–1979).*

Table 2
Costs of the 1970 Potential Design Modification Strategy: High Estimate

calendar year	sales (1,000)	estimated unit cost ($)	estimated total cost ($ million)	present value of estimated costs in 1970 ($ million)
1970	76	18.66	1.418	1.418
1971	328	18.66	6.120	5.564
1972	287	18.66	5.355	4.425
1973	268	18.66	5.001	3.757
1974	192	18.66	3.583	2.447
1975	170	18.66	3.172	1.969
1976	106	18.66	1.978	1.116
		Total		20.696

J. C. Echold, Ford's director of automotive safety, studied the issue of gas tank design in anticipation of government regulations requiring modification. His study, "Fatalities Associated with Crash Induced Fuel Leakage and Fires," included the following cost-benefit analysis:

> The total benefit is shown to be just under $50 million, while the associated cost is $137 million. Thus, the cost is almost three times the benefits, even using a number of highly favorable benefit assumptions.[110]
>
> **Benefits**
>
> Savings—180 burn deaths, 180 serious burn injuries, 2,100 burned vehicles.
> Unit cost—$200,000 per death, $67,000 per injury, $700 per vehicle.
> Total benefits—(180 × $200,000) + (180 × $67,000) + (2,100 × $700) = $49.15 million
>
> **Costs**
>
> Sales—11 million cars, 1.5 million light trucks
> Unit cost—$11 per car, $11 per truck
> Total costs—(11,000,000 × $11) + (1,500,000 × $11) = $137 million

Ford's unit cost of $200,000 for one life was based on a National Highway Traffic Safety Administration calculation developed as shown in Table 3.

A Gas Tank Tragedy

In November 1971, Mr. and Mrs. Gray purchased a 1972 Pinto hatchback manufactured by Ford in October 1971. The Grays had trouble with the car from the outset. During the first few months of ownership, they had to return the car to the dealer for repairs a number of times. The problems included excessive gas and oil consumption, down-shifting of the automatic transmission, lack of power, and occasional stalling. It was later learned that the stalling and excessive fuel consumption were caused by a heavy carburetor float.

[110] *Ralph Drayton, "One Manufacturer's Approach to Automobile Safety Standards,"* CTLA News, *February 8, 1968, p. 11.*

component	1971 costs
Future productivity losses	
Direct	$132,000
Indirect	41,300
Medical costs	
Hospital	700
Other	425
Property damage	1,500
Insurance administration	4,700
Legal and court	3,000
Employer losses	1,000
Victim's pain and suffering	10,000
Funeral	900
Assets (lost consumption)	5,000
Miscellaneous accident cost	200
Total Per Family	$200,725[111]

Table 3
Ford's Unit Cost of $200,000 for One Life

On May 28, 1972, Mrs. Gray, accompanied by 13-year-old Richard Grimshaw, set out in the Pinto from Anaheim for Barstow to meet Mr. Gray. The Pinto was then six months old and had been driven approximately 3,000 miles. Mrs. Gray stopped in San Bernadino for gasoline, then got back onto Interstate 15 and proceeded toward Barstow at sixty to sixty-five miles per hour. As she approached the Route 30 off ramp where traffic was congested, she moved from the outside fast lane into the middle lane. The Pinto then suddenly stalled and coasted to a halt. It was later established that the carburetor float had become so saturated with gasoline that it sank, opening the float chamber and causing the engine to flood. The driver of the vehicle immediately behind Mrs. Gray's car was able to swerve and pass it, but the driver of a 1962 Ford Galaxie was unable to avoid hitting the Pinto. The Galaxie had been traveling from fifty to fifty-five miles per hour but had slowed to between twenty-eight and thirty-seven miles per hour at the time of impact.[112]

The Pinto burst into flames that engulfed its interior. According to one expert, the impact of the Galaxie had driven the Pinto's gas tank forward and caused it to be punctured by the flange or one of the bolts on the differential housing so that fuel sprayed from the punctured tank and entered the passenger compartment through gaps opening between the rear wheel well sections and the floor pan. By the time the Pinto came to rest after the collision, both occupants had been seriously burned. When they emerged from the vehicle, their clothing was almost completely burned off. Mrs. Gray died a few days later of congestive heart failure as a result of the burns. Grimshaw survived, only through heroic medical measures. He underwent numerous and extensive surgeries and skin grafts, some occurring over the ten years after the

[111] *Mark Dowie, "Pinto Madness,"* Mother Jones, *September/October 1977, p. 28.*

[112] *"Who Pays for the Damage?"* Time, *January 21, 1980, p. 61.*

collision. He lost parts of several fingers on his left hand and his left ear, and his face required many skin grafts.[113]

Aftermath of the Pinto: Criminal and Civil Liability

As Ford continued to litigate Mrs. Gray's lawsuit and thousands of other rear-impact Pinto suits, damages reaching $6 million had been awarded to plaintiffs by 1980. In 1979, Indiana filed criminal charges against Ford for reckless homicide. The indictment appears below.

State v. Ford Motor Co.

Indictment in Four Counts Charging Three Counts of Reckless Homicide, a Class D Felony, and One Count of Criminal Recklessness, a Class A Misdemeanor

No. 5324 (1979)

Indiana Superior Court, Elkhart County, Indiana

The Grand Jurors of Elkhart County, State of Indiana, being first duly sworn upon their oaths do present and say:

Count I

That Ford Motor Company, a corporation, on or about the 10th day of August, 1978, in the County of Elkhart, State of Indiana, did then and there through the acts and omissions of its agents and employees acting within the scope of their authority with said corporation recklessly cause the death of Judy Ann Ulrich, a human being, to-wit: that the Ford Motor Company, a corporation, did recklessly authorize and approve the design, and did recklessly design and manufacture a certain 1973 Pinto automobile, Serial Number F3T10X298722F, in such a manner as would likely cause said automobile to flame and burn upon rear-end impact; and the said Ford Motor Company permitted said Pinto automobile to remain upon the highways and roadways of Elkhart County, State of Indiana, to-wit: U.S. Highway Number 33, in said County and State; and the said Ford Motor Company did fail to repair and modify said Pinto automobile; and thereafter on said date as a proximate contributing cause of said reckless disregard for the safety of other persons within said automobile, including, the said Judy Ann Ulrich, a rear-end impact involving said Pinto automobile did occur creating fire and flame which did then and there and thereby inflict mortal injuries upon the said Judy Ann Ulrich, and the said Judy Ann Ulrich did then languish and die by incineration in Allen County, State of Indiana, on or about the 11th day of August, 1978.

And so the Grand Jurors aforesaid, upon their oaths aforesaid, do say and charge that the said Ford Motor Company, a corporation, did recklessly cause the death of the said Judy Ann Ulrich, a human being, in the manner and form aforesaid, and contrary to the form of the statutes in such cases made and provided, to-wit: Burns Indiana Statutes, Indiana Code Section 35-42-1-5; and against the peace and dignity of the State of Indiana.

Counts II and III

P [Counts II and III repeat the allegations of Count I as to the deaths of Donna M. Ulrich and Lynn M. Ulrich, respectively.]

[113] *Adapted from* Grimshaw v. Ford Motor Co., *174 Cal. Rptr. 348 (1981).*

Count IV

That Ford Motor Company, a corporation, on or about the 10th day of August, 1978, and diverse days prior thereto, in the County of Elkhart, State of Indiana, did through the acts and omissions of its agents and employees acting within the scope of their authority with said corporation, recklessly create a substantial risk of bodily injury to the persons of Judy Ann Ulrich, Donna M. Ulrich and Lynn M. Ulrich, human beings, and each of them, to-wit: that the Ford Motor Company, a corporation, did recklessly permit a certain 1973 Pinto automobile, Serial Number F3T10X298722F, designed and manufactured by the said Ford Motor Company to remain upon the highways and roadways of Elkhart County, State of Indiana, to-wit: U.S. Highway Number 33 in said County and State; and said Pinto automobile being recklessly designed and manufactured in such a manner as would likely cause said automobile to flame and burn upon rear-end impact; and that the said Ford Motor Company had a legal duty to warn the general public and certain occupants of said Pinto automobile, namely: Judy Ann Ulrich, Donna M. Ulrich and Lynn M. Ulrich of the dangerous tendency of said Pinto automobile to flame and burn upon rear-end impact; and the said Ford Motor Company did fail to repair and modify said Pinto automobile; and that as a proximate contributing cause of said Ford Motor Company's acts, omissions and reckless disregard for the safety of other persons within said Pinto automobile, including the said Judy Ann Ulrich, Donna M. Ulrich and Lynn M. Ulrich, a rear-end impact involving said Pinto automobile did occur on or about August 10, 1978, in Elkhart County, Indiana, creating fire and flame which did then and there and thereby inflict bodily injury upon the persons of the said Judy Ann Ulrich, Donna M. Ulrich and Lynn M. Ulrich, human beings, and each of them.

And so the Grand Jurors aforesaid, upon their oaths aforesaid, do say and charge that the said Ford Motor Company, a corporation, did recklessly create a substantial risk of bodily injury to the persons of Judy Ann Ulrich, Donna M. Ulrich and Lynn M. Ulrich, human beings, and each of them, in the manner and form aforesaid, and contrary to the form of the Statutes in such cases made and provided, to-wit: Burns Indiana Statutes, Indiana Code Section 35-42-2-2, and against the peace and dignity of the State of Indiana.

A true bill.

Discussion Questions

1. Calculate the total cost if all the "fixes" for the Pinto gas tank problem had been done.
2. What was management's position on the fixes?
3. Who was responsible for Grimshaw's injury? Would Copp have moral responsibility for the accident, death, and injuries involving Mrs. Gray's Pinto?
4. Did the Pinto design violate any laws?
5. Was Ford simply answering a public demand for a small, fuel-efficient, and inexpensive auto?

6. Don't all automobiles present the potential for injuries? Do we assume risks in driving and buying an automobile?

7. If you had held Copp's position, what would you have done differently?

8. The Pinto has become a popular stock car on the racing circuit. Recalled Pintos can be purchased for $50 from junkyards.[114] Should Ford be concerned about such use?

9. In 1996, Ford issued a recall on 8.7 million vehicles because a joint investigation with NHTSA revealed the ignition in certain cars could short circuit and cause a fire. Ford ran full-page ads in major newspapers. The ad from *The Wall Street Journal*, May 8, 1996, p. B7, is reproduced below:

T.J. Wagner
Vice President

Ford Motor Company
Dearborn, MI 48121

Customer Communication & Satisfaction

To Our Ford, Lincoln and Mercury Owners:

As I am sure you have read, Ford Motor Company recently announced a program to voluntarily recall 8.7 million vehicles to replace ignition switches. You should know that at the time we announced the recall, the actual number of complaints which may be related to the ignition switch in question was less than two hundredths of one percent of that total. We regret the inconvenience this has caused the customers who have placed their trust in our products.

Q: *What happened?*

A: Following an intensive investigation in cooperation with the U.S. National Highway Traffic Safety Administration and Transport Canada, we determined that the ignition switch in a very small percentage of certain models could develop a short circuit—creating the potential for overheating, smoke, and possibly fire in the steering column of the vehicle. The factors that contribute to this are a manufacturing process change to the ignition switch in combination with the electrical load through the switch.

Q: *What vehicles are affected by this voluntary recall?*

A: The following model year vehicles are affected:

- 1988 Ford EXP.
- 1988–1990 Ford Escort.
- 1988–1992 Ford Mustang, Thunderbird, Tempo, and Mercury Cougar and Topaz.
- 1993 Ford Mustang, Thunderbird, Tempo, and Mercury Cougar and Topaz models built prior to October 1992.
- 1988–1989 Ford Crown Victoria, Mercury Grand Marquis and Lincoln Town Car.
- 1988–1991 Ford Aerostar, Ford Bronco full-size sport utility and Ford F-Series light truck.

[114] *Gregory A. Patterson, "Downscale Racer: The Pinto Is Junk, But It Sure Is Fast,"* The Wall Street Journal, *June 14, 1990, p. A1.*

Q: *What should I do?*

A: If you own one of these vehicles, you will receive a letter from us instructing you take your vehicle to the Ford or Lincoln/Mercury dealer of your choice and have the switch replaced free of charge. However, you do not have to wait for our letter. You may contact your dealer and arrange to have the switch replaced immediately if you choose, free of charge.

Q: *How long will it take?*

A: The repair procedure should take about one hour. But please contact your dealer in advance to schedule a time that is convenient for you.

Q: *What if I need additional help?*

A: You may contact your dealer anytime, or call our Ford Ignition Switch Recall Customer Information Line at 1-800-323-8400.

We're in business because people believe in or products. We make improvements because we believe we can make our products better. And at times we'll take a major step like this to make sure that people who buy a Ford, Lincoln or Mercury vehicle know that they bought more than a vehicle, they bought a company and a dealer organization that stands behind the cars and trucks they build and sell. This is our *Quality is Job 1* promise to you. Thank you for your patience and support.

Has Ford had a cultural change on product safety?

CASE 7.9

GM and Its Malibu

On July 9, 1999, a Los Angeles jury awarded Patricia Anderson, her four children, and friend, Jo Tigner, $107 million in actual damages and $4.8 billion in punitive damages from General Motors in a lawsuit the six brought against GM because they were trapped and burned in their Chevrolet Malibu when it exploded on impact following a rear-end collision.[115]

A juror, explaining the magnitude of the jury verdict Coleman Thorton, the jury foreman, said, "GM has no regard for the people in their cars, and they should be held responsible for it." Richard Shapiro, an attorney for GM said, "We're very disappointed. This was a very sympathetic case. The people who were injured were innocent in this matter. They were the victims of a drunk driver."[116]

The accident occurred on Christmas eve 1993 and was the result of a drunk driver striking the Anderson Malibu at 70 mph. The driver's blood alcohol level was .20, but the defense lawyers noted they were not permitted to disclose to the jury that the driver of the auto that struck the Malibu was drunk.

[115] *Ann W. O'Neill, Henry Weinstein, and Eric Malnic, "Jury Orders GM to Pay Record Sum,"* Arizona Republic, *July 10, 1999, pp. A1, A2.*
[116] Id.

The discovery process in the case uncovered a 1973 internal "value analysis" memo on "post-collision fuel-tank fires" written by a low-level GM engineer, Edward C. Ivey, in which he calculated the value of preventing fuel-fed fires. Mr. Ivey used a figure of $200,000 for the cost of a fatality and noted that there are 500 fatalities per year in GM auto fuel fire accidents. The memo also stated that his analysis must be read in the context of "it is really impossible to put a value on human life." Mr. Ivey wrote, using an estimate of $200,000 as the value of human life, that the cost of these explosions to GM would be $2.40 per car. After an in-house lawyer discovered the memo in 1981, he wrote:

> Obviously Ivey is not an individual whom we would ever, in any conceivable situation, want identified to the plaintiffs in a post-collision fuel-fed fire case, and the documents he generated are undoubtedly some of the potentially most harmful and most damaging were they ever to be produced.[117]

In the initial cases brought against GM, the company's defense was that the engineer's thinking was his own and did not reflect company policy. However, when the 1981 lawyer commentary was found as part of discovery in a Florida case in 1998, GM lost that line of defense. In the Florida case in which a 13-year-old boy was burned to death in a 1983 Oldsmobile Cutlass station wagon, the jury awarded his family $33 million.

The two documents have become the center of each case. Judge Ernest G. Williams of Los Angeles Superior Court, who upheld the verdict in the $4.9 billion LA case but reduced the damages wrote in his opinion:

> The court finds that clear and convincing evidence demonstrated that defendants' fuel tank was placed behind the axle of the automobiles of the make and model here in order to maximize profits—to the disregard of public safety.[118]

Currently, there are 100 such cases pending around the country. The suits center around GM's mid-size "A-cars," which include the Malibu, Buick Century, Oldsmobile Cutlass, and Pontiac Grand Prix. Approximately 7.5 million cars are equipped with this gas tank design. On appeal, the Los Angeles verdict was reduced from $4.9 billion (total) to $1.2 billion.[119]

Discussion Questions

1. Why do you think the drunk driver was not held responsible for the Los Angeles accident?
2. If you had found the 1973 memo, what would you have done with it?
3. If you had read the 1973 memo prior to the time the Malibu was released for production and to the market, what would you have done with it?
4. What happens as time conceals memos such as this engineer's discussion?

[117] *Milo Geyelin, "How an Internal Memo Written 26 Years Ago Is Costing GM Dearly,"* The Wall Street Journal, *September 29, 1999, pp. A1, A6.*

[118] Id.

[119] *Margaret A. Jacobs, "BMW Decision Used to Whittle Punitive Awards,"* The Wall Street Journal, *September 13, 1999, p. B2.*

CASE 7.10

ATVs: Danger on Wheels

Honda Motor Company, Ltd.; Yamaha Motor Company, Ltd.; Suzuki Motors Company, Ltd.; Kawasaki Heavy Industries, Ltd.; and Polaris Industries all made various types of motorcycles and all-terrain vehicles (ATVs) during the late 1970s and 1980s. Honda was the leading seller of ATVs, offering a full range of three-wheel models. It even made a very small three-wheel ATV for children ages four through ten that it advertised at the height of the market in the mid-1980s. The fat-wheeled vehicles that look like large tricycles were advertised as able to conquer all land surfaces with great ease. Suzuki's ads said its ATV would "embarrass the wind."[120]

The ATV was introduced in 1977 by Honda; several other manufacturers entered the market in the following year. Yamaha and Kawasaki ATVs were larger in size and motor capacity and carried higher price tags than Honda's.

In 1978, based on a complaint from the National Association of Emergency Room Physicians (NAERP) and the American Neurological Society (ANS), the Consumer Product Safety Commission began investigating ATVs and their use and misuse. The commission's reports, which incorporated information from NAERP and ANS, found that:

1. ATV accidents were increasing dramatically:[121]

	ATV-related emergency room admissions	*deaths from ATV accidents*
1982	8,600	26
1983	26,900	85
1984	63,900	153
1985	85,900	246
1986	86,400	268

   Of all the fatalities over the five-year period, 165 involved children ages eleven and younger, while 47 percent of the total involved children ages sixteen and younger.[122]
2. Of all ATV-related injuries, 90 percent involved people under the age of thirty and 70 percent involved those under the age of eighteen.
3. In some areas, ATV-related injuries accounted for 45 percent of all emergency care on weekends.
4. Ninety percent of all injuries happened to experienced ATV riders (those who had logged more than twenty-five hours of riding time).
5. Leg injuries were common, with spiral fractures being the most frequent form.
6. Many injuries requiring emergency care were leg burns caused by riders holding their legs too close to ATV engines.

[120] *Frederick M. Maynard, "Peril in the Path of All-Terrain Vehicles,"* Business and Society Review, *Winter 1987, pp. 48–52.*

[121] *Daniel B. Moskowitz, "Why ATVs Could Land in a Heap of Trouble,"* Business Week, *November 30, 1987, p. 38. The numbers do vary in press releases and according to various groups.*

[122] *James Bolger, "The High Gravity Risk of ATV's,"* Safety & Health, *November 1987, pp. 48–49.*

Dr. Ralph R. Fine, codirector of the National Spinal Cord Injury Statistical Center, testified before a House committee about his concerns: "We were seeing a disproportionate number of spinal cord injuries resulting from three wheeler or ATV crashes. These are dangerously deceptive, deceptively dangerous vehicles."[123]

Honda was aware of the report and submitted a study to the Consumer Product Safety Commission that showed the accidents with injuries happened when ATVs were misused.[124] Referred to in the Honda report as "hotdogging," misuse included driving too fast, climbing hills at ninety-degree angles, going through rapidly moving water, and using ramps for jumping.[125]

Between 1982 and 1986, there were more than 50,000 ATV-related injuries. By 1986, 2.1 million ATVs at an average price of $2,000 each were in use. Between 1982 and 1988, 858 people were killed in ATV accidents, many of them young children. A Consumer Product Safety Commission report concluded, "Children under 12 years of age are unable to operate any size ATV safely."[126] State attorneys general began efforts to regulate ATV use in 1986. Texas Assistant Attorney General Stephen Gardner stated, "These are killer machines. They should not be allowed."[127] The CPSC tried to have the industry sales to sixteen-year-olds and younger banned, but was unsuccessful.[128]

After the report, Yamaha introduced a four-wheel ATV, including one model with two seats. Yamaha also undertook a dealer education program and issued an instruction manual with the vehicles to encourage responsible operation.[129]

Roy Janson of the American All-Terrain Vehicle Association, a subsidiary of the American Motorcyclist Association, stated at congressional hearings on ATVs:

> Problems result primarily from how a vehicle is used rather than from its design. When ATVs are used as intended, they present no unreasonable risk to their operators. The major problems related to three-wheel ATV injuries are the failure of users to wear proper safety equipment while operating ATVs and using these vehicles in areas not recommended for ATV recreation. User education and information programs are clearly the most effective means for addressing the problems relating to misuse.[130]

In 1980, major nationally franchised rental centers ceased renting ATVs because of liability concerns.

In 1986, the Consumer Product Safety Commission published proposed ATV regulations that included these key provisions:

1. No ATVs below certain size limits would be manufactured. ATV riders would have to weigh at least 100 pounds and be at least sixteen years old.

[123] *"Public Safety: All-Terrain Vehicles,"* National Safety and Health News, *August 1985, pp. 78–80.*

[124] *Jeff Riggenbach, "Regulation Not Needed; Danger Is Exaggerated,"* USA Today, *November 6, 1986, p. 10A.*

[125] *"Safety Group Targets Use of ATVs by Young Riders,"* Mesa Tribune, *November 20, 1986, p. A4.*

[126] *Randolph Schmid, "Safety Panel Tackles All-Terrain Cycle Issue,"* Phoenix Gazette, *November 19, 1986, p. A14.*

[127] *Moskowitz, "Why ATVs Could Land in a Heap of Trouble," p. 38.*

[128] *"ATV Makers Warned to Halt Sales to Children or Face Ban,"* Mesa Tribune, *October 2, 1986, p. A2.*

[129] *Alan R. Isley, "Industry Is Emphasizing Safety,"* USA Today, *November 6, 1986, p. 1B.*

[130] *"Public Safety," p. 79.*

2. All ATVs would have four wheels.
3. All manufacturers would undertake educational ad campaigns on the use and dangers of ATVs. No promotional advertising would be permitted in any media form.

While the proposed regulations were being debated, ATV accidents continued to climb steadily. Of particular concern was the marked increase in severe injuries, such as spinal cord and head injuries, to children six to ten years of age. At the same time, some manufacturers continued to provide studies to the Consumer Product Safety Commission indicating misuse, not design, was the primary cause of ATV accidents.

By 1987, the Association of Trial Lawyers of America had established a clearinghouse for the exchange of information on ATV claims, and over 400 lawsuits had been filed. Three-fourths of the suits were being settled for a typical payment of $1 million.

Because of increased, widely publicized objections from consumer groups, as well as a call for action from the American Academy of Pediatrics, the commission recalled three-wheel ATVs in May 1988 and halted their manufacture.[131] Meanwhile, manufacturers accelerated production of four-wheel vehicles. After judicial review of the commission's order and agreements were reached with the five manufacturers, the commission withdrew the recall but successfully implemented the ban on future sales.[132]

Some consumer groups, however, still felt a recall was necessary. James Florio, a Congressman from New Jersey, said, "How can anyone truly concerned with safety in effect say "tough luck' to people who currently own these unsafe vehicles?"[133]

However, the manufacturers did agree to take the following steps:

- Offer cash incentives to encourage owners of ATVs purchased after December 30, 1987, to enroll in training programs.
- Revise warning labels and owner's manuals to outline the dangers of vehicle operation.
- Set up a consumer telephone hotline.
- Restrict sales of ATVs with engine displacements greater than ninety cubic centimeters displacement (CCD) to people sixteen years or older; children under twelve years would not be permitted to operate vehicles with engines greater than seventy CCD.
- Scrap a provision in the preliminary agreement that would have required ATV purchasers to sign a form acknowledging the risks of operating the vehicle.[134]

Honda sent out the following "Safety Alert"[135] to owners of its ATVs in January 1988:

> The Consumer Product Safety Commission has concluded that all-terrain vehicles (ATVs) may present a risk of death or severe injury in certain circumstances. While accidents may occur for many reasons:
>
> - Over 900 people, including many children, have died in accidents associated with ATVs since 1982.

[131] *"We Need Regulation of Dangerous ATVs,"* USA Today, *November 14, 1986, p. 10A.*

[132] *"ATV Makers Agree to Warnings, Vehicle Ban,"* Arizona Business Gazette, *May 9, 1988, Law 3.*

[133] *"Outlawing a Three-Wheeler,"* Time, *January 11, 1988, p. 59.*

[134] *Matt DeLorenzo, "ATV Companies Agree to Warn, Train Owners,"* Automotive News, *March 21, 1988, p. 58.*

[135] *Reprinted with permission of Honda Motor Company, Ltd.*

- Many people have become severely paralyzed or suffered severe internal injuries as a result of accidents associated with ATVs.
- Thousands of people have been treated in hospital emergency rooms every month for injuries received while riding an ATV.

Because of this, the United States government has filed a lawsuit against all manufacturers and distributors of ATVs asking the court to declare that ATVs are hazardous and to order the manufacturers and distributors to take actions to protect ATV riders. The distributors, while contesting the validity of the allegations made by the government, are presently engaged in discussions with the government to resolve these issues without litigation.

You should be aware that an ATV is not a toy and may be dangerous to operate. An ATV handles different from other vehicles, including motorcycles and cars. According to the Consumer Product Safety Commission, at ATV can roll over on the rider or violently throw the rider without warning, and even hitting a small rock, bump, or hole at low speed can upset the ATV.

To avoid death or severe personal injury:

Never drive an ATV without proper instruction. *Take a training course.* Beginning drivers should receive training from a certified instructor. . . .

- *Never* lend your ATV to anyone who has not taken a training course or has not been driving an ATV for at least a year.
- *Always* follow these age recommendations:
    - A child under 12 years old should never drive an ATV with engine size 70 CCD or greater.
    - A child under 16 years old should never drive an ATV with engine size greater than 90 CCD.
- *Never* allow a child under 16 years old to drive an ATV without adult supervision. Children need to be observed carefully because not all children have the strength, size, skills, or judgment needed to drive an ATV safely.
- *Never* drive an ATV after consuming alcohol or drugs.
- *Never* carry a passenger on an ATV; carrying a passenger may upset the balance of the ATV and may cause it to go out of control.
- *Never* drive an ATV on pavement. The vehicle is not designed to be used on paved surfaces and may be difficult to control.
- *Never* drive an ATV on a public road, even a dirt or gravel one, because you may not be able to avoid colliding with other vehicles. Also, driving on a public road with an ATV may be against the law.
- *Never* attempt to do "wheelies," jumps, or other stunts.
- *Never* drive an ATV without a good helmet and goggles. You should also wear boots, gloves, heavy trousers, and a long-sleeve shirt.
- *Never* drive an ATV at excessive speeds.
- *Always* be extremely careful when driving an ATV, especially when approaching hills, turns, and obstacles and when driving on unfamiliar or rough terrain.
- *Always* read the owner's manual carefully and follow the operating procedures described.

Discussion Questions

1. Is the ATV too dangerous to be sold?
2. Are the warnings and the ban on future ATV sales sufficient?
3. If you were in marketing for one of the five firms, could you continue your sales efforts?
4. Should the three-wheel ATV have been recalled?
5. Is the cost of a recall just too high?

CASE 7.11

A. H. Robins and the Dalkon Shield

The Dalkon Shield contraceptive, designed by a doctor and an engineer and commercially introduced in 1969, offered an alternative to the dangers of using birth control pills. The Dalkon Shield, along with the Lippes Loop, was heralded as the ideal modern birth control: safe, cheap, and effective. Dr. Hugh Davis, the shield's inventor, declared it to be a "first-choice method of contraception control." The name "Dalkon" was derived from the names of the inventor, his engineer friend, Irwin Lerner, and Lerner's lawyer, Robert Cohn. "Shield" came from the device's resemblance to a police badge.

In June 1970, A. H. Robins, a 123-year-old Virginia pharmaceutical company, acquired all rights to the Dalkon Shield and sold the device between June 12, 1970, and June 28, 1974. Over 2.2 million of the devices were prescribed for women in the United States, and 1.7 million were shipped abroad. The shield sold for $4.35 but cost only 35 cents to make.[136]

A. H. Robins enjoyed an excellent reputation as a pharmaceutical firm but had had no experience in the birth control market. When it bought the intrauterine device (IUD) from Davis in 1970 for $750,000 plus consulting fees and 10 percent royalties, Robins had never made or sold a medical device or gynecological product and had no obstetricians or gynecologists on staff. At the time of the purchase, there was evidence that Davis's claim of a 1.1 percent contraceptive failure rate for the shield was actually 5 percent. Robins nonetheless used the 1.1 percent figure in its advertising.[137]

In March 1971, Wayne Crowder, the quality control supervisor for the shield, conducted crude experiments that showed the open-ended string on the shield could

[136] *406 F. Supp. 540 (J.P.M.D.L. 1975) (presents a compilation of Dalkon Shield litigation, including the general grounds for these suits).*

[137] *Milo Geyelin, "Criminal Investigation of A. H. Robins, Former Law Firm is Dropped by U.S.,"* The Wall Street Journal, *January 12, 1990, p. B3.*

"wick" bacteria from the vagina into the sterile uterus, which could then result in infections and pelvic inflammation (pelvic inflammatory disease [PID]).[138]

Crowder suggested to Robins officers that either the string tip be sealed with heat or the string be replaced with a safer monofilament string. Crowder explained that he could not "in good conscience" approve of "something that I felt could cause infections."[139] Crowder's boss replied that "conscience didn't pay his salary." Crowder was eventually fired.[140]

An estimated 2.8 million shields were sold in the United States between 1970 and 1974. The shield produced documented injuries to women, including septic abortion, tubal pregnancy, perforation of the uterine wall, PID, and death. In many cases, complete hysterectomies were required because of perforations and tissue masses. Damage to kidneys, intestines, and the colon were frequent. The most common injury was PID.[141]

When injuries resulting from the shield were reported, the FDA initiated a series of public and private fact-finding hearings. A. H. Robins stopped production of the shield on June 28, 1974. In August 1974, the FDA formally recommended that Robins halt sales.

In October 1974, the FDA's Advisory Committee on Obstetrics and Gynecology voted to lift the recommendation and allow sales to resume. It reversed this decision on November 7, 1974, when new defects in the shield were discovered.[142, 143] On December 20, 1974, the FDA acted against the advisory committee's advice and sanctioned the sale of the shield. All of the events were reported in national papers, such as *The New York Times* and the *Washington Post.* Most major city newspapers also carried stories.

The Dalkon Shield package and insert did not mention the possible dangers of using the device and did not recommend a fixed removal date, which is customary manufacturer practice.

During the FDA hearings on the Medical Device Amendments of 1973, one physician admonished:

> I would like to point out without reservation that it is not only time for regulation of IUD testing, manufacture, and advertising, but it is long overdue. Parenthetically, I must question how 14 years have elapsed since the introduction of the plastic IUDs into women commenced without responsible organizations and experts demanding regulatory standards.[144]

[138] *Note,* The Intrauterine Device: A Criticism of Governmental Complaisance and an Analysis of Manufacturer and Physician Liability, *24 Cle. St. L. Rev. 247 (1975).*

[139] Id.

[140] Id.

[141] *Milo Geyelin, "Risks Grow for Dissatisfied Dalkon Users,"* The Wall Street Journal, *April 30, 1993, p. B4; see also "A. H. Robbins Hauls a Judge into Court,"* Business Week, *July 16, 1984, pp. 27–28.*

[142] *21 C.F.R. 7.45 (a).*

[143] *21 U.S.C. 301–392, Food, Drug and Cosmetic Act.*

[144] *Catherine Breslin, "Day of Reckoning,"* Ms., *June 1989, p. 46; see also Medical Device Amendment Hearing before the Subcommittee on Health of the Committee on Labor and Public Welfare, 93d Cong., 1st Sess. (1973) (statement of Russel J. Thomsen, M.D.).*

> It remains even more astonishing that because of the benign silence of these usually concerned parties, the protection of women users of IUDs was neglected for over a decade by a Federal agency which has rather specific obligations to deal with the safety of health-related products. The fact that the Food and Drug Administration has never been given specific legislative authority over medical devices is a matter of record, but that seems a mute excuse for inaction.[145]

Nearly 11,000 suits were filed against A. H. Robins for injuries from the shield. In one such suit, U.S. District Judge Miles W. Lord required Robins's CEO, E. Claiborne Robins, Jr.; its general counsel, William A. Forest, Jr.; and its research director to read a speech on ethics in his courtroom. Lord then noted:

> If one poor young man were by some act of his to inflict such damage upon one woman, he would be jailed for a good portion of the rest of his life. And yet your company, without warning to women, invaded their bodies by the millions and caused them injuries by the thousands. And when the time came for these women to make their claims against your company, you attacked their characters. . . . You have taken the bottom line as your guiding beacon and the low road as your route. This is corporate irresponsibility at its meanest.[146]

In attempting to counter the claims by former Dalkon Shield users that the device caused PID, Robins claimed that the disease can be caused by sexually transmitted diseases and probed into the intimate details of the claimants' sex lives to establish this defense.[147]

In 1974, the FDA ordered Robins to remove the shield from the market. It was not until 1984 that Robins urged women to have the shields removed at the firm's expense.[148]

By 1984, lawsuits were being filed against the IUD manufacturer at a rate of three hundred per month. Robins's stock price was depressed, and the company's establishment of a $615 million reserve for the claims resulted in Robins being the biggest money loser in the Fortune 500 for 1985.[149, 150, 151, 152, 153]

By the time Robins filed for Chapter 11 bankruptcy in 1985, 334,863 claims were pending. Class action litigation continued raucously (with thirty-eight attorneys on the Dalkon Shield Claimants' Committee alone) until a new committee of five, including three claimants, was appointed. A. H. Robins was purchased by American Home Products in January 1988. American Home Products agreed to pay $2.375

145 Id.

146 *Geyelin, "Risks Grow for Dissatisfied Dalkon Users," p. B4; see also "A. H. Robbins Hauls a Judge into Court," pp. 27–28.*

147 *Paul Blustein, "Out of Court: How 2 Young Lawyers Got Rich by Settling IUD Liability Claims, Appert and Pyle Face Probe of Tactics Used in a Bevy of Dalkon Shield Cases, A Tie to Insurance Adjuster?"* The Wall Street Journal, *February 24, 1982, pp. A1, A12.*

148 *Breslin, "Day of Reckoning," p. 46–52.*

149 *406 F. Supp. 540 (J.P.M.D.L. 1975) (presents a compilation of Dalkon Shield litigation, including the general grounds for these suits).*

150 AMP v. Gardner, *389 F.2d 825 (2d Cir. 1968).*

151 *In* Re A. H. Robins Co., Inc., *850 F.2d 709 (4th Cir. 1989).*

152 National Confectioners Association v. Califano, *569 F.2d 690 (D.C. Cir. 1978).*

153 U.S. v. An Article of Drug . . . Bacto-Unidisk, *394 U.S. 784 (1969).*

billion to the claimants for compensatory but no punitive damages.[154] A $2.3 billion trust was established to cover an estimated 197,000 claims.[155, 156]

The vast majority of Dalkon Shield users accepted settlements from the trust, but 2,500 claimants rejected settlement offers as inadequate.[157] Those who challenged the offers found in the trials on their claims that attorneys for the trust delved into their sexual history. Even claimants who opted for arbitration ended up in full-blown hearings on the fundamental issue of whether the shield was defective.[158] Only 244 claimants took their cases to trial or arbitration.[159]

Discussion Questions

1. What moral standards were in conflict in the Dalkon Shield case?
2. What moral standards would be involved if the banned inventory of the shields were sold to third world countries?
3. Explain, from a utilitarian perspective, the long-term benefits and costs of Robins's liability to the women who used the Dalkon Shield.
4. If you were an executive with Robins from 1972 to 1974, would you feel morally responsible for the injuries some women experienced from the Dalkon Shield?
5. Are the lawyers for the trust behaving ethically in their responses to users' claims?

CASE 7.12

E. Coli, Jack-in-the-Box, and Cooking Temperatures

On January 11, 1993, young Michael Nole and his family ate dinner at a Jack-in-the-Box restaurant in Tacoma, Washington, where Michael enjoyed his $2.69 "Kid's Meal." The next day, Michael was admitted to Children's Hospital and Medical Center in Seattle with severe stomach cramps and bloody diarrhea. Several days later, Michael died of kidney and heart failure.[160]

[154] *Kenneth Labich, "Lawsuits by the Thousand,"* Fortune, *April 29, 1985, p. 258.*

[155] *Tamar Lewin, "Pacifying Step in Robins Case,"* The New York Times, *April 1, 1986, p. 30.*

[156] *Note,* The Intrauterine Device: A Criticism of Governmental Complaisance and an Analysis of Manufacturer and Physician Liability, *24 Cle. St. L. Rev. 247 (1975).*

[157] *Phillip Elmer-DeWitt, "A Bitter Pill to Swallow: Birth Control in the U.S. Is Out of Date—and Getting More So." Reported by Georgia Harbison/New York and Dick Thompson/Washington,* Time, *February 26, 1990, p. 44.*

[158] *Geyelin, "Criminal Investigation of A. H. Robins," p. B3.*

[159] *Labich, "Lawsuits by the Thousand," p. 258.*

[160] *Catherine Yang and Amy Barrett, "In a Stew over Tainted Meat,"* Business Week, *April 12, 1993, p. 36.*

At the same time, 300 other people in Idaho, Nevada, and Washington who had eaten at Jack-in-the-Box restaurants were poisoned with E. coli bacteria, the cause of Michael's death. By the end of the outbreak, over 600 people nationwide were affected.[161]

Jack-in-the-Box, based in San Diego, was not in the best financial health, having just restructured $501 million in debt. The outbreak of poisonings came at a difficult time for the company.

Federal guidelines require that meat be cooked to an internal temperature of 140 degrees Fahrenheit. Jack-in-the-Box followed those guidelines. In May 1992 and September 1992, the state of Washington notified all restaurants, including Jack-in-the-Box, of new regulations requiring hamburgers to be cooked to 155 degrees Fahrenheit. The change would increase restaurants' costs because cooking to 155 degrees slows delivery of food to customers and increases energy costs.

At a news conference one week after the poisonings, Jack-in-the-Box president Robert J. Nugent criticized state authorities for not notifying the company of the 155-degree rule. A week later, the company found the notifications, which it had misplaced, and issued a statement.

After the Jack-in-the-Box poisonings, the federal government recommended that all states increase their cooking temperature requirements to 155 degrees. Burger King cooks to 160 degrees; Hardee's, Wendy's, and Taco Bell to 165 degrees. The U.S. Agriculture Department also changed its meat inspection standards.[162, 163]

The poisonings cut sales at Jack-in-the-Box by 20 percent.[164] Three store managers were laid off, and the company's plan to build five new restaurants was put on hold until sales picked up. Jack-in-the-Box scrapped 20,000 pounds of hamburger patties produced at meat plants where the bacteria was suspected to have originated. It also changed meat suppliers and added extra meat inspections of its own at an expected cost of $2 million a year.[165]

Consumer groups advocated a 160-degree internal temperature for cooking and a requirement that the meat no longer be pink or red inside.

A class action law suit brought by plaintiffs with minor E-Coli effects was settled for $12 million. Two other suits, brought on behalf of children who went into comas, were settled for $3 million and $15.6 million, respectively.[166] All of the suits were settled by the end of 1997, most of the settlements coming from a pool of $100 million established by the company's ten insurers.[167]

[161] *Fred Bayles, "Meat Safety,"* USA Today, *October 8, 1997, p. 1A.*

[162] *Richard Gibson and Scott Kilman, "Tainted Hamburger Incident Heats Up Debate over U.S. Meat-Inspection System,"* The Wall Street Journal, *February 12, 1993, pp. B1, B7.*

[163] *Martin Tolchin, "Clinton Orders Hiring of 160 Meat Inspectors,"* The New York Times, *February 12, 1993, p. A11.*

[164] *Ronald Grover, Dori Jones Yang, and Laura Holson, "Boxed in at Jack-in-the-Box,"* Business Week, *February 15, 1993, p. 40.*

[165] *Adam Bryant, "Foodmaker Cancels Expansion,"* The New York Times, *February 15, 1993, p. C3.*

[166] *"Jack-in-the-Box Ends E-Coli Suits,"* National Law Journal, *November 17, 1997, p. A8.*

[167] *Bob Van Voris, "Jack in the Box Ends E-Coli Suits,"* National Law Journal, *November 17, 1997.*

Discussion Questions

1. In 1993 Jack-in-the-Box adopted tougher standards for its meat suppliers than those required by the federal government so that suppliers test more frequently for E. coli. Could Jack-in-the-Box have done more after the outbreak occurred?
2. The link between cooking to a 155-degree internal temperature and the destruction of E. coli bacteria has been publicly known for five years. The federal Centers for Disease Control tests showed Jack-in-the-Box hamburgers were cooked to 120 degrees. Should Jack-in-the-Box have increased cooking temperatures voluntarily and sooner?
3. What does the misplacement of the state health department notices on cooking temperature say about the culture at Jack-in-the-Box?
4. Are there moral issues involved in deciding what temperature to cook meat to?
5. A plaintiff's lawyer praised Jack-in-the-Box saying, "They paid out in a way that made everybody walking away from the settlement table think they had been treated fairly." What do we learn about the company from this statement?

7C

Product Social Issues

Sometimes the product is legal, the quality is good and, yet, the product does have its issues. In this section, the issues are ones of social responsibility.

CASE 7.13

The Mommy Doll

Villy Nielsen, APS, a Danish toy company, introduced the Mommy-To-Be doll in the United States. The doll, named Judith, looks like it is pregnant. When its belly is removed, a baby is revealed inside that can be popped out. Once the baby is removed, the doll's original stomach pops into place. The new stomach is flat and instantly restores Judith's youthful figure.

Teenage girls are intrigued by the doll, and call it "neat." However, Diane Welsh, the president of the New York chapter of the National Organization for Women, stated, "A doll that magically becomes pregnant and unpregnant is an irresponsible toy. We need to understand having a child is a very serious business. We have enough unwanted children in this world."[168]

Mommy-To-Be comes with Charles, her husband, and baby accessories. An eleven-year-old shopper said of the doll, "I don't think she looks like a mommy. . . . She looks like a teenager."[169]

Discussion Questions

1. Is the doll a socially responsible toy?
2. Would you carry the doll if you owned a toy store?
3. Would you want your children to have the doll?

[168] *"Mommy Doll Makes Birth a Snap,"* Mesa Tribune, *May 9, 1992, p. A7.*

[169] Id.

CASE 7.14

Rock Music Warning Labels

In the summer of 1985, Tipper Gore, the wife of then-Senator Albert Gore of Tennessee, and Susan Baker, the wife of former U.S. Treasury Secretary James Baker, formed a citizens' group called the Parents Resource Music Center (PMRC). The group's concern was that rock music advocates "aggressive and hostile rebellion, the abuse of drugs and alcohol, irresponsible sexuality, sexual perversions, violence and involvement in the occult." Gore began the group after she listened to the song "Darling Nikki" from her eleven-year-old daughter's *Purple Rain* album by Prince. The song is about a girl masturbating as she looks at a magazine. Gore then discovered Sheena Easton singing about "genital arousal," Judas Priest singing about oral sex at gunpoint, and the lyrics in Motley Crue's top-selling *Shout at the Devil* album describe killing a person and watching his face turn blue.

PMRC's strategy was to work with record companies to reach a mutually agreeable solution to the problem. PMRC met with the Recording Industry Association of America to request a ratings system for records, similar to that used for movies, and a requirement that printed lyrics be included with all records so that disc jockeys would know what they are sending out over the airwaves. In the first month after PMRC was organized, it received over 10,000 letters of support and inquiry. PMRC maintains a database with the following information:

- Teenagers listen to their music four to six hours per day for a total of 10,000 hours between grades seven and twelve.
- Of all violent crimes, 70 percent are committed by youths under the age of seventeen.
- Teenage suicide has increased by 300 percent since 1955.
- U.S. teenage pregnancy rates are the highest in the world.[170]

When PMRC failed to reach an agreement with the record industry, congressional hearings were held on a proposed bill to require labeling on records. Susan Baker and Tipper Gore testified, as did musicians Frank Zappa, former member of the Mothers of Invention, and Dee Snider of Twisted Sister. Zappa stated, "Putting labels on albums is the equivalent of treating dandruff by decapitation."[171]

Though nothing came of the hearings, by 1990 bills were pending in thirty-five state legislatures to require labeling of records. PMRC backed state groups lobbying for the legislation.[172] In Arizona, a reporter for *New Times* asked a sponsor of a labeling bill, Senator Jan Brewer, to read some of the objectionable lyrics. The reporter recorded the reading, set it to music, and played the tape over the speakers in the Capitol.[173]

In May 1990, with the state legislative debates on the label requirements still in progress, the Recording Industry Association of America introduced a uniform label for albums with explicit lyrics and expressed hope that its voluntary use by industry

[170] *William A. Henry, "Did the Music Say Do It?"* Time, *July 30, 1990, p. 65.*

[171] *"Musicians Mock Senators' Wives at Hearing,"* Mesa Tribune, *September 20, 1995, p. A4.*

[172] *"Record Firm to Back Stores with Legal Aid,"* Mesa Tribune, *June 5, 1990, p. A2.*

[173] *Ed Foster, "Music-Label Bill Shelved,"* Arizona Republic, *March 24, 1990, p. A1.*

members would halt the passage of legislation.[174] The black-and-white label appears in the lower right-hand corner of the album and reads: "Parental Advisory—Explicit Lyrics."[175] The label is to be used on albums with lyrics relating to sex, violence, suicide, drug abuse, bigotry, or satanic worship. Use of the label is the decision of the record company and the artist.[176]

The PMRC and the National Parent and Teacher Association endorsed the warning system and asked state legislators to consider dropping proposed label legislation.[177]

Controversy continued to surround rock music lyrics. In the summer of 1990, parents of a teenager who committed suicide sued the rock group Judas Priest, alleging that its lyrics resulted in murderous mind control and the death of their son.[178] Their subliminal persuasion argument was unsuccessful.[179]

By 1995, the record industry's then ten-year-old warning label program was reviewed with the conclusion that parents don't know what the explicit-lyrics labels are.[180] A meeting between the Recording Industry Association of America and the National Association of Recording Merchandisers resulted in new plans to help the system work better.[181] The provisions included:

- Display signs in stores explaining the "Parental Advisory Explicit Lyrics" logo.[182]
- Ensure that record companies use the correct size (1-inch by 1/2-inch) and placement (lower right) on the record's permanent packaging.
- Alert reviewers of each record's sticker status.
- Encourage inclusion of a record's warning label in ads and promotional materials.

The attention to gangsta rap music also resulted in increased attention to lyrics. Recording company MCA was targeted in 1996 for marketing "death and degradation." MCA refused to make changes other than complying with warning labels and called Mr. William Bennett, a former secretary of Education and author, a "warden of morality." Wal-Mart refused to stock explicit lyric music.

In late November 1997, the Senate began exploring the effects of music on children. One parent testified that his 15-year-old son committed suicide after listening to the Marilyn Manson album, "Antichrist Superstar."

The issues of rock music, lyrics, and artists' rights had its usual cycle of relative quiet between 1997 and 2000. However, during the presidential election of 2000, the issues again surfaced because Mr. Gore was running for president and his wife Tipper again was in the news along with the issues that concerned her. In addition, George W.

[174] *"Warning: Rock Music Ahead,"* Time, *May 21, 1990, p. 69.*

[175] *Robert M. Andrews, "Records Get Uniform Warning Tag,"* Arizona Republic, *May 10, 1990, p. A1.*

[176] *Carrie White, "Rating Rock Music,"* Mesa Tribune, *December 12, 1995, p. D1.*

[177] *"Record Firm to Back Stores with Legal Aid," p. A2.*

[178] *David Stout, "Senate Hearing Is Told Lyrics Led to Suicide,"* The New York Times, *November 7, 1997, p. A1.*

[179] *Henry, "Did the Music Say Do It?" p. 65.*

[180] *Edna Gundersen, "Explicit Lyrics Warning Just Aren't Sticking,"* USA Today, *October 25, 1995, p. 1D.*

[181] *Julia Malone, "Washington Wives Use Influence to Target Sex, Drugs in Rock Music,"* Christian Science Monitor, *August 23, 1995, pp. 1, 36.*

[182] *"MCA 'Peddling Filth,' Critics Say,"* Arizona Republic, *December 11, 1996, p. A7.*

Bush chose Dick Cheney as his running mate. Mr. Cheney is married to Dr. Lynne Cheney, who was the head of the Council on Humanities for Presidents Reagan and Bush, holds a PhD in literature, and is a resident scholar at the American Enterprise Institute.

During the presidential campaign of 2000, both Mrs. Cheney and Mrs. Gore became vocal about the lyrics of rock star Eminem. Eminem released his "The Marshall Mathers LP," which became the fastest-selling release ever, selling 5.2 million copies in two months. The album sold 8 million copies in nine months.[183] Mrs. Cheney stunned Congress when she read lyrics from Eminem's song, most too crude to reproduce here, but which included phrases such as:

> Beat your bitches [sic] ass while your kids stare in silence
>
> Went up inside the First National Bank broke, and left rich
>
> Walking bio-hazard causing wreckage

His lyrics were described by various critics and commentators:

> "Vile and full of frightening calls to violence." Jim Fouratt, *Billboard*
>
> "In the hands of a more capable artist (say, Frank Zappa or Richard Pryor), this vitriol might be taken to such an extreme to make it a subversive farce; in Em's ego-fueled tirade, it's merely sickeningly offensive . . . about as funny as kiddie porn . . ." *Sonic Net.com*
>
> "The first great pop record of the 21st Century . . . A-minus for artistry, D-plus for moral responsibility." *Entertainment Weekly*
>
> "Crude, hostile, bigoted lyrics." Michael Medved, *USA Today*[184]

Discussion Questions

1. What are the ethical issues in the production of songs with explicit lyrics?
2. Will voluntary regulation work for the recording industry?
3. If you were a record producer, would your company sign artists who sing explicit lyrics?
4. If you were a record producer, would you feel an obligation to do more than put a warning label on albums with explicit lyrics?
5. You have just been informed that a teenager committed suicide while listening to the music of one of the artists your company produces. The music suggested suicide as an alternative to unhappiness. Would you feel morally responsible for the suicide? Should the artist feel morally responsible?
6. Does the reemergence of Eminem establish that rock music lyrics will always be an issue? Is there a danger that the bar is lowered with each discussion? For example,

[183] *Edna Gundersen, "Eminem: What's With This Guy?"* USA Today, *July 27, 2000, p. 1D.*

[184] *Mim Udovitch, "Visible Man,"* New York Times Magazine, *February 18, 2001, pp. 9–10.*

in this edition of the book, the Eminem lyrics are simply too crude to include whereas the lyrics from the last round could be included. Is this decline evidence of a decline in the social responsibility of record companies and artists?

CASE 7.15
Stem-Cell Research

During the summer of 2001, there was extensive debate over stem-cell research because President George W. Bush was faced with the decision of whether to allow federal funding for the extraction of stem cells from human embryos.

Stem-cell research has strong advocates in the medical and scientific community because of their belief that the research holds great potential for cures for Alzheimer's disease, cancer, spinal cord injuries, Parkinson's, diabetes, and a range of other related illnesses.[185] The advocates had strong support from Mrs. Nancy Reagan, wife of President Ronald Reagan, who has suffered from Alzheimer's for nearly a decade, and Christopher Reeve, a Hollywood actor with a spinal cord injury.

However, stem-cell research has its strong opponents among those who believe that life begins at conception and that the "harvesting" of stem cells from embryos is the taking of life, and that encouraging such research is likely to result in the creation of human embryos for purposes of harvesting the cells. These opponents tout adult stem-cell research as an alternative that has been pursued with some success and a solution that avoids what they see as a moral dilemma. They also fear the likelihood of the slippery slope to cloning.[186] Indeed, the House voted to ban human cloning during this time period because of concerns that any federal funding that would be approved might lead to further experimentation.[187] Richard M. Doerflinger, of the U.S. Conference of Catholic Bishops, has called the research "grotesque," and said, "Those who have become accustomed to destroying 'spare' embryos for research now think nothing of taking the next horrible step, creating human life for the purpose of destroying it."[188]

During the time of the debate, the media revealed that the Jones Institute, a private fertility clinic in Norfolk, Virginia, was mixing eggs and sperm to create human embryos.[189]

Mr. Bush, as a compromise position on a hotly debated issue, approved limited federal funding for lines of research on stem cells that were already "harvested." His reasoning was that the cells should not be thrown away.

[185] *Robert P. George, "Don't Destroy Human Life,"* The Wall Street Journal, *July 30, 2001, p. A16.*

[186] *David Baltimore, "Don't Impede Medical Progress,"* The Wall Street Journal, *July 30, 2001, p. A16.*

[187] *Sheryl Gay Stolberg, "House Backs Ban on Human Cloning for Any Objective,"* The New York Times, *August 1, 2001, pp. A1, A11.*

[188] *Laurie McGinley, "Nancy Reagan Urges GOP to Back Stem-Cell Research,"* The Wall Street Journal, *July 12, 2001, p. B2.*

[189] *Sheryl Gay Stolberg, "Bioethicists Find Themselves the Ones Being Scrutinized,"* The New York Times, *August 2, 2001, pp. A1, A14.*

While the public continued its debate, biotech businesses were gearing up for what they felt would be the new direction for medical research and treatment. For example, Advanced Cell Technology, Inc. began acquiring eggs from female donors for purposes of future research.[190] Later in 2001, Advanced Cell Technology announced that it has successfully cloned a human embryo.[191]

Universities such as Georgetown and Michigan, with extensive cancer research programs, stand to benefit substantially from federal research dollars. Upon President Bush's announcement of his partial approval, biotech stocks soared.

Discussion Questions

1. Is it ethical for the Jones Institute to create embryos? What of Advanced Cell Technology's cloning?
2. One bioethicist has questioned the role of bioethicists in the debate raising the question, "Are we being ethical even as we say what is ethical?" What if they are funded by hospitals, biotech companies, and pharmaceutical firms in their research or at their colleges and universities?
3. Is stem-cell research a moral issue that breaks down along religious lines or are there implications for each side's position?
4. Pope John Paul II, believed to suffer from Parkinson's, has taken a strong position against stem-cell research and indicated "the end never justifies the means."[192] What does he mean? Are businesses using this rationalization?
5. Would you work for a company that creates human embryos? That conducts stem-cell research? Why or why not?

[190] *"Cloning of Embryos for Research Raises Ethics Questions,"* The Wall Street Journal, *July 12, 2001, p. B2.*

[191] *Sheryl Gay Stolberg, "Cloning Executive Presses Senate,"* The New York Times, *December 5, 2001, p. A22.*

[192] *Robert A. Sirico, "No Compromise on Stem Cells,"* The Wall Street Journal, *July 11, 2001, p. A16.*

unit 8

Business and Government

Businesses are regulated by government agencies, but they also provide goods and services to those same agencies. Unique ethical dilemmas arise on both sides when the private and public sectors cross.

> *"I want a society that is based on truth. That means no longer hiding what we used to hide."*
>
> Boris Yeltsin

> *Dishonesty by government officials and employees not only costs us money, it undermines our faith in their integrity and that of our public institutions. Ethical breaches by government employees have far-reaching effects because they are so public.*
>
> Michael Josephson

8a

Government Employees

CASE 8.1

A Club in My Name

The Keds Corporation paid $7.2 million to the fifty state attorneys general to settle a complaint that the shoemaker had engaged in price fixing involving several lines of Keds' girls and womens shoes. The attorneys general each received a portion of the $7.2 million and had agreed to give the money to charities. Most donated the funds to Boys and Girls Clubs in their states.

Arizona's attorney general, Grant Woods, donated his state's share, $85,500, to the Mesa Boys and Girls Club, which used the money to help build a $3 million clubhouse that it then named after Woods.

A state representative noted:

> It is a very good cause and I support the Boys and Girls Club, but that is not the point. The money is public money. It is not [Woods's] money.
>
> My point is that no agency or director should be able to direct money to any specific personal cause or for personal use.[1]

Discussion Questions

1. What issues of propriety are raised?
2. Is it bad form to raise ethical issues when all the money went to charity?
3. How could the state representative's reaction have been anticipated?

[1] *Kirk Mitchell, "Mesa Club Got Funds,"* Mesa Tribune, *January 7, 1995, pp. A1, A6.*

CASE 8.2

The Fireman and His Family

Robert "Hoot" Gibson served with the Phoenix Fire Department for nearly four decades. He was serving as deputy chief when he retired immediately after a four-month investigation revealed the following:

- Holiday pay of $5,000 to employees who had not actually worked those holidays;
- Three employees were permitted to store their pontoon boat at a city property;
- Design 10, a company owned by Gibson's wife and three children, had the contract for clothing sales to the fire department;
- Gibson's son was hired to open the department's print shop; and
- Relatives of Gibson and other employees were hired as temporary employees without going through standard hiring procedures.[2]

Discussion Questions

1. What ethical breaches could you see in this conduct?

2. What tests could have been applied to prevent these decisions from being made?

CASE 8.3

Commodities, Conflicts, and Clintons

In October 1978, Hillary Rodham Clinton, wife of then-attorney general of Arkansas and gubernatorial candidate William Jefferson Clinton, opened a margin account with a $1,000 investment at Refco, a commodities brokerage firm. Commodities market regulators had disciplined Robert L. "Red" Bone, Mrs. Clinton's chief broker at Refco, for his practice of allocating trades among his customers only after learning whether the actual trades made were positive or negative.[3]

Mrs. Clinton was given advice on her trades by James B. Blair, corporate counsel for Tyson Foods, Inc., which is the nation's largest producer of frozen chicken patties and pieces for grocery market sales and fast food franchises.[4] Like any poultry processor, Tyson is subject to strict federal and state regulation. Don Tyson, then-CEO of Tyson Foods, contributed to Mr. Clinton's campaigns for public office. Mr. Blair has stated that Mrs. Clinton alone decided the size of her commodities trades but that they discussed whether her trades should be short or long.

[2] *Chris Fiscus, "Key Official Forced to Retire,"* Arizona Republic, *October 18, 1996, pp. A1, A12.*

[3] *Michael K. Frisby and Bruce Ingersoll, "First Lady Turned $1,000 Investment Into a $98,000 Profit, Records Show,"* The Wall Street Journal, *March 30, 1994, p. A1.*

[4] *"Hillary in the Pits,"* The Wall Street Journal, *March 30, 1994, p. A18.*

Between October 1978 and October 1979, Mrs. Clinton's $1,000 investment grew as follows:

Day 1—First Trade—profit of $5,300

October 1978—December 31, 1978—	$49,069—profits
	$22,548—losses
	$26,541—net profit
January 1979—July 1979—	$109,600—profits
	$36,600—losses
	$72,996—net profit[5]

After Mr. Clinton was elected governor of Arkansas in November 1978, he appointed several Tyson executives to state government positions, and Tyson received favorable regulatory decisions on several actions pending in state agencies. Tyson awarded its outside legal work to the Rose Law Firm in Little Rock, where Mrs. Clinton was a partner.[6] A Tyson spokesman has stated, "There is absolutely no evidence that Jim Blair's relationship with Bill or Hillary Clinton had any impact on our treatment."[7]

Commented a commodities trader: "The idea that Mrs. Clinton could turn $1,000 into $100,000 trading a cross-section of markets such as cattle, soybeans, sugar, hogs, copper and lumber just isn't believable. To make 100 times your money is possible, but it's difficult to understand how a newcomer could do it. I don't care who is advising her. It just isn't very likely."[8]

In 1992, Mr. Clinton was elected president of the United States. For more information on the role of Tyson at the federal government level following Mr. Clinton's election, see Case 8.4.

Discussion Questions

1. Did Mr. Blair have a conflict of interest in providing Mrs. Clinton with assistance on her trades?
2. Did Mrs. Clinton have a conflict of interest in accepting Mr. Blair's assistance on the trades?
3. Is there evidence of a quid pro quo?
4. Did Mr. Clinton have a conflict of interest?
5. Did Tyson's employment of the Rose Law Firm as outside counsel constitute a conflict of interest?
6. Evaluate all these decisions using the front-page-of-the-newspaper test.

[5] *Frisby and Ingersoll, "First Lady Turned $1,000 Investment Into a $98,000 Profit, Records Show," p. A1.*

[6] *"O Tempora! O Mores!"* The Wall Street Journal, *March 21, 1994, p. A18.*

[7] *Bruce Ingersoll, "Agriculture Chief's Handling of Chicken Industry Revives Questions About Clinton's Ties to Tyson,"* The Wall Street Journal, *March 17, 1994, p. A16.*

[8] *Frisby and Ingersoll, "First Lady Turned $1,000 Investment Into a $98,000 Profit, Records Show," p. A1.*

7. What questions from Laura Nash's analysis provide insight into the ethical issues here?

8. Is the Tyson spokesperson's statement about there being no evidence of Mr. Blair's conduct having any influence relevant in determining whether a conflict of interest existed?

CASE 8.4

The Secretary of Agriculture, Chicken Processors, and Football Skybox Seats

Former President Bill Clinton appointed Mike Espy as Secretary of Agriculture in 1993. Mr. Espy accepted from Tyson Foods, Inc., the world's largest producer of fresh and processed poultry products, a ride on a Tyson corporate jet, free lodging at a lakeside cabin owned by Tyson, and seats in Tyson's skybox at a Dallas Cowboys/New York Giants playoff game. Later, a car paid for by the company took Mr. Espy and his friend, Pat Dempsey, shopping, then to the airport for the return trip to Washington.

Mr. Espy went to the 1994 Super Bowl at government expense, saying he made the trip because Smokey the Bear was being honored in public service announcements at the game. Additionally, Mr. Espy's girlfriend, Pat Dempsey, received a $1,200 college scholarship from Tyson Foods.[9] At the time, Tyson and other regulators were fighting proposed Department of Agriculture guidelines (ultimately not implemented for poultry processors and withdrawn for other meat processors) that would have imposed a "zero tolerance" on the presence of fecal matter during processing. Tyson Foods also provided lodging at its management center in Russellville, Arkansas, to Mr. Espy and Pat Dempsey, while Mr. Espy was in the state to speak before the Arkansas Poultry Federation. A Tyson plane flew them back to Washington. Mr. Espy did reimburse Tyson for the cost of a first-class ticket from Washington, D.C., to Russellville and he also paid back the value of all the other flights and gifts he received from Tyson and others he regulated. These paybacks for flights, gifts such as luggage, limousine rides, and games brought the total of the benefits Mr. Espy received to $33,228.

As a former member of Congress, Mr. Espy felt the benefits he had accepted were so small in terms of monetary value that his accepting them was not an issue. However, public reaction to Mr. Espy's relationship with Tyson, despite the paybacks, was so intense that he was urged by the Clinton White House to resign. He did tender his resignation as Secretary of Agriculture as of December 31, 1994.[10, 11, 12, 13] Donald

[9] *Bruce Ingersoll, "Agriculture Chief's Handling of Chicken Industry Revives Questions About Clinton's Ties to Tyson,"* The Wall Street Journal, *March 17, 1994, p. A16.*

[10] *Richard Benedetto, "Calls Ethics Accusations Distracting,"* USA Today, *October 4, 1994, p. 1A.*

[11] *Richard Benedetto, "A Personnel Loss for Clinton,"* USA Today, *October 4, 1994, p. 3A.*

[12] *David Johnston, "Agriculture Chief Quits as Scrutiny of Conduct Grows,"* The New York Times, *October 4, 1994, pp. A1, A11.*

[13] *Bruce Ingersoll and Jeffrey H. Birnbaum, "Agriculture Secretary Espy Resigns Under Pressure From the White House,"* The Wall Street Journal, *October 4, 1994, p. A3.*

Smaltz was appointed as a special prosecutor to investigate the legality of Mr. Espy's acceptance of the things Tyson had offered and whether he had granted any favors to Tyson in exchange.[14]

As Mr. Smaltz conducted his investigation there was an expanding web of issues involving others beyond Mr. Espy. Ronald Blackley, who became Mr. Espy's chief of staff at the Agriculture Department, has acknowledged that while a congressional aide to Mr. Espy, he was also on the payroll of farmers seeking support payments from the government. Mr. Blackley did close his consulting business before joining the Agriculture Department. While Mr. Espy was still secretary, Mr. Blackley ordered aides to stop work on proposals for tougher standards for poultry inspections.[15]

Mr. Smaltz also found benefits from other companies. For example, the chief executive of Quaker Oats, William D. Smithburg, gave Mr. Espy a ticket to a June 18, 1993, Chicago Bulls playoff game. The company indicated that it had received a request for the ticket from the Secretary of Agriculture's office.

Because Henry Espy, brother of Mike Espy, ran an unsuccessful campaign to take over his his brother's Mississippi congressional seat, Mr. Smaltz examined campaign contributions in that run for office to determine the scope of contributions from agribusinesses to Mr. Espy's brother.[16]

All those who had given or offered Mr. Espy flights, tickets, and other benefits were also investigated. Richard Douglas, a longtime friend of Mr. Espy who was also the chief lobbyist for Sun-Diamond Growers of California, an almond and raisin cooperative based in California, and others were investigated largely because of a lavish birthday party Sun-Diamond paid for for Mr. Espy. The inspector general of the Department of Agriculture also investigated the party to determine whether any of the 150 Sun-Diamond employees in attendance were pressed for contributions to cover the party's cost.[17, 18]

As a result of the special prosecutor's investigation, the following charges, verdicts, and pleas occurred:

party	*charge*	*result*
Arthur Schaffer III	Executive of Tyson charged with making illegal gifts	Convicted; judge granted judgment NOV; appellate court reinstated conviction
Sun-Diamond	Charged with making illegal gifts to Mr. Espy and illegal campaign contributions to Henry Espy ($4,000)	Convicted; fine of $1.5 million; conviction reversed; *U.S. v. Sun-Diamond Growers of California*, (1999), because the criminal statute required

[14] *Bruce Ingersoll, "Espy Inquiry Focuses on Mystery Memo to Learn If Coverup Occurred Over Industry Favoritism," The Wall Street Journal, January 16, 1995, p. A14.*

[15] Id.

[16] *Jerry Seper, "Payments to Espy Brother Bring Big Fine,"* Washington Times, *January 25, 1998, p. 10.*

[17] *Bruce Ingersoll, "Former Lobbyist for Sun-Diamond Gets Split Decision in Trial on Aiding Espys,"* The Wall Street Journal, *November 26, 1997, p. B2.*

[18] *Bruce Ingersoll, "Lobbyist for Tyson Indicted in Espy Probe,"* The Wall Street Journal, *September 18, 1996, p. B5.*

party	charge	result
		proof of some connection between the gifts and a specific pending matter, not a generic desire to seek goodwill
Richard Douglas (lobbyist for Sun-Diamond Growers of California)	Charged with making illegal gifts (luggage plus a trip to the U.S. Open tennis tournament that cost $4,590)	Convicted[19, 20]
	Charged with furnishing Mr. Espy's girlfriend with a $3,100 plane ticket so that she could accompany him to Greece	Jury deadlocked
James Lake (Washington lobbyist for Sun-Diamond)	Wire fraud, violations of Federal Election Campaign Act (a $4,000 gift to Henry Espy)	Convicted[21]
Crop Growers Corp.	Concealment of corporate campaign contributions to Henry Espy ($46,000)	Convicted[22]
American Family Life Assurance Co.	Illegal corporate conduit for campaign contributions to Henry Espy	Civil penalty of $80,000
John Hemmingson (Chairman of Crop Growers Corporation)	Fraud/money laundering; illegal campaign contributions to Henry Espy	Convicted
Tyson Foods, Inc.	Charged with making illegal gifts ($12,000 in tickets, travel, and lodging)	Guilty plea; $4 million in fines plus costs of the investigation ($2 million)[23, 24]
Jack Williams (lobbyist for Tyson Foods)	Four-count indictment for bribery and illegal gifts involving Mr. Espy; two counts for making false statements to regulators	Conviction; reversed on appeal; new trial ordered
Don Tyson (CEO of Tyson Foods)		Granted immunity for everything except perjury in exchange for his testimony

[19] *Jerry Seper, "Lobbyist for Tyson Indicted,"* Washington Times, *October 12, 1997, p. 7.*

[20] *Bruce Ingersoll, "Sun-Diamond Gets Fine of $1.5 Million in Espy Affair,"* The Wall Street Journal, *May 14, 1997, p. B7.*

[21] *Seper, "Lobbyist for Tyson Indicted," p. 7.*

[22] *Seper, "Payments to Espy Brother Bring Big Fine," p. 10.*

[23] *John Godrey, "Tyson Foods is Fined $6 Million,"* Washington Times, *January 11, 1998, pp. 1, 22.*

[24] *Jerry Seper, "Tyson Foods is Named a Target in Espy Investigation,"* Washington Times, *July 6, 1997, p. 8.*

party	charge	result
Henry Espy (Mike Espy's brother)	Defrauding election authorities; false statements in loan applications	Charges dismissed for lack of evidence[25]
Ron Blackley (Mike Espy's chief of staff at Agriculture)	Lying to government authorities	Convicted/ sentenced to 27 months in prison
Mike Espy	39-count indictment; accepting and soliciting gifts and favors (including Super Bowl tickets, a crystal bowl gift, and the $1,200 scholarship) from agribusinesses; witness tampering; procuring illegal campaign contributions	9 counts dismissed; pleaded innocent; acquitted on all 30 counts[26]

Mr. Smaltz obtained indictments against twenty individuals as part of his investigation and obtained more than fifteen convictions and $11 million in penalties.[27] However, many called for the elimination of the independent counsel statute that authorized these investigations of officials in the executive branch (the statute has since lapsed).

Discussion Questions

1. Is the value of these items an issue in determining whether Mr. Espy acted ethically? In a statement released by Tyson Foods upon its indictment was the following sentence: "The company deplores the independent counsel's apparent view that acts of hospitality—consisting of a couple of meals and a football game—can rise to the level of criminal conduct." Is this a sound view for government relations?

2. Does Mr. Espy's reimbursement change the ethical issues?

3. What tests could Mr. Espy have used prior to accepting these items that would have required him to refuse them on ethical grounds?

4. Did Mr. Espy create a conflict of interest?

5. Evaluate each of the matters the special prosecutor investigated. Are there ethical breaches regardless of any illegality?

6. Evaluate each of the following statements from an ethical perspective.

   a. "They used Mr. Espy's fondness for sports to get on his good side. He was easy pickings for companies that wanted to slip him something special," said Mr. Espy's attorney, Theodore Wells, in his opening statement in Mr. Espy's trial.

[25] *Seper, "Payments to Espy Brother Bring Big Fine," p. 10.*

[26] *"Espy to Court,"* USA Today, *September 11, 1997, p. 6A.*

[27] *Terry Eastland, "How Justice Tried to Stop Smaltz,"* The Wall Street Journal, *December 22, 1997, p. A19.*

Mr. Wells also noted, "He's completely innocent. He did not commit any criminal acts. He's not a crook."

b. "I recall him saying something like in passing, in a very social setting . . . 'It's a bunch of junk. I'm going to do like I did in Congress.'" Former EPA Administrator, Carol Browner, during her testimony in Mr. Espy's trial when asked if he had ever discussed the Clinton Administration ethics rules with her. Ms. Browner said she could not remember the exact words but testified that Mr. Espy referred to the rules as "a bunch of junk."

c. In sentencing Ronald Blackley for lying about his sources of income on a disclosure form and to investigators who asked him about the form, Judge Royce Lambreth said, "This court has a duty to send a message to other high government officials that there is a penalty to be paid for making false statements under oath." The judge ignored a sentencing recommendation of probation and sentenced Mr. Blackley to 27 months. An appellate court rejected his appeal.

7. Mr. Smaltz spent $11 million on his investigation. Is this amount justified for the size of the gifts? Mr. Smaltz stated when Tyson Foods entered its guilty plea, "Such conduct must continue to invite outrage, never passivity, from those who are regulated, the public, and our lawmakers." Is Mr. Smaltz correct?

Sources

"Asides," *The Wall Street Journal*, December 30, 1997, p. A10.

Behar, Richard, "On Fresh Ground," *Time*, December 26, 1994, p. 111.

Behar, Richard, and Michael Kramer, "Something Smells Fowl," *Time*, October 17, 1994, pp. 42–44.

Cauchon, Dennis, "Millionaire Tyson Stretches Political Limits," *USA Today*, October 5, 1994, p. 4A.

Clark, Kim, "Tough Times for the Chicken King," *Fortune*, October 28, 1996, pp. 88–97.

"Espy Quits with Push from Clinton," *Arizona Republic*, October 4, 1994, pp. A1, A9.

Fields, Gary, and Tom Squiteri, "Tough Term Is Warning in Intern Scandal," *USA Today*, March 19, 1998, p. 1A.

Ingersoll, Bruce, "Espy Case Figure, John Hemmingson, Is Indicted Again," *The Wall Street Journal*, August 7, 1996, p. B2.

Nichols, Bill, "Espy's Once-Promising Political Career Probably Over," *USA Today*, August 28, 1997, p. 4A.

Nichols, Bill, "Ex-Cabinet Member Indicted," *USA Today*, August 28, 1997, p. 1A.

Novak, Viveca, "The Peril of Prosecutorial Passion," *Time*, June 16, 1997, p. 42.

Seper, Jerry, "Illegal Gifts, Cover-Up Charged in Espy Indictment," *Washington Times*, September 7, 1997, p. 11.

Seper, Jerry, "Judge OK's Tyson Foods' Plea Deal," *Washington Times*, January 25, 1998, p. 10.

Stout, David, "Inquiry on Espy Leads to Indictment of Former Chief Aide," *The New York Times*, April 23, 1997, p. A12.

CASE 8.5

The City Council Member with Clout

The following chronology details the actions of Mr. Jim Stapley, a former member of the Mesa City Council.

March 1994

Stapley printed a photograph of him and former President Reagan in a campaign brochure for the City Council primary election. The photo was taken with a cardboard cutout of the former president, however.

April 1996

Councilwoman Joan Payne leaked word of a 15-month-old memo to the city manager in which she accused Stapley of putting his hand on her knee during a helicopter ride and of mailing her pornographic material. She asked the city manager to order Stapley to stay away from her.

In response, Stapley issued his own memo a few days later, saying that Payne touched his knee.

May 1997

Stapley called a Mesa justice of the peace about an eviction case proceeding against his son William. The case was later transferred to another Mesa Justice Court, but the judge said the two actions were not related.

June 1997

Stapley sought to have disorderly conduct charges dropped against Lee Watkins, a friend and political ally. In addition, Stapley sought to have the city prosecutor fired.[28] The council voted to censure Stapley after this incident, minutes after a measure to oust him failed by two votes.

July 1997

Stapley filed a lawsuit against Payne, saying she defamed him in two radio appearances by calling him a "pervert in polyester" and a "racist." The suit was settled in October. Terms were not made public.

August 1997

Stapley possibly violated his censure by placing several calls to Mesa Firefighters Union President Chris Medrea about a $1,000 donation the union made to Payne's

[28] *Art Thomason, "Red Beets Less Luster in Scandal,"* Arizona Republic, *June 19, 1997, p. EV1; see also Dan Nowicki, "Council Rebukes Stapley,"* Mesa Tribune, *June 19, 1997, pp. A1, A4.*

legal defense fund, established after Stapley sued her for defamation. Stapley said he feels he didn't violate the censure because he was contacting Medrea in his role with the union, not as a city firefighter.

October 1997

A memo surfaced in which Stapley was accused of impersonating a Pinal County sheriff's detective at a Florence courthouse in February 1995. Police records say Stapley flashed a police badge and said he was a detective when he visited the clerk's office at Pinal County Superior Court. He was looking for a search warrant affidavit on a narcotics case involving his son, Kenneth.

Stapley circulated petitions at a meeting attended by city employees. The action may have been unethical, since city policy forbids candidates to ask city employees to sign petitions in city buildings on city time.

Following the October 1997 impersonation, Mr. Stapley resigned.[29]

Discussion Questions

1. What ethical breaches do you feel occurred?

2. What impact would Mr. Stapley's conduct have on employees?

3. Would Mr. Stapley's involvement affect the wheels of justice?

4. Do you think employees would be comfortable complaining?

CASE 8.6

IRS Employees and Sensitive Data

In 1997, the IRS disciplined hundreds of employees for using agency computers and records to browse through the tax records of friends, relatives, and celebrities. The IRS fired 23 employees, disciplined 349, and provided counseling for 472.

During 1996 and 1997, the IRS investigated 1,515 cases of "snooping" among its 102,000 employees. Half of the employees have computer access to taxpayer returns.

Those employees who were counseled said they did not believe that what they did was wrong nor that there would be any sanctions for doing it. The law is not violated by "snooping," it is violated only if the information is disclosed to others. However, in a case that reached the appellate level just as the IRS employees were disciplined, a court reached a different conclusion.

Richard Czubinski, an IRS employee in its Boston office, was a member of the IRS's Taxpayer Services Division and had full access to taxpayer files. He could retrieve taxpayer information on anyone in the United States who has filed a federal income tax return.

29 *Chris Moeser, "Stapley Quits Mesa Council," Mesa Tribune, November 1, 1997, p. A1.*

During lunch hours and breaks, Czubinski retrieved the tax returns of the following:

- An assistant district attorney in Boston who was prosecuting Czubinski's father
- A woman he was dating
- David Duke (at the time he was a presidential candidate)

Czubinski was charged with violations of the Computer Fraud and Abuse Act and convicted. The appellate court held that because he did not use the information to make up any dossiers, disclose the information to anyone, or even use the information beyond just looking at it, he had not violated the federal laws. The court added the following cautionary note at the end of its opinion:

> We add a cautionary note. The broad language of the mail and wire fraud statutes are both their blessing and their curse. They can address new forms of serious crime that fail to fall within more specific legislation. On the other hand, they might be used to prosecute kinds of behavior that, albeit offensive to the morals or aesthetics of federal prosecutors, cannot reasonably be expected by the instigators to form the basis of a federal felony. The case at bar falls within the latter category. Also discomforting is the prosecution's insistence, before trial, on the admission of inflammatory evidence regarding the defendant's membership in white supremacist groups purportedly as a means to prove a scheme to defraud, when, on appeal, it argues that unauthorized access in itself is a sufficient ground for conviction on all counts. Finally, we caution that the wire fraud statute must not serve as a vehicle for prosecuting only those citizens whose views run against the tide, no matter how incorrect or uncivilized such views are.[30]

Discussion Questions

1. What is so bad about snooping?
2. Should the law be the only standard?
3. What if the snooping was used only for clues to help in litigation?
4. What distinction does the most recent decision noted make between criminal violations, the law, and ethics?

CASE 8.7

The Generous and Profitable Foundation Board

Peggie Jean Gambarana was a real estate investor in the Las Vegas area whose substantial holdings enabled her to become one of the community's most generous philanthropists. Upon her death, her will provided that $1.5 million in cash and property be given to the University of Nevada at Las Vegas Foundation to benefit the James R. Dickinson Library.

[30] U.S. v. Czubinski, *106 F.3d 1069 (1st Cir. 1997).*

The $1.5 million testate donation, the largest ever for the library, included $350,000 in cash, three properties, and a leasehold interest in a souvenir shop located at Fourth and Fremont Streets in downtown Las Vegas. However, by the time the funds and properties were converted to permanent library endowments, their value had been reduced by one-third. The reduction in value was the result of three real estate deals that involved members of the foundation.

The foundation sold all three donated properties below their appraised values. The Gambarana family home was sold to Arthur Nathan, who was moving from New Jersey to become the human resources director for the Mirage Hotel. The UNLV Foundation's chairwoman, Elaine Wynn, is an executive in Mirage Resorts, Inc., and her husband, Steve Wynn, is the corporation's chairman. Nathan purchased the home, which had an appraised value of $170,000, for $157,500. Golden Nugget, Inc., which later became Mirage Resorts, Inc., loaned Nathan the funds for the purchase. Wynn said she was not involved in the negotiations:

> It's possible for me to represent both interests without . . . creating a conflict of interest in this, especially since I didn't benefit personally nor did Mr. Nathan benefit personally.[31]

Ms. Wynn signed the sale documents for the property transaction.

The second property the foundation sold was appraised at $270,000 and sold for $206,628. The third property was appraised at $490,000 and sold for $320,000. After paying real estate commissions, the foundation received $296,200 from the sales. The commissions were paid to Madison Graves, a candidate for university regent in 1992 and a longtime friend of the foundation's director, Lyle Rivera. Rivera was also a broker for Graves' Flamingo Realty, the agency that handled the sales. Rivera saw no conflict of interest because Graves probably lost money on the sales, given the time it took to sell the property:

> We always ask them to do it at a lesser commission than standard so most of these guys don't relish doing business with the foundation.[32]

One of the purchasers of the third property was Shelli Lowe, who had also performed the appraisal on the property. Finally, with regard to the Las Vegas souvenir shop, the foundation lost $235,000 because it failed to exercise its option to renew the lease on the shop.

Discussion Questions

1. Was there a conflict of interest in the Nathan sale?
2. How would you have handled the Nathan sale differently?
3. Was there a conflict in having Madison Graves as the listing broker for the property appraised at $490,000?

[31] *John Gallant, "UNLV's Gift Fails to Meet Projections,"* Las Vegas Review Journal, *June 26, 1992, pp. 1A, 3A.*
[32] Id.

4. Does a conflict exist when an appraiser purchases a property for which she has furnished the appraisal?
5. Did the foundation manage the funds as if they were its personal funds? Is this right or wrong?
6. What things would you have done differently if you had been a foundation member responsible for managing the gift?
7. Would disclosure forms and processes help the foundation's image?

8b

Government Contracts

The existence of unlimited sources of funds often is used to justify behavior. In government contracts, the supply of funds seems endless, and the competition is stiff. These benefits and pressures often cause poor resolutions of ethical dilemmas. Pay particular attention to the impact of media coverage in the cases.

CASE 8.8

Stanford University and Government Overhead Payments

Included in government research grants to universities are indirect cost payments designed to compensate for the researchers' use of the schools' facilities.

Stanford University received approximately $240 million in federal research funds annually. About $75 million went to actual research, while Stanford billed the federal government $85 million, or 20 percent of its operating budget, for its overhead.[33] The rest of the research funds went toward employee benefits. An audit of Stanford's research program in 1990 by U.S. Navy accountant Paul Biddle revealed that the school billed the government $3,000 for a cedar-lined closet in president Donald Kennedy's home (Hoover House), $2,000 for flowers, $2,500 for refurbishing a grand piano, $7,000 for bedsheets and table linens, $4,000 for a reception for trustees following Kennedy's 1987 wedding, and $184,000 for depreciation for a seventy-two-foot yacht as part of the indirect costs for federally funded research.[34]

In response to the audit, Stanford withdrew requests for reimbursement totaling $1.35 million as unallowable and inappropriate costs. Stanford's federal funds were cut by $18 million per year.[35, 36]

[33] *Colleen Cordes, "Universities Review Overhead Charges; Some Alter Policies on President's Home,"* Chronicle of Higher Education, *April 3, 1991, p. A1.*

[34] *Maria Shao, "The Cracks in Stanford's Ivory Tower,"* Business Week, *March 11, 1991, pp. 64–65.*

[35] *Gary McWilliams, "Less Gas for the Bunsen Burners,"* Business Week, *May 20, 1991, pp. 124–126.*

[36] *Courtney Leatherman, "Stanford's Shift in Direction,"* Chronicle of Higher Education, *September 7, 1994, p. A29.*

Kennedy issued the following statements as the funding crisis evolved:

December 18, 1990: What was intended as government policy to build the capacity of universities through reimbursement of indirect costs leads to payments that are all too easily misunderstood.

Therefore, we will be reexamining our policies in an effort to avoid any confusion that might result.

At the same time, it is important to recognize that the items currently questioned, taken together, have an insignificant impact on Stanford's indirect-cost rate. . . .

Moreover, Stanford routinely charges the government less than our full indirect costs precisely to allow for errors and disallowances.

—From a university statement

January 14, 1991: We certainly ought to prune anything that isn't allowable—there isn't any question about that. But we're extending that examination to things that, although we believe are perfectly allowable, don't strike people as reasonable.

I don't care whether it's flowers, or dinners and receptions, or whether it's washing the table linen after it's been used, or buying an antique here or there, or refinishing a piano when its finish gets crappy, or repairing a closet and refinishing it—all those are investments in a university facility that serves a whole array of functions.

—From an interview with the Stanford Daily

January 23, 1991: Because acute public attention on these items threatens to overshadow the more important and fundamental issue of the support of federally sponsored research, Stanford is voluntarily withdrawing all general administration costs for operation of Hoover House claimed for the fiscal years since 1981. For those same years, we are also voluntarily withdrawing all such costs claimed for the operations of two other university-owned facilities.

—From a university statement

February 19, 1991: I am troubled by costs that are perfectly appropriate as university expenditures and lawful under the government rules but I believe ought not be charged to the taxpayer. I should have been more alert to this policy issue, and I should have insisted on more intensive review of these transactions.

—From remarks to alumni

March 23, 1991: Our obligation is not to do all the law permits, but to do what is right. Technical legality is not the guiding principle. Even in matters as arcane as government cost accounting, we must figure out what is appropriate and act accordingly. Over the years, we have not hesitated to reject numerous lawful and attractive business proposals, gifts, and even federal grants because they came with conditions we thought would be inappropriate for Stanford. Yet, with respect to indirect-cost recovery, we pursued what was permissible under the rules, without applying our customary standard of what is proper. . . .

The expenses for Hoover House—antique furniture, flowers, cedar closets—should have been excluded, and they weren't. That the amounts involved were relatively small is fortunate, but it doesn't excuse us. In our testimony before the subcommittee I did deal with this issue, but I obviously wasn't clear enough. I explained that we were removing Hoover House and some similar accounts from the cost pools that drew indirect-cost recovery because they plainly included inappropriate items. What came out in the papers was that Stanford removed the costs because it was forced to, not because it was wrong. . . . That is not so. To repeat, the allocation of these expenses to indirect-cost pools is inappropriate, regardless of its propriety under the law.

—From remarks to alumni[37]

By July 1991, Kennedy announced his resignation, effective August 1992, stating, "It is very difficult . . . for a person identified with a problem to be a spokesman for its solution."[38] Gerhard Casper, who was hired as Stanford's new president, said, "I just want this to remain one of the great universities in the world. I ask that we question what we are doing every day." Kennedy remains at Stanford, teaching biology.[39]

Stanford's donations declined that year; 1999 was the first time it saw an uptick in its donations since the time of this government overhead issue.[40]

Discussion Questions

1. Did Kennedy's ethics evolve during the crisis? Contrast his March 23, 1991, ethical posture with his December 18, 1990, assessment.
2. Is legal behavior always ethical behavior?
3. Do Casper's remarks reflect an ethical formula for Stanford's operations?

CASE 8.9

Casino Leases and the County Supervisor

Yvonne Atkinson Gates, the chairperson of the Clark County, Nevada, Commission, an elected office, also operated her own daiquiri business. Many of the new and expanding hotels in Clark County, where Las Vegas is located, have retail space available for shops and restaurants. Ms. Atkinson Gates, as a commissioner, makes decisions on whether proposed hotels and expansions will be approved.

Ms. Atkinson Gates was alleged to have approached executives from five casinos about leasing space for her daiquiri franchises. Ms. Atkinson Gates acknowledges the contacts but that they "were made in passing and cannot be considered solicitations."[41] She acknowledged actually seeking an arrangement with MGM Grand Resorts.

[37] *Karen Grassmuch, "What Happened at Stanford: Key Mistakes at Crucial Times in a Battle with the Government over Research Costs,"* Chronicle of Higher Education, *May 15, 1991, p. A26.*

[38] *"Embattled Stanford President to Quit,"* Mesa Tribune, *July 30, 1991, p. A6.*

[39] *Associated Press, "Stanford's Chief Resigns over Billing Controversy,"* Arizona Republic, *July 30, 1991, p. A8.*

[40] *Leatherman, "Stanford's Shift in Direction," p. A29.*

[41] *Susan Green, "Official Defines Role in Venture,"* Las Vegas Review Journal, *October 4, 1997, pp. 1A, 2A.*

Sheldon Adelson, the chairperson of Las Vegas Sands, Inc. said, "I was shocked, absolutely shocked that Yvonne would come to me directly. I felt she was pressuring me to agree. And when I didn't, I think she went out of her way to vote against my project."[42] Adelson wanted to build a Sands Venetian Mall, but his proposal was not approved by the commission.

The state Ethics Commission is investigating Ms. Atkinson Gates' conduct with her daiquiri business.

Discussion Questions

1. Is there a conflict in Ms. Atkinson Gates' solicitations?
2. How should she handle the business solicitations?
3. What conclusions did Mr. Adelson draw? Is he justified?
4. Ms. Atkinson Gates says she is a silent partner. Does this status help?

CASE 8.10

Bids, Employees, and Conflicts

The state of Arizona awarded the contract for indemnity insurance for the state's 55,000 employees to Intergroup of Arizona. An investigation by the Attorney General's office found that the Department of Administration, the agency responsible for reviewing bids and awarding contracts, permitted a state employee who is the wife of an Intergroup executive to make key decisions about the insurance bids and the process.[43]

By the time the investigation was completed, the contract had been awarded.

Discussion Questions

1. What problems do you see with the process?
2. Why do you think no one said anything until the investigation was conducted?
3. How will Intergroup fare in the next round of contract bids?

[42] *Susan Green, "Official Sought Casino Leases,"* Las Vegas Review Journal, *October 3, 1997, pp. 1A, 2A.*

[43] *Jodie Snyder, "AG: Insurer Chosen Unfairly,"* Arizona Republic, *August 2, 1991, pp. B1, B2.*

8C

Government Responsibilities

How careful must government be with our money? The accountability of government employees for managing funds and resources is a critical area of focus in ethics.

CASE 8.11

Orange County: Derivative Capital of the United States

On December 6, 1994, Orange County, California, filed for bankruptcy protection.[44, 45, 46] The chairman of the Orange County Board of Supervisors said the step was necessary to prevent local agencies from withdrawing their funds from the county's investment fund of $7.5 billion, which might force a fire sale of the fund's assets.[47]

The investment pool had substantial holdings in risky financial instruments known as derivatives (see Case 5.12 for more information) that would provide returns only if interest rates continued to fall. Interest rates rose, and Orange County had large debts from borrowing to invest in derivatives. As a result, the county could not pay its creditors and its investment pool lost $2.5 billion. The investments had been masterminded by County Treasurer Robert Citron.

Twelve different brokerage houses were left with loans to Orange County that might not be repaid.[48] The announcement of the county's bankruptcy caused the stock market to plunge fifty points. Litigation is pending by school districts and other

[44] *"Orange County Seeks Protection under Bankruptcy Law,"* Mesa Tribune, *December 7, 1994, p. A7.*

[45] *Karen Donovan, "Chapter 9: The Next Page,"* National Law Journal, *December 26, 1994, p. A6.*

[46] *Sallie Hofmeister, "In Rare Move, California County Files for Bankruptcy Protection,"* The New York Times, *December 7, 1994, pp. C1, C5.*

[47] *Del Jones, "County Seeks Bankruptcy Protection,"* USA Today, *December 7, 1994, pp. 1C, 2C.*

[48] *"Orange County Fallout Hits Stocks,"* Arizona Republic, *December 8, 1994, p. C3.*

government entities against the brokers who handled the derivatives sales. Hiring was frozen in the county, and many people with disabilities whose funds were in the Orange County investment pool could not withdraw their money because of the bankruptcy.[49] Mr. Citron and others entered pleas to various charges.

A report by the California state Bureau of Audits concludes as follows:

> The Orange County (county) treasurer is responsible for receiving and keeping safe all funds belonging to the county and other monies deposited with the treasurer. However, we found that the former treasurer pursued an investment strategy that violated the basic principles of prudent investing, which are safety, liquidity, and yield, in that order. In fact, his investment strategies were diametrically opposed to these principles. The former treasurer's investments were unsafe, highly risky, and extremely volatile, and they lacked the liquidity needed to meet the portfolio's objectives. Further, he sacrificed safety and liquidity in a failed strategy to capture higher yields.[50] The former treasurer did this by leveraging the portfolio more than 2.7 times and purchasing highly volatile inverse floaters and other structured securities that comprised more than 40 percent of his investments.[51]

Discussion Questions

1. Should government investment decisions be based on factors different from those used in making private investment decisions?
2. List all the groups of people affected by the losses in Orange County.
3. What impact will Orange County's bankruptcy have on the ability of other government entities to sell their bonds?
4. Would you invest your own money in derivatives?
5. Should Orange County voters and investment pool participants have been given more information on the risk?
6. Should brokers who made the investments be held liable for advising Orange County to purchase unsuitable securities for its funds?
7. One of the recommendations of the Bureau of Audits report done by the state of California was as follows:

   > In addition, we recommend that the board of supervisors establish strict rules regarding ethics, conflict of interest, and asset safekeeping for all the county's investment activities, and adopt and approve the treasurer's comprehensive investment policies.[52]

   Why are ethics and conflicts of interest important in preventing this from happening again?

[49] *"As Orange County Investments Flop, Kids' Money Is Frozen,"* Mesa Tribune, *December 10, 1994, p. A9.*

[50] *David J. Lynch, "How Golden Touch Turned into Crisis,"* USA Today, *December 23, 1994, p. 1B.*

[51] *http://www.bsa.ca.gov/bsa/summaries/94026sum.html*

[52] Id.

Sources

Coffee, John C., "The Suitability Doctrine Revisited: Can Orange County Sue Its Broker for Recommending the Purchase of Unsuitable Securities for Its Funds?" *National Law Journal*, January 16, 1995, pp. B4, B6.

Craig, David, "Dow Plunges 50 as Investors Skitter," *USA Today*, December 9, 1994, p. 1B.

Craig, David, "Orange County Freezes Hiring as Markets Feel the Heat," *USA Today*, December 9, 1994, p. 1A.

Greenwald, John, "The California Wipeout," *Time*, December 19, 1994, p. 55.

Jereski, Laura, "How a Rescue Mission Failed, Just Barely, in Orange County," *The Wall Street Journal*, December 22, 1994, pp. A1, A14.

Jereski, Laura, "Orange County Fund Losses Put at $2.5 Billion," *The Wall Street Journal*, December 12, 1994, pp. A3, A5.

Jereski, Laura, "Who Bears Loss Becomes Critical Orange County Issue," *The Wall Street Journal*, January 10, 1995, p. C1.

Johnson, Kevin, and David J. Lynch, "California County Seeks Court Help on Debt," *USA Today*, December 7, 1994, p. 1A.

Memmott, Mark, "Orange County's Woes Won't Sway Fed's Course," *USA Today*, December 8, 1994, p. 1B.

Stevens, Amy, "Attorneys May Share Blame by Not Disclosing Risk in Orange County," *The Wall Street Journal*, December 16, 1994, p. B3.

Taylor, Jeffrey, "Hard-Charging Broker Draws the Spotlight in Orange County Miss," *The Wall Street Journal*, December 12, 1994, pp. A1, A7.

CASE 8.12

Cars and Conflicts

Maricopa County supervisors, Mary Rose Wilcox and Ed King (elected officials), turned in the county cars that they had been taking home with them. King's chief administrator also turned in his car. County policy is that employees may check out cars but should not drive them home without prior authorization, which is given only for night hearings or activities and next-day trips where distance to a car pick-up at the motor pool makes it time prohibitive.

Their use of vehicles was revealed in a public meeting by another supervisor who said it was "feeding off the taxpayers and sending the wrong message to county employees."[53]

[53] *David Schwartz, "2 Supervisors, Aide Turn in County Cars,"* Arizona Republic, *May 4, 1994, pp. B1, B5.*

Discussion Questions

1. Mrs. Wilcox apologized and said, "Sometimes, you get so immersed in things that you don't see what's right. I made a mistake, and for that, I'm sorry." What could have helped her see the issue?
2. What operational dangers for government agencies arise when elected officials don't follow the rules?

unit 9

Ethics and Nonprofits

Good intentions are not necessarily the same as good ethics. In this final segment of the book, we take a look at good intentions gone amuck. These organizations had the goodwill and donations of others but abused that trust, with resulting consequences that had far-reaching effects.

9a

Ethics and Nonprofits

CASE 9.1

Giving and Spending the United Way

The United Way, which evolved from the local community chests of the 1920s, is a national organization that funnels funding to charities through a payroll-deduction system.

Ninety percent of all charitable payroll deductions in 1991 were for the United Way. This system, however, has been criticized as coercive. Bonuses, for example, were offered for achieving 100 percent employee participation. Betty Beene, president of United Way of Tristate (New York, New Jersey, and Connecticut), commented, "If participation is 100 percent, it means someone has been coerced."[1] Tristate discontinued the bonuses and arm-twisting.

United Way's system of spending also came under fire through the actions of William Aramony, president of the United Way from 1970 to 1992. During his tenure, United Way receipts grew from $787 million in 1970 to $3 billion in 1990. But some of Aramony's effects on the organization were less positive.

In early 1992, the *Washington Post* reported that Aramony:

- Was paid $463,000 per year.
- Flew first class on commercial airlines.
- Spent $20,000 in one year for limousines.
- Used the Concorde for trans-Atlantic flights.[2]

The article also revealed that one of the taxable spin-off companies Aramony had created to provide travel and bulk purchasing for United Way chapters had bought a $430,000 condominium in Manhattan and a $125,000 apartment in Coral Gables, Florida, for his use. Another spin-off had hired Aramony's son, Robert Aramony, as its president.

When Aramony's expenses and salary became public, Stanley C. Gault, chairman of Goodyear Tire & Rubber Company, asked, "Where was the board? The outside au-

[1] *Susan Garland, "Keeping a Sharper Eye on Those Who Pass the Hat,"* Business Week, *March 16, 1992, p. 39.*

[2] *As reported in "Ex-executives of United Way Indicted,"* Arizona Republic, *September 14, 1994, p. A6.*

ditors?"[3] Aramony resigned after fifteen chapters of the United Way threatened to withhold their annual dues to the national office.

Said Robert O. Bothwell, executive director of the National Committee for Responsive Philanthropy, "I think it is obscene that he is making that kind of salary and asking people who are making $10,000 a year to give 5 percent of their income."[4]

In August 1992, the United Way board of directors hired Elaine Chao, the Peace Corps director, to replace William Aramony at a salary of $195,000, with no perks.[5] She reduced staff from 275 to 185 and borrowed $1.5 million to compensate for a decline in donations. By 1995, United Way donations had still not returned to their 1991 $3.2 billion. Ms. Chao left the United Way and was eventually appointed as Labor Secretary for the Bush Administration In 2001. Ms. Chao is married to Republican Senator Mitch McConnell of Kentucky.

In September 1994, William Aramony and two other United Way officers, including the chief financial officer, were indicted by a federal grand jury for conspiracy, mail fraud, and tax fraud. The indictment alleged the three officers diverted more than $2.74 million of United Way funds to purchase an apartment in New York City for $383,000, interior decorating for $72,000, a condominium, vacations, and a lifetime pass on American Airlines. In addition, $80,000 of United Way funds were paid to Aramony's girlfriend, a 1986 high school graduate, for consulting, even though she did no work.

On April 3, 1995, Aramony was found guilty of twenty-five counts of fraud, conspiracy, and money laundering. Two other United Way executives were also convicted.

By April, 1998, donation levels were still not completely reinstated, but did increase (up 4.7 percent) for the first time since the 1992 Aramony crisis. Relationships between local chapters and the national organization were often strained and the recent Boy Scouts of America boycott has created additional tension. United Way's donations fell 11 percent since 1991 while overall charitable giving was up 9 percent.

In January 2000, a federal district court judge awarded Mr. Aramony the full value of his deferred compensation plan, or $4.2 million. Judge Shira Scheindlin ruled in favor of Mr. Aramony because she said there was no clause for forfeiting the money if Mr. Aramony committeed a felony. Such a so-called "bad boy" clause had been discussed by the board when it was in the process of approving the deferred compensation plan for Mr. Aramony and other United Way executives. However, the "bad boy" clause never made it into the final agreement.[6]

However, Judge Scheindlin also ruled that United Way could withhold $2.02 million of the amount due to cover salary, investigation costs, and interest on those amounts. She did not award Mr. Aramony attorneys' fees for having to bring the suit against United Way to collect his deferred compensation.

[3] *Garland, "Keeping a Sharper Eye on Those Who Pass the Hat," p. 39.*

[4] *Felicity Barringer, "United Way Head Is Forced Out in a Furor over His Lavish Style,"* The New York Times, *February 28, 1992, p. A1.*

[5] *Desda Moss, "Peace Corps Director to Head United Way,"* USA Today, *August 27, 1992, p. 6A; Sabra Chartrand, "Head of Peace Corps Named United Way President,"* The New York Times, *August 27, 1992, p. A8.*

[6] *David Cay Johnston, "Ex-United Way Chief Owed $4.2 Million,"* The New York Times, *January 5, 2000, p. C4.*

Discussion Questions

1. Was there anything unethical about Aramony's expenditures?
2. Was the board responsible for the expenditures?
3. Is the perception as important as the acts themselves?
4. If Aramony were a CEO of a for-profit firm, would your answers change?
5. What obstacles did Chao face as she assumed the United Way helm?
6. Do you think Mr. Aramony should have asked for his deferred compensation funds?

Sources

Allen, Frank E., and Susan Pulliam, "United Way's Rivals Take Aim at Its Practices," *The Wall Street Journal*, March 6, 1992, pp. B1, B6.

Barringer, Felicity, "Ex-Chief of United Way Vows to Fight Accusations," *The New York Times*, April 10, 1992, p. A13.

Duffy, Michael, "Charity Begins at Home," *Time*, March 9, 1992, p. 48.

"Ex-executives of United Way Indicted," *Arizona Republic*, September 14, 1994, p. A6.

Kinsley, Michael, "Charity Begins with Government," *Time*, April 6, 1992, p. 74.

Moss, Desda, "Change Is Focus of United Way Meeting," *USA Today*, August 19, 1992, p. 7A.

Moss, Desda, "Former United Way Chief Charged with Looting Funds," *USA Today*, September 14, 1994, p. 1A.

Moss, Desda, "United Way's Ex-Chief Guilty of Using Funds," *USA Today*, April 14, 1995, p. 1A.

CASE 9.2

New Era—If It Sounds Too Good to Be True, It Is Too Good to Be True

The Foundation for New Era Philanthropy was founded in 1989 by Mr. John G. Bennett, Jr. New Era took in over $200 million between 1989 and May 1995, when the SEC brought suit against New Era and the foundation went into bankruptcy.

Mr. Bennett is a charismatic individual who was able to bring in many individual and institutional investors (most of them nonprofit organizations that included many colleges and universities) with the promise of a double-your-money return. Mr. Bennett often met personally with investors or their representatives and opened and closed his sessions with them with prayer.[7] Among the individual investors in New Era were Laurance Rockefeller, Pat Boone, then-president of Procter & Gamble John Pepper, and former Treasury Secretary William Simon. The institutional investors included the University of Pennsylvania, the Nature Conservancy, and the National Museum of American Jewish History.[8]

In 1991, Melenie and Albert Meyer moved from their native South Africa to Michigan, where Mr. Meyer took a tenure-track position as an accounting professor at Spring Arbor College. Because there were only three accounting majors at the time he was hired, Mr. Meyer was also required to work part-time in the business office.[9]

During his first month in the business office, Mr. Meyer found that the college had transferred $294,000 to Heritage of Values Foundation, Inc. He connected the term "Heritage" with Reverend Jim Bakker and went to the library to research Heritage of Values Foundation, Inc. While he found no connection to Jim Bakker, he could find no other information on the foundation. Mr. Meyer asked his supervisor, the vice president for business affairs, Ms. Janet M. Tjepkema, about Heritage of Values and the nature of the transfer. She explained that Heritage was the consultant that had found the New Era Foundation and had advised the college to invest in this "double your investment" fund.

Mr. Meyer attempted to research New Era but could find no registration for it in Pennsylvania, its headquarters location. He could not obtain information from New Era (there was no registration in Pennsylvania ever filed and no tax returns were filed until 1993). Mr. Meyer continued to approach administrators of the college, but they seemed annoyed. He continued to collect information about New Era for the next two years. He gathered income tax returns and even spoke directly with Mr. Bennett. Mr. Meyer remained silent during the time that he gathered information because he was untenured and on a temporary work visa.[10]

After he had collected files of information on New Era, which he labeled "Ponzi File," Mr. Meyer wrote a letter to the president of Spring Arbor as well as the chairman of the board of trustees for the college warning them about his concerns regarding New Era. Mr. Meyer had also tried to talk with his colleagues about the information he had uncovered. He felt shunned by administrators and his colleagues and, by April 1994, he and his wife were no longer attending any social functions held by the college. He was told by administrators that raising funds was tough enough without his meddling. He repeatedly tried to convince administrators not to place any additional funds with New Era. His advice was ignored and Spring Arbor invested an additional $1.5 million in New Era in 1994. At that time, Spring Arbor College's total endowment was $6 million. The $1.5 million would later be lost as part of the New Era bankruptcy.

In March 1995, Mr. Meyer received tenure and began to try to help others by warning them about his concerns about New Era. He wrote to the SEC and detailed his information and concerns. The SEC then notified Prudential Securities, which was holding $73 million in New Era stock. Prudential began its own investigation and found resistance from New Era officers in releasing information. New Era began to

[7] *Steve Wulf, "Too Good to Be True,"* Time, *May 29, 1995, p. 34.*

[8] *Steve Secklow, "A New Era Consultant Lured Rich Donors Over Pancakes, Prayer,"* The Wall Street Journal, *June 2, 1995, pp. A1, A4.*

[9] *Barbara Carton, "Unlikely Hero: A Persistent Accountant Brought New Era's Problems to Light,"* The Wall Street Journal, *May 19, 1995, pp. B1, B10.*

[10] Id.

unravel and by June 1995 it was in bankruptcy. There were 300 creditors named and net losses were $107 million. New Era was nothing but a Ponzi scheme. It was able to pay out double the investment, but only so long as it could recruit new participants. When it could no longer recruit participants, it was unable to pay on demands for withdrawal.

Mr. Bennett was indicted on 82 counts of fraud, money laundering, and tax code violations in March 1997.[11] He entered a no contest plea.[12] He was sentenced to twelve years in prison in October 1997. The judge departed from the 24 1/2 years dictated by the federal sentencing guidelines in ordering a reduced sentence because Mr. Bennett had been "extraordinarily cooperative" in the investigation and because he had voluntarily turned over $1.5 million in assets to the bankruptcy court to be distributed to New Era participants.[13] The judge also noted what he felt was Mr. Bennett's diminished capacity.[14] The judge, in particularly harsh language, lectured Mr. Bennett on the egregious nature of his conduct: "It is possible for an ostensibly good and reverent person who is a true believer to engage in egregiously reprehensible and societally disruptive behavior."[15]

Discussion Questions

1. Why did Mr. Meyer have so much difficulty convincing his college administrators that there was a problem with New Era?
2. Did Mr. Meyer follow the right steps in trying to bring New Era to the attention of the college officials?
3. What impact did Mr. Meyer's personal situation (visa and tenure issues) have on his desire to carry through with his concerns?
4. Why were administrators so reluctant to hear Mr. Meyer out? Mr. Bennett notified Spring Arbor College officials when Mr. Meyer called him and asked administrators to keep Mr. Meyer quiet. How would you read this kind of request? What would you do if you were an administrator?
5. About forty of the nonprofit organizations that had invested in New Era and withdrawn their funds and earnings prior to its collapse voluntarily agreed to return their money to the bankruptcy pool.[16] An administrator from Lancaster Bible College, in explaining the return of his college's funds to the trustee, quoted St. Paul's letter to the Philippians, "Let each of you look not only to his own interest, but also to the interests of others." Hans Finzel, head of CB International, a missionary fund, said his organization would not be returning the money: "It's true

[11] *Steve Secklow, "Retired Judge Will Sort Out New Era Mess,"* The Wall Street Journal, *June 29, 1995, pp. B1, B16.*

[12] *Steve Secklow, "How New Era's Boss Led Rich and Gullible Into a Web of Deceit,"* The Wall Street Journal, *May 19, 1995, pp. A1, A5.*

[13] *Dinah Wisenberg Brin, "Philanthropy Scam Nets 12 Years,"* USA Today, *September 23, 1997, p. 2A.*

[14] *Carton, "Unlikely Hero," pp. B1, B10.*

[15] *Joseph Slobodzian, "Bennett Gets 12 for New Era Scam,"* National Law Journal, *October 6, 1997, p. A8.*

[16] *Andrea Gerlin, "Among the Few Given Money by New Era, Many See Blessings in Giving It Back,"* The Wall Street Journal, *June 20, 1995, pp. B1, B10.*

that it's tainted money, but it's also true that we received it in good faith."[17] Compare and contrast the positions of the parties. Would you return the money?

6. Bennett M. Weiner, head of the Philanthropic Advisory Service of the Council of Better Business Bureaus, says, "There's tremendous pressure on charities today to increase their revenues to meet expenses and growing public needs. Unfortunately, this can influence some organizations to take financial risks because of potential rewards."[18] Is this an indication that nonprofits operate as businesses and are susceptible to the same business ethics issues? Should nonprofits have ethics programs and training for their staff and volunteers?

Sources

Bloom, Michael A., "Key in New Era Settlement," *National Law Journal*, July 15, 1996, p. A4.

Davis, Ann, "Charity's Troubles Put Dechert in Bind," *National Law Journal*, May 29, 1995, p. A6.

Lambert, Wade, "Trustee in New Era Bankruptcy May Pursue 'Donations,'" *The Wall Street Journal*, May 22, 1995, p. B3.

Secklow, Steve, "A New Era Consultant Lured Rich Donors Over Pancakes, Prayers," *The Wall Street Journal*, June 2, 1995, pp. A1, A4.

Secklow, Steve, "New Era's Bennett Gets 12-Year Sentence," *The Wall Street Journal*, September 23, 1997, p. B13.

Secklow, Steve, "Prudential Securities Agrees to Settle New Era Suits by Paying $18 Million," *The Wall Street Journal*, November 18, 1996, p. A4.

Secklow, Steve, and Joseph Rebello, "IRS Is Studying Whether New Era's Donors Committed Fraud on Deductions," *The Wall Street Journal*, May 24, 1995, p. A3.

Slobodzian, Joseph, "New Era Founder Says: God Made Him Do It," *National Law Journal*, March 17, 1997, p. A9.

CASE 9.3

The Red Cross, New York, and Ground Zero

Following the September 11, 2001, attacks on the World Trade Center and their collapse, there were many who had lost loved ones, their homes or businesses, or both.

[17] *Michael A. Bloom, "Key in New Era Settlement,"* National Law Journal, *July 15, 1996, p. A4.*

[18] *William M. Bulkeley, "Charities Coffers Easily Become Crooks' Booty,"* The Wall Street Journal, *June 5, 1995, pp. B1, B3.*

The outpouring of support from the American public was overwhelming. The public donated $543 million for the September 11 disaster relief fund.[19] However, the Red Cross indicated it would use the funds for infrastructure support and not necessarily all of it would go to victims and their families.

When the decision to use the funds in this manner was made, Dr. Bernadine Healy resigned as president of the Red Cross, giving up her $450,010 annual salary and position.

The American public was outraged and demanded that the funds go to the victims and their families. The Red Cross eventually relented, admitted an error in judgment, and agreed to the limited and intended use of the funds.

Discussion Questions

1. Did the Red Cross commit an ethical violation in its initial decision?
2. What do you think of Dr. Healy's decision? Is she a whistleblower?
3. What policies should the Red Cross establish for the future in fund-raising and fund disbursement?

[19] *Marvin Olasky, "Charity Doesn't Have to Mean Bureaucracy,"* The Wall Street Journal, *November 21, 2001, p. A15.*

Business Discipline Index

ACCOUNTING

ADVERTISING

BUSINESS COMMUNICATIONS

BUSINESS LAW

COMPLIANCE PROGRAMS

CONFLICTS OF INTEREST

CORPORATE GOVERNANCE

CYBERLAW

ECONOMICS

EMPLOYEE RIGHTS AND RESPONSIBILITIES

FINANCE

GOVERNMENT

HEALTH CARE

HONESTY

INTERNATIONAL

LABOR LAW

MANAGEMENT

MARKETING

NONPROFIT MANAGEMENT

ORGANIZATIONAL BEHAVIOR

PURCHASING

QUALITY MANAGEMENT

REGULATION

SOCIAL RESPONSIBILITY

STRATEGY

SUPPLY CHAIN MANAGEMENT

WHISTLE-BLOWING

Product/Company/Individuals/Subject Index

NATIONAL CAR RENTAL

NATIONAL ORGANIZATION FOR WOMEN (NOW)

NESTLÉ

NIKE

NINOS AND NINAS

NORTH TEXAS TOYOTA DEALERS ASSOCIATION

NUTRI/SYSTEM

OPTIFAST

ORANGE COUNTY

PAINE WEBBER

PEPSI

PHAR-MOR

PHILIP MORRIS

Topic Index

ADVERTISING

AFFIRMATIVE ACTION

AGENCY

APPROPRIATION

AUDITORS

BANKRUPTCY

BILLING

BRIBERY

CHRISTIAN CONSEQUENTIALISM

COMPENSATION

COMPETITION

CONFLICTS OF INTEREST

CONTRACTS

CONTRIBUTIONS

COPYRIGHT INFRINGEMENT

DEONTOLOGY

DERIVATIVES

DISCRIMINATION

DOWNSIZING

EGOISM

ENVIRONMENT

EQUITY

EXECUTIVE PAY

FINANCE

FOREIGN COUNTRIES— DIFFERING BUSINESS PRACTICES

GIFTS

GOVERNMENT CONTRACTS

GOVERNMENT EMPLOYEES

GREASE PAYMENTS

HEALTH

HONESTY

INSIDE INFORMATION

INTERNAL AUDIT/CONTROLS

INTUITIONISM

MISREPRESENTATION

MORAL RESPONSIBILITY

PATENTS

PAY

See Compensation, Executive Salaries

PLANT CLOSINGS

PRICING

PRIVACY

PRODUCT SAFETY

PRODUCT QUALITY

PROPERTY RIGHTS

PURCHASING AGENTS

RIGHTS

SCREENING

SECURITIES FRAUD

SEXUAL HARASSMENT

SHAREHOLDER PROPOSALS

SOCIAL RESPONSIBILITY

TECHNOLOGY

UTILITARIANISM

WHISTLE-BLOWING

WORKPLACE SAFETY